INTRODUCTION TO

Hospitality Management

FIFTH EDITION

John R. Walker

McKibbon Professor of Hotel and Restaurant Management,
University of South Florida, Sarasota–Manatee and Fulbright
Senior Specialist.

PEARSON

Boston   Columbus   Indianapolis   New York   San Francisco
Amsterdam   Cape Town   Dubai   London   Madrid   Milan   Munich   Paris   Montreal   Toronto
Delhi   Mexico City   São Paulo   Sydney   Hong Kong   Seoul   Singapore   Taipei   Tokyo

Executive Editor: Daryl Fox
Editorial Director: Andrew Gilfillan
Program Manager: Susan Watkins
Project Manager: Maria Reyes
Development Editor: Kay Ueno
Editorial Assistant: Lara Dimmick
SVP Field Marketing: David Gesell
Senior Marketing Manager: Darcy Betts
Field Marketing Manager: Thomas Hayward
Senior Marketing Coordinator: Les Roberts
Senior Art Director: Diane Y. Ernsberger

Procurement Specialist: Deidra Skahill
Media Production and Development Project Manager: Leslie Brado
Cover Art: Shutterstock, © ClimberJAK
Cover Designer: Cenveo Publishing Services
Full-Service Project Management: Nancy Kincade, Lumina Datamatics
Composition: Lumina Datamatics
Printer/Binder: RR Donnelley, Willard
Cover Printer: Phoenix Color Corp.

Credits and acknowledgments borrowed from other sources and reproduced, with permission, in this textbook appear on the appropriate page within text

Library of Congress Cataloging-in-Publication Data

Names: Walker, John R., 1944-
Title: Introduction to hospitality management / John R. Walker, McKibbon
   Professor of Hotel and Restaurant Management, University of South Florida,
   Sarasota—Manatee, and Fulbright Senior Specialist.
Other titles: Hospitality management
Description: Fifth edition. | Boston : Pearson, [2017] | Includes
   bibliographical references and index.
Identifiers: LCCN 2015037250| ISBN 9780134151908 (alk. paper) | ISBN
   0134151909 (alk. paper)
Subjects: LCSH: Hospitality industry—Management.
Classification: LCC TX911.3.M27 W3515 2017 | DDC 647.94068—dc23
LC record available at http://lccn.loc.gov/2015037250

10 9 8 7 6 5 4 3 2 1

ISBN-13: 978-0-13-415190-8
ISBN-10:   0-13-415190-9

To You: the professors and students who are dedicating yourselves to the future of Hospitality and Hospitality Management.

BRIEF CONTENTS

CONTENTS

Chapter 2   The Hotel Business   51

Chapter 4 Food and Beverage   151

Chapter 6   The Restaurant Business   235

Part III Tourism, Recreation, Attractions, Clubs, and Gaming   349

Chapter 9 Tourism   351

Part IV Assemblies, Events, Attractions, Leadership, and Management 485

Chapter 16 Organizing

Chapter 17 Communication and Decision Making   651

Chapter 18 Control   685

Thank you to the professors and students who have used the previous editions of this text. This new fifth edition of *Introduction to Hospitality Management* focuses on hospitality operations and has been written in response to professors and students who wanted a broader view of the world's largest industry. *Introduction to Hospitality Management* complements *Introduction to Hospitality* and *Exploring the Hospitality Industry*, also written by John R. Walker. Adopters may select the title best suited to their needs. This text offers a comprehensive overview of the industry.

This text is designed for the hospitality management professionals of tomorrow. By involving readers in each step of this exciting journey, *Introduction to Hospitality Management* invites students to share the unique enthusiasm and passion surrounding the hospitality industry. Each chapter has been vetted by industry professionals and includes several hands-on examples that help students understand the how-to aspects of the hospitality industry.

The primary goals and objectives of this text are to:

- Prepare students to advance in their hospitality career by offering a foundation of knowledge about the hospitality industry presented in a lively, interesting manner with an extensive array of features to facilitate the learning process.
- Assist students in learning the details of the hospitality industry by offering chapters on the operational areas of the industry.
- Offer students information on the array of careers available in the various segments of the hospitality industry.
- Facilitate learning by offering a student-friendly text to students and an outstanding instructional package to professors.

Organization of the Text

This fifth edition has been divided into four parts:

Part I   Introducing Hospitality and Lodging
Part II   Beverages, Restaurants, and Managed Services
Part III   Tourism, Recreation, Attractions, Clubs, and Gaming
Part IV   Assemblies, Events, Attractions, Leadership, and Management
Part V   Managerial Areas of the Hospitality Industry

New to this edition:

1. An interesting How To feature added to each chapter that highlights and examines an essential function or issue within the Hospitality industry
2. A new section on spas added to Chapter 3
3. A Learning Objective at the beginning of each major section throughout a chapter helps focus students in their reading
4. A new case study added to MyHospitalityLab for each chapter
5. Trivia questions added to MyHospitalityLab that are designed to help students score better on multiple choice test questions

New and continuing features include:

1. Revision of each chapter with current facts, figures, new photos, and new page layouts
2. Chapter 1: Addition of a section on hospitality in the twenty-first century, and an update of the salaries figure
3. Chapter 2: Extension of timeline beyond the year 2000, plus the addition of new hotels by price segment, and a revised Focus on Development by Dr. Chad Gruhl
4. Chapter 6: Reduced "The Restaurant Business" chapter by removing material related to developing a restaurant
5. Updated Corporate, Personal, and "Day in the Life . . . " profiles in each chapter
6. Case Studies: Updated questions for each chapter case available via MyHospitalityLab
7. Added insights by Dr. Greg Dunn to the Trends section of each chapter
8. New Technology Spotlight sections in relevant chapters
9. "Sustainability" section as it relates to the hospitality industry added to every chapter
10. A Check Your Knowledge feature throughout each chapter aids in checking reading comprehension of learning objectives
11. Key words and concepts set in boldface in text, listed at the ends of chapters, and defined in the Glossary
12. Review Questions
13. Internet Exercises
14. Apply Your Knowledge questions
15. Summaries at the ends of chapters that correspond to chapter Learning Objectives
16. Suggested Activities

Supplements Package

1. Professional PowerPoint presentation is available online to qualified text adopters
2. Updated Online Test Bank of class-tested questions
3. Online Instructors Manual
4. MyHospitalityLab course

To access supplementary materials online, instructors need to request an instructor access code. Go to **www.pearsonhighered.com/irc**, where you can register for an instructor access code. Within 48 hours after registering, you will receive a confirming e-mail, including an instructor access code. Once you have received your code, go to the site and log on for full instructions on downloading the materials you wish to use.

Dear Future Hospitality Professional:

This textbook is written to empower you and help you on your way to becoming a future leader of this great industry. It will give you an in-depth overview of the world's largest and fastest growing business. Each chapter contains **profiles of industry practitioners and leaders**, **case studies**, and **corporate profiles**. Additionally, industry experts speak on their area of specialization in **focus boxes**.

Read the Book

Read and study the text, including the profiles, focus boxes, applications, and case studies. Answer the Check Your Knowledge questions and review questions. By using the many tools throughout this textbook—including boldface key words and concepts—you will be amazed at how much more you get out of class by preparing ahead of time.

Use the Resources Accompanying This Book

Make use of the excellent **MyHospitalityLab** (www.myhospitalitylab.com) course with its unique Hospitality and Tourism Interactive Activities, Dynamic Study Modules, case studies with graded questions, lecture note PowerPoints, and flashcards. By doing so, you will improve your chances of achieving success in this class and will find that you enjoy learning.

Success in the Classroom

Faculty constantly say that the best students are the ones who come to class prepared. I know that, as a hospitality student, you have many demands on your time: work, a heavy course load, family commitments, and, yes, fun—plus a lot of reading and studying for your other courses. With these thoughts in mind, I tried to make this book as visually appealing, easy, and engaging to read and enjoyable as possible.

Wishing you success in your studies and career.

Sincerely,
John Walker D.B.A., CHA., FMP.

Take some time to turn the page and review descriptions of all the features and tools in this book and find out how they will facilitate your reading and understanding of the concepts. **Discover** the exciting opportunities in the numerous and varied segments of the hospitality industry.

Boxed Features Connect You to the Real World

These boxed features introduce you to *real people* who describe their experiences *on the job* in the world of hospitality management.

Introducing . . . and A Day in the Life of . . .

INTRODUCING VALERIE FERGUSON

Senior Vice President, Operations, Denihan Hospitality Group and Past Chair of the American Hotel & Lodging Association

To most, "making it big" seems like a regular statement and a task easily achieved. Ferguson, well, it comes with a lot of work, dedication, and heart. She speaks often ab opportunities and adding self-interest to what you do for your career.

For this African American woman, life wasn't always easy. As the managing direct Philadelphia Hotel and regional vice president of Loews Hotels, she had a lot to say got her to where she is now.

One of her most important role models was her father, Sam Ferguson. She says, and I had a great relationship in which he supported me, but in which he never put an

A DAY IN THE LIFE OF DENNY BHAKTA

Revenue Manager, Hilton Hotels San Diego

Revenue management is a strategic function in maximizing room revenue (REV PAR) along with growing market share. REV PAR and market share are the two primary barometers used in the industry to grade a revenue manager's competency. It is essential for revenue managers to have a system in place for daily business reviews to formulate winning strategies. Daily duties include:

1. Analyzing Data: A revenue manager must develop a reporting system for daily monitoring. In recent years, the larger hotel brands have developed proprietary revenue management systems that provide on-demand reporting of historical data, future position, and the ability to apply real-time pricing changes to future nights. Understanding past performance can uncover various business trends over high and low demand periods. It is critical to understand the effectiveness of previous pricing strategies to better position the hotel on future nights.

The general public can view rates and book rooms up to 365 days into the future. Therefore, the revenue

You're introduced to industry practitioners' careers, the issues and challenges they encounter, and their achievements and contributions. These features give a "from-the-heart," up-close and personal view of their work. From dreams to reality—follow the career path to success for industry leaders and learn from their experiences.

Corporate Profiles

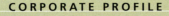

CORPORATE PROFILE

Wyndham Worldwide—A Collection of Hotel Brands

Wyndham Hotels and Resorts, Wyndham Grand Hotels and Resorts, Wyndham Garden, Days Inn, Howard Johnson, Ramada, Knights Inn, Super 8, Travelodge, Baymont Inns & Suites, Microtel Inns and Suites, Hawthorn Suites, Wingate by Wyndham, TRYP by Wyndham, Dream Hotels, and Night Hotels, totalling more than 7,340 hotels in 66 countries.[12]

As a franchisor, the company licenses the owners and operators of independent businesses to use Wyndham brand names, without taking on big business risks and expenses. Wyndham does not operate hotels, but instead provides coordination and services that allow franchisees to retain local control of their activities. At the same time, franchisees benefit from the economies of scale of widely promoted brand names and well-established standards of service

Learn about the practices, growth, and scope of leading corporations and organizations. For example, Marriott International did not start out as a multibillion-dollar company; the company began as a nine-seat root beer stand in 1927.

Focus on . . .

FOCUS ON ROOMS DIVISION

Rooms Division with Charlie Adams

From the early days of primitive inns to our modern super hotels, like the Izmailovo Hotel with 7,500 rooms in Moscow, employees are the crucial ingredient to hotel or motel success. Even with extraordinary advances in technology and the globalization of lodging in the twenty-first century, lodging remains fundamentally a people business and it is the employees who are responsible for the appearance, image, and reputation of a lodging facility.

The rooms division is considered the "center" of hotel activity because it is accountable for revenue, customer service, and departmental forecasting. Room sales are the primary source of income for most hotels and almost 100 percent of the revenue for many select service or budget hotels. The rooms division has the most guest contacts because it is comprised of reservations, front office, housekeeping, and uniformed services. The reservations department provides the needed accurate information for other departments to use to forecast for upcoming events and guest needs along with scheduling the proper staffing levels in the hotel.

Starting your career in the rooms division of a hotel is an exciting, demanding, and rewarding experience. You will be part of a team whose overall responsibility is the well-being of guests and ensuring that their expectations are met and that they have

Written by contributing expert authors, these boxes offer unique personal perspectives on chapter topics.

How To . . .

HOW TO GET A STEP AHEAD IN THE INDUSTRY

Courtesy of **James McManemon**, M.S., University of South Florida Sarosta—Manatee

Josh Medina, who recently earned his degree in hospitality management at the University of South Florida, recognized at the outset that for the majority of department management positions prior experience working in lower-level and/or supervisory positions is necessary, while moving into upper-management positions beyond, would require both experience in lower-level positions, plus an undergraduate and/or graduate degree (a business-related or hospitality degree is ideal) as well. Josh's choice was to study hospitality management as an undergraduate, and work nights as a server/bartender at a fine-dining restaurant. After a single year at this night job, Josh was promoted to head-server, which allowed him to train new servers, expedite food, assist with making schedules, and manage payroll. Upon graduation, Hyatt Regency in Sarasota, Florida, hired him as assistant restaurant manager. Though Josh had no prior experience as a restaurant manager, his experience working as a head-server and bartender, combined with his educational knowledge of management, gave him the necessary tools to get a step

This feature focuses on a specific issue related to a central function within various sectors of the hospitality industry and how that issue was (or might be) addressed and resolved.

Technology Spotlights

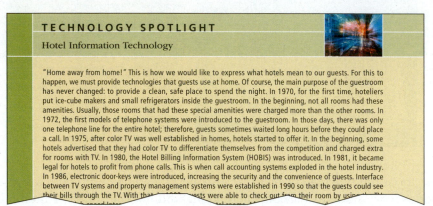

TECHNOLOGY SPOTLIGHT

Hotel Information Technology

"Home away from home!" This is how we would like to express what hotels mean to our guests. For this to happen, we must provide technologies that guests use at home. Of course, the main purpose of the guestroom has never changed: to provide a clean, safe place to spend the night. In 1970, for the first time, hoteliers put ice-cube makers and small refrigerators inside the guestroom. In the beginning, not all rooms had these amenities. Usually, those rooms that had these special amenities were charged more than the other rooms. In 1972, the first models of telephone systems were introduced to the guestroom. In those days, there was only one telephone line for the entire hotel; therefore, guests sometimes waited long hours before they could place a call. In 1975, after color TV was well established in homes, hotels started to offer it. In the beginning, some hotels advertised that they had color TV to differentiate themselves from the competition and charged extra for rooms with TV. In 1980, the Hotel Billing Information System (HOBIS) was introduced. In 1981, it became legal for hotels to profit from phone calls. This is when call accounting systems exploded in the hotel industry. In 1986, electronic door-keys were introduced, increasing the security and the convenience of guests. Interface between TV systems and property management systems were established in 1990 so that the guests could see their bills through the TV. With that

Here you'll learn about the wide variety of technological processes, systems, and products used within the hospitality industry.

Timelines

Trends

Trends in Hotel and Rooms Division Operations

Courtesy of Dr. Greg Dunn, Senior Lecturer & Managing Director, University of Florida, Eric Friedheim Tourism Institute.

- *Diversity of work force.* All the pundits are projecting a substantial increase in the number of women and minorities who will not only be taking hourly paid positions, but also supervising and management positions as well.

- *Increase in use of technology.* Reservations are being made by individuals over the Internet. Travel agents are able to make reservations at more properties. There is increasing simplification of the various PMSs and their interface with POS systems. In the guest room, increasing demand for high-speed Internet access, category 5 cables, and in some cases equipment itself is anticipated.

- *Continued quest for increases in productivity.* As pressure mounts from owners and mana...   ...s, hotel mana...   ...looking f...

Dr. Greg Dunn has revised and updated the Trends section in each chapter to give you an up-to-date and realistic picture of factors currently shaping the future of that segment of the industry.

Hone Your Critical Thinking Skills

Case Studies

CASE STUDY

Overbooked: The Housekeeping Perspective

It is no secret that in all hotels the director of housekeeping must be able to react quickly and efficiently to any unexpected circumstances that arise. Stephen Rodondi, executive housekeeper at the Hyatt Regency La Jolla usually starts his workday at 8:00 A.M. with a department meeting. These morning meetings help him and the employees to visualize their goals for the day. On this particularly busy day, Rodondi arrives at work and is told that three housekeepers have called in sick. This is a serious challenge for the hotel because it is overbooked and has all its 400 rooms to service.

Discussion Question

1. What should Stephen do to maintain standards and ensure that all the guest rooms are serviced?

In this edition, you will find a new case study written for each chapter—all based on industry scenarios. You will be challenged to test your skills and knowledge as you address and recommend appropriate actions in each situation.

Internet Exercises

Internet Exercises

1. Organization: **Hyatt Hotels Corporation**
   Summary: Hyatt Hotels Corporation is a multibillion-dollar hotel management company. Together with Hyatt International, the company has about eight percent of the hotel industry market share. Hyatt is recognized for its decentralized management approach, in which general managers are given a great deal of the management decision-making process.
   Click the "About Hyatt" tab, and click "Careers" under the "For Job Seekers" section. Click on "University Recruiting," and then click on "Mgmt Training Program" to learn
   ~~~ this program ~~~

   (a) What is Hyatt's management training program?
   (b) What requisites must applicants meet to qualify for Hyatt's management training program?

2. Organization: **Hoteljobs.com**
   Summary: Hoteljobs.com is a Web site that offers information to recruiters, employers, and job seekers in the hospitality industry.
   (a) What different jobs are being offered under "Job Search," and which one, if any, interests you?
   (b) Post your résumé online.

Surf the Internet to uncover answers to specific hospitality questions. The Internet Exercises challenge you to learn more and prepare you for a career in this fascinating industry.

Apply Your Knowledge

> ### Apply Your Knowledge
>
> 1. If you were on the executive committee of a hotel, what kinds of things would you be doing to ensure the success of the hotel?
>
> 2. Your hotel has 275 rooms. Last night, 198 were occupied. What was the occupancy percentage?

Apply the knowledge and skills learned in each chapter to real-life industry topics.

Important Memory Tools

Learning Objectives

> ### CHAPTER 3
>
> # Rooms Division
>
> **LEARNING OBJECTIVES**
>
> After reading and studying this chapter, you should be able to:
>
> • Outline the duties and responsibilities of key executives and department heads.
>
> • Draw an organizational chart of the rooms division of a hotel and identify the executive committee members.
>
> • Describe the main functions of the rooms division departments.
>
> • D_____ management ___ ___ disc__

> **LEARNING OBJECTIVE 1**
> Describe a restaurant's front of the house.
>
> ## Front of the House
>
> Restaurant operations are generally divided between what is commonly called **front of the house** and **back of the house**. The front of the house includes anyone with guest contact, from the hostess to the busser. The sample organization chart in Figure 7–1 shows the differences between the front- and back-of-the-house areas.
>
> The restaurant is run by the general manager, or restaurant manager. Depending on the size and sales volume of the restaurant, there may be more managers with special responsibilities, such as kitchen manager, bar manager, and dining room manager. These managers are usually cross-trained to relieve each other.
>
> In the front of the house, restaurant operation begins with creating and maintaining what is called **curbside appeal**, or keeping the restaurant looking attractive and welcoming. Ray Kroc of McDonald's once spent a couple of hours in a good suit with one of his restaurant managers cleaning up the parking lot of one of his restaurants. Word soon got around to the other stores that management *begins* in the parking lot and *ends* in the bathrooms. Most restaur_____ _____ have checklists that each m_____ager uses. In the f___

Helping students keep track *of* and focus *on* the essential information they must take away from each chapter is an essential pedagogical tool. In this edition, a bulleted list of Objectives is featured on the opening page of each chapter, thus providing a "heads up" with regard to chapter coverage and organization; however, in this new edition, you also will be reminded of the relevant objective to be covered in each major section by a *numbered* Learning Objective to help you focus and organize your thoughts as you read through the chapter. Ultimately this feature provides a map of what you need to know after studying the chapter and doing the exercises, case questions, and Apply Your Knowledge questions.

Check Your Knowledge

▶ **Check Your Knowledge**

1. What is the role of the general manager?
2. What topics do the members of an executive committee usually address in their weekly meetings?

Every few pages, the Check Your Knowledge section helps you review and reinforce the material that has just been covered.

Chapter Summary

The chapter summary highlights the most important points in the chapter. It provides a brief review of the chapter and reinforces the main terms, concepts, and topics.

Key Words and Concepts

Highlighted in bold with easy-to-understand definitions in the Glossary, the key words and concepts help you recall the importance of and meaning of these important terms. Master the key words and concepts of the text and improve your test scores.

Review Questions

By answering these review questions, you will reinforce your mastery of the materials presented in the text and most likely improve your test scores.

Visuals

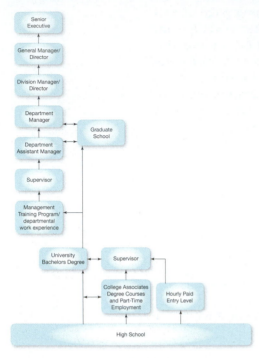

Figure 1–1 • A Possible Career Path in the Hospitality Industry. Is Education Worth It? You Bet! Just Think—Over a Career, the Difference in Salary between an Associate and a Bachelor's Degree is $500,000. Yes, That's Half a Million Bucks!

(*Source:* U.S. Census Bureau Average Lifetime Earnings— Different Levels of Education.)

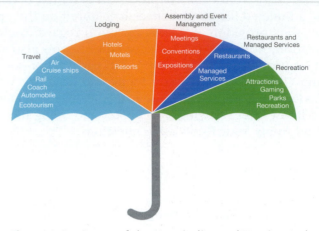

Figure 1–2 • Scope of the Hospitality and Tourism Industries.

Figure 1–3 • The Interrelated Nature of Hospitality, Travel, and Tourism.

The interrelated nature of hospitality and tourism means that we could fly here, stay in a hotel, and eat in a restaurant.

Color format with lively photographs, drawings, and tables maintain your interest and provide visual aids to learning.

Additional Student Resources

MyHospitalityLab, www.myhospitalitylab.com

This online course has been designed specifically to help you review, reinforce, and apply the concepts presented in the book. This interactive site features chapter-specific study modules, case studies with questions, interactive activities, and lecture note PowerPoint slides.

Message from John Walker

It is our goal to help you succeed in your career. If you have any suggestions for improving upon the material in the book or in MyHospitalityLab, or additional information you would like to see, e-mail me at *jwalker@sar.usf .edu* or *johnniewalkergold@hotmail.com*.

ACKNOWLEDGMENTS

Thanks to the students and professors, especially those who have made valuable contributions to this edition, and to the industry professionals who contributed to this text. Special thanks to Dr. Greg Dunn for adding his trends insights to this edition; James McManemon, MS, who contributed most of the How To features; Nicholas Thomas, who contributed an update to the gaming entertainment chapter and a How To feature for it. To my Program Manager Susan Watkins, I am deeply grateful for all your hard work and dedication to this project.

Thanks to all of my CHRIE colleagues, many of whom encouraged me to undertake this project and made valuable suggestions. I would like to thank the following contributing authors, who graciously allowed their materials and expertise to be included in this edition: James McManemon, William B. Martin, Ryan Lashway, Greg Dunn, Joseph Moreta, Chad Gruhl, Valerie Ferguson, Jason Samson, Charlie Adams, Jay Schrock, Denny Bhakta, George Goldhoff, Jose Martinez, Catherine Rabb, Rob Westfall, Richard Melman, Jim Inglis, Chris Marrero, Sarah Stegner, John Self, Tim Brady, Chris Della-Cruz, Steve Dobrowolski, Reg Washington, Allie Hire, Fred DeMicco, JT Watters, Patti Roscoe, Ann-Marie Weldon, Ed Shaughnessy, Bart Bartlett, Margie Martin, Nicholas Thomas, David Schwartz, Stephen Wynn, Jill Moran, Alexandra Stout, Amanda Alexander, Suzanne Bailey, Tina Stoughton, Horst Schulze, Bill Fisher, Stephanie Summerall, Jessica Leibovich, Tim Mulligan, Andrea Kazanjian, Patricia Engfer, Patricia Tam, Suzanne Seder, Cherry Cerminara, Michael Thorpe, and Kay Ueno.

I am indebted to the following reviewers, who provided constructive comments and suggestions during the development of the fifth edition: Janeen Hill, California State University, East Bay; Woody Kim, Florida State University; Michael Oshins, Boston University; Heidi Sung, St. John's University; Baker Ayoun, Auburn University; Joseph Lema, The Richard Stockton College of New Jersey; Lori Pennington, University of Florida; Donna Yancey, University of North Alabama; and Alvin Hung-Chih Yu, St. Cloud State University.

Sincere thanks to the following friends and colleagues who helped with advice and contributions: Bart Bartlett, Michael Brizek, David De Salvo, Stephen Deucker, Ben Dewald, Charlotte Jordan, John Lee, Edward O'Schaughnessy, Mary Jo Ross, Eva Smith, and Karl Titz. Gary Ward, thank you for your work on the Instructor's Manual, PowerPoints, and the TestGen. It was a pleasure working with you.

ABOUT THE AUTHOR

Dr. John R. Walker, DBA, FMP, CHA, is the McKibbon Professor of Hotel and Restaurant Management at the University of South Florida and a Fulbright Senior Specialist. John's years of industry experience began with management training at the Savoy Hotel London. This was followed by terms as food and beverage manager, assistant rooms division manager, catering manager, and general manager with Grand Metropolitan Hotels, Selsdon Park Hotel, Rank Hotels, Inter-Continental Hotels, and the Coral Reef Resort, Barbados, West Indies.

John has taught at two- and four-year schools in Canada and the United States. In addition to being a hospitality management consultant and text author, he has been published in *The Cornell Hotel Restaurant Administration Quarterly*, *The Hospitality Educators Journal*, and the *New York Times*. He is a 10-time recipient of the President's Award for teaching, scholarship, and service, and he has received the Patnubay Award for exemplary professional performance through teaching and authorship of tourism and hospitality publications.

John is an editorial advisory board member for Progress in Tourism and Hospitality Research. He is a past president of the Pacific Chapter of the Council on Hotel, Restaurant, and Institutional Education (CHRIE). He is a certified hotel administrator (CHA) and a certified foodservice management professional (FMP).

John is married to Josielyn T. Walker, and they have twins, Christopher and Selina. The Walkers live in Sarasota, Florida.

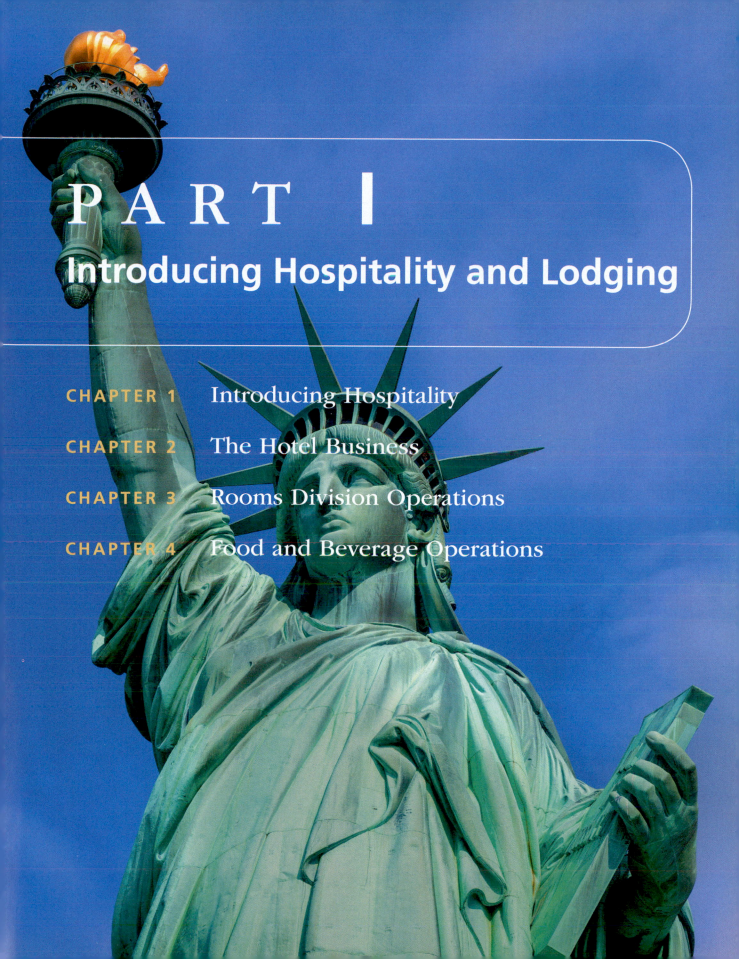

PART I
Introducing Hospitality and Lodging

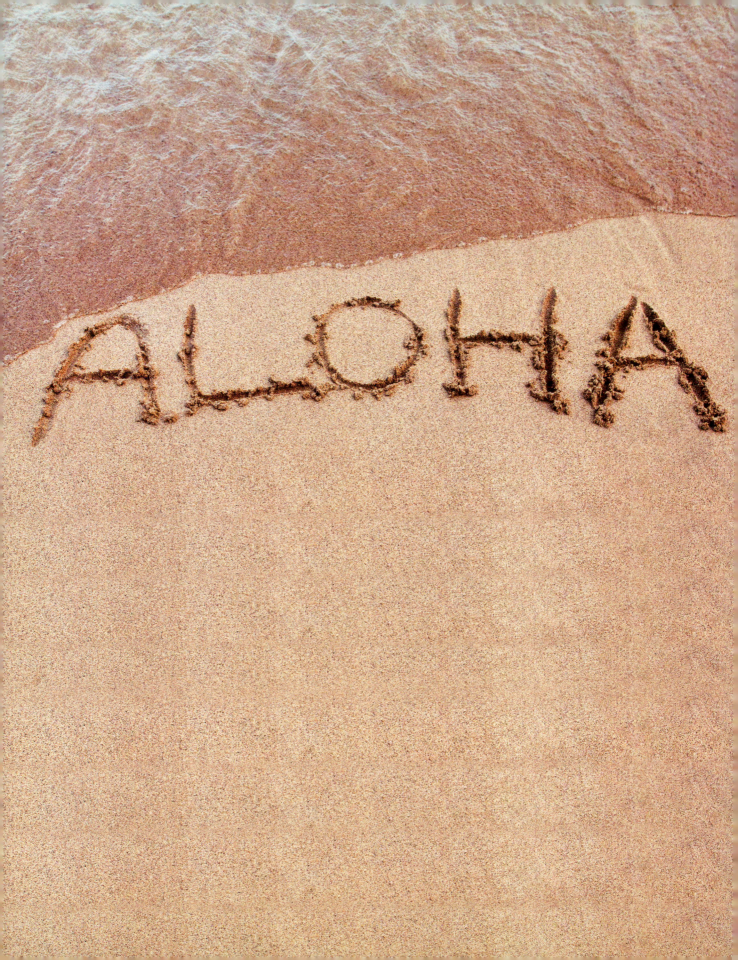

CHAPTER 1

Introducing Hospitality

LEARNING OBJECTIVES

After reading and studying this chapter, you should be able to:

- Discuss the history of hospitality through the ages.

- Describe the characteristics of the hospitality industry.

- Explain corporate philosophy and Total Quality Management.

- Discuss the many facets of service and why it has become such an important part of the hospitality industry.

- Suggest ways to improve service.

- Discuss current trends in the hospitality industry.

Prelude

Interested in a six-figure income? Read on, this book and the hospitality industries can take you there. We begin with a brief overview of how we got to where we are today.

Hospitality through the Ages[1]

The concept of hospitality is as old as civilization itself. Its development from the ancient custom of breaking bread with a passing stranger to the operations of today's multifaceted hospitality conglomerates makes fascinating reading, and interesting comparisons can be made with today's hospitality management.

The word **hospitality** comes from *hospice*, an old French word meaning "to provide care/shelter for travelers." The most famous hospice is the Hospice de Beaune in the Burgundy region of France, also called the Hotel Dieu or the House of God. It was founded as a charity hospital in 1443 by Nicolas Rolin, the Chancellor of Burgundy, as a refuge for the poor.

The hospital is still functioning, partly because of its role in the wine world. Throughout the centuries, several Burgundian landowners have donated vineyards to the Hospice to help pay for maintaining its costs. Every fall, the wines from these vineyards—about a hundred acres of vines—are sold at a colorful wine auction on the third Thursday in November, which determines the prices for the next year's Burgundy wines.

Ancient Times

The Sumerians (who lived in what is now Iraq) were the first to record elements of hospitality in about 4,500 years Before the Common Era (B.C.E.). They moved from being hunter-gatherers to growing crops, which, due to surpluses, they were able to trade. More time became available for other activities such as writing, inventing money, creating pottery, making tools, and producing beer, which was probably safer to drink than water! Taverns served several beers, and as with today, provided a place for locals to relax and enjoy each other's company.

Between 4000 and 2000 B.C.E., early civilizations in Europe, China, Egypt, and India all had some elements of hospitality offerings, such as taverns and inns along the roadside.

Famous "Hospices de Beaune" in Burgundy, France.

Greece and Rome

Mention of hospitality—in the form of taverns—is found in writings dating back to ancient Greece and Rome, beginning with the Code of Hammurabi (circa 1700 B.C.E.). The Code required owners to report guests who planned crimes in their taverns. The penalty for not doing so was death, making tavern-keeping a hazardous occupation. The death penalty could also be imposed for watering the beer!

Increased travel and trade made some form of overnight accommodations an absolute necessity. Because travel was slow and journeys long and arduous, many travelers depended solely on the hospitality of private citizens.[2] In the Greek and Roman empires, inns and taverns sprang up everywhere. The

The Beautiful Pavilion in Black Dragon Pool Park, Lijiang, Yunnan Province China.

Romans constructed elaborate and well-appointed inns on all the main roads. They were located about 25 miles apart. To ensure that fresh horses were available for officials and couriers of the Roman government, these inns could only be used with special government documents granting permission. By the time Marco Polo traveled to the Far East, there were 10,000 inns, the best of which were in China.[3]

Some wealthy landowners built their own inns on the edges of their estates. These inns were run by household slaves. Nearer the cities, inns and taverns were run by freemen or by retired gladiators who would invest their savings in the "restaurant business" in the same way that so many of today's retired athletes open restaurants. The first "business lunch" is reputed to have been the idea of Seqius Locates, a Roman innkeeper; in 40 B.C.E. Locates devised the idea for ships' brokers, who were often too busy to go home for their midday meals.

Medieval Times

On the European continent, Charlemagne established rest houses for pilgrims in the eighth century; the sole purpose of several orders of knighthood was to protect pilgrims and to provide hospitality for pilgrims on their routes. One such rest house, an abbey at Roncesvalles, advertised services such as a warm welcome at the door, free bread, a barber and a cobbler, cellars full of fruit and almonds, two hospices with beds for the sick, and even a consecrated burial ground.

In 1282, the innkeepers of Florence, Italy, incorporated a guild, or an association, for the purpose of business. The inns belonged to the city, which sold three-year leases at auction. They must have been profitable, because by 1290, there were 86 innkeepers as members of the guild.

In England, the stagecoach became the favored method of transportation. A journey from London to the city of Bath took three days, with several stopovers at inns or taverns that were also called post houses. Today, the journey from London to Bath takes about one and a half hours by car or train. As travel and travelers increased during the Middle Ages, so did the number of wayside inns in Europe; yet, they were primitive affairs by today's standards. Guests often slept on mattresses in what today would be the inn's lobby. As the quality of the inns improved, more people began to travel. Many of the travelers were wealthy people, accustomed to the good life; their expectations demanded that inns be upgraded.

In the late sixteenth century, a type of eating place for commoners called an *ordinary* began to appear in England. These places were taverns serving a fixed-price, fixed-menu meal at a long common table. "Ordinary" diners could not be choosy, nor did they often question what they were eating. Frequently, the main dish served was a long-cooked, highly seasoned meat-and-vegetable stew. Culinary expertise was limited by the availability and cost of certain ingredients. Few diners had sound teeth—many had no teeth at all—so the meal had to be able to be gummed as well as being edible. Fresh meat was not always available; spoiled meat was often the rule rather than the exception. Spices helped not only to preserve meat but also to disguise the flavor of gamey or "high" meat.

Coffee Houses

During the sixteenth century, two "exotic" imports began to influence the culinary habits of Western Europe: coffee and tea. These beverages, so integrated into the twenty-first century way of life, were once mere curiosities. Travelers to Constantinople (now Istanbul, Turkey) enjoyed coffee there and brought it back to Europe.

During the seventeenth century, coffeehouses sprang up all over Europe. By 1675, the city-state of Venice had dozens of coffee houses, including the famous Café Florian on the Piazza San Marco, still filled to capacity today. The first English coffee house was opened in 1652. Coffee houses, the social and literary centers of their day and the predecessor of today's cafés and coffee shops, served another, even more useful (though less obvious), purpose: They helped to sober up an entire continent.

In a day when water was vile, milk dangerous, and carbonated beverages centuries in the future, alcoholic drinks were the rule, rather than the exception. Adults drank amounts measured in gallons. Queen Elizabeth I's ladies-in-waiting, for instance, were allowed a breakfast allowance of two gallons of ale. Drunkenness was rampant.

Café Florian, St. Mark's Square, Venice, Italy.

The New World

There is some evidence that a tavern was built in Jamestown, Virginia, during the early days of the settlement. It was in Boston where the first "ordinary" was recorded—Cole's Ordinary—in 1663. After Cole's, the next recorded "ordinary" was Hudson's House, in 1640.[4] The Dutch built the first known tavern in New York—the Stadt Huys—in 1642. Early colonial American inns and taverns are steeped as much in history as they are in hospitality. The next year, Kreiger's Tavern opened on Bowling Green in New York City. During the American Revolution, this tavern, then called the King's Arms, became the Revolutionary headquarters of British General Gage.

The even more famous Frauncis Tavern was the Revolutionary headquarters of General George Washington and was the place where he made his famous Farewell Address. It is still operating today. As the colonies grew from scattered settlements to towns and cities, more and more travelers appeared, along with more accommodations to serve them. The inn, tavern, or "ordinary" in the colonies soon became a gathering place for residents, a place where they could catch up on the latest gossip, keep up with current events, hold meetings, and conduct business. The innkeeper was often the most respected member of the community and was always one of its more substantial citizens. The innkeeper usually held some local elected office and sometimes rose much higher than that. John Adams, the second president of the United States, owned and managed his own tavern between 1783 and 1789.

The Revolutionary War did little to change the character of these public places. They maintained their position as social centers, political gathering places, newsrooms, watering holes, and travelers' rests; now, however, these places were going by different names—hotels—that reflected a growing French influence in the new nation.

The French Revolution

The French Revolution took place at approximately the same time as the American colonies were fighting for their independence. Among many other effects, the French Revolution helped to change the course of culinary history. M. Boulanger, "the father of the modern restaurant," sold soups at his all-night tavern on the Rue Bailleul. He called these soups *restorantes* (restoratives), which is the origin of the word *restaurant*. One dish was made of sheep's feet in a white sauce, another was *boulangere* potatoes—a dish in use today—made of sliced potatoes cooked in stock, which was baked in the bread baker's oven after the bread was done.[5]

The French Revolution, 1789–1799, changed the course of culinary history. Because nearly all the best chefs worked for the nobility, who were deposed or literally "lost their heads," the chefs lost their employment. Many chefs immigrated to America, especially to New Orleans, a French enclave in America. Others scattered throughout Europe or immigrated to Quebec, a French-speaking province of Canada. The chefs brought their culinary

The Court of the Two Sisters, New Orleans, Louisiana.

traditions with them. Soon the plain, hearty fare of the British and the primitive cooking of the Americans were laced with *sauces piquantes* (sauces having a pleasantly sharp taste or appetizing flavor) and *pots au feu* (French beef stew). In 1784, during a five-year period as an envoy to France, Thomas Jefferson acquired a taste for French cuisine. He later persuaded a French chef to come to the White House to lend his expertise. This act stimulated interest in French cuisine and enticed U.S. tavern owners to offer better quality and more interesting food.

Over time, New Orleans was occupied by Britain, Spain, France, and America, and one interesting restaurant there, the Court of the Two Sisters, has the names of prisoners of various wars inscribed on the walls of its entrance.

The Nineteenth Century

Restaurants continued to flourish in Europe. In 1856, Antoine Carême published *La Cuisine Classique* and other volumes detailing numerous dishes and their sauces. The grande cuisine offered a carte (or list) of suggestions available from the kitchen. This was the beginning of the à la carte menu. In 1898, the Savoy Hotel opened in London. The general manager was the renowned César Ritz (today, the Ritz-Carlton hotels bear his name) and the chef de cuisine was August Escoffier. Between them, they revolutionized hotel restaurants. Escoffier was one of the greatest chefs of all time. He is best known for his classic book *Le Guide Culinaire*, which simplified the extraordinary works of Carême. He also installed the brigade de cuisine system in the kitchen.

Americans used their special brand of ingenuity to create something for everyone. By 1848, a hierarchy of eating places existed in New York City. At the bottom was Sweeney's "sixpenny eating house" on Ann Street, whose proprietor, Daniel Sweeney, achieved questionable fame as the father of the "greasy spoon." Sweeney's less than appetizing fare ("small plate sixpence, large plate shilling") was literally slid down a well-greased counter to his hungry guests, who cared little for the social amenities of dining.

The famous Delmonico's was at the top of the list of American restaurants for a long time. The Delmonico family owned and operated the restaurant from 1827 until 1923, when it closed due to Prohibition. The name *Delmonico's* was synonymous with fine food, exquisitely prepared and impeccably served—the criteria by which all like establishments were judged. Delmonico's served Swiss-French cuisine and became the focal point of American gastronomy (the art of good eating). Delmonico's is also credited with the invention of the bilingual menu, Baked Alaska, Chicken à la King, and Lobster Newburg. The Delmonico steak is named after the restaurant. More and more, eating places in the United States and abroad catered to residents of a town or city and less to travelers; the custom of eating out for its own sake had arrived.

Thirty-five restaurants in New York City have now celebrated their one-hundredth birthdays. One of them, P. J. Clarke's, established in 1884, is a restaurant-bar that has changed little in its hundred years of operation. On entering, one sees a large mahogany bar, its mirror tarnished by time, the original tin ceiling, and the tile mosaic floor. Memorabilia ranges from celebrity pictures to Jessie, the house fox terrier that customers had stuffed when she died, who now stands guard over the ladies' room door. Guests still write down their own checks at lunchtime, on pads with their table numbers on them (this goes back to the days when one of the servers could not read or write and struggled to remember orders).[6]

Many American cities had hotel palaces: Chicago had the Palmer House, New Orleans had the St. Charles, St. Louis had the Planter's Hotel, Boston had The Lenox, and San Antonio had The Menger. As the railroads were able to transport passengers to exotic locations like South Florida, hotels such as The Breakers in Palm Beach were built to accommodate the guests.

P. J. Clarke's, in New York City, established in 1884 and still going strong.

The Twentieth Century

In 1921, Walter Anderson and Billy Ingraham began the White Castle hamburger chain. The name White Castle was selected because "white" stood for purity and "castle" for strength. These eye-catching restaurants were nothing more than stucco building shells, a griddle, and a few chairs. People came in droves, and within 10 years, White Castle had expanded to 115 units.[7]

The Four Seasons restaurant opened in 1959 as the first elegant American restaurant that was not French in style. The Four Seasons was the first restaurant to offer seasonal menus. With its modern architecture and art as a theme, Joe Baum, the developer of this and many other successful restaurants, understood why people go to restaurants—to be together and to connect to one another. It is very important that the restaurant reinforce why guests chose it in the first place. Restaurants exist to create pleasure, and how well a restaurant meets this expectation of pleasure is a measure of its success.[8]

Following World War II, North America took to the road. There was a rapid development of hotels, motels, fast food, and coffee shops. The 1950s and 1960s also saw an incredible growth in air transportation. Cross-continental flights were not only more frequent, but took much less time. Many of the new jets introduced in this period helped develop tourism worldwide.

The Breakers, Palm Beach, Florida, a legendary resort destination built by Standard Oil Company magnate Henry Flagler and family who developed railroads to the east coast of Florida.

Hotels and restaurant chains sprang up to cater to the needs of the business and leisure traveler as well as city residents.

In the 1980s, hospitality, travel, and tourism continued to increase dramatically. The baby boomers began to exert influence through their buying power. Distant exotic destinations and resorts became even more accessible. The 1990s began with the recession that had started in 1989. The Gulf War continued the downturn that the industry had experienced. As hospitality and tourism companies strived for profitability, they downsized and consolidated. From 1993 until 9/11, the economic recovery proved very strong and hospitality businesses expanded in North America and abroad, particularly in Europe and China.

The Twenty-First Century

In the twenty-first century, we have already had 9/11, war, epidemics, and a great recession—all in just a few years. As we emerge from the recession, the hospitality industry continues to mature with increased market segmentation and consolidation. Companies are increasing their focus on security, health, sustainability, and lifestyles. More people are traveling, especially from and to China, Brazil, and India. Technology will improve the facilitation of guests' needs and "Big Data" will prove a challenge. The recession slowed the industry, but as we emerge from it occupancies are up along with revenue per available room. Now companies are driving the margins to squeeze out a reasonable profit.

Welcome to You, the Future Hospitality Industry Leaders!

The hospitality industry is a fascinating, fun, and stimulating one in which to enjoy a career, plus you get compensated quite well and have excellent advancement opportunities. We often hear from industry professionals that it (the industry) gets in your blood—meaning we become one with the hospitality industry. On countless class industry visits, the persons speaking to the class said that they wouldn't change their job—even if they had a chance.

Only one speaker said, "You must be nuts if you want to work in this industry"—of course, he was joking! But there are some realities you need to be aware of, and they are discussed in the section titled, "Characteristics of the Hospitality Industry," found later in this chapter. Many examples exist of people graduating and being offered positions that enable them to gain a good foundation of knowledge and experience in the industry. Possible career paths are illustrated in Figure 1–1. In most cases, it does not take long for advancement opportunities to come along. Let's begin our journey with a look at *service spirit*, which plays a crucial role in the success of our industry, no matter what your position or title.

HOW TO GET A STEP AHEAD IN THE INDUSTRY

Courtesy of **James McManemon**, M.S., University of South Florida Sarosta—Manatee

Josh Medina, who recently earned his degree in hospitality management at the University of South Florida, recognized at the outset that for the majority of department management positions prior experience working in lower-level and/or supervisory positions is necessary, while moving into upper-management positions beyond, would require both experience in lower-level positions, plus an undergraduate and/or graduate degree (a business-related or hospitality degree is ideal) as well. Josh's choice was to study hospitality management as an undergraduate, and work nights as a server/bartender at a fine-dining restaurant. After a single year at this night job, Josh was promoted to head-server, which allowed him to train new servers, expedite food, assist with making schedules, and manage payroll. Upon graduation, Hyatt Regency in Sarasota, Florida, hired him as assistant restaurant manager. Though Josh had no prior experience as a restaurant manager, his experience working as a head-server and bartender, combined with his educational knowledge of management, gave him the necessary tools to get a step ahead in his career immediately after graduating. Next for Josh, who has ambitions of hotel manager, regional vice president, or any position that requires significant strategic management, long-term planning, and top-notch leadership/management skills, is a post-graduate degree in a business-related or hospitality field. Josh remarks, "It may take longer than two years since I am going to school part time, while working full time, but it will be worth it in the long run."

Ever think about why Marriott International is so successful? Well, one of the reasons is given by Jim Collins writing in the foreword of Bill Marriott's book, *The Spirit to Serve: Marriott's Way*. Collins says Marriott has *timeless core values and enduring purpose*, including the belief that its people are number one: "Take care of Marriott people and they will take care of the guests." Also, Marriott's commitment to continuous improvement and good old-fashioned dedication to hard work, and having fun while doing it, provide a foundation of stability and enduring character. Collins adds that Marriott's core purpose—making people away from home feel that they are among friends and are really wanted—serves as a fixed point of guidance and inspiration.

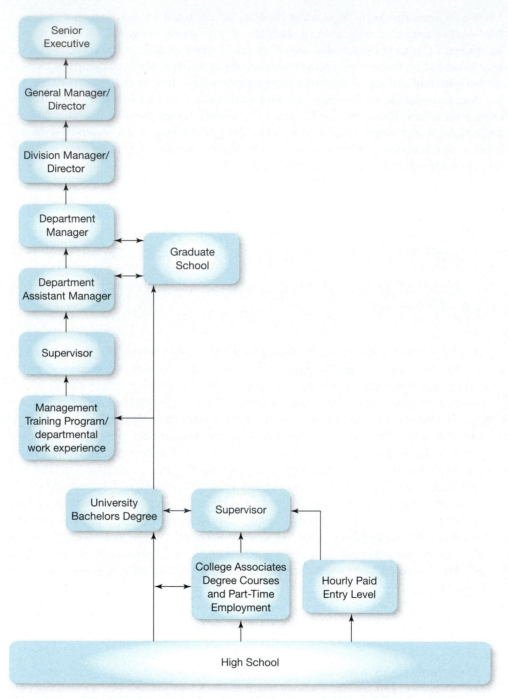

Figure 1–1 • A Possible Career Path in the Hospitality Industry. Is Education Worth It? You Bet! Just Think—Over a Career, the Difference in Salary between an Associate and a Bachelor's Degree is $500,000. Yes, That's Half a Million Bucks!

(*Source:* U.S. Census Bureau Average Lifetime Earnings—Different Levels of Education.)

So, where does *hospitality spirit* fit into all this? It's simple—it begins with each and every time we have a guest encounter. People with a *service spirit* are happy to do something extra to make a guest's experience memorable. The hospitality spirit means that it is our passion to give pleasure to others, or as one human resources director, Charlotte Jordan, calls it, "creating memorable experiences for others and being an ambassador of the world, adding warmth and caring."[9] Every day we encounter guests who rely on us for service, which can make or break their experience. We want to "wow" guests and have them return often with their friends. Yes, we are in the people business, and it's "we the people" who succeed in the hospitality industry when we take pride. In the words of the Ritz-Carlton hotel company: We are ladies and gentlemen taking care of ladies and gentlemen.

The **National Restaurant Association (NRA)** forecasts a need for thousands of supervisors and managers for the hospitality and tourism industries. Are you wondering if there's room in this dynamic industry for you? You bet! There's room for everyone. The best advice is to consider what you love to do most and get some experience in that area—to see if you really like it—because our industry has some distinct characteristics. For starters, we are in the business of giving service. When Kurt Wachtveilt, 30-year veteran former general manager of the Oriental Hotel in Bangkok, Thailand—considered by many to be one of the best hotels in the world—was asked, "What is the secret of being the best?" he replied, "Service, service, service!" To serve is to "provide goods and services for" and "be of assistance to." With thousands of guest encounters each day, it is critical to give our guests exceptional service at each encounter. And that's the challenge!

The hospitality industry can also be a good choice for entrepreneurs who prefer to do their own thing, whether it be running a bar, catering company, restaurant, or night club; being involved in event management; or being a tour guide or wedding planner or whatever. The prospects are good for starting a successful endeavor. Think about it: You could begin with one restaurant concept, open a second, and then begin to franchise. Whatever your dreams and goals, the hospitality industry likely has an opportunity for you.

Consider that a company like Marriott International started out as a small root beer place, in Washington, D.C., with a counter and a few stools. And that an immigrant, who opened up a hot dog stand outside Dodger Stadium in Los Angeles later became the multimillionaire owner of a chain restaurant (Karl Kartcher, owner of Carl's Jr.). And that a former dishwasher, Ralph Rubio, now owns the successful chain of Rubio's Fresh Mexican Grill quick-service restaurants, which have sold more than 50 million fish tacos since the opening of the first restaurant in 1983. Then there is Peter Morton, who, in the early 1970s, lived in London, and, missing American food, borrowed $60,000 from family and friends to open the Great American Disaster. It was an immediate success, with a line of customers around the block. Morton quickly realized that London needed a restaurant that not only served American food but also embodied the energy and excitement of music past and present. He opened the Hard Rock Cafe and offered a hearty American meal at a reasonable price in an atmosphere charged with

The pineapple is the symbol of hospitality.

energy, fun, and the excitement of rock and roll.[10] More recently, Howard Schultz, who while in Italy in the early 1980s was impressed with the popularity of espresso bars in Milan, saw the potential to develop the coffee bar culture in the United States and beyond. There are now more than 18,000 Starbucks locations.[11] Any ideas on what the next hot entrepreneurial idea will be?

The Pineapple Tradition

The pineapple has enjoyed a rich and romantic heritage as a symbol of welcome, friendship, and hospitality. Pineapples were brought back from the West Indies by early European explorers during the seventeenth century. From that time on, the pineapple was cultivated in Europe and became the favored fruit to serve to royalty and the elite. The pineapple was later introduced into North America and became a part of North American hospitality as well. Pineapples were displayed at doors or on gateposts, announcing to friends and acquaintances: "The ship is in! Come join us. Food and drink for all!"

Since its introduction, the pineapple has been internationally recognized as a symbol of hospitality and a sign of friendliness, warmth, cheer, graciousness, and conviviality.

The Interrelated Nature of Hospitality and Tourism

The hospitality and **tourism** industry is the largest and fastest-growing industry groupings in the world. In fact, the U.S. Bureau of Labor Statistics estimates that there are approximately 14 million people working in the leisure and hospitality industry.[12] One of the most exciting aspects of this industry is that it is made up of so many different professions. What picture comes to mind when you think about a career in hospitality and tourism? Do you picture a chef, a general manager, owners of their own businesses, a director of marketing, or an event manager? The possibilities are many and varied, ranging from positions in restaurants, resorts, air and cruise lines, theme parks, attractions, and casinos, to name a few of the several sectors of the hospitality and tourism industries (see Figures 1–2 and 1–3).

James Reid, a professor at New York City Technical College, contributed his thoughts to this section. As diverse as the hospitality industry is, there are some powerful and common dynamics, which include the delivery of services and products and the guests' impressions of them. Whether an employee is in direct contact with a guest (**front of the house**) or performing duties behind the scenes (**heart of the house**), the profound and most challenging reality of working in this industry is that hospitality employees have the ability to affect the human experience by creating powerful impressions—even

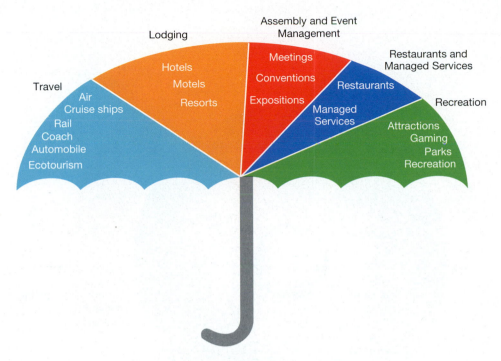

Figure 1–2 • Scope of the Hospitality and Tourism Industries.

brief moments of truth—that may last a lifetime. (A "moment of truth" is an industry expression used to describe a guest and an associate meeting, as when a guest walks into a hotel or restaurant.)

Imagine all the reasons why people leave their homes temporarily (whether alone or with others) to go to other places near and far.

People travel for many reasons. A trip away from home might be for vacation, for work, to attend a conference, or maybe even to visit a college campus, just to name a few. Regardless of the reason, under the umbrella of travel and tourism, many professions are necessary to meet the needs and wants of people away from home. Think of the many people who provide services to travelers and who have the responsibility of representing their communities and creating experiences that, when delivered successfully, are pleasurable and memorable for travelers. These people welcome, inform, comfort, and care for tourists and are collectively a part of a process that can positively affect human lives and well-being.

The hotel business provides career opportunities for many associates who help make reservations and greet, assist, and serve guests in hospitality operations of varied sizes and in locations all over the world. Examples include a husband and wife who operate their own bed and breakfast (B&B) in upstate Vermont. This couple provides the ideal weekend retreat for avid skiers during a frosty February, making their guests want to return year after year. Another example is the hundreds of employees necessary to keep the 5,505-room MGM Grand in full swing 365 days a year! Room attendants, engineers, front-desk agents, food servers, and managers are just a few of

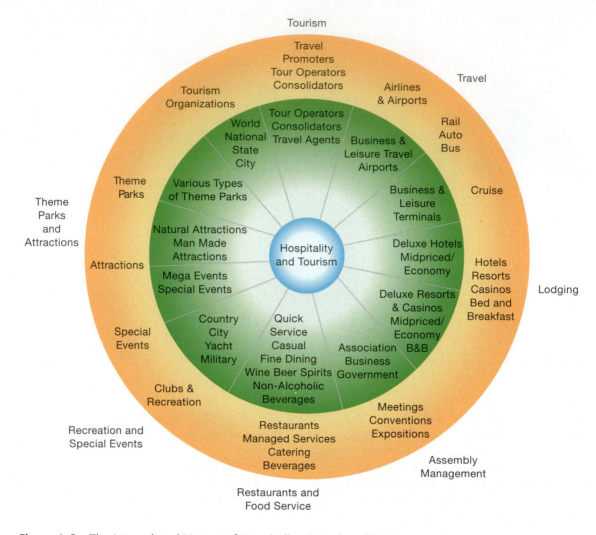

Figure 1–3 • The Interrelated Nature of Hospitality, Travel, and Tourism.

The interrelated nature of hospitality and tourism means that we could fly here, stay in a hotel, and eat in a restaurant.

the positions that are vital to creating experiences for visitors who come to Las Vegas from around the globe.

The restaurant business is also a vital component under the travel and tourism umbrella. People go to restaurants to fulfill diverse needs and wants. Eating is a biological need that restaurants accommodate, but restaurants and the people who work in them fulfill numerous other human desires, such as the need to socialize and to be entertained.

Gramercy Tavern restaurant in New York City may be the perfect location for a certain group of friends to celebrate a

21st birthday. The individual guest who turned 21 may remember this fête for a lifetime because the service and food quality were excellent and added value to the experiences for all the celebrants. For this kind of collective and powerful impression to be made, many key players are needed to operate and support the service-delivery system: several front-of-the-house staff members, such as the food servers, bartenders, greeters, managers, and bus attendants; plus the back-of-the-house employees, such as the chefs, dishwashers, food purchaser, and stewards (to name a few). All these people had to coordinate a

Gramercy Tavern, a Danny Meyer, Union Square Hospitality Group Restaurant.
(Photographer: Maura McEvoy)

variety of activities and responsibilities to create this dynamic, successful, and, for the restaurant ownership, profitable event.

In managed services, foodservices are provided for airlines, military facilities, schools, colleges and universities, health care operations, and business and industry. These foodservice operations have the dual challenge of meeting the needs and wants of both the guests and the client (i.e., the institution that hired the foodservices). The employees who are part of foodservices enterprises have responsibilities very much like those of other restaurant operations. The quality of food products delivered in an airline, for example, may be the key to winning passengers back in the future and creating positive word-of-mouth promotion that attracts new customers.

Since history has been recorded, beverages have provided a biological need that has expanded the beverage menu far beyond water alone! Whether it is the cool iced tea garnished with lemon and mint served poolside at a Riviera resort or the champagne toast offered at a 50th wedding anniversary party in Boston, beverages play a major role in satisfying people and adding to the many celebrations of life.

As with food products, the creation and delivery systems for beverage products are vital components of the hospitality industry. These operations involve many people who consumers rarely see: the farmer in Napa Valley who tends to the vineyard every day of the year, the coffee bean harvester in Colombia, the sake server in Tokyo, or the orchard owner who crates oranges in Florida. These individuals behind the scenes have diverse and crucial responsibilities so that guests, whether in a resort, an office, a hospital, a college, or a roadside snack bar, can have the quality of products they want.

TECHNOLOGY SPOTLIGHT

The Increasing Importance of Technology to the Hospitality Industry

Courtesy of **James McManemon**, M.S., University of South Florida Sarasota–Manatee

Think about the last travel reservation that you made—did you book your travel online? Did you check consumer reviews on the hotel or restaurant? Studies show that as many as 57 percent of consumers now use the Internet to book their travel, a percentage that vastly changes the landscape of the hospitality industry. In fact, technology could be the thin line between a successful business and bankruptcy for many organizations. In 2013, only four out of every 10 restaurants that open will still be operating in three years. One of the main reasons for the high failure rate is the lack of control in a slim profit-margin industry. With technology, hospitality and tourism businesses can attempt to control costs and generate success. Technology used to be accepted as a cost center by hospitality and tourism organizations. However, in today's world, technology is a strategic enabler. Technology has become such a vital tool that it is hard to imagine a hotel, resort, theme park, cruise ship, restaurant, or airline company running without it.

In each chapter of this book, we will try to show technology applications and uses for each different part of the hospitality and tourism business. Consider this: In a typical full-service hotel, there are about 65 different technology applications. This number is around 35 for a limited-service hotel. Hotels are finding new ways to use technology for a strategic advantage. Consider this example: Mandarin Oriental is keeping track of the fruits eaten by the guest. These records are kept in the guest's profile. Next time the guest visits the hotel, when a fruit basket is sent, it is dominated by the fruits that guest likes. This creates a "wow" factor since it is not directly solicited, but, rather, quietly observed and recorded with the help of proper training and technology.

Similarly, restaurants use more than 30 different technology applications to provide faster, more cost efficient and productive business operations for guests and staff. Airline companies use complex central reservation and yield-management tools. Travel agencies depend on global reservation system networks to operate. Cruise ships employ different technology and navigation systems to operate in an efficient and fast way. Theme parks use different biometric technologies to keep track of their guests and staff members.

The airline industry became a commodity a long time ago. In the contemporary age, travelers do not necessarily care about which carrier will take them from point A to point B. Price seems to be the most important factor in selecting an air carrier. The hotel industry is showing similar symptoms. In the age where hospitality and tourism products are becoming a commodity, technology is becoming a true differentiator. Hoteliers, as in the example of Mandarin Oriental, are turning to technology to differentiate themselves so that they do not become a commodity in the eyes of guests. Many studies already showed that high-speed Internet is one of the most important in-room amenities that enable guest satisfaction in a hotel. In this new age of technology, it is very important for hospitality and tourism students to understand all the different technology applications out there in order to compete in a tough market environment.

Characteristics of the Hospitality Industry

LEARNING OBJECTIVE 2
Describe the characteristics of the hospitality industry.

Hospitality businesses are open 365 days a year and 24 hours a day. No, we don't have to work every one of those 365 days, but we do tend to work longer hours than people in other industries. Those on their way to senior positions in the hospitality industry, and many others for that matter, often work 10 hours a day. However, because of managerial burnout, there is a trend in the industry of reducing working hours of managers to attract and retain members of Generation X and the Millennial Generation. Evenings and weekends are included in the workweek—so we have to accept that we may be working when others are enjoying leisure time.

The hospitality industry depends heavily on shift work. Early in your career, depending on the department, you will likely work on a particular shift. Basically, there are four shifts, beginning with the morning shift, so you may be getting up as early as 6:00 A.M. to get to the shift that starts at 7:00 A.M. The midshift is usually from 10:00 A.M. to 7:00 P.M.; the evening shift starts at 3:00 P.M. and goes on until 11:00 P.M.; and finally there is the night shift that begins at 11:00 P.M. and lasts until 7:30 A.M. Supervisors and managers often begin at 8:00 A.M. and work until 6:00 or 8:00 P.M. Success does not come easily.

In the hospitality industry, we constantly strive for outstanding **guest satisfaction**, which leads to guest loyalty and, yes, profit. Our services are mostly **intangible**, meaning the guest cannot "test drive" a night's stay or "taste the steak" before dining. Our product is for the guest's *use* only, not for possession. Even more unique, for us to produce our product—hospitality—we must get the guest's input. Imagine General Electric building a refrigerator with the customer in the factory, participating in the actual construction of the product! Seems preposterous, yet we do it every single day, numerous times per day, and in a uniquely different way each time. This is referred to as the **inseparability** of production and consumption of the service product, which presents a special challenge because each guest may have his or her own requests and in our business, we essentially produce and consume the hospitality product at the same time.

Another unique dimension of our industry is the **perishability** of our product. For example, we have 1,400 rooms in inventory—that is, available to sell—but we sell only 1,200 rooms. What are we to do with the 200 unsold rooms? Nothing. We have permanently lost the opportunity to sell those 200 room-nights and their revenue. As a hotelier, we can try and make up the lost room revenue in other ways, but the room inventory for sale has perished. The same goes for restaurant seats not filled during a shift, airline seats unsold on a flight that has departed, and cruise ship berths going empty as a ship sails to sea.

Related to the idea that the hospitality product is simultaneously produced and consumed, one other unique characteristic of the hospitality industry to consider is the **variability** inherent within those that produce and consume. For instance, on the production side of the equation, each employee has different levels of skill, knowledge, ability, and passion for what they do and therefore we often see variability in the quality of work. On the consumer side of the equation, each guest has different levels of experience, understanding, and expectations in what they are seeking to buy and therefore we often see variability in the ability and way that guests consume the hospitality product. The variability within employees and guests, combined with the fact that the hospitality product is highly perishable and simultaneously produced and consumed, makes for a more complex buyer–seller relationship than found in other industries. This example illustrates that in the hospitality industry, we are in business to make a **return on investment** for owners and/or shareholders and society. People invest money for us to run a business, and they expect a fair return on their investment. Now, the amount that constitutes a fair return can be debated and will depend on the individual business circumstances. The challenge increases when there is an economic downturn or, worse, a recession, such as we have recently experienced. Then, the struggle is to make more money than is spent, known as keeping one's head above water!

▶ Check Your Knowledge

1. Identify and explain two differences between the hospitality business and other business sectors.

2. List and describe the four shifts in the hospitality industry.

3. Identify some of the highlighted characteristics of the hospitality industry.

Each year, the NRA invites the best and brightest students from universities and colleges to participate in the annual restaurant show in Chicago. The highlight of the show is the "Salute to Excellence" day when students and faculty attend forums, workshops, and a gala award banquet with industry leaders. Coca-Cola and several other corporations involved in the industry sponsor the event.

During the day, students are invited to write their dreams on a large panel, which is later displayed for all to enjoy. So what are your dreams and goals? Take a moment to think about your personal dreams and goals. Keep them in mind and look back on them often. Be prepared to amend them as you develop your career.

Careers

There are hundreds of career options for you to consider, and it's fine if you are not yet sure which one is for you. In Figure 1–3 you saw the major hospitality industry segments: lodging, restaurants and foodservice, recreation and special events, assembly management, theme parks and attractions, travel, and tourism. For instance, lodging provides career opportunities for many associates who make reservations, greet, assist, and serve guests in hotels, resorts, and other lodging operations all over the world. Among the many examples are the operators of a B&B in upstate New York who cater to seasonal guests. Another example is the hundreds of employees necessary to keep the City Center in Las Vegas operational. Throughout the chapters of this text we will explore the important segments of the hospitality industry.

Figures 1–4, 1–5, and 1–6 show a career ladder for lodging management and food and beverage management and the rooms division in mid-sized and large hotels. Figure 1–7 shows a career ladder for restaurant management. Information relating to careers comes from the 2011 American Community Survey (ACS) released by the Census Bureau statistics of lifetime earnings, which indicates that high school graduates earn $1.4 million.[13] Associate degree holders earn more than $1.6 million, but less than both bachelor's degree holders who earn $2.1 million, and master's degree holders who earn over $2.5 million.[14] Figure 1–8 shows the income for different levels of education.

Speaking of salaries, not everyone follows these steps; some move from front-of-the-house positions to heart-of-the-house positions to "round out" their experiences. Figure 1–8 is a current salary guide for hospitality positions. Please note that these figures (2015) are a guide and may vary by company and location.

Figure 1–4 • Lodging Management Career Ladder.

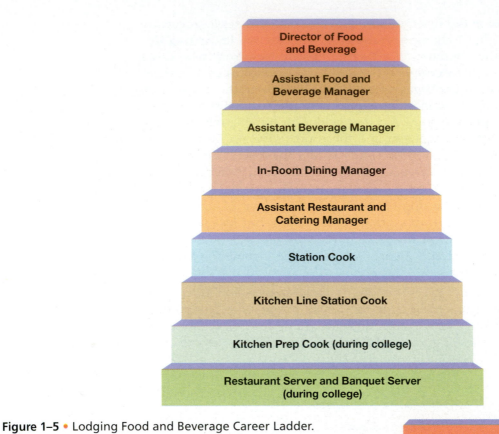

Figure 1–5 • Lodging Food and Beverage Career Ladder.

Figure 1–6 • Lodging Rooms Division Career Ladder.

Figure 1–7 • Restaurant Management Career Ladder.

Hospitality Salaries	
President of a Chain Lodging Company	$350,000–1,000,000+
President of a Chain Restaurant Company	$175,000–450,000+
Vice President of a Lodging Company	$250,000–500,000+
Hotel/Resort General Manager	$75,000–375,000+
Country Club General Manager	$100,000–750,000+
Vice President of a Restaurant Company	$75,000–250,000+
Restaurant General Manager	$40,000–100,000+
Hotel or Resort Rooms Division Director	$70,000–120,000+
Hotel/Resort Human Resources Director	$50,000–80,000+
Hotel or Resort Food and Beverage Director	$55,000–125,000+
Hotel/Resort Catering Manager	$50,000–90,000+
Assistant Restaurant Manager	$25,000–45,000+
Hotel Front Office Manager	$30,000–60,000+
Hotel/Resort Executive Housekeeper	$30,000–75,000+
Hotel/Resort Assistant Food and Beverage Manager	$35,000–60,000+
Hotel/Resort Executive Chef	$60,000–120,000+
Restaurant Chef	$30,000–80,000+
Front Desk Agent	$20,000–30,000+
Servers	$25,000–50,000+
Cooks	$20,000–35,000+

Figure 1–8 • A Guide to Hospitality Salaries 2015. (These salaries may vary by location or company.)

Hospitality Industry Philosophy

LEARNING OBJECTIVE 3
Explain corporate philosophy and Total Quality Management.

Current **hospitality industry philosophy** has changed from one in which managers plan, organize, implement, and measure to that in which managers counsel associates, giving them resources and helping them to think for themselves. The outcome is a more participative management style, which results in associate **empowerment**, increased productivity, and guest and employee satisfaction. For example, Ritz-Carlton associates are empowered to spend up to $2,000 to make a guest completely happy. Imagine a bride-to-be arriving at a hotel and sending her wedding dress to be pressed. Unfortunately, the iron burns the dress. Luckily, the concierge comes to the rescue by taking the bride to a wedding dress store, where they select a gorgeous dress for around $1,800, and the bride is happy because it is a nicer dress than the original. Corporate philosophy has strong links to quality leadership and the **total quality management (TQM)** process. (TQM is discussed in a later section.)

Corporate philosophy embraces the values of the organization, including ethics, morals, fairness, and equality. The new paradigm in corporate American hospitality is the shift in emphasis from the production aspect of our business to the focus on guest-related services. The philosophy of "whatever it takes" is winning over "it's not my job." Innovation and creativity are winning over "that's the way we've always done it." Successful organizations are those that are able to impart corporate philosophies to employees and guests alike. Disney Corporation, as discussed later in the chapter, is a good example of a corporation that has a permeating corporate philosophy.

Service Philosophy Is a Way of Life

J. W. (Bill) Marriott Jr. is chairman of the board of directors of Marriott International. Marriott's Web site defines the "Marriott Way" as "about serving the associates, the guest, and the community." These ideals serve as the cornerstone for all Marriott associates who strive to fulfill the "Spirit to Serve."[15] The values originate from deep inside the people themselves—authentic, bone deep, and passionately held. Marriott's **core values** include the belief that people are number one ("Take care of Marriott people and they'll take good care of Marriott guests"), a commitment to continuous improvement and overcoming adversity, and a good old-fashioned dedication to hard work and having fun while doing it.

Marriott's core values drive the culture. Similarly, regardless of which service organization we work for, our culture influences the way we treat associates, guests, and the community, and that affects the success of everyone. In the words of J. W. Marriott, Jr., "Culture is the life-thread and glue that links our past, present, and future."[16]

Sustainable Hospitality

Sustainable development is a holistic concept based on a simple principle. As outlined in the 1987 Brundtland Commission Report titled, "Our Common Future," the Brundtland Commission, formally the World Commission on Environment and Development, was convened by the United Nations to address the growing concern "about the accelerating deterioration of the human environment."[17] The concept of sustainability involves "development that meets the needs of the present without compromising the ability of future generations to meet their own needs."

Sustainability is the ability to achieve ongoing economic prosperity while protecting the natural resources of the planet and maintaining an ideal quality of life for its people and future generations.[18] Operators of hospitality businesses have generally embraced the concept of sustainable hospitality and are increasingly making it a part of their operation. As an example in the lodging industry, the Willard InterContinental's Sustainable Development initiative is showing substantial results. The program's chief goals are based on profits, people, and planet. The first goal is to find ways to operate the hotel according to the idea of a "triple bottom line," which embodies profitable operation combined with attention to the people who use and work in the hotel and with a focus on careful stewardship of resources.[19] More on making sustainable hospitality operational as it relates to water, solid waste, construction, sourcing, use of alternative power, and reduction of energy will be presented in each chapter in the text.

▶ Check Your Knowledge

1. Describe Marriott's "Spirit to Serve."

2. Define the term corporate philosophy and how it is currently understood, especially in the hospitality industry.

3. What is sustainability, and how does it relate to the hospitality industry?

Success in Service

LEARNING OBJECTIVE 4
Discuss the many facets of service and why it has become such an important part of the hospitality industry.

What must happen to achieve success in service? Given that approximately 70 percent of the U.S. and Canadian economies and an increasing percentage of other countries' are engaged in **service industries**, it is critical to offer guests exceptional service, but what is exceptional service? *Service* is defined in *Webster's New World Dictionary* as "the act or means of serving." To serve is to "provide goods and services for" and "be of assistance to."

This is the *age of service*, and the hospitality industry is getting revamped because guest expectations have increased and the realization is that "we buy loyalty with service."[20] With thousands of guest encounters, or moments of truth, each day, it is critical to incorporate service excellence in each hospitality organization. Some corporations adopt the expression, "If you're not serving the guest, you had better be serving someone who is." This is the essence of teamwork: Someone in the **back of the house** (also called the heart of the house) is serving someone in the front of the house, who is serving the guest.

A guest is anyone who receives or benefits from the output of someone's work. The external guest is the guest most people think of in the traditional sense. The satisfaction of external guests ultimately measures a company's success, because they are the people who are willing to pay for its services. The internal guests are the people inside a company who receive or benefit from the output of work done by others in the company, for example, the server or busser preparing the restaurant to serve lunch has been "served" by the dishwasher, who has prepared clean plates, knives, forks, spoons, and glassware.

For success in service, we need to do the following:

1. Focus on the guest.
2. Understand the role of the guest-contact employee.
3. Weave a service culture into education and training systems.
4. Emphasize high touch as well as high tech.
5. Thrive on change—constantly improve the guest experience.

As hospitality professionals, we need to recognize a variety of guest-related situations and act to relieve them or avoid them. Imagine how an associate can win points by showing empathy—that is, putting him- or herself in someone else's shoes—in the following situation: A party of two ladies arrives for lunch one cool January day at an upscale Florida waterfront hotel. They decide it would be nice to have lunch on the terrace. A server from the adjacent lounge notices the guests, and upon learning of their request to have lunch on the terrace, quickly lays up a table for them, brings them hot tea, takes their order, and then goes to the laundry to have two blankets put in the dryer for a couple of minutes to take out to the ladies to keep them warm. Little did the server realize who the guests were—travel writers for the *New York Times*, who described their outstanding experience in an article that brought praise to the hotel and its service.

Another key objective in the service equation is to encourage guest loyalty. We not only need to keep guests happy during their stay but also to

INTRODUCING J. W. (BILL) MARRIOTT, JR.

Chairman and Chief Executive Officer, Marriott International

Bill Marriott is the son of J. W. Marriott, founder of Marriott International, a company that began as a nine-stool root beer stand in Washington, D.C., in 1927. Bill was an Eagle Scout and recipient of the Distinguished Eagle Scout Award who, during and after high school, worked various positions in his parents' Hot Shoppes restaurant chain. He graduated from the University of Utah with a Bachelor of Science degree in finance and served as an officer in the Navy before joining the Marriott Corporation in 1956.

Bill Marriott has had an enormous influence on the hospitality industry with years of dedicated service. He is an example of the Spirit to Serve, the title of his well-worth-reading book. Under Marriott's lead, Marriott International has grown from a family restaurant business to a global lodging company of over 4,000 managed and franchised properties of 18 brands, ranging from economy limited-service brands up to full-service luxury hotels and resorts, as well as executive apartments, conference centers, and golf courses in 80 countries and territories.[21]

Mr. Marriott continues his father's tradition of visiting two to three hundred hotels a year. He is passionate about quality and service and can quickly tell how good a general manager (GM) is by the reaction of associates to him or her when the GM is walking the halls of the property. If the associates smile and greet the GM with a cheerful good morning, he knows he has a great GM, but if the associates look down and don't say anything, he knows that there is a problem.

Bill Marriott also cares passionately about Marriott associates by giving them the best possible working conditions, competitive wages and salaries, and excellent benefits. Marriott also provides outstanding training programs to help associates do a great job and to retain the best associates. One of the often used quotes from Mr. Marriott is, "I want our associates to know that there really is a guy named Marriott who cares about them."[22] A central part of Marriott's core values is that attention to detail, quite simply, leads to high customer satisfaction, to repeat business—and to good profits and attractive returns for stockholders and property owners.[23]

keep them returning—with their friends, we hope! It costs several times more to attract new guests than it does to retain existing ones. Imagine how much more profitable a hospitality business would be if it could retain just 10 percent of its guests as loyal guests. Losing a guest equates to losing much more than one sale; it has the potential to be a loss of a lifetime guest. Consider a $40 restaurant dinner for two people. If the guests return twice a month over several years—say, 10—the amount they have contributed to the restaurant quickly becomes huge ($9,600). If they bring their friends, this amount is even higher. Can you remember your worst service experience? Also, can you remember your best service experience?

We know that service is a complex yet critical component of the hospitality industry. In their book, *Service America!*, Albrecht and Zemke suggest two basic kinds of service: "Help me!" and "Fix it."[24] "Help me!" refers to guests' regular and special needs, such as, "Help me find the function room" or, "Help me to get a reservation at the best restaurant in town." "Fix it" refers to services such as, "Please fix my toilet; it won't flush" or, "Please fix the TV so that we can watch the World Series."

Moments of Truth

"Moments of truth" is a term coined by Jan Carlson. When Carlson became president of Scandinavian Airlines (SAS), it was ranked at the bottom of the European airline market. He quickly realized that he had to spend a lot of time on the front line coaching SAS associates in how to handle guest encounters, or as he called them, "moments of truth." As a result of his efforts, SAS was soon ranked at the top of the European airlines for service. Service commitment is a total organizational approach that makes the quality of service, as perceived by the customer, the number one driving force for the operation of the business.[25]

FOCUS ON SERVICE

Hospitality Is Offering a Cup of Kindness

William B. Martin, Cal Tech–Monterey Bay

Guest service is a central focus of hospitality. It is what hospitality is all about—what we do. If you are interested in a hospitality career, it is important to understand and learn as much as possible about guest service and particularly how to be successful at it. Your success will come from a complete understanding of hospitality.

Let's begin by exploring why we provide hospitality. Why are hospitality businesses in business? What is the primary purpose of a foodservice operation? A lodging establishment? A travel- or tourism related business? Is it just for the money? Many of you might answer an easy yes to this question. But as you will see, hospitality is much more than just about money. Money is important, but it is important as a means and as a necessary ingredient to help us get to where we want to go. Money is not the primary reason for hospitality. Then what is the primary purpose of hospitality?

Our job, first and foremost, is to enhance the lives of those people (guests, passengers, etc.) to whom we are dedicated to serve. Yes, it is that simple (and complex at the same time). Our job is to make the lives of others better in a small way or big way; it makes no difference. Whatever it is, we are out to make people's lives on this planet a little bit better, or maybe even a lot better. This is our purpose. It is where we find meaning. We in the hospitality industry are about enhancing the lives of others—period. Ultimately, that is what makes it all worthwhile.

With that said, where does guest service fit in? Good question. If you are a sharp student, you've already got it. You can readily see that if the purpose of hospitality is to enhance the lives of others, the way we do that is through service. And what is service? It is how we go about treating our guests—how we make (or fail to make) their lives better by how we treat them. And we can go a long way toward treating them well by simply offering them a cup of kindness.

What does this mean? What does it take to be kind? What do we have to do? How do we enhance the lives of others through kindness? We begin by *understanding* what it is that they need. The problem is that all of our guests come to us with many needs. Some we can meet, some we can't. But of all the needs they come with, four of them are specifically hospitality related. If you can work toward helping them satisfy these needs, you can go a long way toward making their lives better through kindness. Quality guest service demands that service providers understand what it is that guests want. Kindness, after all, comes through understanding. Kindness is demonstrated by making everyone feel *welcome*.

Quality guest service requires that we make all guests feel *comfortable*—that we provide the assurance that they will be taken care of, and follow through. They don't need to worry; they are in good hands. In short, when

FOCUS ON SERVICE *(Continued)*

we can do this we are filling their cups with more kindness. Whether they deserve it or not, they should be made to feel important. Why? Because, we all have a *need to feel important*. This is a part of our job. Moreover, it is another important way we can show kindness to our guests.

We need to stay focused on the primary purposes of hospitality. We need to understand the power of kindness and the importance of satisfying the four basic service needs of our guests. In the final analysis, hospitality and guest service success are found in our ability to enhance the lives of others through how we treat them—with a little cup of kindness.

Every hospitality organization has thousands of moments of truth every day. This leads to tremendous challenges in maintaining the expected levels of service. Let's look at just some of the moments of truth in a restaurant dining experience:[26]

1. Guest calls the restaurant for a table reservation.
2. Guest tries to find the restaurant.
3. Guest parks.
4. Guest is welcomed.
5. Guest is informed that the table is not ready.
6. Guest either waits or goes to the lounge for a cocktail.
7. Guest tries to attract the bartender's attention for a cocktail because there are no seats available.
8. Guest is called over a loudspeaker or paged.
9. Guest is seated at the table.
10. Server takes order.
11. Server brings beverages or food.
12. Server clears food or beverages.
13. Server brings check.
14. Guest pays for meal.
15. Guest departs restaurant.

From your own experiences, you can imagine just how many moments of truth there are in a restaurant dining experience.

▶ Check Your Knowledge

1. Explain why service in the hospitality industry is so important. Give an example from your own experience as a guest, if possible.
2. List the five things required for success in service.
3. What is a moment of truth?

The Focus on Service

LEARNING OBJECTIVE 5
Suggest ways to improve service.

Giving great service is a very difficult task; few businesses give enough priority to training associates in how to provide service. We suffer from an overreliance on technology so that service providers are often not motivated to give great service. For example, when checking a guest into the hotel, the front-desk associate may greet the guest but then look down at the computer for the remainder of the service encounter, even when asking for the guest's name. Or consider the reservations associate who says nothing when asked for a specific type of guest room because he is waiting for the computer to indicate availability.

To help improve service in the hospitality industry, the Educational Foundation of the NRA, one of the hospitality industry's leading associations, developed a number of great programs that will enhance your professional development. Further information may be obtained from the NRA's Web site (www.restaurant.org).

Among the various programs and courses is one titled Foodservice Leadership. Effective leaders are those who make things happen because they have developed the knowledge, skills, and attitude required to get the most out of the people in their operation. Leadership involves change; in fact, change is the one thing we can be sure of in the coming years. Our guests are constantly changing; so is technology, product availability, and, of course, our competition.

The American Hotel & Lodging Association (AH&LA) offers a great variety of information on service-related topics including **best practices**, which give details of the most effective techniques in lodging operations. One area of interest is the Green Resource, where innovative means of going green are shared to improve the carbon footprint and the "bottom line."[27]

One way in which leaders involve employees in the process of improving guest service is through TQM and empowerment.

Service and Total Quality Management

The increasingly open and fiercely competitive marketplace is exerting enormous pressure on service industries to deliver superior service. Inspired by rising guest expectations and competitive necessity, many hospitality companies have jumped on the service quality bandwagon. W. Edwards Deming is credited with launching the Total Quality Management movement. He was best known for his work in Japan, where in the 1950s and onward, the quality of Japanese products was not good. He taught top Japanese management how to improve design—through the use of statistical methods he reduced the number of defects—and thus service, product quality, testing, and sales. Dr. Deming made a significant contribution to the improvement of Japanese products.[28]

The Malcolm Baldrige National Quality Award is the highest level of national recognition for quality that a U.S. company can receive. Named after former commerce secretary Malcolm Baldrige, who was a champion of quality movement as a way of improving U.S. commerce, the award promotes an understanding of quality excellence, greater awareness of quality as a critical competitive element, and the sharing of quality information and strategies.

The Ritz-Carlton Hotel Company, the only hospitality company to win not just one but two Malcolm Baldrige National Quality Awards, in 1992 and 1999, was founded on principles of excellence in guest service. The essence of this philosophy was refined into a set of core values collectively called the Gold Standards. The credo is printed on a small laminated card that all employees must memorize or carry on their person at all times when on duty.

The quality movement began at the turn of the twentieth century as a means of ensuring consistency among the parts produced in the different plants of a single company so that they could be used interchangeably. In the area of service, TQM is a participatory process that empowers all levels of employees to work in groups to establish guest service expectations and determine the best way to meet or exceed these expectations. Notice that the term *guest* is preferred over the term *customer*. The inference here is that if we treat customers like guests, we are more likely to exceed their expectations. One successful hotelier has insisted for a long time that all employees treat guests as they would like to be treated themselves.

TQM is a continuous process that works best when managers are also good leaders. A successful company will employ leader–managers who create a stimulating work environment in which guests and employees (sometimes called internal guests: One employee serves another employee, who in turn serves a guest) become integral parts of the mission by participating in **goal** and objective setting.

Implementing TQM is exciting because after everyone becomes involved, there is no stopping the creative ways employees will find to solve guest-related problems and improve service. Other benefits include cost reductions and increased guest and employee satisfaction, leading ultimately to increased profits.

Top executives and line managers are responsible for the success of the TQM process; when they commit to ownership of the process, it will be successful. Focused commitment is the foundation of a quality service initiative, and leadership is the critical component in promoting commitment. Achieving TQM is a top-down, bottom-up process that must have the active commitment and participation of all employees, from the top executives down to those at the bottom of the corporate ladder. The expression "If you are not serving the guest, then you had better be serving someone who is" still holds true today.

The difference between TQM and quality control (QC) is that QC focuses on error detection, whereas TQM focuses on error prevention. QC is generally based on industrial systems and, because of this, tends to be product oriented rather than service oriented. To the guest, services are experiential; they are felt, lived through, and sensed. The moment of truth is the actual guest contact.

A DAY IN THE LIFE OF RYAN LASHWAY

Assistant Manager, Mar Vista Dockside Restaurant, Longboat Key, Florida

To describe a typical day of work for me at the Mar Vista, I must first tell you a little bit about the restaurant. Located on Sarasota Bay on the north end of Longboat Key in historic Longbeach Village, the Mar Vista has existed for over 60 years. Built in the early 1940s, "The Pub" was originally a bait and tackle shop until the 1950s, when the owners started selling hamburgers and beer to the local fishermen crowd. The Mar Vista operated like this until coming under the ownership of Ed Chiles of the Chiles Group Corporation in 1990. Chiles is the son of former governor of Florida, Lawton Chiles, and also owns the Beachhouse and Sandbar restaurants on Anna Maria Island. The Mar Vista is an authentic part of Old Florida, and our history and ambiance make it a fun and relaxing place. Our goal at the Mar Vista is to provide our guests with the finest in food and courteous, prompt service. For further information about the Chiles Group Corporation, visit our Web site at www.groupersandwich.com.
A typical day for a manager at the Mar Vista goes like this:

8:30 A.M. Arrive and check the premises for any unusual activity. Unlock the doors and turn on all lights and A/C units. Check to see that the overnight cleaning crew has done a thorough job, especially in the kitchen, restrooms, and behind the bars. Then, look at the schedules to see which employees are working on any given day and make ready for the kitchen staff's arrival at 9:00 A.M.

9:00 A.M. Upon arrival, the kitchen staff is entered into our in-house computer system so that their hours for the day will be recorded. Towels and cleaning materials must also be supplied for the entire staff. The restrooms must be checked and stocked with hand towels, liquid soap, and toilet paper. The premises are then walked again and the grounds checked for trash. All windows and mirrors must be cleaned.

10:30 A.M. The wait staff and bar staff arrive. The cash banks for the bar must be counted and paired up for daily use. The safe in the manager's office must then be opened and the money from the previous day made ready for pickup by our financial officer. The kitchen manager must then be met with to discuss the daily specials. Upon agreement of the best use for food items, the specials must then be printed and inserted into the menus.

11:30 A.M. Open for lunch business. Throughout the day, management focuses on customer relations and making sure the restaurant runs smoothly. Incoming paperwork from deliveries for the kitchen and bar must be fully documented, and all incoming orders must be checked in and signed for. Any problems with food orders or guest service must be handled in such a way that the customer is never scorned; return business is the primary focus. In general, the customers are always right, and in this business we must do whatever is necessary to keep them happy.

3:00 P.M. Toward the end of the lunch shift, servers are finishing their daily work and will require checkout forms to do their money drops. Managers must check each server out individually and make sure that all side work is completed and that the restaurant will be ready for the next shift crew arriving at 4:00 P.M. Managers must meet with the kitchen manager again and prepare the dinner specials. The P.M. bartender will also be arriving and will require a night bank, while the A.M. bartender will need to be checked out and his or her bank checked for correct money transactions.

5:00 P.M. Dinner begins and the night manager arrives. Discuss the events and highlights of the day with the P.M. manager and notify him or her of any problems.

Then it's off to rest up and prepare to do it again tomorrow!

The nature of business has changed. Leaders empower employees who welcome change. Empowerment is a feeling of partnership in which employees feel responsible for their jobs and have a stake in the organization's success. Empowered employees tend to do the following:

• Speak out about their problems and concerns.

• Take responsibility for their actions.

• Consider themselves a network of professionals.

• Accept the authority to make their own decisions when serving guests.

To empower employees, managers must do the following:

1. Take risks.
2. Delegate.
3. Foster a learning environment.
4. Share information and encourage self-expression.
5. Involve employees in defining their own vision.
6. Be thorough and patient with employees.

CORPORATE PROFILE

Marriott International, Inc.[29]

Marriott International is a leading worldwide hospitality company. Its heritage is traced back to a root beer stand opened in Washington, D.C., in 1927, by J. Willard and Alice S. Marriott. Today, Marriott International has more than 4,000 lodging properties in the United States and 80 other countries and territories. Marriott International operates and franchises hotels under the following tiers of brands:

Luxury Tier:

Bulgari Hotels and Resorts, a collection of sophisticated, intimate luxury properties tucked away in exclusive destinations.

The Ritz-Carlton Hotel Company, LLC: The worldwide symbol for the finest in hotel and resort accommodations, dining, and service. Two-time recipient of the Malcolm Baldrige National Quality Award, offering signature service amenities, fine dining, 24-hour room service, twice-daily housekeeping, fitness centers, business centers, and concierge services.

JW Marriott Hotels and Resorts: The most elegant and luxurious Marriott brand, offering business and leisure travelers a deluxe level of comfort and personal service.

Gaylord Hotels: One of the leaders in resort accommodations, offering scenic vacation destinations and convention opportunities. From beauty to efficiency, you'll find "everything in one place."[30]

Autograph Collection: A collection of high-personality, independent hotels, powered by the world-class platforms of Marriott International.

CORPORATE PROFILE *(Continued)*

Lifestyle/Boutique:

EDITION was created in partnership with boutique hotel pioneer Ian Schrager to introduce a new brand with as many as one hundred hotels that have perfected a highly personal, intimate, and rarified experience for each guest.

Renaissance Hotels invite guests to "stay interesting" at distinctive hotels offering unique, locally relevant architecture and design, destination restaurants and bars, and off-the-radar travel experiences worldwide.

Signature Brand:

Marriott Hotels and Resorts: The flagship brand of quality-tier, full-service hotels and resorts with features such as fully equipped fitness centers, gift shops, swimming pools, concierge levels, business centers, meeting facilities, and high-speed Internet.

Select Service & Extended Stay Brands:

Courtyard by Marriott: A moderately priced lodging brand designed by business travelers for business travelers that has recently increased the number of downtown locations, often through conversions of historical buildings. Features include 80–150 guest rooms, high-speed Internet access, restaurants, lounges, meeting spaces, central courtyards, exercise rooms, swimming pools, and 24-hour access to food.

SpringHill Suites by Marriott: A moderately priced, all-suite lodging brand that offers up to 25 percent larger-than-standard hotel rooms. Features include complimentary continental breakfast, self-serve business centers, indoor pools, whirlpool spas, high-speed Internet access, and exercise rooms.

Fairfield Inn by Marriott: A consistent, quality lodging at an affordable price. Features include spacious guest rooms, daily complimentary breakfast, and swimming pools. Future plans call for exercise rooms.

Residence Inn by Marriott: Designed as a home away from home for travelers staying five or more nights, it includes a residential atmosphere with spacious accommodations. Features include complimentary hot breakfasts, evening hospitality hours, swimming pools, sport courts, personalized grocery shopping, guest suites with separate living and sleeping areas, fully equipped kitchens, and work spaces with data ports and voice mail.

TownePlace Suites by Marriott: A midpriced, extended-stay brand that provides all the comforts of home in a residential atmosphere.

Marriott Executive Apartments: A corporate housing brand designed to meet the needs of business executives on an overseas assignment for 30 days or more by offering residential accommodations with hotel-like amenities.

In addition to these brands there are also several Vacation Clubs, which are offered on a fractional ownership basis.

Marriott has been ranked the number-one most admired company in the lodging industry 13 times by *Fortune*, including each of the past six years, as well as one of the "100 Best Companies to Work For" for the past eight years.

▶ Check Your Knowledge

1. What is the Malcolm Baldrige National Quality Award?
2. Explain Total Quality Management.
3. List several ways a leader can empower employees.

The Disney Approach to Guest Service

The Disney mission statement is simple: "We create Happiness." Disney is regarded as one of the most excellent corporations throughout the text. The following discussion, adapted from a presentation given by Susan Wilkie to the Pacific chapter of the Council on Hotel Restaurant and Institutional Education (CHRIE) conference outlines Disney's approach to guest service.

When conceiving the idea to build Disneyland, Walt Disney established a simple philosophical approach to his theme park business, based on the tenets of quality, service, and show. The design, layout, characters, and magic of Disneyland grew out of Walt's successful experience in the film industry. With Disneyland, he saw an opportunity to create a whole new form of entertainment: a three-dimensional live show. He wanted Disneyland to be a dynamic, ever-changing experience.

To reinforce the service concept, Disney has *guests*, not *customers*, and *cast members*, not *employees*. These terms set the expectations for how guests will be served and cared for while at the park or resort. This commitment to service means the following:

- Disney clearly understands its product and the meaning of its brand.
- It looks at the business from the guests' perspective.
- It considers creating an exceptional experience for every individual who enters its gates to be its responsibility.

Disney executives say, "our inventory goes home at night." Disney's ability to create a special brand of magic requires the talents of thousands of people fulfilling many different roles. But the heart of it is the frontline cast members who go out of their way to greet and welcome each guest with a smile and to always provide exceptional guest service help when needed.

Disney has used profile modeling but says it all comes down to a few simple things:

- Interpersonal relationship–building skills
- Communication
- Friendliness

Disney uses a 45-minute team approach to interviewing called *peer interviews*. In one interview, there may be four candidates and one interviewer. The candidates may include a homemaker returning to the workforce, a teacher looking for summer work, a retiree looking for a little extra income, and a teenager looking for a first job. All four candidates are interviewed in the same session. The interviewer is looking for how they individually answer questions but also how well they interact with each other—a good indicator of their future onstage treatment of guests.

The most successful technique used during the 45 minutes is to *smile*. The interviewer smiles at the people being interviewed to see if they *return the smiles*. If they don't, it doesn't matter how well they interview—they won't get the job.

On the first day at work, every new Disney cast member participates in a one-day orientation program at the Disney University, "Welcome to Show Business." The main goal of this experience is to learn the Disney approach to helpful, caring, and friendly guest service.

How does this translate into action? When a guest stops a street sweeper to ask where to pick up a parade schedule and the sweeper not only answers the question but recites the parade times from memory, suggests the best viewing spots on the parade route, offers advice on where to get a quick meal before parade time, *and* ends the interaction with a pleasant smile and warm send-off, people can't help but be impressed. It also makes the sweepers feel their jobs are interesting and important—which they are!

I AM YOUR GUEST

We can all find inspiration from these anonymous words about people who make our business possible:

✓ *I am your guest.* Satisfy my needs, add personal attention and a friendly touch, and I will become a "walking advertisement" for your products and services. Ignore my needs, show carelessness, inattention, and poor manners, and you will cease to exist as far as I am concerned.

✓ *I am sophisticated.* Much more so than I was a few years ago. My needs are more complex. It is more important to me that you appreciate my business; when I buy your products and services, I'm saying you are the best.

✓ *I am a perfectionist.* When I am dissatisfied, take heed. The source of my discontent lies in something you or your products have failed to do. Find that source and eliminate it or you will lose my business and that of my friends as well. For when I criticize your products or services, I will talk to anyone who will listen.

✓ *I have other choices.* Other businesses continually offer "more for my money." You must prove to me again and again that I have made a wise choice in selecting you and your company above all others.

The Show is why people go to Disneyland. Each land tells a unique story through its theme and attention to detail, and the cast members each play a role in the Show. The most integral component of the training is the traditions and standards of guest service. The first of these is called the *Personal Touch*. The cast members are encouraged to use their own unique style and personality to provide a personal interaction with each guest. One of the primary ways Disney accomplishes this is through name tags. Everyone, regardless of position, goes by his or her first name. This tradition was started by Walt and continues today. It allows cast members to interact on a more personal level with guests. It also assists internally, by creating an informal environment that facilitates the flow of open communication and breaks down some of the traditional barriers.

Opening Disneyland

Imagine what Walt Disney had to overcome to open Disneyland. Disneyland opened on July 17, 1955, to the predictions that it would be a failure. And, in truth, everything that could go wrong did. Just to give an example, here is what happened on opening day:

* Plumbers went on strike.
* Tickets were duplicated.
* Attractions broke down.
* There was a gas leak in Fantasyland.
* The asphalt on Main Street didn't harden in time, so in the heat of July, horses' hooves and women's high heels stuck in the street.

As Walt once said, "You may not realize it when it happens, but a kick in the teeth might be good for you." Walt had his fair share of challenges, one of which was obtaining financing to develop Disneyland—he had to deal with more than 300 banks.

Service always begins with a smile at Disney and ends with a "thank you." Cast members are trained to be respectful of guests and to always maintain eye contact. They greet each guest with their own sense of Disney magic and go out of their way to be helpful, at times approaching guests first before they have a chance to seek out help. These basic steps are at the core of Disney's culture. After initial cast member training is completed, these concepts must be applied and continually reinforced by leaders who possess strong coaching skills. Disney uses a model called the *Five Steps of Leadership* to lead the cast member performance.

Each step in the leadership model is equally important in meeting service and business goals. Each leader must do the following:

1. Provide clear expectations and standards.
2. Communicate these expectations through demonstration, information, and examples.
3. Hold cast members accountable for their feedback.
4. Coach through honest and direct feedback.
5. Recognize, reward, and celebrate success.

Cinderella's castle soaring above tourists at Walt Disney World, Orlando, Florida.

To supplement and reward the leadership team, Disney provides technical training to every new manager and assistant manager. In addition, the management team also participates in classes at the Disney University to learn the culture, values, and the leadership philosophy necessary to be successful in the Disney environment.

Disney measures the systems and reward process by distributing 1,000 surveys to guests as they leave Disneyland and 100 surveys to guests who stayed at each of the Disney hotels. The guests are asked to take the surveys home and mail them back to Disney. In return, their names are entered for a drawing for a family weekend package at the park and hotel.

Feedback from the surveys has been helpful in improving the guest experience. For example, as a result of the surveys, the entertainment division realized that the opportunity to interact with a character was a key driver to guest satisfaction. So, the entertainment team designed a brochure, "The Characters Today," which is distributed at the main entrance daily. This brochure allows guests to maximize their opportunity to see the characters. This initiative has already raised guest satisfaction by 10 percentage points.

Cast members are also empowered to make changes to improve service. These measures are supplemented by financial controls and "mystery shoppers" (when people use the services like any other guest, but they are really employed to sample the service and report their findings) that allow Disney to focus resources on increasing guest satisfaction. The reward system does not consist of just the hard reward system we commonly think of, such as bonuses and incentive plans, important though they are. Recognition is not a one-size-fits-all system. Disney has found that noncash recognition is as powerful as, if not more powerful than, a recognition tool in many situations. Some examples follow:

- Disney recognizes milestones of years of service. They use pins and statues and have a formal dinner for cast members and guests to reinforce and celebrate the value of their experience and expertise at serving Disney's guests.
- Throughout the year, Disney hosts special social and recreational events that involve the cast members and their families in the product.
- Disney invites cast members and their families to family film festivals featuring new Disney releases to ensure that they are knowledgeable about the latest Disney products.
- The Disneyland management team hosts the Family Christmas Party in the park after hours. This allows cast members to enjoy shopping, dining, and riding the attractions. Management dresses in costumes and runs the facilities.

Career Paths

Now that we know that the hospitality industries are the largest and arguably the fastest growing in the world, let's explore some of the many **career paths** available to graduates. The concept of career paths describes the career progression available in each segment of the hospitality industry. A career path does not always go in a straight line, as sometimes described in a career ladder. You could liken it to jumping into a swimming pool: You get wet whichever end you jump in and then you might swim over to the other side—but not always in a straight line. It's like that in the hospitality industry, also. We may begin in one area and later find another that is more attractive. Opportunities come our way and we need to be prepared to take advantage of them. To illustrate, take Barbra. A few years ago, she was a hospitality management graduate who was not very outgoing, so she decided to take a position in the hotel accounting office. A few years later, we visited the hotel where she was working, and to our pleasant surprise, we found a smiling Barbra welcoming us as the front office manager. After a few more years, she moved into the food and beverage department and then the marketing department, and is now a general manager.

Progression means that we can advance from one position to another. In the hospitality industry we don't always use straight-line career ladders because we need experience in several areas before becoming, say, a general manager, director of human resources, catering manager, meeting planner, or director of marketing. The path to general manager in a hotel may go through food and beverage, rooms division, marketing, human resources, or finance and accounting, or, more likely, a combination of these, because it is better to have experience in several areas (cross-training). The same is true for restaurants. A graduate with service experience will need to spend some time in the kitchen learning each station and then bartending before becoming an opening or closing assistant or manager, general manager, area manager, regional director, vice president, and president.

Sometimes we want to run before we can walk. We want to progress quickly. But remember to enjoy the journey as much as the destination. If you advance too quickly, you may not be ready for the additional responsibility, and you may not have the skills necessary for the promotion. For instance, you cannot expect to become a director of food and beverage until you really know "food and beverage": this means spending a few years in the kitchen. Otherwise, how can you relate to an executive chef? You have to know how the food should be prepared and served. You have to set the standards—not have them set for you. Be prepared because you never know when an opportunity will present itself.

Career Goals

You may already know that you want to be a director of accounting, an event manager, a director of marketing, or of food and beverage, or a restaurant owner. If you are not sure of which career path to pursue, that's OK. Now is the time to explore the industry to gain the information you need to decide which career path to follow. A great way to do this is through internships and work experience. Some suggest trying a variety of jobs rather than sticking to the same one.

If we follow the interrelated nature of hospitality, travel, and tourism in Figure 1–2 or 1–3, we can see some of the numerous career options in various industry segments.

Is the Hospitality Industry for You?

In this chapter, we described some characteristics of the hospitality industry. Due to the size and scope of the hospitality industry, career prospects are gradually improving. We also know that it is an exciting and dynamic industry with growth potential, especially when the economy is strong. In the hospitality industry we are often working when others are at leisure—think of the evening or weekend shift; however, in some positions and careers, many evenings and weekends can be yours to enjoy as you wish. (Accounting, marketing and sales, human resources, and housekeeping are some examples.)

The hospitality industry is a service industry; this means that we take pride in caring about others as well as ourselves. Ensuring that guests receive outstanding service is a goal of hospitality corporations. This is a business that gets into your blood! It is mostly fun, exciting, and seldom dull, and an industry in which almost everyone can succeed. So, what does it take to be successful in the hospitality industry? The personal characteristics, qualities, skills, and abilities you'll need are honesty, hard work, being a team player, being prepared to work long hours spread over various shifts, the ability to cope with stress, good decision-making skills, good communication skills, being dedicated to exceptional service, and having a passion and desire to exceed guest expectations. Leadership, ambition, and the will to succeed are also important and necessary for career success.

Recruiters look for *service-oriented* people, who "walk their talk," meaning they do what they say they're going to do. Good work experience, involvement in on-campus and professional organizations, a positive attitude, a good grade point average—all show a commitment to an individual's studies. Career-minded individuals who have initiative and are prepared to work hard and make a contribution to the company, which has to make a profit, are what companies are looking for.

Self-Assessment and Personal Philosophy

The purpose of completing a self-assessment is to measure our current strengths and weaknesses and to determine what we need to improve on if we are going to reach our goals. Self-assessment helps establish where we are now and shows us the links to where we want to go, our goals. In a self-assessment, we make a list of our positive attributes. For example, we may have experience in a guest-service position; this will be helpful in preparing for supervisory and managerial positions. Other positive attributes include our character and all the other things that recruiters look for, as listed previously.

We also make a list of areas where we might want to make improvements. For example, we may have reached a certain level of culinary expertise, but need more experience and a course in this specialty. Or you may want to improve your Spanish-language skills because you will be working with Spanish-speaking colleagues. Your *philosophy* is your beliefs and the way you treat others and your work. It will determine who you are and what you stand for. You may state that you enjoy giving excellent service by treating others as you would like to be treated and that you believe in honesty and respect.

A great web resource for self-assessment is www.queendom.com; this site provides self-assessment quizzes.

Now Is the Time to Get Involved

For your own enjoyment and personal growth and development, it is very important to get involved with on-campus and professional hospitality and tourism organizations and participate in the organization of events. Recruiters notice the difference between students who have become involved with various organizations and students who have not, and they take that into consideration when assessing candidates for positions with companies. Becoming involved will show your commitment to your chosen career and will lead you to meet interesting peers and industry professionals who can potentially help you along your chosen career path. You will develop leadership and organizational skills that will help you in your career.

Professional Organizations

Professional organizations include becoming a student member of CHRIE (www.chrie.org). You can also access the excellent Web zine *Hosteur*, which is published especially for students; CHRIE offers its members free access. The NRA is another organization to join. You will likely find several NRA magazines and publications to be very helpful. The NRA and your state restaurant association are affiliated, and both have trade shows; the NRA hosts the Salute to Excellence, a day of activities that culminates with a gala dinner. Only two students from each school are invited to this special event; make sure you're one of them, as it is well worth it. The AH&LA (www.ahla.com) is a good organization to belong to if you are interested in a career in the lodging segment of the industry. Benefits of AH&LA memberships include access to the organization's career center, which is powered by Hcareers.com, the largest online database of career opportunities in the lodging industry; a subscription to *Lodging* magazine, a leading industry publication with news, product information, and current articles on industry-related topics; subscriptions to *Lodging News*, *Lodging Law*, and *Lodging H/R* e-newsletters; and use of the AH&LA's information center—helpful for those pesky term papers! And you can receive scholarship information, too!

The International Special Events Society (ISES; www.ises.com) includes over 3,000 professionals representing special event producers, from festivals to trade shows. Membership brings together professionals from a variety of special events disciplines. The mission of ISES is to educate, advance, and promote the special events industry and its network of professionals, along with related issues.

The Professional Convention Management Association (PCMA; www.pcma.org) is a great resource for convention management educational offerings and networking opportunities. The National Society of Minorities in Hospitality (NSMH; www.nsmh.org) has a membership of several hundred minority hospitality majors who address diversity and multiculturalism as well as career development via events and programs.

Trends in Hospitality and Tourism

LEARNING OBJECTIVE 6
Discuss current trends in the hospitality industry.

Courtesy of Dr. Greg Dunn, Senior Lecturer & Managing Director, University of Florida, Eric Friedheim Tourism Institute.

Since the Great Recession ended two years ago, there has been healthy growth in the hospitality and tourism industry globally. There are a number of trends that will continue to have a significant impact on the hospitality industry. Here, in no particular order, are some of the major trends to consider as a hospitality professional. You will find these trends and others discussed further in the chapters of this text.

- *Globalization.* Globalization is occurring faster than ever and international knowledge and experience is in high demand. According to the World Travel & Tourism Council, the Travel and Tourism industry is currently among the largest and fastest-growing industries worldwide, and is expected to provide more than 328 million jobs, or 10 percent of the world's workplace by the year 2022. In the United States, the hospitality and tourism industry is one of the top 10 industries and provides one out of eight jobs. In 2013 alone, the United States added approximately 55,000 hospitality related jobs per month, with increases expected into the next year. We have truly become the global village that was described a few years ago. We have the opportunity to work or vacation in other countries, and more people than ever travel freely around the world. With an increase in average household incomes, more middle-class households, interests to explore, and more traveler-friendly visa requirements to leave a host country or enter the United States, we will expect to see more international visitors over the next several years into the United States—especially from China, India, and Brazil.

- *Health, Safety, and Security.* Visitor, employee, and resident safety remain important topics worldwide. Perceived or real threats to visitor and guest safety have immediate impacts on a destination's reputation and can dramatically affect visitation and patronage. If guest health and safety are not well thought-out and managed, adverse incidents can significantly impact an individual hospitality business, community, or destination. Moreover, and since September 11, 2001, we have all become more conscious of our personal safety and have experienced increased scrutiny at airports and federal and other buildings. But it goes beyond that; over the last several years we have witnessed an increase in the number of kidnapping of tourists from airports, tours, and resorts to be held for ransom, while other tourists have experienced muggings or assaults. Security of all types of hospitality and tourism operations is critical, and disaster plans should be made for each kind of threat. Personal health, safety, and security of visitors and guests must be the first priority of destinations and hospitality and tourism organizations; they have the responsibility of having well-thought-out and actionable crisis management plans and programs.

- *Diversity and Changing Demographics.* The U.S. population continues to become more diverse. The use of the term "minority," to describe racial and ethnic groups in the United States, will need to be rethought according to the Census Bureau (2013). By the end of this decade no single racial or ethnic group will constitute a majority of children under 18. And in about three decades, no single group will constitute a majority of the country as a whole. We can also expect the U.S. population to grow more slowly than anticipated, with the elderly making up a growing share of the population, and we will become more racially and ethnically diverse. All of these trends will have a significant impact on the hospitality and tourism industry in terms of the types of employees we hire and guests we serve.

- *Service*. It is no secret that service is at the top of guests' expectations, yet few companies offer exceptional service. World-class service does not just happen; training is important in delivering the services that guests have come to expect.

- *Technology*. Technology is a driving force of change that presents opportunities for greater efficiencies and integration for improved guest service. However, the industry faces great challenges in training employees to use the new technology and in standardization of software and hardware design. Some hotels have several systems that do not talk to each other, and some reservation systems bounce between seven and 10 percent of sales nationally.

- *Sustainability and Green Travel*. Sustainability is the new standard in hospitality, and more companies are environmentally conscious. Eco-friendly practices are becoming the norm, rather than the exception. We should expect to see more green practices, products, and services available to travelers and guests. More and more guests are expecting their hospitality provider to be environmentally conscious and the majority does not expect to pay more for it. Green tourism, also known as nature-based tourism or sustainable tourism, is in great demand and will continue its growth in the future. The majority of travelers are aware of the negative impact tourism may have on the environment and have become more responsible with regard to sustainability and with whom they choose to do business.

- *Legal Issues*. The hospitality industry as a whole, and various sectors within the industry in particular, continue to face challenges arising from changes in the local, regional, national, and international marketplace. For instance, in this post recession era, there are more stringent laws, regulations, and agreements between owners, management companies, and franchisees as a result of the many bankruptcies, defaults, and closings of hospitality businesses. There are also continuing legal issues between parties with respect to the licensing of hospitality brands and granting of geographic exclusivity for hospitality brand franchisees and management companies. Lawsuits are not only more frequent, but they cost more whether defending or losing a case. More than one hospitality company has spent several million dollars just to defend a case over the past several years. Increasing government regulations and the added complexity of owner and employee relations create increased challenges for hospitality operators.

- *Travel with a Purpose*. Another important future trend in the hospitality industry is the desire on behalf of travelers who are looking for travel that offers added value rather than just a classic lazy sun and sea vacation. While nearly all travelers are looking for a great price-value vacation, many are now looking for authentic travel experiences that enrich their learning and understanding of other cultures. While some seek out travels that involve volunteering, for others this may be learning a new language, exploring new culinary techniques, attending a seminar, a concert, or an event that enriches their lives in some other way.

- *Social Media and Mobile.* We have witnessed an unprecedented rise of social media in many different forms such as in collaborative projects (e.g., Wikipedia), blogs and micro-blogs (e.g., Twitter), content communities (e.g., YouTube), social networking sites (e.g., Facebook), etc. We have also witnessed a complimentary rise in the adoption and use of mobile phones in the United States and around the world. We can expect to see a greater merging of social media and mobile phone use. People create social media updates from their phones, while tagging their friends or checking in. Content communities such as YouTube and Pinterest will continue to play a more important role in social media as photo and video sharing becomes more popular and powerful in the way they enable people to communicate and share lifestyle and travel experiences.

CASE STUDY

Being Promoted from Within

One month ago, Tom was promoted from line cook to kitchen manager. It was a significant step up in his life. He felt that his promotion was well deserved, as he had always been a hard worker. Tom never had a second thought about going the extra mile for his employer. He felt that since he had seniority in the kitchen and was friendly with everyone in the back of the house, he would be sure to get the respect he deserved from everyone for whom he had responsibility. About three weeks into his new position, Tom found that this was not the case. Several back-of-the house employees had become careless about their responsibilities after Tom was promoted. They were coming to work late, wearing unlaundered uniforms, and becoming sloppier with their plate presentations. Every day at work, Tom was becoming more frustrated and upset. He knew that the employees were never careless about these matters with their previous supervisor.

Discussion Questions

1. What are some possible reasons for the back-of-the house employees' carelessness?
2. How should Tom assess the current situation?
3. If you were Tom's supervisor, what advice would you have given him before he started his new position?

Career Information

Do you know exactly where you want to be in five or 10 years? The best advice is to follow your interests. Do what you love to do and success will soon come. Often, we assess our own character and personality to determine a suitable path. Some opt for the accounting and control side of the tourism business; others, perhaps with more outgoing personalities, vie for sales and marketing;

others prefer operations, which could be either in back or in front of the house. Creating your own career path can be an exciting and a challenging task. However, the travel and tourism industry is generally characterized as dynamic, fun, and full of challenges and opportunities. And remember, someone has to run Walt Disney World, Holland American Cruise Lines, Marriot Hotels and Resorts, B&Bs, restaurants, and be the airport manager.

The anticipated growth of tourism over the next few years offers today's students numerous career opportunities in each section of the industry, as well as increasing job stability. Every chapter in this book will list and describe some of the career possibilities for that specific sector. However, there are many general things that can be said about a career in the hospitality industry. For example, a regular 8:30 A.M. to 4:30 P.M. job is not the norm; nearly all sectors operate up to 24 hours a day, 365 days a year—including evenings, weekends, and holidays. The good news is that nearly all sectors are experiencing growth and should continue to do so over the next few years.

CASE EXAMPLE

How to Treat Prospective Associates

A recent hospitality graduate, Stacy Sanford, started her hospitality career working for a major hotelier in New York, where she experienced firsthand how a world-class human resources (HR) department executed a well-devised HR plan. She describes the hotel:

It is a 500-room hotel that is full service and always busy. We have about 25 to 30 employees in the kitchen alone; the banquet and service staff represents another 40 people, and there are probably another 100 people employed as housekeepers, room service, front desk, a bellman, maintenance, HR, and management. Stacy's first experience with this employer was its HR department. She applied to the job from a listing at the school she was attending in Hyde Park, New York. The listing stated they needed a cook to work long weekend hours and they would accept applications Monday through Friday between 2:00 and 4:00 P.M. She arrived on a Tuesday and was greeted by one of the HR employees. After filling out the paperwork, she thought that they would probably contact her at a later date if they were interested, but as she turned to leave, the HR employee asked her to stay. Patricia, the HR director, asked her to come into the office for a prescreening, where she was asked questions about prior experience, education, and plans for the future. Patricia kept using terms like *team members* and *family*. After a short time, Patricia had the sous chef come down to talk to Stacy, and he asked questions about Stacy's passions and hobbies. She began to feel as if they might hire her, but the sous chef said he needed to send the chef down to talk to her. By now, Stacy had been in the HR office for over an hour. The chef came down and asked her to take a trip up to the restaurant on the top floor. He told his story about how he made it to where he is today. Stacy began to realize the entire staff was sizing her up to see if they wanted her to work with them. After her talk with the chef, he said there was one more person she would need to talk to. She was walked down to the office of the hotel manager. The hotel manager stood up, introduced himself, and asked Stacy why she chose their hotel. She answered that it was because of the company's excellent reputation. After finishing all of her impromptu interviews, Stacy was escorted back down to Patricia, who finished her paperwork, took her on an extended tour of the hotel, and introduced her to the entire staff. As she walked through the hotel, there was not one person she passed who did not say hi and introduce themselves.

(continued)

CASE EXAMPLE *(continued)*

Stacy realized that her experience with human resources was just part of the company's mission to make sure they had the right person for the job. The planning to make sure that every applicant was interviewed by at least three managers and the interest in her future goals and future with the company was very impressive. Stacy was trained in her job for two weeks before she went solo, and Patricia checked on her several times throughout her first two weeks. Stacy saw that the employees at this hotel loved their jobs and did not have to be prodded to do what they were supposed to do. They all felt grateful to be working with a company that cared so much about their employees. The quality of work that the employees produced was incredible, and everyone watched everyone else to make sure that the standards stayed high and that guest satisfaction was the main focus.

In the planning stages of this HR department, the long-term or strategic plan was to hire only the right person for each position; they also took extra care in the hiring process to make sure that the person fit the team. The personnel were chosen by the managers of HR and were handpicked; when they found a person to fit the mold they took extra time with the applicant to make sure everything lined up. This hotel used the exemption form of management and was able to use this style because of the quality of the employees they hired. The job descriptions were clearly defined so that employees knew what their job entailed, and all employees were thoroughly trained.

Having a plan in place allows companies to choose the best people, they become proactive instead of reactive, they are ready to hire a good person because the system is in place to allow the interviews, and the training is in place so the employee does not become frustrated. The HR manager knows that checking on the employee in the first week helps build confidence in the employee that if he or she has problems he or she has somewhere to go.

Summary

1. The hospitality and tourism industries are the largest and fastest-growing industries in the world.
2. Now is a great time to pursue a career in the hospitality and tourism field because thousands of supervising managers are needed for this dynamic industry.
3. Common dynamics in the hospitality industry include delivery of services and guest impressions of them.
4. Hospitality businesses are open 365 days a year, 24 hours a day, and are likely to require shift work.
5. One essential difference between the hospitality business and other businesses is that in hospitality we are selling an intangible and perishable product.
6. Corporate philosophy is changing from managers who plan, organize, implement, and so on, to that of managers who counsel associates, give them resources, and help them to think for themselves.
7. Corporate philosophy embraces organizational values that stress ethics, morals, fairness, and equality. Within this context, the philosophy of "do whatever it takes" to serve your guests properly is critical for success.
8. Corporate culture refers to the overall style or feel of the company, or how people relate to one another and their jobs.

9. A mission statement is a statement of central purposes, strategies, and values of the company. It should answer the question, "What business are we in?"
10. A goal is a specific target to be met; objectives or tactics are the actions needed to accomplish the goal.
11. Total Quality Management has helped improve service to guests by empowering employees to give service that exceeds guest expectations.
12. Globalization and the rapid changes in technology are two of the current trends faced by the hospitality and tourism industry.

Key Words and Concepts

back of the house
best practices
career path
core values
corporate philosophy
empowerment
front of the house
goal

guest satisfaction
heart of the house
hospitality
hospitality industry philosophy
inseparability
intangible
National Restaurant Association (NRA)

perishability
return on investment
service industries
sustainability
total quality management (TQM)
tourism
variability

Review Questions

1. Why is service so critical in the hospitality and tourism industries?
2. Describe and give an example of the following:
   Mission statement
   Moment of truth
3. What is the Disney service model?
4. Explain the significance behind Ritz-Carlton winning the Malcolm Baldrige award and how they were able to accomplish this.
5. What are some trends in the hospitality and tourism industry?

Internet Exercises

1. Organization: **World Travel and Tourism Council**
   Summary: The World Travel and Tourism Council (WTTC) is the global business leaders' forum for travel and tourism. It includes all sectors of industry, including accommodation, catering, entertainment, recreation, transportation, and other travel-related services. Its central goal is to work with governments so that they can realize the full potential economic impact of the world's largest generator of wealth and jobs: travel and tourism.
   (a) Find the latest statistics or figures for the global hospitality and tourism economy.

2. Organization: **The Ritz-Carlton Hotels**
   Summary: The Ritz-Carlton is renowned for its elegance, sumptuous surroundings, and legendary service. With 74 hotels in 23 countries worldwide, a majority of them award-winning, the Ritz-Carlton reflects one hundred years of tradition.
   (a) What is it about the Ritz-Carlton that makes it such a great hotel chain?

3. Organization: **Disneyland and Walt Disney World**
   (a) Compare and contrast Disneyland's and Walt Disney World's Web sites.

Apply Your Knowledge

1. Write your personal mission statement.

2. Suggest ways to improve service in a hospitality business.

Suggested Activities

1. Where are you going? Take a moment to think about your future career prospects. Where do you want to be in five, 10, or 20 years?

2. Prepare some general hospitality- and career-related questions, and interview two supervisors or managers in the hospitality industry. Share and compare the answers with your class next session.

Endnotes

1. This section draws on: *Hospitality through the Ages* (Corning, NY: Corning Foodservice Products: Corning Foodservice Products, February 1972), 2–34.

2. William S. Gray and Salvatore C. Liquori, *Hotel and Motel Management and Operation* (Englewood Cliffs, NJ: Prentice Hall, 1980), 4–5, quoted in John R. Walker, *Introduction to Hospitality*, 2nd ed. (Upper Saddle River, NJ: Prentice Hall, 1999), P5.

3. John R. Walker, *Introduction to Hospitality*, 2nd ed. (Upper Saddle River, NJ: Prentice Hall, 1999), P5.

4. Garvin R. Nathan, *Historic Taverns of Boston: 370 Years of Tavern History in One Definitive Guide* (Lincoln, NE: iUniverse, 2006), 3.

5. Linda Glick Conway, ed., *The Professional Chef*, 5th ed. (Hyde Park, NY: The Culinary Institute of America, 1991), 5.

6. Ibid.

7. John Mariani, *America Eats Out* (New York: William Morrow, 1991), 122–124.

8. Martin E. Dorf, *Restaurants That Work* (New York: Whitney Library of Design, 1992), 9.

9. Personal conversation with Charlotte Jordan, May 6, 2007.

10. Nathan Cobb, *Boston Globe Magazine*, June 4, 1989, quoted in John R. Walker, *The Restaurant from Concept to Operation*, 6th ed. (New York: John Wiley and Sons, 2012), 59.

11. Starbucks Coffee Company, *Our Heritage* and Starbucks Coffee Company, *Company Profile*, www.starbucks.com. Go to About Us and click on Our Company (accessed January 14, 2011 and accessed July 22, 2014, respectively).

12. Industries at a Glance. Leisure and Hospitality. Retrieved on February 4, 2014. http://www.bls.gov. Go to Tools and click on Industries at a Glance.

13. Tiffany Julian, *Work-Life Earnings by Field of Degree and Occupation for People With a Bachelor's Degree: 2011*. http://www.census.gov. Go to Library and click on Publications to search for this article (accessed November 4, 2013).

14. Robert Longley, *Lifetime Earnings Soar with Education: Masters Degree Worth $2.5 Million Income Over a Lifetime*, http://www.about.com. Go to More, click on News & Issues, find U.S. News and click on US Government, and then search for "Lifetime Earnings Soar with Education" (accessed February 3, 2011).

15. Marriott International, Inc., *Core Values*, www.marriott.com. Click on About Marriott and then click on Core Values & Heritage (accessed January 18, 2015).

16. Marriott, *Marriott Culture*, www.marriott.com. Click on About Marriott and then click on Core Values & Heritage (accessed January 18, 2015).

17. NGO Committee on Education, United Nations, *Our Common Future, Chairman's Foreword*, http://www.un-documents.net. Type in the search term "ocf-cf" to find this article (accessed February 15, 2015).

18. *Green Living*. www.rwu.edu. Go to Campus Life, click on Campus & Beyond, and then click on Green Living (accessed November 5, 2015).

19. Hervé Houdré, Center for Hospitality Research, *Sustainable Hospitality: Sustainable Development in the Hotel Industry*, www.cornell.edu. Go to Academics, click on Colleges & Schools, and then click on School of Hotel Administration (SHA). Perform a search for "Sustainable Hospitality" to find this article (accessed February 14, 2015).

20. Mohamed Gravy, General Manager Holiday Inn Sarasota, address to University of South Florida students, Tampa, Florida, February 8, 2010.

21. Marriott International Company Profile. http://www.marriott.com. Click on About Marriott, click on Marriott News Center, and then click on Company Profile (accessed July 21, 2014).

22. Ibid.

23. John W. Marriott Jr. and Kathi Ann Brown, *The Spirit to Serve: Marriott's Way* (New York: Harper Collins, 1997), 34.

24. Karl Albrecht and Ron Zemke, *Service America!* (Homewood, IL: Dow Jones-Irwin, 1985), 2.

25. Karl Albrecht, *At America's Service* (New York: Warner Books, 1992), 13.

26. Karl Albrecht, *At America's Service*, 27.

27. American Hotel & Lodging Association, *AH&LA Green Resource Center*, http://www.ahla.com. Click on programs & initiatives, and then click on Green (accessed February 3, 2011).

28. *The Fourteen Points for the Transformation of Management,* https://www.deming.org. Click on The Man, click on Theories & Teachings, and then click on The Fourteen Points For The Transformation of Management (accessed May 20, 2015).

29. Marriott International, Inc., *Brands*, http://www.marriott.com. Click on About Marriott, click on Hotel Development, and then click on Brands (accessed August 10, 2011).

30. Experience it all with Gaylord Hotels: Vacations, conventions, reunions & more http://www.marriott.com. Click on Destination Entertainment, and then click on Gaylord Hotels (accessed on May 20, 2015).

CHAPTER 2

The Hotel Business

LEARNING OBJECTIVES

After reading and studying this chapter, you should be able to:

- Describe hotel ownership and development via hotel franchising and management contracts.

- Explain the diamond rating classification of hotels.

- Classify hotels by rating system type, location, and price.

- Discuss the concept and growth of vacation ownership.

- Discuss sustainable/green lodging.

- Identify trends influencing the hotel business.

A Brief History of Innkeeping in the United States[1]

1634—Samuel Coles Inn opens on Washington Street and is the first tavern in Boston; it is later named the Ship Tavern.

1642—The City Tavern in New York City is built by the West India Company.

1775—The Green Dragon in Boston becomes the meeting place of American Revolutionaries. Patrick Henry calls the taverns of colonial America the "cradles of liberty."

1790—The first use of the word *hotel* in America is at Carre's Hotel, 24 Broadway, New York City.

1801—The Francis Union Hotel in Philadelphia opens in a former presidential mansion.

1801–1820—Taverns are rechristened as *hotels* following a surge in popularity of all things French.

1824—The Mountain House, the first of the large resort hotels in the Catskills, eventually has 300 rooms and accommodates 500 persons.

1829—The Tremont House in Boston appears. Designed from cellar to eaves to be a hotel, it has three stories and 170 rooms. This hotel is known for several firsts: the first bellboys, the first inside water closets (toilets), the first hotel clerk, the French cuisine on a Yankee menu, the first menu card in this country, the first annunciators in guest rooms, the first room keys given to the guests, and the first guests checked in at a dedicated reception area—previously they checked in at the bar.

1834—The Astor House, New York City's first palatial hotel, has rooms furnished in black walnut and Brussels carpeting.

1846—The first centrally heated hotel, the Eastern Exchange Hotel, opens in Boston.

1848—Safety deposit boxes are provided for guests by the New England Hotel in Boston.

1852—Electric lights dazzle guests for the first time in New York City's Hotel Everett and at Chicago's Palmer House in 1894.

1859—The first passenger elevator goes into operation in the Old Fifth Avenue Hotel; upper rooms are sometimes more expensive than those on lower floors.

1875—The Palace Hotel in San Francisco is billed as the "world's largest hotel"; floor clerks are installed along with four elevators.

1880–1890s—There is a resort boom in Florida, New England, Virginia, Pennsylvania, and Atlantic City.

1887—The Ponce de León Hotel, in St. Augustine, is built; it is the first luxury hotel in Florida.

1888—The Del Coronado Hotel is built; it is the first luxury resort in California.

1892—The Brown Palace Hotel in Denver is built with "gold money" to be as fine as any hotel back east. The Brown Palace focuses on catering to business people and is regarded as one of the first convention hotels.

1908—The Statler Hotel in Buffalo, New York, is established by Elsworth Milton Statler, and is considered by many to be the premier hotelier of all time (his story makes interesting reading—try Googling him). The Statler hotel is the first to introduce keyholes for safety, electric light switches, private baths, ice water, and the delivery of a morning newspaper. The hotel is also constructed so as to have bathrooms backing onto each other; this enables the plumbing to go up or down one shaft along with protected electrical wiring. The Statler Inn at Cornell University is built with money from the Statler foundation.

1919—Conrad Hilton opens the Mobley Hotel in Cisco, Texas.

1920—There are 12 million cars in America, and auto camping becomes a national pastime as cities open up camps for people to stay at.

1922—Cornell University begins a hotel and restaurant program.

1929–1945—During the Great Depression and World War II, hotel occupancy drops and several hotels are lost by owners—others just manage to survive.

1946—The Golden Nugget and the Flamingo open in Las Vegas, prompting a boom in hotel construction that continues to this day.

1950s and 1960s—More interstate highways are constructed and more motels and hotels are established for the ordinary person, not just the rich.

1954—Kemmons Wilson opens the first Holiday Inn.

1960s—Westin introduces 24-hour room service.

1966—The ice and vending machines make their debuts in InterContinental hotels.

1967—The Atlanta Hyatt Regency Hotel, designed by John Portman with an atrium and an indoor garden, opens.

1960s and 1970s—Hotels begin to develop internationally.

1970s—Hotels are hit hard by the energy crisis—there is little development. Cable TV arrives; it later evolves into Internet access.

1975—Hyatt introduces concierge lounges for its VIP guests.

1980s—The electric key card is introduced, and hotels begin to accept major credit cards as payment.

1980s and 1990s—Hotel chains develop more rapidly internationally. Hotels are developed in several tiers/price points to appeal to different market segments.

1990s—Voice mail and in-room Internet connections are introduced.

THE AMERICAN HOTEL & LODGING ASSOCIATION

Dedicated to Serving the Interests of Hoteliers

For over 100 years, the American Hotel & Lodging Association (AH&LA) has been an advocate for all matters relating to lodging. The AH&LA represents 52,887 properties with 4,926,543 guestrooms, $163 billion in sales, $68.64 revenue per available room (Rev Par), and an average occupancy rate of 62.2 percent.[4] As a nonprofit trade association, the AH&LA exists to help the lodging industry prosper, with national advocacy on Capitol Hill, public relations and image management, education, research, and information. The AH&LA also has several programs that benefit members, among which are a comprehensive Green Resource Center; diversity programs and advice for helping members improve their diversity initiatives; technology resources and initiatives to help members improve their technology efforts; social media advice, including resources for Facebook, blogs, Twitter, Yelp (the number-one travel application for the iPhone), Four Square (another way for consumers to write reviews, leave suggestions, and talk about hotels), LivingSocial, Groupon, and Buy With Me; Traveler-Generated Content (user-generated data for gathering travel information); and online resources for leveraging the collective buying power to which more than 20 million people subscribe, with electronic promotions sent daily.

The AH&LA has conventions, the main one being in New York City in November. Additionally, there are state chapters and conventions that are recommended for you to attend as they offer several interesting presentations and discussions on lodging topics.

2000s—Boutique hotels come of age, and LEED (Leadership in Energy and Environmental Design) hotels are constructed. Sustainability becomes increasingly more important. Social media starts to appear and continuously increases presence in hotels, while the Internet continues to reach wider audiences. Internet destination marketing and online hotel bookings increase.

2013—Mobile devices reach greater online access than desktops or laptops. Hotel and destination marketers look at increased ways to profit on mobile applications, as social media and mobile devices become inseparable. Everything is going social.[2]

2014—Meta-search marketing allows people to compare between hotels and other lodging options based on a variety of real-time factors such as room rates, availability, promotions, and other factors. Meta-search marketing provides guests with relevant and succinct information about location, amenities, and guest reviews at any given time.[3]

LEARNING OBJECTIVE 1
Describe hotel ownership and development via hotel franchising and management contracts.

Hotel Development and Ownership

The lodging industry is a more than $155 billion industry that includes approximately 53,000 properties with almost five million guestrooms. This is an industry that continues to flourish predominantly by way of franchising

FOCUS ON DEVELOPMENT

Dr. Chad M. Gruhl, Professor at Metropolitan State University of Denver.

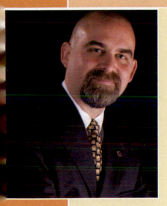

Dr. Gruhl is a hotel expert working for such places as the Waldorf Astoria in New York City, Trump Plaza Hotel and Casino in Atlantic City, Hotel Intercontinental in Chicago, and Residence Inn by Marriott in three states.

There has been a tremendous amount of development in the hotel industry in the past 40 years. The large hotel corporations discovered that if they targeted specific markets, they would be able to increase market share for particular segments. For example, in the early 1940s until the 1970s, Hilton Hotels focused primarily on their major hotel chain, full-service Hilton Hotels. Later in the 1970s, Hilton began expanding and developing other concepts in order to capture a larger market share:

1970—Purchased the Flamingo Hotel and the Las Vegas International, making them big players in the gaming industry

1984—The first Embassy Suites (all-suite brand) and Hampton Inn (mid-economy segment) opened under the Hilton umbrella

1989—Hilton opens the first Homewood Suites Hotel (extended-stay segment)

1990—Hilton Garden Inn debuts four hotels (mid-economy segment)

2002—Hilton becomes involved with Vacation Ownership (resort segment)

2009—Expansions into 76 countries making Hilton the largest full-service hotel brand in the world (full-service brand)

2011—Home2 Suites (extended-stay segment) opens in Fayetteville, NC

Today, Hilton also owns the Waldorf Astoria Collection, Conrad Hotels and Resorts, Canopy, Curio, and Double-Tree. Hilton flies a total of 12 flags with over 4,200 hotels (698,000 rooms) in 93 countries and territories.

Do these large companies do it all themselves? Meaning, do they operate, own, and expand the corporate name all by themselves? The answer is, absolutely not. The largest hotel companies have expanded at very fast rates through franchising. This is one of the primary sources of income for most large hotel and restaurant companies.

For example, to apply for an InterContinental Hotel and Resorts flag (the right to use their name), it costs $500 per room with a $75,000 minimum for the initial cost and application fee. After the hotel opens, it costs five percent of revenue for royalty fees and another three percent for marketing fees. In other words, it is very expensive to fly a major hotel flag. So why would anyone develop a hotel where they fly another company's flag? The answer is simple: The major hotel companies have very large reservation systems and brand recognition that brings people to that hotel once the hotel opens its doors.

There are eight large corporate hotel companies that fly approximately 75 percent of all U.S. hotels. Behind each large corporation are only a few of the larger flags that they own:

1. **Wyndham Hotels and Resorts:** Days Inn, Howard Johnson's, Ramada, Super 8, Travelodge
2. **Choice Hotels:** Comfort Inn, Quality Inn, Clarion, Econo Lodge, Sleep Inn

(continued)

FOCUS ON DEVELOPMENT *(Continued)*

3. **Accor:** Sofitel, Novotel, Mercure, Ibis, Adagio
4. **InterContinental Hotel Group:** Crowne Plaza, Holiday Inn, Staybridge Suites, Candlewood Suites, Hotel Indigo, InterContinental, Even, Hualuxe
5. **Marriott International:** The Ritz-Carlton, Marriott Hotels & Resorts, Renaissance Hotels & Resorts, Courtyard, Fairfield Inn, Residence Inn, Bulgari Hotels & Resorts
6. **Blackstone:** Hilton Hotels, Waldorf Astoria Hotels & Resorts, DoubleTree by Hilton, Embassy Suites Hotels, Hampton Inn
7. **Carlson Rezidor Hotel Group:** Radisson, Country Inns & Suites, Park Inn, Park Plaza
8. **Starwood:** Sheraton Hotels & Resorts, Four Points by Sheraton, St. Regis Hotels & Resorts, Le Méridien, W Hotels, Westin Hotels & Resorts

There are many development and franchising opportunities in the hotel and restaurant world. You, too, can make your mark on the industry.

and management contracts, which are the two main driving forces in the development and operation of the hotel business.[5] After the potential of franchising caught on, there was no stopping American ingenuity. In about a half century, the hotel business was changed forever, and here is how it happened.

Franchising

Franchising in the hospitality industry is a concept that allows a company to expand more rapidly by using other people's money rather than acquiring its own financing. The company, or franchisor, grants certain rights to the franchisee—for example, the rights to use its trademark, signs, proven operating systems, operating procedures and, possibly, its reservations system, marketing know-how, purchasing discounts, and so on—for a fee. In return, the franchisee agrees by signing the franchise contract to operate the restaurant, hotel, or franchised outlet in accordance with the guidelines set by the franchisor. Franchising is a way of doing business that benefits both the franchisor—who wants to expand the business rapidly—and the franchisee—who has financial backing but lacks specific expertise and recognition. Some corporations franchise by individual outlets and others by territory. North America is host to more than 180 hotel brand extensions and franchised hotel brands.

Franchising hotels in the United States began in 1907, when the Ritz Development Company franchised the Ritz-Carlton name in New York City.[6] Howard Johnson began franchising his hotels in 1954—he had successfully franchised the "red roof" restaurants since 1927. Holiday Inn (now a part of InterContinental Hotels Group [IHG], one of the largest lodging enterprises in the world) also grew by the strategy of franchising: In 1952, Kemmons

Wilson, a developer, had a disappointing experience while on a family vacation when he had to pay for an extra room for his children. Therefore, Wilson decided to build a moderately priced family-style hotel.

Each room was comfortably sized and had two double beds; this enabled children to stay for free in their parents' rooms. In the 1950s and early 1960s, as the economy grew, Holiday Inn grew in size and popularity. Holiday Inns eventually added restaurants, meeting rooms, and recreational facilities. They upgraded the furnishings and fixtures in the bedrooms and almost completely abandoned the original concept of being a moderately priced lodging operation.

One of the key factors in the successful development of Holiday Corporation was that it was one of the first companies to enter the midprice range of the market. These inns, or motor hotels, were often located away from the expensive downtown sites, near important freeway intersections and the more reasonably priced suburbs. Another reason for their success was the value they offered: comfort at a reasonable price, avoiding the expensive trimmings of luxury hotels.

At about this time, a new group of budget motels emerged. Motel 6 (so named because the original cost of a room was $6 a night) in California slowly spread across the country, as did Days Inn and others. Cecil B. Day was in the construction business and found Holiday Inns too expensive when traveling on vacation with his family. He bought cheap land and constructed buildings of no more than two stories to keep the costs down. These hotels and motels, primarily for commercial travelers and vacationing families, were located close to major highways and were built to provide low-cost lodging without frills. Some of these buildings were modular constructions. Entire rooms were built elsewhere, transported to the site, and placed side by side.

It was not until the 1960s that Hilton and Sheraton began to franchise their names. Franchising was the primary growth and development strategy of hotels and motels during the 1960s, 1970s, and 1980s. However, franchising presents two major challenges for the franchisor: maintenance of quality standards and avoidance of financial failure on the part of the franchisee.

It is difficult for the franchise company to state in writing all the contingencies that will ensure that quality standards are met. Recent franchise agreements are more specific in terms of the exterior maintenance and guest service levels. Franchise fees vary according to the agreements worked out between the franchisor and the franchisee; however, an average agreement is based on three or four percent of room revenue.

The world's leading franchisors of hotels are InterContinental Hotels and Resorts with 688,517 rooms in 4,704 hotels;[7] Wyndham Worldwide with 627,440 rooms in 7,340 hotels;[8] and Choice Hotels International with 500,000 rooms in 6,300 hotels.[9] Franchising

The colorful lobby of a Hotel Indigo, a franchised InterContinental Hotels Group concept.

provides both benefits and drawbacks to the franchisee and franchisor. The benefits to the franchisee are as follows:

- A set of plans and specifications from which to build
- National advertising
- A centralized reservation system (CRS)
- Participation in volume discounts for purchasing furnishings, fixtures, and equipment
- Listing in the franchisor's directory
- Low fee percentage charged by credit card companies

The drawbacks to the franchisee are as follows:

- Franchisees must pay high fees, both to join and ongoing.
- Central reservations generally produce between 17 and 26 percent of reservations.
- Franchisees must conform to the franchisor's agreement.
- Franchisees must maintain all standards set by the franchisor.

The benefits to the franchise company are as follows:

- Increased market share and recognition
- Up-front fees

The drawbacks to the franchise company are as follows:

- The need to be very careful in the selection of franchisees
- Difficulty in maintaining control of standards

Franchising continues to be a popular form of expansion both in North America and the rest of the world. However, there are always a few properties that lose their right to franchise by not maintaining standards.

Factors propelling franchise growth include the following:

- Fresh looks (curb appeal)
- Location near highways, airports, and suburbs
- Expansion in smaller cities throughout the United States
- New markets located in proximity to golf courses and other attractions
- Foreign expansion and a move to increase brand awareness

Is There a Franchise in Your Future?[10]

Many of you may not realize the pervasiveness of franchised operations in the United States. Predictions are that more than 50 percent of all retail sales in the United States (including restaurants) will soon be transacted through franchised units. Furthermore, franchises are available not only in the hotel, restaurant, travel, and recreation industries, but also in a large variety of other businesses that might interest you. These businesses include automotive tires and parts, retailing of all kinds, mail and copy services, janitorial and decorating services, personnel agencies, and so on. Today, many franchises can be operated from home by those interested in lifestyle changes.

If you end up working for a hospitality-related organization after graduation, chances are that your career will be influenced by franchising. You may work directly for a franchisor (the company that sells a franchised concept to an entrepreneur), whether on the corporate staff (e.g., training and franchise consulting) or in an operations position in a franchisor-owned unit. Many franchisors own their own units, which they use to test new operational or marketing ideas and to demonstrate the viability of the business to potential franchisees (the entrepreneurs who buy the franchised unit).

Alternatively, you may work for a franchisee. Some franchisees are small businesses, owning only one or a few units. Other franchisees are large corporations, owning hundreds of units and doing hundreds of millions, and now, upwards of one billion dollars in sales every year. For instance, Flynn Restaurant Group, the country's largest franchisee, owns and operates more than 500 restaurants in 23 states, including 470 Applebee's and 170 Taco Bell franchises. The nation's largest franchisees are more inclined to operate some of the better known quick service and fast casual restaurants, such as McDonald's, Burger King, Wendy's, Arby's, and Applebee's.[11]

A third way that franchising may involve you is through ownership. Rather than starting your own independent business after college, you may want to consider buying a franchise. Several advantages can result. First, by working with a larger company you get the benefits of its experience in running the business that you have chosen to enter. Many of the mistakes that a new entrepreneur may make have already been overcome by your franchisor. The company might provide cash flow. The company might also provide other support services at little or no cost, such as marketing and advertising, site selection, construction plans, assistance with financing, and so on. All this assistance leads to a second key reason for buying a franchise—reducing your risk of failure. Franchising is probably less risky than starting your own business from scratch.

Consider the following factors that many franchisors seek. Are you strongly motivated to succeed and do you have a past history of business success, even if it is in a different business? Do you have a significant sum of money as well as access to credit? Are you willing to accept the franchisor's values, philosophy, and ways of doing business, as well as its technical assistance? Do you have the full support of your immediate family as you develop your business? Are you willing to devote substantially all of your working time to the business?

Franchising does have some disadvantages, as noted by many former franchisees. Your expectations of success may not be met. Perhaps the business did not have the potential that you expected, or perhaps you were not willing to invest the time needed. In a few cases, an overzealous or dishonest franchisor representative has misled franchisees.

As a franchisee, your freedom is somewhat restricted. You must operate within the constraints set out by your franchise agreement and the operational standards manual. Although there may be some room for you to express your creativity and innovation, it is generally limited. This may mean that, over time, the work might become monotonous and unchallenging, yet you have a long-term commitment to the company because of the franchise agreement that you signed. Your failure to consistently follow the

CORPORATE PROFILE

Wyndham Worldwide—A Collection of Hotel Brands

Wyndham Hotels and Resorts, Wyndham Grand Hotels and Resorts, Wyndham Garden, Days Inn, Howard Johnson, Ramada, Knights Inn, Super 8, Travelodge, Baymont Inns & Suites, Microtel Inns and Suites, Hawthorn Suites, Wingate by Wyndham, TRYP by Wyndham, Dream Hotels, and Night Hotels, totalling more than 7,340 hotels in 66 countries.[12]

As a franchisor, the company licenses the owners and operators of independent businesses to use Wyndham brand names, without taking on big business risks and expenses. Wyndham does not operate hotels, but instead provides coordination and services that allow franchisees to retain local control of their activities. At the same time, franchisees benefit from the economies of scale of widely promoted brand names and well-established standards of service, national and regional direct marketing, co-marketing programs, and volume purchasing discounts.

All brands share extensive market research, use proprietary reservation systems and a room inventory tracking system, which is extremely technology intensive and eliminates waste. By monitoring quality control and extensively promoting the brand names, Wyndham offers its independent franchise owners franchise fees that are relatively low compared to the increased profitability they gain.

Through franchising, the company limits its own risks and is able to keep overhead costs low. Wyndham also limits the volatility in the business as best as they can because fees come from revenue, not the franchisee's profitability. A further advantage of being a franchiser of such dimension is that the company is even more protected from the cyclical nature of the economy than are other franchise ventures.

Wyndham Vacation Ownership is the largest vacation ownership business when measured by the number of vacation ownership interests. Wyndham Vacation Ownership develops, markets, and sells vacation ownership interests and provides consumer financing to owners through its three primary consumer brands: Wyndham Vacation Resorts, WorldMark by Wyndham, and Wyndham Vacation Resorts Asia Pacific.[13]

Wyndham Vacation Ownership has developed or acquired approximately 185 vacation ownership resorts throughout the United States, Canada, Mexico, the Caribbean, and the South Pacific that represent approximately 23,000 individual vacation ownership units and more than 900,000 owners of vacation ownership interests.[14]

Wyndham Exchange and Rentals helps to deliver vacations to more than 3.7 million members in approximately 100 countries. Wyndham provides exclusive access for specified periods to more than 106,000 vacation properties, including vacation ownership condominiums, traditional hotel rooms, villas, cottages, bungalows, campgrounds, city apartments, second homes, fractional resorts, private residence clubs, condominium hotels, and yachts. With a portfolio of more than 30 brands, Wyndham delivers unique vacation experiences to over four million leisure-bound families each year.[15]

Wyndham has been named to the Diversity Inc. 25 noteworthy companies that are raising diversity management leaders. Wyndham has also been ranked among the best 100 greatest companies in America by *Newsweek* magazine, who also ranked Wyndham among the top 100 greenest companies in America.

franchisor's methods for running the business could result in the termination of your contract and your forced removal from the business.

Finally, the franchisor may not be performing well, thereby hurting your local business. Also, they may allow other franchisees to open units so near to your operation that your business is adversely affected.

Buying a franchise can be a very rewarding business experience in many ways. But like any other business venture, it requires research and a full discussion with family, friends, and business advisors, such as your accountant and attorney. You should carefully weigh whether you are psychologically suited to be a franchisee. Perhaps you perform more effectively in a corporate structure as an employee. Perhaps you are better suited to starting your own business from scratch. A careful analysis can help you make an informed decision. Buying a franchise such as Subway, Cold Stone Creamery, or Sea Master cruises is a lot cheaper—as in a few thousand dollars—compared to $1 million-plus for a hotel or even a McDonald's. A key question to be answered before you buy a franchise is whether you are better suited to being a franchisee or an independent entrepreneur.

Referral Associations

Referral associations offer similar benefits to properties as franchises, albeit at a lower cost. Hotels and motels with a referral association share a CRS and a common image, logo, or advertising slogan. In addition, referrals may offer group-buying discounts to members, as well as management training and continuing education programs. Each independent hotel refers guests to each of the other member hotels. Hotels and motels pay an initial fee to join a referral association. Size and appearance standards are less stringent than those in a franchise agreement; hence, guests may find more variation between the facilities than between franchise members.

Preferred Hotels and Resorts Worldwide is a consortium of 185 independent, luxury hotels and resorts united to compete with the marketing power of chain operations. It promotes the individuality, high standards, hospitality, and luxury of member hotels. It also provides marketing support services and a reservation center.

With the decrease in airline commissions, referral organizations—especially those at the luxury end of the market—are well placed to offer incentives to agents to book clients with the referral group's hotels. An example is awarding trips to the property for every 10 rooms booked. Another, for instance, is when the referral hotels offer, for instance, a 20 percent commission to travel agents during slow periods.

Three luxury Boston-area preferred properties— the Boston Harbor Hotel, the Bostonian Hotel, and the Charles Hotel in Cambridge, Massachusetts— joined together in promoting a St. Patrick's Day weekend package. Preferred Hotels in Texas—the Mansion on Turtle Creek and Hotel Crescent Court

The Ciragan Kempinski Palace Hotel Istanbul, Turkey.

in Dallas, La Mansion del Rio South in San Antonio, and the Washington Hotel in Fort Worth—launched a major, year-long promotion that includes a tie-in with major retail, credit card, and airline partners.

In addition to regional marketing programs, the referral associations that handle reservations for members have joined Galileo International's Inside Availability Service. This gives agents access to actual rates and room availability that are not always available on the standard CRS databases.

Leading Hotels of the World (LHW) was set up in 1928 as Luxury Hotels of Europe and Egypt by 38 hotels, including the London Savoy; the Hotel Royal in Evian, France; and the Hotel Negresco in Nice, France—each was interested in improving its marketing. The organization operated by having hotels advise their guests to use the establishments of fellow members. It then opened a New York office to make direct contact with wealthy American and Canadian travelers wishing to visit Europe and Egypt.

LHW, which is controlled by its European members, acts as an important marketing machine for its members, especially now, with offices around the world providing reservations, sales, and promotional services. All the hotels and offices are connected by a central computer reservation system called ResStar. The number of reservations members receive from Leading Hotel members varies from place to place, but with more than 430 member hotels, it must be beneficial.

Like LHW, Small Luxury Hotels of the World (SLH) is another marketing consortium in which 79 independently owned and managed hotels and resorts are members. For more than 35 years, it has sought to market and sell its membership to the travel industry and to provide an inter-hotel networking system for all members. Each hotel is assessed and regularly checked to ensure that it maintains the very highest standards.

Management Contracts

Management contracts have been responsible for the hotel industry's rapid boom since the 1970s. They became popular among hotel corporations because little or no up-front financing or equity is involved. Hotel management companies often form a partnership of convenience with developers and owners who generally do not have the desire or ability to operate the hotel. The management company provides operational expertise, marketing, and sales clout, often in the form of a CRS.

Some companies manage a portfolio of properties on a cluster, regional, or national basis. Even if the hotel corporation is involved in the construction of the hotel, ownership generally reverts to a large insurance company or other large corporation. This was the case with the La Jolla, California, Marriott Hotel. Marriott Corporation built the hotel for about $34 million, and then sold it to Paine Webber, a major investment banking firm, for about $52 million on completion. Not a bad return on investment!

The management contract usually allows for the hotel company to manage the property for a period of five, 10, or 20 years. For this, the company receives as a management fee, often a percentage of gross and/or net operating profit, usually about 2–4.5 percent of gross revenues. Lower fees in the two-percent range are more prevalent today, with an increase in the incentive fee based on profitability. Some contracts begin at two percent for the first year, increase to 2.5 the second, and to 3.5 the third and for the remainder of the contract.[16]

Today, many contracts are for a percentage of sales and a percentage of operating profit. This is normally 2 + 2 percent. Increased competition among management companies has decreased the management contract fees in the past few years. In recent years, hotel companies increasingly have opted for management contracts because considerably less capital is tied up in managing as compared with owning properties. This has allowed for a more rapid expansion of both the U.S. and international markets.

Recent management contracts have called for an increase in the equity commitment on the part of the management company. In addition, owners have increased their operational decision-making options to allow them more control over the property. General managers have increased responsibility to owners who also want their share of profit.

Hyatt Hotels operates most of its hotels by management contract rather than owning them all.

Today, hotel management companies exist in an extremely competitive environment. They have discovered that the hotel business, like most others, has changed and they are adapting accordingly. Today's hotel owners are demanding better bottom-line results and reduced fees. Management companies are seeking sustainability and a bigger share of the business. With international expansion, a hotel company entering the market might actively seek a local partner or owner to work within a form of joint venture.

▶ Check Your Knowledge

1. What main factor changed the nature of the hotel industry? What impact does it have today?

2. What are some of the benefits and drawbacks to being a franchisee?

3. In your own words, define *franchising* and *management contracts*.

4. Explain the nature of a referral association and some of the benefits such an arrangement offers.

Real Estate Investment Trust

Real estate investment trusts (REITs) have existed since the 1960s. In those early days, they were mostly mortgage holders. But in the 1980s, they began to own property outright, often focusing on specific sectors such as hotels, office buildings, apartments, malls, and nursing homes. An REIT must have at least 75 percent of its assets in real estate. Today, about 300 REITs, with a combined market value of $70 billion, are publicly traded. Investors like them because they do not pay corporate income tax and, instead, are required to distribute at least 95 percent of net income to shareholders. In addition, because they trade as stocks, they are much easier to get into or out of than are limited partnerships or the direct ownership of properties. In the hotel industry, REITs are clearly where the action is. As with any investment, the investor is looking for a reasonable return on the investment. Anyone can buy stocks of REITs or other publically traded companies; first, it is wise to ensure that the company is well managed and financially sound before putting any money down. The leading REIT corporations are Patriot American Hospitality, Wyndham Hotels, and Starwood Lodging Trust.

INTRODUCING CONRAD HILTON AND HILTON HOTELS CORPORATION

"King of Innkeepers" and Master of Hotel Finance

Before he was 18, Conrad Hilton had worked as a trader, a clerk, a bellboy, and a pianist. By age 25, he had worked in politics and banking.

In 1919, while visiting Cisco, Texas, Conrad Hilton had intended to take advantage of the oil boom by buying a small bank. Instead, he found bank prices prohibitive and hotels so overbooked he could not find a place to sleep. When one owner in Cisco complained he would like to sell his property in order to take advantage of the oil boom, Hilton struck a deal. He bought the Mobley Hotel with an investment of $5,000. Hilton rented rooms to oil industry prospectors and construction workers. Because of high demand for accommodations and very little supply, Hilton rented rooms in eight-hour shifts, for 300-percent occupancy. On some occasions, he even rented out his own room and slept in a lobby chair.

Because Hilton knew the banking business well and had maintained contacts who would lend him money for down payments on properties, he quickly expanded to seven Texas hotels. Hilton's strategy was to borrow as much money as possible to expand as rapidly as possible. This worked well until the Great Depression of the early 1930s. Hilton was unable to meet the payments on his properties and lost several of them but did not declare bankruptcy.[17]

Hilton, like many great leaders, even during the Depression years had the determination to bounce back. To reduce costs, he borrowed money against his life insurance and even formed an alliance with the National Hotels Corporation.

Hilton's success was attributed to two main strategies: (1) hiring the best managers and letting them have total autonomy and (2) being a careful bargainer who, in later years, was careful not to overextend his finances. Conrad Hilton had begun a successful career in the banking business before he embarked on what was to become one of the most successful hotel careers ever.

Hilton's business and financial acumen is legendary. The *New York Times* described Conrad Hilton as "a master of finance and a cautious bargainer who was careful not to overfinance" and as someone who had "a flawless sense of timing."[18] In 1954, Conrad acquired the Statler Hotel Company for $111 million, which at the time was the world's most expensive real estate transaction.

Hilton was the first person to notice vast lobbies with people sitting in comfortable chairs but not spending any money. So he added the lobby bar as a convenient meeting place and leased out space for gift shops and newsstands. Most of the additional revenue from these operations went directly to the bottom line. Today, Hilton Hotels Corporation includes Conrad Hotels, DoubleTree, Embassy Suites Hotels, Hampton Inn and Hampton Inns & Suites, Hilton Hotels, Hilton Garden Inn, Hilton Grand Vacation, Homewood Suites by Hilton, and the Waldorf Astoria Collection. These brands total thousands of hotels in cities all over the world, and "Be my guest" is still the gracious and warm way guests are received. There are 4,100 Hilton brand hotels today, and they are owned by the Blackstone Group.[19]

Hotel Development

Hotel ownership and development is very **capital intensive**. It takes millions of dollars to develop a property. New hotels are built as a business venture by a developer, and because the developer expects to make a **fair return on the** (substantial) **investment**, a **feasibility study** is done to assess the viability of the project—this is generally required by lenders. The feasibility study examines the market area's demand and supply, including any potential or real competition in the pipeline. The feasibility study determines the degree to which the proposed hotel project would be financially successful. Revenue projections based on anticipated occupancy, average daily rate, and revenue per available room are presented. The feasibility study also helps determine the type of hotel that would best suit the market and is used by the developer to obtain financing for the project. One of the most important documents is a **Summary Operating Statement**, which details revenues and expenses for a period; an example of a Summary Operating Statement is given in Figure 2–1. Also of interest is the source and disposition of the industry dollar. An example is given in Figure 2–2.

In Figure 2–1, note that close to 70 percent of a hotel's revenue and most of the profit comes from the sale of rooms. About 26 percent of revenue comes from food and beverage sales. In Figure 2–2 we can see that the average hotel room revenue is slightly different, at 66.6 percent. Each hotel will have a slight variation on these figures according to its own individual circumstances. Note in Figure 2–2 how high the percentage of wages, salaries, and benefits are at 46.7 percent.

Obviously, there needs to be a gap in the market in which a segment is currently not being served (e.g., the hip, lifestyle boutique hotels such as Hotel Indigo), plus a new hotel is expected to take some business away from existing properties if the room rates are close in price. There are two views on new hotels versus remodeled hotels as far as room rates and profits are concerned. It is often difficult for a new property to make a profit for a few years because of the higher cost of construction and the need to become known and to gain a good market share. On the other hand, a remodeled hotel has the cost of remodeling to pay for plus higher operating costs for energy and maintenance, so the two options tend to almost cancel each other out.

Today, many larger hotels are developed as part of a mixed-use project. The hotel could be near or next to a convention center, business, or

	2014 Dollars Per Available Room	Change From Prior Year	2014 Percent of Revenue	2014 Dollars Per Occupied Room
Revenue				
Rooms	$ 45,360	7.6 %	71.3 %	$ 166.05
Food and Beverage	15,526	5.9	24.4	56.84
Other Operated Departments	2,177	4.3	3.4	7.97
Rentals and Other Income	590	4.8	0.9	2.16
Total Revenue	$ 63,653	7.0 %	100.0 %	$ 233.01
Departmental Expenses*				
Rooms	$ 11,893	5.9 %	26.2 %	$ 43.54
Food and Beverage	11,585	4.1	74.6	42.41
Other Operated Departments	1,530	2.1	70.3	5.60
Total Departmental Expenses	$ 25,008	4.8 %	39.3 %	$ 91.55
Total Departmental Income	$ 38,645	8.5 %	60.7 %	$ 141.47
Undistributed Operating Expenses				
Administrative and General	$ 5,566	4.4 %	8.7 %	$ 20.37
Sales and Marketing	5,228	5.8	8.2	19.14
Property Operations and Maintenance	2,784	3.8	4.4	10.19
Utilities	2,241	5.1	3.5	8.20
Total Undistributed Expenses	$ 15,818	4.9 %	24.8 %	$ 57.90
Gross Operating Profit	$ 22,827	11.2 %	35.9 %	$ 83.56
Management Fees	$ 2,278	8.7 %	3.6 %	$ 8.34
Income Before Fixed Charges	$ 20,550	11.5 %	32.3 %	$ 75.23
Fixed Charges				
Property and Other Taxes	$ 2,245	2.5 %	3.5 %	$ 8.22
Insurance	614	4.0	1.0	2.25
Total Fixed Charges	$ 2,859	2.8 %	4.5 %	$ 10.47
Net Operating Income**	$ 17,690	13.0 %	27.8 %	$ 64.76
Percentage of Occupancy	74.8 %	3.1 %		
Average Daily Rate	$ 166.05	4.3 %		
RevPAR	$ 124.27	7.6 %		
Average Size (Rooms)	248	(0.2)%		

* Expressed as a percent of departmental revenue.
** Before deduction for rent.

Figure 2–1 • A Full-Service Hotel Summary Operating Statement.

(Courtesy of PKF Hospitality Research.)

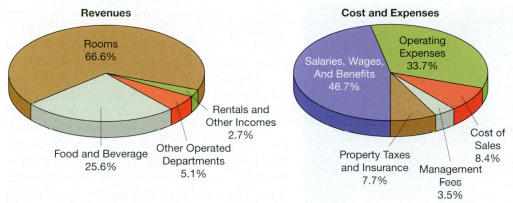

Figure 2–2 • Source and Disposition of the Industry Dollar.
(Courtesy of PKF Hospitality Research.)

attraction. The hotel may also have a residential component (as in residencies if it's a Ritz-Carlton or a condotel) and may include a spa.

Older hotels are generally renovated about every seven years. This is because they become dated and would otherwise likely lose market share, which equals decreased profit—or even a loss. Older hotels have an advantage over new ones—or should have an advantage as a result of positive recognition in the market. Additionally, most if not all of their mortgage may be paid off, so their debt service is likely easier on the cash flow than it is for a new hotel. Older hotels may have more charm, but they are more expensive to maintain. Older hotels should also have built up repeat business through guest loyalty, something a new hotel needs to do.

Kimpton hotels have an amazing collection of boutique properties. In 1981, Bill Kimpton pioneered the boutique hotel concept in the United States. His dream was to provide weary travelers with a haven of comfort, service, security, and style. (Kimpton hotels were bought by Inter-Continental Hotels Group in 2015). According to Market Metrix Hospitality Index™, Kimpton has the highest customer satisfaction scores (higher than 93 percent) and emotional attachment scores (89 percent) of any hotel company operating in the United States.[20]

Hotel chains are introducing new brands to their portfolio as they identify market segment needs. Marriott has the Autograph collection of diverse independent hotels—boutique Arts, Iconic historic, Boutique Chic, Luxury Redefined, and Retreat properties.[21] Starwood has almost 140 Aloft hotels. Hyatt has introduced Andaz, a boutique-style hotel that is vibrant yet relaxed, with each hotel reflecting the unique cultural scene and spirit of the surrounding neighborhood.[22] Hyatt has also introduced Ziva and Zilara properties for the inclusive market that have unusual amenities like floating fire pits, dolphin experiences, and interactive dining.

The Economic Impact of Hotels

Hotels provide substantial **direct** and **indirect economic impact** to the communities in which they are located. For direct impact, consider a hotel that has an average of 240 guests a night, each of whom spends $250 at the hotel

Aloft Tempe, Arizona.

and in restaurants and stores in the community per day. That would mean $240 × $250 × 365 days = $21.9 million a year infused into the local economy.

The indirect impact comes from the ripple effect, which we describe in the tourism chapter; this is where money is spent by the employees (wages and salaries) of the hotel in the community. It is also money used by the hotel to purchase all the items to service the guests. Communities also benefit from the Transient Occupancy Tax (TOT), otherwise known as the bed tax. Interestingly, the TOT tax averages 12.62 percent in the United States, or $12.39 a night nationwide.[23] In addition, the hotel and its guests and employees also pay local taxes on the purchases they make. This all adds up to a considerable economic impact. Every dollar collected by a hotel eventually recycles, or multiplies itself, creating many levels of economic activity in communities. This multilevel economic activity generated by a hotel's business is estimated by using economic multipliers for revenues, wages, salaries, and employment. If we take just the revenue impact, we can see that if a hotel's annual sales are $4,250,000 and the revenue multiplier for that area is 1.979, then the total revenue impact for the year would be $8,410,750. If we consider the employment impact, we note that if the example hotel has 160 employees and the employment multiplier for the area is 1.62, then the hotel will generate 259 jobs in the area.[24] Figure 2–3 illustrates the multiplier effect of hotels.

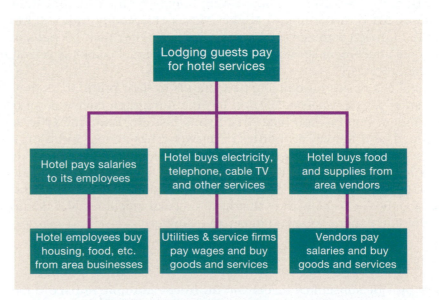

Figure 2–3 • The Multiplier Effect of Hotel Dollars on a Community.
(Courtesy of the American Hotel and Lodging Association.)

▶ **Check Your Knowledge**

1. Explain a Real Estate Investment Trust (REIT).

2. What is the difference between direct and indirect economic impact?

3. Identify the two views with regard to new hotel versus remodeled hotel development.

Classification of Hotels and Lodging Properties

LEARNING OBJECTIVE 2
Explain the diamond rating classification of hotels.

According to the AH&LA, as of year-end 2013, the U.S. lodging industry consisted of 52,887 hotels and motels, with a total of 4,926,543 guest rooms with $163 billion in sales. The average revenue per available room was $68.64 and the average occupancy was 62.2 percent.[25]

The Lodging Industry

Hotels may be classified in several ways and may have one or more affiliations. For instance, hotels may be classified using the Smith Travel Research (STR) hotel classification system, the Forbes Travel Guide Five-Star rating process, and the American Automobile Association (AAA) Five-Diamond award system. Smith Travel, Forbes, and AAA have all expanded their rating practices outside the United States.

Smith Travel Research, founded in the United States in 1985, is the industry leader in the collection, analysis, and dissemination of hotel performance data and research. Smith Travel Research collects data on hotel properties, competitive set, and the industry within and outside the United States and issues STAR reports, which summarize hotel and market performance on a weekly, monthly, and annual basis. Smith Travel Research classifies hotels using a scale system such as luxury, upper upscale, upscale, upper midscale, midscale, and economy.

Hotel Affiliations

A hotel may have multiple affiliations including being part of a chain, parent company, operation (such as corporation, franchise, or independent), management company, owner, asset management company, and/or a member of a membership or marketing group.

When a hotel belongs to a chain, it is affiliated with a specific hotel brand. In 2013, there were 22 chains in the United States, with 50,000 or more rooms and 24 chains in the world with 75,000 or more rooms. Parent hotel companies such as Marriott International, Hilton Worldwide,

HOW TO EARN A FIVE-DIAMOND AWARD *(Continued)*

Step 5: Employee **RECOGNITION** is given when an employee is caught doing something right in order to encourage that behavior.

That's it; simple, but effective. This process is used to ensure all new employees are polite, knowledgeable about their job responsibilities, and fulfill guest requirements. In addition, a guest's needs are anticipated by offering or performing extra services in every interaction. Service must be quick, seamless, and unobtrusive.

- One-diamond properties have simple roadside appeal and the basic lodging needs.
- Two-diamond properties have average roadside appeal, with some landscaping and a noticeable enhancement in interior décor.
- Three diamonds carry a degree of sophistication through higher service and comfort.
- Four diamonds have excellent roadside appeal and service levels that give guests what they need before they even ask for it.
- Five-diamond properties have the highest service levels, sophistication, and offerings.

Similar to the system used by AAA, Forbes Travel Guide classifies hotels using a five-star rating system. Out of the 50,000 hotels in the United States, Forbes rates and recommends about 8,000 properties a year. Of those, only a few dozen earn the five-star rating. Only facilities that meet the Forbes Travel Guide rigorous standards are rated and listed in both the travel guides and on the Forbes Travel Guide Web site. Deteriorating or poorly managed establishments are deleted from the list. The Forbes Travel Guide Star Award classification is as follows:

- Five-star properties are exceptional hotels that provide a memorable experience through virtually flawless service and the finest of amenities. Staff are intuitive, engaging, and passionate and eagerly deliver service above and beyond the guests' expectations. Hotels were designed with the guest's comfort in mind, with particular attention paid to craftsmanship and quality of product.
- Four-star properties provide a distinctive setting with many interesting and inviting elements to enjoy throughout the property. Attention to detail is prominent from design concept to quality of products provided. Staff are accommodating and take pride in catering to the guest's specific needs.
- Recommended properties are well-appointed hotels with enhanced amenities that provide travelers with a strong sense of location, whether for style or function. They may have a distinguishing style and ambience in both the public spaces and guest rooms.[27]

	◇	◇◇	◇◇◇	◇◇◇◇	◇◇◇◇◇
General	Simple roadside appeal — Limited landscaping	Average roadside appeal — Some landscaping	Very good roadside appeal — Attractive landscaping	Excellent roadside appeal — Professionally planned landscaping	Outstanding roadside appeal — Professional landscaping with a variety of foliage and stunning architecture
Lobby	Adequate size with registration, front desk, limited seating, and budget art, if any	Medium size with registration, front desk, limited seating, carpeted floors, budget art, and some plants	Spacious with front desk, carpeted seating area arranged in conversation groupings, good-quality framed art, live plants, luggage carts, and bellstation	Spacious or consistent with historical attributes; registration and front desk above average with solid wood or marble; ample seating area with conversation groupings and upscale appointments including tile, carpet, or wood floors; impressive lighting fixtures; upscale framed art and art objects; abundant live plants; background music; separate check-in/-out; bellstation	Comfortably spacious or consistent with historical attributes; registration and front desk above average; ample seating with conversation groupings and upscale appointments; impressive lighting fixtures; variety of fine art; abundant plants and fresh floral arrangements; background music; separate check-in/-out; bellstation that may be part of concierge area; concierge desk
Guestrooms	May not reflect current industry standards	Generally reflect current industry standards	Reflect current industry standards	Reflect current industry standards and provide upscale appearance	Reflect current standards and provide luxury appearance
Service	Basic attentive service	More attentive service	Upgraded service levels	High service levels and hospitality	Guests are pampered by flawless service executed by professional staff

Figure 2–4 • Summary of AAA Diamond Rating Guidelines.

(Reprinted from http://www.aaasouth.com, by permission of AAA.)

Hotels may also be classified according to geography, location, price, and type of services offered. This allows guests to make a selection on these categories as well as personal criteria.

Using a geographic orientation, hotels may be classified as world, continent, subcontinent, country, market, or submarket. According to the United Nations World Tourism Organization (UNWTO), there are four continents in the world: Americas, Europe, Mideast/Africa, and Asia Pacific. Each continent has several subcontinents. The Americas includes North America, South America, Central America, and the Caribbean. The subcontinent North America has a number of regions, including New England, Middle Atlantic, South Atlantic, East North Central, East South Central, West North Central, West South Central, Mountain, and Pacific.

Besides being part of a continent, subcontinent, or region, a hotel will also be classified as belonging to a market. The market in which a hotel belongs to is one of the most important geographic categories for a hotel general manager. A market is usually thought of as a city, but sometimes a market is thought to represent other areas such as rural areas outside of major cities. It is important for hotel owners and management to understand the market they operate in, as the performance of a hotel is measured against other properties in their market and sometimes against properties operating in other markets. Worldwide, the top 35 metro markets for hotels include Shanghai, China; Beijing, China; Las Vegas, Nevada, USA; Orlando, Florida, USA; and London, England. The top 25 markets in the United States in 2012 included Orlando; Chicago; Washington, DC/Maryland/Northern Virginia; New York; and the Los Angeles–Long Beach markets.

In addition to being classified in a specific market, hotels may be classified as belonging to a tract or submarket. In the United States, there may be multiple tracts in a market. In a metro market, there is often a tract for the downtown area, sometimes referred to as the central business district, and other tracts for other parts of a city such as north or south parts of the city.

While the Forbes Five-Star and AAA Five-Diamond categorizations are popular for consumers to understand how a hotel is classified, the Smith Travel Research scale categorization is popular for the hotel industry to classify hotels. Smith Travel uses a seven-scale categorization, with six categories for chain hotels (e.g., economy, midscale, upper midscale, upscale, upper upscale, and luxury) and one scale category for independent hotels.

Smith Travel Research focuses on hotel ADR rather than features or amenities when positioning chains into a scale group. It is important to note that luxury hotels are often found in larger, urban cities or resort communities, upper upscale hotels are often located in larger cities and urban or suburban locations where there is more business conducted, and economy and midscale hotels in smaller cities, rural, and roadside locations.

The hotel industry also classifies hotels by location or features and benefits. A hotel may be located in an urban or city center, suburban, airport, interstate or freeway, resort, small town/rural, casino, full-service, extended-stay, all-suite, convention, or bed and breakfast.

Following is a list of hotel classifications:

City Center and Suburban: May include luxury, first-class, full-service, convention, midscale, economy, boutique, extended stay, corporate housing, and all-suite hotels.

Resort: May include luxury, midscale, economy suites, condominium, timeshare, convention, boutique, all-suite, all-inclusive, or a mixed-use hotel (e.g., includes a full-service hotel, condominiums, homes, and fractional ownership/timeshare units on property).

Airport: May include luxury, full-service, midscale, economy, and all-suite hotels.

Freeway: May include midscale, economy, and all-suite hotels.

Casino: May include luxury, upper upscale, and midscale hotels with an attached casino operation.

Rural and Small Town: May include a mix of midscale, economy, and bed and breakfast hotels.

Alternatively, the hotel industry may be segmented according to price. Figure 2–5 gives an example of a national or major regional brand-name hotel chain in each segment.

City Center and Suburban Hotels

LEARNING OBJECTIVE 3
Classify hotels by rating system type, location, and price.

City center and suburban hotels, by virtue of their location, meet the needs of the traveling public for business or leisure reasons. These hotels could be luxury, midscale, business, suites, economy, or residential. They offer a range of accommodations and services. Luxury hotels offer the ultimate in décor, butler service, concierge and special concierge floors, secretarial services, the latest Wi-Fi or in-room technology, computers, fax machines, beauty salons, health spas, 24-hour room service, swimming pools, tennis courts, valet service, ticket office, airline office, car rental, and doctor/nurse on duty or on call. Figure 2–5 shows hotels by price segment.

Generally, they offer a signature restaurant, coffee shop, or an equivalent recognized name restaurant; a lounge; a named bar; meeting and convention rooms; a ballroom; and possibly a fancy night spot. The Drake Hotel in Chicago is an example of a city center luxury hotel. An example of a midpriced hotel in New York City is the Ramada Hotel; an economy hotel is the Day's Inn; and a suites property is the Embassy Suites.

Resort Hotels

Destination resorts appeal to both leisure and group travelers. They are often a destination unto themselves and are developed to be all-encompassing, where the guest may not ever need to go off-property for entertainment, recreation, meeting, or relaxing. There are approximately 350 destination resorts in the United States. Resort hotels came of age with the advent of rail travel. Increasingly, city dwellers and others had the urge to vacation in locations they found appealing. Traveling to these often

Economy $55–$89	Midprice $149–$220	Upscale $169–$249	Luxury $259–$659	All-Suites $159–$249
Holiday Inn Express	Holiday Inn Fairfield Inn		Crowne Plaza Hotel InterContinental	
Fairfield Inn	Courtyard Inn Residence Inn	Marriott	Marriott Marquis Ritz-Carlton	Marriott Suites
Days Inn		Omni	Renaissance	
EconoLodge	Radisson Inn	Radisson		Radisson Suites
Ramada Limited	Ramada Inn	Ramada		Ramada Suites
	Sheraton Inn Four Points	Sheraton	Sheraton Grande	Sheraton Suites
Sleep Inn	American Inn	Hyatt	Grand Hyatt Hyatt Regency Hyatt Park	Hyatt Suites
Comfort Inn	Quality Inn Wingate	Clarion Hotels		Quality Suites Comfort Suites
Extended Stay America	Hilton Inn	Hilton	Hilton Towers	Hilton Suites
Thrift Lodge	DoubleTree Club	DoubleTree		DoubleTree Suites
Travelodge Hotels	Travelodge Hotels	Forte Hotels	Forte Hotels	
Motel 6	Country Inn & Suites	Westin	Westin	Spring Hill Suites
Super 8	La Quinta Red Roof Inn Best Western Hampton Inn			Homewood Suites by Hilton Hampton Suites Embassy Suites

Note: Some brands' price ranges may overlap because of location and seasonal pricing.

Figure 2–5 • Hotels by Price Segment.

Beijing, China Oriental Plaza facade of Grand Hyatt hotel.

more exotic locations became a part of the pleasure experience. In the late 1800s, luxury resort hotels were developed to accommodate the clientele that the railways brought. Such hotels include the famous Greenbrier at White Sulphur Springs, West Virginia; the Hotel del Coronado near San Diego, California; the Breakers in Florida; and the Homestead at Hot Springs, Virginia.

The leisure and pleasure travelers of those days were drawn by resorts, beaches, or spectacular mountain scenery. At first, many of these grand resorts were seasonal. However, as automobile and air travel made even the remote resorts more accessible and an increasing number of people could afford to visit, many resorts became year-round properties.

Resort communities sprang up in the sunshine belt from Palm Springs to Palm Beach. Some resorts focus on major sporting activities such as skiing, golf, or fishing; others offer family vacations. Further improvements in both air and automobile travel brought

Copper Mountain, Colorado.

exotic locations within the reach of the population. Europe, the Caribbean, and Mexico became more accessible. As the years passed, some of the resorts suffered because the public's vacation plans changed.

The traditional family month-long resort vacation gave way to shorter, more frequent getaways of four to seven days. The regular resort visitors became older; in general, the younger guests preferred the mobility of the automobile and the more informal atmosphere provided by the newer and more informal resorts.

Hyatt hotels have organized a program consisting of a variety of activities for children, thereby giving parents an opportunity either to enjoy some free time on their own or join their children in fun activities. Many resort hotels began to attract conventions, conferences, and meetings so that they could maintain or increase occupancy, particularly during the low and shoulder seasons.

Guests go to resorts for leisure and recreation. They want a good climate—summer or winter—in which they can relax or engage in recreational activities. Because of the remoteness of many resorts, guests are a kind of "captured clientele," who may be on the property for days at a time. This presents resort managers with some unique operating challenges. Another operating challenge concerns seasonality: Some resorts either do not operate year-round or have periods of very low occupancy. Both present challenges in attracting, training, and retaining competent staff.

Many guests travel considerable distances to resorts. Consequently, they tend to stay longer than they do at transient hotels. This presents a challenge to the food and beverage manager to provide quality menus that are varied and are presented and served in an attractive, attentive manner. To achieve this, resorts often use a cyclical menu that repeats itself every 14–21 days. Also, they provide a wide variety and number of dishes to stimulate interest. Menus are now more health conscious—lighter and low in saturated fats, cholesterol, salt, and calories.

The food needs to be presented in a variety of ways. Buffets are popular because they give guests the opportunity to make choices from a display of foods. Barbecues, display cooking, poolside dining, specialty restaurants, and reciprocal dining arrangements with nearby hotels give guests even more options.

With increased global competition, not only from other resorts but also from cruise lines, resort managers are challenged to both attract guests and to turn those guests into repeat business, which traditionally has been the foundation of resort viability.

To increase occupancies, resorts have diversified their marketing mix to include conventions, business meetings, sales meetings, incentive groups, sporting events, additional sporting and recreational facilities, spas, adventure tourism, ecotourism, and more.

Because guests are cocooned in the resort, they expect to be pampered. This requires an attentive, well-trained staff; hiring, training, and retaining a competent staff present a challenge in some remote areas and in developing countries.

There are a number of benefits to operating resorts. The guests are much more relaxed in comparison to those at transient hotels, and the resorts are located in scenically beautiful areas. This frequently enables staff to enjoy a better quality of life than do their transient hotel counterparts. Returning guests tend to treat associates like friends. This adds to the overall party-like atmosphere, which is prevalent at many of the established resorts.

INTRODUCING VALERIE FERGUSON

Senior Vice President, Operations, Denihan Hospitality Group and Past Chair of the American Hotel & Lodging Association

To most, "making it big" seems like a regular statement and a task easily achieved. To Valerie Ferguson, well, it comes with a lot of work, dedication, and heart. She speaks often about seizing opportunities and adding self-interest to what you do for your career.

For this African American woman, life wasn't always easy. As the managing director of Loews Philadelphia Hotel and regional vice president of Loews Hotels, she had a lot to say about what got her to where she is now.

One of her most important role models was her father, Sam Ferguson. She says, "My father and I had a great relationship in which he supported me, but in which he never put any images in front of me about what I should shoot for."

The leisure and pleasure travelers of those days were drawn by resorts, beaches, or spectacular mountain scenery. At first, many of these grand resorts were seasonal. However, as automobile and air travel made even the remote resorts more accessible and an increasing number of people could afford to visit, many resorts became year-round properties.

Resort communities sprang up in the sunshine belt from Palm Springs to Palm Beach. Some resorts focus on major sporting activities such as skiing, golf, or fishing; others offer family vacations. Further improvements in both air and automobile travel brought exotic locations within the reach of the population. Europe, the Caribbean, and Mexico became more accessible. As the years passed, some of the resorts suffered because the public's vacation plans changed.

Copper Mountain, Colorado.

The traditional family month-long resort vacation gave way to shorter, more frequent getaways of four to seven days. The regular resort visitors became older; in general, the younger guests preferred the mobility of the automobile and the more informal atmosphere provided by the newer and more informal resorts.

Hyatt hotels have organized a program consisting of a variety of activities for children, thereby giving parents an opportunity either to enjoy some free time on their own or join their children in fun activities. Many resort hotels began to attract conventions, conferences, and meetings so that they could maintain or increase occupancy, particularly during the low and shoulder seasons.

Guests go to resorts for leisure and recreation. They want a good climate—summer or winter—in which they can relax or engage in recreational activities. Because of the remoteness of many resorts, guests are a kind of "captured clientele," who may be on the property for days at a time. This presents resort managers with some unique operating challenges. Another operating challenge concerns seasonality: Some resorts either do not operate year-round or have periods of very low occupancy. Both present challenges in attracting, training, and retaining competent staff.

Many guests travel considerable distances to resorts. Consequently, they tend to stay longer than they do at transient hotels. This presents a challenge to the food and beverage manager to provide quality menus that are varied and are presented and served in an attractive, attentive manner. To achieve this, resorts often use a cyclical menu that repeats itself every 14–21 days. Also, they provide a wide variety and number of dishes to stimulate interest. Menus are now more health conscious—lighter and low in saturated fats, cholesterol, salt, and calories.

The food needs to be presented in a variety of ways. Buffets are popular because they give guests the opportunity to make choices from a display of foods. Barbecues, display cooking, poolside dining, specialty restaurants, and reciprocal dining arrangements with nearby hotels give guests even more options.

With increased global competition, not only from other resorts but also from cruise lines, resort managers are challenged to both attract guests and to turn those guests into repeat business, which traditionally has been the foundation of resort viability.

To increase occupancies, resorts have diversified their marketing mix to include conventions, business meetings, sales meetings, incentive groups, sporting events, additional sporting and recreational facilities, spas, adventure tourism, ecotourism, and more.

Because guests are cocooned in the resort, they expect to be pampered. This requires an attentive, well-trained staff; hiring, training, and retaining a competent staff present a challenge in some remote areas and in developing countries.

There are a number of benefits to operating resorts. The guests are much more relaxed in comparison to those at transient hotels, and the resorts are located in scenically beautiful areas. This frequently enables staff to enjoy a better quality of life than do their transient hotel counterparts. Returning guests tend to treat associates like friends. This adds to the overall party-like atmosphere, which is prevalent at many of the established resorts.

INTRODUCING VALERIE FERGUSON

Senior Vice President, Operations, Denihan Hospitality Group and Past Chair of the American Hotel & Lodging Association

To most, "making it big" seems like a regular statement and a task easily achieved. To Valerie Ferguson, well, it comes with a lot of work, dedication, and heart. She speaks often about seizing opportunities and adding self-interest to what you do for your career.

For this African American woman, life wasn't always easy. As the managing director of Loews Philadelphia Hotel and regional vice president of Loews Hotels, she had a lot to say about what got her to where she is now.

One of her most important role models was her father, Sam Ferguson. She says, "My father and I had a great relationship in which he supported me, but in which he never put any images in front of me about what I should shoot for."

After high school, Valerie applied to and was accepted at the University of San Francisco, where she earned a degree in government. Eventually realizing that law wasn't where her heart was, she decided to move out to Atlanta where she got a job as a night-time desk clerk at the Hyatt Regency. She fell in love with the hotel industry and saw it as a challenge. Soon enough, though, she realized that the challenges she was really facing were issues of race and gender. She explains, "I was raw in my approach to the business world, but I soon came to realize that it takes more than working hard. To succeed, a person must be able to proclaim his or her goals."

Through the years, Valerie has managed several hotels for Hyatt and Ritz-Carlton. Her outstanding work and devotion to the hospitality and lodging industry have not gone unrewarded. Ed Rabin, executive vice president of Hyatt and an early Ferguson mentor, says, "From the get-go, she demonstrated an ability and willingness to understand and learn the business and win over guests, colleagues, and peers in the process."

When Loews was being opened, Valerie was thrilled with the adventure of being with a still-growing company. President and CEO of Loews, Jonathan Tisch, became a close friend as they served together on the board of the American Hotel and Lodging Association (AH&LA). In 1994, Valerie ran for a seat on the AH&LA's executive committee and eventually succeeded Tisch as chair. She was the first African American and second woman to serve as AH&LA chair.

She comments on the hospitality industry: "The hospitality industry is one of the last vestiges of the American dream, where you can enter from very humble beginnings and end up a success." The great relationship she has with people has been a great contribution to her well-deserved success.

Ferguson has come a long way in her career and is now SVP of Operations at Denihan where she provides leadership support to five hotels. She is proud of what she is doing and doesn't believe that she has stopped climbing the ladder of success. She is fighting to make other women and minority members realize that there is a whole world of opportunities out there and they should set their goals high. She believes that equality of opportunity "should not come as the result of a mandate of the federal government or as the result of pressure from groups outside this industry. The impetus for change must come from within the hearts and souls of each of us."

Sources: *Lodging* 23, no. 5 (January 1998); Loews Hotels and Resorts, *Welcome to Loews Hotels*, www.loewshotels.com (accessed October 26, 2011); American Hotel & Lodging Association; Robert A. Nozar, "Newsmaker Interview: Valerie Ferguson."

Airport Hotels

Many airport hotels enjoy high occupancy because of the large number of travelers arriving and departing from major airports. The guest mix in airport hotels consists of business, group, and leisure travelers. Passengers with early or late flights may stay over at the airport hotel, whereas others rest while waiting for connecting flights.

Airport hotels are generally in the 200- to 600-room size and are full service. To care for the needs of guests who may still feel as if they are in different time zones, room service and restaurant hours may be extended or even offered around the clock. More moderately priced hotels have vending machines.

As competition at airport hotels intensified, some added meeting space to cater to businesspeople that want to fly in, meet, and fly out. Here, the airport hotel has the advantage of saving the guests from having to go downtown. Almost all airport hotels provide courtesy van transportation to and from the airport.

Convenient locations, economical prices, and easy and less costly transportation costs to and from the airport are some reasons why airport hotels are becoming intelligent choices for business travelers. Airport hotels can mean a bargain for groups, especially considering that the transportation to the hotel and back from the airport is usually free or is very inexpensive, says Brian Booth, director of sales and marketing at the Dallas Hyatt Regency Airport Hotel. One of the most conveniently located hotels in the country is the Miami International Airport Hotel, which is located within the airport itself.

Freeway and Interstate Hotels and Motels

Freeway hotels and motels came into prominence, with the help of the Interstate Highway Act, in the 1950s and 1960s. They are smaller than most hotels—usually fewer than 50 rooms—and are frequently mom-and-pop establishments or franchised (such as Motel 6). As Americans took to the open road, they needed a convenient place to stay that was reasonably priced with few frills. Guests could simply drive up, park outside the office, register, rent a room, and park outside the room. Over the years, more facilities were added: lounges, restaurants, pools, vending machines, game rooms, and satellite TV.

Motels are often clustered near freeway off ramps on the outskirts of towns and cities. Today, some are made of modular construction and have as few as 11 employees per hundred rooms. These savings in land, construction, and operating costs are passed on to the guest in the form of lower rates.

Casino Hotels

The casino hotel industry is now coming into the financial mainstream, to the point that, as a significant segment of the entertainment industry, it is reshaping the U.S. economy. The entertainment and recreation sector has become a very important engine for U.S. economic growth, providing a boost to consumer spending, and thus creating tremendous prosperity for the industry. One of the fastest-growing sectors of the entertainment field is gaming, which is discussed in Chapter 11.

The gaming business is strictly for adults; in addition to gaming, a multinational fine cuisine for dining, health spas for relaxation, dance clubs, and dazzling shows are available. Casino hotels are now marketing themselves as business hotels. They include in their rooms work space, Wi-Fi, a fax, a copier, and computer data ports. Other amenities include a full-service business center, travel bureau, and room service. Larger casino hotels also attract conventions, which represent a lucrative business. There are now more than 150 hotels on Native American tribal land. They cater to an increasing number of guests who want to stay and be entertained as well as gamble.

Conference and Convention Hotels

Conference and convention hotels provide facilities and meet the needs of groups attending and holding conventions. Apart from this segment of the market, conference and convention hotels also attract seasonal leisure travelers. Typically, conference hotels focus on providing conference and meeting facilities and typi-

The Universal Portofino Bay Hotel in Orlando, Florida, is a popular convention hotel modelled after Portofino, Italy.

cally meet the guidelines of the International Association of Conference Centers (IACC). Convention hotels on the other hand, usually have a minimum of 300 guest rooms and a minimum of 20,000 square feet of meeting space and larger public areas to accommodate hundreds of people at any given time. Convention hotels have many banquet areas within and around the hotel complex. These hotels have a high percentage of double occupancies, and rooms have double queen-sized beds. Convention hotels may also offer a concierge floor to cater to individual guest needs. Round-the-clock room service, an in-house laundry, a business center, a travel desk, and an airport shuttle service are other amenities found in convention hotels.

Full-Service Hotels

Another way to classify hotels is by the degree of service offered: full-service, economy, extended-stay, and all-suite hotels. Full-service hotels offer a wide range of facilities, services, and amenities, including many that were mentioned under the luxury hotel category: multiple food and beverage outlets including bars, lounges, and restaurants; both formal and casual dining; and meeting, convention, and catering services. Business features might include a business center, secretarial services, fax, in-room computer hookups, and so on.

Most of the major North American cities have hotel chain representation, such as Four Seasons, Hilton, InterContinental, Choice, Hyatt, Marriott, Omni, Wyndham, Radisson, Loews, and Starwood. Each of these

A La Quinta Inn.

chains has a portfolio of brands in different market segments: deluxe, such as Marriott's Ritz-Carlton and the JW Marriott; luxury, such as Renaissance; and luxury boutique, such as Edition and Autograph, a collection of high-personality independent hotels.

Economy/Budget Hotels

After enjoying a wave of growth for most of the last 20 years, the economy hotel segment may be close to the saturation point. There are about 25,000 properties in this segment with many market categories. The economic law of supply and demand rules: If an area has too many similar properties, then price wars usually break out as they try to attract guests. Some will attempt to differentiate themselves and stress value rather than discounting. This adds to the fascination of the business.

An economy or budget hotel offers clean, reasonably sized and furnished rooms without the frills of full-service hotels. Popular brands in this market sector are Hampton Inn, Fairfield Inn, Holiday Inn Express, Best Western, Travelodge, Motel 6, Microtel, Days Inn, Choice's Sleep Inn, Roadway Inn and Econo Lodge, Wingate, Super 8, Baymont Inn, and Country Inn. These properties do not have restaurants or offer substantial food and beverages, but they do offer guests a continental breakfast in the lounge or lobby.

These chains became popular by focusing on selling beds, not meals or meetings. This enabled them to offer rates about 30 percent lower than the midpriced hotels can. Economy properties, which represent about 15 percent of total hotel rooms, have experienced tremendous growth.

Boutique Hotels

Boutique hotels offer a different lodging experience compared to mid- to large chain hotels. Boutique hotels have a unique architecture, style, décor, and size. Hotels in this category often promote themselves as stylish, cool, hip, and luxurious. As of 2012, there were approximately 700 boutique hotels in the United States and more than 2,500 in the world. They are smaller than their chain competitors, with about 25–125 rooms and a high level of personal service. Some examples of boutique hotels are the trendy South Beach retro types, Kimpton Hotels, Rosewood, Kessler Collection, Joie de Vivre Hotels, Edition from Marriott, and the avant-garde hotel George in Washington, D.C.

A DAY IN THE LIFE OF JASON SAMSON

General Manager, Hilton Garden Inn, Sarasota, Florida

Hospitality has been in my blood ever since I began working at Rosen Hotels and Resorts while I was at the Rosen College at UCF. I worked at the front desk and as VIP concierge for two years. After graduation, I worked for Hilton in Ft. Lauderdale at DoubleTree. There, I worked as front office manager, housekeeping manager, and in sales and marketing. Later, I transferred to an ownership group and worked in a variety of positions and locations as well as in asset management at the corporate level.

I have been in this market since 2005 managing a 121-room property overseeing all facets from sales and marketing to food and beverage and property operations, as well as in accounting/profit and loss generations, as an ambassador for the property in the community, and with the chamber of commerce and visitor's bureau.

Not that there is such a thing as an average day in this business, but normally I arrive and "walk" the property to check on the departments and their staffing levels. I begin with the restaurant, and I help out if needed. If help is not needed, I continue on to housekeeping. I try to maintain a presence in the housekeeping department and will check several rooms every day. I'll then return to the restaurant and "walk tables." I usually talk to guests, but on weekends they are busier so I will help out. I also spend time in the lobby as hotel ambassador greeting and saying farewell to guests.

At 10 A.M. I have a quick stand-up meeting with department heads in my office to go over the day and review any important topics. Afterward, I check my e-mail. If I have not done so already, I'll review the reports from the previous day's business. Naturally, I do spend time on human resource–related issues and on corporate items such as forecasting, budgeting, accounts receivable, and accounts payable. I also focus on revenue management with the director of sales. We do daily, weekly, and monthly revenue strategies and ensure that all booking channels are live. Finally, I review our service scores and reply to guest's correspondence. Then it's out to the front desk and lobby once more to meet and greet incoming guests.

Courtesy of Christopher Walker.

A good example of a chain boutique hotel is Hotel Indigo, part of the InterContinental Hotels Group. Hotel Indigo provides an oasis where guests can escape the hectic pace of travel and think more clearly, work more productively, and rest more refreshingly. It offers an environment that doesn't just shelter guests but inspires and re-energizes them. That's the idea behind Hotel Indigo.[28]

Extended-Stay Hotels and All-Suites
Extended-Stay Hotels

Some hotels cater to guests who stay for an extended period. They do, of course, take guests for a shorter time when space is available; however, the majority of guests are long term. Guests take advantage of a reduction in room rates based on the length of their stay. The mix of guests is mainly business and professional/technical guests, or relocating families.

Homewood Suites by Hilton all-suite hotel.

The options for this type of lodging may range from a guest room to a studio or a three-bedroom apartment. Extended-stay properties, otherwise known as corporate housing, often quote weekly or monthly rates and the stay may vary between short- and long-term rentals. Guests often stay between more than one week and less than six months. The units are typically furnished, complete with linens and a stocked kitchen, and the type of extended stay property will dictate the amenities and services it provides. For instance, housekeeping services may be provided, but it may be offered weekly versus daily. Swimming pools, fitness centers, tennis courts, and limited food and beverage may also be offered.

Candlewood Suites, Extended Stay America, Homestead Studio Suites, Hawthorn Suites, Baymont Inns and Suites, Residence Inns, and Homewood Suites are popular brands in this segment of the lodging industry. All-suites extended-stay hotels typically offer approximately 25 percent more space for the same amount of money as the regular hotel in the same price range. The additional space is usually in the form of a lounge and possibly a kitchenette area.

Embassy Suites, owned and operated by Hilton Hotels Corporation; Residence Inns, Fairfield Suites, and Town-Place Suites, all by Marriott; Extended Stay America; Homewood Suites; and Guest Quarters are among the popular brands in the all-suites, extended-stay segment of the lodging industry. Several of the major hotel chains have all-suites extended-stay subsidiaries, including Radisson, Choice Hotels (which dominate the economy all-suites segment with Comfort and Quality Suites), Sheraton Suites, Hilton Suites, Homegate Studios, and Suites by Wyndham Hotels. These properties provide a closer-to-home feeling for guests who may be relocating or attending seminars or who are on work-related projects that necessitate a stay of greater than about five days.

There are now more than 2,500 all-suites extended-stay properties. Many of these properties have business centers and offer services such as grocery shopping and laundry/dry cleaning. The designers of extended-stay properties realize that guests prefer a homelike atmosphere. Accordingly, many properties are built to encourage a community feeling, which allows guests to interact informally.

Condotels, Timeshare, and Mixed-Use Hotels

As the word suggests, a condotel is a combination of a hotel and condominium. Developers build a hotel and sell all, or parts of the property, as condo units, and owners can opt to place their unit into a pool for rental or use and allow access to all resort facilities and amenities. The hotel operating company gets a cut of the money from renting the units and so does the owner. The owner of the condo unit may have exclusive right to the use of the unit for a fixed period of time (usually one month); other than that, the hotel operating company knows that it can rent out the condos.

Some new hotels are developed as mixed-use properties, meaning that a hotel may also have "residences"—real condos that people use, so they are not for renting like condotels—along with amenities such as a spa and sports facilities. Mixed-use hotels can also be a part of a major urban or resort development, which may include office buildings, convention centers, sporting facilities, or shopping malls.

Bed and Breakfast Inns

Bed and breakfast inns, or B&Bs as they are familiarly known, offer an alternative lodging experience to the normal hotel or motel. According to *TravelASSIST* magazine, B&B is a concept that began in Europe and started as overnight lodging in a private home. A true B&B is an accommodation with the owner, who lives on the premises or nearby, providing a clean, attractive accommodation and breakfast, usually a memorable one. The host also offers to help the guest with directions, restaurants, and suggestions for local entertainment or sightseeing.

There are many different styles of B&Bs with prices ranging from about $30 to $300 or more per night. B&Bs may be quaint cottages with white picket fences leading to gingerbread houses, tiny and homey, with two or three rooms available. On the other hand, some are sprawling, ranch-style homes in the Rockies, multistoried town homes in large cities, farms, adobe villas, log cabins, lighthouses, and many stately mansions. The variety is part of the thrill, romance, and charm of the B&B experience.[29]

There are an estimated 25,000 bed and breakfast places in the United States alone. B&Bs have flourished for many reasons. Business travelers are growing weary of the complexities of the check-in/checkout processes at some commercial hotels. With the escalation of transient rates at hotels, an opportunity has been created to serve a more price-sensitive segment of travelers. Also, many leisure travelers are looking for accommodation somewhere between a large, formal hotel and staying with friends. The B&Bs offer a homelike atmosphere. They are aptly called "a home away from home." Community breakfasts with other lodgers and hosts enhance this feeling. Each B&B is as unique as its owner. Décor varies according to the region of location and the unique taste of its owner. The owner of the bed and breakfast often provides all the necessary labor, but some employ full- or part-time help.

A Bed and Breakfast in Yorkshire, England.

▶ Check Your Knowledge

1. What is the role of Smith Travel Research?
2. Identify the characteristics of one through five-diamond, as well as one through five-star, hotels.
3. List the characteristics of each hotel segment highlighted.

Best, Biggest, and Most Unusual Hotels and Chains

So, which is the best hotel in the world? The answer may depend on whether you watch the Travel Channel or read polls taken by a business investment or travel magazine. Magazines like *Travel + Leisure* and Web sites like TripAdvisor invite readers to vote for their favorite hotels and then they publish the list, so it's more of a popularity poll. However, the results are interesting and are not split into several categories: best in Asia, best in the Caribbean, best romantic, best city, and so on. One recent list had the Golden Well Hotel, Prague, Czech Republic as number one, whereas another had The Oberoi Vanyavilas, Rajasthan, India. High on the list was the Fairmont Mara Safari Club, Masai Mara, Kenya and the Earth Lodge at Sabi Sabi Private Game Reserve, Kruger National Park, South Africa. The Mandarin Oriental hotel in Bangkok, Thailand has been rated number one in the world; so, too, has the Intercontinental Hong Kong and the Connaught of London. Each list picks other hotels. The largest hotel in the world is the Izmailovo Hotel in Moscow with 7,500 rooms, followed by the 7,372-room MGM Grand in Las Vegas and the Venetian Hotel, also in Las Vegas, which has 7,117 rooms.

A bedroom in an ice hotel.

The Best Hotel Chains

The Ritz-Carlton and the Four Seasons are generally rated the highest-quality large chain hotels. The Ritz-Carlton Hotel Company has received all the major awards the hospitality industry and leading consumer organizations can bestow. It has received the Malcolm Baldrige National Quality Award from the U.S. Department of Commerce—the first and only hotel company to win the award and the first and only service company to win the award two times, in

1999 and 1992. Ritz-Carlton has long been recognized as the best luxury hotel chain in the industry. Amanresorts has been awarded the Zagat best hotel group in the world, and Rosewood Hotels & Resorts have several outstanding properties.

TECHNOLOGY SPOTLIGHT

The Use of Technology in Property Management

Technology has become an inseparable part of the hotel business. As mentioned in the Technology Spotlight in Chapter 1, there are about 65 different applications in a typical full-service hotel. This number is around 35 for a limited-service hotel. The use of technology starts even before a guest checks in to a hotel. More than half of hotel guests book their hotel rooms electronically. This means that guests use either direct or indirect reservation/distribution channels. Direct reservation/distribution channels include walk-in, phone call to the hotel, hotel's Web site, and hotel chain's Web site (central reservation system). Indirect reservation/distribution channels include online travel agencies such as Expedia.com, Travelocity.com, Orbitz.com, and opaque travel agencies where the consumer does not know the brand of the hotel until after the purchase is completed. These opaque online travel agencies include priceline.com and Hotwire.com. A distribution/reservation system typically performs the following basic functions: (1) selling individual reservations, (2) selling group reservations, (3) displaying room availability and guest lists, (4) tracking advance deposits, (5) tracking travel agent bookings and commissions, and (6) generating confirmation letters and e-mails and various reports.

Each hotel has a property management system (PMS). The functions of the PMS are enabling guest reservations, enabling guest check-in/out, enabling staff to maintain guest facilities, keeping accounting for a guest's financial transactions, and tracking guest activities. The PMS is often interfaced to central reservation systems and global reservation systems. This way, when a guest makes a reservation from a hotel chain's Web site such as Hilton.com or Marriott.com, the reservation is automatically transferred to the hotel's property reservation system. This interface allows the hotel to control the room inventory on a real-time basis and to manage the revenue management process efficiently. The revenue management module of the PMS also uses advanced technology systems. Hotels use the revenue management system to calculate the rates, rooms, and restrictions on sales in order to best maximize the return. These systems measure constrained and unconstrained demand along with pace to gauge which restrictions—for example, length of stay, nonrefundable rate, or close to arrival. Revenue management teams in the hotel industry have evolved tremendously over the last 10 years, and in this global economy, targeting the right distribution channels, controlling costs, and having the right market mix plays an important role in yield management. Yield management in hotels is selling rooms and services at the right price, at the right time, to the right people.

The use of technology continues after the reservation. When the guest checks in, the reservation details are found in the PMS and an electronic key card is cut. The guest can use this electronic card to access his or her room and other general areas of the hotel such as fitness room, pool area, and concierge club. There are many more technology applications in the guest room. We will cover those in the next chapter.

The Most Unusual Hotels

Among the world's most unusual hotels are ones like the Treetops Hotel in one of Kenya's wild animal parks—literally in the treetops. The uniqueness of the hotel is that it is built on the tops of trees overlooking a wild animal watering hole in the park.

Another magnificent spectacle is the ICEHOTEL, situated on the shores of the Torne River in the old village of Jukkasjärvi in Swedish Lapland. The ICEHOTEL is built from scratch on an annual basis with a completely new design, new suites, new departments, even the "Absolut Ice Bar," a bar carved in ice with ice glasses and ice plates. The ICEHOTEL can accommodate more than 100 guests, with each room having its own distinct style. The hotel also has an ice chapel, an ice art exhibition hall, and, believe it or not, a cinema.

Australia boasts an underwater hotel at the Great Barrier Reef, where guests have wonderful underwater views from their rooms.

Japan has several unusual hotels. One is a cocoon-like hotel, called a capsule hotel, in which guests do not have a room as such. Instead, they have a space of about 4 feet × 7 feet. In this space is a bed and a television— which guests almost have to operate with their toes! Such hotels are popular with people who get caught up in the obligatory late-night drinking with the boss and with visiting professors, and who find them the only affordable place to stay in expensive Tokyo.

One of the highest hotels in the world, in terms of altitude, is the Hotel Everest View. It is nestled in the Himalayan mountain range at an altitude of 13,000 feet. Weather permitting, there is a marvelous view of Mount Everest. As many as 80 percent of the guests suffer from nausea, headaches, or sleeplessness caused by the altitude. No wonder the hottest-selling item on the room-service menu is oxygen—at $1 a minute.

LEARNING OBJECTIVE 4
Discuss the concept and growth of vacation ownership.

Timeshare, Vacation Ownership, and Fractional Ownership

From its beginnings in the French Alps in the late 1960s, the timeshare industry, otherwise known as **vacation ownership** or fractional ownership, has become the fastest-growing segment of the U.S. travel and tourism industry, increasing in popularity at the rate of about 15 percent each year. Vacation or fractional ownership is a form of real estate ownership or right to use a property in part. These types of properties are often resort or urban condominiums, town homes, or single family homes, in which multiple parties own and have rights to the property and amenities. Ownership and access are designated in defined periods of time (e.g., one week, two weeks, a month, etc.), and the units may be owned forever or on a specified period of time lease or right-to-use basis.

Vacation ownership offers consumers the opportunity to purchase fully furnished vacation accommodations in a variety of forms, such as weekly intervals or in points-based systems, for a percentage of the cost of ownership. For a one-time purchase price and payment of a yearly maintenance fee, purchasers own their vacation either in perpetuity (forever) or for a predetermined number of years. Owners share both the use and cost of upkeep of their unit and the common grounds of the resort property. Vacation ownership purchases are typically financed through consumer loans of five to 10 years duration, with terms dependent on the purchase price and the amount of the buyer's down payment. The average cost of a vacation ownership is $14,800–$18,500.[30]

Vacation clubs, or point-based programs, provide the flexible use of accommodations in multiple resort locations. With these products, club members purchase points that represent either a travel-and-use membership or a deed real

Condos in Cabo San Lucas.

estate product. These points are then used like money to purchase accommodations during a season, for a set number of days at a participating resort. The number of points needed to access the resort accommodation varies by the members' demand for unit size, season, resort location, and amenities.

Henry Silverman, formerly of Avis Budget—which owns the Indianapolis, Indiana–based Resort Condominiums International (RCI)—said that a **timeshare** is really a two-bedroom suite that is owned rather than a hotel room that is rented for a transient night. A vacation club, on the other hand, is a "travel-and-use" product. Consumers do not buy a fixed week, unit size, season, resort, or number of days to vacation each year. Instead, they purchase points that represent currency, which are used to access the club's vacation benefits. An important advantage to this is the product's flexibility, especially when tied to a point system. Disney Vacation Club is one major company that uses a point system. General manager Mark Pacala states, "The flexibility of choosing among several different vacation experiences is what sets the Disney Vacation Club apart from many similar plans. The vacation points system allows members to select the type of vacation best suited to their needs, particularly as those needs change from year to year." Each year, members choose how to use their vacation points, either for one long vacation or for a series of short getaways.[31]

The World Tourism Organization has called timeshares one of the fastest-growing sectors of the travel and tourism industry. Hospitality companies are adding brand power to the concept with corporations such as Marriott Vacation Club International, the Walt Disney Company, Hilton Hotels, Hyatt Hotels, Choice Hotels, InterContinental, and even the Ritz-Carlton and Four Seasons participating in an industry that has grown rapidly in recent years. Still, only about four percent of all U.S. households hold vacation ownership.

RCI estimates that the figure could rise to 10 percent within the next decade for households with incomes of more than $75,000. It is not surprising that hotel companies have found this to be a lucrative business.

RCI, the largest vacation ownership exchange (that allows members to exchange vacations with other locations), has more than 3.7 million member families living in 100 countries. There are more than 4,500 participating resorts, and members can exchange vacation intervals for vacations at any participating resort, and to date, RCI has arranged exchange vacations for more than 54 million people.[32] Vacation ownership is popular at U.S. resorts from Key West in Florida to Kona in Hawaii and from New York City and Las Vegas to Colorado ski resorts.

Interval International is a vacation exchange network made up of more than 2,900 resorts and more than two million member families in over 80 nations worldwide.[33] Interval does not own or manage any of the resorts, but rather provides members—vacation owners from around the world—with a variety of exchange services to enhance their vacation experiences. Members can exchange a stay at their home resort for a stay at one of the timeshares supported by Interval International.

By locking in the purchase price of accommodations, vacation ownership helps ensure future vacations at today's prices at luxurious resorts with amenities, service, and ambience that rival any of the world's top-rated vacation destinations. Through vacation exchange programs, timeshare owners can travel to other popular destinations around the world. With unparalleled flexibility and fully equipped condominiums that offer the best in holiday luxury, vacation ownership puts consumers in the driver's seat, allowing them to plan and enjoy vacations that suit their lifestyle.

Timeshare resort developers today include many of the world's leading hoteliers, publicly held corporations, and independent companies. Properties that combine vacation ownership resorts with hotels, adventure resorts, and gaming resorts are among the emerging timeshare trends. The reasons for purchasing most frequently cited by current timeshare owners are the high standards of quality accommodations and service at the resorts where they own and exchange, the flexibility offered through the vacation exchange opportunities, and the cost effectiveness of vacation ownership. Nearly one-third of vacation owners purchase additional intervals after experiencing ownership. This trend is even stronger among long-time owners: More than 40 percent of those who have owned for eight years or longer have purchased additional intervals within the timeshare.

Travel the World through Exchange Vacations

Vacation ownership offers unparalleled flexibility and the opportunity for affordable worldwide travel through vacation ownership exchange. Through the international vacation exchange networks, owners can trade their timeshare intervals for vacation time at comparable resorts around the world. Most resorts are affiliated with an exchange company that administers the exchange service for its members. Typically, the exchange company directly solicits annual membership. Owners individually elect to become members of the affiliated exchange company. To exchange, the owner places his or her interval into the exchange company's pool of resorts and weeks available for exchange and, in turn, chooses an available resort and week from that pool. The exchange company charges an exchange fee, in addition to an annual membership fee, to complete an exchange. Exchange companies and resorts frequently offer their members the additional benefit of saving or banking vacation time in a reserve program for use in a different year.

International Perspective

We are all part of a huge global economy that is splintered into massive trading blocks, such as the European Union (EU) and the North American Free Trade Agreement (NAFTA) among Canada, the United States, and Mexico, with a total population of 444.1 million consumers.[34]

The European Union (EU), with a population of more than 509 million people in 28 nations, is an economic union that has removed national boundaries and restrictions not only on trade but also on the movement of capital and labor.[35] The synergy developed between these 28 member nations is beneficial to all and is a form of self-perpetuating development. As travel, tourism, commerce, and industry have increased within the European Economic Community (EEC), which could soon expand by another five nations, and more in the future, so has the need for hotel accommodations.

In the Middle East, in countries like Dubai and Abu Dhabi, United Arab Emirates, several very impressive hotels and resorts have been added as part of a strategy to encourage more tourism to and within the region and the world. Once the airport is capable of handling several international flights daily, then soon hotels are built to cater to the traveler's needs. Now, these cities are gateways to the region and host international conferences.

NAFTA will likely be a similar catalyst for hotel development in response to increased trade and tourism among the three countries involved. But Argentina, Brazil, Chile, and Venezuela may also join an expanded NAFTA, which would become known as the Americas Trading Bloc.

Burj Al Arab hotel, Dubai, United Arab Emirates.

It is easy to understand the international development of hotels given the increase in international tourism trade and commerce. The growth in tourism in Pacific Rim countries is expected to continue at the same rate as in recent years. Several resorts have been developed in Indonesia, Malaysia, Thailand, and Vietnam, and China and India have both seen hotel growth. Further international hotel development opportunities exist in Eastern Europe, Russia, and the other republics of the former Soviet Union, where some companies have changed their growth strategy from building new hotels to acquiring and renovating existing properties. Hotel development in China has

Raffles Singapore, a world-famous classic hotel.

exploded with nearly all the major companies rushing to establish themselves in this important emerging market.

In Asia, Hong Kong's growth has been encouraged by booming economies throughout Southeast Asia and the kind of tax system for which supply-siders hunger. The Hong Kong government levies a flat 16.5 percent corporate tax, a 15 percent individual income tax, and no tax on capital gains or dividends. Several hotel corporations have their headquarters in Hong Kong. Among them are Mandarin Oriental Hotel Group, The Peninsula Hotels, and Shangri-La Hotels and Resorts, all world-renowned for their five-star status. They are based in Hong Kong because of low corporate taxation and the ability to bring in senior expatriate executives with minimal bureaucratic difficulty.[36]

In developing countries, once political stability has been sustained, hotel development quickly follows as part of an overall economic and social progression. An example of this is the former Eastern European countries and former Soviet republics that for the past few years have offered development opportunities for hotel corporations.

LEARNING OBJECTIVE 5
Discuss sustainable/green lodging.

Sustainable or Green Lodging

Today, of necessity, developers are more environmentally conscious because it can cost far more not only to build a lodging facility but also to run it if it is not sustainable. By using local materials, a new hotel or resort can save money on the cost of materials plus the cost of transporting those materials from a distance, or even importing them. Given the weak U.S. dollar, it increases costs if materials must be imported.

The cost of energy has increased so much in recent years that lodging construction now incorporates ways of using natural lighting and building energy-efficient buildings. Energy-efficient buildings require far less air-conditioning than do conventional buildings because they use materials such as darkened glass and lower-wattage lighting that produces lower temperatures.

How can hotels, motels, lodges, and resorts become more sustainable? There are many ways in which to assess how to save energy and recycle.

There are eight steps you can take to start an effective, sustainable lodging program including:

1. Organize a waste reduction team;
2. Conduct a waste assessment;
3. Establish waste reduction goals;
4. Secure recycling markets;
5. Set up a collection and storage system;
6. Buy recycled products.

Lighting can account for 30–40 percent of commercial electricity consumption. This can be reduced by the following strategies:

- Use lighting only when necessary—employ motion detectors.
- Use energy-efficient fixtures and lamps.
- Use low-wattage lighting for signs and décor.
- Avoid over-lighting wherever possible.

Water conservation is another method that can greatly reduce waste. Today, many hotels are replacing showerheads, toilets, and faucets with low-flow water devices. Low-flow showerheads can save 10 gallons of water every five minutes of showering. That means a savings of over $3,000 annually if 100 people shower each day, and water and sewer costs are one cent per gallon.[37] Other water conservation methods include only washing full loads of dishes and laundry, serving drinking water by request only, asking guests to consider reusing towels, and restricting lawn watering.

Fairmont Hotels and Resorts[38] are among the leading sustainable lodging companies whose projects fall into three key areas: (1) minimizing the company's impact on the environment by making ongoing operational improvements, mainly in waste management and energy and water conservation; (2) working at a corporate level to foster high-profile partnerships and accreditations that help promote environmental issues and to share its stewardship message; and (3) to follow best practices, which include working at individual properties to develop innovative ways to reduce the carbon footprint of hotels.

Career Information

A variety of career options are directly and indirectly related to hotel development and classification. Some examples include working in the corporate office to develop hotels or searching out locations, negotiating the deals, and/or organizing the construction or alterations. This involves knowledge of operations plus expertise in marketing, feasibility studies, finance, and planning. Similarly, consulting firms like PKF Consulting have interesting positions for consultants who provide specialized services in feasibility studies, marketing, human resources, and accounting and finance due diligence (a check to ensure that the cost of purchasing a property is reasonable and that all systems are in working order). Working for a consulting firm usually requires a master's degree plus operational experience in an area of specialty. AAA and Mobil both have inspectors who check hotel standards. Inspectors are required to travel and write detailed reports on the properties at which they stay.

Good advice comes from Jim McManemon, general manager of the Ritz-Carlton, Sarasota, Florida: "It is important to have a love of people, as there is so much interaction with them. I also suggest working in the industry to gain experience. Actually, it is a good idea to work in various departments while going to school so you can either join a management-training program or take a supervisory or assistant management position upon graduation. Work hard, be a leader, and set an example for the people working with you."[39]

Trends in Hotel Development and Management

LEARNING OBJECTIVE 6
Identify trends influencing the hotel business.

Courtesy of Dr. Greg Dunn, Senior Lecturer & Managing Director, University of Florida, Eric Friedheim Tourism Institute.

- *Capacity control*. Refers to who will control the sale of inventories of hotel rooms, airline seats, auto rentals, and tickets to attractions. Presently, owners of these assets are in control of their sale and distribution, but increasingly control is falling into the hands of those who own and manage global reservation systems and/or negotiate for large buying groups. Factors involved in the outcome will be telecommunications, software, available satellite capacity, governmental regulations, limited capital, and the travel distribution network.

- *Safety and security*. Important aspects of safety and security are terrorism, the growing disparity between the haves and have-nots in the world, diminishing financial resources, infrastructure problems, health issues, the stability of governments, and personal security.

- *Assets and capital*. The issues concerning assets and capital are rationing of private capital and rationing of funds deployed by governments.

- *Technology*. An example of the growing use of *expert systems* (a basic form of artificial intelligence) would be making standard operating procedures available online, 24 hours a day, and establishing yield management systems designed to make pricing decisions. Other examples include increasing numbers of smart hotel room and communications ports to make virtual office environments for business travelers and the impact of technology on the structure of corporate offices and individual hotels.

- *New management.* The complex forces of capacity control, safety and security, capital movement, and technology issues will require a future management cadre that is able to adapt to rapid-paced change across all the traditional functions of management.

- *Globalization.* A number of U.S. and Canadian chains have developed and are continuing to develop hotels around the world. International companies are also investing in the North American hotel industry.

- *Consolidation.* As the industry matures, corporations are either acquiring or merging with each other.

- *Diversification within segments of the lodging industry.* The economy segment now has low-, medium-, and high-end properties. The extended-stay market has a similar spread of properties, as do all the other hotel classifications.

- *Rapid growth in vacation ownership.* Vacation ownership is the fastest-growing segment of the lodging industry and is likely to continue growing as the baby boomers enter their fifties and sixties.

- *An increase in the number of spas and the treatments offered.* Wellness and the road to nirvana are in increasing demand as guests seek release from the stresses of a fast-paced lifestyle.

- *Gaming.* An increasing number of hotels are coming online that are related to the gaming industry.

- *Mixed-use properties.* An increasing number of hotels are being developed as multiuse properties, meaning hotels with residences (condominiums), spas, and recreational facilities.

- *Sustainable lodging development.* There is increasing development of lodging facilities with environmental designs, construction, and operating procedures.

- *Culinary selectiveness.* There is a rise in the development of appearance, ambience, and food quality at restaurants within hotels with hoteliers realizing the potential for increased revenue through food and beverage outlets. Additionally, dining has become a more interactive experience with consumers becoming more knowledgeable and interested about their food selections. Chefs are required to focus more on sustainability, organic and local ingredients, low-calorie meals, and popular culinary trends. Current trends include "farm to table," "small-plate," and "snackification."[40]

▶ Check Your Knowledge

1. Explain timeshare, vacation, and fractional ownership.

2. Identify several sustainable or green lodging strategies.

3. List and explain some trends in hotel development.

CASE STUDY

Condotels

In recent years, several new lodging brands have been introduced by leading hotel chains to the market. Among the names of these brands are DoubleTree, Candlewood Suites, Homewood Suites, Mainstay, Spring Hill Suites, and so on. In addition, there is Hyatt, which recently purchased AmeriSuites, which it has renovated and now calls Hyatt Place.

A hot trend in lodging development is condo hotels, called condotels. With condotels, a developer can more quickly raise the funds necessary from investors than from other traditional sources such as banks and finance houses. As a result, it makes sense for developers to encourage investors by offering an arrangement for owners to have exclusive use of the unit for a fixed number of days a year (typically 30–60 days) and for the hotel company to rent out the units/rooms for the remainder of the year. The cost of development is high and ranges from an average of $800–$900 per square foot up to a high of $1,400.

Despite the rave reviews on Wall Street for condotels, there are some unresolved issues. With time, who will develop and pay for the replacement of furniture, fixtures, and equipment (FF&E)? What are the association dues, and what form will the relationship take between the owners, the developer, and the hotel company? There are the additional complexities for the hotel operator—such as space for meetings, restaurants, and recreation—and how many rooms will be available on any given night. Yet, the payoffs for both individual investors—owners and hotel operating companies—are good to great. With 78 million baby boomers ready to retire, the prospects look very good to all concerned.

Discussion Questions

1. So what is in a name? Is Hyatt right to use the name Hyatt Place?

2. Is InterContinental or Hilton wrong not to include their name, as in Hilton Hampton Inn or Hampton Inn by Hilton? What is your opinion?

3. Which other areas of the United States are good potential locations for condotels, and why?

4. Will condotels split into various segments like other lodging properties have?

Summary

1. Improved transportation has changed the nature of the hotel industry from small, independently owned inns to big hotel and lodging chains that are operated using concepts such as franchising and management contracts.

2. Hotels can be classified according to location (city center, resort, airport, freeway), types of services offered (casino, convention), and price (luxury, midscale, budget, and economy). Hotels are rated by Mobil and AAA (five-star or five-diamond rankings).

3. Vacation ownership offers consumers the opportunity to purchase fully furnished vacation accommodations, similar to condominiums, sold in a variety of forms, such as weekly intervals or point-based systems, for only a percentage of the cost of full ownership. According to the World Tourism Organization, timeshares are one of the fastest-growing sectors of the travel and tourism industry.

4. Every part of the world offers leisure and business travelers a choice of unusual or conservative accommodations that cater to personal ideas of vacation or business trips.

5. The future of tourism involves international expansion and foreign investment, often in combination with airlines, and with the goal of improving economic conditions in developing countries. It is further influenced by increased globalization, as evidenced by such agreements as NAFTA.

Key Words and Concepts

capital intensive
corporate hotel
fair return on investment
feasibility study
franchise hotel
franchising

direct economic impact
independent hotel
indirect economic impact
management company
management contracts

real estate investment trusts (REITs)
referral associations
summary operating statement
timeshare
vacation ownership

Review Questions

1. What are the advantages of (a) management contracts and (b) franchising? Discuss their impacts on the development of the hotel industry.
2. Explain how hotels cater to the needs of business and leisure travelers in reference to the following concepts: (a) resorts, (b) airport hotels, and (c) vertical integration.
3. What are the different types of timeshare programs available for purchase?

Internet Exercises

1. Organization: **Hilton Hotels**
Summary: Hilton Hotels Corporation and Hilton International have a worldwide alliance to market Hilton. Hilton is recognized as one of the world's best-known hotel brands. Collectively, Hilton offers more than 3,600 hotels in more than 66 countries, truly a major player in the hospitality industry.

(a) What are the different hotel brands that can be franchised through Hilton Hotels Corporation?
(b) What are your views on Hilton's portfolio and franchising options? Click on "Hilton Worldwide Brands."

2. Organization: ***Hotels* Magazine**
Summary: *Hotels* magazine is a publication that offers vast amounts of information on the hospitality industry with up-to-date

industry news, corporate trends, and nationwide developments.

    (a) What are some of the top headlines currently being reported in the industry?
    (b) Go to "Print Magazine Archives," click on the icon for the October 2010 edition, and then go to page 22 of the online magazine. Browse through the corporate rankings and industry leaders. List the top five hotel corporations and note how many rooms each one has.

Apply Your Knowledge

1. From a career perspective, what are the advantages and disadvantages of working in each type of hotel?

2. If you were going into the lodging sector, which type of property would you prefer to work at and why?

Suggested Activities

1. Identify a career pathway to a senior position in the lodging industry.

Endnotes

1. Arjun Kumar Bhatia, *Tourism Development: Principles and Practice* (New Delhi: Sterling Publishers Pvt. Ltd., 2002), 173; Donald E. Lundberg, *The Hotel and Restaurant Business*, 6th ed. (New York: Van Nostrand Reinhold, 1994), 28–29; John Caprarella, et al.: *The History of Lodging: The Hotel in America*, 2002.

2. Hotelcluster.com, *8 Emerging Hospitality Industry Trends in 2013*, http://www.hotelcluster.com, click on Blog and search for the article "8 Emerging Hospitality Industry Trends in 2013" (accessed November 5, 2014).

3. Hotelcluster.com, *8 Emerging Hospitality Industry Trends in 2014*, http://www.hotelcluster.com, click on Blog and search for article "8 Emerging Hospitality Industry Trends in 2014" (accessed on July 22, 2014).

4. American Hotel & Lodging Association, *2013 At-a-Glance Statistical Figures*, http://www.ahla.com (accessed July 22, 2014).

5. American Hotel & Lodging Association, *2013 Lodging Industry Profile*, http://www.ahla.com (accessed February 4, 2015).

6. New York Architecture, *The Plaza Hotel*, www.nyc-architecture.com (accessed October 26, 2011).

7. IHG Hotel & Room World Stats, http://www.ihgplc.com (accessed July 22, 2014).

8. Hospitalitynet, *Franchise Companies*, http://www.hospitalitynet.org (accessed July 22, 2015).

9. Choice Hotels Media Center, http://www.choice-hotels.com, click on Media Center (accessed July 22, 2015).

10. This section is courtesy of Robert Kok, Professor, Johnson and Wales University.

11. Black Enterprise, *Nation's Largest Restaurant Franchisees Grew in Size & Scope in 2012*, http://www.blackenterprise.com, click on Small Business (accessed November 5, 2014).

12. Wyndham Worldwide, *Wyndham Hotel Group*, http://www.wyndhamworldwide.com, go to About Wyndham and click on Wyndham Hotel Group (accessed November 5, 2014).

13. WorldMark by Wyndham, *About Wyndham*, www.worldmarkbywyndham.com, click on About Wyndham (accessed February 22, 2011).

14. Club Wyndham, *Wyndham Hotel Group*, https://www.wyndhamvacationresorts.com, click on About Club Wyndham (accessed July 22, 2014).

15. Wyndham Worldwide, *Wyndham Vacation Ownership*, http://www.wyndhamworldwide.com, go to About Wyndham, click on Wyndham Vacation Ownership (accessed November 5, 2014).

16. Personal conversation with Bruce Goodwin, President of Goodwin and Associates hotel consultants, May 4, 2015.

17. Paul R. Dittmer and Gerald G. Griffen, *The Dimensions of the Hospitality Industry: An Introduction* (New York: Van Nostrand Reinhold, 1993), 91–92; Conrad Hilton, *Be My Guest* (New York: Prentice Hall Press, 1957), 184–199.

18. Joan Cook, "Conrad Hilton, Founder of Hotel Chain, Dies at 92," *New York Times*, January 5, 1979, sec. 11.

19. Hilton Worldwide, *About Us*, http://www.hilton-worldwide.com, click on About Us (accessed July 22, 2014).

20. Kimpton Hotels & Restaurants, *About Us*, www.kimptonhotels.com, click on Kimpton History (accessed February 22, 2015).

21. Marriott International, Inc., *Our Brands: Autograph Collection*, www.marriott.com, click on Lifestyle/Collections (accessed February 18, 2015).

22. Hyatt Corporation, *Our Brands: Andaz*, www.hyatt.com, click on About Hyatt, and then click on Andaz (accessed February 18, 2015).

23. American Hotel & Lodging Association, *Press Release: 2008 Study on Hotel Room Taxes Quantifies Economic Impact*, www.ahla.com (accessed on February 24, 2015).

24. Adapted from the American Hotel & Lodging Association's Economic Impact of Hotels and Motels.

25. American Hotel & Lodging Association, *2014 Lodging Industry Profile*, http://www.ahla.com (accessed July 22, 2014).

26. NewsRoom, *Diamond Ratings: Five Diamond*, http://newsroom.aaa.com, click on Diamond Ratings (accessed November 5, 2014).

27. Forbes Travel Guide, *Forbes Travel Guide's Ratings*, http://www.forbestravelguide.com, click on About and then Star Ratings (accessed August 25 2015).

28. InterContinental Hotels Group, *Hotel Indigo: Our Story*, www.ihg.com (accessed October 26, 2014).

29. "What Is a Bed and Breakfast Inn?," *TravelASSIST*, January 1996, www.travelassist.com, click on TravelASSIST Magazine (accessed October 26, 2014).

30. Great Escapes, *Home Page*, www.greatescapes-online.com (accessed February 19, 2011); Resort Condominiums International, *About Us*, www.rci.com (accessed February 19, 2011).

31. Lynn Sheldon, "Timeshare Concept Adopted by Hotel Industry," *Rhode Island Roads*, http://riroads.com, click on News to search through their articles (accessed November 5, 2014).

32. Resort Condominiums International, *RCI Milestones*, http://www.rci.com (accessed July 21, 2014).

33. Interval International, Home Page, http://www.intervalworld.com (accessed July 22, 2014).

34. NAFTANOW.org, *Fast Facts: North American Free Trade Agreement*, www.naftanow.org, click on About NAFTA, and then click on Fast Facts (accessed November 5, 2014).

35. European Union Demographics Profile 2013, http://www.indexmundi.com, click on Europe, click on European Union, and then click on Demographics (accessed July 22, 2014).

36. Personal conversation with Leonard Gordon, March 15, 2006.

37. Ibid.

38. Fairmont Hotels & Resorts, Green Partnership Program, www.fairmont.com, click on Corporate Responsibility, and then click on Environment & Ecosystem (accessed February 25, 2011).

39. Personal interview with Jim McManemon, General Manager, Ritz-Carlton, Sarasota, Florida, and Chris Bryant, Guest Services Manager, Grand Hyatt, Tampa Bay, Florida, February 26, 2011.

40. Top ten boutique hotel future trends for 2014. http://www.boutiquehotelnews.com and search for "boutique hotel future trends 2014" (accessed on January 5, 2015).

CHAPTER 3

Rooms Division

LEARNING OBJECTIVES

After reading and studying this chapter, you should be able to:

- Outline the duties and responsibilities of key executives and department heads.

- Draw an organizational chart of the rooms division of a hotel and identify the executive committee members.

- Describe the main functions of the rooms division departments.

- Describe property management systems and discuss yield management.

- Calculate occupancy percentages, average daily rates, and actual percentage of potential rooms revenue.

- Outline the importance of the reservations and guest services functions.

- List the complexities and challenges of the concierge, housekeeping, and security/loss prevention departments.

This chapter examines the function of a hotel and the many departments that constitute a hotel. It also helps to explain why and how the departments are interdependent in successfully running a hotel.

The Functions and Departments of a Hotel

The primary function of a hotel is to provide lodging accommodation. A large hotel is run by a general manager (GM) and an executive committee that consists of the key executives who head the major departments: rooms division director, food and beverage (F&B) director, marketing and sales director, human resources director, chief accountant or controller, and chief engineer or facility manager. These executives generally have a regional or corporate counterpart with whom they have a reporting relationship, although the general manager is their immediate superior.

A hotel is made up of several businesses or **revenue centers** and **cost centers**. A few thousand products and services are sold every day. Each area of specialty requires dedication and a quality commitment for each department to get little things right all the time. Furthermore, hotels need the cooperation of a large and diverse group of people to perform well. James McManemon, the GM of the elegant Ritz-Carlton, Sarasota hotel, calls it "a business of details."[1]

Hotels are places of glamour that may be awe-inspiring. Even the experienced hotel person is impressed by the refined dignity of a beautiful hotel like a Ritz-Carlton or the artistic splendor of a Hyatt. The atmosphere of a hotel is stimulating to a hospitality student. Let us step into an imaginary hotel to feel the excitement and become a part of the rush that is similar to show business, for a hotel is live theater and the GM is the director of the cast of players.

Hotels, whether they are chain affiliated or independent properties, exist to serve and enrich society and at the same time make a profit for the owners. Frequently, hotels are just like pieces of property on a Monopoly board. They often make or lose more money with equity appreciation or depreciation than through operations. Hotels have been described as "people palaces." Some are certainly palatial, and others are more functional. Hotels are meant to provide all the comforts of home to those away from home.

Management Structure

Management structure differs among larger, midscale, and smaller properties. The midscale and smaller properties are less complex in their management structures than are the larger ones. However, someone must be

The Grand Hall in the Willard InterContinental, Washington, D.C. It was at this hotel that the term *lobbyist* was coined when then-President Grant would retire after dinner to an armchair in the lobby. People would approach him and try to gain his support for their causes.

responsible for each of the key result areas that make the operation successful. For example, a small property may not have a director of human resources, but each department head will have general day-to-day operating responsibilities for the human resources function. The manager has the ultimate responsibility for all human resources decisions. The same scenario is possible with each of the following areas: engineering and maintenance, accounting and finance, marketing and sales, food and beverage management, and so on.

Role of the Hotel General Manager

Hotel general managers have a lot of responsibilities. They must provide owners with a reasonable return on investment, keep guests satisfied and returning, and keep employees happy. This may seem easy, but because there are so many interpersonal transactions and because hotels are open every day, all day, the complexities of operating become challenges that the general manager must face and overcome. The GM not only focuses on leading and operating the hotel departments but also on aspects of the infrastructure, from room atmosphere to security.

Larger hotels can be more impersonal. Here, the general manager may only meet and greet a few VIPs. In the smaller property, it is easier—though no less important—for the GM to become acquainted with guests to ensure that their stay is memorable and to secure their return. One way that experienced GMs can meet guests, even in large hotels, is to be visible in the lobby and F&B outlets at peak times (checkout, lunch, check-in, and dinner time). Guests like to feel that the GM takes a personal interest in their well-being. Max Blouet, who was general manager of the famous Four Seasons Hotel George V, Paris for more than 30 years, was a master of this art. He was always present at the right moment to meet and greet guests during the lunch hour and at the evening check-in. Great hoteliers always remember they are hosts.

The GM is ultimately responsible for the performance of the hotel and the employees. The GM is the leader of the hotel. As such, she or he is held accountable for the hotel's level of profitability by the corporation or owners.

To be successful, GMs need to have a broad range of personal qualities. Among those most often quoted by GMs are the following:

- Leadership
- Attention to detail
- Follow-through—getting the job done
- People skills
- Patience
- Ability to delegate effectively

A General Manager discussing the "forecast" with a Rooms Division Director.

INTRODUCING CESAR RITZ

Cesar Ritz was a legend in his own time; like so many of the early industry leaders, he began at the bottom and worked his way up through the ranks. In his case, it did not take long to reach the top because he quickly learned the secrets of success in the hotel business. His career began as an apprenticed hotel keeper at the age of 15. At 19, he was managing a Parisian restaurant. Suddenly, he quit that position to become an assistant waiter at the famous Voisin restaurant. There he learned how to pander to the rich and famous. In fact, he became so adept at taking care of the guests—remembering their likes and dislikes, even their idiosyncrasies—that a guest would ask for him and would only be served by him.

At the age of 22, Ritz became manager of the Grand Hotel National in Lucerne, Switzerland, one of the most luxurious hotels in the world. The hotel was not very successful at the time he became manager, but Ritz, with his ingenuity and panache, was able to attract the "in" crowd to complete a turnaround. After 11 seasons, he accepted a bigger challenge at The Savoy Hotel in London, which had been open only a few months and which was not doing well. Cesar Ritz became manager of one of the most famous and luxurious hotels in the world at the age of 38.

Once again, the flair and ability of Ritz to influence society quickly made a positive impression on the hotel. To begin with, he made the hotel a cultural center for high society. Together with Escoffier as executive chef, he created a team that produced the finest cuisine in Europe in the most elegant of surroundings. He made evening dress compulsory and introduced orchestras to the restaurants. Cesar Ritz would spare no expense to create the lavish effect he sought. On one occasion, he converted a riverside restaurant into a Venetian waterway, complete with small gondolas and gondoliers singing Italian love songs.[2]

Both Ritz and Escoffier were dismissed from the Savoy in 1897. Ritz was implicated in the disappearance of over 3,400 pounds of wine and spirits.[3] In 1898, Ritz opened the celebrated Hôtel Ritz in the Place Vendôme, Paris, France. The Hotel Ritz in Madrid, Spain, opened in 1910, inspired by King Alfonso XIII's desire to build a luxury hotel to rival the Ritz in Paris. Ritz enjoyed a long partnership with Escoffier, the famous French chef and father of modern French cooking.[4]

Ritz considered the handling of people as the most important of all qualities for an hotelier. His imagination and sensitivity to people and their wants contributed to a new standard of hotel keeping. The Ritz name remains synonymous with refined, elegant hotels and service.[5] However, Ritz drove himself to the point of exhaustion, and at age 52, he suffered a nervous breakdown. This is a lesson for us not to drive ourselves to the point of exhaustion.

A successful GM selects and trains the best people. A former GM of Four Seasons Hotel Chicago deliberately hired division heads who knew more about the job for which they were hired than he did. The GM sets the tone—a structure of excellence—and others try to match it. Once the structure is in place, each employee works to define the hotel's commitment to excellence. General managers need to understand, empathize, and allow for the cultures of both guests and employees. Progressive general managers empower associates to do anything legal to delight the guest.

The Executive Committee

The general manager, using input from the **executive committee** (Figure 3–1), makes all the major decisions affecting the hotel. This committee, which includes the directors of human resources, food and beverage, rooms division, marketing and sales, engineering, and accounting, compile the hotel's occupancy forecast together with all revenues and expenses to make up the budget. They generally meet once a week for one or two hours—although the Ritz-Carlton has a daily lineup at 9 A.M.—and might typically cover some of the following topics:

LEARNING OBJECTIVE 2
Draw an organizational chart of the rooms division of a hotel and identify the executive committee members.

- Guest satisfaction
- Employee satisfaction
- Total quality management
- Occupancy forecasts
- Sales and marketing plans
- Training
- Major items of expenditure
- Renovations
- Ownership relations
- Energy conservation
- Recycling
- New legislation
- Profitability

Some GMs rely on input from the executive committee more than others do, depending on their leadership and management style. These senior executives determine the character of the property and decide on the missions, goals, and objectives of the hotel. For a chain hotel, this will be in harmony with the corporate mission.

In most hotels, the executive committee is involved with the decisions, but the ultimate responsibility and authority rest with the GM. One major role of the committee is that of communicator, both up and down the line of authority. This helps build interdepartmental cooperation. Not all lodging operations will have an executive committee—obviously there is no need for one at a small motel, lodge, or a bed and breakfast (B&B).

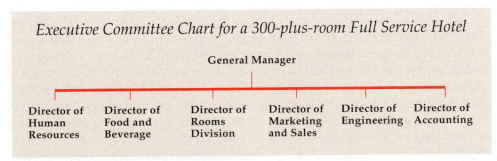

Executive Committee Chart for a 300-plus-room Full Service Hotel

General Manager

Director of Human Resources | Director of Food and Beverage | Director of Rooms Division | Director of Marketing and Sales | Director of Engineering | Director of Accounting

Figure 3–1 • Executive Committee Chart.

► Check Your Knowledge

1. What is the role of the general manager?
2. What topics do the members of an executive committee usually address in their weekly meetings?

The Departments

In larger hotels, the rooms division has several departments that all work together to please guests. In midsize and smaller properties, those departments may be reduced in size and number, but they still need to serve guests.

Rooms Division

LEARNING OBJECTIVE 3
Describe the main functions of the rooms division departments.

The rooms division director is held responsible by the GM for the efficient and effective leadership and operation of all the rooms division departments. They include concerns such as the following:

- Financial responsibility for rooms division
- Employee satisfaction goals
- Guest satisfaction goals
- Guest services
- Guest relations
- Security
- Gift shop

The **rooms division** consists of the following departments: front office, reservations, housekeeping, concierge, guest services, security, and communications. Figure 3–2 shows the organizational chart for a 300-plus-room hotel rooms division.

The guest cycle in Figure 3–3 shows a simplified sequence of events that takes place from the moment a guest calls to make a reservation until he or she checks out.

Front Office

The front-office manager's (FOM) main duty is to enhance guest services by constantly developing services to meet guest needs. An example of how some FOMs enhance guest services is to have a guest service associate (GSA) greet guests as they arrive at the hotel, escort them to the front desk, and then personally allocate the room and take the guest and luggage to the room. This innovative way of developing guest services looks at the operation from the guest's perspective. There is no need to have separate departments for doorperson, bellperson, front desk, and so on. Each guest associate is cross-trained in all aspects of greeting and rooming the guest. This is now being

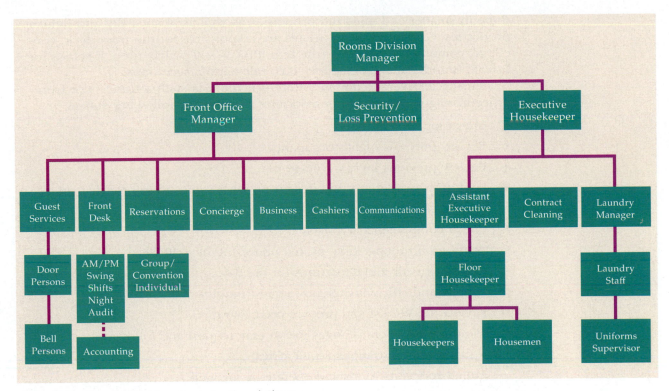

Figure 3–2 • Rooms Division Organizational Chart.

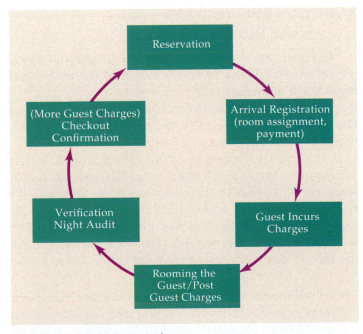

Figure 3–3 • The Guest Cycle.

done in smaller and midsized properties as well as at specialty and deluxe properties. Guest service associates are responsible for the front desk, concierge, communications/PBX (the term PBX is still widely used; it stands for Private Brand Exchange), bellpersons, valet, and reservations.

During an average day in a hotel—if there is such a thing—the front-office manager and his or her associates perform the following duties:

- Check night clerk report.
- Review previous night's occupancy.
- Review previous night's average rate.
- Look over market mix and determine what rooms to sell at what price.
- Handle checkouts and check-ins.
- Check complimentary rooms.
- Verify group rooms to be picked up for the next 30 days.
- Review arrivals and departures for the day.
- Politely and efficiently attend to guest inquiries.
- Review the VIP list and prepare preregistration.
- Organize any room changes guests may request and follow up.
- Arrange preregistrations for all arrivals.
- Attend rooms divisions and operations meeting.
- Advise housekeeping and room service of flowers/fruit for VIPs.
- Review arrivals and departures for the next day.
- Make staffing adjustments needed for arrivals and departures.
- Note any important things in the log book.
- Check issuing and control of keys.
- Review scheduling (done weekly).
- Meet with lead GSAs (done daily).

In some hotels, the reservations manager and associates report to the director of sales. These positions report to the chief accountant: night auditor, night audit associates, and cashiers.

The front office has been described as the hub or nerve center of the hotel. It is the department that makes a first impression on the guest and one that the guest relies on throughout his or her stay for information and service. Positive first impressions are critical to the successful guest experience. Many guests arrive at the hotel after long, tiring trips. They want to be met by someone with a warm smile and a genuine greeting. If a guest should have a negative experience when checking into a hotel, he or she will be on guard in encounters with each of the other departments. The position description for a guest service agent details the work performed. Position descriptions for the three main functions of the front office are as follows:

1. *To sell rooms.* The hotel departments' personnel work like a team in a relay race. Sales or reservations staff make up room sales until the evening before the guest's arrival. At 6:00 P.M., when the reservations office

closes, all the expected arrivals and available rooms are then handed over to the front desk P.M. shift. Reservations calls after 6:00 P.M. may either be taken by the front-desk staff or the 1-800 number. The front-desk team will try to sell out (achieve 100 percent occupancy) by selling the remaining rooms to call-in or walk-in guests—and of course the frantic calls from preferred guests who need a favor!

Upselling occurs when the guest service agent/front-desk clerk suggestively sells the features of a larger room, a higher floor, or perhaps a better view. **Yield management** originated in the airline industry where demand also fluctuates. Basically, a percentage of guests who book and send in a

A front-office manager taking care of a guest request.

deposit in advance will be able to secure a room at a more reasonable price than can someone booking a room with just three days' notice. The price will be even higher for the booking at three days' notice if demand is good.

Many other factors influence the hotel's ability to sell out. Chief among these are *demand*—the number of people needing rooms—and *supply*—the number of available rooms. A good example is the International Hotel, Motel + Restaurant Show. This event takes place in a city that has a high demand for hotel rooms in proportion to its inventory (number of available rooms). Because there is a fairly constant demand for rooms in New York, special events tend to increase demand to a point that forces up **room rates**. (See Figure 3–4.) Another example comes from the airline industry, which always seems to raise prices at the peak travel times (Thanksgiving, Christmas, Easter, and the summer vacation times). They only offer special fares when school is in session. Revenue management is explained in more detail later in this chapter.

2. *To maintain balanced guest accounts.* This begins with advance deposits, opening the guest folio (account), and posting all charges from the various departments. Most hotels have **property management systems (PMS)** (property management systems are explained in more detail later in this chapter) and point-of-sale (POS) terminals, which are online to the front office.

This means that guest charges from the various outlets are directly debited to the guest's folio. Payment is either received on guest checkout or transferred to the **city ledger** (a special account for a company that has established credit with the hotel). This means that the account will be sent and paid within a specified time period.

3. *To offer services such as handling mail, faxes, messages, and local and hotel information.* People constantly approach the front desk with questions. Front-desk employees need to be knowledgeable about the

FOCUS ON ROOMS DIVISION

Rooms Division with Charlie Adams

From the early days of primitive inns to our modern super hotels, like the Izmailovo Hotel with 7,500 rooms in Moscow, employees are the crucial ingredient to hotel or motel success. Even with extraordinary advances in technology and the globalization of lodging in the twenty-first century, lodging remains fundamentally a people business and it is the employees who are responsible for the appearance, image, and reputation of a lodging facility.

The rooms division is considered the "center" of hotel activity because it is accountable for revenue, customer service, and departmental forecasting. Room sales are the primary source of income for most hotels and almost 100 percent of the revenue for many select service or budget hotels. The rooms division has the most guest contacts because it is comprised of reservations, front office, housekeeping, and uniformed services. The reservations department provides the needed accurate information for other departments to use to forecast for upcoming events and guest needs along with scheduling the proper staffing levels in the hotel.

Starting your career in the rooms division of a hotel is an exciting, demanding, and rewarding experience. You will be part of a team whose overall responsibility is the well-being of guests and ensuring that their expectations are met and that they have a memorable experience. As a rooms division employee you will be part of several interconnected functions that include: front desk, housekeeping, reservations, concierge, guest services, security, and communications. The following are some important tips for success in fulfilling the company's promise to each guest:

Front Desk   Here is where the first and last impressions are always made! At the front desk it is important to be personable, confident, and patient because your guests will vary in temperament, needs, and expectations. Always remember a friendly, calm, and positive attitude are your best tools even in trying situations. Multitasking becomes an art form at the front desk, calling upon all of your communication, typing, and computer skills.

Housekeeping   Perception is reality and cleanliness is always at the top of a guest's expectations. In housekeeping it is the attention to details, the eye for the out of place, the worn or frayed that keeps it real for guests. It is a demanding work area with much physical labor that is essential to guest satisfaction. Your work is done mostly behind the curtain, out of guest view, but noticed and appreciated when they enter to fresh towels, a made bed, and a flawlessly clean room. This is where you should start your lodging management career because it is the most demanding and least popular department among new hospitality graduates, and yet it is the best training ground for early lodging management success!

Reservations   How do you convey a smile over the phone? You must do so as you begin the process of the guest cycle. Reservations calls for total command of the keyboard, awareness of hotel revenue goals, upcoming events, room availability, but above all listen, truly **listen**, to the guest so you can match their requests with the hotel's services. The promise begins with you and you must never write a check that the front desk can't cash at check-in.

Concierge   A job that calls for diplomacy, ability to wheel-n-deal, and just a touch of magic. Your role is to accommodate the guest needs during their stay. It calls for an encyclopedic memory of restaurants, theater offerings, key points of interest, and current city events. The ability to develop a vast network of connections throughout the hospitality community in your area is essential to serve your guests and see to their every wish. Your reward as a successful concierge is that no two days are ever the same and there are always new and different challenges, opportunities, and rewards.

Guest Services   Also referred to as uniformed services; consists of valet, doorperson, and bellperson positions. All jobs essential to first and last impressions set the tone for the quality of service. A congenial disposition that projects a true spirit of helpfulness will disarm any initial guest trepidation. It also calls for thorough comprehension of the hotel, its layout, rooms, and amenities. It is work that demands immaculate grooming (especially the uniform), standing for long hours, and physical activity. In uniform, you *are* the hotel to the guest.

Major hotel chains offer a number of different room rates, including the following:

rack rate
corporate
association rate
government
encore
cititravel
entertainment cards
AAA
AARP (American Association of Retired Persons)
wholesale
group rates
promotional special

The rack rate is the rate that is used as a benchmark quotation of a hotel's room rate. Let us assume that the Hotel California had a rack rate of $135. Any discounted rate may be offered at a percentage deduction from the rack rate. An example would be a corporate rate of $110, an association rate of $105, and AARP rate of $95—certain restrictions may apply. Group rates may range from $95 to $125 according to how much the hotel needs the business.

Throughout the world there are three main plans on which room rates are based:

AP/American Plan—room and three meals a day
MAP/Modified American Plan—room plus two meals
EP/European Plan—room only, meals extra

Figure 3–4 • The Types of Room Rates Offered by Hotels.

various activities in the hotel. The size, layout, and staffing of the front desk will vary with the size of the hotel. The front-desk staff size of a busy 800-room city center property will naturally differ from that of a country inn. The front desk is staffed throughout the 24 hours by three shifts. The evening shift duties include the following:

• Check the log book for special items. (The log book is kept by guest contact; associates at the front office note specific and important guest requests and occurrences such as requests for room switches or baby cribs.)

• Check on the room status, number of expected checkouts still to leave, and arrivals by double-checking registration cards and the computer so that they can update the forecast of the night's occupancy. This will determine the number of rooms left to sell. Nowadays, this is all part of the capability of the PMS.

- Handle guest check-ins. This means notifying the appropriate staff of any special requests guests may have made (e.g., nonsmoking room or a long bed for an extra-tall guest).
- Take reservations for that evening and future reservations after the reservations staff have left for the day.

Night Auditor

A hotel is one of the few businesses that balances its accounts at the end of each business day. Because a hotel is open 24 hours every day, it is difficult to stop transactions at any given moment. The **night auditor** and his or her team wait until the hotel quiets down at about 1:00 A.M., and then begins the task of balancing the guests' accounts receivable. The process of night auditing is as follows:

1. The night audit team runs a preliminary reconciliation report that shows the total revenue generated from room and tax, banquets and catering, food and beverage outlets, and other incidentals (phone, gift shop, etc.).
2. All errors on the report are investigated.
3. All changes are posted and balanced with the preliminary charges.
4. A comparison of charges is carried out, matching preliminary with actual charges.
5. Totals for credit card charges, rooms operations, food and beverages, and incidentals are verified.
6. The team "rolls the date"—they go forward to the next day.
7. Post any charges that the evening shift was not able to post.
8. Pass discrepancies to shift managers in the morning. The room and tax charges are then posted to each folio and a new balance shown.
9. Run backup reports so that if the computer system fails, the hotel will have up-to-date information to operate a manual system.
10. Reconcile point-of-sale and PMS to guest accounts. If this does not balance, the auditor must balance it by investigating errors or omissions. This is done by checking that every departmental charge shows up on guest folios.
11. Complete and distribute the daily report. This report details the previous day's activities and includes vital information about the performance of the hotel.
12. Determine areas of the hotel where theft could potentially occur.

Larger hotels may have more than one night auditor, but in smaller properties these duties may be combined with night manager, desk, or night watchperson duties.

CORPORATE PROFILE

Hyatt Hotels

When Nicholas Pritzker emigrated with his family from the Ukraine to the United States, he began his career by opening a small law firm. His outstanding management skills led to the expansion of the law firm, turning it into a management company. Pritzker purchased the Hyatt House motel next to the Los Angeles International Airport in 1957.

Today, Hyatt is an international brand of hotels within the Hyatt Hotels Corporation, a multibillion-dollar hotel management and development company. It is among the leading chains in the hotel industry, with close to eight percent of the market share.[6] Hyatt has earned worldwide fame as the leader in providing luxury accommodations and high-quality service, targeting especially the business traveler, but strategically differentiating its properties and services to identify and market to a very diverse clientele. This differentiation has resulted in the following types of hotels:

1. *Grand Hyatt* features distinctive luxury hotels in major gateway cities.
2. The *Hyatt Regency* hotels represent the company's core product. They are usually located in business city centers and are often regarded as four- and five-star hotels.
3. *Hyatt Resorts* are vacation retreats. They are located in the world's most desirable leisure destinations, offering the "ultimate escape from everyday stresses."
4. The *Park Hyatt* hotels are smaller, European-style, luxury hotels. They target the individual traveler who prefers the privacy, personalized service, and discreet elegance of a small European hotel.
5. *Hyatt Place* locations are lifestyle 125- to 200-room properties located in urban, airport, and suburban areas. Signature features include The Gallery, which offers a coffee and wine bar and a 24/7 kitchen where travelers can find freshly prepared food.
6. *Hyatt Zilara* and *Hyatt Ziva* are all-inclusive luxury resorts that provide guests with unique experiences and entertainment options. Additionally, Hyatt Zilara offers guests adult-only lodgings for a relaxing kids-free getaway.
7. *Hyatt House* is an extended-stay brand of 125- to 200-room all-suite properties that provide the feel of a residency. Hyatt House offers a casual hospitality experience, and features complimentary breakfast with a build-your-own omelette station. Locations are urban, airport, and suburban.
8. *Andaz* is a casual, stylish, boutique-style hotel; each hotel reflects the unique cultural scene and spirit of the surrounding neighborhood.
9. *Hyatt Residence Club* offers vacation ownership, vacation rentals, and mini vacations in sensational destinations throughout the United States.

The Hyatt Hotels Corporation is characterized by a decentralized management approach, which gives the individual general manager a great deal of decision-making power, as well as the opportunity to use personal creativity and, therefore, stimulate differentiation and innovation. The development of novel concepts and products is perhaps the

CORPORATE PROFILE *(Continued)*

key to Hyatt's outstanding success. For example, the opening of the Hyatt Regency Atlanta with its atrium lobby gave the company instant recognition throughout the world. The property's innovative architecture, designed by John Portman, revolutionized the common standards of design and spacing, thus changing the course of the lodging industry.

A further positive aspect of the decentralized management structure is the fact that the individual manager is able to be extremely guest responsive by developing a thorough knowledge of the guests' needs and thereby providing personalized service—fundamental to achieving customer satisfaction. This is, in fact, the ultimate innkeeping purpose, which Hyatt attains at high levels.

The other side of Hyatt's success is the emphasis on human resources management. Employee satisfaction, in fact, is considered to be a prerequisite to external satisfaction. Hyatt devotes enormous attention to employee training and selection. What is most significant, however, is the interaction among top managers and operating employees.

The company operates 554 hotels and resorts in 47 countries worldwide.

The **daily report** contains key operating ratios such as **room occupancy percentage (ROP)**, which is the number of rooms occupied divided by the number of rooms available:

$$\frac{\text{Rooms Occupied}}{\text{Rooms Available}}$$

Thus, if a hotel has 850 rooms and 622 are occupied, the occupancy percentage is $622 \div 850 = 73$ percent.

The **average daily rate (ADR)** is calculated by dividing the rooms revenue by the number of rooms sold:

$$\frac{\text{Rooms Revenue}}{\text{Rooms Sold}}$$

If the rooms revenue is $75,884 and the number of rooms sold is 662, then the ADR is $114.63. The ADR is, together with the occupancy percentage, one of the key operating ratios that indicates the hotel's performance. See Figure 3–5 for an example of a daily report.

Room occupancy percentage (ROP):

If total available rooms are	850
And total rooms occupied are	622

Then:

Occupancy percentage = $(622/850) \times 100 = 73\%$

Average daily rate:

If rooms revenue is	$75,884
And total number of rooms sold is	622

Then:

$$\textbf{Average daily rate} = \frac{\textbf{75,884}}{\textbf{662}} = \textbf{\$114.63}$$

Weather
Stormy

Daily Revenue Report
Monday, March 17, 2014

ROOM SALES	TODAY Sales	# Rooms Sold	Avg Rate	M-T-D ACTUAL Sales	# Rooms Sold	Avg Rate	M-T-D BUDGET Sales	# Rooms Sold	Avg Rate	MTD FORECAST Sales	# Rooms Sold	Avg Rate	MTD Last Year Sales	# Rooms Sold	Avg Rate	2013
RACK	3,357.00	20	$167.85	81,659.16	387	$211.01	60,327.40	300	$201.09	75,925.26	384	$197.72	38,765.48	206	$188.01	
CONSORTIUM	2,298.00	12	$191.50	17,349.00	85	$204.11	13,835.95	72	$192.17	13,453.63	75	$179.38	14,034.32	75	$186.80	
NATIONAL CORPORATE	1,059.00	8	$132.38	22,330.06	152	$146.91	24,925.00	187	$133.29	20,088.84	139	$144.52	14,583.81	105	$139.24	
LOCAL CORPORATE	4,116.30	26	$158.32	38,526.50	262	$147.05	33,180.00	237	$140.00	28,987.85	202	$143.50	26,904.42	186	$144.72	
GOVERNMENT/MILITARY	1,262.00	8	$157.75	10,457.00	68	$153.78	6,109.00	41	$149.00	10,483.87	71	$147.66	10,476.39	65	$160.54	
DISCOUNTS	5,033.17	31	$162.36	102,276.26	623	$164.17	110,759.98	665	$166.56	111,637.19	688	$162.26	78,261.97	512	$152.96	
PACKAGE	(315.48)	3	($105.16)	23,470.14	129	$181.94	14,818.59	87	$170.33	21,817.82	116	$188.08	13,226.00	77	$172.27	
WHOLESALE	141.75	1	$141.75	283.50	2	$141.75		0	$0.00	-	0	$0.00	520.97	5	$95.00	
CONTRACT/OTHER	-	0	$0.00	-	0	$0.00		0	$0.00	-	0	$0.00	-	0	$0.00	
TOTAL TRANSIENT ROOM SALE	16,951.74	109	$155.52	296,351.62	1,708	$173.51	263,955.92	1,589	$166.11	282,394.46	1,675	$168.59	196,773.35	1,231	$159.83	
GROUP CORPORATE	-	0	$0.00	3,490.50	13	$268.50		0	$0.00	2,506.00	14	$179.00	77,736.61	513	$151.45	
GROUP ASSOCIATION	-	0	$0.00	-	0	$0.00		0	$0.00	-	0	$0.00	-	0	$0.00	
GROUP GOVT/MILITARY	-	0	$0.00	-	0	$0.00		0	$0.00	-	0	$0.00	-	0	$0.00	
GROUP SMERF	-	0	$0.00	28,631.27	177	$161.76	46,512.00	298	$156.08	31,419.10	194	$161.95	17,619.68	117	$150.14	
GROUP TOUR/TRAVEL	-	0	$0.00	-	0	$0.00		0	$0.00	-	0	$0.00	1,210.84	0	$0.00	
GROUP CONTRACT/OTHER	-	0	$0.00	773.83	9	$85.98		0	$0.00	891.00	9	$99.00	-	18	$0.00	
TOTAL GROUP ROOM SALES	-	0	$0.00	32,895.60	199	$165.30	46,512.00	298	$156.08	34,816.10	217	$160.44	96,567.13	648	$148.98	
COMPLIMENTARY ROOM		0	$0.00		3	$0.00		0	$0.00		0	$0.00		0	$0.00	
OUT OF ORDER ROOM		0	$0.00		6	$0.00		0	$0.00		0	$0.00		0	$0.00	
TOTAL ROOM SALES	16,951.74	109	$155.52	329,247.22	1,907	$172.65	310,467.92	1,887	$164.53	317,210.56	1,892	$167.66	293,340.48	1,879	$156.09	
REVENUE OCC % TOTAL OCC%	94.8%	/	94.8%	97.5%	/	97.7%	96.5%	/	96.5%	96.8%	/	96.8%	96.1%	/	96.1%	

Outlet I	Sales	Covers	Avg Check	Sales	Covers	Avg Check	Sales	Covers	Avg Check	Sales	Covers	Avg Check	Sales	Covers	Avg Check	
BREAKFAST	415.26	48	$8.65	5,652.29	568	$9.95	4,545.03	434	$10.46	4,577.94	438	$10.46	4,813.55	1,154	$4.17	
LUNCH	0.00	0	$0.00	361.45	0	$0.00	0.00	0	$0.00	0.00	0	$0.00	0.00	0	$0.00	
DINNER	375.80	28	$13.42	3,764.02	315	$11.95	3,340.23	252	$13.27	4,335.00	280	$15.50	3,149.85	247	$12.76	
LITE FARE / OTHER	0.00	0	$0.00	0.00	0	$0.00	0.00	0	$0.00	0.00	0	$0.00	0.00	0	$0.00	
Total Food	791.06	76	$10.41	9,777.76	883	$11.07	7,885.26	686	$11.49	8,912.94	717	$12.43	7,963.40	1,401	$5.69	
LIQUOR	168.50			3,191.75			2,250.03			2,250.03			2,206.16			
BEER	60.00			1,134.00			1,252.52			1,398.39			1,227.84			
WINE	66.00			1,441.00			1,017.26			1,206.45			987.63			
Total Beverage	294.50			5,766.75			4,519.81			4,854.87			4,421.63			
TOTAL REST SALES	1,085.56	76	$14.28	15,544.51	883	$17.60	12,405.06	686	$18.08	13,767.81	717	$19.19	12,385.03	1,401	$8.84	

Room Service	Sales	Covers	Avg Check	Sales	Covers	Avg Check	Sales	Covers	Avg Check	Sales	Covers	Avg Check	Sales	Covers	Avg Check	
BREAKFAST	0.00	0	$0.00	0.00	0	$0.00	0.00	0	$0.00	0.00	0	$0.00	0.00	0	$0.00	
LUNCH	0.00	0	$0.00	0.00	0	$0.00	0.00	0	$0.00	0.00	0	$0.00	0.00	0	$0.00	
DINNER	96.95	5	$19.39	887.93	53	$16.75	1,095.87	86	$12.81	1,095.68	63	$17.37	1,053.77	84	$12.56	
LITE FARE / OTHER	0.00	0	$0.00	0.00	0	$0.00	0.00	0	$0.00	0.00	0	$0.00	0.00	0	$0.00	
Total Food	96.95	5	$19.39	887.93	53	$16.75	1,095.87	86	$12.81	1,095.68	63	$17.37	1,053.77	84	$12.56	
LIQUOR	0.00			0.00			0.00			0.00			0.00			
BEER	0.00			0.00			0.00			0.00			0.00			
WINE	0.00			0.00			0.00			0.00			0.00			
Total Beverage	0.00			0.00			0.00			0.00			0.00			
TOTAL REST II SALES	96.95	5	$19.39	887.93	53	$16.75	1,095.87	86	$12.81	1,095.68	63	$17.37	1,053.77	84	$12.56	

BANQUET	Sales	Covers	Avg Check	Sales	Covers	Avg Check	Sales	Covers	Avg Check	Sales	Covers	Avg Check	Sales	Covers	Avg Check	
BREAKFAST	190.00	19	$10.00	430.00	39	$11.03	485.52	49	$9.94	658.06	66	$10.00	469.23	48	$9.84	
LUNCH	0.00	0	$0.00	905.70	42	$21.56	830.81	45	$18.48	830.81	45	$18.48	792.17	43	$18.29	
DINNER	0.00	0	$0.00	521.70	22	$23.71	304.90	12	$26.48	945.97	41	$23.00	284.61	11	$25.95	
BREAKS	0.00	0	$0.00	50.00	16	$3.13	146.97	22	$6.70	146.97	22	$6.70	146.47	22	$6.68	
RECEPTION	0.00	0	$0.00	0.00	0	$0.00	164.52	33	$5.00	164.52	33	$5.00	150.81	32	$4.74	
OTHER	0.00	0	$0.00	0.00	0	$0.00	0.00	0	$0.00	0.00	0	$0.00	0.00	0	$0.00	
Total Food Sales	190.00	19	$10.00	1,907.40	119	$16.03	1,932.52	160	$12.07	2,746.32	207	$13.28	1,843.29	156	$11.84	
LIQUOR	0.00			0.00			8.23			8.23			0.00			
BEER	0.00			0.00			16.45			27.42			6.17			
WINE	0.00			0.00			16.45			32.90			12.36			
Total Beverage	0.00			0.00			41.13			68.55			18.54			
TOTAL BANQUET	190.00	19	$10.00	1,907.40	119	$16.03	1,973.65	160	$12.33	2,814.87	207	$13.62	1,861.83	156	$11.95	
TOTAL FOOD SALES	1,078.00			12,573.09			10,913.65			12,754.94			10,860.46			
TOTAL BEVERAGE SALES	294.50			5,766.75			4,560.94			4,923.42			4,440.17			
MEETING ROOM SALES	400.00			3,000.00			1,919.35			2,303.23			4,393.95			
BANQUET MISC SALES	0.00			70.00			191.94			191.94			459.24			
BANQUET GRATUITY CHARGE	38.00			381.48		21,791.32	137.10			685.48			104.58			
TOTAL F & B REVENUE	1,810.51			21,791.32			17,722.97			20,859.00			20,258.41			

OTHER INCOME	Sales		PER OCC RM	Sales		PER OCC RM	Sales		PER OCC RM	Sales		PER OCC RM	Sales		PER OCC RM	
TELEPHONE	86.74		$0.80	143.42		$0.08	120.65		$0.06	120.65		$0.06	57.15		$0.03	
GTD NO SHOW/ATTRICION	0.00		$0.00	0.00		$0.00	274.19		$0.15	82.26		$0.04	0.00		$0.00	
ATTRICION - FOOD	0.00		$0.00	0.00		$0.00	0.00		$0.00	0.00		$0.00	0.00		$0.00	
PARKING	0.00		$0.00	0.00		$0.00	0.00		$0.00	0.00		$0.00	0.00		$0.00	
ROOF/STORE RENTALS	84.15		$0.77	1,342.81		$0.70	0.00		$0.00	0.00		$0.00	0.00		$0.00	
MOVIES	93.86		$0.86	1,200.07		$0.63	1,039.19		$0.55	932.26		$0.49	1,128.57		$0.60	
OTHER INCOME	40.36		$0.37	944.19		$0.50	1,794.87		$0.95	1,819.00		$0.96	2,166.22		$1.15	
TOTAL OTHER INCOME	305.11		$2.80	3,630.49		$1.90	3,228.90		$1.71	2,954.16		$1.56	3,351.94		$1.78	

| TOTAL PROPERTY | 19,067.36 | | | 354,669.03 | | | 331,419.79 | | | 341,023.72 | | | 316,950.83 | | | |

	Today	MTD Change
Guest Ledger	33,895.69	4,011.62
City Ledger	49,345.65	(22,742.07)
Advance Deposit	(11,379.39)	1,184.22
Total	71,861.95	(17,546.23)

Cash Receipts	791.38	12,517.84
Credit Card Receipts	19,850.05	362,315.10

Figure 3–5 • A Hotel Daily Report.

A more recently popular ratio to gauge a hotel rooms division's performance is the percentage of potential room's revenue, which is calculated by determining potential rooms revenue and dividing the actual revenue by the potential revenue.

While these figures are of great importance to running a successful hotel, the most important of the lodging ratios is **revenue per available room (REV PAR)**, which is discussed in the next section.

LEARNING OBJECTIVE 4
Describe property management systems and discuss yield management.

LEARNING OBJECTIVE 5
Calculate occupancy percentages, average daily rates, and actual percentage of potential rooms revenue.

Revenue Management

Revenue management is used to maximize room revenue at the hotel. It is based on the economics of supply and demand, which means that prices rise when demand is strong and drop when demand is weak. Naturally, management would like to sell every room at the highest rack rate. However, this is not a reality, and rooms are sold at discounts from the rack rate. An example is the corporate or group rate. In most hotels, only a small percentage of rooms are sold at rack rate. This is because of conventions and group rates and other promotional discounts that are necessary to stimulate demand.

What revenue management does is allocate the right type of room to the right guest at the right price so as to maximize revenue per available room.[7] Thus, the purpose of revenue management is to increase profitability. Generally, the demand for room reservations follows the pattern of group bookings, which are made months or even years in advance of arrival, and individual bookings, which mostly are made a few days before arrival. Figures 3–6 and 3–7 show the pattern of individual and group room reservations. Revenue management examines the demand for rooms over a period of a few years and determines the extent of demand for a particular room each night. This includes busy periods, slow periods, and holidays. The computer program figures out a model of that demand, which is then used to guestimate future demand so that management can determine pricing levels to set.

Because group reservations are booked months, even years, in advance, revenue management systems can monitor reservations and, based on previous trends and current demand, determine the number and type of rooms to sell at what price to obtain the maximum revenue.

The curve in Figure 3–6 indicates the pattern of few reservations being made 120 days prior to arrival. Most of the individual room bookings are made in the last few days before arrival at the hotel. The revenue management program monitors the demand and supply and recommends the number and type of rooms to sell for any given day, and the price for which to sell each room.

With revenue management, not only will the time before arrival be an important consideration in the pricing of guest rooms, but also the type of room to be occupied.

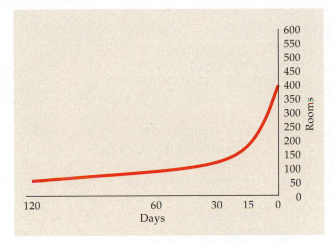

Figure 3–6 • Individual Room Booking Reservations Curve.

(*Source:* Personal correspondence with Jay R. Schrock, May 18, 2015.)

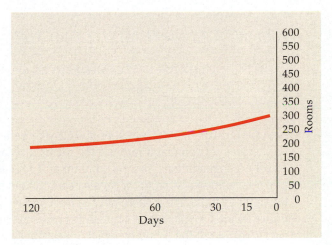

Figure 3–7 • Group Booking Curve.

The application of revenue management in hotels is still being refined to take into consideration factors such as multiple nights' reservations and incremental food and beverage revenue. If the guest wants to arrive on a high-demand night and stay through several low-demand nights, what should the charge be?

Revenue management has some disadvantages. For instance, if a business person attempts to make a reservation at a hotel three days before arrival and the rate quoted to maximize revenue is considered too high, this person may decide to select another hotel and not even consider the first hotel when making future reservations.

REV PAR was developed by Smith Travel Research. It is calculated by dividing room revenue by the number of rooms available.

For example, if room sales are $50,000 in one day for a hotel with 400 available rooms, then the REV PAR formula is $50,000 divided by 400, or a REV PAR of $125.

Hotels use REV PAR to see how they are doing compared to their competitive set of hotels. Hotel operators use REV PAR as an indicator of a hotel's revenue management program. One of the ways that REV PAR is used is for comparison to other properties in a competitive set on the Smith Travel Star Report.

Smith Travel Report (STR Global) is the publisher of the STAR reports, a benchmarking suite that tracks one hotel's occupancy, average daily rate, and REV PAR against a competitive set of hotels for comparison purposes. The information provided helps identify if a particular property is gaining or losing market share and helps the organization make necessary corrections to its management, marketing, and sales strategies. The STR STAR reports are used extensively in the lodging industry as the best tool for revenue management.[8]

HOW TO ANALYZE THE STAR PROGRAM

Courtesy of **James McManemon**, M.S., University of South Florida Sarasota–Manatee

Lynn Clifton, the general manager and 22-year veteran of a well-known hotel chain, who has worked her way up the chain of command through the rooms division, discussed the importance of Smith Travel's STAR (Smith Travel Accommodations Report) program as it relates to her particular hotel, as well as the hospitality industry as a whole. The STAR program serves as a confidential comparison between hotels, which is most important to the hotel operator, the owner(s) of the hotel property, and the bank that finances the asset. The private owners of Lynn's hotel use the report to analyze how well the property is being managed, as well as to determine if they ever want to sell the property, which is essentially an asset that they would like to turn a profit on. The report analyzes a hotel's REV PAR and its REV PAR index. REV PAR is a universal term used in the hospitality industry because it creates a level playing field between all hotels regardless of their brand, size, number of rooms, location, and so on. The REV PAR index analyzes an individual hotel's REV PAR compared with the total revenue generated by all the hotels in its competitive set. If a competitive set (determined by the hotel operator and their team) of five hotels has an equal share of available revenue, each hotel would get approximately 20 percent fair share of revenue. If one of those hotel's REV PAR index is 25 percent, then that hotel is getting 20 percent fair share, plus an additional 5 percent of the competitive set's share. A hotel operator's goal is to grow their index by a certain amount each year by taking a bigger piece of the set's available revenue. The general manager is tasked with setting strategies both short- and long-term to continuously improve results, much of which is based on the STAR program. As the general manager, it is important for Lynn to determine what works and what doesn't work for her hotel. "You can't look at these reports once a week or once a month and expect to see positive results at the end of the year; it is an everyday thing. You have to look at the numbers and understand what might have impacted either winning or losing on any given day." Lynn has coined the terms "market-centric" and "egocentric" pricing for the purposes of understanding her pricing model. Egocentric pricing is what you would like to charge in an ideal world, whereas market-centric pricing is what the market drives realistically. If you charge too much for your daily rate your occupancy is going to be low, which can negatively affect your REV PAR. Additionally, if you charge too little for your daily rate, you can also negatively affect your REV PAR. You have to find a balance between average daily rate and occupancy that allows you to maximize revenue to its highest potential.

▶ Check Your Knowledge

1. What are the principal concerns of a rooms division director?

2. Describe the duties performed by the front-office manager.

3. What is the rack rate, and what other types of room rates are there?

4. How do you calculate the room occupancy percentage and the average daily rate?

Energy Management Systems

Technology is used to extend guest in-room comfort by means of an energy management system. Passive infrared motion sensors and door switches can reduce energy consumption by 30 percent or more by automatically switching off lights and air-conditioning, thus saving energy when the guest is out of the room. Additional features include the following:

- Room occupancy status reporting
- Automatic lighting control
- Minibar access reporting
- Smoke detector alarm reporting
- Central electronic lock control
- Guest control amenities

Because of increasing energy costs, some operators are installing software programs that will turn off nonessential equipment during the peak billing times of day (utility companies' charges are based on peak usage). Hospitality operators can save money by utilizing this type of energy-saving software to reduce their energy costs.

Call Accounting Systems

Call accounting systems (CAS) track guest room phone charges. Software packages can be used to monitor where calls are being made and from which phones on the property. To track this information, the CAS must work in conjunction with the PBX (telephone) and the PMS. Call accounting systems today can be used to offer different rates for local guest calls and long-distance guest calls. The CAS can even be used to offer discounted calling during off-peak hours at the hotel.

Guest Reservation Systems

Before hotels started using the Internet to book reservations, they received reservations by letters, telegrams, faxes, and phone calls. Airlines were the first industry to start using **global distribution systems (GDS)** for reservations. Global distribution systems are electronic markets for travel, hotel, car rental, and attraction bookings.

A **central reservation system (CRS)** houses the electronic database in the **central reservation office (CRO)**. Hotels provide rates and availability information to the CRO usually by data communication lines. This automatically updates the CRS so that guests get the best available rate when they book through the central reservation office. Guests instantly receive confirmation of their reservation or cancellation. The hotel benefits from using a central reservation system. With such a system, hotels can avoid overselling rooms by too large a

Access control and management system for hotels.

margin. The CRS database can also be used as a chain or individual property marketing tool because guest information can easily be stored. A CRS can also provide yield management information for a hotel. The more flexible a central reservation system is, the more it will help with yield management. For example, when demand is weak for a hotel, rates will need to drop to increase reservations and profitability. When demand is higher, the hotel can sell room rates that are closer to the rack rate (*rack rate* is the highest rate quoted for a guestroom, from which all discounts are offered).

A CRS can be used in several areas of a hotel. If a hotel has a reservations department, the terminals or personal computers in that department can be connected to the central reservation system. It is also important for front-desk employees to have access to the CRS so that they know what the hotel has available because they may need to book rooms for walk-ins who don't have reservations. Constant communication back and forth is needed between the central reservation system and the front-office and reservations department. Managers who are the decision makers in the hotel will also use the system to forecast and set pricing for rooms and different amenities.

Hotels can use other forms of technology to facilitate reservation systems. Several companies offer an **application service provider (ASP)** environment that can deliver a complete booking system tied to the hotel's inventory in real time via the Web. One operator, Paul Wood of the El Dorado Hotel in Santa Fe, New Mexico, says that he simply went to the ASP Web site and put in a promotional corporate rate for the summer, and the same day he started seeing reservations coming in with that code. After a few months, bookings were up three percent over the previous year.

Billing Guests

Hospitality businesses today seek to obtain the most high-speed and reliable computer systems they can afford that they can use to bill their guests without delay. Fast access to guests' accounts is required by large hotels because of their high priority of guest satisfaction (no lineups at checkout).

Billing guests has become much easier with the aid of computers. Billing guests can be a long process if information technologies are not used to complete transactions. PMSs aid large hotels to make faster transactions and provide a more efficient service to their guests. These systems help the hospitality associates bill their guests within seconds.

Some hotels utilize software that enables guests to check and approve their bills by using the TV and remote control, thus avoiding the need to line up at the cashier's desk to check out. A copy of the final bill is then mailed to the guest's home address.

Security

Each business in the hospitality industry offers some sort of security for its guests and employees. Peace of mind that the hotel or restaurant is secure is a key factor in increasing guest satisfaction. Security is one of the highest concerns of guests who visit hospitality businesses. Hospitality information technology systems include surveillance systems in which cameras are installed in many different areas of the property to monitor the grounds and help ensure guest safety. These cameras are linked directly to computers, televisions, and digital recorders, which helps security teams keep an eye on the whole property.

Recent technological advances have produced electronic door locking systems, some of which even offer custom configurations of security and safety. Guest room locks are now capable of managing information from both magstripe and smart cards simultaneously. From the hotel's point of view, a main advantage of this kind of key is that the hotel knows who has entered the room and at what time because the system can trace anyone entering the room.

In-room safes can now be operated by key cards. Both systems are an improvement on the old metal keys. Even smarter safes use biometric technology such as the use of thumbprints or retina scans to verify a user's identity.

Guest Comfort and Convenience

Hotels provide guest comfort and convenience to maintain a home-away-from-home feeling for their guests. Hotels receive recognition when they provide many additional in-room services and amenities for their guests, such as dining, television, telephones, Internet connections, minibars, and hygiene products. These amenities help provide a cozy experience for the guest. Many other services can be provided outside of the rooms, such as swimming pools, massages, fine dining, postal services, and meeting space. Other services are provided to suit the demands of all types of guests; a concierge and business center is one example.

Hotels communicate with many entities to provide services for their guests. Some companies offer creative solutions to hotels for enhanced in-room services for guests. Sprint InSite with KoolConnect Interactive Media has created a product that provides many services to the guest from just one supplier. Services include Internet access and e-mail; movies, music, and games on demand; hotel and concierge services; special promotions; advertising; travel planning; feedback from guests; and customer support. All these services aid hotels in fulfilling guest demands. Sprint states, "Build loyalty and promote business retention by enhancing the overall quality-of-visit for your guest."[9] PlayStations and video games are also a part of the technology-based guest amenities.

▶ Check Your Knowledge

1. What functions does the PMS perform?
2. What is revenue management? How is revenue management applied in the hotel industry?

TECHNOLOGY SPOTLIGHT

Hotel Information Technology

"Home away from home!" This is how we would like to express what hotels mean to our guests. For this to happen, we must provide technologies that guests use at home. Of course, the main purpose of the guestroom has never changed: to provide a clean, safe place to spend the night. In 1970, for the first time, hoteliers put ice-cube makers and small refrigerators inside the guestroom. In the beginning, not all rooms had these amenities. Usually, those rooms that had these special amenities were charged more than the other rooms. In 1972, the first models of telephone systems were introduced to the guestroom. In those days, there was only one telephone line for the entire hotel; therefore, guests sometimes waited long hours before they could place a call. In 1975, after color TV was well established in homes, hotels started to offer it. In the beginning, some hotels advertised that they had color TV to differentiate themselves from the competition and charged extra for rooms with TV. In 1980, the Hotel Billing Information System (HOBIS) was introduced. In 1981, it became legal for hotels to profit from phone calls. This is when call accounting systems exploded in the hotel industry. In 1986, electronic door-keys were introduced, increasing the security and the convenience of guests. Interface between TV systems and property management systems were established in 1990 so that the guests could see their bills through the TV. With that, in 1993, guests were able to check out from their room by using the TV. In 1995, high-speed Internet access was available in hotel rooms. After 2000, hotels started to use Voice over Internet Protocol (VoIP) phoning systems, high-definition TV, wireless Internet access, interactive entertainment systems, smart-energy management systems, and many other systems.

In today's modern hotel rooms, it is possible to see the following technologies that make the guest stay a more comfortable one: (1) electronic locking system, (2) energy management and climate control systems, (3) fire alarm and security systems, (4) in-room minibars, (5) in-room safe boxes, (6) guestroom phone systems, (7) voice-mail/wake-up systems, (8) in-room entertainment systems, (9) guestroom control panels, and (10) self check-in/check-out systems.

Let's look into the future to see what the guestroom might look like:

You just booked a hotel room from your smartphone with a voice command. When you go to check in to the hotel, you see that check-in desk is replaced with a "hospitality desk." As soon as you arrive at the hotel, your phone is showing you a map of the hotel rooms, asking you to make a choice. Once you make your choice, your phone becomes your electronic key card. When you wave your phone, the door opens and the 100-per-cent sustainable room welcomes you with your preferred wall color (thanks to nanopaint) and your favorite song. When you turn on the TV with your voice command, you see your favorite and local TV channels (thanks to Internet TV) and your video library from your home phone. The picture frame shows the pictures from your Facebook page. Your sheets and towels will be changed based on "green" preferences, such as to change the bed sheets and towels every three days and bring the temperature of the room 10 degrees down or up based on the season when you are not in the room. When you need help, you connect to a virtual concierge to get any kind of information about the hotel and the area. The wardrobe door generates power when you open and close the door for lighting. When you use the restroom, the smart toilet checks your health and sends you a digital report to your e-mail. Does this sound like a nice dream? Actually, this is a description of a next-generation hotel.

Reservations

LEARNING OBJECTIVE 6
Outline the importance of the reservations and guest services functions.

The reservations department is headed by the reservations manager who, in many hotels today, is on the same level as the front-office manager and reports directly to the director of rooms division or the director of sales. This emphasizes the importance of the sales aspects of reservations and encompasses yield management. Reservations is the first contact for the guest or person making the reservation for the guest. Although the contact may be by telephone, a distinct impression of the hotel is registered with the guest. Because of this, exceptional telephone manners and telemarketing skills are necessary. Because some guests may be shopping for the best value, it is essential to sell the hotel by emphasizing its advantages over the competition. Figure 3–8 shows the sequence and relationship of a hotel guest reservation.

The reservation department generally works from 8:00 A.M. to 6:00 P.M. Depending on the size of the hotel, several people may be employed in this important department. The desired outcome of the reservations department is to exceed guest expectations when they make reservations. This is achieved by selling all of the hotel rooms for the maximum possible dollars and avoiding possible guest resentment of being overcharged. Reservations originate from a variety of sources:

1. The Internet
2. Corporate/1-800 numbers
3. Travel agents
4. Telephone to the same property
    a. Fax
    b. Letter
    c. Cable
5. Meeting planners
6. Tour operators
7. Referral from another company property
8. Airport telephone
9. Walk-in

Clearly, reservations are of tremendous importance to the hotel because of the potential and actual revenue realized. Many hotel chains have a 1-800 number that a prospective guest may call without charge to make a reservation at any of the company properties in the United States and internationally. The corporate central reservations system allows operators to access the inventory of room availability of each hotel in the chain. Once a reservation has been made, it is immediately deducted from the inventory of rooms for the duration of the guest stay. The central reservations system interfaces with the hotel's inventory and simultaneously allows reservations to be

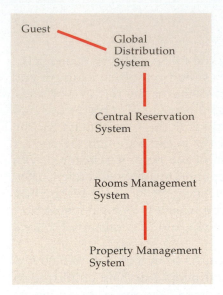

Figure 3–8 • The Sequence and Relationships of a Hotel Guest Reservation.

made by the individual hotel reservations personnel. A number of important details need to be recorded when taking reservations.

Confirmed reservations are reservations made with sufficient time for a confirmation slip to be returned to the client by mail or fax. Confirmation is generated by the computer printer and indicates confirmation number, dates of arrival and departure, type of room booked, number of guests, number of beds, type of bed, and any special requests. The guest may bring the confirmation slip to the hotel to verify the booking.

Guaranteed reservations are given when the person making the reservation wishes to ensure that the reservation will be held. This is arranged at the time the reservation is made and generally applies in situations when the guest is expected to arrive late. The hotel takes the credit card number, which guarantees payment of the room, of the person being billed. The hotel agrees to hold the room for late arrival. The importance of guaranteed reservations is that the guest will more likely cancel beforehand if unable to show up, which gives more accurate inventory room count and minimizes no-shows.

Another form of guaranteed reservations is advance deposit/advance payment. In certain situations, for example, during a holiday, to protect itself against having empty rooms (no-shows), the hotel requires that a deposit of either one night or the whole stay be paid in advance of the guest's arrival. This is done by obtaining the guest's credit card number, which may be charged automatically for the first night's accommodation. This discourages no-shows. Corporations that use the hotel frequently may guarantee all of their bookings so as to avoid any problems in the event a guest arrives late, remembering that in cities where the demand is heavy, hotels release any nonguaranteed or nonpaid reservations at 4:00 P.M. or 6:00 P.M. on the evening of the guest's expected arrival.

Communications CBX or PBX

The communications CBX or PBX includes in-house communications; guest communications, such as pagers and radios; voice mail; faxes; messages; and emergency center. Guests often have their first contact with the hotel by telephone. This underlines the importance of prompt and courteous attention to all calls because first impressions last.

The communications department is a vital part of the smooth running of the hotel. It is also a profit center because hotels generally add a 50 percent charge to all long-distance calls placed from guest rooms. Local calls cost about $0.75–$1.25, plus tax, but many hotels offer local calls for free.

Communications operates 24 hours a day, in much the same way as the front office does, having three shifts. It is essential that this department be staffed with people who are trained to be calm under pressure and who follow emergency procedures.

Guest Services/Uniformed Services

Because first impressions are very important to the guest, the guest service or uniformed staff has a special responsibility. The guest service department or **uniformed staff** is headed by a guest services manager who may also happen to be the bell captain. The staff consists of door attendants and bellpersons and the concierge, although in some hotels the concierge reports directly to the front-office manager.

Door attendants are the hotel's unofficial greeters. Dressed in impressive uniforms, they greet guests at the hotel front door, assist in opening/closing automobile doors, removing luggage from the trunk, hailing taxis, keeping the hotel entrance clear of vehicles, and giving guests information about the hotel and the local area in a courteous and friendly way. People in this position generally receive many gratuities (tips); in fact, years ago, the position was handed down from father to son or sold for several thousand dollars. Rumor has it that this is one of the most lucrative positions in the hotel, even more lucrative than the general manager's.

The bellperson's main function is to escort guests and transport luggage to their rooms. Bellpersons also need to be knowledgeable about the local area and all facets of the hotel and its services. Because they have so much guest contact, they need a pleasant, outgoing personality. The bellperson explains the services of the hotel and points out the features of the room (lighting, TV, air-conditioning, telephone, wake-up calls, laundry and valet service, room service and restaurants, and the pool and health spa).

Concierge

LEARNING OBJECTIVE 7
List the complexities and challenges of the concierge, housekeeping, and security/loss prevention departments.

The **concierge** is a uniformed employee of the hotel who has her or his own separate desk in the lobby or on a special concierge floor. The concierge is a separate department from the front-office room clerks and cashiers.

A DAY IN THE LIFE OF DENNY BHAKTA

Revenue Manager, Hilton Hotels San Diego

Revenue management is a strategic function in maximizing room revenue (REV PAR) along with growing market share. REV PAR and market share are the two primary barometers used in the industry to grade a revenue manager's competency. It is essential for revenue managers to have a system in place for daily business reviews to formulate winning strategies. Daily duties include:

1. Analyzing Data: A revenue manager must develop a reporting system for daily monitoring. In recent years, the larger hotel brands have developed proprietary revenue management systems that provide on-demand reporting of historical data, future position, and the ability to apply real-time pricing changes to future nights. Understanding past performance can uncover various business trends over high and low demand periods. It is critical to understand the effectiveness of previous pricing strategies to better position the hotel on future nights.

The general public can view rates and book rooms up to 365 days into the future. Therefore, the revenue manager must monitor daily pickup in reservations and regrets for future nights and make necessary adjustments to enhance speed to market. Each hotel will have different booking windows (or lead times) for their transient and group business. For example, the San Diego market has a majority of transient bookings that occur within 120 days to arrival, whereas the group business is booked many months out, and in some cases several years in advance. The primary booking window must be analyzed on a daily basis and adjusted accordingly. The longer booking windows can be analyzed periodically with the director of sales to equip the Sales team with rates to book group business based on the hotel's revenue goals.

2. Mix of Business Assessment: Finding the right balance of occupancy and ADR could yield the greatest REV PAR and is greatly influenced by the mix of business. It is composed of two primary customer segments: Transient (individual travelers for business or leisure) and Groups, which are bookings with 10 more rooms per night (i.e., conventions, company meetings, etc.). Hotels can differ with mixes of business based on location, number of rooms, and event space. Convention hotels may have a desired mix of 80 percent group and 20 percent transient to achieve their optimum point of profit, whereas small to midsize hotels may have a need for greater transient business, all of which are key factors in formulating effective pricing strategies. Although the majority of group business will be booked further in advance, those rates are also determined by the revenue manager and director of sales based on historical trends and future business needs.

3. Competitor Analysis: It is always valuable to know what the competition is doing. Revenue management is part science and part craft. With the advancement in technology, companies such as Smith Travel Research and The Rubicon Group have created essential tools that allow hoteliers and revenue managers to determine their position in the marketplace. Smith Travel Research produced the STAR report that is routed on a weekly and monthly basis. This report allows a hotel to choose a competitive set, which then compares the hotel's actualized results by segment versus the competitive set, resulting in market share indexes for occupancy, ADR, and REV PAR. Although it is every hotel's goal to capture fair market share (dollar for dollar), it is a greater priority to gain share by outperforming the competition. The Rubicon Group created a "Market Vision" tool that provides competitors' rates and occupancy levels up to 365 days into the future, which can determine peaks and valleys in market demand.

4. Distribution Channels: It is crucial to know where the business is coming from, and how to increase production from the right channels. Most hotel brands have a central reservations system, which is powered by their Web site and land-based call centers. In addition, there are thousands of travel agencies that

(continued)

A DAY IN THE LIFE OF DENNY BHAKTA *(Continued)*

book rooms into hotels, which includes: online agencies (i.e., Expedia and Travelocity) and land-based agencies (i.e., AAA Travel and American Express Travel). The major agencies will have regional market managers that will supply market share data along with insight on any future developments that could be very beneficial to a hotel's strategy. A great revenue manager will establish daily communications with the large agencies to gain knowledge and to leverage hotel placement on their Web sites. Customers will not book you if they can't find you. The same applies to land-based travel agents, which are generally serviced by the hotel's sales and marketing team, who can be great resources in looking into the future. Greater market intelligence can equate to sound decision making.

5. Pricing Strategies: There is no right and wrong to the number of times rates should be adjusted on any given night. However, a greater understanding of market dynamics will come from a balance of historical knowledge and future market intelligence.

Lastly, this question will always be asked: Could we have done something different to maximize REV PAR? It is the revenue manager's responsibility to answer the question with integrity. Successful general managers will appreciate the honesty and will have greater confidence level in a revenue manager that can determine both strengths and weaknesses in their own strategies.

Luxury hotels in most cities have concierges. New York's Plaza Hotel has over 400 rooms and a battery of 10 concierges. The concierge assists guests with a broad range of services such as the following:

- Tickets to the hottest shows in town, even for the very evening on the day they are requested. Naturally, the guest pays up to about $150 per ticket.
- A table at a restaurant that has no reservations available
- Advice on local restaurants, activities, attractions, amenities, and facilities
- Airline tickets and reconfirmation of flights
- VIP's messages and special requests, such as shopping

Less frequent requests are:

- Organize a wedding on two days' notice
- Arrange for a member of the concierge department to go to a consulate or embassy for visas to be stamped in guests' passports
- Handle business affairs

Concierges serve to elevate a property's marketable value and its image. They provide the special touch services that distinguish a "top property."

Concierges assist guests with a variety of services.

To make sure they can cater to a guest's precise needs, concierges should make sure that they know precisely what the guest is looking for budget-wise, as well as any other parameters. Concierges must be very attentive and must anticipate guest needs when possible. In this age of highly competitive top-tier properties and well-informed guests, only knowledgeable concierge staff can provide the services to make a guest's stay memorable. As more properties try to demonstrate enhanced value, a concierge amenity takes on added significance.

The concierge needs not only a detailed knowledge of the hotel and its services, but also of the city and even international details. Many concierges speak several languages; most important of all, they must want to help people and have a pleasant, outgoing personality. The concierges' organization, which promotes high professional and ethical standards, is the Union Professionelle des Portiers des Grand Hotels (UPPGH), more commonly called the *Clefs d'Or*® (pronounced clays-dor) because of the crossed gold-key insignia concierges usually wear on the lapels of their uniforms.

Housekeeping

The largest department in terms of the number of people employed is housekeeping. Up to 50 percent of the hotel employees may work in this department. Because of the hard work and comparatively low pay, employee turnover is very high in this essential department. The person in charge is the executive housekeeper or director of services. Her or his duties and responsibilities call for exceptional leadership, organization, motivation, and commitment to maintaining high standards. The logistics of servicing large numbers of rooms on a daily basis can be challenging. The importance of the housekeeping department is underlined by guest surveys that consistently rank cleanliness of rooms number one. Figure 3–9 shows the house-keeping department organization chart.

The four major areas of responsibilities for the executive housekeeper are as follows:

1. Leadership of people, equipment, and supplies
2. Cleanliness and servicing the guest rooms and public areas
3. Operating the department according to financial guidelines prescribed by the general manager
4. Keeping records

An example of an executive housekeeper's day might be as follows:

7:45 A.M.   **Walk the lobby and property with the night cleaners and supervisors**

Check the housekeeping logbook

Check the forecast house count for number of checkouts

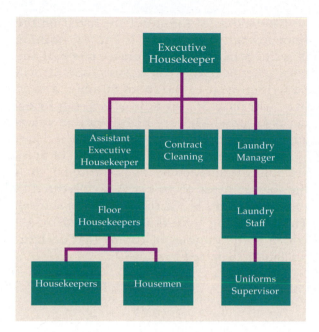

Figure 3–9 • Housekeeping Department Organization Chart.

Check daily activity reports, stayovers, check-ins, and VIPs to ensure appropriate standards

Attend housekeepers' meeting

Meet challenges

Train new employees in the procedures

Meet with senior housekeepers/department managers

Conduct productivity checks

Check budget

Approve purchase orders

Check inventories

Conduct room inspections

Review maintenance checks

Interview potential employees

6:00 P.M.   **Attend to human resource activities, counseling, and employee development**

Perhaps the biggest challenge of an executive housekeeper is the leadership of all the employees in the department. Further, these employees are often of different nationalities. Depending on the size of the hotel, the executive housekeeper is assisted by an assistant executive housekeeper and one or more housekeeping supervisors, who in turn supervise a number of room attendants or housekeeping associates (see Figure 3–9). The assistant executive housekeeper manages the housekeeping office. The first important daily task of this position is to break out the hotel into sections for allocation to the room attendants' schedules.

A housekeeper at work. Attention to detail is important in maintaining standards.

The rooms of the hotel are listed on the floor master. If the room is vacant, nothing is written next to the room number. If the guest is expected to check out, then SC will be written next to the room number. A stay-over will have SS, on hold is AH, out of order is OO, and VIPs are highlighted in colors according to the amenities required.

If 258 rooms are occupied and 10 of these are suites (which count as two rooms), then the total number of rooms to be allocated to room attendants is 268 (minus any no-shows). The remaining total is then divided by 17, which is the number of rooms that each attendant is expected to make up.

Total number of rooms occupied	258
Add 10 for the suites	+10
Less any no-shows	−3
Total number of rooms and suites occupied	265
Divided by 17 for the number of rooms that each attendant is expected to make up	$265 \div 17 = 16$

Therefore, 16 attendants are required for that day.

Figure 3–10 shows a daily attendant's schedule. To reduce payroll costs and encourage room attendants to become "stars," a number of hotel corporations have empowered the best attendants to check their own rooms. This has reduced the need for supervisors. Notice in Figure 3–10 how the points are weighted for various items. This is the result of focus groups of hotel guests who explained the things about a room that are important to them. The items with the highest points were the ones that most concerned the guests.

The housekeeping associates clean and service between 15 and 20 rooms per day, depending on the individual hotel characteristics. Servicing a room takes longer in some older hotels than it does in some of the newer properties. Also, service time depends on the number of checkout rooms versus stayovers because servicing checkouts takes longer. Housekeeping associates begin their day at 8:00 A.M., reporting to the executive or assistant executive housekeeper. They are assigned a block of rooms and given room keys, for which they must sign and then return before going off duty.

The role of the executive housekeeper may vary slightly between the corporate chain and the independent hotel. An example is the purchasing of furnishings and equipment. A large independent hotel relies on the knowledge and experience of the executive housekeeper to make appropriate selections, whereas the chain hotel company has a corporate purchase agent (assisted by a designer) to make many of these decisions.

The executive housekeeper is responsible for a substantial amount of record keeping. In addition to the scheduling and evaluation of employees, an

Housekeeper's Guest Room Self–Inspection Rating
Inspection Codes:

| P – POLISH | R – REPLACE | E – WORK ORDER | S – SOAP SCUM | SM – SMEAR |
| SA – STAIN | H – HAIR | D – DIRT | DU – DUST | M – MISSING |

PART I – GUEST ROOM		S			U	COMMENTS
Entry, door, frame, threshold, latch				1		
Unusual odor OR smoke smell				3		
CLOSET, doors, louvers–containing				1		
Hangers, 8 suits, 4 skirts, 2 bags w/ invoices				2		
Two (2) robes, with info card				2		
Extra TP & FACIAL				1		
One (1) luggage rack				1		
Current rate card				1		
VALET	Shoe Horn & Mitt			2		
DRESSER	LAMP/ SHADE/ BULB			2		
	ICE BUCKET, LID, TRAY			2		
	TWO (2) WINE GLASSES			2		
	Room Service MENU			2		
MINIBAR	TOP, FRONT, 2 Wine glasses/ price list			1		
SAFE	KEY IN SAFE, SIGN			5		
CHECK BEHIND DRESSER				2		
DRAWERS	BIBLE AND BUDDHIST BOOK			1		
	PHONE BOOKS, ATT DIRECTORY			1		
TELEVISION	ON & OFF, CH 19 BEHIND			1		
COFFEE TABLE	REMOTE CONTROL/TEST 1			2		
	T.V. LISTINGS/BOOK MARK			1		
	GLASS TOP/LA JOLLA BOOK			1		
CARPET	VACUUM, SPOTS?			2		
SOFA	UNDER CUSHION/ BEHIND			2		
3 W LAMP	BULB, SHADE, & CORD			1		
WINDOWS	GLASS, DOOR, LATCH—C BAR?			2		
CURTAINS	Pull — check seams			1		
PATIO	2 CHAIRS, TABLE & DECK			3		
DESK	2 CHAIRS, TOP, BASE, & LAMP/SHADE			5		
	GREEN COMPENDIUM			3		
	Waste paper can			1		
BED	Tight, Pillows, bedspread			5		
	Check Under/SHEETS, PILLOWS			3		
HVAC	Control, setting, vent			1		
SIDE TABLES	Lamps & shade			2		
	Telephone, MESSAGE LIGHT			1		
	Clock Radio CORRECT TIME?			1		
MIRRORS	LARGE MIRROR OVER DRESSER			1		
PICTURES	ROOM ART WORK			1		
WALLS	Marks, stains, etc.			3		

Numbers in rating column range from 1 (least important) to 5 (most important).

Figure 3–10 • Housekeeper's Guest Room Self-Inspection Form.

Housekeeper's Guest Room Self–Inspection Rating

Inspection Codes:

P – POLISH	R – REPLACE	E – WORK ORDER	S – SOAP SCUM	SM – SMEAR
SA – STAIN	H – HAIR	D – DIRT	DU – DUST	M – MISSING

PART II – BATHROOM		S			U		COMMENTS
BATH TUB/SHOWER							
	GROUT/TILE & EDGE			2			
	ANTISLIP GRIDS			2			
	SIDE WALLS			1			
	SHOWER HEAD			1			
	WALL SOAP DISH			1			
	CONTROL LEVER			1			
	FAUCET			1			
	CLOTHESLINE			1			
	SHOWER ROD, HOOKS			1			
	SHOWER CURTAIN/ LINER			2			
VANITY	TOP, SIDE, & EDGE			1			
	SINK, TWO FAUCETS			3			
	3 GLASSES, COASTERS			2			
	WHITE SOAP DISH			1			
	FACIAL TISSUE & BOX			1			
AMENITY BASKET							
	1 SHAMPOO			1			
	1 CONDITIONER			1			
	1 MOISTURIZER			1			
	2 BOXED SOAP			1			
	1 SHOWER CAP			1			
MIRROR	LARGE & COSMETIC			2			
WALLS, CEILING, & VENT				2			
TOILET	TOP, SEAT, BASE, & LIP			2			
OTHER	TOILET PAPER, fold			1			
	SCALE AND TRASH CAN			2			
	FLOOR, SWEPT AND MOPPED			3			
	TELEPHONE			1			
BATH LINENS, racks							
	THREE (3) WASH CLOTHS			1			
	THREE (3) HAND TOWELS			1			
	THREE (3) BATH TOWELS			1			
	ONE (1) BATH MAT			1			
	ONE (1) BATH RUG			1			
LIGHT SWITCH				1			
DOOR	FULL LENGTH MIRROR			1			
	HANDLE/LOCK			1			
	THRESHOLD			1			
	PAINTED SURFACE			1			

Figure 3–10 • Housekeeper's Guest Room Self-Inspection Form. *(continued)*

inventory of all guest rooms and public area furnishings must be accurately maintained with the record of refurbishment. Most of the hotel's maintenance work orders are initiated by the housekeepers who report the maintenance work. Many hotels now have a computer linkup between housekeeping and engineering and maintenance to speed the process. Guests expect their rooms to be fully functional, especially at today's prices. Housekeeping maintains a perpetual inventory of guest room amenities, cleaning supplies, and linens.

Amazingly, it took about 2,000 years, but hotels have finally figured out that guests spend most of their stay on a bed, so they have introduced wonder beds and heavenly beds to allow guests to enjoy sweet dreams—but hopefully not miss that pesky wake-up call. Around the country, guest rooms are getting a makeover that includes new mattresses with devices that allow one side to be set firmer than the other side or on an incline. Other room amenities include new high-definition or plasma TVs, Wi-Fi services, and room cards that activate elevators.

Productivity in the housekeeping department is measured by the person-hours per occupied room. The labor costs per person-hour for a full-service hotel ranges from $2.66 to $5.33, or 20 minutes of labor for every occupied room in the hotel. Another key ratio is the labor cost, which is expected to be 5.1 percent of room sales. Controllable expenses are measured per occupied rooms. These expenses include guest supplies such as soap, shampoo, hand and body lotion, sewing kits, and stationery. Although this will vary according to the type of hotel, the cost should be about $2.00 per room. Cleaning supplies should be approximately $0.50 and linen costs $0.95, including the purchase and laundering of all linen. These budgeted costs are sometimes hard to achieve. The executive housekeeper may be doing a great job controlling costs, but if the sales department discounts rooms, the room sales figures may come in below budget. This would have the effect of increasing the costs per occupied room.

Another concern for the executive housekeeper is accident prevention. Insurance costs have skyrocketed in recent years, and employers are struggling to increase both employee and guest safety. It is necessary for accidents to be carefully investigated. Some employees have been known to have an accident at home but go to work and report it as a work-related injury to be covered by workers' compensation. To safeguard themselves to some extent, hotels keep sweep logs of the public areas; in the event that a guest slips and falls, the hotel can show that it does genuinely take preventative measures to protect its guests.

The **Occupational Safety and Health Administration (OSHA)**, whose purpose is to ensure safe and healthful working conditions, sets mandatory job safety and health standards, conducts compliance inspections, and issues citations when there is noncompliance. Additionally, the U.S. Senate Bill 198, known as the **Employee Right to Know**, has heightened awareness of the storage, handling, and use of dangerous chemicals. Information about the chemicals must be made available to all employees. Great care and extensive training is required to avoid dangerous accidents.

The executive housekeeper must also minimize loss prevention. Strict policies and procedures are necessary to prevent losses from guest rooms.

A beautiful king-size bed in a tropical hotel bedroom ready for guests.

Some hotels require housekeeping associates to sign a form stating that they understand they may not let any guest into any room. Such action would result in immediate termination of employment. Although this may seem drastic, it is the only way to avoid some hotel thefts.

▶ Check Your Knowledge

1. Describe the different types of reservations that guests make at hotels.
2. What is the role played by uniformed services?
3. Explain the responsibilities of an executive housekeeper.

Spas

Who does not like to be pampered? The spa business has four mantras: decompression, revitalization, beauty, and spiritual uplift, not necessarily in that order. The objective is to achieve maximum relaxation, renewal, and recreation for the client. The ultimate goal is to achieve an ascent into a realm devoid of anxiety where the natural healing power of the client's body has free reign. For some, the road to nirvana comes with a gentle walk and communion with nature. With others it is experienced in being kneaded, mangled and massaged, bathed in aromatic oils, wrapped in a seaweed mixture, or immersed in a special mud (ask any warthog!).

The spa has never been more popular. Hundreds are in the United States. Nearly every major hotel has a spa of sorts where beauty treatments, exercise equipment, and other paraphernalia invite the guest to relax or to exercise away anxieties. Many people, perhaps most, see the spa as a time of renewal or decompression chambers and for pampering and mental adjustment, increase in physical strength, and intellectual and spiritual enrichment. The herbal wrap and hairstyle are fine, but getting in touch with the soul is even better.

Soaking in hot water was popular as early as the fifth century B.C. in Greece and on some Aegean islands. Later the Romans spread the spa idea as they expanded their empire. The hot mineral springs in Bath, England were used by the Romans in the first century A.D. About 2,000 years ago the Roman emperor philosopher, Marcus Aurelius, found the waters of what is now Baden-Baden (translates to bath), Germany, remarkable for moderating his arthritis. The great majority of spas are day spas, followed by resort spas, then medical spas, club spas, destination spas, cruise ship spas, and mineral spas. All these spas offer an array of services to suit the needs of their clients.

Spa treatments include hydrotherapy, the use of water as in a sauna, mineral springs, whirlpools, tubs, and steam rooms. Many spa treatments originated in Asia where Ayurveda, a holistic (whole body) healing system developed in India thousands of years ago. Ayurveda is based on the belief that health and wellness depend on a delicate balance between the mind, body, and spirit. The primary focus of Ayurvedic medicine is to promote good health rather than fight disease.[10]

Other spa treatments are based on traditional Chinese medicine (TCM) and the yin-yang and five elements theories. Typical TCM therapies include acupuncture, herbal medicine, and qigong exercises. These therapies are different in approach yet they share the same underlying set of assumptions and insights in the nature of the human body and its place in the universe.

The term "spa cuisine" suggests beautiful food and limited calories, served in beautiful surroundings. Spa guests expect to leave slimmer and trimmer. The spa may have a named chef, small portions of fish and chicken rather than beef or pork, and of course, oodles of salad greens. A full-time nutritionist may be on hand with diet suggestions. The dietician's role is not to lead the spa guest into the land of milk and honey but to a regime of low-calorie polyunsaturated fats, designed to lower blood cholesterol and based largely on grains, vegetables, fruit, and nonfat dairy products.

There are a variety of staffing positions in a spa ranging from aestheticians, massage therapists, nail technicians, cosmetologists, fitness instructors, and personal trainers.

Laundry

Increasingly, hotels are operating their own laundries. This subdepartment generally reports to the executive housekeeper. The modern laundry operates computerized washing/drying machines and large presses. Dry cleaning for both guests and employees is a service that may also come under the laundry department. Hotels are starting to get away from in-house dry cleaning because of environmental concerns.

Sustainable Lodging

Green Hotel Initiatives

The environmentally conscious companies are not only helping to avoid further environmental degradation but are also saving themselves money while being good corporate citizens. Operationally, hotels have been recycling for years and saving water and chemicals by leaving cards in guest rooms saying that sheets will be changed every third day unless otherwise requested. Some hotels move the top sheet down to the bottom on the second or third day. Likewise, a card in the bathroom explains to guests that if they want a towel changed to leave it on the floor. Hotels have been quick to realize that the life of sheets and towels has been greatly extended, thus increasing savings.

The wattage of lighting has been reduced and long-life and florescent bulbs are saving thousands of dollars a year per property. Air-conditioning units can now control the temperature of a room through body-motion sensing devices that even pick up people's breathing. These devices can automatically shut off the air-conditioning unit when guests are out of their rooms. Savings are also being made with low-flow toilets and showerheads that have high-pressure, low-volume flows of water.

Ecoefficiency, also generally termed *green*, is based on the concept of creating more goods and services while using fewer resources and creating less waste and pollution. In other words, it means doing more with less. So what does this have to do with your bottom line? Ecoefficiency helps hotels provide better service with fewer resources; reducing the materials and energy-intensity of goods and services lowers the hotel's ecological impact and improves the bottom line. It's a key driver for overall business performance.[11] Figure 3–11 shows a model for the implementation of sustainable lodging practices.

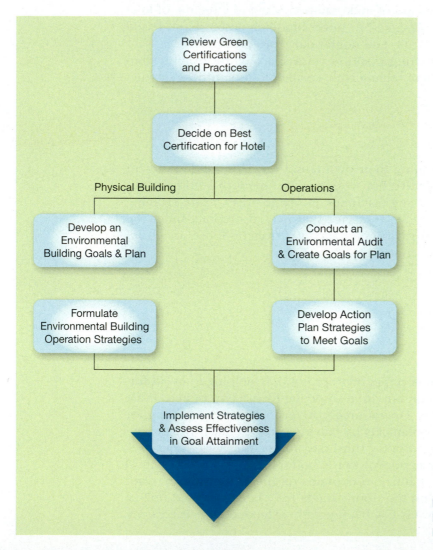

Figure 3–11 • A Model for the Implementation of Sustainable Lodging Practices.

Triple bottom line, sometimes called the TBL or 3P approach (people, planet, and profits), requires thinking in three dimensions, not one. It takes into account ecological and societal performance in addition to financial. Today, quantifiable environmental impacts include consumption of finite resources, energy usage, water quality and availability, and pollution emitted. Social impacts include community health, employee and guest safety, education quality, and diversity.[12]

Sustainable lodging, also known as green hotels, has become a powerful movement. The American Hotel and Lodging Association (AH&LA) and various state associations are leading the way with operational suggestions for best practices that lead to a green certification. Both corporations and independent properties are increasingly becoming greener in their operating practices. Sustainable Lodging & Restaurant–certified facilities develop goals and identify people in their organizations to find new opportunities to improve their operations through education, employee ideas, and guest feedback.

J.D. Power and Associates' 2009 North America Hotel Guest Satisfaction Index Study, which surveyed over 66,000 guests who stayed in North American hotels between May 2008 and June 2009, found that guests' awareness of their hotel's green programs increased significantly in 2009. Sixty-six percent of guests said they were aware of their hotel's conservation efforts, up from 57 percent the previous year.[13]

Ray Hobbs, a member of EcoRooms & EcoSuites' board of advisors and a certified auditor for Green Globe International, said, "In the hospitality industry, we're seeing a wave of new government mandates stating that employees can only stay in or host meetings in green hotels. But there are only 23 states with official green certification programs, and the industry is still attempting to find the certification process that best serves its needs."[14]

Being green is also financially good for certified properties. By saving energy and water, reducing waste, and eliminating toxic chemicals, green properties lower their operating costs, which allows them to provide enhanced services to their guests and a healthier environment for both their guests and employees. Sustainable properties are doing the following to become more sustainable in their operating practices[15]:

- Reducing energy needs by doing the following:

  Installing motion sensors in public areas and occupancy sensors in guestrooms

  Installing energy-efficient lighting, dimmers, and timers to reduce energy consumption

  Installing LED (light-emitting diode) exit signs

  Installing Energy Star appliances

  Increasing building insulation

  Using natural day lighting whenever possible

Tightening the property shell, with added/better insulation, eliminating leaks, replacing windows

- Conserving water by doing the following:

Installing aerators on faucets

Installing water diverters on existing toilets or installing low-flow toilets

Installing low-flow showerheads

Implementing towel and linen reuse programs

Landscaping with native plants

Using timers/moisture sensors in landscape watering

Changing lawn watering to encourage deeper root growth

- Reducing waste by doing the following:

Providing recycling areas for guests and staff

Purchasing postconsumer recycled paper and buying in bulk

Serving meals with cloth napkins and reusable china and dinnerware

Using refillable soap/shampoo dispensers in bathrooms

Recycling usable furniture and other items at "dump stores" or through charity

Reusing old towels and linens as cleaning rags

Asking vendors to minimize packaging

Recycling cooking grease

Composting food and lawn waste

- Reducing hazardous waste by doing the following:

Properly disposing of fluorescent lighting, computers, and other electronic equipment

Participating in local hazardous waste collection days

Using low-VOC (volatile organic compound) paints, carpets, and glues

Using rechargeable batteries

Using energy-efficient shuttle vans

Using environmentally friendly cleaning products

Guest Shuttle

Free shuttle service to area attractions is provided; the vehicle is either a hybrid car or a 15-passenger van for bigger groups.

Guest Bicycles

Bicycles are available for guest use in warm weather. Excellent bicycle-route maps are provided for those who want to explore the city on two wheels.

Greening the Guestroom

Guest rooms offer an opportunity for greening. Sustainable hotels do the following[16]:

- Give guests an option to have the towels and linens changed every other day, or less frequently, rather than every day. Surveys have shown that more than 90 percent of guests like the option.

- Encourage staff to close drapes and turn off lights and air conditioning when rooms are unoccupied.

- Install water-efficient fixtures, such as showerheads, aerators, and low-flow toilets in each room.

- Use refillable soap and shampoo dispensers.

- Encourage guests to recycle by providing clearly marked recycling bins for cans, bottles, and newspapers.

- Install energy-efficient lighting fixtures in each room. Compact fluorescent fixtures can be screwed into many existing lamps and ceiling fixtures. To prevent theft, many hotels are installing new fixtures with compact fluorescent lamps hardwired into the fixture.

- Consider purchasing Energy Star–labeled TVs and other energy-efficient appliances.

- Clean rooms with environmental cleaners to improve indoor air quality and reduce emissions of VOCs.

- Use placards in the room to inform your guests about your green efforts. Why not tell them a hotel can save 13.5 gallons of fresh water by choosing not to replace bath towels and linen daily?

- Use an opt-out approach to linen and towel reuse (this can save a 250-room hotel more than $15,000 per year).

- If a hotel adopts these and other measures every year, it would amount to savings of thousands of dollars. Consider also the gains for hotels that adopt and practice sustainable operations. In the case of Washington, D.C., it has been estimated that the hotel gained $800,000 of incremental group business as a result of having sustainable meeting and event management at the property.

Security/Loss Prevention

Providing guest protection and loss prevention is essential for any lodging establishment regardless of size. Violent crime is a growing problem, and protecting guests from bodily harm has been defined by the courts as a reasonable expectation from hotels. The security/loss division is responsible for maintaining security alarm systems and implementing procedures aimed at protecting the personal property of guests and employees and the hotel itself.

A comprehensive security plan must include the following elements:

Security Officers

- These officers make regular rounds of the hotel premises, including guest floors, corridors, public and private function rooms, parking areas, and offices.
- Duties involve observing suspicious behavior and taking appropriate action, investigating incidents, and cooperating with local law enforcement agencies.

Equipment

- Two-way radios between security staff are common.
- Closed-circuit television cameras are used in out-of-the-way corridors and doorways, as well as in food, liquor, and storage areas.
- Smoke detectors and fire alarms, which increase the safety of the guests, are a requirement in every part of the hotel by law.
- Electronic key cards offer superior room security. Key cards typically do not list the name of the hotel or the room number. So, if lost or stolen, the key is not easily traceable. In addition, most key card systems record every entry in and out of the room on the computer for further reference.

Safety Procedures

- Front-desk agents help maintain security by not allowing guests to re-enter their rooms once they have checked out. This prevents any loss of hotel property by guests.
- Security officers should be able to gain access to guest rooms, store rooms, and offices at all times.
- Security staff develop **catastrophe plans** to ensure staff and guest safety and to minimize direct and indirect costs from disaster. The catastrophe plan reviews insurance policies, analyzes physical facilities, and evaluates possible disaster scenarios, including whether they have a high or low probability of occurring. Possible disaster scenarios may include fires, bomb threats, earthquakes, floods, hurricanes, and blizzards. The well-prepared hotel develops formal policies to deal with any possible scenario and trains employees to implement chosen procedures should they become necessary.

Identification Procedures

- Identification cards with photographs should be issued to all employees.
- Name tags for employees who are likely to have contact with guests not only project a friendly image for the property, but are also useful for security reasons.

Trends in Hotel and Rooms Division Operations

Courtesy of Dr. Greg Dunn, Senior Lecturer & Managing Director, University of Florida, Eric Friedheim Tourism Institute.

- *Diversity of work force.* All the pundits are projecting a substantial increase in the number of women and minorities who will not only be taking hourly paid positions, but also supervising and management positions as well.

- *Increase in use of technology.* Reservations are being made by individuals over the Internet. Travel agents are able to make reservations at more properties. There is increasing simplification of the various PMSs and their interface with POS systems. In the guest room, increasing demand for high-speed Internet access, category 5 cables, and in some cases equipment itself is anticipated.

- *Continued quest for increases in productivity.* As pressure mounts from owners and management companies, hotel managers are looking for innovative ways to increase productivity and to measure productivity by sales per employee.

- *Increasing use of revenue management.* The techniques of revenue management will increasingly be used to increase profit by effective pricing of room inventory.

- *Greening of hotels and guest rooms.* Recycling and the use of environmentally friendly products, amenities, and biodegradable detergents will increase. Energy management technology is used for the reduction of energy costs by setting back temperature and shutting off power in vacant rooms through control sensors that regulate the HVAC system.[17]

- *Security.* Guests continue to be concerned about personal security. Hotels are constantly working to improve guest security. For example, one hotel has instituted a women-only floor with concierge and security. Implementation of security measures will increase.

- *Diversity of the guest.* More women travelers are occupying hotel rooms. This is particularly a result of an increase in business travel.

- *Compliance with the ADA.* As a result of the Americans with Disabilities Act (ADA), all hotels must modify existing facilities and incorporate design features into new constructions that make areas accessible to persons with disabilities. All hotels are expected to have at least four percent of their parking space designated as "handicapped." These spaces must be wide enough for wheelchairs to be unloaded from a van. Guest rooms must be fitted with equipment that can be manipulated by persons with disabilities. Restrooms must be wide enough to accommodate wheelchairs. Ramps should be equipped with handrails, and meeting rooms must be equipped with special listening systems for those with hearing impairments.

- *Use of hotels' Web sites.* Hotel companies will continue to try to persuade guests to book rooms using the hotel company Web site rather than via an Internet site such as Hotels.com because the hotel must pay about $20 for each room booking from such sites.

- *In-room technology upgrades.* The increase in personal devices such as smartphones, iPads, and other portable technology presents hotels with a need to facilitate the use of these devices in guestrooms. Some hotels are now offering personal iPads for use while staying in guestrooms, some of which act as the guest's personal concierge.[18]

- *Television service upgrades.* The steady increase in Netflix subscribers and other streaming devices causes a need to beef up television content and offerings to guests. This has also led to a decrease in "pay-per-view" movies. Some hotels are offering technology featuring free HD movies and television, as well as the ability to connect to the Internet over the television screen, or through an inclusive connectivity panel, guests are able to connect their own electronic devices to their television set.[19]

Career Information

Hotel management is probably the most popular career choice among seniors who are graduating from hospitality educational programs. The reason for this popularity is tied to the elegant image of hotels and the prestige associated with being a general manager or vice president of a major lodging chain. Managing a hotel is a complex balancing act that involves keeping employees, guests, and owners satisfied while overseeing a myriad of departments, including reservations, front desk, housekeeping, maintenance, accounting, food and beverage, security, concierge, and sales. To be a general manager, a person must understand all of the various functions of a hotel and how their interrelationship makes up the lodging environment. The first step down this career path is to get a job in a hotel while you are in college.

Once you become proficient in one area, volunteer to work in another. A solid foundation of broad-based experience in the hotel will be priceless when you start your lodging career. Some excellent areas to consider are the front desk, night audit, food and beverage, and maintenance. Another challenging but very important place to gain experience is in housekeeping. It has been said that if you can manage the housekeeping department, the rest of lodging management is easy. An internship with a large hotel chain property can also be a powerful learning experience. There is simply no substitute for being part of a team that operates a lodging property with several hundred rooms. You may hear about graduates being offered "direct placement" or "manager in training" (MIT) positions. (There are several name variations for these programs.) Direct placement means that when you graduate, you are offered a specific position at a property. An MIT program exposes you to several areas of the hotel over a period of time. Then you are given an assignment based on your performance during training. Neither one is better from a career standpoint.

Another important consideration of a lodging career is your wardrobe. In a hotel environment, people are judged based on their appearance. A conservative, professional image is a key to success. Clothes are the tools of the lodging professional's trade, and they are not inexpensive. Begin investing in clothes while you are in school. Buy what you can afford, but buy items of quality. Stay away from trendy or flashy clothes that will quickly be out of fashion.

When you take a position, you can expect to work around 50 hours per week. The times you work may vary. You can expect to have a starting salary of between $30,000 and $34,000. Some hotel chains will assist with moving expenses and may even offer a one-time signing bonus. However, try not to focus too much on the money; instead, try to find a company that you feel comfortable with and that will allow you opportunities for advancement. Figure 3–12 shows a career path in lodging management.

Bob Weil, director of food and beverage at the Longboat Key Club and Resort, Sarasota, Florida, offers the following advice: "Be passionate about what you do and be in touch with the people you work with. I tour the property every day to get a feeling for the challenges our team may have—it's important to be in tune with what's going on." Another piece of advice is "to never stop cooking and to maintain your fitness so that you can be a high-energy person. Students can expect many rewards in the hospitality business, but remember it's a long journey, a process. You need to experience all levels in order to become a complete leader."

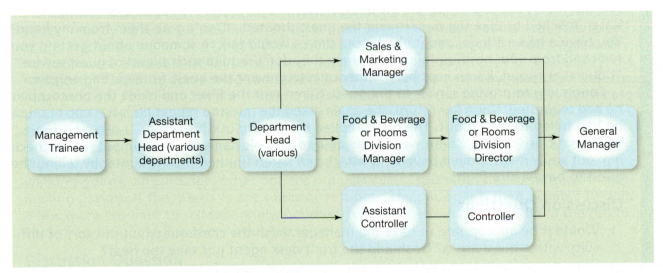

Figure 3–12 • A Career Path in Lodging Management.
(Courtesy of Dr. Charlie Adams, Texas Tech University.)

CASE STUDY

Overbooked: The Housekeeping Perspective

It is no secret that in all hotels the director of housekeeping must be able to react quickly and efficiently to any unexpected circumstances that arise. Stephen Rodondi, executive house-keeper at the Hyatt Regency La Jolla usually starts his workday at 8:00 A.M. with a department meeting. These morning meetings help him and the employees to visualize their goals for the day. On this particularly busy day, Rodondi arrives at work and is told that three housekeep-ers have called in sick. This is a serious challenge for the hotel because it is overbooked and has all its 400 rooms to service.

Discussion Question

1. What should Stephen do to maintain standards and ensure that all the guest rooms are serviced?

Source: Courtesy of Stephen Rodondi, Executive Housekeeper, Hyatt Regency La Jolla, CA.

Summary

1. A big hotel is run by a general manager and an executive committee, which is rep-resented by the key executives of all the major departments, such as rooms division, food and beverage, marketing, sales, and human resources.

2. The general manager represents the hotel and is responsible for its profitability and performance. Because of increased job consolidation, he or she also is expected to attract business and to empathize with the cultures of both guests and employees.

3. The rooms division department consists of front office, reservations, housekeeping, con-cierge, guest services, and communications.

4. The front desk, as the center of the hotel, sells rooms and maintains balanced guest accounts, which are completed daily by the night auditor. The front desk constantly must meet guests' needs by offering ser-vices such as mailing, faxing, and mes-sages.

5. PMSs, centralized reservations, and yield management have enabled hotels to work more efficiently and to increase profitability and guest satisfaction.

6. The communications department, room service, and guest services (such as door attendants, bellpersons, and the concierge) are vital parts of the personality of a hotel.

7. Housekeeping is the largest department of the hotel. The executive housekeeper is in charge of inventory, cleaning, employees, and accident and loss prevention. The laun-dry may be cleaned directly in the hotel or by a hired laundry service.

8. The electronic room key and closed-circuit television cameras are basic measures provided to protect the guests and their property.

9. Spas are now a popular feature of many U.S. hotels, offering a variety of beauty treatments, exercise equipment, and other means for guest relaxation.

Key Words and Concepts

application service provider (ASP)

average daily rate (ADR)

call accounting systems (CAS)

catastrophe plans

central reservation office (CRO)

central reservation system (CRS)

city ledger

concierge

confirmed reservations

cost centers

daily report

Employee Right to Know

executive committee

global distribution systems (GDS)

guaranteed reservations

night auditor

Occupational Safety and Health Administration (OSHA)

productivity

property management systems (PMS)

revenue management

revenue centers

revenue per available room (REV PAR)

room occupancy percentage (ROP)

room rates

rooms division

uniformed staff

yield management

Review Questions

1. Briefly define the purpose of a hotel. Why is it important to empathize with the culture of guests?
2. List the main responsibilities of the front-office manager.
3. What are the advantages and disadvantages of yield management?
4. Why is the concierge an essential part of the personality of a hotel?
5. Explain the importance of accident and loss prevention. What security measures are taken to protect guests and their property?

Internet Exercises

1. Organization: **Hyatt Hotels Corporation**
   Summary: Hyatt Hotels Corporation is a multibillion-dollar hotel management company. Together with Hyatt International, the company has about eight percent of the hotel industry market share. Hyatt is recognized for its decentralized management approach, in which general managers are given a great deal of the management decision-making process.
   Click the "About Hyatt" tab, and click "Careers" under the "For Job Seekers" section. Click on "University Recruiting," and then click on "Mgmt Training Program" to learn more about this program that Hyatt offers.

   (a) What is Hyatt's management training program?
   (b) What requisites must applicants meet to qualify for Hyatt's management training program?

2. Organization: **Hoteljobs.com**
   Summary: Hoteljobs.com is a Web site that offers information to recruiters, employers, and job seekers in the hospitality industry.

   (a) What different jobs are being offered under "Job Search," and which one, if any, interests you?
   (b) Post your résumé online.

Apply Your Knowledge

1. If you were on the executive committee of a hotel, what kinds of things would you be doing to ensure the success of the hotel?

2. Your hotel has 275 rooms. Last night, 198 were occupied. What was the occupancy percentage?

Suggested Activities

1. Go to a hotel's Web site and find the price of booking a room for a date of your choice. Then, go to one of the Web sites (Hotels .com, Expedia, Travelocity, etc.) that "sell" hotel rooms and see how the price there compares with the price on the hotel's Web site.

Endnotes

1. James E. McManemon, General Manager The Ritz-Carlton Sarasota, address to University of South Florida students, March 26, 2010.
2. Richard A. Wentzel, "Leaders of the Hospitality Industry or Hospitality Management," *An Introduction to the Industry*, 6th ed. (Dubuque, IA: Kendall/Hunt, 1991), 29.
3. Allen Brigid, "Ritz, César Jean (1850–1918)," *Oxford Dictionary of National Biography* (Oxford: Oxford University Press, 2006).
4. William F. Ashburner, "Escoffier, Georges Auguste (1846–1935)," *Oxford Dictionary of National Biography* (Oxford: Oxford University Press, 2006).
5. Donald E. Lundberg, *The Hotel and Restaurant Business*, 4th ed. (New York: Van Nostrand Reinhold, 1984), 33–34.
6. Personal conversation with Rollie Teves, July 20, 2014.
7. Personal correspondence with Jay R. Schrock, Ph.D., Dean, School of Hotel and Restaurant Management, University of South Florida, Sarasota-Manatee, January 18, 2011.
8. STR Global, *Products*, http://www.strglobal.com, click on Products (March 3, 2011).
9. Personal conversation with Bruce Lockwood, March 16, 2006.
10. WebMD, www.webmd.com, search for "ayurvedic treatments" (February 9, 2015).
    Susan Patel, *Triple Bottom Line and Eco-Efficiency: Where to Start?*, EcoGreenHotel, www.ecogreenhotel.com/, click on Contact, click on Blog, and then search for "Triple Bottom Line" to view this article, (accessed February 26, 2015).
11. Ibid.
12. Scott Parisi, CHA and Ray Burger, CHA, "Green Hotel Certification Programs Snowball, Sparks Confusion," *Sustainable Travel*, January 19, 2010, http://blog.sustainabletravel.com, search for "Green Hotel Certification Programs Snowball" (February 26, 2015).

13. Ibid.
14. New Hampshire Sustainable Lodging & Restaurant Program, Home Page, www.nhslrp.org/ (February 26, 2015).
15. BUILDINGS.com, *Greening Your Hotel*, http://www.buildings.com/ (May 22, 2015).
16. Debra Walsh, *Temp Control at Half the Cost, Hospitality Technology (HT)*, http://hospitalitytechnology.edgl.com, search for "Temp Control at Half the Cost" (February 7, 2015).
17. Christina Volpe, *2011 Guestroom Tech Trends, Hospitality Technology (HT)*, http://hospitalitytechnology.edgl.com, search for "2011 Guestroom Tech Trends" (February 7, 2015).
18. Ibid.

CHAPTER 4

Food and Beverage

LEARNING OBJECTIVES

After reading and studying this chapter, you should be able to:

- Describe the duties and responsibilities of a food and beverage director and other key department heads.

- Describe a typical food and beverage director's day.

- State the functions and responsibilities of the food and beverage departments.

- Perform computations using key food and beverage operating ratios.

LEARNING OBJECTIVE 1
Describe the duties and
responsibilities of a food and
beverage director and other
key department heads.

Food and Beverage Management

In the hospitality industry, the food and beverage division is led by the **director of food and beverage**. He or she reports to the general manager (GM) and is responsible for the efficient and effective operation of the following departments:

- Kitchen/catering/banquet
- Restaurants/room service/minibars
- Lounges/bars/stewarding

Figure 4–1 illustrates a food and beverage organization chart.

The position description for a director of food and beverage is both a job description and a specification of the requirements an individual needs to do the job. In recent years, the skills needed by a food and beverage director have grown enormously, as shown by the following list of responsibilities:

- Exceeding guests' expectations in food and beverage offerings and service
- Leadership
- Identifying trends
- Finding and keeping outstanding employees
- Training
- Motivation
- Budgeting

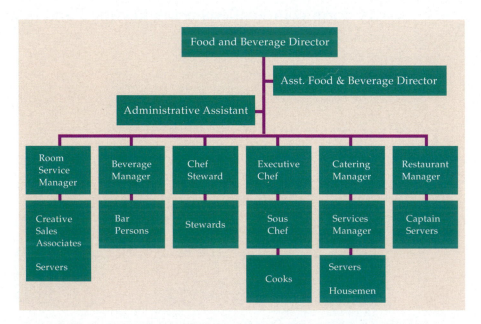

Figure 4–1 • Food and Beverage Division Organization Chart for a Large Hotel.

- Cost control
- Finding profit from all outlets
- Having a detailed working knowledge of the front-of-the-house operations

These challenges are set against a background of stagnant or declining occupancies and the consequent drop in room sales. Therefore, greater emphasis has been placed on making food and beverage sales profitable. Traditionally, only about 20 percent of the hotel's operating profit comes from the food and beverage divisions. In contrast, the current acceptable profit margin from a hotel's food and beverage division is generally considered to be 25–30 percent. This figure can vary according to the type of hotel. For example, according to Pannell Kerr Forster, an industry consulting firm, all-suite properties achieve a seven percent food and beverage profit (probably because of the complimentary meals and drinks offered to guests). It is interesting to note that U.S. hotels have fewer food and beverage outlets compared to their Asian and European counterparts. The reason is likely profit in the United States and culture in Asia and Europe where hotels are used more as meeting places and the bars and restaurants are well frequented by nonresidents.

A typical food and beverage director's day might look like the following:

LEARNING OBJECTIVE 2
Describe a typical food and beverage director's day.

8:30 A.M.	Check messages and read logs from outlets and security. Tour outlets, especially the family restaurant (a quick inspection).
	Check the breakfast buffet, reservations, and the shift manager.
	Check daily specials.
	Check room service.
	Check breakfast service and staffing.
	Meet the executive chef and purchasing director.
	Meet executive steward's office to ensure that all equipment is ready.
	Meet banquet service office to check on daily events and coffee break sequence.
10:00 A.M.	Work on current projects: new summer menu, pool outlet opening, conversion of a current restaurant with a new concept, remodeling of ballroom foyer, installation of new walk-in freezer, and analysis of current profit-and-loss (P&L) statements. Plan weekly food and beverage department meetings.
11:45 A.M.	Visit kitchen to observe lunch service and check the "12:00 line," including banquets.
	Confer with executive chef.
	Check restaurants and banquet luncheon service.

1:00 P.M.	Lunch in employee cafeteria with executive chef, director of purchasing, and/or director of catering to review any outstanding issues.
1:30 P.M.	Meet with human resources to discuss current incidents.
2:30 P.M.	Check messages and return calls. Telemarket to attract catering and convention business.
	Conduct hotel daily menu meeting.
3:00 P.M.	Go to special projects/meetings.
5:30 P.M.	Tour cocktail lounges.
	Check for staffing.
	Review any current promotions.
	Check entertainment lineup.
6:00 P.M.	Check special food and beverage requests/requirements of any VIPs staying at the hotel.
	Tour kitchen.
	Review and taste.
8:00 P.M.	Review dinner specials.
	Check the restaurant and lounges.

A food and beverage director's typical day starts at 8:00 A.M. and ends at 8:00 P.M., unless early or very late events are scheduled, in which case the working day is even longer. Usually, the food and beverage director works Monday through Saturday. If there are special events on Sunday, then he or she works on Sunday and takes Monday off. In a typical week, Saturdays are used to catch up on reading or specific projects.

The director of food and beverage eats in his or her restaurants at least twice a week for dinner and at least once a week for breakfast and lunch. Bars are generally visited with clients, at least twice per week. The director sees salespersons regularly because they are good sources of information about what is going on in the industry and they can introduce leads for business. The director attends staff meetings, food and beverage meetings, executive committee meetings, interdepartmental meetings, credit meetings, and P&L statement meetings.

To become a food and beverage director takes several years of experience and dedication. One of the best routes is to gain work experience or to participate in an internship in several food and beverage departments while attending college. This experience should include full-time, practical kitchen work for at least one to two years to master the core concepts, followed by varying periods of a few months in purchasing, stores, cost control, stewarding, and room service. Stewarding is responsible for back-of-the-house areas such as dishwashing and issuing and inventorying china, glassware, and cutlery. Stewarding duties include maintaining cleanliness in all areas. Additionally, a year spent in each of the following work situations is helpful: restaurants, catering, and bars. After these departmental experiences, and once you master the core competencies, you can likely serve as a department manager, preferably in a different hotel from the one in which the departmental experience was gained. This prevents the awkwardness of being manager of a department in which the person was once an employee and also offers the employee the opportunity to learn different things at different properties.

▶ Check Your Knowledge

1. What are the skills and responsibilities of a food and beverage director?
2. Describe a food and beverage director's day.

INTRODUCING GEORGE GOLDHOFF

President and CEO of Pure Canadian Gaming, Alberta, Canada.

Being hired as the pot washer for the Old Homestead Country Kitchen at the early age of 15 hardly seemed to herald the beginnings of an auspicious career in the hospitality industry. But to George Goldhoff, with his high energy and natural leadership skills, he had found the perfect environment in which to excel. The sense of family and camaraderie between the staff members and the interaction with guests, mixed with the intensity of performance and deadlines, have never lost their appeal. Excellence in service would become his lifelong pursuit.

Fast-forward 20 years. As director of food and beverage at Bellagio of MGM Resorts International in Las Vegas, George was responsible for the quality assurance, personnel development, and financial performance of 17 restaurants and 10 bars, with 3,000 employees and more than $200 million in revenues. As one of the original members of the opening team for the Bellagio, George drew from his extensive and varied food and beverage background to make the Bellagio's opening a success.

George earned his B.S. degree in hotel, restaurant, and travel administration from the University of Massachusetts, a big accomplishment for a young man without a high school diploma who was often characterized as wild and rebellious. It was a revelation, an awakening of his potentials and the realization that he could accomplish great things. This accomplishment instilled in George the self-confidence in his abilities and the technical skills necessary to achieve his goals. His introduction to corporate culture was as an assistant front-office manager and Hyatt corporate trainee in Savannah, Georgia.

Upon completion of his training, George moved to Tahoe in 1988, where he was able to combine his love for restaurants and sports. An all-around athlete, he pursued speed skiing competitions at the highest levels. George's ambitions led him to The Plaza Hotel in New York, where he started as an assistant beverage director. At The Plaza, George immersed himself in his new position with his usual high-voltage energy and infectious enthusiasm. Within six months, he was promoted to manager of the stately Oak Room, the youngest manager in the restaurant's 90-year history. Within a two-year period, he was promoted to managing four of The Plaza Hotel's five à la carte restaurants.

(continued)

INTRODUCING GEORGE GOLDHOFF *(Continued)*

In 1993, he realized one of his dreams—the opportunity to work with the legendary Joe Baum—managing the famous Rainbow Room in Rockefeller Center. George's commitment to service, the evident pride he takes in his work, and his high standard of ethics earned him praise from Joe Baum as being his best maître d' ever. In 1997, he left the Rainbow Room to enroll in the MBA program at Columbia University. With the same self-confidence, resourcefulness, and ability to focus on multiple tasks, George, not surprisingly, took first place in Columbia's Business Plan competition and was the recipient of the prestigious Eugene Lang Entrepreneurial Initiative Fund. Armed with his MBA degree and newly acquired business skills, he was ready for his next adventure. George went on to become General Manager of Gold Strike Casino Resort and is now President and CEO of PURE Canadian Gaming Corp., based in Edmonton, Alberta, Canada.

For George, it's all about service. Excellence in guest satisfaction and a genuine concern for his staff and coworkers have been his guiding principles. The ability to instill in those around him the desire to strive beyond and stretch past their comfort zones is just one of his leadership characteristics. George has great expectations for himself and those around him and is not afraid of hard work. In fact, he works with a passion. The long hours and the intensity do not faze him. His adaptability to different situations, his ability to relate to a variety of personalities and temperaments, and his keen sense of humor serve him well both in front and back of the house. With his winning smile and straightforward demeanor, George sets his sights on a promising future and the many adventures ahead.

LEARNING OBJECTIVE 3
State the functions and responsibilities of the food and beverage departments.

Kitchen

A hotel kitchen is under the charge of the **executive chef** or chef in smaller and medium-sized properties. This person, in turn, is responsible to the director of food and beverage for the efficient and effective operation of kitchen food production. The desired objective is to exceed guests' expectations in the quality and quantity of food—its presentation, taste, and portion size—and to ensure that hot food is served hot and cold food is served cold. The executive chef operates the kitchen in accordance with company policy and strives to achieve desired financial results.

Some executive chefs are now called **kitchen managers**; they even serve as food and beverage directors in midsized and smaller hotels. This trend toward "right-sizing," observed in other industries, euphemistically refers to restructuring organizations to retain the most essential employees. Usually, this means cutting labor costs by consolidating job functions. For example, Michael Hammer is executive chef and food and beverage director at the 440-room Hilton La Jolla Torrey Pines. Mike is typical of the new breed of executive chefs: His philosophy is to train his sous chefs, *sous* being a French word meaning "under," to make many of the operating decisions. He delegates ordering, hiring, and firing decisions; sous chefs are the ones most in control of the production and the people who work on their teams. By delegating more of the operating decisions, he is developing the *chefs de partie* (or stations chefs) and empowering them to make their own decisions. As he puts it, "No decision is wrong—but in case it is unwise, we will talk about it later."

Mike spends time maintaining morale, a vital part of a manager's responsibilities. The kitchen staff is under a great deal of pressure and frequently works against the clock. Careful cooperation and coordination are the keys to success. He explains that he does not want his associates to "play the tuba"—he wants them to conduct the orchestra. He does not hold food and beverage department meetings; instead he meets with groups of employees frequently, and problems are handled as they occur. Controls are maintained with the help of software that costs their standard recipes, establishes **perpetual inventories**, and calculates potential food cost per outlet. Today, executive chefs and food and beverage directors look past food cost to the actual profit contribution of an item. For example, if a pasta dish costs $3.25 and sells for $12.95, the contribution margin is $9.70. Today, there are software programs such as ChefTec that offer software solutions for purchasing, ordering, inventory control, and recipe and menu costing; ChefTec Plus offers perpetual inventory, sales analysis, theoretical inventory reports, and multiple profit centers.

The executive chef of a large hotel manages the kitchen and may not do much cooking—mostly administration.

Controlling costs is an essential part of food and beverage operations and, because labor costs represent the most significant variable costs, staffing becomes an important factor in the day-to-day running of the food and beverage locations. Labor cost benchmarks are measured by covers-per-person-hour. For example, in stewarding, it should take no more than one person per hour to clean 37.1 covers. Mike and his team of outlet managers face interesting challenges, such as staffing for the peaks and valleys of guest needs at breakfast. Many guests want breakfast during the peak time of 7:00–8:30 A.M., requiring organizations to get the right people in the right place at the right time to ensure that meals are prepared properly and served in a timely manner.

At the Hilton La Jolla Torrey Pines, Executive Chef Hammer's day goes something like the following:

1. Arrive between 6:00 and 7:00 A.M. and walk through the food and beverage department with the night cleaners.
2. Check to make sure the compactor is working and the area is clean.
3. Check that all employees are on duty.
4. Ask people what kind of challenges they will face today.
5. Sample as many dishes as possible, checking for taste, consistency, feel, smell, and overall quality.
6. Check walk-ins.
7. Recheck once or twice a day to see where the department stands production-wise—this helps reduce or eliminate overtime.
8. Approve schedules for food and beverage outlet.
9. Keep a daily update of food and beverage revenues and costs.
10. Forecast the next day's, week's, and month's business based on updated information.
11. Check on final numbers for catering functions.

Financial results are generally expressed in ratios, such as **food cost percentage**—the cost of food divided by the amount of food sales. A simple example is the sale of a hamburger for $1.00. If the cost of the food is $0.30, then the food cost percentage is 30 percent, which is about average for many hotels. The average might be reduced to 27 percent in hotels that do a lot of catering. As discussed later in this section, in determining the food and beverage department's profit and loss, executive chefs and food and beverage directors must consider not only the food cost percentage, but also the **contribution margin** of menu items. The contribution margin is the amount contributed by a menu item toward overhead expenses and is the difference between the cost of preparing the item and its selling price.

Another important cost ratio for the kitchen is labor cost. The **labor cost percentage** may vary depending on the amount of convenience foods purchased versus those made from scratch (raw ingredients). In a kitchen, the labor cost percentage may be expressed as a **food sales percentage**. For example, if food sales total $1,000 and labor costs total $250, then labor costs may be expressed as a percentage of food sales by the following formula:

$$\frac{\text{Labor Cost}}{\text{Food Sales}}, \text{ therefore } \frac{\$250}{\$1,000} = 25\% \text{ labor cost}$$

Labor management is controlled with the aid of programs such as TimePro from Commeg Systems. TimePro is a time, attendance, and scheduling package that provides an analytical tool for managers and saves time on forecasting and scheduling.

An executive chef has one or more **sous chefs**. Because so much of the executive chef's time is spent on administration, sous chefs are often responsible for the day-to-day running of each shift. Depending on size, a kitchen may have several sous chefs: one or more for days, one for evenings, and another for banquets.

CORPORATE PROFILE

Marilyn Carlson Nelson, Former Chairman and CEO, Carlson

Based in Minneapolis, Carlson's brands and services employ about 100,000 people in nearly 150 countries and territories.[1] Formerly led by Chairman Marilyn Carlson Nelson and now led by her daughter, Chair Diana Nelson, Carlson continues to build on a cornerstone set by Marilyn's father, Curtis Carlson, over 75 years ago: developing long-lasting relationships with clients.

The history of Carlson is one of the classic business success stories in the American free-enterprise system. Starting in 1938 with merely an idea and $55 of borrowed capital, entrepreneur Curtis L. Carlson founded the Gold Bond Stamp Company in his home city of Minneapolis, Minnesota. His trading stamp concept, designed to stimulate sales and loyalty for food stores and other merchants, proved to be right for the times and swept the nation in a wave of dramatic growth.

Through the years, Carlson diversified into hotels, travel, and other related businesses. In the 1960s, Carlson and several other partners collectively bought an interest in the original Radisson

Hotel in downtown Minneapolis. Eventually, Carlson became sole owner of the hotel brand and expanded it around the globe.

Among the names in the Carlson family of brands and services are Radisson Hotels & Resorts, Park Plaza Hotels & Resorts, Country Inns & Suites by Carlson, Park Inn, Quorvus Collection, Radisson Blu, Radisson Red, and Carlson Wagonlit Travel.

Carlson Worldwide encompasses 1,370 hotels in 150 countries and territories, and is the world's leading Travel Management Company. Under the banner of Looking Forward, Vision 20/20 has goals of creating sustainable businesses, driving growth, and building shareholder wealth. Vision 20/20 has the strategic objectives of developing the right talent; fostering a culture of innovation and collaboration; creating customer bright spots; and delivering results.

In addition to global business success, Carlson is also recognized as a top employer by receiving numerous workplace awards and recognitions and is among the leadership in responsible business practices for people, community, and environment.

Under the sous chefs is the **chef tournant** (relief cook). This person rotates through the various stations to relieve the **station chef** heads. These stations are organized according to production tasks, based on the classic "brigade" introduced by Escoffier. The **brigade** includes the following:

Sauce chef, who prepares sauces, stews, sautés, and hot hors d'oeuvres

Roast chef, who roasts, broils, grills, and braises meats

Fish chef, who cooks fish dishes

Soup chef, who prepares all soups

Cold larder/pantry chef, who prepares all cold foods: salads, cold hors d'oeuvres, buffet food, and dressings

Banquet chef, who is responsible for all banquet food

Pastry chef, who prepares all hot and cold dessert items

Vegetable chef, who prepares vegetables (this person may be the fry cook and soup cook in some smaller kitchens)

Soup, cold larder, banquets, pastry, and vegetable chefs' positions may be combined in smaller kitchens.

A pastry chef decorating a cake.

▶ Check Your Knowledge

1. What is a food cost percentage, and how is it calculated?

2. What is a contribution margin?

3. How is labor cost percentage calculated?

A DAY IN THE LIFE OF CHEF JOSE MARTINEZ

Chef-Owner, La Maison Blanche, Longboat Key, Florida

Chef Jose Martinez apprenticed with three legendary, three-star Michelin French chefs and restaurateurs: Joël Robuchon at Restaurant Jamin in Paris; Alain Senderens, a founder of New French cuisine; and chef Michel Guérard at Les Prés d'Eugénie at Eugenie les Bains, France. Chef Martinez was awarded his own Michelin star for Maison Blanche in Paris, and then moved his family to Longboat Key, Florida, where La Maison Blanche is now among the best restaurants in the United States.

Chef Martinez arrives between 9:00 and 10:00 A.M. and does paperwork in the mornings. He orders and organizes supplies for the kitchen and meets with local farmers and small suppliers who, he says, understands his needs better than the large companies. He also works on the wine list by talking with suppliers and ensuring a good pairing with the menu items. By late morning he is planning and organizing the *mise en place* requirements for the evening dinner. At 1:00 P.M. he welcomes staff and gives their assignments. Chef Martinez always remembers that he must be able to do and be responsible for everything. There is no separation between owner and staff in this size of restaurant.

The afternoon is entirely devoted to preparation for the completion of the *mise en place.* This is a routine operation with a lot of discipline. The discipline is necessary to execute the *mise en place* correctly. At 5:00 P.M. the staff have their dinner before the opening at 5:30 P.M., when everything must be ready to go!

Chef Martinez's philosophy is: "There is no alternative to excellence." And he adds, "Capturing excellence in a dining experience begins and ends with the food. I have great respect for the production of food and the privilege bestowed on me being able to use it and apply my talent and focus on creating the most excellent product possible."

Food Outlets

A hotel may have several restaurants or no restaurant at all; the number and type of restaurants varies as well. A major chain hotel generally has two restaurants: a signature or upscale formal restaurant and a casual coffee shop–type restaurant. These restaurants cater to both hotel guests and to the general public. In recent years, because of increased guest expectations, hotels have placed greater emphasis on food and beverage preparation and service. As a result, there is an increasing need for professionalism on the part of hotel personnel.

Hotel restaurants are run by **restaurant managers** in much the same way as other restaurants. Restaurant managers are generally responsible for the following:

- Exceeding guest service expectations
- Hiring, training, and developing employees
- Setting and maintaining quality standards

- Marketing
- Banquets
- Coffee service
- In-room dining, minibars, or the cocktail lounge
- Presenting annual, monthly, and weekly forecasts and budgets to the food and beverage director

Café at the Paris Casino and Hotel in Las Vegas.

Some restaurant managers work on an incentive plan with quarterly performance bonuses. Hotel restaurants present the manager with some interesting challenges because hotel guests are not always predictable. Sometimes they will use the hotel restaurants, and other times they will dine out. If they dine in or out to an extent beyond the forecasted number of guests, problems can arise. Too many guests for the restaurants results in delays and poor service. Too few guests means that employees are underutilized, which can increase labor costs unless employees are sent home early. A restaurant manager keeps a diary of the number of guests served by the restaurant on the same night the previous week, month, and year.

The number (house count) and type of hotel guest (e.g., the number of conference attendees who may have separate dining arrangements) should also be considered in estimating the number of expected restaurant guests for any meal. This figure is known as the **capture rate**, which, when coupled with historic and banquet activity and hotel occupancy, will be the restaurant's basis for forecasting the number of expected guests.

Most hotels find it difficult to coax hotel guests into the restaurants. However, many hotels continuously try to convert foodservice from a necessary amenity to a profit center. The Royal Sonesta New Orleans offers restaurant coupons worth $5 to its guests and guests of nearby hotels. Another successful strategy, adopted by the Hotel Plaza Athénée in New York, is to show guests the restaurants and explain the cuisine before they go to their rooms. This has prompted more guests to dine in the restaurant during their stay. At some hotels, the restaurants self-promote by having cooking demonstrations in the lobby: The "on-site" chefs offer free samples to hotel guests. Progressive hotels, such as the Kimco Hotel in San Francisco, ensure that the hotel restaurants look like freestanding restaurants with separate entrances.

FOCUS ON LODGING

Gracious Hospitality

Catherine Rabb, Johnson and Wales University

I find great pleasure in seeing a well-managed hotel handling full occupancy, special events, and busy dining rooms with seemingly effortless grace. How welcoming it is for the traveler or for the guest at a special event to be served by professionals who embody the true spirit of gracious hospitality.

What the guest doesn't see is the complex network of interlocking relationships and intensive training necessary behind the scenes to make each day successful at any hotel. It has been said that hotels need to be like ducks—appearing to glide effortlessly along the surface, while paddling like the devil underneath! Every person in our operation is a critical component of our business. We sell food and beverages in a variety of ways, but in hospitality operations, the interaction with the guest becomes part of the product, with no room for returns if service is defective. We are only as good as our last meal, our last event, or our last contact with a guest. Service itself *is* the product.

As you will learn in this chapter, many different departments and people with diverse skills must work together efficiently. Hotels of different sizes and styles exist, so some operations need more people, and some need less, but for all hotels a dedication to providing the best available services and products is critical. This diverse group of people must work together to create a service product whose appearance is seamless. The coordination of people, talents, schedules, and needs is a complex ballet of intricate steps choreographed to create a seamless whole. A successful operation needs the talents of every member of the staff and welcomes the varied skills, energies, and ideas that their team brings to the table. Everyone, from the newest part-time employee to the manager, needs to be at the top of his or her game to reach the goal of service excellence.

The term *multitasking* has perhaps been overused in recent years; however, nowhere is the term better suited than to describe the routine tasks done by so many industry professionals. Whether we are chefs, bartenders, stewards, catering managers, or food and beverage directors, we all need a wide variety of skills and abilities to be successful in this challenging industry. We need the technical skills necessary to do the job: correct service techniques, food preparation skills, the ability to mix a perfect drink, or to set a room properly for a special event. We must also possess the ability to interact with our team members, each of whom is responsible for a different set of tasks performed under pressure. It is critical that we understand and master the fact that our business must make a profit, and we work hard to blend effective budgets and cost controls with our service goals. We continuously provide extensive, thorough, effective, and ongoing training for ourselves and our staff so that our team is knowledgeable, trained, and empowered to act in the best interest of the guest and, ultimately, our operation. Our knowledge of the legalities of operating a business must be extensive so that our operations and our staff are protected. We are competitive because our market is changing and challenging, and we continually strive to position our businesses to be competitive. We must be strong because the physical demands of the business can be demanding, and we must be self-aware, for doing a challenging job well means that we are able to take care of ourselves and our lives outside the hotel. We lead by example to inspire our teammates to do the very best job they can, whatever the circumstances. Terrific service requires terrific people who possess the ability to integrate these characteristics into every workday.

What type of people are drawn to this business? People who love a challenge. People who enjoy other people. People who love their work and take pride in their ability to create a beautiful banquet, a perfect soup, or a well-designed training program. People with a work ethic, honesty, and integrity that make them an example to others. People who love to learn. People who enjoy the fact that every day is different and brings different challenges. Perhaps someone like you!

Bars

Hotel bars allow guests to relax while sipping a cocktail after a hectic day. This opportunity to socialize for business or pleasure is advantageous for both guests and the hotel. Because the profit percentage on all beverages is higher than it is on food items, bars are an important revenue source for the food and beverage departments. The cycle of beverages from ordering, receiving, storing, issuing, bar stocking, serving, and guest billing is complex, but, unlike restaurant meals, a beverage can be held over if not sold. An example of a world-famous hotel bar is the King Cole Bar in The St. Regis Hotel in New York City. This bar has been a favored New York "watering hole" of the rich and famous for many years. The talking point of the bar is the painted mural of Old King Cole, the nursery rhyme character.

Bars are run by bar managers. The responsibilities of a bar manager include the following:

- Supervising the ordering process and storage of wines
- Preparing a wine list
- Overseeing the staff
- Maintaining cost control
- Assisting guests with their wine selection
- Proper service of wine
- Knowledge of beers and liquors and their service

Bar efficiency is measured by the **pour/cost percentage**. Pour cost is obtained by dividing the cost of depleted inventory by sales over a period of time. Food and beverage directors expect a pour cost of between 16 and 24 percent. Generally, operations with lower pour costs have more sophisticated control systems and a higher-volume catering operation. An example of this is an automatic system that dispenses the exact amount of beverage requested via a pouring gun, which is fed by a tube from a beverage store. These systems are expensive, but they save money for volume operations by being less prone to pilferage, overpouring, or other tricks of the trade. Their greatest savings comes in the form of reduced labor costs; fewer bartenders are needed to make the same amount of drinks. However, the barperson may still hand pour premium brands for show.

Hotel bars are susceptible to the same problems as other bars. The director of food and beverage must set strict policy and procedure guidelines and see to it that they are followed. In today's litigious society, the onus is on the operator to install and ensure **responsible alcoholic beverage service**, and all beverage service staff should receive training in this important area because it might limit the bar's liability. (The National Restaurant Association (NRA) offers ServSafe Alcohol.) If a guest becomes intoxicated and is still served alcohol or a minor is served alcohol and is involved in an accident involving someone else, then the server of the beverage, the barperson, and the manager may be liable for the injuries sustained by the person who was harmed, the third party.

Another risk bars encounter is **pilferage**. Employees have been known to steal or tamper with liquor. They could, for example, dilute drinks with water

A server carries Singapore Slings in the Long Bar at Raffles Hotel Singapore.

or colored liquids, sell the additional liquor, and pocket the money. There are several other ways to defraud a bar. One of the better known ways is to overcharge guests for beverages. Another is to underpour, which gives guests less for their money. Some bartenders overpour measures to receive larger tips. The best way to prevent these occurrences is to have a good control system, which should include **shoppers**—people who are paid to use the bar like regular guests, except they are closely watching the operation.

In a large hotel there are several kinds of bars:

Lobby bar. This convenient meeting place was popularized when Conrad Hilton wanted to generate revenue out of his vast hotel lobby. Lobby bars, when well managed, are a good source of income.

Restaurant bar. Traditionally, this bar is away from the hubbub of the lobby and offers a holding area for the hotel's signature restaurant.

Service bar. In some of the very large hotels, restaurants and room service have a separate backstage bar. Otherwise, both the restaurant and room service are serviced by one of the regular beverage outlets, such as the restaurant bar.

Catering and banquet bar. This bar is used specifically to service all the catering and banquet needs of the hotel. These bars can stretch any operator to the limit. Frequently, several cash bars must be set up at a variety of locations; if cash wines are involved with dinner, it becomes a race to get the wine to the guest before the meal, preferably before the appetizer. Because of the difficulties involved in servicing a large number of guests, most hotels encourage inclusive wine and beverage functions, in which the guests pay a little more for tickets that include a predetermined amount of beverage service. Banquet bars require careful inventory control. The bottles should be checked immediately after the function, and, if the bar is very busy, the bar manager should pull the money just before the bar closes. The breakdown of function bars should be done on the spot if possible to help prevent pilferage.

The banquet bar needs to stock not only large quantities of the popular wines, spirits, and beers, but also a selection of premium spirits and after-dinner liqueurs. These are used in the ballroom and private dining rooms, in particular.

Pool bar. A pool bar is popular at resort hotels where guests can enjoy a variety of exotic cocktails poolside. Resort hotels that cater to conventions often put on theme parties one night of the convention to allow delegates to kick back. Popular themes that are catered around the pool might be a Hawaiian luau, a Caribbean reggae night, a Mexican fiesta, or Country and Western events. Left to the imagination, one could conceive of a number of theme events.

Minibar. The minibar, sometimes called an honor bar, is a small, refrigerated bar placed in each guest room. It offers the convenience of having beverages available at all times. For security, the minibar has a separate key, which may be either included in the room key envelope at check-in or withheld, according to the guest's preference. Minibars are typically checked and replenished on a daily basis. Charges for items used are automatically added to the guest folio.

Night club. Some hotels offer guests evening entertainment and dancing. Whether formal or informal, these food and beverage outlets offer a full beverage service. Live entertainment is very expensive. Many hotels are switching to operations with a DJ or a bar that itself is the entertainment (e.g., a sports bar). Directors of food and beverage are now negotiating more with live bands, offering them a base pay (below union scale) and a percentage of a cover charge.

Sports bar. The sports bar has become a popular hotel feature. Almost everyone identifies with a sporting theme, which makes for a relaxed atmosphere that complements contemporary lifestyles. Many sports bars have a variety of games such as pool, football, bar basketball, and so on, which, together with satellite-televised sporting events, contribute to the atmosphere.

Casino bar. Casino bar and beverage service is intended to keep people gambling by offering low-cost or free drinks. Some casino bars have lavish entertainment and light food offerings, which entice guests to enjoy the gaming experience, even when sustaining heavy losses.

Different types of bars produce revenue according to their location in the hotel and the kind of hotel in which they are located. Nightclubs, sports bars, and banqueting departments see bulk consumption of alcoholic beverages, and restaurant bars usually see more alcohol consumption than minibars and lounge bars.

▶ Check Your Knowledge

1. What departments does the food and beverage director oversee?
2. What are the specific responsibilities of a food and beverage director on a day-to-day basis?
3. Explain how the pour/cost percentage is used in a bar to measure efficiency.

A chief steward checking the inventory.

Stewarding Department

The **chief steward** is responsible to the director of food and beverage for the following functions:

- Cleanliness of the back of the house (all the areas of the backstage that hotel guests do not see)
- Maintaining clean glassware, china, and cutlery for the food and beverage outlets
- Maintaining strict inventory control and monthly stock check
- Maintenance of dishwashing machines
- Inventory of chemical stock
- Sanitation of kitchen, banquet aisles, storerooms, walk-ins/freezers, and all equipment
- Pest control and coordination with exterminating company
- Forecasting labor and cleaning supplies

In some hotels, the steward's department is responsible for keeping the kitchen(s) clean. This is generally done at night to prevent disruption of the food production operation. A more limited cleaning is done in the afternoon between the lunch and dinner services. The chief steward's job can be an enormous and thankless task. In hotels, this involves cleaning up after several hundred people three times a day. Just trying to keep track of everything can be a headache. Some hotels have different patterns of glasses, china, and cutlery for each outlet. The casual dining room frequently has an informal theme, catering and banqueting a more formal one, and the signature restaurant, very formal place settings. It is difficult to ensure that all the pieces are returned to the correct places. It is also difficult to prevent both guests and employees from taking souvenirs. Strict inventory control and constant vigilance help keep pilferage to a minimum.

TECHNOLOGY SPOTLIGHT

Courtesy of **James McManemon**, M.S., University of South Florida Sarasota–Manatee

Full-service hotels have several food and beverage operations. These may include breakfast, lunch, and dinner restaurants; lobby, pool, fitness club, spa, and snack bars; a night club and discothèque; and banquet/event rooms. In addition, hotels may have outlets such as a gift shop. All of these transactions are managed by point-of-sale (POS) systems. A POS system can enhance decision-making, operational control, guest services, and revenues. A POS system is a network of cashier and server terminals that typically handles food and beverage orders, transmission of orders to the kitchen and bar, guest-check settlement, timekeeping, and interactive charges posting to guest folios. POS information can also be imported to accounting and food-cost/inventory software packages. A variety of reports can be generated, including open check (list of outstanding checks), cashier, voids/comps, sales analysis, menu mix, server sales summary, tip, labor cost, and so forth. Sophisticated POS systems can generate as many as 200 management reports. The advantages of using a POS system in a food and beverage operation include the following:

1. **Elimination of arithmetic errors:** A POS system may eliminate manual arithmetic calculations, therefore increasing guest satisfaction and tips. A study concluded that restaurants using handwritten checks have lower tipping and a substantial loss of potential revenue.

2. **Improved guest check control:** In an industry where the failure rate among restaurants is about 60 percent within the first three years, controlling costs and revenue is critical. A POS system allows for all transactions to be recorded, allowing less room for fraud. Failure to audit missing checks and to reconcile guest check sales with cash register readings often results in a lower sales volume and higher cost ratios. With a POS system, a server must place the order through a server terminal for it to be printed in the kitchen or bar. This ensures the recording of all sales and provides line cooks with legible orders. It also electronically tracks open checks, settled checks, voids, comps, discounts, and sales for each server, as well as employee meals.

3. **Increased average guest check:** Since orders are transmitted to the kitchen printer, travel time to the kitchen is reduced. This allows more time for suggestive selling and servicing guests. Also, a POS system provides a detailed summary for each server, listing average guest check, items sold, and total sales. This information can be used for job evaluations, motivational programs (e.g., wine contest), and assessing merchandising skills (e.g., average guest check and item sales), and server efficiency (e.g., sales per hour).

4. **Faster reaction to trends:** A POS system can provide a wealth of information on a real-time basis. Most POS systems can easily track sales and cost information by time period (e.g., hourly, daily, and weekly), employee, meal period, register, outlet, table, and menu item. This allows a restaurant operator to quickly spot and react to problematic areas affecting profitability, such as a declining average guest check during lunch, excessive labor hours in the kitchen, a changing menu mix, or sluggish liquor sales.

5. **Reduced labor costs and greater operational efficiency:** An efficient POS system should be able to increase operational efficiency, therefore allowing staff members to have higher levels of productivity. In the long term, this may result in reduced labor costs.

In addition to the POS system, some of the applications for a restaurant include table management systems, home delivery, frequent-dining and gift card programs, inventory control systems, and menu management systems. We will cover them in the future chapters.

Catering Department

Throughout the world's cultural and social evolution, numerous references have been made to the breaking of bread together. Feasts or banquets are one way to show one's hospitality. Frequently, hosts attempted to outdo one another with the extravagance of their feasts. Today, occasions for celebrations, banquets, and catering include the following:

- State banquets, when countries' leaders honor visiting royalty and heads of state
- National days
- Embassy receptions and banquets
- Business and association conventions and banquets
- Gala charity balls
- Company dinner dances
- Weddings

The term *catering* has a broader scope than does the term *banquet*. **Banquet** refers to groups of people who eat together at one time and in one place. **Catering** includes a variety of occasions when people may eat at varying times. However, the terms are often used interchangeably.

For example, catering departments in large, city-center hotels may service the following events in just one day:

- A Fortune 500 company's annual shareholders' meeting
- An international loan-signing ceremony
- A fashion show
- A convention
- Several sales and board meetings
- Private luncheons and dinner parties
- A wedding or two

Naturally each of these events requires different and special treatment. Hotels in smaller cities may cater the local chamber of commerce meeting, a high school prom, a local company party, a regional sales meeting, a professional workshop, and a small exhibition.

A caterer oversees an event.

Catering may be subdivided into on-premise and off-premise. In off-premise catering, the event is catered away from the hotel. The food may be prepared either in the hotel or at the event. The organizational chart in Figure 4–2 shows how the catering department is organized. The dotted lines show cooperative reporting relationships, and continuous lines show a direct reporting relationship. For example, the banquet chef reports directly to the executive chef, but must cooperate with the **director of catering (DOC)** and the catering service manager.

The DOC is responsible to the food and beverage director for selling and servicing, catering, banquets, meetings, and exhibitions in a way that exceeds guests' expectations and produces reasonable profit. The director of catering has a close working relationship with the rooms division

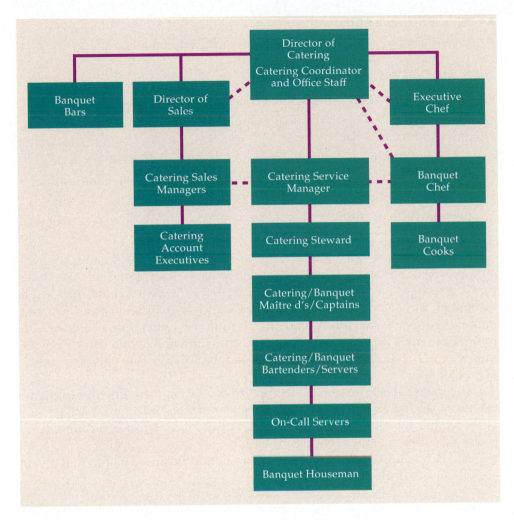

Figure 4–2 • Organization of the Catering Department.

manager because the catering department often brings conventions, which require rooms, to the hotel. There is also a close working relationship with the executive chef. The chef plans the banqueting menus, but the catering manager must ensure that they are suitable for the clientele and practical from a service point of view. Sometimes they work together in developing a selection of menus that will meet all the requirements, including cost and price.

Position Profile of a Director of Catering

The director of catering must be a leader *and* possess a thorough going knowledge of food and beverage management. The profile of a person holding this position would be as follows:

Leadership

- Lead a team of employees
- Set departmental mission, goals, and objectives

- Set service standards
- Ensure that the catering department is properly maintained

Skills and Abilities

- An ability to sell conventions, functions, and banquets
- An ability to develop individual and department sales and cost budgets, and produce a profit
- An ability to train department members in all facets of the operation
- Possess creativity, as well as knowledge, about food, wine, and service
- Possess a useful knowledge of the likes, dislikes, and dietary restrictions of various ethnic groups, especially Jewish, Middle Eastern, and European

The catering department is extremely complex and demanding; the tempo is fast and the challenge to be innovative is always present. The director of catering in a large city hotel should, over the years, build up a client list and an intimate knowledge of the trade shows, exhibitions, various companies, groups, associations, and social, military, education, religious, and fraternal market (SMERF) organizations. This knowledge and these contacts are essential to the director of catering's success, as is the selection of the team members.

The main sales function of the department is conducted by the DOC and catering sales managers (CSMs). Their jobs are to optimize guest satisfaction and revenue by selling the most lucrative functions and exceeding guests' food and beverage and service expectations.

The DOC and catering sales managers obtain business leads from a variety of sources, including the following:

Hotel's director of sales. He or she is a good source of event bookings because he or she is selling rooms, and catering is often required by meetings and conventions.

General managers. These people are good sources of leads because they are very involved in the community.

Corporate office sales department. If, for example, a convention were held on the East Coast one year at a Marriott hotel, and by tradition the association goes to the West Coast the following year, the Marriott hotel in the chosen city can contact the client or meeting planner. Some organizations have a selection of cities and hotels bid for major conventions. This ensures a competitive rate quote for accommodations and services.

Convention and visitors bureau. Here is another good source of leads because its main purpose is to seek out potential groups and organizations to visit that city. To be fair to all the hotels, they publish a list of clients and brief details of their requirements, which the hotel catering sales department may follow up on.

Reading the event board of competitive hotels. The event board is generally located in the lobby of the hotel and is frequently read by the competition. The CSM then calls the organizer of the event to solicit the business the next time.

Rollovers. Some organizations, especially local ones, prefer to stay in the same location. If this represents good business for the hotel, then the DOC and GM try to persuade the decision makers to use the same hotel again.

Cold calls. During periods of relative quiet, CSMs call potential clients to inquire if they are planning any events in the next few months. The point is to entice the client to view the hotel and the catering facilities. It is amazing how much information is freely given over the telephone.

The most frequent catering events in hotels are the following:

- Meetings
- Conventions
- Dinners
- Luncheons
- Weddings

For meetings, a variety of room setups are available, depending on a client's needs. The most frequently selected meeting room setups are as follows:

Theater style. Rows of chairs are placed with a center group of chairs and two aisles. Figure 4–3 shows a **theater-style room seating** setup with equipment centered on an audiovisual platform. Sometimes multimedia presentations, requiring more space for reverse-image projections, reduce the room's seating capacity.

Classroom style. As the name suggests, tables, usually slim 18-inch ones, are used because meeting participants need space to take notes. **Classroom-style seating** usually takes about three times as much space as theater style and takes more time and labor to set up and break down. Figure 4–4 shows a classroom-style setup.

Horseshoe style. **Horseshoe-style room seating** (Figure 4–5) is frequently used when interaction is sought among the delegates, such as training sessions and workshops. The presenter or trainer stands at the open end of the horseshoe with a black or white board, flip chart, overhead projector, and video monitor and projector.

Dinner style. Dinners are generally catered at round tables of eight or 10 persons for large parties and on boardroom-style tables for smaller numbers. Of course, there are variations of the **dinner-style room seating** setup (see Figure 4–6).

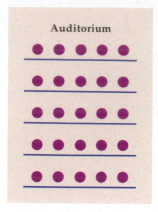

Figure 4–3 • Theater-Style Seating.

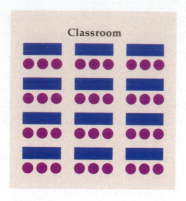

Figure 4–4 • Classroom-Style Seating.

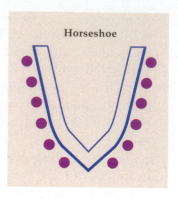

Figure 4–5 • Horseshoe-Style Seating.

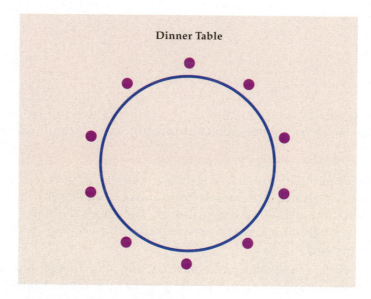

Figure 4–6 • Dinner-Style Seating.

Catering Event Order

A **catering event order (CEO)**, which may also be called a **banquet event order (BEO)**, is prepared/completed for each function to inform not only the client but also the hotel personnel about essential information (what needs to happen and when) to ensure a successful event.

The CEO is prepared based on correspondence with the client and notes taken during the property visits. Figure 4–7 shows a CEO and lists the room's layout and décor, times of arrival, if there are any VIPs and what special attention is required for them, bar times, types of beverages and service, cash or credit bar, time of meal service, the menu, wines, and service details. The catering manager or director confirms the details with the client.

THE GRANDE TORREY PINES HOTEL
BANQUET EVENT ORDER

POST AS: WELCOME BREAKFAST
EVENT NAME: MEETING
GROUP: GRUHL AND ASSOCIATES
ADDRESS: 41 MAIN ST
DENVER, CO
PHONE: (619) 635-4627
FAX: (619) 635-4528
GROUP CONTACT: Dr. Chad Gruhl
ON-SITE-CONTACT: same

CHERI WALTER

BILLING:

DIRECT BILL

Amount Received:

DAY	DATE	TIME	FUNCTION	ROOM	EXP	GTE	SET	RENT
Fri	January 25, 2013	7:30 AM – 12:00 PM	Meeting	Palm Garden	50			250.00

BAR SET UP:

N/A

MENU:

7:30 AM CONTINENTAL BREAKFAST

Freshly Squeezed Orange Juice, Grapefruit Juice, and
 Tomato Juice
Assortment of Bagels, Muffins, and Mini Brioche
Cream Cheese, Butter, and Preserves
Display of Sliced Seasonal Fruits
Individual Fruit Yogurt
Coffee, Tea, and Decaffeinated Coffee

PRICE:_____

11:00 AM BREAK

Refresh Beverages as needed

WINE:

FLORAL:

MUSIC:

AUDIO VISUAL:
–OVERHEAD PROJECTOR/SCREEN
–FLIPCHART/MARKERS
–VCR/MONITORS

PARKING:

HOSTING PARKING, PLEASE PROVIDE VOUCHERS

LINEN:
HOUSE

SETUP:
–CLASSROOM-STYLE SEATING
–HEAD TABLE FOR 2 PEOPLE
–APPROPRIATE COFFEE BREAK SETUP
–(1) 6' TABLE FOR REGISTRATION AT ENTRANCE
  WITH 2 CHAIRS, 1 WASTEBASKET

All food and beverage prices are subject to an 18% service charge and 7% state tax. Guarantee figures, cancellations, changes must be given 72 hours prior or the number of guests expected will be considered the guarantee. To confirm the above arrangements, this contract must be signed and returned.

ENGAGOR SIGNATURE _____   DATE _____

BEO # 003069

Figure 4-7 • Catering Event Order.

Usually, two copies are sent, one for the client to sign and return and one for the client to keep.

An accompanying letter thanks the client for selecting the hotel and explains the importance of the function to the hotel. The letter also mentions the **guaranteed-number policy**. This is the number of guests the hotel will prepare to serve and will charge accordingly. The guaranteed number is given about seven days prior to the event. This safeguards the hotel from preparing for 350 people and having only 200 show up. The client, naturally, does not want to pay for an extra 150 people—hence, the importance of a close working relationship with the client. Contracts for larger functions call for the client to notify the hotel of any changes to the anticipated number of guests in increments of 10 or 20.

Experienced catering directors ensure that there will be no surprises for either the function organizer or the hotel. This is done by calling to check on how the function planning is going. One mistake catering directors sometimes make is accepting a final guest count without inquiring as to how that figure was determined. This emphasizes the fact that the catering director should be a consultant to the client. Depending on the function, the conversion from invitations to guests is about 50 percent. Some hotels have a policy of preparing for about 3–5 percent more than the anticipated or guaranteed number. Fortunately, most events have a prior history. The organization may have been at a similar hotel in the same city or across the country. In either case, the catering director or manager will be able to receive helpful information from the catering director of the hotel where the organization's function was held previously.

The director of catering holds a daily or weekly meeting with key individuals who will be responsible for upcoming events. Those in attendance should be the following:

- Director of catering
- Executive chef and/or banquet chef
- Beverage manager or catering bar manager
- Catering managers
- Catering coordinator
- Director of purchasing
- Chief steward
- Audiovisual representative

The purpose of this meeting is to avoid any problems and to be sure that all key staff know and understand the details of the event and any special needs of the client.

Catering Coordinator

The **catering coordinator** has an exacting job in managing the office and controlling the "bible," or function diary, now on computer. He or she must see that the contracts are correctly prepared and must check on numerous last-minute details, such as whether flowers and menu cards have arrived.

Web-enabled technology tools such as Newmarket International's Delphi system (which is used at more than 4,000 properties) is a leader in delivering group, sales, catering, and banquet software for global travel and entertainment groups. One of the latest hotels to adopt the Delphi system is the Wynn Las Vegas, which installed the sales and catering systems Delphi Diagrams, MeetingBroker, and eProposal. The Delphi system can keep inventory current in real time because of its ability to interface with the property management system. The suite of Delphi products allows function space to be clearly and concisely managed, which increases guest satisfaction and profitability.

An elegant banquet room at a hotel.

A DAY IN THE LIFE OF JAMES McMANEMON

Food and Beverage Manager, Hyatt Regency

Friday—Start of a Busy Weekend

6:30 A.M.–8:00 A.M. (opening manager) Upon arrival, I will first walk through the restaurant to ensure prompt opening. I make sure tables are properly set, the carpet is clean, lighting is set, and that nothing is broken. I check for all the little things that may seem trivial but that don't go overlooked by our more observant guests.

Next, I walk through the breakfast buffet to make sure it's fully stocked and meets corporate standards. Afterward, I make my way over to the coffee bar to make sure that the barista is set up and ready to go for the coffee rush. I will spend the next 15 minutes talking to guests and conducting quality checks at each table to ensure that all of our guests' needs are being fulfilled and that they are enjoying their dining experience.

8:00 A.M.–8:30 A.M. At the daily meeting for operations managers, the managers of each operation in the hotel meet in the general manager's office to recap the previous day's business and discuss activity in each department that day. This meeting will include the food and beverage manager, banquets manager, housekeeping manager, front-office manager, sales and catering manager, executive chef, and general manager.

I will routinely discuss amenities that need to be sent up to guests' rooms that day, groups in-house, and reservations or parties we are expecting in the restaurant. It just so happens that today the restaurant will be hosting a four-course dinner for 30 people, carefully crafted and paired with unique wines by our executive chef.

(continued)

A DAY IN THE LIFE OF JAMES McMANEMON *(Continued)*

8:30 A.M.–11:00 A.M.   Balance managing the breakfast shift with preparation paperwork. Besides managing the floor during the breakfast shift, I must manage daily paperwork, which includes updated employee's schedules and time clocks for payroll, purchase inventory for the outlets, and respond to e-mails from employees, clients, and so on.

11:00 A.M.–12:00 P.M.   Once breakfast ends at 11 A.M., I will conduct a post-shift with my employees (servers, room service attendants, barista), where I discuss how I felt the breakfast shift went that morning, along with anything else they would need to know for the upcoming lunch shift that day. I will make sure that side work is completed in a timely manner and will then meet with incoming employees who are about to start their shift for the day.

12:00 P.M.–4:00 P.M.   Manage the lunch shift and finish paperwork. This entails expediting food, conducting quality checks with guests, and assisting staff when business picks up. Once the lunch rush slows down, I will complete any unfinished paperwork, and then begin preparing for the four-course menu for this evening. Here is an idea of what we will be serving:

First course: Lemon verbena smoked scallops with a cantaloupe caviar, micro mint leaves, and black lava sea salt, paired with a Chardonnay from Santa Barbara, California.

Second course: Watermelon steak crusted with a warm and smoky spice blend, wild arugula, Humboldt fog cheese and aged balsamic, paired with a Rose of Syrah from Colchagua Valley, Chile.

Third course: Espresso braised short rib with forest mushroom polenta and burnt leek chocolate pesto, paired with a Meritage from Paso Robles, California. This is a bold and rounded red wine that blends Cabernet Sauvignon, Cabernet Franc, Merlot, and Petit Verdot.

Fourth course: Cinnamon plum tea panna cotta with amarena cherries, paired with a Muscat from California. This wine serves as the perfect accompaniment to the thick panna cotta and rich, syrupy cherries.

After the menu has been created, I will show the servers how the restaurant should be set for this event. There should be a different glass for each wine, and the table decorum should be elegant but simple. We don't want to overwhelm our guests with gaudy decorations; the food and wine will speak for itself.

4:00 P.M.–10:00 P.M. (closing manager)   Manage the dinner rush. In addition to the party of 30, there will be plenty of other guests in the restaurant for dinner this evening who will expect to receive a wonderful dining experience. The manager must balance all activity to ensure a smooth and successful operation. This is the challenge in managing food and beverage operations, but it is also where the excitement lies.

10:00 P.M.–12:00 A.M.   Once the dinner rush is over, it's time to conduct a walk through and make sure the space is properly set for the following morning, then finish closing paperwork and call it a day. Although one manager does not typically stick around from sunrise until midnight, it has been known to happen on occasion. This is an industry that requires sacrifice of your time, and sometimes your patience. Describing a day in the life of a food and beverage manager is somewhat challenging, because each day is so different—and that's what I love about it.

Catering Services Manager

The **catering services manager (CSM)** has the enormous responsibility of delivering higher-than-expected service levels to guests. The CSM is in charge of the function from the time the client is introduced to the CSM by the director of catering or catering manager. This job is very demanding because several functions always occur simultaneously. Timing and logistics are crucial to the success of the operation. Frequently, there are only a few minutes between the end of a day meeting and the beginning of the reception for a dinner dance.

The CSM must be liked and respected by guests and at the same time be a superb organizer and supervisor. This calls for a person of outstanding character and leadership—management skills that are essential for success. The CSM has several important duties and responsibilities, including the following:

- Directing the service of all functions
- Supervising the catering housepersons in setting up the room
- Scheduling the banquet captains and approving the staffing levels for all events
- Cooperating with the banquet chef to check menus and service arrangements
- Checking that the client is satisfied with the room setup, food, beverages, and service
- Checking last-minute details
- Making out client bills immediately after the function
- Adhering to all hotel policies and procedures that pertain to the catering department, including responsible alcoholic beverage service and adherence to fire code regulations
- Calculating and distributing the gratuity and service charges for the service personnel
- Coordinating the special requirements with the DOC and catering coordinator

▶ Check Your Knowledge

1. What is the difference between banquets and catering?
2. What does SMERF stand for?
3. Where do the director of catering and the catering sales manager obtain their information?
4. What are the various styles used when setting up a meeting room? Give examples of when each style might be used.

Room Service/In-Room Dining

The term **room service** has for some time referred to all service to hotel guest rooms. Recently, some hotels have changed the name of room service to *in-room dining* to present the service as more upscale. The intention is to bring the dining experience to the room with quality food and beverages but also by providing *quality service.*

A survey of members of the American Hotel & Lodging Association showed that 56 percent of all properties offer room service and that 75 percent of airport properties provide room service. Generally, the larger the hotel and the higher the room rate, the more likely it is that a hotel will offer room service.

Economy and several midpriced hotels avoid the costs of operating room service by having vending machines on each floor and food items such as pizza or Chinese food delivered by local restaurants. Conversely, some hotels prepare menus and lower price structures that do not identify the hotel as the provider of the food. As a result, the guests may have the impression that they are ordering from an "outside" operation when they are in fact ordering from room service.

The level of service and menu prices will vary from hotel to hotel. The Hilton La Jolla Torrey Pines in California has butler service for all guest rooms without additional charge.

A few years ago, room service was thought of as a necessary evil, something that guests expected, but which did not produce profit for the hotel. Financial pressures have forced food and beverage directors to have this department also contribute to the bottom line. The room service manager has a difficult challenge running this department, which is generally in operation between 16 and 24 hours a day. Tremendous effectiveness is required to make this department profitable. Nevertheless, it can be done. Some of the challenges in operating room service are as follows:

- Delivering orders on time—this is especially important for breakfast, which is by far the most popular room service meal

- Making room service a profitable food and beverage department

- Avoiding complaints of excessive charges for room service orders

There are many other challenges in room service operation. One is forecasting demand. Room service managers analyze the front-desk forecast, which gives details of the house count and guest mix—convention, group, and others for the next two weeks. The food and beverage forecast will indicate the number of covers expected for breakfast, lunch, and dinner. The convention résumés will show where the convention delegates are having their various meals. For example, the number of in-house delegates attending a convention breakfast can substantially reduce the number of room service breakfast orders.

Experience enables the manager to check if a large number of guests are from different time zones, such as the West or East Coasts or overseas. These guests have a tendency to get up either much earlier or much later than the average guest. This could throw room service demands off balance. Demand also fluctuates between weekdays and weekends; for example, city hotels may cater to business travelers, who tend to require service at about the same time. However, on weekends, city hotels may attract families, who will order room service at various times.

To avoid problems with late delivery of orders, a growing number of hotels have dedicated elevators to be used only by room service during peak periods. At some hotels, rapid action teams (RATs) are deployed. These are designated food and beverage managers and assistants who can be called on when room service orders are heavy.

Westin Hotels recently introduced Service Express, an innovation that allows a customer to address all needs (room service, housekeeping, laundry, and other services) with a single call. In addition, new properties are designed with the room service kitchen adjacent to the main kitchen so that a greater variety of items can be offered.

Meeting the challenge of speedy and accurate communication is imperative to a successful room service operation. This begins with timely scheduling and ends with happy guests. In between is a constant flow of information that is communicated by the guest, the order taker, the cook, and the server.

Another challenge is to have well-trained and competent employees in the room service department. From the tone of voice of the order taker and the courteous manner with which the order is taken to the panache of the server for the VIP dinners, training makes the difference between ordinary service and outstanding service. With training, which includes menu tasting with wine and suggestive selling, an order taker becomes a room service salesperson. This person is now able to suggest cocktails or wine to complement the entree and can entice the guest with tempting desserts. The objective of this is to increase the average guest check. Training also helps the setup and service personnel hone their skills to enable them to become productive employees who are proud of their work.

HOW TO CREATE A NEW SET OF SERVICE STANDARDS

Courtesy of **James McManemon**, M.S., University of South Florida Sarasota–Manatee

Troy Williams, a food and beverage operations consultant, shared his experience consulting for a large hospital that wanted its food and beverage operations to run more like a hotel room service department. After inspecting the hospital's existing food and beverage operation through several observation periods, Troy determined that a set of service standards were warranted. Two particular areas of the hospital's operation were problematic, both of which would be specific concerns addressed by any high-quality hotel room service department:

(continued)

HOW TO CREATE A NEW SET OF SERVICE STANDARDS
(Continued)

- Food tray presentation
- Food service attendant's approach when entering a patient's room, including appearance, delivery of food, and interaction with patient, as well as departure

The new set of service standards were created based on the ideal service delivery common in many high quality hotels and adapted to the hospital setting as follows:

Approach

- **Professional Appearance**: Make sure you are in proper uniform and your name badge is facing front.
- **Ensure**: Check the food tray to ensure all items and condiments are included, drinks are standing upright, and the tray is attractively presented.
- **Knock**: Always knock before entering.
- **Sanitize**: Always wash hands or use hand sanitizer upon entering a room.

Interaction

- **Posture**: Stand upright, not leaning, and make direct eye contact with the patient.
- **Positive Attitude**: Greet every guest with a smile and provide an authentic and friendly interaction, using the patient's name in the process.
- **Setup**: Make sure the tray is properly set for dining on the patient's bedside table, napkins and cutlery are placed in an orderly fashion, offer to unwrap or open drinks for patients.

Familiarity

- **Identification**: "Good (morning/afternoon/evening), (*patient's name*). I am (*your name*) from Food and Nutrition Services. I have your meal for you." If you cannot pronounce their last name, ask, "Can you tell me your last name?"
- **Description**: Offer a brief description of all items on the tray to ensure that the order is accurate.

Personalization

- **Quality Check**: After you have given a brief description of the meal, ask, "Does everything look fine?" If the patient asks you to assist, please do.
- **Offer Additional Assistance**: Ask if you can assist the patient with any additional needs.
- **Closure**: Use the phrase, "Enjoy your meal, (*Mr./Mrs. patient's name*)."

Sustainable Food and Beverage

Practicing sustainable food and beverage operations can and does lead to a better bottom line. When operators save water and electricity, recycle, and purchase local produce, they help lessen the footprint of the operation.

Guests are increasingly aware of the importance of sustainable operations of a food and beverage facility. They are pleased to see the greening of food and beverage operations and the use of local natural products, which helps reduce the cost of transportation and adds local flavor.

Michelle Leroux, director of sales and marketing at the Delta Chelsea Hotel in Toronto, has noticed a shift in the booking inquiries: "It isn't so much that having a 'green' or 'sustainable' meeting package sells additional pieces of business—it is more along the line that certain groups will not book at your hotel if you can't demonstrate knowledge and experience with sustainable meetings."[2]

According to Brita Moosmann, a consultant,[3] the best way to start the process of making food and beverage more sustainable and profitable is to conduct a comprehensive audit or evaluation of your food and beverage operation in order to provide a baseline in terms of energy efficiency and carbon footprint; they should be part of an overriding strategy that will provide an in-depth analysis of the organization's sustainable position. This evaluation also should measure the impact of the various elements on the organization's stakeholders and have a total quality approach regarding customer satisfaction. It is also advisable to obtain feedback to understand what is important to the local community.

Trends in Lodging Food and Beverage

- Hotels are using branded restaurants instead of operating their own restaurants.

- Hotels are opting not to offer food and beverage outlets. These are usually smaller to midsized properties that may have restaurants on the same lot or nearby.

- Restaurants and beverage outlets are being made more casual.

- Restaurants are being developed or remodeled with a theme. For example, one major hotel chain has adopted a northern Italian theme in all its restaurants.

- Menus are being standardized for all hotel restaurants in a chain.

- Many hotels are converting one of the beverage outlets into a sports-themed bar.

- Technology is being used to enhance guest services and control costs in all areas of a hotel, including guest ordering and payment, food production, refrigeration, marketing, management control, and communication.

- More low-fat and low-carb items are being added to menus:

  - Healthier menu items with less salt and sugar.

  - Hotel restaurants are offering more locally sourced produce and an occasional herb garden.

CASE STUDY

Ensuring Guest Satisfaction

The Sunnyvale Hotel is operated by a major hotel management corporation. To ensure guest satisfaction, 300 survey forms, each containing 65 questions, are mailed to guests each month. Usually, about 70 of the forms are returned. The hotel company categorizes the guest satisfaction scores obtained into colored zones, with green being the best, then clear and yellow, and red being the worst. Scores can be compared with those of equivalent hotels.

The most recent survey indicated a significant decline for the Sea Grill Restaurant, with scores in the red zone. Guests' concerns were in the following areas: hostess attentiveness, spread of service, and quality of food.

On investigation, the director of food and beverage also realized that the name of the restaurant, Sea Grill, was not appropriate for the type of restaurant being operated. When asked, some guests commented "it's a bit odd to eat breakfast in a fish place."

Discussion Question

1. What would you do, as director of food and beverage, to get the guest satisfaction scores back into the clear or green zones?

CASE STUDY

Friday Evening at the Grand Hotel's Casual Restaurant

Karla Gomez is the supervisor at the Grand Hotel's casual restaurant. Karla's responsibilities include overseeing five servers and two bussers, seating guests, and taking reservations. One Friday evening, the restaurant was very busy—all 20 tables were occupied, there was a substantial wait list, and there were people on standby. The service bar was almost full of guests, and most of the seated guests in the dining area had finished their entrées or were just beginning their desserts. They were not leaving, however, in part because of cold, rainy weather outside. The guests did not seem to be in a rush to leave the restaurant, but several of the guests waiting for tables were complaining about the long wait.

Discussion Question

1. What can Karla do to solve the problem?

Summary

1. The food and beverage department division is led by the director of food and beverage, who is responsible for the efficient operation of kitchen, catering, restaurants, bars, and room service; in addition, the director has to keep up with trends and preplan for special events.

2. A hotel kitchen is the responsibility of the executive chef, who is in charge of the quality and quantity of food, organization of the kitchen and his or her sous chefs, administrative duties, and careful calculation of financial results.

3. A hotel usually has a formal and a casual restaurant, which are either directly connected to the hotel or operated separately.

4. Bars are an important revenue source for a hotel, but they must adhere to strict guidelines to be profitable. Commensurate with its size, a hotel might have several kinds of bars, such as a lobby bar, a restaurant bar, a minibar, or even a night club.

5. The chief steward has the often unrewarded job of cleaning the kitchen, cutlery, plates, glasses, and backstage of the hotel and is in charge of pest control and inventory.

6. Catering is subdivided into on-premise and off-premise occasions, which may include meetings, conventions, dinners, luncheons, and weddings. According to the occasion, the type of service and room setup may vary. Catering involves careful planning and the interaction and cooperation of many people.

7. Room service offers the convenience of dining in the room, with quality food and beverage service, at a price acceptable to both the guest and the hotel.

Key Words and Concepts

banquet
banquet event order (BEO)
brigade
capture rate
catering
catering coordinator
catering event order (CEO)
catering services manager (CSM)
chef tournant
chief steward
classroom-style seating

contribution margin
dinner-style room seating
director of catering (DOC)
director of food and beverage
executive chef
food cost percentage
food sales percentage
guaranteed-number policy
horseshoe-style room seating
kitchen manager
labor cost percentage
perpetual inventory

pilferage
pour/cost percentage
responsible alcoholic beverage service
restaurant manager
room service
shopper
sous chef
station chef
theater-style room seating

Review Questions

1. Briefly describe the challenges a food and beverage director faces on a daily basis.

2. List the measures used to determine the food and beverage department's profit and loss.

3. Explain the problems a hotel faces in making the following departments profitable: restaurants, bars, and room service.

4. Explain the importance of the catering department for a hotel and list the responsibilities of a catering sales manager (CSM).

Internet Exercises

1. Organization: **Foodservice.com**
   Summary: Foodservice.com is a Web site that focuses on the foodservice industry. It has links to employment, industry resources, foodservice, technology innovations, and much more.
   (a) Click the "Forums and Chat" icon. Go to the "Chef and Cooks Corner," and look at some of the latest posts. Bring your favorite one to the table (discuss in class).
   (b) Look at the most current articles on the food safety forum. What are the major concerns being addressed?

2. Organization: **National Restaurant Association**
   Summary: The National Restaurant Association is an organization devoted to representing, educating, and promoting the restaurant/hospitality industry.
   (a) Look under the "Education & Networking" tab. What does it mean to be "FMP Certified," and what are the eligibility requirements?
   (b) What are some of the upcoming events and what do they have to offer?

Apply Your Knowledge

1. If a casual dining restaurant in a four-star hotel forecasts 100 covers, how many servers, bussers, hosts, and assistant managers would you schedule on that particular day? Calculate the labor cost of these associates for that day if the manager(s) work from 1:00 P.M. to 11:00 P.M., the server(s) work from 4:00 P.M. to 11:00 P.M., the busser(s) work from 4:30 P.M. to 11:30 P.M., and the host(s) works from 4:00 P.M. to 11:00 P.M.

   Use minimum wage of $5.75 for calculations. Use the rate of $12 per hour for the assistant manager(s) and $6.50 for hosts.

2. Kitchen labor costs are an important ratio used to determine the efficiency of the food and beverage department. The labor cost for a banquet meal is $126.45 and the revenue for the banquet is $505.80. What is the labor cost percentage?

Suggested Activities

1. Contact a bar manager in your area. Discuss with him or her how to monitor pilferage and overpouring. Ask what the expected and actual pouring cost percentages are and how the manager deals with any variances.

2. Visit a hotel restaurant in your area. Make a note of how busy the establishment is. Does it seem to be staffed with the appropriate number of employees? Are guests being served in a timely manner? Think about why this specific restaurant may be overly crowded or overly vacant. What could or should be done differently? What seems to be working well?

Endnotes

1. Carlson. Our Company. http://www.carlson.com/our-company/index.do (accessed May 22, 2015).
2. Brita Moosmann, *Sustainable F&B Operations Can Create Valuable Profit Partner*, http://hotelnewsnow.com/, search for "Sustainable F&B Operations Can Create Valuable Profit Partner" to view this article (accessed March 9, 2015).
3. Ibid.

PART 2

Beverages, Restaurants, and Managed Services

CHAPTER 5

Beverages

This chapter offers an overview of alcoholic and nonalcoholic beverages in the hospitality industry. Be sure that you realize the utmost importance of responsible beverage consumption and service. Arrange for a designated driver if you intend to have a drink. If you do drink alcoholic beverages, then stay with the same drink—don't mix them. The two different types are grape (wine) and grain (beer and spirits). That's when trouble really begins and hangovers are bad. Remember that moderation is the key to enjoying beverages, whether at a get-together with friends at a local restaurant or on a getaway for spring break. Examine the tragic alcohol-related auto and other accidents that too many people are involved in each year. Enjoy, but do not overindulge.

Serving beverages is traditional throughout the world. According to his or her culture, a person might welcome a visitor with coffee or tea—or bourbon. Beverages are generally categorized into two main groups: alcoholic and nonalcoholic. **Alcoholic beverages** *are further categorized as wines, beer, and spirits. Figure 5–1 shows these three categories.*

LEARNING OBJECTIVE 1
List and describe the main grape varieties.

Wines

Wine is the fermented juice of freshly gathered ripe grapes. Wine may also be made from other sugar-containing fruits, such as blackberries, cherries, or elderberries. In this chapter, however, we will confine our discussion to wine made from grapes. Wine may be classified first by color: red, white, or pink (rose). Wines are further classified as light beverage wines, still wines, sparkling wines, dessert and fortified wines, and aromatic wines.

Light Beverage Wines

White, red, or rose table wines are "still" light beverage wines; such still table wines may come from a variety of growing regions around the world. In the United States, the premium wines are named after the grape varietal, such as chardonnay, cabernet sauvignon, and merlot. In Europe, wines were traditionally named for their region, such as Pouilly-Fuissé and Chablis, two regions in France; however, some European wine producers are now naming their wines after the grape varietal.

Wine	Beer	Spirits
Still	Top fermenting	Grapes/fruit
Natural	Lager	Grains
Fortified	Bottom fermenting	Cactus
Aromatic	Ale	Sugar cane/molasses
Sparkling	Stout	
	Lager	
	Pilsner	
	Porter	

Figure 5–1 • Alcoholic Beverages.

Sparkling Wines

Champagne, sparkling white wine, and sparkling rose wine are called **sparkling wines**. Sparkling wines contain carbon dioxide, which causes them to bubble, like any carbonated beverage. The carbon dioxide may be either naturally produced or mechanically infused into the wine. The best-known sparkling wine is Champagne, which has become synonymous with celebrations and happiness.

Champagne became the drink of fashion in France and England in the seventeenth century. The wine owed its unique sparkling quality to a secondary **fermentation**—originally unintentional—occurring in the bottle itself. This process became known as *Méthode Champenoise*.

The Benedictine monk Dom Perignon (1638–1715) was the cellar master for the Abbaye Hautvillers and an exceptional wine connoisseur. He was the first to experiment with blending different wines to achieve the so-called *cuvée* (a method of pressing grapes to extract the finest juice), denoting the basis of Champagne production. He also revolutionized wine by retaining the resulting carbon dioxide in the bottles. Dom Perignon's methods were refined throughout the centuries and led to the modern method used in champagne production.

Champagne may, by law, only come from the Champagne region of France. The term Champagne is safeguarded by the European law, Protected Designation of Origin (PDO), for the purpose of labeling wine. Sparkling wines from other countries have *Méthode Champenoise* written on their labels to designate that a similar method was used to make that particular sparkling wine. Figure 5–2 explains how to handle and serve champagne. It is strongly recommended to avoid mixing drinking wine and spirits at the same time or within a few hours because it may seriously affect you with a terrible hangover. The same goes for beer and wine. As the saying goes, beer before wine is ok but beer after wine, look out!

Remember not to point the cork from a bottle of champagne at anyone when opening the bottle; point it at the ceiling. In fact, a napkin should be placed over the cork, which is then held there while the bottle is gently twisted open. Champagne is served chilled in fluted glasses, which help the bouquet and effervescence last longer.

▶ Check Your Knowledge

1. Why is champagne served in fluted glasses?

2. How are alcoholic beverages categorized?

3. Why should you avoid mixing grape (wine) and grain (spirits) drinks?

4. Where should you point the cork of a champagne bottle when opening it?

Champagne should be stored horizontally at a temperature between 50 and 55 degrees Fahrenheit. However, it should be served at a temperature between 43 and 47 degrees Fahrenheit. This is best achieved by placing the bottle in an ice bucket.

When serving champagne, there are some recommended steps to take to achieve the best results, as listed below.

1. If the bottle is presented in a champagne cooler, it should be placed upright in the cooler, with fine ice tightly packed around the bottle.
2. The bottle should be wrapped in a cloth napkin. Remove the foil or metal capsule to a point just below the wire, which holds the cork securely.
3. Hold the bottle firmly in one hand at a 45-degree angle. Unwind and remove the wiring. With a clean napkin, wipe the neck of the bottle and around the cork.
4. With the other hand, grasp the cork so that it will not fly out. Twist the bottle and ease the cork out.
5. When the cork is out, retain the bottle at an angle for about five seconds. The gas will rush out and carry with it some of the champagne if the bottle is held upright.
6. Champagne should be served in two motions: pour until the froth almost reaches the brim of the glass. Stop and wait for the foam to subside. Then finish filling the glass to about three-quarters full.

Figure 5–2 • Handling and Serving Champagne.

Fortified Wines

Sherries, ports, Madeira, and Marsala are **fortified wines**, meaning that they have had brandy or wine alcohol added to them. The brandy or wine alcohol imparts a unique taste and increases the alcohol content to about 20 percent. Most fortified wines are sweeter than regular wines. Each of the groups of fortified wines has several subgroups with myriad tastes and aromas.

Aromatic Wines

Aromatized wines are fortified and flavored with herbs, roots, flowers, and barks. These wines may be sweet or dry. Aromatic wines are also known as aperitifs, which generally are consumed before meals as digestive stimulants. Among the better-known brands of aperitif wines are Dubonnet Red (sweet), Dubonnet White (dry), vermouth red (sweet), vermouth white (dry), Byrrh (sweet), Lillet (sweet), Punt e Mes (dry), St. Raphael Red (sweet), and St. Raphael White (dry).

The History of Wine

Wine has been produced for centuries. The ancient Egyptians and Babylonians recorded using the fermentation process. The very first records of winemaking date back about 7,000 years. The Greeks received the vine from the Egyptians, and later the Romans contributed to the popularization of wine in Europe by planting vines in the territories they conquered.

The wine produced during these times was not the cabernet or chardonnay of today. The wines of the past were drunk when they were young and likely to be highly acidic and crude. To help offset these deficiencies, people added

Sherry can be dry (fino), medium, or sweet. Pictured here are bottles of dry sherry with a glass. The lighter the color, the drier the sherry.

different spices and honey, which made the wine at least palatable. To this day, some Greek and German wines have added flavoring.

Good winemaking is dependent on the quality of the grape variety, type of soil, climate, preparation of vineyards, and the method of winemaking. Thousands of grape varietals exist, thriving in a variety of soil and climate conditions. Different plants thrive on clay, chalky, gravelly, or sandy soil. The most important wine-making grape varietal is the *Vitis vinifera*, which yields cabernet sauvignon, gamay, pinot noir, pinot chardonnay, and Riesling.

Port wines are generally red, fortified, and sweet. Vintage port is the most prized by port lovers. Port is typically served with cheese and biscuits at the end of a meal.

Matching Wine with Food

The combination of food and wine is one of life's great pleasures. We eat every day, so a gourmet will seek out not only exotic foods and **vintage** wines but also simple food that is well prepared and accompanied by an unpretentious, yet quality, wine.

LEARNING OBJECTIVE 2
Suggest appropriate pairings of wine with food.

Over the years, traditions have developed a how-to approach to the marrying of wines and food. Generally, the following traditions apply:

- White wine is best served with white meat (chicken, pork, or veal), shellfish, and fish.
- Red wine is best served with red meat (beef, lamb, duck, or game).
- The heavier the food, the heavier and more robust the wine should be.
- Champagne can be served throughout the meal.
- Port and red wine go well with cheese.
- Dessert wines best complement desserts and fresh fruits that are not highly acidic.
- When a dish is cooked with wine, it is best served with that wine.
- Regional food is best complemented by wines of the region.
- Wine experts suggest that wine should not accompany salads with vinegar dressings; the taste will clash or be overpowering.
- Sweet wines should be served with foods that are less sweet.

White grapes make white wines; the main white grapes are chardonnay, sauvignon blanc, Riesling, pinot blanc, and gewürztraminer.

Figure 5–3 matches some of the better-known varietal wines with food.

Food and wine are described by texture and flavor. Textures are the qualities in food and wine that we feel in the mouth, such as softness, smoothness, roundness, richness, thickness, thinness, creaminess, chewiness, oiliness, harshness, silkiness, coarseness, and so on.

Red grapes make red wine; the main red grapes are cabernet sauvignon, merlot, merlot/cabernet sauvignon, pinot noir, and Shiraz.

Textures correspond to sensations of touch and temperature, which can be easy to identify—for example, hot, cold, rough, smooth, thick, or thin. Regarding the marrying of food and wine, light food with light wine is always a reliable combination. Rich food with rich wine can be wonderful as long as the match is not too rich. For example, full-bodied red wines like a Cabernet Sauvignon or Rosso Piceno go well with chocolate or pepperoni pizza. However, very sweet foods like pralines or very spicy foods like Chinese mapo tofu do not pair well. The two most important qualities to consider when choosing the appropriate wine are richness and lightness.

Flavors are food and wine elements perceived by the olfactory nerve as fruity, minty, herbal, nutty, cheesy, smoky, flowery, earthy, and so on. A person often determines flavors by using the nose as well as the tongue. The combination of texture and flavor is what makes food and wine a pleasure to enjoy; a good match between the food and wine can make occasions even more memorable. Figure 5–4 suggests the steps to be taken in **wine tasting**.

▶ Check Your Knowledge

1. What are the names of the main white and red grape varieties used to make wine?
2. Cabernet sauvignon is best served with _____.
3. Chardonnay is best served with _____.
4. Why does a wine taster swirl the wine around the glass before tasting it?
5. What is the general guideline for serving wine with food?

Sniffing the bouquet of the wine.

Major Wine-Growing Regions

Europe

Germany, Italy, Spain, Portugal, and France are the main European wine-producing countries. Germany is noted for the outstanding Riesling wines from the Rhine and Moselle river valleys. Italy produces the world-famous Chianti. Spain makes good wine but is best known for making sherry. Portugal also makes good wine but is better known for its port.

France is the most notable of the European countries, producing not only the finest wines but also champagne and cognac. The two most famous wine-producing areas in France are the Bordeaux and Burgundy regions. The vineyards, villages, and towns are steeped in the history of centuries devoted to the production of the finest quality wines. They represent some of the most beautiful countryside in Europe and are well worth visiting.

FOCUS ON WINES

Wine and Food Pairing

Jay R. Schrock, Professor Emeritus, University of South Florida

The combination of food and wine is as old as the making of wine. It is truly one of the great pleasures in life. Food and wine are natural accompaniments and enhance the flavor and enjoyment of each other. The flavor of a wine consumed by itself will taste different than when it is imbibed with food. Much of the wine taste experience is actually perceived from the nose; hence, you will hear that "the wine has a good nose." In fact, wine experts, called *sommeliers*, say that 80 percent of the taste—of nuts, oak, fruits, herbs, spices, and the other words used to describe wine—comes via one's nose. To improve the smell and taste of wine, we often decant it and serve it in stemware with large openings. The wine taster often swirls the wine to increase the aromas entering the nose.

Over the years, traditions have developed as to how to approach **wine and food pairing**. Remember, these are traditions and that food and wine pairing is a highly subjective and an inexact process. The traditional rules basically state that red wines are served with red meat and white wines are served with fish and poultry. These rules are still generally valid, but they don't take into consideration the complexity of today's multiethnic fusion cuisines, with their wide range of flavors and the corresponding wide range of wines from around the world that are now readily available to everyone. Today, you are more likely to hear of food and wine pairing suggestions rather than the hard-and-fast traditional rules of the past.

A new tradition has begun:

1. When serving more than one wine at a meal, it's best to serve lighter wines before full-bodied ones. The drier wines should be served before sweeter wines. The exception is if a sweet-flavored food is served early in the meal. Serve wines with lower alcohol content before wines with higher alcohol content.

2. Pair light-bodied wines with lighter food and fuller-bodied wines with heaver, richer, or more flavorful foods. This is a restatement of the old red wine with red meat and white wine with fish and chicken suggestion.

3. Match flavors. A pinot noir goes well with duck, prosciutto, and mushrooms, while a gewürztraminer is a well-suited accompaniment for ham, sausage, curry, and Thai and Indian food. Beware of pairing a wine with food that is sweeter than the wine. Most people agree that chocolate is the one exception. It seems to go with almost anything.

4. Delicately flavored foods that are poached or steamed should be paired with delicate wines.

5. Match regional wines with regional foods; they have been developed together and have a natural affinity for each other. The red sauces of Tuscany and the Chianti wines of the Tuscany region in Italy are an unbeatable combination.

6. Soft cheese such as Camembert and Brie pair well with a variety of red wine, including cabernet sauvignon, zinfandel, and red burgundy. Cabernet sauvignon also goes well with sharp, aged cheddar cheese. Pungent and intensely flavored cheeses, such as a blue cheese, are better with the sweeter eiswein (or icewine) or late-harvest dessert wines. Sheep and goat cheeses pair well with dry white wines, while red wine with fruit flavors goes best with milder cheeses.

Many of your restaurant guests may want to have wine with their dinner but are intimidated by the process or are afraid of the price. Set your guests' minds at ease when they are ordering wine. The know-it-all attitude will not work here; you are not trying to sell a used car or life insurance. You are trying to improve your guests' experience, the check average, and your tip. Make an honest suggestion, and try to explain the differences in wine choices. If guests are pondering two wines by the glass, do not just suggest the more expensive one; bring two glasses and let them taste. They will decide for themselves.

WINE	SMELL AND TASTE ASSOCIATED WITH WINE	FOOD PAIRING
Gewürztraminer (Alsace in France)	grapefruit, apple, nectarine, peach, nutmeg, clove, cinnamon	Thai, Indian, Tex-Mex, Szechuan, ham, sausage, curry, garlic
Chardonnay Chablis (Burgundy in France)	citrus fruit, apple, pear, pineapple, other tropical fruit	pork, salmon, chicken, pheasant, rabbit
Sauvignon Blanc Sancerre (Loire in France)	citrus fruit, gooseberry, bell pepper, black pepper, green olives, herbs	goat cheese, oysters, fish, chicken, pork, garlic
Pinot Blanc	citrus fruit, apple, pear, melon	shrimp, shellfish, fish, chicken
Pinot Noir Côte d' Or (Burgundy in France)	strawberry, cherry, raspberry, clove, mint, vanilla, cinnamon	duck, chicken, turkey, mushrooms, grilled meats, fish and vegetables, pork
Merlot Gamay (Beaujolais in France)	cherry, raspberry, plum, pepper, herbs, mint	beef, lamb, duck, barbecued meats, pork ribs
Cabernet Sauvignon Médoc (Bordeaux in France)	cherry, plum, pepper, bell pepper, herbs, mint, tea, chocolate	beef; lamb; braised, barbecued and grilled meats; aged cheddar; chocolate
Late harvest white wines	citrus fruit, apple, pear, apricot, peach, mango, honey	custard, vanilla, ginger, carrot cake, cheesecake, cream puffs, apricot cobbler

Figure 5–3 • Matching Wine with Food.
(Courtesy of Jay R. Schrock.)

Many restaurants have introduced wine tastings as special marketing events to promote the restaurant itself, or a particular type or label of wine. Wine tasting is more than just a process—it is an artful ritual. Wine offers a threefold sensory appeal: color, aroma, and taste. Wine tasting, thus, consists of three essential steps.

1. Hold the glass to the light. The color of the wine gives the first indication of the wine's body. The deeper the color, the fuller the wine will be. Generally, wines should be clear and brilliant.
2. Smell the wine. Hold the glass between the middle and the ring finger in a "cup-like" fashion and gently roll the glass. This will bring the aroma and the bouquet of the wine to the edge of the glass. The bouquet should be pleasant. This will tell much about what the taste will be.
3. Finally, taste the wine by rolling the wine around the mouth and by sucking in a little air—this helps release the complexities of the flavors.

Figure 5–4 • Wine Tasting.

In France, wine is named after the village in which the wine is produced. In recent years, the name of the grape varietal has also been used. The name of the wine grower is also important; because the quality may vary, reputation understandably is very important. A vineyard might also include a chateau in which the wine is made.

Within the Bordeaux region, wine growing is divided into five major districts: Médoc, Graves, Saint-Émilion, Pomerol, and Sauternes. The wine from each district has its own characteristics.

There are several other well-known wine-producing regions of France, such as the Loire Valley, Alsace, and Côtes du Rhône. French people regard wine as an important part of their culture and heritage.

United States and Canada

In California, viticulture began in 1769 when Junípero Serra, a Spanish friar, began to produce wine for the missions he started. At one time, the French considered California wines to be inferior. However, California is blessed with a near-perfect climate and excellent vine-growing soil. In the United States, the name of the grape varietal is used to name the wine, not the village or chateau as used by the French. The better-known varietal white wines in the United States are chardonnay, sauvignon blanc, riesling, and chenin blanc; varietal red wines are cabernet sauvignon, pinot noir, merlot, Syrah, and zinfandel.

California viticulture areas are generally divided into the following three regions:

1. North and central coastal region
2. Great central valley region
3. Southern California region

The north and central coastal region produces the best wines in California. A high degree of use of mechanical methods allows for efficient, large-scale production of quality wines. The two best-known areas within this region are the Napa and Sonoma Valleys. The wines of the Napa and Sonoma Valleys resemble those of Bordeaux and Burgundy. In recent years, the wines from the Napa and Sonoma Valleys have rivaled and even exceeded the French and other European wines. The chardonnays and cabernets are particularly outstanding.

The Napa and Sonoma Valleys are the symbols as well as the centers of the top-quality wine industry in California.

Several other states and Canadian provinces provide quality wines. New York, Oregon, and Washington are the other major U.S. wine-producing states. In Canada, the best wineries are in British Columbia's Okanagan Valley and southern Ontario's Niagara peninsula. Both of these regions produce excellent wines.

Australia

Australia has been producing wines for about 150 years, but it is only in the last half-century that these wines have achieved the prominence and recognition they rightly deserve. Australian winemakers traveled to Europe and California to perfect the winemaking craft. Unlike France, with many rigid laws controlling wine growth and production, Australian winemakers use high technology to produce excellent wines, many of which are blended to offer the best characteristics of each wine.

A Napa Valley vineyard.

Wine and Health

A glass of wine may be beneficial to health. This perspective was featured in the CBS news program *60 Minutes*, which focused on a phenomenon called the French paradox. The French eat 30 percent more fat than Americans do, smoke more, and exercise less, yet they suffer fewer heart attacks—about one-third as many as Americans. Ironically, the French drink more wine than people of any other nationality—about 75 liters per person a year. Research indicates that wine attacks platelets, which are the smallest of the blood cells that cause the blood to clot, preventing excess bleeding. However, platelets also cling to the rough, fatty deposits on arterial walls, clogging and finally blocking arteries and causing heart attacks. Wine's flushing effect removes platelets from the artery wall. After the *60 Minutes* program was broadcast, sales of wine, particularly red wine, in the United States increased dramatically.[3]

Sustainable Wine Production[4]

Environmentally and socially responsible grape growing and winemaking is not new, but what was once labeled a trend is now becoming an industry standard. Organic is a term given to environmentally friendly methods that use no chemicals or pesticides. Sustainability is defined as a holistic approach to growing and food production that respects the environment, the ecosystem, and even society.

The California Association of Wine Grape Growers has prepared a *Code of Sustainable Winegrowing Practices*; this is a 490-page voluntary self-assessment workbook covering everything from pest management to wine quality to water conservation to environmental stewardship. This tool allows growers and vintners to gauge how they are doing, and then to design and implement their own action plans.

A good example of sustainable winemaking is the Viansa Winery in California. It has long boasted a natural antipest team of bats, barn owls, and insectaries to keep its bug populations under control. The winery uses organic fungicide and has eliminated all herbicides.

LEARNING OBJECTIVE 3
Identify the various types of beer.

Beer

Beer is a brewed and fermented beverage made from malted barley and other starchy cereals and flavored with hops. *Beer* is a generic term for a variety of mash-based, yeast-fermented brewed malt beverages that have an alcohol content mostly between 3.8 and 8 percent.[5] The term **beer** includes the following:

- Lager, the beverage that is normally referred to as beer, is a clear, light-bodied, refreshing beer.
- Ale is fuller bodied and more bitter than lager.
- Stout is a dark ale with a sweet, strong, malt flavor.
- Pilsner is not really a beer. The term *pilsner* means that the beer is made in the style of the famous beer brewed in Pilsen, Czech Republic.

The Brewing Process

Beer is brewed from water, **malt**, **yeast**, and **hops**. The brewing process begins with water, an important ingredient in the making of beer. The mineral content and purity of the water largely determine the quality of the final product. Water accounts for 85–89 percent of the finished beer.

Next, grain is added in the form of malt, which is barley that has been ground to a coarse grit. The grain is germinated, producing an enzyme that converts starch into fermentable sugar.

The yeast is the fermenting agent. Breweries typically have their own cultured yeasts, which to a large extent determine the type and taste of the beer.

Mashing is the term for grinding the malt and screening out any bits of dirt. The malt then goes through a hopper into a mash tub, which is a large stainless steel or copper container. Here the water and grains are mixed and heated.

A brewer adds hops to the beer as it boils in the kettle of a microbrewery.

The liquid is now called **wort** and is filtered through a mash filter or lauter tub. This liquid then flows into a brewing kettle, where hops are added and the mixture is boiled for several hours. After the brewing operation, the hop wort is filtered through the hop separator or hop jack. The filtered liquid then is pumped through a wort cooler and into a fermenting vat where pure-culture yeast is added for fermentation.[6] The brew is aged for a few days prior to being barreled for draught beer or pasteurized for bottled or canned beer.

Today, marketing and distribution partnerships promote an even greater choice of beers for consumers. Among those available from Anheuser-Busch distributors are Löwenbräu and Beck's from Germany; Stella Artois and Hoegaarden from the Netherlands; Staropramen and Czechvar from the Czech Republic; Harbin from China; and Landshark from Florida. Other interesting beverages include Michelob ULTRA Dragon Fruit Peach, Michelob Ultra Fruit Pomegranate Raspberry, and Michelob Ultra Fruit Lime Cactus.

Organic and Craft Beers, Microbreweries, and Brewpubs

The U.S. Department of Agriculture (USDA) established the National Organic Program in 1997, opening the door for organic beer. The guidelines for organic beer are the same as for all organic foods: The ingredients must be grown without toxic and persistent pesticides or synthetic fertilizers and in soil that has been free from such chemicals for at least three years. No genetically modified ingredients can be used in the brewing process. Studies show that organic farming reduces erosion and ground water pollution and that it significantly reduces negative impacts on wildlife.[7]

The organic requirements lend themselves well to smaller breweries. An American craft brewery is a small, independent, and traditional brewery.[8]

Craft beer showcases the different areas of the country and their seemingly distinct styles of beer and craft beer scenes. You can get an India pale ale (IPA) from anywhere, but there's a reason people will refer to a super hoppy, dry IPA as a "west coast IPA." Also, a lot of craft breweries only distribute in a small- to medium-sized area.[9] As craft brewers have come of age, little did the world know that their full-flavored craft beers would generate such passion and excitement.

Today is a great time to be a beer lover, and as a nation, we now have more beer styles and beer brands to choose from than any other market in the world.[10] Traditionally, a brewer has either an all-malt flagship (the beer that represents the greatest volume sold among that brewer's brands) or has at least 50 percent of its volume represented by either all-malt beers or by beers that use adjuncts to enhance rather than lighten flavor.[11]

The Brewers Association describes a microbrewery as a brewery that produces a limited amount (less than 15,000 barrels) of beer a year. A brewpub brews and sells beer on the premises and may also be known as a microbrewery if 75 percent of the production is distributed beyond the premises.[12]

Sustainable Brewing

Breweries use a lot of resources yet have the potential to significantly reduce their environmental footprint. Here is how some brewers are reducing their footprint:[13]

- Efficient brewhouse: The brewery is as sustainable and efficient as possible, starting with the parts of the building that were reclaimed and recycled such as when the Full Sail brewery first opened in the old Diamond Fruit cannery in Oregon. Full Sail utilizes measures such as energy-efficient lighting and air compressors, and compresses the work week into four very productive days, which helps reduce water and energy consumption by 20 percent.

- Sustainable brew process: Pure water literally flows from the peaks that surround the brewery, so Full Sail takes care to conserve this precious resource. While average breweries consume six to eight gallons of water for every gallon of beer produced, Full Sail has reduced its consumption to a mere 3.45 gallons and operates its own on-site wastewater treatment facility. Local farms supply the other essential ingredients for award-winning brews: 85 percent of hops and 95 percent of barley come straight from Northwest farms.

- Reduce–Reuse–Recycle: Full Sail uses 100 percent recycled paperboard on all its packaging (and was one of the first in the industry to commit to long-term purchasing of recycled paper products). Everything from office paper to glass to stretch wrap to wooden pallets is recycled. Even dairy cows are beneficiaries of brewery waste: 4,160 tons of spent grain and 1,248 tons of spent yeast are sent back to farmers every year to use as feed for cows.

- Community-wide practices: Full Sail purchases 140 blocks of Pacific Power Blue Sky renewable energy per month. This practice results in the reduction of 168 tons of carbon dioxide emissions, the equivalent of planting 33,000 trees. Full Sail also supports over 300 events and charities each year, with a focus on those in Oregon. Employees at the company have inspired environmental change among other businesses in the Hood River area as well. Full Sail was a founding member of the Hood River Chamber of Commerce's "Green Smart" program, an initiative that helps businesses and organizations within the Hood River watershed increase their productivity and profitability by improving resource efficiency and by reducing waste and pollution.

As the push for sustainability gains momentum, one only needs to look down at the pint or mug he or she is holding to see how breweries are joining the growing green movement! Beer is the third most-consumed beverage in the world behind water and tea. Upon surveying a number of breweries and sustainable brewing documents, BlueMap Inc. has determined 10 green steps every brewery should consider.[14]

Utilize Biochar Processing to Reuse Spent Grains

Processing spent grains through pyrolysis (a process that burns grains to create biochar, a valuable soil amendment) is a carbon-negative process: it creates heat and syngas while sequestering carbon. By doing so, pyrolysis decreases a brewery's carbon footprint.

Implement Water Use Reduction Measures

Water is one of the largest inputs in brewing. A brewery can conserve water by reducing lost steam, increasing the efficiency of wort production, increasing the life of water in boiler systems, and altogether preventing waste.

Implement Variable-Speed Fans or Motors

Many brewery processes have variable loads that are more efficiently served by variable-speed motors, fans, and drives. Where applicable, an upgrade in a brewery's fans and motors can offer substantial savings and have favorable pay back periods. Savings are only observed if loads vary.

Ensure a Regular Maintenance Regime

A regular maintenance regimen is a great way to cut down on energy inefficiencies. Regularly scheduled maintenance allows breweries to catch problems sooner and address them before excess energy is wasted. Also, keeping a system tuned up means that motors and pumps run at optimum speeds, controls are set properly, and control systems are turned on.

Capture Methane at On-Site Water Treatment Facilities

For breweries that process wastewater on site, methane capture is a great way to regain value from a waste stream. Currently, closed systems and pond cover methane capture exist. These systems purify and burn methane onsite, which typically offsets the brewery's fuel costs while cutting costs.

whisky, the spirit must conform to the standards of the Scotch Whisky Act; only whisky made with this process can be called Scotch whisky. Some of the better-known quality-blended Scotch whiskies are Chivas Regal and Johnnie Walker Black, Gold, and Blue Labels.

A single malt Scotch whisky is the product of one specific distillery and has not been mixed with whisky from any other distilleries. Some whisky aficionados prefer a single malt Scotch, from which there are several brands to choose, for example, Laphroaig and Macallan, two of the better known single malts.

Irish Whiskey

Irish whiskey is spelled with an *e* and is produced from malted or unmalted barley, corn, rye, and other grains. The malt is not dried like it is in the production of Scotch whisky, which gives Irish whiskey a milder character, yet an excellent flavor. Two well-known Irish whiskies are Bushmills Black Bush and Jameson's 12 Year Old Special Reserve.

Bourbon Whisky

Liquor was introduced in America by the first settlers, who used it as a medicine. Bourbon has a peculiar history. In colonial times in New England, rum was the most popular distilled spirit. After the break with Britain, settlers of Scottish and Irish background predominated. They were mostly grain farmers and distillers, producing whisky for barter. When George Washington levied a tax on this whisky, the farmers moved south and continued their whisky production. However, the rye crop failed, so they decided to mix corn, particularly abundant in Kentucky, with the remaining rye. The result was delightful. This experiment occurred in Bourbon County—hence the name of the new product.

Bourbon whisky is produced mainly from corn; other grains are also used, but they are of secondary importance. The distillation processes are similar to those of other types of whisky. Charred barrels provide bourbon with its distinctive taste. It is curious to note that barrels can only be used once in the United States to age liquor. Aging, therefore, occurs in new barrels after each distillation process. Bourbon may be aged up to six years to improve its mellowness. Among the better-known bourbon whiskies are Jack Daniels, Maker's Mark, and George Dickel.

Canadian Whisky

Like bourbon, Canadian whisky is produced mainly from corn. It is characterized by a delicate flavor that nonetheless pleases the palate. Canadian whisky must be at least four years old before it can be bottled and marketed. It is distilled at 70–90 percent alcohol by volume. Among the better-known Canadian whiskies are Seagram's and Canadian Club.

White Spirits

Gin, rum, vodka, and tequila are the most common of the spirits that are called **white spirits**. Gin, first known as Geneva, is a neutral spirit made from juniper berries. Although gin originated in Holland, it was in London that the word

Geneva was shortened to *gin*, and almost anything was used to make it. Often gin was made in the bathtub in the morning and sold in hole-in-the-wall dram shops all over London at night. Obviously, the quality left a lot to be desired, but the poor drank it to the point of national disaster.[17] Gin also was widely produced in the United States during Prohibition. In fact, the habit of mixing something else with it led to the creation of the cocktail. Over the years, gin became the foundation of many popular cocktails (e.g., martini, gin and tonic, gin and juice, Tom Collins).

Rum can be light or dark in color. Light rum is distilled from the fermented juice of sugarcane, and dark rum is distilled from molasses. Rum comes mainly from the Caribbean islands of Barbados (Mount Gay), Puerto Rico (Bacardi), and Jamaica (Myers). Rums are mostly used in mixed frozen and specialty drinks such as rum and Coke, rum punches, daiquiris, and piña coladas.

Tequila is distilled from the *Agave tequilana* (a type of cactus), which is called *mezcal* in Mexico. Official Mexican regulations require that tequila be made in the area around the town of Tequila because the soil contains volcanic ash, which is especially suitable for growing the blue agave cactus. Tequila may be white, silver, or golden in color. The white is shipped unaged, silver is aged up to three years, and golden is aged in oak from two to four years. Tequila is mainly used in the popular margarita cocktail or in the tequila sunrise (made popular in a song by the Eagles rock group).

Vodka can be made from many sources, including barley, corn, wheat, rye, or potatoes. Because it lacks color, odor, and flavor, vodka generally is combined with juices or other mixers whose flavors predominate. To offer consumers more choices, vodka producers have popularized flavored vodkas with lemon, pepper, vanilla, raspberry, peach, pears, and mango, among others. Brand names of vodka producers are Absolut from Sweden, Stolichnaya (or Stoli for short) from Russia, Grey Goose from France, TRU Organic from the United Sates, and Van Gogh from the Netherlands.

A glass of Cognac.

Other Spirits

Brandy is distilled from wine in a fashion similar to that of other spirits. American brandy comes primarily from California, where it is made in column stills and aged in white-oak barrels for at least two years. The best-known American brandies are made by Christian Brothers and Ernest and Julio Gallo. Their brandies are smooth and fruity with a touch of sweetness. The best brandies are served as after-dinner drinks, and ordinary brandies are used in the well for mixed drinks.

Cognac is regarded by connoisseurs as the best brandy in the world. It is made only in the Cognac region of France, where the chalky soil and humid climate combine with special distillation techniques to produce the finest brandy. Only brandy from this region may be called cognac. Most cognac is aged in oak casks from two to four years or

A martini cocktail served in a martini glass.

more. Because cognacs are blends of brandies of various ages, no age is allowed on the label; instead, letters signify the relative age and quality.

Brandies labeled as *VSOP* must be aged at least four years. All others must be aged in wood at least five years. Five years, then, is the age of the youngest cognac in a blend; usually, several others of older age are added to lend taste, bouquet, and finesse. About 75 percent of the cognac shipped to Canada and the United States is produced by four companies: Courvoisier, Hennessy, Martell, and Rémy Martin.

Cocktails

The first cocktails originated in England during the Victorian era, but it wasn't until the 1920s and 1930s that cocktails became popular.

Cocktails are usually drinks made by mixing two or more ingredients (wines, liquors, fruit juices), resulting in a blend that is pleasant to the palate, with no single ingredient overpowering the others. Cocktails are mixed by stirring, shaking, or blending. The mixing technique is particularly important to achieve the perfect cocktail. Cocktails are commonly divided into two categories according to volume: short drinks (up to 3.5 ounces) and tall drinks (generally up to 8.5 ounces).

The secret of a good cocktail lies in several factors such as the following:

- The balance of the ingredients: No single ingredient should overpower the others.
- The quality of the ingredients: As a general rule, cocktails should be made from a maximum of three ingredients.
- The skill of the bartender: The bartender's experience, knowledge, and inspiration are key factors in making a perfect cocktail.

A good bartender should understand the effect and the "timing" of a cocktail. It is not a coincidence that many cocktails are categorized by when they are best served. There are aperitifs, digestifs, corpse-revivers, pick-me-ups, and so on. Cocktails can stimulate an appetite or provide the perfect conclusion to a fine meal.

▶ Check Your Knowledge

1. Describe the different types of beer.
2. Describe the various spirits.

Nonalcoholic Beverages

Nonalcoholic beverages are increasing in popularity. In the 1990s and 2000s, a radical shift has occurred from the free-love 1960s and the singles bars of the 1970s and early 1980s. People are, in general, more cautious about the consumption of alcohol. Lifestyles have become healthier, and organizations such as Mothers Against Drunk Driving (MADD) have raised the social conscience about responsible alcohol consumption. Overall consumption of alcohol has decreased in recent years, with spirits declining the most.

In recent years, several new beverages have been added to the nonalcoholic beverage list. From Goji juice to passion fruit green tea, the nonalcoholic beverage world has been innovative in creating flavored teas and coffees and an ever-increasing variety of juices to satisfy all our tastes. The rise in popularity of craft beverages has fashioned a heightened interest in craft soda production from independent beverage companies and craft beer producers to larger producers that distribute their products nationwide. Whether it's for the taste or for the trendiness, craft sodas, while not the newest thing to hit the market, are certainly one of the most exciting nonalcoholic beverages worth trying.

Nonalcoholic Beer

Guinness, Anheuser-Busch, and Miller, along with many other brewers, have developed beer products that have the same appearance as regular beer but that have a lower calorie content and approximately 95–99 percent of the alcohol removed, either after processing or after fermentation. The taste, therefore, is somewhat different from regular beer.

Coffee

Coffee is the drink of the present. People who used to frequent bars are now patronizing coffeehouses. The U.S. coffee market brings in $18 billion per year. It is also estimated that there are more than 24,000 coffee cafés nationwide.[18]

Coffee first came from Ethiopia and Mocha, which is in the Yemen Republic. Legends say that Kaldi, a young Abyssinian goatherd, accustomed to his sleepy goats, noticed that after chewing certain berries, the goats began to prance about excitedly. He tried the berries himself, forgot his troubles, lost his heavy heart, and became the happiest person in "happy Arabia." A monk from a nearby monastery surprised Kaldi in this state, decided to try the berries, too, and invited the brothers to join him. They all felt more alert that night during prayers![19]

In the Middle Ages, coffee found its way to Europe via Turkey, but not without some objections. In Italy, priests appealed to Pope Clement VIII to have the use of coffee forbidden among Christians. Satan, they said, had forbidden his followers, the infidel Moslems, the use of wine because it was used in the Holy Communion and had given them instead his "hellish black brew." Apparently, the pope liked the drink, for he blessed it on the spot, after which coffee quickly became the social beverage of Europe's middle and upper classes.[20]

The coffeehouses were nicknamed *penny universities*, where any topic could be discussed and learned for the price of a pot of coffee. The men of the period not only discussed business but actually conducted business. Banks, newspapers, and the Lloyd's of London Insurance Company began at Edward Lloyd's coffeehouse.

Coffeehouses were also popular in other areas of Europe. In Paris, Café Procope, which opened in 1689 and still operates today, has been the meeting place of many a famous artist and philosopher, including Rousseau and Voltaire (who are reputed to have drunk 40 cups of coffee a day).

The Dutch introduced coffee to the United States during the colonial period. Coffeehouses soon became the haunts of the revolutionary activists plotting against King George of England and his tea tax. John Adams and Paul Revere planned the Boston Tea Party and the fight for freedom at a coffeehouse. This helped establish coffee as the traditional democratic drink of Americans.

Brazil produces more than 30 percent of the world's coffee, most of which goes into canned and instant coffee. Coffee connoisseurs recommend beans by name, such as arabica and robusta beans. In Indonesia, coffee is named for the island on which it grows; the best is from Java and is rich and spicy with a full-bodied flavor. Yemen, the country in which coffee was discovered, names its best coffee for the port of Mocha. Its fragrant, creamy brew has a rich, almost chocolaty aftertaste. Coffee beans are frequently blended by the merchants who roast them; one of the best blends, mocha java, is the result of blending these two fine coffees.

Coffee may be roasted from light to dark according to preference. Light roasts are generally used in canned and institutional roasts, and medium is the all-purpose roast most people prefer. Medium beans are medium brown in color, and their surface is dry. Although this brew may have snappy, acidic qualities, its flavor tends to be flat. Full, high, or Viennese roast is the roast preferred by specialty stores, where balance is achieved between sweetness and sharpness. Dark roasts have a fancy, rich flavor, with espresso the darkest of all roasts. Its almost-black beans have shiny, oily surfaces. All the acidic qualities and specific coffee flavor are gone from espresso, but its pungent flavor is a favorite of espresso lovers.

Decaffeinating coffee removes the caffeine with either a solvent or water process. In contrast, many specialty coffees have things added. Among the better-known specialty coffees are café au lait or caffè latte. In these cases, milk is steamed until it becomes frothy and is poured into the cup together with the coffee. A cappuccino is made with espresso, hot milk, and milk foam, which may then be sprinkled with powdered chocolate and cinnamon.

Tea

Tea is a beverage made by steeping in boiling water the leaves of the tea plant, an evergreen shrub, or small tree, native to Asia. Tea is consumed as either a hot or cold beverage by approximately half of the world's population, yet it is second to coffee in commercial importance because most of the world's tea crop is consumed in the tea-growing regions. Tea leaves contain 1–3 percent caffeine. This means that weight for weight, tea leaves have more than twice as much caffeine as coffee beans. However, a cup of coffee generally has more caffeine than a cup of tea because one pound of

CORPORATE PROFILE

Starbucks Coffee Company

Operations

Starbucks Coffee Company (named after the first mate in Herman Melville's *Moby-Dick*) is the leading retailer, roaster, and brand of specialty coffee in North America. More than 7 million people visit Starbucks stores each week. In addition to its more than 18,000 retail locations, the company supplies fine dining, foodservice, travel, and hotel accounts with coffee and coffee-making equipment and operates a national mail-order division.

Locations and Alliances

Starbucks currently has more than 18,000 stores in 50 U.S. states and in 64 countries.[21] Starbucks has strategic alliances with United Airlines and is now the exclusive supplier of coffee on every United flight.

In addition, Specialty Sales and Marketing supplies Starbucks coffee to the health care, business and industry, college and university, and hotel and resort segments of the foodservice industry; to many fine restaurants throughout North America; and to companies such as Costco, Nordstrom, Starwood, Barnes and Noble, Hilton Hotels, Sodexho, ARAMARK, Compass, Wyndham, Borders, Radisson, Sysco, Safeway, Albertson's, Kraft Foods, PepsiCo, and Marriott International.

Product Line

Starbucks roasts more than 30 varieties of the world's finest arabica coffee beans. The company's retail locations also feature a variety of espresso beverages and locally made fresh pastries. Starbucks specialty merchandise includes Starbucks private-label espresso makers, mugs, plunger pots, grinders, storage jars, water filters, thermal carafes, and coffee makers. An extensive selection of packaged goods, including unique confections, gift baskets, and coffee-related items, are available in stores and online.

Starbucks introduced Frappuccino blended beverages, a line of low-fat, creamy, iced coffee drinks. This product launch was the most successful in Starbucks history. The company also has a bottled version of Frappuccino, which is currently available in grocery stores and in many Starbucks retail locations.

A long-term joint venture between Starbucks Coffee and Breyer's Grand Ice Cream dishes up a premium line of coffee ice creams, with national distribution of several different flavors to leading grocery stores. Starbucks has become the number-one brand of coffee ice cream in the United States. Currently, ice cream lovers can choose from eight delectable flavors or two ice cream bars.

Community Involvement

Starbucks contributes to a variety of organizations that benefit AIDS research, child welfare, environmental awareness, literacy, and the arts. The company encourages its partners (employees) to take an active role in their own neighborhoods.

Starbucks fulfills its corporate social responsibility mission by reducing its environmental footprint on the planet. The company addresses three high-impact areas: sourcing of coffee, tea, and paper; transportation of people and products; and design and operations (energy, water, waste reduction, and recycling). Starbucks has developed relations with organizations that support the people and places that grow its coffee and tea, such as Conservation International, CARE, Save the Children, and the African Wildlife Foundation. Additionally, Starbucks

CORPORATE PROFILE *(Continued)*

has entered into a partnership with the U.S. Agency for International Development (USAID) and Conservation International to improve the livelihoods of small-scale coffee farmers through private sector approaches within the coffee industry that are environmentally sensitive, socially responsible, and economically viable. In 2005, Starbucks received the World Environment Center's Gold Medal for International Corporate Achievement in Sustainable Development.

Starbucks has received numerous awards for quality innovation, service, and giving.

tea leaves makes 250–300 cups of tea, whereas one pound of coffee beans makes only 40 cups of coffee.

The following list shows where the different types of tea originate:

China—oolong, orange pekoe

India—Darjeeling, Assam (also known as English breakfast tea), Dooars

Indonesia—Java, Sumatra

Carbonated Soft Drinks and Energy Drinks

Coca-Cola and Pepsi have long dominated the carbonated soft drink market. In the early 1970s, Diet Coke and Diet Pepsi were introduced and quickly gained popularity. The diet colas now command about a 10-percent market share. Caffeine-free colas offer an alternative, but they have not, as yet, become as popular as diet colas. In order to curb obesity, former New York Mayor Michael R. Bloomberg championed a restriction on the sale of large sugary drinks and the city Board of Health voted to approve it.

Energy drinks are beverages that are designed to give the consumer a burst of energy by using a combination of methylxanthines (including caffeine), B vitamins, and exotic herbal ingredients. Energy drinks commonly include caffeine, guarana (extracts from the guarana plant), taurine, various forms of ginseng, maltodextrin, inositol, carnitine, creatine, glucuronolactone, and ginkgo biloba. Some contain high levels of sugar, while most brands also offer an artificially sweetened version. Red Bull is an example of a popular energy drink that originated in Thailand and that has a Japanese heritage. It was adapted to Australian tastes and in only a few years has become popular around the world. The claims are that Red Bull vitalizes the body and mind by supplying tired minds and exhausted bodies with vital substances that have been lost, while reducing harmful substances. It purports to provide immediate energy and vitamins to the consumer. Red Bull has a large market share in more than 160 countries.

Sales of energy drinks and shots are soaring, even as there are growing health concerns given the popularity of the high-caffeine drinks among young people. The dollar value of energy-drink sales continue to rise each year, thanks in part to energy-shot sales at convenience stores, according to a report from the market research firm SymphonyIRI Group.[22] Former American

Beverage Association Senior Vice President of Science Policy Maureen Storey says energy drinks are no worse than coffee. A 16-ounce cup of Starbucks' Pike Place coffee, for instance, has 330 mg of caffeine. That size of latte has 160 mg—the same as a 16-ounce can of the energy drink Monster Energy, which bills itself as "a killer energy brew" that "you can really pound down." The federal Food and Drug Administration limits caffeine in soft drinks to 71 mg for 12 ounces but doesn't regulate the caffeine in energy drinks, coffee, or tea.[23]

A juice bar.

Juices

Popular juice flavors include orange, cranberry, grapefruit, mango, papaya, and apple. Nonalcoholic versions of popular cocktails made with juices have been popular for years and are known as virgin cocktails.

Juice bars have established themselves as places for quick, healthy drinks. Lately, "smart drinks" that are supposed to boost energy and improve concentration have become popular. The smart drinks are made up of a blend of juices, herbs, amino acids, caffeine, and sugar and are sold under names such as Plasma Energy Drink and IQ Energy.

Other drinks have jumped on the healthy drink bandwagon, playing on the consumer's desire to drink something refreshing, light, and healthful. Often, these drinks are fruit flavored, giving the consumer the impression of drinking something healthier than sugar-filled sodas. Unfortunately, these drinks usually just add the flavor of the fruit and rarely have any nutritional value.

In addition, some drinks are created by mixing different fruit flavors to arrive at new, exotic flavors such as Passion–Kiwi–Strawberry and Mango–Banana Delight. Some examples of such drinks are Snapple and Tropicana Twister.

Sports enthusiasts also find drinks that professional athletes use and advertise available in stores. These specially formulated isotonic beverages are intended to help the body regain the vital fluids and minerals that are lost during heavy physical exertion. The National Football League sponsors Gatorade and encourages its use among its athletes. The appeal of being able to drink what the professionals drink is undoubtedly one of the major reasons for the success of Gatorade's sales and marketing. Other brands of isotonic beverages include Powerade and All Sport, which is sponsored by the National Collegiate Athletics Association.

Bottled Water

Bottled water was popular in Europe years ago when it was not safe to drink tap water. In North America, the increased popularity of bottled water has coincided with the trend toward healthier lifestyles.

In the 1980s, it was chic to be seen drinking Perrier (a sparkling water) or some other imported bottled water. Perrier, which comes from France, lost market share a few years ago when an employee tampered with the product. Now the market leader is Evian (a spring water), which is also French. Domestic bottled water is as good as imported and is now available in various flavors that offer the consumer a greater selection.

Bottled waters are available as sparkling, mineral, and spring waters. Bottled water is a refreshing, clean-tasting, low-calorie beverage that will likely increase in popularity as a beverage on its own or to accompany another beverage such as wine or whisky.

Bars and Beverage Operations

From an operating perspective, bar and beverage management follows much the same sequence as does food management, as shown in the following list:

- Forecasting
- Determining what to order
- Selecting the supplier
- Placing the order
- Receiving the order
- Storing
- Issuing
- Serving
- Accounting
- Controlling

Bar Setup

Whether a bar is part of a larger operation (restaurant) or a business in its own right, the physical setup of the bar is critical to its overall effectiveness. There is a need to design the area in such a way that it not only is pleasing to the eye but it also is conducive to a smooth and efficient operation. This means that bar stations—where drinks are filled—are located in strategic spots, and that each station has everything it needs to respond to most, if not all, requests. All well liquors should be easily accessible, with popular call brands not too far out of reach. The brands that are less likely to be ordered (and more likely to be high priced) can be farther away from the stations. The most obvious place for the high-priced, premium brands is the back bar, a place of high visibility. Anyone sitting at the bar will be looking directly at the back bar, giving the customers a chance to view the bar's choices.

As for beer coolers, their location depends on the relative importance of beer to the establishment. In many places, beer is kept in coolers under the bar or below the back bar, and sample bottles or signs are displayed for

HOW TO EFFECTIVELY MANAGE A BAR

Courtesy of **James McManemon**, M.S., University of South Florida Sarasota–Manatee

Jeanne Kearney, an assistant restaurant manager for a boutique hotel chain, who is responsible for managing two separate bars, along with the restaurant and in-room dining departments, shared her insight on three aspects of effective bar management in multiple food and beverage outlets.

"First," Jeanne remarked, "as bar manager, know how to bartend yourself because you will more than likely be behind the bar 25–50 percent of the time during peak business hours and rushes. You don't need to be a professional mixologist, but a solid working knowledge of making drinks is necessary to effectively assist your bartenders when they are in the weeds." (See Jeanne's personal list of drinks that she recommends as good basic knowledge at the end of this feature.)

The second area Jeanne pointed to is the importance of staffing enough bartenders and/or a "bar back" to continuously keep inventory—garnishes, ice, and fresh bar glasses—stocked at all times. "The last thing you want is to run out of necessary items and have your bartenders flustered and scrambling to cut limes, haul ice from the freezer to the bar, or search through the storage room for a bottle of liquor here and there, while guests complain about waiting for their drinks." She pointed out that when managing multiple bars, it is often necessary to work your way between bars and station yourself at the bar that is busier. This way you can more effectively manage the flow of traffic and gauge areas where you can help out or assist guests.

"Finally," Jeanne cautioned, "always be aware of your environment and the people occupying it, especially when alcohol is involved. Be alert and aware of who is being served drinks and how much alcohol is being consumed. There will come a time when you will more than likely need to handle a situation that requires a quick and levelheaded response. The rest, you will learn as you go, so hopefully you are the type of person who likes to think on their feet."

Jeanne's suggested list of drinks reflect a good basic bartending knowledge. An effective bar manager should possess the following:

- **Pouring a draft beer**: Take a clean, slightly chilled glass, hold it at a 45-degree angle just below the draft faucet, and quickly pull the handle toward you in one motion. As the glass fills, straighten it until it is upright, which is close to the same time when the glass should be full. Snap the handle back away from you. Don't forget a coaster!

- **Basic cocktails**: When in doubt, pour one part liquor to three parts mixer in a glass filled with ice (rum and coke, gin and tonic, screwdriver, vodka soda, and so on).

- **Martini** (traditionally gin, more often than not vodka): Fill the mixer with ice. Pour five counts of gin or vodka. Add a dash of vermouth. Stir or swirl briskly 30–50 times (shake if you must). Strain into a chilled martini glass. Garnish with an olive or a twist of lemon.

- **Manhattan**: Ingredients include: 2 oz. rye whiskey, ½ oz. sweet vermouth, 2–3 dashes of Agostino bitters, maraschino cherry to garnish. In shaker with ice: pour, stir, strain, garnish. Rob Roy is to scotch what Manhattan is to whisky.

- **Margarita** (on the rocks): Pour salt on a small plate. Rub the rim of the glass with lime and roll it in the salt for a salted rim. Fill the mixer with ice. Pour ½ full with sweet and sour mix, or substitute lime juice.

HOW TO EFFECTIVELY MANAGE A BAR *(Continued)*

Pour four counts of gold tequila. Pour two counts of triple sec and two counts of Grand Marnier (or another orange liqueur). Mix and pour into glass with salted rim.

- **Bloody Mary**: Fill the mixer with ice. Fill ⅔ full with tomato juice. Pour four counts of vodka. Squeeze ½ a lemon. Add several hefty dashes of Worcestershire sauce. Add several dashes of hot sauce. Pour a splash of olive juice. Mix and pour into a glass. Garnish with a celery stick, spear of olives, lemon wedges, or whatever you think looks festive for the occasion.

customers. However, in many places, beer is the biggest seller, and bars may offer numerous brands from around the world. In such places, other setups may be used, such as standup coolers with glass doors so that customers can easily see all the varieties available. This is also true for draft beers.

Inventory Control

The beverage profitability of an organization is not a matter of luck. Profits result largely from the implementation and use of effective **inventory controls** by management and employees. Training is also important to ensure that employees treat inventory as cash and that they handle it as if it were their own money. Management's example will be followed by employees. If employees sense a lax management style, they may be tempted to steal. No control system can guarantee the prevention of theft completely. However, the better the control system, the less likely it is that there will be a loss.[23]

To operate profitably, a beverage operation manager needs to establish what the expected results will be. For example, if a bottle of gin contains 25 one-ounce measures, it would be reasonable to expect 25 times the selling price in revenue. When this is multiplied for each bottle, the total revenue can be determined and compared to the actual revenue.

One of the critical areas of bar management is the design, installation, and implementation of a system to control possible theft of the bar's beverage inventory. Theft may occur in a number of ways, including the following:

- Giving away drinks
- Overpouring alcohol
- Mischarging for drinks
- Selling a call liquor at a well price
- Outright stealing of bar beverages by employees

As is the case with food operations, anticipated profit margin is based on the ratio of sales generated to related beverage costs. Bar management must be able to account for any discrepancies between expected and actual profit margins.

All inventory control systems require an actual physical count of the existing inventory, which may be done on a weekly or monthly basis, depending on the needs of management. This physical count is based on units. For liquor and wine, the unit is a bottle, either 0.750 or 1.0 liter; for bottled beer, the unit is a case of 24 bottles; for draft beer, the unit is one keg. The results of the most current physical count are then compared to the prior period's physical count to determine the actual amount of beverage inventory consumed during the period. This physical amount is translated into a cost or dollar figure by multiplying the amount consumed for each item by its respective cost per unit. The total cost for all beverages consumed is compared to the sales generated to result in a profit margin, which is then compared to the expected margin.

Management should design forms that can be used to account for all types of liquor, beer, and wine available at the bar. The listing of the items should follow their actual physical setup within the bar to facilitate easy accounting of the inventory. The forms should also have columns where amounts of each inventory item can be noted. A traditional way to account for the amount of liquor in a bottle is by using the "10" count, where the level of each bottle is marked by tenths; thus, a half-full bottle of well vodka would be marked as "0.5" on the form. Similarly, for kegs of draft beer, a breakdown of 25, 50, 75, and 100 percent may be used to determine their physical count.

Beverage Management Technology

Technology for beverage management has improved with products from companies such as Scannabar (**en.scannabar.com**), which offers beverage operators a system that accounts for every ounce, with daily, weekly, or monthly results. The ongoing real-time inventory allows viewing results at any time and place, with tamperproof reliability interfaced with major point-of-sale (POS) systems.

The Scannabar liquor module has a bar-coded label on each bottle, making it easy to track bottles from purchase to recycle bin. Each bottle variety has the same bar code, allowing for easy calibration. The barcoded ribbon is used as a measuring tool to give accurate results. Inventory taking is done with a portable handheld radio frequency bar code reader. Once the label is scanned, the level of alcohol in the bottle is recorded and the data are sent from the user's handheld reader to the computer in the office for real-time results.[25]

The wine module keeps control of all wines by region, variety, or vintage. After the wines have been configured within the directory, the procedure is that, when a wine is received, the variety is identified by scanning the bar code already on the bottle or is selected directly from the portable handheld radio frequency bar code reader. A bar-coded tag is placed around the collar, which creates a unique identity for each bottle. Once the bottle is ready to be served, either at the table or at the bar, the bar-coded tag is removed from the bottle and scanned out of inventory. Scanning the tag around the neck of the bottle accomplishes inventory taking.[26]

The beverage system from Azbar Plus offers a POS system that runs the operations behind the bar. It rings up the charge as the beverage is being poured while automatically removing the product from inventory.

TECHNOLOGY SPOTLIGHT *(Continued)*

bartender pours in to a glass, each pour is registered, therefore allowing full control of the beverage sales and keeping inventory. The disadvantage of this system is the low speed of service in a busy bar environment.

A new generation of beverage-dispensing control systems is the radio-frequency identification (RFID)–based systems. In this system, an RFID spout is assigned to each bottle in the bar, and every drink dispensed is automatically tracked in real time. The Capton beverage tracking solution uses RFID-enabled free-pour spouts, allowing bartenders to pour liquor without adjusting normal bar operations. Each spout contains an RFID microchip that wirelessly transmits pour data via radio frequency to a receiver. Every RFID microchip has a unique serial code, so each spout can be tracked individually. These spouts are completely self-contained and hold the battery, electronics, transmitter, and microchip. They are water resistant and impact resistant so they can be cleaned like any other pour spout. They fit all major brands of liquor and are completely reprogrammable through a simple software update. Every event, including pours, placement on bottle, and placement off bottle, is date and time stamped and transmitted in real time. The wireless spouts transmit on a low-range AM spectrum (433 megahertz). With this system, the management can know the perpetual inventory (total inventory—all sales) at a given time.

Instead of holding up bottles and guessing what is left in them or even weighing each bottle at the end of shifts, the AZ-200 controller can at any time give a report of what was sold, who completed the transaction, how the system was used, and what the actual profits are by brand, transaction, or product group. The system can be remotely monitored from home or other locations by dialing into the bar location; this is handy for making price changes and monitoring sales activity.

The AZ-200 is the heart of a dispensing system that interfaces with a variety of products: "spouts," a cocktail tower, beer, wine, juice, soft drink machines, and soda guns. The system even runs cocktail programming, so if the bartender does not know what goes into a certain drink, he or she can hit the cocktail button, and the system will tell the bartender what liquor bottle to pick up and will control the recipe pour amounts.[27]

Personnel Procedures

Another key component of internal control is having procedures in place for screening and hiring bar personnel. Employees must be experienced in bartending and cocktail serving, and they also must be honest because they have access to the bar's beverage inventory and its cash.

Bar managers may also implement several other procedures to control inventory and reduce the likelihood of employee theft. One popular method is the use of *spotters*, who are hired to act like typical bar customers, but who are actually observing the bartenders and/or cocktailers for inappropriate behavior, such as not taking money from customers or overpouring. Another method for checking bar personnel is to perform a bank switch in the middle of the shift. In some cases, employees steal from the company by taking money from customers without ringing it up on the register. They keep the extra money in the cash drawer until the end of the shift when they are cashing out, at which point they retrieve the stolen funds. To do a bank switch, the manager must "z-out" a bartender's cash register, take the cash drawer, and replace it with a new bank. The manager then counts the money in the drawer, subtracts the starting bank, and compares that figure to the one on the register's tape. If there is a significant surplus of funds, it is highly likely that the employee is stealing. If there is less than what is indicated on the tape, the employee may be honest but careless when giving change or hitting the buttons on the register. Either way, there is a potential for loss.

Restaurant and Hotel Bars

In restaurants, the bar is often used as a holding area to allow guests to enjoy a cocktail or aperitif before sitting down to dinner. This allows the restaurant to space out the guests' orders so that the kitchen can cope more effectively; it also increases beverage sales. The profit margin from beverages is higher than the food profit margin.

In some restaurants, the bar is the focal point or main feature. Guests feel drawn to having a beverage because the atmosphere and layout of the restaurant encourages them to have a drink. Beverages generally account for about 25–30 percent of total sales. Many restaurants used to have a higher percentage of beverage sales, but the trend toward responsible consumption of alcoholic beverages has influenced people to decrease their consumption.

Bars carry a range of each spirit, beginning with the *well* package. The well package is the least expensive pouring brand that the bar uses when guests simply ask for a "scotch and water." The *call* package is the group of spirits that the bar offers to guests who are likely to ask for a particular name brand. For example, guests may call for Johnnie Walker Red Label. An example of a premium scotch is Johnnie Walker Black Label, and a super premium scotch is Chivas Regal.

A popular method of costing each of the spirits poured is to calculate cost according to the following example:

A premium brand of vodka such as Grey Goose costs $41.25 per liter and yields twenty-five 1¾-oz shots that each sell for $7.25. Therefore, the bottle brings in $181.25. The profit margins produced by bars may be categorized as follows:

Beach restaurant at dusk.

Liquor Pouring Cost % (approx.)	12
Beer	25
Wine	38

When combined, the sales mix may have an average pouring cost of 16–20 percent.

Most bars operate on some form of par stock level, which means that for every spirit bottle in use, there is a minimum par stock level of one, two, or more bottles available as a backup. As soon as the stock level falls to a level below the par level, more is automatically purchased.

Nightclubs

Nightclubs have long been a popular place to go to get away from the stresses of everyday life. From the small club in a suburban neighborhood to the world-famous clubs of New York, Las Vegas, and Miami's South Beach, all clubs have one thing in common: People frequent them to kick back, relax, and, more often than not, enjoy a wild night of dancing and partying with friends and strangers alike.

Like restaurant ownership, starting up a nightclub is a very risky business. But with the right education and proper planning, nightclub ownership can be a very profitable endeavor. As with most businesses in the hospitality industry, many believe that experience is more important than education and that you can learn as you go. However, when embarking on a journey as involved as owning a nightclub, a person with a degree and a high level of education is well ahead of the game.

The ability to read the market is key in developing a nightclub. When investing anywhere from $300,000 to $1 million in start-up costs, it is of utmost importance to be sure that the right spot is chosen and that a relevant market is within reach. Great nightclubs result from an accurate and calculated read of a marketplace, not by virtue of good luck. In fact, the number one cause of early nightclub failure stems from an inaccurate read on the marketplace. For example, if an entrepreneur is interested in opening up a country line–dancing nightclub in an urban neighborhood, he or she may want to do extensive market research to be sure that members of the community even like country music.

When considering the prospect of a new nightclub, it is important to invest considerable time in the study of demographics, market attitude, and social dynamics of the proposed target. Many people tend to come up with a concept they are dead set on pursuing without really digging into the market. One should take all markets into account, even if the other markets may not seem relevant at the time. In the future, it may be these same markets that are being divided to come to the newer clubs that have just opened.

A new and exciting concept is a highly important factor in creating a nightclub. Some people feel that if one nightclub is doing well down the street, they will open the same type and be equally successful. This is not true. Variety is one of the keys to successful business. By offering patrons a fresh new opportunity, one can draw clientele away from the old clubs and into the new club.

Budgeting is another big factor in developing a nightclub. Although such an undertaking can be very costly, cutting corners in building and design will only hurt the business later. It is better to spend the money now and do it right than to have to spend more money for repairs later. Creating a budget should include all aspects of the operation, including, but not limited to, food and beverage, staffing and labor, licenses, building ramifications, décor, lighting, and entertainment.

Be sure to know all the legal issues that come with running a nightclub. For example, many laws exist on the sale and distribution of alcohol. In many instances, if a problem occurs involving a patron who was last drinking at the club, the problem can be considered the fault of the operation's management. Lawsuits can arise fairly easily, and it is highly important to be aware of such possibilities.

Nightclubs can be great experiences for both the patrons and the owner because revenues can be very high. However, it is important to remember the risks involved and work to minimize them.

Although this is only a brief discussion of the creation of a nightclub, the points given are quite important to successful operation. As with all business endeavors, the more one knows about the industry with which he or she is getting involved, the better off the business will be. For more information regarding the nightclub industry, go to **www.nightclub.com** or **www .nightclubbiz.com**.

Brewpubs and Microbreweries

Brewpubs are a combination brewery and pub or restaurant that brews its own fresh beer onsite to meet the taste of local customers. Microbreweries are craft breweries that produce up to 15,000 barrels (or 30,000 kegs) of beer a year. The North American microbrewery industry trend revived the concept of small breweries serving fresh, all-malt beer. Although regional breweries, microbreweries, and brewpubs account for only a small part of the North American brewing industry in terms of total beer production (less than 5 percent), they have a potentially large growth rate. One reason for the success of microbreweries and brewpubs is the wide variety of styles and flavors of beer they produce. On one hand, this educates the public about beer styles that have been out of production for decades and, on the other hand, helps brewpubs and restaurants meet the individual tastes and preferences of their local clientele.

Starting a brewpub is a fairly expensive venture. Although brewing systems come in a wide range of configurations, the cost of the equipment ranges from $200,000 to $800,000. Costs are affected by factors such as annual production capacity, beer types, and packaging. The investment in microbreweries and brewpubs is well justified by the enormous potential for returns. Microbreweries can produce a wide variety of ales, lagers, and other beers, the quality of which depends largely on the quality of the raw materials and the skill of the brewer. There are several regional brewpub restaurants of note, including Rock Bottom, which built its foundation on a tradition of fresh handcrafted beers and a diverse menu. It promotes itself as a place to gather with friends, drink the best beer around, enjoy a great meal, and share good times. John Harvard's has a famous selection of ales and lagers that are brewed on the premises according to the old English recipes brought to America in 1637 by John Harvard, after whom Harvard University is named. Gordon Biersch has several excellent brewery restaurants also offering handcrafted ales and beers along with a varied menu.

Sports Bars

Sports bars have always been popular but have become more so with the decline of disco and singles bars. They are places where people relax in the sporting atmosphere, so bar/restaurants such as Characters at Marriott hotels have become popular "watering holes." Satellite TV coverage of the top sporting events helps sports bars to draw crowds. Sports bars have evolved over the years into much more than corner bars featuring the game of the week. In the past, sports bars were frequented by die-hard sports fans and were rarely visited by other clientele. Today, the sports bar is more of an entertainment concept and is geared toward a more diverse base of patrons.

Sports bars were originally no more than a gathering spot for local sports fans when the home team played on TV. Now, such places have been transformed into mega-sports adventures, featuring musical entertainment, interactive games, and hundreds of TVs tuned in to just about every sport imaginable. "There are no more watering holes," says Zach Strauss, general manager of Sluggers World Class Sports Bar in Chicago. "Things have changed. People are more health conscious; nobody really drinks, drinks, drinks anymore… . You have to offer more than booze. People expect sports bars to have more personality, better food, and better service."[28]

Today's sports bars are attracting a much more diverse clientele. Now, more women and families are frequenting these venues, which provide a new prospect for revenue for bar owners. Scott Estes, founding partner of Lee Roy Selmon's restaurant in Tampa, Florida, has recognized that women are an increasing revenue force in the industry and has made adjustments to his restaurant to be sure to capitalize on this rapidly expanding market. Sports bars are also making changes in their establishments to become more family oriented. Lee Roy Selmon's main dining room, for example, is a TV-free environment. Many families go into sports bars and request a room with no TVs, so, recognizing that, an increasing number of owners have chosen to set aside a special place where families can eat uninterrupted by the noise of TV.

Sports bar.

Another method of attracting bar patrons on slower nights is to offer games and family-friendly menus. Franklin Park in Brooklyn attracts families with its indoor and outdoor spaces. Kids are entertained by skee ball, photo booth, and pop-a-shot. Sports bars have also become the latest version of the traditional arcade. Many bars offer interactive video games where friends and families can compete against one another. Virtual reality games such as Indy 500 and other sports games are available at many establishments. Some venues have even gone a step farther and offer batting cages, bowling alleys, and basketball courts for their patrons to enjoy.

Another aspect of the sports bar that has changed drastically is the menu. Sports bars have a reputation for serving spicy chicken wings, hamburgers, and other typical bar fare. But just as sports bars have evolved in their entertainment offerings, so too have their menus. People's tastes have changed, causing sports bars to offer a more diverse menu. Today, guests can dine on a variety of foods, from filet mignon to fresh fish, to gourmet sandwiches and pizza. Now people frequent sports bars as much for the great meal they will have as for the entertainment. In the past, sports bars usually had a few TVs that showcased games that would appeal to the area and big games such as the Super Bowl. The sudden increase in technology and TV programming available has made game viewing very different. The popularity of satellites and digital receivers has allowed bars to tune in to virtually dozens of events at any given time. Bars now have hundreds of TVs, and fans can watch games featuring every sport, team, and level of play around the world at any time of the day or night.

Burbank, California–based ESPN Zone has about 200 TVs in each of its locations so that fans can catch all the action. A handful of TVs are placed in the restaurant's bathrooms because the evolution of sports bars has turned the smoky corner bar into an exciting dining and sports experience. Customers who once rarely frequented the establishments, such as women and families, are now some of the biggest patrons, increasing both attendance and revenue at sports bars.

Coffee Shops

Another fairly recent trend in the beverage industry in the United States and Canada is the establishment of coffeehouses, or coffee shops. Coffeehouses originally were created based on the model of Italian bars, which reflected the deeply rooted espresso tradition in Italy. The winning concept of Italian bars lies in the ambiance they create, which is suitable for conversation of a personal, social, and business nature. A talk over a cup of coffee with soft background music and maybe a pastry is a typical scenario for Italians. Much of the same concept was re-created in the United States and Canada, where there was a niche in the beverage industry that was yet to be acknowledged and filled. The original concept was modified, however, to include a much wider variety of beverages and styles of coffee to meet the tastes of North American consumers. Consequently, the typical espresso/cappuccino offered by Italian bars has been expanded in North America to include items such as iced mocha, iced cappuccino, and so forth.

Students as well as businesspeople find coffeehouses a place to relax, discuss, socialize, and study. The success of coffeehouses is reflected in the establishment of chains such as Starbucks, as well as family-owned, independent shops.

Wireless cafés are a recent trend in the coffeehouse sector. Wireless cafés offer the use of computers, with Internet capability, for about $6 per hour. Guests can enjoy coffee, snacks, or even a meal while online. Reasonable rates allow regular guests to have e-mail addresses.

▶ Check Your Knowledge

1. Describe the bar setup.

2. How is inventory control conducted?

3. What is the average beverage pouring cost percentage?

4. What is a trend in sports bars?

LEARNING OBJECTIVE 5
Explain a restaurant's liability in terms of serving alcoholic beverages.

Liquor Liability and the Law

Owners, managers, bartenders, and servers may be liable under the law if they serve alcohol to minors or to persons who are intoxicated. The extent of the liability can be very severe. The legislation that governs the sale of alcoholic beverages is called **dram shop legislation**. The dram shop laws, or civil damage acts, were enacted in the 1850s and dictated that owners and operators of drinking establishments are liable for injuries caused by intoxicated customers.

Some states have reverted back to the eighteenth-century common law, removing liability from vendors except in cases involving minors. Nonetheless, most people recognize that as a society we are faced with major problems of underage drinking and drunk driving.

To combat underage drinking in restaurants, bars, and lounges, a major brewery distributed a booklet showing the authentic design and layout of each state's driver's licenses. Trade associations such as the National Restaurant Association and the American Hotel & Lodging Association, together with major corporations, have produced a number of preventive measures and programs aimed at responsible alcohol beverage service. The major thrust of these initiatives is awareness programs and mandatory training programs, such as ServSafe Alcohol, that promote responsible alcohol service. ServSafe Alcohol is sponsored by the National Restaurant Association and is a certification program that teaches participants about alcohol and its effects on people, the common signs of intoxication, and how to help customers avoid drinking too much.

Other programs for responsible alcohol service and consumption include designated drivers, who only drink nonalcoholic beverages to ensure that they can drive friends home safely. Some operators give free nonalcoholic beverages to the designated driver as a courtesy.

One positive outcome of the responsible alcohol service programs for operators is a reduction in the insurance premiums and legal fees for beverage establishments, which had skyrocketed in previous years.

Trends in the Beverage Industry

Courtesy of Dr. Greg Dunn, Senior Lecturer & Managing Director, UF Eric Friedheim Tourism Institute

- *Seasonal lattes.* Restaurants and bars are spicing up their coffee and tea drink offerings beyond the traditional vanilla, mocha, and caramel flavors. For instance, fast food and casual dining stores are offering pumpkin spice, toffee nut, and gingerbread lattes during the holidays. Others have added red velvet (cake-flavored) lattes, peppermint mocha, and white chocolate cheesecake.

- *Cocktails.* The profession of bartending is constantly developing to keep up with the increasing interest in crafting cocktails. The art of mixing, infusing, and pairing liquors with a number of other ingredients is constantly evolving to new experimental and even scientific heights. Mixologists are always seeking out new ways to turn the average martini or basic mixed cocktail into a new and exciting concoction that not only looks cool, but also sends your taste buds racing and truly raises your spirit! Outlined below are some of the trendy ingredients, accompaniments, and mixing methods that you're sure to start seeing more of:

  - It's all about the ice. Mixologists know that the amount of ice used and the way ice is shaped makes a difference in the look and taste of the end product. Cubed, cracked, crushed, chipped, shaved, spherical, and smoky: the shape of ice and the amount that is used determine the rate of dilution. Some of the more advanced include a dense spherical shape of ice used for keeping the alcohol cool when you don't want the ice to dilute the drink at a rapid rate. Additionally, dry ice is used to create a thick smoke, often reminiscent of a volcano erupting in your glass.

  - Less mixer is more. Mixologists are replacing the typical sugary mixer, such as margarita mix, fountain sodas, and concentrated fruit juices, with natural, organic, and fresh mixers. By using fresh squeezed fruit juices, homemade syrups, tonics, and bitters, and muddled fruits, vegetables, and herbs, your favorite drinks can be made fresher, less manufactured, and lower in calories.

  - Infusing spirits with fresh flavor. Spirits can be infused with fruits, vegetables, herbs, spices, and a number of other flavors to create a product that can be enjoyed on its own or as a mixed drink. With infused spirits, single flavors and simple combinations are known to work best; think chile and lime, lemon and basil, chocolate and cherries, or any one of those ingredients unaccompanied. Infused spirits can also be paired with foods to create a heightened culinary experience.

  - Cocktails synched with food concepts. For instance, seafood restaurants are introducing beach drinks and "moonshine" cocktails while others such as Brazilian steakhouses are offering variations of their traditional caipirinha.

  - Different and unique Scotches, herbaceous liquors, and bitters. Mixologists are introducing and reinventing craft cocktails by combining upscale and small batch liquors with homemade mixers using old-school techniques in order to create premier cocktails full of flavor, balance, and aesthetic appeal.

Summary

1. Beverages are categorized into alcoholic and nonalcoholic beverages. Alcoholic beverages are further categorized into spirits, wines, and beer.
2. Wine is the fermented juice of ripe grapes. It is classified as red, white, and rose, and we distinguish between light beverage wines, sparkling wines, and aromatic wines.
3. The six steps in making wine are crushing, fermenting, racking, maturing, filtering, and boiling. France, Germany, Italy, Spain, and Portugal are the main European wine-producing areas, and California is the main American wine-producing area.
4. Beer is a brewed and fermented beverage made from malt. Different types of beer include ale, stout, lager, and pilsner.
5. Spirits have a high percentage of alcohol and are served before or after a meal. Fermentation and distillation are parts of their processing. The most popular white spirits are rum, gin, vodka, and tequila.
6. Today people have become more health conscious about consumption of alcohol; nonalcoholic beverages such as coffee, tea, soft drinks, juices, and bottled water are increasing in popularity.
7. Beverages make up 20–30 percent of total sales in a restaurant, but managers are liable if they serve alcohol to minors. Programs such as designated drivers, ServSafe Alcohol, and the serving of virgin cocktails have increased.

Key Words and Concepts

alcoholic beverage
beer
brandy
champagne
cognac
dram shop legislation
fermentation
fortified wines
hops

inventory control
liquor
malt
mashing
nonalcoholic beverage
Prohibition
proof
sparkling wine
spirit

vintage
white spirits
wine
wine and food pairing
wine tasting
wort
yeast

Review Questions

1. What is the difference between fortified and aromatic wines? In what combination is it suggested to serve food and wine and why?
2. Describe the brewing process of beer. What is the difference between a stout and a pilsner?
3. Name and describe the main types of spirits.
4. Why have nonalcoholic drinks increased in popularity, and what difficulties do bar managers face when serving alcohol?
5. Describe the origin of coffee.
6. Describe the proper procedure for handling and serving champagne.
7. Describe the origin of cocktails. What constitutes a cocktail?
8. Describe a typical bar setup.

Internet Exercises

1. Organization: **Clos Du Bois**
   Summary: Clos Du Bois is one of America's well-known and loved wineries and is a premier producer of wines from Sonoma County in California. The winery was started in 1974 and since then has acquired many more vineyards and a name for itself. It now sells about a million cases of premium wine annually.
   (a) Look at the suggested food and wine pairings. What can you serve with the Clos Du Bois North Coast sauvignon blanc? Compare it to what you already know about what to eat with sauvignon blanc.
   (b) Clos Du Bois has been named Wine of the Year for nine years by *Wine & Spirits*. What is it about this wine that makes it so different from others?

2. Organization: **Siebel Institute of Technology**
   Summary: Siebel Institute of Technology is recognized for its training and educational programs in brewing technology.
   (a) What are some of the services that the Siebel Institute of Technology offers its students?
   (b) List the career path options available through Siebel Institute of Technology.

Apply Your Knowledge

1. In groups, do a blindfold taste test with cans of Coke and Pepsi. See if your group can identify which is which.

2. Complete a class survey of preference for Coke or Pepsi and share the results with your classmates.

3. Request a local wine representative to demonstrate the correct way of opening and serving a bottle of nonalcoholic wine. Then practice opening a bottle yourself.

4. What type of wine would be recommended with the following:
   a. Pork
   b. Cheese
   c. Lamb
   d. Chocolate cake
   e. Chicken

Suggested Activities

1. Search the Internet for underage drinking statistics and related highway deaths in your state.

2. Mothers Against Drunk Driving (MADD) is a nonprofit organization working to stop drunk drivers and support victims of drunk drivers. Find out what impact MADD has had on society.

3. Create an outline for a sports bar concept.

Endnotes

1. Personal correspondence with Jay R. Schrock, Dean, School of Hotel and Restaurant Management, University of South Florida, March 26, 2011.

2. Ibid.

3. Dr. Vino, "60 Minutes on red wine, 1991," http://www.drvino.com. Search for "60 minutes on red wine" (accessed August 31, 2015).

4. This section draws on Sarah Berkley, "Organic and Sustainable Wine Production Expanding Rapidly in California," Organic Consumers Association, http://www.organicconsumers.org/organic/wine012104.cfm (retrieved March 12, 2015).

5. Budweiser Brewing Company presentation, University of South Florida, Tampa, Florida, September 7, 2004.

6. Ibid.

7. Greg Hottinger, "Organic Beer: Tapping a New Market," BestNaturalFoods.com, http://bestnaturalfoods.com/newsletter/organic_beer.html (accessed May 27, 2015).

8. Craft Beer, *Small, Independent Traditional*, www.craftbeer.com. Go to blogs, click on Craft Beer Muses, search for "Small Independent Traditional," and click on the Craft Breweries: Small, Independent and Traditional article (accessed March 21, 2015).

9. Drink Craft Beer, *Home Page*, www.drinkcraftbeer.com/ (accessed March 21, 2015).

10. Craft Beer, *Small, Independent Traditional*, www.craftbeer.com. Go to blogs, click on Craft Beer Muses, search for "Small Independent Traditional," and click on the "Craft Breweries: Small, Independent and Traditional" article (accessed March 21, 2015).

11. Ibid.

12. Brewers Association, *Home Page*, www.brewersassociation.org (accessed November 13, 2014).

13. Jonny Fullpint, "Oregon Honors Full Sail Brewing for Sustainability," The Full Pint, January 6, 2009, http://thefullpint.com. Click on Beer News and search for "Oregon Honors Full Sail Brewing" (accessed March 14, 2015).

14. "10 Must-Do Steps for Sustainable Homebrewing," *The Beer Apostle* (blog), Thursday, April 2, 2015, http://www.thebeerapostle.com/ (accessed April 15, 2015).

15. New Belgium Brewing Company, Inc. (2009). Sustainability Management System. New Belgium Brewing Company, 27. Retrieved from http://www.newbelgium.com/. Click on Sustainability, click on Environmental Metrics, click on New Belgium's S.M.S. to view this file (accessed September 13, 2015).

16. Odell Brewing Company, "Sustainability Around The Brewery," Odell Brewing Company (blog), April 22, 2015, http://odellbrewing.com/. Click on Blog, click on Sustainability, click on Sustainability Around The Brewery to view the article (accessed September 13, 2015).

17. Costas Katsigiris and Mary Porter, *The Bar and Beverage Book*, 3rd ed. (New York: John Wiley and Sons, 2002), 139.

18. "Coffee Statistics," *E-Importz*, http://www.e-importz.com. Click on Coffee Statistics (accessed November 13, 2014).

19. "The History of Coffee," *National Coffee Association USA*, http://www.ncausa.org. Click on Knowledge Bank, All About Coffee, The History of Coffee (accessed March 21, 2015).

20. Ibid.

21. "Starbucks Company Statistics–Statistic Brain," *2014 Statistic Brain Research Institute, publishing as Statistic Brain*, Research Date: April 20, 2015, http://www.statisticbrain.com/, search for "Starbucks company statistics" (accessed May 22, 2015).

22. Elaine Watson, "Energy Drinks, Coffee and Bottled Water: The Top Performers in the Center of the Store," *FoodNavigator-USA,* January 3, 2013, http://www.foodnavigator-usa.com/. Search for "Energy drinks, coffee and bottled water" to find this article (accessed May 27, 2015).

23. "Energy Drink Dollar Sales Grow 13.3%," *CSP Daily News*, March 17, 2011, http://www.cspnet.com/. Search for "Energy Drink Dollar Sales Grow 13" for this article (accessed May 27, 2015).

24. Belverd Needles, Marian Powers, and Susan Crosson, *Financial and Managerial Accounting*, 10th ed. (Boston: Cengage Learning, 2013), 331.

25. Scannabar, *Liquor Inventory Software*, http://en.scannabar.com/. Go to Products and click on Liquor Inventory (accessed March 19, 2015).

26. Scannabar, *Wine Inventory Software*, http://en.scannabar.com. Go to Products and click on Wine Inventory (accessed March 19, 2015).

27. Azbar Plus, *Home*, www.azbarplus.com (retrieved March 19, 2015).

28. Personal conversation with Zach Strauss, General Manager of Sluggers World Class Sports Bar in Chicago, May 4, 2007.

The Restaurant Business

Restaurants are a vital part of our everyday lifestyles; because we are a society on the go, we patronize them several times a week to socialize as well as to eat and drink. Restaurants offer a place to relax and enjoy the company of family, friends, colleagues, and business associates and to restore our energy level before heading off to the next class or engagement. Actually, the word *restaurant* derives from the word *restore*. Today, there are more than 990,000 restaurants in the United States, with sales of $683.4 billion and 13.5 million employees (marking the restaurant business as the largest employer apart from the government!). The restaurant industry's share of the food dollar has risen to 47 percent. On a typical day, restaurant industry sales average $1.8 billion.[1]

As a society we spend an increasing amount, approaching 50 percent, of our food dollar away from home. Restaurants are a multibillion-dollar industry that provides employment and contributes to the nation's social and economic well-being. No discussion of restaurants can continue without talking about the main ingredient: food. So, let's take a brief look at our culinary heritage.

Classical Cuisine

LEARNING OBJECTIVE 1
Discuss the significance of classical cuisine.

North America gained most of its culinary legacy from France. Two main events were responsible for our culinary legacy coming from France. First was the French Revolution in 1793, which caused the best French chefs of the day to lose their employment because their bosses lost their heads! Many chefs came to North America as a result, bringing with them their culinary talents. The second event was when Thomas Jefferson, who starting in 1784 spent five years as envoy to France, brought a French chef to the White House when he became president. This act stimulated interest in French cuisine and enticed U.S. tavern owners to offer better quality and more interesting food.

No mention of classical cuisine can be made without talking about the two main initiators: Marie-Antoine Carême (1784–1833), who is credited as the founder of classical cuisine, and Auguste Escoffier, who is profiled later in this chapter. Carême was abandoned on the streets of Paris as a child, and then worked his way up from cook's helper to become the chef to the Prince de Talleyrand and the Prince Regent of England. He also served as head chef to the future King George IV of England, Tsar Alexander of Russia, and Baron de Rothschild. His goal was to achieve "lightness," "grace," "order," and "perspicuity" of food. Carême dedicated his career to refining and organizing culinary techniques. His many books contain the first really systematic account of cooking principles, recipes, and menu making.[2]

The other great contributor to classical cuisine, Auguste Escoffier (1846–1935), unlike Carême, never worked in an aristocratic household. Instead, he held forth in the finest hotels of the time: the Place Vendôme in Paris and the Savoy and Carlton hotels in London. Escoffier is noted for his many contributions to cuisine, including simplifying the Grand Cuisine of Carême by reducing the number of flavors and garnishes and even simplifying the number of sauces to five "mother" or leading sauces. Escoffier brought simplicity and harmony to the Grand Cuisine. His many cookbooks are still in use today: *Le Guide Culinaire* (1903) is a collection of more than 5,000 classic cuisine recipes; in *Le Livre des Menus* (1912), he compares a great meal with a symphony; and *Ma Cuisine* (1934) contains more than 2,000 timeless recipes. All of his books emphasize the importance of mastering the techniques of cooking.[3]

This is an exciting time to be involved in the culinary arts and restaurant industry. Not only are new restaurant concepts and themes to fit a variety of tastes and budgets appearing on the scene, the culinary arts are being developed by several creative and talented chefs. It is important to realize that in this industry, we are never far from food. So, let's take a look at the recent development of **culinary arts**.

The main "ingredient" in a restaurant is cuisine, and one of the main foundations of classical French cooking, on which much of American cuisine is based, is the five **mother sauces**: bechamel, velouté, espagnole, tomato, and hollandaise. These elaborate sauces were essential accompaniments for the various dishes on the menu. Until about 1900, all menus were written in French—some still are—and regardless of whether a person was dining in a good hotel or restaurant in London or Lisbon, the intention was that the dish should be prepared in the same manner and taste similar to the French version. The travelers of the day either spoke French or had a knowledge of menu French.

Classical French cuisine was the norm until the late 1960s and early 1970s, when **nouvelle cuisine** became popular. Nouvelle cuisine is a lighter cuisine than the classical French and is based on simpler preparations—with the aid of processors, blenders, and juicers—using more natural flavors and ingredients. Instead of thickening a sauce with a flour-based **roux**, a **purée** of vegetables could be used instead. Fresh is in, and this includes herbs for flavor. Nouvelle cuisine combines classical techniques and principles with modern technology and scientific research. "Simpler, quicker" quickly became more stylish, with plate presentation becoming a part of the chef's art. North American cooking had arrived. The bounties of Canada and the United States provided the basis for regional cuisine to flourish nationally. **Fusion**, the blending of flavors and techniques from two cuisines, became popular. For example, New England and Italian or Californian and Asian cuisines can be blended, or a Japanese recipe might be blended with a Mexican one to create a new hybrid recipe.

Many great chefs have influenced our recent culinary development. Among them are Julia Child, whose television shows did much to take the mystique out of French cooking and encourage a generation of homemakers to elevate their cooking techniques and skills. More recently, Anthony Bourdain's *No Reservations* and *Parts Unknown* along with Andrew Zimmern's *Bizarre Foods* garnered the public's interest by combining culinary delicacies with travel to unique and exotic locations, while Food Network personalities like Emeril Lagasse, Bobby Flay, Guy Fieri, Adam Richman, and Robert Irvine have popularized cooking and the gourmand lifestyle with shows that range from uncovering the hottest *Diners, Drive-Ins and Dives* to giving failing restaurants a complete makeover in just a few days. Additionally, programs like *Chopped* and *Cutthroat Kitchen* have also become popular.

Culinary schools have done an excellent job of producing a new generation of chefs who are making significant contributions to the evolving culinary arts. For example, Alice Waters, chef/owner of Chez Panisse in Berkeley, California, is credited with the birth of California cuisine. Waters uses only fresh produce from local farmers. Paul Prudhomme is another contemporary chef who has energized many aspiring chefs with his passion for basic cooking, especially Cajun style.

Charlie Trotter, former chef/owner of Charlie Trotter's in Chicago, was considered by many to be one of America's finest chef/owners and king of fusion. He has said in one of his books:

After love there is only cuisine! It's all about excellence, or at least working towards excellence. Early on in your approach to cooking—or in running a restaurant—you have to determine whether or not you are willing to commit fully and completely to the idea of the pursuit of excellence. I have always looked at it this way: if you strive for perfection—an all out assault on total perfection—at the very least you will hit a high level of excellence, and then you might be able to sleep at night. To accomplish something truly significant, excellence has to become a life plan.[4]

Chef Trotter brought his knowledge and exposure together into a coherent view on what the modern fine-dining experience could be. He said, "I thought the blend of European refinement regarding the pleasures of the table, American ingenuity and energy in operating a small enterprise, Japanese minimalism and poetic elegance in effecting a sensibility, and a modern approach to incorporating health and dietary concerns would encompass a spectrum of elements through which I could express myself fully. Several years later, I find I am even more devoted than ever to this approach."[5] Charlie Trotter tragically died of a stroke at the age of 54.

▶ Check Your Knowledge

1. Discuss the significance of classical cuisine.
2. From which country did America gain most of its culinary legacy?

Food Trends and Practices

LEARNING OBJECTIVE 2
Identify food trends and practices.

As the level of professionalism rises for the chef of the twenty-first century, chefs will need a strong culinary foundation with a structure that includes multicultural cooking skills and strong employability traits, such as passion, dependability, cooperation, and initiative. Additional management skills include strong supervisory training, sense of urgency, accounting skills, sanitation/safety knowledge, nutritional awareness, and marketing/merchandising skills.

Not only are trans fats banned from many city menus but, according to the National Restaurant Association's (NRA) research, nearly three out of four Americans say they are trying to eat more healthfully in restaurants than they did two years ago. The HealthyDiningFinder.com Web site is a great resource for those looking to make smart choices when dining out.[6] Among the early program members are Arby's, P. F. Chang's, Buca di Beppo, Cracker Barrel, Round Table Pizza, El Pollo Loco, and Famous Dave's. Several other

INTRODUCING AUGUSTE ESCOFFIER (1846–1935)[7]

"Emperor of the World's Kitchens"

Auguste Escoffier is considered by many to be the patron saint of the professional cook. Called the "emperor of the world's kitchens," he is considered a reference point and a role model for all chefs. His exceptional culinary career began at the age of 13, when he apprenticed in his uncle's restaurant, and he worked until 1920, and retired to die quietly at home in Monaco in 1935. Uneducated, but a patient educator and diligent writer, he was an innovator who remained deeply loyal to the regional and bourgeois roots of French cookery. He exhibited his culinary skills in the dining rooms of the finest hotels in Europe, including the Place Vendôme in Paris and the Savoy and Carlton hotels in London.

When the Prince of Wales requested something light but delicious for a late dinner after a night in a Monte Carlo casino, Auguste Escoffier responded with *Poularde Derby*, a stuffed chicken served with truffles cooked in champagne, alternating with slices of butter-fried *foie gras*, its sauce basted with the juices from the chicken and truffles. Another interesting anecdote regarding the chef's originality in making sauces tells of a special dinner for the Prince of Wales and Kaiser Wilhelm. Escoffier was asked to create a special dish to honor such an occasion. Struggling with an apparent loss of creativity until the night before the event, the chef finally noticed a sack of overripe mangos, from which he created a sauce that he personally came out from the kitchen to serve. As he placed the plate on the table, he looked at the Kaiser and with a wicked smile said, "*zum Teufel*"—to the devil. Thus was born sauce diable, today a favorite classic sauce. Escoffier's insistence on sauces derived from the cooking of main ingredients was revolutionary at the time and in keeping with his famous instruction: *faités simple*—keep it simple.

In fact, in his search for simplicity, Escoffier reduced the complexity of the work of Carême, the "cook of kings and king of cooks," and aimed at the perfect balance of a few superb ingredients. In *Le Livre des Menus* (1912), Escoffier makes the analogy of a great dinner as a symphony with contrasting movements that should be appropriate to the occasion, the guests, and the season. He was meticulous in his kitchen, yet wildly imaginative in the creation of exquisite dishes. In 1903, Escoffier published *Le Guide Culinaire*, an astounding collection of more than 5,000 classic cuisine recipes and garnishes. Throughout the book, Escoffier emphasizes technique, the importance of a complete understanding of basic cookery principles, and ingredients he considers essential to the creation of great dishes.

Escoffier's refinement of Carême's *grande cuisine* was so remarkable it developed into a new cuisine referred to as *cuisine classique*. His principles have been used by successive generations, most emphatically by the *novelle cuisine* brigade. Francois Fusero, *chef de cuisine* at the Hotel Hermitage, Monte Carlo, and many others, regard Escoffier as their role model.

TECHNOLOGY SPOTLIGHT

Restaurant Technology: Front-of-house, Back-of-house, and Guest Experience

In the restaurant industry, the front-of-house and back-of-house operations are all about striving to provide high levels of guest satisfaction through consistency of products and customer service delivered. Over the years, technology has provided operators with the tools to offer a quicker and more consistent operation, which on the surface may seem simpler, but technology also has provided an expansion of the ways that consumers think about restaurant products and customer service. In this section, we will explore some of the newest and trendiest front-of-house, back-of-house, and guest experience technology and what this means for both restaurant operators and consumers in the fast-paced and ever-changing restaurant industry.

Some of the most popular guest experience technological advancements in the restaurant industry include smartphone apps and mobile payment. Recent studies have been conducted estimating that more than 30 percent of consumers would prefer to pay their restaurant bill with a mobile payment option rather than a physical credit/debit card or the cash payment option. The increase in consumer dependency on smartphone devices has forced restaurants to implement the capability to accept mobile payments.[8] Additionally, technology at the table allows consumers to order food and drinks from a tablet or kiosk provided by the restaurant, and, in some cases, directly from their smartphone. This front-facing technology allows for less wait time at the restaurant, which is desired by the current and future generation of consumers, as well as a decrease in wages spent by the restaurant, which is beneficial to the operator.

Tablet technology is on the rise, and this once experimental technology, first introduced by trendy and independent restaurant concepts, such as Carmel Kitchen & Wine Bar, is constantly gaining momentum and is now in the process of being implemented by larger restaurant chains, such as Applebee's, Chili's, and Buffalo Wild Wings. Additionally, some fast casual and **quick-service restaurants (QSRs)**, such as Pizza Hut and Chipotle, are beginning to test out touch screen and tablet technology and will begin efforts to implement this technology into their operations in the near future. Tablet technology has been named one of the hottest current trends in the industry by the National Restaurant Association, and it could potentially transition from a trend to a standard restaurant operational component in years to come.[9]

Smartphone apps are constantly gaining in popularity as more companies begin creating their own apps. Some of the most popular apps and reasons for consumers downloading apps include the following:

- Locating a restaurant or making a reservation (OpenTable, Urbanspoon, MenuPages)
- Reading reviews about restaurants (Yelp, TripAdvisor, Citysearch)
- Looking up the health content of menu items (HealthyOut, Gluten Free Fast Food)
- Promotions and discounts (LivingSocial, Groupon)
- Delivery services (Delivery.com, GrubHub, Seamless)
- Payment apps (PayPal, BarTab)[10]

These apps are helpful for both the consumer, because they provide quick reference points for easy dining out information, and for the operator, because they assist with promoting the restaurant and providing customer feedback on the dining experience.

POS (point of sale) systems are continuously increasing in capability with each model that is released into the market. The number of companies offering POS products is rapidly growing and with the current technological developments in the restaurant industry, there is much more to consider now with regard to payment processing, management features, and customer care when investing in a new POS system. For example, when considering payment processing, which is the most fundamental component of a POS system, it is important to consider whether the system supports most types of payments, mobile payments, online ordering, and bank association. Newly implemented management features can now support inventory and vendor data, loyalty programs, employee and customer profiles, remote access, and online store integration. Additionally, it is important to consider fees associated with POS systems, including monthly subscription fees, PCI compliance fees, and hardware support fees. Finally, POS systems are now produced in a variety of hardware formats for mobile or tablet products.[11]

One of the biggest technological buzzwords in the restaurant industry right now is "big data," which essentially refers to the large amount of data created from the restaurant's internal sources such as the POS system, kitchen inventory and revenue software, or other software used by the restaurant, as well as outside data sources (social media, Internet sites, or other sources providing information about or regarding the restaurant). Restaurants are currently attempting to combine the internal and external data to take full advantage of tracking marketing dollars spent, controlling costs, increasing revenue, and enhancing the overall dining experience.[12] Internet sites for companies like eBay, Amazon, and Overstock.com use big data to track online search and buying patterns, which allows them to make recommendations and suggestions for products and services using predictive analytics.[13]

The combination of internal and external technology use provides restaurateurs with the means to determine where to focus investing money to increase their brand perception, achieve operational efficiency, or enhance their product and service offerings. Ultimately, the decision to use this array of technology depends on the restaurant concept, customer demographics, and market competition, among other factors. With the constant increase in technology, fast paced industry, and wealth of information provided to consumers, it can be difficult to determine what is most important to enhance the customer experience and most often requires conducting significant market research. However, new technology also provides an opportunity for restaurateurs to experiment with new ideas, and with luck, they could be the first to implement the next big trend in the industry.

restaurants are removing additives from ingredients used in menus and some are avoiding genetically modified organisms (GMOs).

The term *back-to-basic cooking* has been redefined to mean taking classical cooking methods and infusing modern technology and science to create healthy and flavorful dishes. Some examples of this include the following:

- Thickening soups and sauces by processing and using the food item's natural starches instead of traditional thickening methods
- Redefining the basic mother sauces to omit the béchamel and egg-based sauces and add or replace them with coulis, salsas, or chutneys
- Pursuing more cultural culinary infusion to develop bold and aggressive flavors
- Experimenting with sweet and hot flavors
- Taking advantage of the shrinking globe and disappearance of national borders to bring new ideas and flavors to restaurants
- Evaluating recipes and substituting ingredients for better flavor; that is, flavored liquid instead of water, infused oils and vinegars instead of nonflavored oils and vinegars
- Substituting herbs and spices for salt

- Returning to one-pot cooking to capture flavors
- Offering more healthy dining choices in restaurants

Today, being a chef is considered a profession that offers a variety of opportunities in every segment of the hospitality industry and anywhere in the world.

Culinary Practices

In this new millennium, we are seeing culinary education setting the pace for dining exploration.[14] As you prepare for a career in the hospitality industry, you will find it imperative that you develop a strong culinary foundation. Within the structure of this you will need to develop cooking skills, strong employability traits, people skills, menu development skills, nutrition knowledge, sanitation/safety knowledge, accounting skills, and computer skills.

Before you can become a successful chef, you have to be a good cook. To be a good cook, you have to understand the basic techniques and principles of cooking. The art of cooking has not changed much in thousands of years—we still use fire for cooking; grilling, broiling, and simmering are still popular methods of cooking. However, science and technology have allowed us to improve the methods of food preparation.

To become a successful chef, you will need to learn all of the basic cooking methods in order to understand flavor profiles. As you look at recipes to cook, try to enhance the basic ingredient list to improve the flavor. As an example, always try to substitute a flavored liquid if water is called for in a recipe. It is also important to understand basic ingredient flavors so that you can improve flavor. The idea behind back-to-basic cooking means you evaluate your recipe and look for flavor improvement with each item.

Employability traits are those skills that focus on attitude, passion, initiative, dedication, sense of urgency, and dependability. These traits are not always traits that can be taught, but a good chef can demonstrate them by example. Most of the employers with job opportunities for students consider these skills to be more important than technical skills. The belief is that if you have strong employability traits, your technical skills will be strong.

One of the most important things to realize about the restaurant industry is that *you can't do it alone*. Each person in your operation must work with each of the others for you to be successful. The most important ingredient in managing people is to *respect them*. Many words can be used to describe a manager (coach, supervisor, boss, mentor), but whatever term is used, you have to be in the game to be effective. Managing a kitchen is like coaching a football team—everyone must work together to be effective. The difference between a football team and a kitchen is that chefs/managers cannot supervise from the sidelines; they have to be in the game. One of my favorite examples of excellent people management skills is that of the general manager of a hotel who had the ware-washing team report directly to him. When asked why, he indicated that they are the people who know what is being thrown in the garbage, they are the people who know what the customers are not eating, and they are the people most responsible for the sanitation and safety of an operation. There are many components to managing people—training, evaluating, nurturing, delegating, and so on—but the most important is respect.

INTRODUCING RICHARD MELMAN

Chairman of the Board and Founder, Lettuce Entertain You Enterprises, Inc.

Lettuce Entertain You Enterprises

Richard Melman is founder and chairman of Lettuce Entertain You Enterprises, a Chicago-based corporation that owns and licenses over 100 restaurants nationwide.

The restaurant business has been Melman's life work, beginning with his early days in a family-owned restaurant and later as a teenager working in fast-food eateries and a soda fountain and selling restaurant supplies. After realizing that he wasn't cut out to be a college student and failing to convince his father that he should be made a partner in the family business, Melman met Jerry A. Orzoff, a man who immediately and unconditionally believed in Melman's ability to create and run restaurants. In 1971, the two opened R.J. Grunts, a hip burger joint that soon became one of the hottest restaurants in Chicago. Here, Melman and Orzoff presented food differently and with a sense of humor, creating the youthful and fun restaurant that was a forerunner in the trend toward dining out as entertainment that swept this country in the early 1970s.

Melman and Orzoff continued to develop restaurant concepts together until Orzoff's death in 1981. Through his relationship with Orzoff, Melman formulated a philosophy based on the importance of partners, of sharing responsibilities and profits with them, and of developing and growing together.

To operate so many restaurants well, Lettuce has needed to hire, train, and develop people, and then to keep them happy and focused on excellence. Melman's guiding philosophy is that he is not interested in being the biggest or the best known—only in being the best he can be. He places enormous value on the people who work for Lettuce Entertain You Enterprises and feels tremendous responsibility for their continued success.[1] Melman says, "We hire people with creativity, passion, and the drive to be the best. That's the idea behind all of our restaurants, with authentic, ethnic concepts ranging from five-diamond French to upscale Italian, from Spanish Tapas to quick-serve Asian."

Today, he has 40 working partners, most of whom came up through the organization, and has 7,000 people working with him. Over the years, Melman has stayed close to the guests by using focus groups and frequent-diner programs. "We've had the ability to give people what they want almost before they know they want it. You can call it trendsetting. I prefer to call it the ability to listen to people."[2]

The group's training programs are rated among the best in the business, and Melman's management style is clearly influenced by team sports. He says, "There are many similarities between running a restaurant and a team sport. However, it's not a good idea to have 10 all-stars; everybody can't bat first. You need people with similar goals—people who want to win and play hard."[3] He places enormous value on the approximately 7,000 people who work for Lettuce Entertain You, and feels tremendous responsibility for their continued success. Melman's commitment now is to develop the young leaders of Lettuce to ensure that the company will be around for another 43 years. Melman's personal life revolves around his family. He and his wife Martha have been married for 39 years and have three children who are now successful restaurateurs themselves.[4]

[1]Marilyn Alva, "Does He Still Have It?" *Restaurant Business* 93, no. 4 (March 1, 1994), 104–111.

[2]Emily Clark, *A Taste of Lettuce Entertain You 2015*, Lettuce Entertain You Restaurants, http://www.leye.com. Click on News, Press Room, Press Kit (accessed February 16, 2015).

[3]*Home Page*, Lettuce Entertain You Restaurants, www.leye.com (accessed February 15, 2015).

[4]*Home Page*, Lettuce Entertain You Restaurants, www.leye.com (accessed February 16, 2015).

► Check Your Knowledge

1. Give examples of food trends and culinary practices.

2. What were Escoffier's most important culinary contributions?

3. Describe how Richard Melman became so successful in operating restaurants.

LEARNING OBJECTIVE 3
Describe the different characteristics of franchise, chain, and independent restaurants.

Franchises

There are several major restaurant brands that utilize business format franchising; this includes both the product and the service. Franchising is a great method for growing a particular business to multiple locations with the same or similar products or service. This is especially true for individuals who wish to run a business but prefer not to go through the process of starting a concept from scratch.

Through a contractual agreement, the franchisor grants the franchisee the rights to use their designs and plans, sell their products, and use their logos, promotional materials, and operational services. The franchisor normally supplies the operational systems, menus and recipe design, and management expertise. The franchisee must agree to maintain the standards set by the franchisor, who will also want the franchisee to meet the following qualifications:

1. Share their vision, mission, values, and business practices
2. Have been successful in other business or aspects of life
3. Have the motivation to succeed
4. Have enough money
5. Be prepared to undergo training
6. Have the time to devote to the franchise

The franchisee benefits by joining a proven successful restaurant concept, which is more likely to succeed than an unproven concept. However, the increased likelihood of success does incur costs. Franchise costs include a franchising fee, a royalty fee, and advertising royalties and requires lots of personal net worth. For example, a Taco Bell franchise requires a commitment to build three restaurants over three years. A stand-alone restaurant runs between $1,200,000 and $1,700,000 and does not include land or lease costs. For a Subway franchise, the estimated cost is between $101,000 and $285,000. This includes the complete investment in setting up a Subway franchise, and also operating expenses for the first three months. After opening, franchisees pay a royalty fee, which is 8 percent of gross sales.[15] The franchisee has total responsibility for operating the restaurant, including supervision of those they may hire to manage the restaurant.

There is also a disadvantage to becoming a franchisee. Because they must adhere to the franchisor's policies, procedures, and standards, the franchisee may feel a loss of operational independence. They may not be able to make certain business decisions, even if they think it would be better for the operation. Sometimes this loss of control by the franchisee appears too limiting, especially if they have an entrepreneurial spirit.

Chain Restaurants

Chain restaurants are a group of restaurants, each identical in market, concept, design, service, food, and name—the largest concentration is found in the quick service segment. Chains grew out of successful independent restaurants, first into a small group, and then, often by franchising, into a concept "with legs" (as they say in the industry) that spread across several states and eventually nationwide. Chain restaurants have proven more successful and more numerous with quick-service or fast casual concepts. A chain restaurant is owned by the parent company, a franchise company, or an independent operator sometimes called an operating partner. By the time a restaurant chain is established, the operators have figured out the best way of doing operational things and can make system-wide savings in design, layout, operating methods, staffing, menus, purchasing, inventory turnover, marketing, and promotions. With chain restaurants most of the important managerial decisions are made at the corporate office. Suggestions and ideas do often come from the restaurants and their guests. One of the biggest challenges is to maintain high quality and consistency with the food offerings.

Being associated with a chain has several benefits. First, if managed correctly, the chain can have outlets in various geographic locations. This global presence enables a chain operator to have a visible presence with a larger number of markets when compared to an independently owned and operated restaurant. A larger market reach gives a chain operator the ability to use national, as well as international, forms of advertising to potential customers.

Second, a chain operation allows a parent company to have multiple streams to generate revenue. This access to cash means that chains may be able to grow more rapidly when compared to its nonchain counterparts, the independently owned and operated restaurant. This multiple revenue stream model that chain restaurants create is one of the primary reasons the foodservice segment of the hospitality industry has seen rapid growth over the past few decades.

Independent Restaurants

Independent restaurants (also called indies) are typically owned by one or more owners who are usually involved in the day-to-day operation of the business. Even if the owners have more than one store (restaurant-speak for a "restaurant"), each usually functions independently. These restaurants are not affiliated with any national brand or name. They offer the owner independence, creativity, and flexibility, but are generally accompanied by more risk. For example, the restaurant may not be as popular as the owners hoped it would be, the owners lacked the knowledge and expertise necessary for success in the restaurant business, or the owners did not have the cash flow to last several months before a profit could be made. You only have to look around your neighborhood to find examples of restaurants that failed for one reason or another.

▶ **Check Your Knowledge**

1. Summarize the different characteristics of franchise restaurants.

Sustainable Restaurants

The average American meal has a shockingly large carbon footprint, usually traveling 1,500 miles to the plate and emitting large amounts of CO_2 in the process, according to the Leopold Center for Sustainable Agriculture.[16] Each meal created produces 275 pounds of waste a day, making restaurants the worst aggressors of greenhouse gas emissions in retail industry, says the Boston-based Green Restaurant Association (GRA), a nonprofit organization that works to create an ecologically sustainable restaurant industry.[17]

A recent NRA study shows that utility costs are a big line item for restaurateurs, accounting for a median of between 2.3 and 3.6 percent of sales, depending on the type of operation. According to *Zagat's America's Top Restaurants*, 65 percent of surveyors said they would pay more for food that has been sustainably raised or procured. According to National Restaurant Association research, 62 percent of adults said they would likely choose a restaurant based on its environmental friendliness.[18]

Does greening a restaurant sound challenging, time-consuming, and costly? According to the Green Restaurant Association, it doesn't have to be any of those things. The GRA was founded almost 20 years ago with the mission of creating an ecologically sustainable restaurant industry, and it has the world's largest database of environmental solutions for the restaurant industry.[19] The GRA strives to simplify things because it realizes that restaurateurs have enough on their plates without worrying what kind of paper towel to order, or where they'll get next month's supply of ecofriendly dish soap.[20]

Menu Planning

LEARNING OBJECTIVE 4
Summarize menu planning.

The menu may be the most important ingredient in a restaurant's success. A restaurant's menu must agree with the concept; the concept must be based on what the guest in the target market expects; and the menu must exceed those expectations. The type of menu will depend on the kind of restaurant being operated.

There are six main types of menus:

À la carte menus. These menus offer items that are individually priced.

Table d'hôte menus. Table d'hôte menus offer a selection of one or more items for each course at a fixed price. This type of menu is used more frequently in hotels and in Europe. The advantage is the perception guests have of receiving good values.

Du jour menus. Du jour menus list the items "of the day."

Tourist menus. These menus are used to attract tourists' attention. They frequently stress value and food that is quickly prepared, inexpensive, and reflective of regional tastes.

California menus. These menus are so named because, in some California restaurants, guests may order any item on the menu at any time of the day.

Cyclical menus. Cyclical menus repeat themselves over a period of time.

A menu generally consists of perhaps six to eight appetizers, two to four soups, a few salads—both as appetizers and entrées—eight to sixteen entrées, and about four to six desserts.

The many considerations in menu planning attest to the complexity of the restaurant business. Considerations include the following:

- Needs and desires of guests
- Capabilities of cooks
- Equipment capacity and layout
- Consistency and availability of menu ingredients
- Price and pricing strategy (cost and profitability)
- Nutritional value
- Accuracy in menu
- Menu analysis (contribution margin)
- Menu design
- Menu engineering
- Chain menus

Needs and Desires of Guests

In planning a menu, the needs and desires of the guests are what is important—not what the owner, chef, or manager thinks. If it is determined that there is a **niche** in the market for a particular kind of restaurant, then the menu must harmonize with the theme of the restaurant.

The Olive Garden restaurants are a good example of a national chain that has developed rapidly during the past few years. The concept has been positioned and defined as middle of the road with a broad-based appeal. During the concept development phase, several focus groups were asked their opinions on topics from dishes to décor. The result was extremely successful until sales fell in 2013 and 2014. A new board will now have to set the menu.[21]

Several other restaurants have become successful by focusing on the needs and desires of the guest. Among them are Darden Restaurants, Panera Bread, Chipotle, Hard Rock Café, Lettuce Entertain You, Union Square Hospitality Group, Blooming Brands, and Applebee's.

method will result in the same expected food cost percentage for each item. It would be great if we lived in such a perfect world. The problem is that if some items were priced out according to a 30-percent food cost, they might appear to be overpriced according to customers' perceptions. For example, some of the more expensive meat and fish would price out at $18–$21, when the restaurant would prefer to keep entrée prices under $15. To balance this, restaurants lower the margin on the more expensive meat and fish items—as long as there are only one or two of them—and raise the price on some of the other items, such as soup, salad, chicken, and pasta. This approach is called the **weighted average**, whereby the factors of **food cost percentage**, **contribution margin**, and **sales volumes** are weighted.

Menu Engineering

Menu engineering is a sophisticated approach to setting menu prices and controlling costs. It operates on the principle that the food cost percentage of each menu item is not as important as the total contribution margin of the menu as a whole. Usually this means that the food cost percentage of a menu item could be larger than desired, yet, the total contribution margin of the menu will increase. Through menu engineering, menu items that should be repositioned, dropped, repriced, or simply left alone can be identified.

Menu Design and Layout

Basic menus can be recited by the server. Casual menus are sometimes written on a chalk or similar type board. Quick-service menus are often illuminated above the order counter. More-formal menus are generally single page, or folded with three or more pages. Some describe the restaurant and type of food offered; most have beverage suggestions and a wine selection. The more upscale American-Continental restaurants have a separate wine list.

Some menus are more distinctive than others, with pictures of the items or at least enticing descriptions of the food. Research indicates that there is a focal point at the center of the right-hand page; this is the spot in which to place the star or signature item.[27]

Like a brochure for the hotel, a menu is a sales tool and motivational device. A menu's design can affect what guests order and how much they spend. The paper, colors, and artwork all play an important role in influencing guest decisions and help to establish a restaurant's image and **ambiance**.

As you can see, a number of factors make for a successful restaurant. Help is available from the U.S. Small Business Association (go to **www.sba.gov** and click on Learning Center in the top navigation bar), which has several courses and other information for those interested in developing a business plan for a restaurant. Now, let's look at the classifications of restaurants.

▶ ## Check Your Knowledge

1. Summarize menu planning.
2. Select a popular restaurant and identify its pricing strategy.

Classifications of Restaurants

There is no single definition of the various classifications of restaurants, perhaps because it is an evolving business. Most experts would agree, however, that there are two main categories: **independent restaurants (indies)** and **chain restaurants**. Other categories include designations such as *fine dining, casual dining and dinner house restaurants, family, fast-casual,* and *quick-service restaurants*. Some restaurants may even fall into more than one category—for instance, a restaurant can be both quick service and ethnic, such as Taco Bell. Fast-casual restaurants combine elements of both casual dining and quick-service restaurants. This category is continuously increasing its presence of different chains and concepts. Some of the most popular include Chipotle Mexican Grill, Firehouse Subs, Five Guys Burgers and Fries, and Pei Wei Asian Diner.

Anthony Bourdain, owner and chef of Les Halles, sits at one of its tables. Bourdain is the top-selling author of *Kitchen Confidential* and *A Cook's Tour* and is star of his own TV shows, *No Reservations* and *Parts Unknown*.

The National Restaurant Association's figures indicate that Americans are spending a lot of food dollars away from home at various foodservice operations. Americans are eating out up to five times a week—and on special occasions such as birthdays, anniversaries, Mother's Day, and Valentine's Day. The most popular meal eaten away from home is lunch, which brings in approximately 50 percent of fast-food restaurant sales.[28]

Part of the marketing strategy of a chain restaurant is to remove uncertainty from the dining experience. The same menu, food quality, level of service, and **atmosphere** can be found in any one of the restaurants, regardless of location. Large companies or entrepreneurs are likely chain restaurant owners. For example, Applebee's is a restaurant chain; some stores are company-owned, but the majority are franchised by territory.

Fine Dining

A **fine-dining restaurant** is one where a good selection of menu items is offered; generally at least 15 or more different entrées can be cooked to order, with nearly all the food being made on the premises from scratch using raw or fresh ingredients. Full-service restaurants may be formal or casual and may be further categorized by price, décor/atmosphere, level of formality, and menu. Most fine-dining restaurants may be cross-referenced into other categories, as mentioned previously. Many of these restaurants serve **haute cuisine** (pronounced *hote*), which is a French term meaning "elegant dining," or literally "high food." Many of the fine restaurants in the United States are based on French or northern Italian cuisines, which, together with fine Chinese cuisine, are considered by many Western connoisseurs to be the finest in the world.

▶ Check Your Knowledge

1. Summarize menu planning.

LEARNING OBJECTIVE 5
Identify some of the top chain
and independent restaurants.

Most fine-dining restaurants are independently owned and operated by an entrepreneur or a partnership. These restaurants are in almost every city. In recent years, fine dining has become more fun because creative chefs offer guests fine cuisine as an art. At places like Union Square Café and Gramercy Tavern in New York, Danny Meyer is looking for guests who want spectacular meals without the fuss. Many cities have independent fine-dining restaurants that offer fine dining for an occasion—a birthday, an "expense account" (business entertaining), or other celebration.

Marco Maccioni, son of Sirio Maccioni of the famed Le Cirque, says that the sons did not want simply to clone Le Cirque. For the menu, they sought inspiration from mama's home cooking—pizza, pasta, and comfortable, braised dishes.

Many cities have independent fine-dining restaurants that pursue those who are not content with wings and deep-fried cheese. Chefs are therefore making approachable, yet provocative food; each course is expertly prepared and may be served with wine.

A DAY IN THE LIFE OF CHRIS MARRERO

General Manager, Pei Wei Asian Diner

Pei Wei is an Asian-themed fast casual restaurant that is owned by P. F. Chang's China Bistro, which is a subsidiary of Wok Parent LLC. Pei Wei has about 190 locations and offers a different menu and dining atmosphere than its parent company. Pei Wei utilizes counter ordering where the guest orders, pays, and then takes a number to a table so the food runner can see where to bring the order.

Chris Marrero has been with Pei Wei for six years. He trained, then became kitchen assistant manager, assistant front-of-the-house manager, and finally was promoted to general manager. He leads a team of 45 associates. Chris generally works about 50 hours a week. He begins between 8:00 and 9:00 A.M. with a walk through the restaurant and a check of the online "red books"—an electronic logbook into which managers enter important details as a part of necessary communication. Chris will order the food, create the schedule, do inventories, and oversee the food preparation. With wok-seared cooking, everything is fresh with supplies coming six days a week. During the early morning, Chris checks the prep list to ensure the correct quantities are prepared. At 10:00 A.M. he conducts a line check where all the temperatures are checked. At 11:00 A.M. it's "all hands on deck" and no one leaves the line until 1:00 P.M. when one or two cooks go back to prepping. At 3:00 P.M. there is another line check for temperatures and freshness. At 4:00 P.M. there is a shift change with continued prepping until 5:00 P.M. when it's again all hands on deck. By 8:00 P.M. staff begin the breakdown of equipment and clean. By 9:30 P.M. the cash drawers are cleared and the deposits made.

Several types of restaurants are included in the fine-dining segment: various steakhouses, ethnic, celebrity, and theme restaurants. The upscale steakhouses, such as Morton's of Chicago, Ruth's Chris, and Houston's, continue to attract the expense account and "occasion" diners. Naturally, they are located near their guests and in cities with convention centers or attractions that draw big crowds.

A few ethnic restaurants are considered fine dining—most cities have a sampling of Italian, French, and other European, Latin, and Asian restaurants. Some even have fusion (a blend of two cuisines—e.g., Italian and Japanese). Fusion restaurants must pay particular attention when blending two unique ethnic flavors. If successful, the dish could turn out to be the latest craze; if unsuccessful, it could be disastrous!

Celebrity chef-owned fine-dining restaurants of interest include Wolfgang Puck's Spago, in four locations; Chinois in Santa Monica, California; CUT, in four locations; Wolfgang Puck Pizzeria & Cucina in Las Vegas; and Alice Waters's Chez Panisse in Berkeley, California. Both chefs have done much to inspire a new generation of talented chefs. Alice Waters has been a role model for many female chefs and has received numerous awards and published several cookbooks, including one for children.

The level of service in fine-dining restaurants is generally high, with a hostess or host to greet and seat patrons. Captains and food servers advise guests of special items and assist with the description and selection of dishes during order taking. If there is no separate sommelier (wine waiter), the captain or food server may offer a description of the wine that will complement the meal and can assist with the order taking. Some upscale or luxury full-service restaurants have tableside cooking and French service from a gueridon cart (a wheelable cart used to add flair to tableside service; it is also used for flambé dishes). The decor of a full-service restaurant is generally compatible with the overall ambiance and theme that the restaurant is seeking to create. These elements of food, service, and décor create a memorable experience for the restaurant guest.

Celebrity Restaurants

Celebrity-owned restaurants have been growing in popularity. Some celebrities, such as Wolfgang Puck, come from a culinary background, whereas others, such as Naomi Campbell, Claudia Schiffer, and Elle Macpherson (owners of the Fashion Café), do not. A number of sports celebrities also have restaurants. Among them are Michael Jordan, Dan Marino, John Elway, and Wayne Gretzky. Television and movie stars have also gotten into the act. Oprah Winfrey was part owner of the Eccentric in Chicago for a number of years. She said she bought the restaurant because she liked a sandwich she had there, but was told that the place was closing. So she stepped in and bought it! Matt Damon and Ben Affleck once owned the Continental, and Dustin Hoffman and Henry Winkler were investors in Campanile, a popular Los Angeles restaurant. Dive, in Century City (Los Angeles),

Wolfgang Puck.

HOW TO PROVIDE AN EXCEPTIONAL DINING EXPERIENCE

Courtesy of **James McManemon**, MS University of South Florida Sarasota–Manatee

Beth Dickinson, a food and beverage operations consultant shared her view of an exceptional dining experience in a renowned five-diamond restaurant based upon her own personal experience as a diner. Beth hoped that by describing a personal experience and sharing it with hospitality students she would be providing insights into the proper way to provide an exceptional dining experience through service.

Ms. Dickinson remarked that within 30 seconds of taking her seat the server greeted her congenially, introduced himself, and placed the dinner menu on the table, along with a special three-course menu. Quickly and unobtrusively the server removed the extra place settings on the table while conversing with her and inquired whether she would prefer sparkling or bottled water, then quickly returned with the consultant's selection. The server then ascertained whether Beth would prefer a glass of wine, a cocktail, or an additional beverage and explained the specials for that evening.

Upon conversing with Ms. Dickinson, the server determined that she was uncertain whether she was interested in having a vegetarian dish, chicken, fish, or red meat, and so he suggested several of his own favorite menu items, along with a suitable wine pairing for each, from which Beth made her selections: a bison tenderloin with a cocoa espresso rub, and a red zinfandel. The server was thoughtful in inquiring about his guest's cooking preferences for the main dish, and then suggested and described several of his favorite appetizers. Though an appetizer was declined, the server congenially removed the menus and departed, returning shortly to present a basket of warm bread and a small plate of butter, explaining that the warm cheddar biscuits were freshly baked in-house.

Delivering the entrée and wine 15 minutes later, the server explained the items on the plate, ensured that nothing else was needed and wished his guest an enjoyable meal. The server returned during the meal to conduct a quality check, thus ensuring that the meal was to the consultant's liking and refilling the water glass, which was three-quarters empty.

Once the meal was finished, the server promptly removed the soiled dishes and asked if Ms. Dickinson would like to see a dessert menu, offering a description of his favorite dessert item, the chocolate lava cake. The offer was declined, and the server departed and quickly returned with the check, wishing his guest "a wonderful evening," thanked her for coming, and asked her to "please return soon." Beth remarked upon this dining experience as one that "exceeded my expectations and provided me with my most memorable dining experience."

INTRODUCING SARAH STEGNER

Chef–Owner, Prairie Grass Café

Sarah Stegner opened Prairie Grass Café in Northbrook, Illinois, with her partner, former executive chef George Bumbaris of the Ritz-Carlton Chicago, in 2004. A little history.... .

Stegner, an Evanston, Illinois, native, grew up in a family devoted to food. Her grandmother was a caterer "before women did those kinds of things," and her grandfather was an avid backyard vegetable gardener. The table was the center of the family and was where Stegner's passion for food emerged.

INTRODUCING SARAH STEGNER *(Continued)*

After a year spent studying classical guitar at Northwestern University, Stegner followed her heart and enrolled at the Dumas Pere cooking school. She graduated with a chef's certificate one year later and was hired as an apprentice at the Ritz-Carlton Chicago.

In 1990, after six years of working in various culinary capacities (including a first job of cleaning fish for 12 hours a day), Stegner was promoted to chef of the Dining Room. She worked for years under the guiding hands of Fernand Gutierrez, former executive chef and director of food and beverage at the Ritz-Carlton Chicago, and current food and beverage director at Four Seasons Mexico City. Since then, Stegner has distinguished herself as one of America's most creative young chefs.

As a result of her talents, she has captured many national honors. Chef Stegner was named Best Chef of the Midwest in 1998 by the prestigious James Beard Foundation, and the Dining Room was named one of the top five restaurants in Chicago in 1999 by *Gourmet* magazine, and it received four stars from the *Chicago Tribune*. In addition, it was rated best hotel dining room in Chicago in 1999 by the prestigious Zagat Chicago Restaurant Guide and was named Best Restaurant in Chicago in 1996 by *Gourmet*, one of the top 13 hotel dining rooms in the United States in 1996 by *Bon Appétit*, and one of the top 10 hotel restaurants in the world in 1996 by *Hotels* magazine.

Chef Stegner is recipient of the 1995 Robert Mondavi Culinary Award of Excellence and captured the national title of 1994 Rising Star Chef of the Year in America by the James Beard Foundation. She also holds the title of Prix Culinaire International Pierre Taittinger 1991 U.S. Winner, where she represented the United States in the finals in Paris and was the only female chef present at the global competition.

In recent years, Chef Stegner has enjoyed periodic training in France, under the expertise of Chef Pierre Orsi at his two-star Michelin Pierre Orsi Restaurant in Lyon, France, and with chefs Bertolli and Berard Bessin in Paris.

She also finds time to donate her talents to charitable causes. Six years ago, she founded The Women Chefs of Chicago, comprising the city's top female chefs who donate cuisine for numerous events throughout the city to raise money for charity. Under her direction, The Women Chefs of Chicago have helped raise more than $500,000 for Chicagoland charities in the past few years.

Sarah's support of her state's agriculture is reflected in her food: she uses the finest seasonal produce from Midwest vegetable farmers and cheesemakers. She works with her husband, Rohit Nambiar, who manages the front of house at Prairie Grass Café. Her mother, Elizabeth Stegner, makes the pies served at Prairie Grass Café. Sarah feels right at home in her new restaurant.

was owned by Steven Spielberg; Dan Aykroyd was one of the co-founders of the House of Blues; Robert De Niro, Christopher Walken, and others own Ago; Kevin Costner, Robert Wagner, Jack Nicklaus, and Fred Couples owned the Clubhouse; and musicians Kenny Rogers and Gloria Estefan are also restaurant owners.

Celebrity restaurants generally have an extra zing to them—a winning combination of design, atmosphere, food, and perhaps the thrill of an occasional visit by the owner(s).

Steak Houses

The steak restaurant segment is quite buoyant despite nutritional concerns about red meat. The upscale steak dinner houses, such as Fleming's Prime Steakhouse & Wine Bar of Chicago, Ruth's Chris, and Houston's, continue to attract the expense account and "occasion" diners. Some restaurants are adding additional value-priced items such as chicken and fish to their menus to attract more guests. Steak restaurant operators admit that they are not expecting to see the same customer every week but hopefully every two or three weeks. The Chart House chain is careful to market its menu as including seafood and chicken, but steak is at the heart of the business, with most of its sales from red meat.

Outback Steakhouse, which is profiled in this chapter, owns and operates about a thousand Outback restaurants and about 30 Fleming's Prime Steakhouse & Wine Bars. Other restaurants in this segment include Stuart Anderson's Black Angus, Golden Corral, and Western Sizzlin', which all have sales of more than $300 million each. In fact, chains have the biggest share of the segment.

Casual Dining and Dinner-House Restaurants

LEARNING OBJECTIVE 6
Name the classifications of restaurants.

The types of restaurants that can be included in the casual dining restaurants category are as follows:

Midscale casual restaurants. Romano's Macaroni Grill, Olive Garden

Family restaurants. Cracker Barrel, Coco's Bakery, Bob Evans, Carrows

Fast Casual. Panera Bread, Chipotle, Carmel Kitchen and Wine Bar, PDQ, Qdoba Mexican Grill, Five Guys Burgers and Fries

Ethnic restaurants. Thai Flavor, Cantina Latina, Panda Express

Theme restaurants. Hard Rock Café, TGI Fridays, Roy's

Quick-service/fast-food restaurants. McDonald's, Burger King, Pizza Hut, Ponderosa, Popeyes, Subway, Taco Bell

As implied, **casual dining** is relaxed and could include restaurants from several classifications: chain or independent, ethnic, or theme. Hard Rock Café, TGI Fridays, Olive Garden, Houston's, Romano's Macaroni Grill, and Red Lobster are good examples of casual dining restaurants.

Houston's, which is owned by the Hillstone Restaurant Group, is a leader in the casual restaurant segment, with about $5.5 million average per unit sales in its restaurants. The menu is limited to about 40 items and focuses on American cuisine, with an $18 average per-person ticket for lunch and a cost of $40–$45 for dinner. While encouraging local individuality in its restaurants and maintaining exceptional executive and unit general manager stability, it succeeds with no franchising and virtually no advertising.

Over the past few years, the trend in **dinner house restaurants** has been toward more casual dining. This trend merely reflects the mode of society. Dinner house restaurants have become fun places to let off steam. A variety of restaurant chains call themselves dinner house restaurants. Some of them could even fit into the theme category.

Many dinner house restaurants have a casual, eclectic décor that may promote a theme. Chart House Seafood Restaurant, for example, is a steak and seafood chain that has a nautical theme. TGI Fridays is an American bistro dinner house with a full menu and a décor of bric-a-brac that contributes

CORPORATE PROFILE

Outback Steakhouse

The founders of Outback Steakhouse have proved that unconventional methods can lead to profitable results. Such methods include opening solely for dinner, sacrificing dining-room seats for back-of-the-house efficiency, limiting servers to three tables each, and handing 10 percent of cash flow to the restaurants' general managers.

March 1988 saw the opening of the first Outback Steakhouse. Outback's founders, Chris Sullivan, Robert Basham, and Tim Gannon, know plenty about the philosophy "No rules, just right" because they have lived it since day one. Even the timing of their venture to launch a casual steak place came when many pundits were pronouncing red meat consumption dead in the United States.

The chain went public and has since created a track record of strong earnings. It was evident that the three founders were piloting one of the country's hottest restaurant concepts. The trio found themselves with hundreds of restaurants, instead of the five they originally envisioned.

Robert Basham was given the Operator of the Year award at the Multi-Unit Foodservice Operators Conference (MUFSO). He helped expand the chain, a pioneer in the steakhouse sector of the restaurant business, to more than a thousand restaurants with some of the highest sales per unit in the industry despite the fact that they serve only dinner (although they now serve lunch at some locations).

Perhaps the strongest indication of what this company is about lies in its corporate structure, or lack thereof. Despite its rapid growth, the company has no public relations department, no human resources department, and no recruiting apparatus. In addition, the Outback Steakhouse headquarters is very different from that of a typical restaurant company. There is no lavish tower—only modest office space in an average suburban complex. Instead of settling into a conservative chair and browsing through a magazine-lined coffee table (as is the case in most reception areas), at Outback you must belly up to an actual bar, brass foot rail and all, to announce your arrival.

Also, Outback's dining experience—large, highly seasoned portions of food for moderate prices—is so in tune with today's dining experience that patrons in many of its restaurants experience hour-long dinner waits seven nights a week. The friendly service is notable, from the host who opens the door and greets guests, to the well-trained servers, who casually sit down next to patrons in the booths and explain the house specialties featured on the menu.

Using such tactics and their "No rules, just right" philosophy, the founders have accomplished two main goals: discipline and solid growth. Good profits and excellent marketing potentials show just how successful the business has become. Bonefish Grill, Fleming's Prime Steakhouse & Wine Bar, Carrabba's Italian Grill, and Outback Steakhouse make up the Bloomin' Brands, Inc. company.

to the fun atmosphere. TGI Fridays is a chain that has been in operation for 50 years, so the concept has stood the test of time.

Family Restaurants

Family restaurants evolved from the coffee shop style of restaurant. In this segment, most restaurants are individually or family operated. Family restaurants are generally located in or with easy access to the suburbs. Most offer an informal setting with a simple menu and service designed to please all the family. Some of these restaurants offer alcoholic beverages, which mostly consist of beer, wine, and perhaps a cocktail special. Usually, there is a hostess/cashier standing near the entrance to greet and seat guests while food servers take the orders and bring the plated food from the kitchen. Some family restaurants have incorporated salad and dessert bars to offer more variety and increase the average check.

The lines separating the various restaurants and chains in the family segment are blurring as operators upscale their concepts. Flagstar's acquisition of Coco's Bakery and Carrows family restaurant brands has created the high-end niche of family dining—somewhere between traditional coffee shops and the casual dining segment. The value-oriented operator in the family dining segment is Denny's. The more upscale family concepts include Perkins, Marie Callender's, and Cracker Barrel, all of which are sometimes referred to as the "relaxed" segment. These chains tend to have higher check averages than do traditional and value-oriented family chains, and compete not only with them, but also with moderately priced, casual-themed operators, such as Applebee's and TGI Fridays.

Karen Brennan, Synergy Restaurant Consultants, says that people's use of restaurants is very different from five years ago. Consumers are thinking in terms of "meal solutions." The operators in this segment are seeking to capitalize on two trends affecting the industry as a whole: the tendency of families to dine out together more often, and the quest among adults for higher-quality, more flavorful food offerings.

Ethnic Restaurants

The majority of **ethnic restaurants** are independently owned and operated. The owners and their families provide something different for the adventurous diner or a taste of home for those of the same ethnic background as the restaurant. The traditional ethnic restaurants sprang up to cater to the taste of the

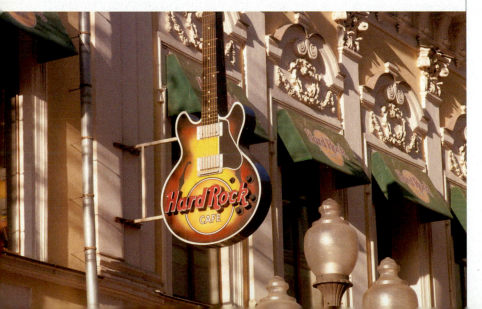

Hard Rock Café offers first-rate, moderately priced casual American fare with, of course, a side of rock and roll.

various immigrant groups—Italian, Chinese, and so on.

Perhaps the fastest growing segment of ethnic restaurants in the United States, popularity wise, is Mexican. Mexican food has a heavy representation in the southwestern states, although, because of near-market saturation, the chains are spreading east. Taco Bell is the Mexican quick-service market leader, with a 60-percent share. This *Fortune 500* company has achieved this incredible result with a value-pricing policy that has increased traffic in all units. There are more than 6,000 units with sales of about $7 billion. Other large Mexican food chains are Del Taco, La Salsa, and El Torito. These Mexican food chains can offer a variety of items on a value menu. Our cities offer a great variety of ethnic restaurants, and their popularity is increasing.

Guests being served at a Mexican restaurant.

Theme Restaurants

Many **theme restaurants** are a combination of a sophisticated specialty and several other types of restaurants. They generally serve a limited menu but aim to wow the guest by the total experience. Of the many popular theme restaurants, two stand out. The first highlights the nostalgia of the 1950s, as done in the T-Bird and Corvette Diners. These restaurants serve all-American food such as the perennial meatloaf in a fun atmosphere that is a throwback to the seemingly more carefree 1950s. The mostly female food servers appear in short polka-dot skirts with gym shoes and bobby socks.

The second popular theme restaurant is the dinner house category; among some of the better-known national and regional chains are TGI Fridays, Houlihan's, and Bennigan's. These are casual, American bistro-type restaurants that combine a lively atmosphere created in part by assorted bric-a-brac that decorate the various ledges and walls. These restaurants have remained popular over the past 20 years. In a prime location, they can do extremely well.

People are attracted to theme restaurants because they offer a total experience and a social meeting place. This is achieved through decoration and atmosphere and allows the restaurant to offer a limited menu that blends with the theme. Throughout the United States and the world, numerous theme restaurants stand out for one reason or another. Among them are decors featuring airplanes, railway, dining cars, rock and roll, 1960s nostalgia, and many others.

Quick-Service/Fast-Food Restaurants

QSRs consist of diverse operating facilities whose slogan is "quick food." The following types of operations are included under this category: hamburger, pizza, chicken, pancakes, sandwich shops, and delivery services.

The quick-service sector is the one that really drives the industry. Recently, the home-meal replacement and fast casual concepts have gained momentum (see Figure 6–1).

Quick-service or fast-food restaurants offer limited menus featuring food such as hamburgers, fries, hot dogs, chicken (in all forms), tacos, burritos, gyros, teriyaki bowls, various finger foods, and other items for the convenience of people on the go. Customers order their food at a counter under a brightly lit menu featuring color photographs of food items. Customers are even encouraged to clear their own trays, which help reduce costs. The following are examples of the different types of quick-service/fast-food restaurants:

Hamburger. McDonald's, Burger King, Wendy's

Pizza. Pizza Hut, Domino's, Godfather's

Steak. Bonanza, Ponderosa

Seafood. Long John Silver's

Chicken. KFC, Church's Chicken, Zaxby's, Kenny Rogers Roasters, Popeyes

Sandwich. Subway

Mexican. Taco Bell, El Torito

Drive-thru/drive-in/delivery. Sonic, Domino's, Pizza Hut

Quick-service restaurants have increased in popularity because of their location strategies. They are found in very convenient locations in every possible area. Their menus are limited, which makes it easy for customers to make quick decisions on what to eat. The world equates time with money these days, and most people do not want to spend time trying to look through long menus to make an eating decision. These restaurants deliver fast service and usually include self-service facilities, too. Such restaurants also use cheaper, processed ingredients, which allow them to have extremely

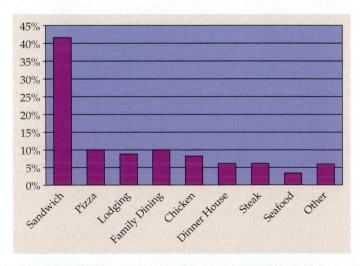

Figure 6–1 • Approximate Market Share of Restaurant Segments.

low, competitive prices. Quick-service restaurants also require minimum use of both skilled and unskilled labor, which increases the profit margins.

In an attempt to raise flat sales figures, more QSR chains are using cobranding at stores and nontraditional locations, including highway plazas and shopping centers. It is hoped that the traffic-building combos will increase sales among the separate brands, such as Carl's Jr. and Green Burrito. Many QSR chains are targeting international growth, mostly in the larger cities in a variety of countries.

Hamburgers

McDonald's is the giant of the entire quick-service/fast-food segment and serves millions of people daily. McDonald's has 35,000 stores in 118 countries with 1.9 million employees and sales of $27.5 billion.[29] This total is amazing because it is more than the next three megachains combined— Burger King, KFC, and Pizza Hut. McDonald's has individual product items other than the traditional burger—for example, chicken McNuggets and burritos as well as salads and fish, which all aim to broaden customer appeal. Customer appeal has also been broadened by the introduction of breakfast and by targeting not only kids but also seniors. Innovative menu introductions have helped stimulate an increase in per-store traffic.

In recent years, because traditional markets have become saturated, McDonald's has adopted a strategy of expanding overseas. It is embarking on a rapid expansion in the world's most populous nation, China, with more than 12,000 restaurants nationwide. The reason for this expansion in China is a rapidly developing middle class with a growing appetite for Western culture and food. McDonald's is now in 118 countries and has a potential audience of 3.2 billion people. Of the company's roughly 35,000 restaurants, approximately 16,000 are outside the United States, serving 70 million people each day.[30]

It is interesting to note that about 50 percent of total profits come from outside of the United States. More than two-thirds of new restaurants added by McDonald's are outside of the United States. McDonald's also seeks out nontraditional locations in the U.S. market, such as on military bases or smaller-sized units in the high-rent districts or gas stations.

McDonald's is taking another step toward being the most convenient foodservice operation in the world by striking deals with gasoline companies Chevron, Star Enterprise, and Mobil to codevelop sites.

It is very difficult to obtain a McDonald's franchise in the United States because they have virtually saturated the primary markets. It often costs between $1 million and $2 million to open a major brand fast-food restaurant. Franchises for lesser-known chains are available for less money (about $35,000) plus the 4 percent of sales royalty fee and 4 percent fee for advertising, but an entrepreneur needs about $125,000 liquid and $400,000 net worth for an upscale, quick-service outlet, not counting land costs.

Each of the major hamburger restaurant chains has a unique positioning strategy to attract their target markets. Burger King hamburgers are flame broiled, and Wendy's uses fresh patties. Some smaller regional chains are succeeding in gaining market share from the big-three burger chains because they provide an excellent burger at a reasonable price. In-N-Out Burger, Sonic, and Rally's are good examples of this.

Pizza

The pizza segment continues to grow, with much of the growth fueled by the convenience of delivery. There are several chains: Pizza Hut, Domino's, Godfather's, Papa John's, and Little Caesar's. Pizza Hut, with more than 13,000 units,[31] has broken into the delivery part of the business over which, until recently, Domino's had a virtual monopoly. Pizza Hut has now developed systemwide delivery units that also offer two pizzas at a reduced price.

In response to the success of Pizza Hut's Stuffed Crust Pizza, Domino's highlighted its Ultimate Deep Dish Pizza and its Pesto Crust Pizza. It is currently advertising its new artisan pizzas, which are intended to look like bistro-style pizzas, with unusual ingredients such as spinach and feta and salami and roasted vegetables.

Chicken

Chicken has always been popular and is likely to remain so because it is relatively cheap to produce and readily available and adaptable to a variety of preparations. It is also perceived as a healthier alternative to burgers.

KFC, with a worldwide total of more than 14,200 units,[32] dominates the chicken segment. Even though KFC is a market leader, the company continues to explore new ways to get its products to consumers. More units now offer home delivery, and in many cities, KFC is teaming up with sister restaurant Taco Bell, selling products from both chains in one convenient location. KFC continues to build menu variety as it focuses on providing complete meals to families. Amazingly, there are now more than a thousand KFC restaurants in China.

Church's Chicken, with over 1,600 units internationally,[33] is the second largest chicken chain. It offers a simple formula consisting of a value menu featuring Southern-style chicken, spicy chicken wings, okra, corn on the cob, coleslaw, biscuits, and other items. Church's focused on becoming a low-cost provider and the fastest to market. To give customers the value they expect day in and day out, it is necessary to have unit economies in order.

Popeyes is another large chain in the chicken segment, with more than 2,000 units, it is owned by AFC Enterprises. Popeyes is a New Orleans–inspired "spicy chicken" chain operating in the United States and 25 countries.[34]

There are a number of up-and-coming regional chains, such as El Pollo Loco, headquartered in Costa Mesa, California. It focuses on a marinated, flame-broiled chicken that is a unique, high-quality product. Kenny Rogers Roasters and Clucker's Charcoal Chicken are also expanding rotisserie chains.

Sandwich Restaurants

Indicative of America's obsession with the quick and convenient, sandwiches have achieved star status. Recently, menu debuts in the sandwich segment have outpaced all others. Classics, such as melts and club sandwiches, have returned with a vengeance—but now there are also wraps and panini.

A sandwich restaurant is a popular way for a young entrepreneur to enter the restaurant business. The leader in this segment is Subway, which

operates more than 42,199 units in 107 countries.[35] Co-for
parlayed an initial investment of $1,000 into one of the
growing chains in the world. Franchise fees are $12,500
fee of $2,500.

The Subway strategy is to invest half of the chai
in national advertising. Franchise owners pay 2.5
marketing fund. As with other chains, Subway is
core 18- to 34-year-old customer base by adding
Choices aimed at capturing the health-conscious n.
added a breakfast menu and flatbread to its bread offering.

Bakery Café

The bakery café sector is headed up by Panera Bread, a 1,880-unit chain
in the United States and Canada, with the mission of "a loaf in every arm"
and the goal of making specialty bread broadly available to consumers
across the United States. Panera focuses on the art and craft of bread-
making, with made-to-order sandwiches, tossed-to-order salads, and soup
served in bread bowls.[36]

▶ Check Your Knowledge

1. Name the different classifications of restaurants, and give examples
   of each.

2. Highlight some of the characteristics that make up the specific
   restaurant types.

Trends in the Restaurant Business

Courtesy of Dr. Greg Dunn, Senior Lecturer & Managing Director, UF Eric
Friedheim Tourism Institute

- *Social Media.* Social-media–based marketing for restaurants continues to
  grow and evolve. More and more people turn to the Internet for information about where to eat. Restaurants will continue to engage social
  media such as Pinterest, Facebook, and Twitter as a key component of
  marketing strategy. Along with registry sites that include a restaurant's
  name, address, phone number, map, and menu, tomorrow's restaurants
  will develop an online profile and participate in online review sites and
  blogs such as TripAdvisor, Yelp, Zagat, and Urbanspoon.

- *Sustainability and Local Foods.* Consumers are increasingly aware of
  where their food is coming from and featuring local foods on menus is
  a great way for restaurants to capitalize on the current trend as well as
  help out your local farmers. While some restauranteurs participate in
  the farm-to-table movement where chefs establish direct relationships

with both local and distant farmers to ensure the highest quality, sustainably farmed products, others operate their own farms and gardens. For instance, as the local sourcing trend continues, so does the hyperlocal subtrend of in-house growing. Beyond restaurant gardens, hyperlocal is extending more fully into house-made, farm-branded, and artisan items. From ice cream to cheese, pickles to bacon, lemonade to beer, restaurants are producing their own signature menu items from scratch.

- *Concerns over Public Health.* Now more than ever, restaurants are being pressured to create healthier meals with natural ingredients, smaller portions, and organic options. Many consumers are considered as overweight and/or plagued by chronic disease such as diabetes, while others suffer from allergies to core menu items that may contain peanut, gluten, or dairy-based ingredients. In response to public demand, more restaurants will offer smaller portion sizes and healthier food options on their regular menu as well as on children's menus. Some restaurants are even transitioning into organic only, grain-free, and GMO-free eateries, while others such as Chipotle, Bareburger, and PDQ feature organic and fresh ingredients into their menus.

- *Environmental Responsibility.* In concert with changes in consumer attitudes and demand for greater sustainability and environmental sensitivity by suppliers, food waste reduction and management is at the forefront of restaurant operations. Composting, recycling, and donating are all tactics of food waste strategies tying into both sustainability and social responsibility. In addition, food costs are expected to continue to rise causing restaurants to take a closer look at minimizing waste and surplus as a cost-management tool.

- *Global Menus.* An evolving trend for the past decades, ethnic cuisine continues its inroads into mainstream menus. As American palates become more sophisticated and adventurous, so do restaurant offerings. Micro-trending in this category includes fusion cuisine cooking, molecular gastronomy, and the blending of local authentic, regional and global foods, spices, and cooking styles, reflecting the breadth and depth of new techniques and flavors being explored. Also, ethnic ingredients, including cheeses, flour, and condiments, are increasingly finding their way into nonethnic dishes. Specific dishes, such as ramen, ethnic streetfood, and kids' entrees are also gaining momentum.

- *Locally Sourced Food.* From meats and seafood to produce, restaurants are more frequently purchasing from local farmers and fishermen, which helps to increase sustainability. Many independent restaurants are practicing hyperlocal sourcing by planting their own restaurant gardens.[37]

- *Healthful Kids' Meals.* Restaurants are creating specialized kids' meals that are not only healthy, but appetizing and aesthetically presented as well. Moving away from the traditional children's fare of fried chicken fingers and fries, hamburgers, and hot dogs, today's menu items are more likely to include a combination of lean protein, colorful fruits and vegetables, whole grains, and light marinades and sauces.[38]

Summary

1. Restaurants offer the possibility of excellent food and social interaction. In general, restaurants strive to surpass an operating philosophy that includes quality food, good value, and gracious service.
2. To succeed, a restaurant needs the right location, food, atmosphere, and service to attract a substantial market. The concept of a restaurant has to fit the market it is trying to attract.
3. The location of a restaurant has to match factors such as convenience, neighborhood, parking, visibility, and demographics. Typical types of locations are downtown, suburban, shopping mall, cluster, or standalone.
4. The menu and pricing of a restaurant must match the market the restaurant wants to attract, the capabilities of the cooks, and the existing kitchen equipment.
5. The main categories of restaurants are independent and chain. Further distinctions can be made as follows: fine dining, casual dining and dinner house, family, ethnic, and quick-service/fast-food. In general, most restaurants fall into more than one category.

Key Words and Concepts

ambiance	ethnic restaurant	niche
atmosphere	family restaurant	nouvelle cuisine
casual dining	fine-dining restaurant	purée
celebrity-owned restaurant	food cost percentage	quick-service restaurant (QSR)
chain restaurant	fusion	roux
contribution margin	haute cuisine	sales volume
culinary arts	independent restaurant (indie)	theme restaurant
dinner house restaurant	mother sauces	weighted average

Review Questions

1. Describe the evolution of American culinary arts.
2. What are the five mother sauces?
3. How are restaurants classified?
4. Explain why there is no single definition of the various classifications of restaurants; give examples.

Internet Exercises

1. Organization: **Panera Bread**
   Summary: Panera Bread has 1,880 bakery-cafes that feature high-quality breads, pastas, pastries, sandwiches, and coffee, reasonably priced food in an inviting comfortable atmosphere.
   (a) How many grams of salt are in each of its soups?

2. Organization: **Olive Garden Restaurants**
   Summary: The Olive Garden is a multiunit chain that primarily serves Italian food. It is currently operated by Darden Restaurants and has about 534 restaurants in the United States and Canada. Olive Garden strives to create a feeling of warmth and caring for every guest, which extends beyond the walls of the restaurants into the community.

Olive Garden participates in civic community service, such as delivering meals during times of crisis, sponsoring charity events, and hosting school tours of the restaurants.

(a) What kind of restaurant does the name Olive Garden represent?

(b) What is the Garden Fare? How is its menu different from the design and layout of the lunch menu?

Apply Your Knowledge

1. In groups, evaluate a restaurant and write out a list of weaknesses. Use the headings outlined in the restaurant chapters. Then, for each of the weaknesses, decide on which actions you would take to exceed guest expectations.

Suggested Activities

1. Identify a restaurant in your neighborhood and identify its catchment area. (A catchment area is the area where guests will be coming from.) How many potential guests live and work in the catchment area?

2. Search the Web for examples of four great restaurant Web sites. Compare them and share your findings in class.

Endnotes

1. National Restaurant Association, *News and Research*. http://www.restaurant.org. Go to News & Research and click on Facts at a Glance (accessed July 22, 2014).
2. Sarah R. Labensky and Alan M. Hause, *On Cooking*, 4th ed. (Upper Saddle River, NJ: Prentice Hall, 2007), 6–7.
3. Ibid.
4. Charlie Trotter, *Charlie Trotter* (Berkeley, CA: Ten Speed Press, 1994), 11.
5. Ibid., 12.
6. Alicia Kelso, "NRA, Healthy Dining Launch Healthy Menu Initiative for Kids," *Fast Casual*, July 12, 2011, www.fastcasual.com. Search "healthy menu initiative for kids" to access article (accessed November 4, 2011).
7. Wikipedia, *Auguste Escoffier*, http://en.wikipedia.org. Search for "Auguste Escoffier" (accessed September 1, 2015).
8. Tim Henschel, "Reflecting on the Technology Trends for the Restaurant Industry in 2015," *NCR Blogs*, March 6, 2015 (9:32 A.M.), http://www.ncr.com. Click on Blogs, Hospitality, and search for "Reflecting on the Technology Trends for the Restaurant Industry" to view this post (accessed May 27, 2015).
9. Skip Cass, "Technology Continues to Transform the Guest Experience," *Restaurant Hospitality*, July 15,

2013, http://restaurant-hospitality.com. Search for "Tablet technology" to view this article (accessed May 27, 2015).

10. Charlie White, "Maximize Your Weekend with the 35 Most Popular Restaurant Apps," *Mashable*, February 16, 2013, http://mashable.com. Search for "Maximize Your Weekend" to view this article (accessed May 27, 2015).

11. Abigail A. Lorden and Dorothy Creamer, "POS Software Trends 2013," *Hospitality Technology (HT)*, December 11, 2012, http://hospitalitytechnology .edgl.com. Search "POS Software Trends 2013" to view this article (accessed July 28, 2015).

12. "Big Data: Get Insights on What It Means for Restaurants," *National Restaurant Association*, February 19, 2015, http://www.restaurant.org. Search "big data insights" to view this article (accessed May 13, 2015).

13. "Wrap Your Arms Around Big Data," *National Restaurant Association*, http://www.restaurant.org. Search for "Wrap your arms around big data" to view this article (accessed May 13, 2015).

14. This section is courtesy of Chef Michael Zema, Elgin Community College, Elgin, IL.

15. Don Daszkowski, "Most Popular Franchises and How Much They Cost," *About.com*, www .about.com. Search for "Most Popular Franchises and How Much They Cost" to view this article (accessed May 11, 2015).

16. Restaurant Reformer, "Cork and Knife – Restaurants Tackle Their Own Incovenient Truth," http:// www.restaurantreformer.com. Search for "restaurants tackle their own inconvenient truth" to view this post (accessed September 1, 2015).

17. Green Restaurant Association, http://www .dinegreen.com (accessed March 8, 2014).

18. Ibid.

19. Green Restaurant Association, "Certification Standards for All Foodservice Operations," http:// www.dinegreen.com. Click on Certification Standards (accessed March 8, 2014).

20. Ibid.

21. Julie Jargon, Joann S. Lublin and David Benoit, New Board Will Set Darden's Menu. The Wall Street Journal October 11-12 2014 p. B3.

22. Chipotle, "Food with Integrity," www.chipotle .com. Click on Food with Integrity (accessed November 4, 2014).

23. Judi Curry, "Restaurant Review: Seasons 52," *San Diego Free Press*, January 9, 2014, www.sandiego freepress.org. Search "Seasons 52" for this article (accessed November 4, 2014).

24. Ibid.

25. U.S. Department of Agriculture, ChooseMyPlate. gov, *About Us*, www.choosemyplate.gov. Click on About Us (accessed November 4, 2011).

26. Dave Pavesic, "How to Win the Menu Pricing Game," *Restaurant Resource Group*, http://rrgconsulting. com. Click on Tips & Articles to find this article (accessed May 27, 2015).

27. Gregg Rapp, "Menu Engineering: How to Raise Restaurant Profits 15% or More," *Menu Cover Depot*, http://www.menucoverdepot.com/. Click on Resource Center and then Articles to view this article (accessed May 27, 2015).

28. Personal conversation with Jay R. Schrock, Dean, School of Hotel and Restaurant Management, University of South Florida.

29. McDonald's, *Our Company*, http://www.mcdonalds .com. Click on Corporate and then click on Our Company (accessed July 22, 2014).

30. Ibid.

31. Yum! Brands, *Pizza Hut*, http://www.yum .com. Go to Our Brands and click on Pizza Hut (accessed November 20, 2013).

32. Yum! Brands, *KFC*, http://www.yum.com. Go to Our Brands and click on KFC (accessed May 27, 2014).

33. Entrepreneur, *Church's Chicken*, http://www .entrepreneur.com/. Search for Church's Chicken (accessed November 20, 2013).

34. Popeyes Louisiana Kitchen, *Company Overview*, www.popeyes.com. Click on Company and then About Popeyes (accessed November 4, 2014).

35. Subway, *Home*, http://www.subway.com (accessed July 22, 2014).

36. Panera Bread, *Our History*, www.panerabread. com. Click on About Panera Bread and then click on Our History (accessed April 1, 2015).

37. Jan Fletcher, "A Case for Sourcing Locally," *QSR*, http://www.qsrmagazine.com. Search for "A Case for Sourcing Locally" to view this article (accessed January 8, 2015).

38. Anita Jones-Mueller, "7 Tips for Healthful Kids' Meals," *National Restaurant Association*, http://www .restaurant.org. Search for "7 tips for healthful kids' meals" to view this article (accessed January 8, 2015).

Front of the House

Restaurant operations are generally divided between what is commonly called **front of the house** and **back of the house**. The front of the house includes anyone with guest contact, from the hostess to the busser. The sample organization chart in Figure 7–1 shows the differences between the front- and back-of-the-house areas.

The restaurant is run by the general manager, or restaurant manager. Depending on the size and sales volume of the restaurant, there may be more managers with special responsibilities, such as kitchen manager, bar manager, and dining room manager. These managers are usually cross-trained to relieve each other.

In the front of the house, restaurant operation begins with creating and maintaining what is called **curbside appeal**, or keeping the restaurant looking attractive and welcoming. Ray Kroc of McDonald's once spent a couple of hours in a good suit with one of his restaurant managers cleaning up the parking lot of one of his restaurants. Word soon got around to the other stores that management *begins* in the parking lot and *ends* in the bathrooms. Most restaurant chains have checklists that each manager uses. In the front of the house, both the parking lot and any greenery, walkways, and steps need to be maintained well. As guests approach the restaurant, hostesses may hold the door open and welcome them to the restaurant or greet them upon entry. At the 15th Street Fisheries restaurant in Ft. Lauderdale, Florida, hostesses welcome the guests by assuring them that "we're glad you're here!"

Once guests are inside, the **host/hostess**, or as TGI Fridays calls him or her, "smiling people greeter" (SPG), greets the guests appropriately, and, if seating is available, escorts them to a table. If there is a wait, the host/hostess will take the guests' names and ask for their table preference.

Aside from greeting the guests, one critical function of the host/hostess is to rotate arriving guests among the sections or stations. This ensures an even and timely distribution of guests—otherwise one section may get

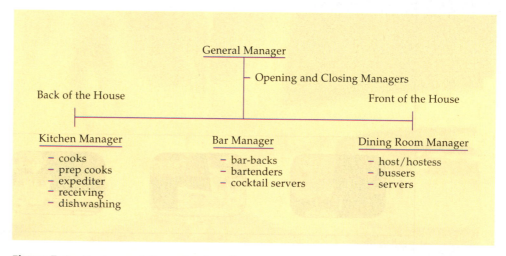

Figure 7–1 • Restaurant Organization Chart.

overloaded. Guests are sometimes asked to wait a few minutes even if tables are available. This is done to help spread the kitchen's workload.

The host/hostess maintains a book, or chart, showing the sections and tables so that they know which tables are occupied, and then escorts guests to the available tables, presents menus, and may explain special sales promotions. Some may also remove excess covers (the number of guests is known as covers in restaurants) from the table.

In some restaurants, servers are allocated a certain number of tables, which may vary depending on the size of the tables and the volume of the restaurant. Usually, five is the maximum. In other restaurants, servers rotate within their section to cover three or four tables.

The server introduces him- or herself, offers a variety of beverages and/or specials, and invites guests to select from the menu. This is known as suggestive selling. The server then takes the entrée orders. Often, when taking orders, the server begins at a designated point and takes the orders clockwise from that point. In this way, the server will automatically know which person is having a particular dish. When the entrées are ready, the server brings them to the table. He or she checks a few minutes later to see if everything is to the guests' liking and perhaps asks if they would like another beverage. Good servers are also encouraged, when possible, to pre-bus tables.

Bussers and servers may clear the entrée plates, while servers suggestively sell desserts by describing, recommending, or showing the desserts. Coffee and after-dinner cocktails are also offered. Suggestions for steps to take in table service are as follows:

1. Greet the guests.
2. Introduce and suggestively sell beverages.
3. Suggest appetizers.
4. Take orders.
5. Check to see that everything is to the guests' liking within two bites of the entrées.
6. Ask if the guests would like another drink.
7. Bring out the dessert tray and suggest after-dinner drinks and coffee.

In addition to the seven steps of the table service, servers are expected to be NCO—neat, clean, and organized—and to help ensure that hot food is served hot and cold food served cold.

For example, during the lunch hour, servers may be scheduled to start at 11:00 A.M. The opening group of two or three people is joined by

A fine-dining restaurant prepares to welcome guests.

HOW TO MYSTERY SHOP AN UPSCALE RESTAURANT

Courtesy of **James McManemon,** M.S., University of South Florida Sarasota–Manatee

Robert Heath, a veteran restaurant "mystery shopper," has performed over 1,000 inspections at various types of dining establishments throughout the country, from quick service to casual and fine dining. Robert recently shared the procedure that so-called mystery shoppers follow, from beginning to end, while performing restaurant "mystery shops."

Robert is registered as an independent contractor for several different mystery shopping companies throughout the United States. Once a mystery shopper is registered with a company, he or she is provided with access to a job board that lists various opportunities to "shop" restaurants. All registered mystery shoppers are required to apply to shop specific restaurants on the job board and make bids on the jobs listed. Once an individual wins a shopping job, they are scheduled to shop on a particular date by the mystery shopping company. A shopper, like Robert, is then provided with a general set of guidelines that he is required to follow when performing the shop. The steps to shopping an upper casual or fine-dining restaurant are listed as follows:

Step 1: The shopper is required to call the restaurant to inquire about making a reservation. During the reservation call, the most important things to test are as follows:

- The number of rings (length of wait) before the call is answered is reasonable.
- The greeting, including "thank you" for calling the restaurant, the name of the reservationist, and an offer of assistance.
- The reservationist was courteous and had a "smile" in their voice during the call.
- The reservationist repeated the reservation details back to the shopper including the name, date and time, and number of guests in the party.
- The reservationist offered a friendly farewell before ending the call.

Step 2: Once a shopper arrives at the restaurant, he or she is required to check in at the host podium, during which time the most important things to test are as follows:

- Did the host acknowledge you with a smile and a welcoming greeting?
- Once the host determined your name for the reservation, your name was used discreetly at some point.
- The host made conversation when escorting you to the table.
- The host provided chair assistance at the table.
- The host presented you with a menu and wished you an enjoyable meal.
- The host offered you a friendly farewell upon departure from the restaurant.

Step 3: A shopper, like Robert, is then required to examine the service provided at the table, during which time the most important things to test are as follows:

- The amount of time it took for the server to greet him was reasonable.
- The server greeted or welcomed him before asking for his drink order.
- The server offered him bottled, sparkling, or regular tap water.

- The server was able to explain the concept and menu, and provided recommendations.
- The server repeated the order back to him.
- The amount of time before each course was delivered was timely, and the courses did not overlap.
- The server announced the dishes when presenting them.
- The server checked on his satisfaction promptly after serving each course.
- The dirty dishes were promptly cleared when he was finished with his meal.
- Drink refills were offered by the server, and water was refilled unprompted.
- The server offered coffee and dessert.
- The check was presented in a timely manner, and payment was promptly processed.
- The server thanked Robert for dining and invited him to return.
- A manager was present throughout the dining area and was seen visiting guests at tables.

Step 4: While dining at the table, the food should be examined, during which time the most important things to test are as follows:

- The food is visually appealing and/or attractively presented.
- The food is served at the correct temperature and properly prepared.
- The food is flavorful and fresh.
- The menu is diverse in offerings.

Step 5: Throughout the course of the restaurant shop, the facility and the atmosphere should be examined, during which time the most important things to test are as follows:

- The outside of the restaurant, including the sidewalk, doors, walls, windows, and landscaping: Are they clean and well maintained?
- The interior windows, walls, floors, and carpet: Are they clean and free of debris, cracks, or stains?
- The podium is neat and organized.
- The table linens are clean and the table settings are uniformly set on the table.
- The china and glassware are clean and free of chips or marks.
- The temperature, lighting, and music are set at comfortable levels.
- The restrooms are clean and well maintained.

Additionally, Robert points out that during the mystery shop, it is important to note in detail the exact times that you interact with each staff member. Also, it is important to record the names and/or descriptions of staff members interacted with; however, it is not advised to ask staff members for their names. Instead, observe name tags if they are worn. If only a description can be determined, make sure to record the staff member's gender, height, hair color/length, and any other distinguishing qualities. All pertinent information can be easily recorded in the notes page on an iPhone, but always remember that subtlety is key.

of the same number at around 11:45 P.M. If the restaurant ... may be phased out early. When the closing group comes in, ... shift meeting, or "alley rally." This provides an opportunity ... sales figures, discuss any promotions, and acknowledge any ... are "eighty-sixed"—the restaurant term for a menu item that is not ... Recognition is also given to the servers during the meetings, serv- ... morale boosters.

Check Your Knowledge

1. Describe the principal functions of the front-of-the-house table server.

2. Why might guests be asked to wait a few minutes even if there are some tables available?

3. What does curbside appeal mean?

LEARNING OBJECTIVE 2
Explain how restaurants forecast their business.

Restaurant Forecasting

Most businesses, including restaurants, operate by formulating a budget that projects sales and costs for a year on a weekly and monthly basis. Financial viability is predicted on sales, and sales budgets are forecasts of expected business.

Forecasting restaurant sales has two components: guest counts, or covers, and the average guest check. **Guest counts**, or **covers**, are the number of guests patronizing the restaurant over a given time period—a week, a month, or a year. To forecast the number of guests for a year, the year is divided into 13 periods: twelve 28-day and one 29-day accounting periods. This ensures that accounting procedures are able to compare equal periods rather than months of unequal days. The accounting periods are then broken down into four 7-day weeks. Restaurant forecasting is done by taking into consideration meal period, day of week, special holidays, and previous forecast materializations.

In terms of number of guests, Mondays usually are quiet; business gradually builds to Friday, which is often the busiest day. Friday, Saturday, and Sunday frequently provide up to 50 percent of revenue. This, however, can vary according to type of restaurant and its location.

The **average guest check** is calculated by dividing total sales by the number of guests. Most restaurants keep such figures for each meal. The number of guests forecast for each day is multiplied by the amount of the average food and beverage check for each meal to calculate the total forecast sales. Each day, actual totals are compared with the forecasts. Four weekly forecasts are combined to form one accounting period; the 13 accounting periods, when totaled, become the annual total.

Restaurant forecasting is used not only to calculate sales projections, but also for predicting staffing levels and labor cost percentages. Much depends on the accuracy of forecasting. Once sales figures are determined, all expenditures, fixed and variable, have to be deducted to calculate profit or loss.[1]

▶ Check Your Knowledge

1. Explain the importance of restaurant forecasting.
2. What formula would a restaurant use to forecast guest counts and guest checks?

Service

LEARNING OBJECTIVE 3
Describe restaurant service.

More than ever, what American diners really want when they eat out is good service. Unfortunately, all too often, that is not on the menu. With increased competition, however, bad service will not be tolerated in American restaurants. Just as American cuisine came of age in the 1970s and 1980s, service is showing signs of maturing in the twenty-first century.

A new American service has emerged. A less formal—yet professional—approach is preferred by today's restaurant guests. The restaurants' commitment to service is evidenced by the fact that most have increased training for new employees. Servers are not merely order takers; they are the salespeople of the restaurant. A server who is undereducated about the menu can seriously hurt business. One would not be likely to buy a car from a salesperson who knew nothing about the car; likewise, guests feel uneasy ordering from an unknowledgeable server.

A server as a salesperson, explaining a dish on the menu to a guest.

Restaurants in the United States, Canada, and many other parts of the world all use American service, in which the food is prepared and appealingly placed onto plates in the kitchen, carried into the dining room, and served to guests. This method of service is used because it is quicker and guests receive the food hot as presented by the chef.

Servers at some San Francisco restaurants role-play the various elements of service such as greeting and seating guests, suggestive selling, correct methods of service, and guest relations to ensure a positive dining experience. A good food server in a top restaurant in many cities can earn $50,000 or more a year.

Good servers quickly learn to gauge the guests' satisfaction levels and to be sensitive to guests' needs; for example, they check to ensure guests have everything they need as their entrée is placed before them. Even better, they anticipate guests' needs. For example, if the guest had used the entrée knife to eat the appetizer, a clean one should automatically be placed to the right side of the guest's plate. In other words, the guest should not receive the entrée and then realize he or she needs another knife.

FOCUS ON RESTAURANT OPERATIONS

The Manager's Role

John T. Self, California State Polytechnic University, Pomona

It seems like only yesterday that I was walking into my first restaurant as a new manager trainee fresh from college. I found the restaurant industry perfect for me. It had plenty of variety, energy, and opportunity that matched my personality. I loved that I would not have to just sit behind a desk doing one thing every day. As a restaurant manager, your day will include accounting, human resources, marketing, payroll, purchasing, personal counseling, and many more functions that will challenge you.

You will be part of a management team that is the foundation of any restaurant, regardless of whether it is a chain or an independent. Managers have a huge sphere of influence, including customer service, sales, and profitability. You will be part of a management team responsible for a multimillion-dollar operation.

When you first become a manager, it is easy to be overwhelmed. You will probably feel that you will never be able to understand all the moving parts of a restaurant. However, as you grow in your management position, you will not only understand how it all works, you will also understand how you influence each part.

Being a restaurant manager offers the opportunity to grow as an individual because you will deal with so many types of people, including employees, peers, supervisors, vendors, and customers. You will learn how to get your team excited and motivated to share common goals. You will find it very rewarding to teach others about the culture of the business and will have many opportunities to make positive impacts on your staff.

The restaurant industry is the epicenter of the people business, and management is at the heart of the restaurant industry. Motivating people, delegating responsibility to people, and leading people is what we are about and what we do.

Whichever company you eventually join, each will present a slightly different environment, career path, hours, days, responsibilities, and opportunities, but all these companies will share an interest in food and in people at their core.

Another example of good service is when the server does not have to ask everyone at the table who is eating what. The server should either remember or do a seating plan so that the correct dishes are automatically placed in front of guests.

Danny Meyer, owner of New York City's celebrated Gramercy Tavern and recipient of both the Restaurant of the Year and Outstanding Service Awards from the James Beard Foundation, gives each of the restaurant's employees—from busser to chef—a $600 annual allowance ($50 each a month) to eat in the restaurant and critique the experience.[2]

At the critically acclaimed Inn at Little Washington in Washington, Virginia, servers are required to gauge the mood of every table and record a number (1–10).[3] Anything below a seven requires a diagnosis. Servers and kitchen staff work together to try to elevate the number to at least a nine by the time dessert is ordered.

Several restaurants are adopting various types of service—among the interesting ones is Chipotle, where guests line up and select their meal from food items displayed in hot containers in a line. After paying, the guests go to a station for a beverage, napkins, sauces, and cutlery, and then seat themselves, all for under $10. At Panera Bread, guests also queue up and order but then are given an electronic pager that is placed on the table so the order can be brought to them. Taking yet another service style, Carmel Kitchen & Wine Bar gives guests tablets with the menu. A description of each dish with photos and a wine selection is provided so guests can place their own orders directly to the kitchen, allowing a server to bring the food and beverages to the table quicker than most other restaurants.

Suggestive Selling

Suggestive selling can be a potent weapon in the effort to increase food and beverage sales. Many restaurateurs cannot think of a better, more effective, and easier way to boost profit margins. Servers report that most guests are not offended or uncomfortable with suggestive selling techniques. In fact, customers may feel special that the server is in tune with their needs and desires. It may be that the server suggests something to the guest that he or she has never considered before. The object here is to turn servers into sellers. Guests will almost certainly be receptive to suggestions from competent servers.

On a hot day, for example, servers can suggest frozen margaritas or daiquiris before going on to describe the drink specials. Likewise, servers who suggest a bottle of fumé blanc to complement a fish dish or a pinot noir or cabernet sauvignon to go with red meat are likely to increase their restaurant's beverage sales.

Upselling takes place when a guest orders a vodka and tonic—for example, instead of serving a lower priced "well" vodka, the server can try to sell the guest on a higher priced vodka like Stoli, Ketel One, or Grey Goose. Another example of the benefits of upselling is if a server is able to upsell a guest on a special by describing the menu item like this: "Our special tonight is a slow-roasted prime Angus beef rib roast, served with roasted potatoes and a medley of fresh vegetables." Now, if this entrée costs $10 more than other items on the menu, the table's check will increase by $10 for every guest who is upsold. If a server has a section of approximately five to six tables with an average of three guests per table and is able to turn those tables four times in a night, the potential increase in sales is between $600 and $720 if each guest is upsold on the special. Obviously every guest is not going to order the special, but each guest that is persuaded to buy a more expensive item increases the restaurant's overall sales.

Additionally, upselling is beneficial for the server as well. We know that a server receives about 15 percent in tips each night. In the scenario above, a server has the potential to make an additional 15 percent of $600 − $720 = $90 − $108 in tips.

▶ **Check Your Knowledge**

1. Describe the different types of restaurant service.
2. Explain the concept of suggestive selling.
3. Name three characteristics of a good server.

Sustainable Restaurant Operations[4]

Sustainability is not just a philosophy about food—it's about people, attitudes, communities, and lifestyles. In the spirit of the theme of the 5th Annual International Chefs Congress—"The Responsibility of a Chef"—the ideas below come from chefs across the country. There's an idea to inspire you each day of the next month; even picking one to consider, or act upon, per week is a good way to start. Almost everywhere one goes, we hear the same message: Small changes and efforts can make a big difference!

1. Go local. It's not possible for everyone all the time. But when it *is* possible, support your local farmers.

2. Take your team to visit a farmer. This is good practice for remembering that each piece of food has a story and a person behind it. (And you can bring back extra produce for a special family meal.)

3. Know your seafood. The criteria for evaluating the sustainability of seafood differ from those for agriculture. Inform yourself using resources like California's Monterey Bay Aquarium's *Seafood Watch Guide*, and demand that your purveyors are informed, too. If they can't tell you where a fish is from and how and when it was caught, you probably don't want to be serving it.

4. Not all bottled water is created equal. Some companies are working to reduce and offset their carbon footprint through a number of innovative measures. Some of the biggest names in the restaurant world (like *The French Laundry*) are moving away from water bottled out of house. In-house filtration systems offer a number of options, including in-house sparkling water.

5. Ditch the Styrofoam. Replace cooks' drinking cups with reusable plastic ones, and replace Styrofoam take-out containers with containers made of recycled paper. BioPac packaging is one option.

6. Support organic, biodynamic viniculture. There are incredible, top-rated biodynamic organic wines from around the world.

7. Support organic bar products. All-natural and organic spirits, beers, and mixers are growing in popularity and availability.

8. Even your kitchen and bar mats can be responsible. Waterhog's Eco Floor Mats are made from 100 percent recycled PET postconsumer recycled fiber reclaimed from drink bottles and recycled tires.

9. Devote one morning per quarter or one morning per month to community service. Send staff to a soup kitchen, bring local kids into the kitchen, teach the kitchen staff of the local elementary school a few tricks, or spend a few hours working in the sun at a community garden.

10. The kitchen equipment of the future is green! Major equipment producers, like Hobart and Unified Brands, are developing special initiatives to investigate and develop greener, cleaner, energy-smart machines (that also save you money in the long run).

11. Shut down the computer and **point-of-sale (POS) systems** when you leave at night. When the computer system is on, the juice keeps flowing—shutting it down can save significant energy bill dollars over the course of a year.

12. Check the seals on your walk-in. If they're not kept clean and tight, warm air can seep in, making the fridge work harder to stay cool.

13. Compact fluorescent light bulbs (CFLs) use 75 percent less energy than incandescent bulbs. CFLs also last 10 times longer, giving them the environmental *and* economic advantage.

14. Consider wind power. Ask your energy provider about options—Con Ed, for example, offers a wind power option. Though it tends to cost 10 percent more than regular energy, there's an incentive to bring the bill down by implementing other energy-saving techniques to offset the higher cost of wind power.

15. Look into solar thermal panels to heat your water. Solar Services, one of the oldest and biggest companies, will walk you through the process— from paperwork to tax credits. With the money saved on a water heater, the system will have paid for itself in two to three years.

16. Green your cleaning routine. Trade astringent, nonbiodegradable, potentially carcinogenic chemical kitchen cleaners for biodegradable, eco-safe products.

17. Use nontoxic pest control. The options are increasing, and even some of the major companies have green options.

18. Consider purchasing locally built furniture. See if there are any artisans in your state working with reclaimed wood (from trees that have fallen naturally because of storms or age).

19. Recycle your fryer oil. Biofuel companies across the country will pick it up and convert it.

20. Grow your own. Consider a rooftop garden or interior/exterior window boxes for small plants and herbs. EarthBoxes are one low-maintenance solution.

21. Cut down on shipping materials. Request that purveyors send goods with the least amount of packing materials possible. Request that Styrofoam packaging not be used.

22. Trade in white toilet paper, c-folds, and restroom paper towels. Instead, use products made of chlorine-free, unbleached, recycled paper.

23. Need new toilets? There are a number of water-saving options that save anywhere from half a gallon to more than a gallon per flush.

The old-fashioned brick technique is a good start, too: place a brick in the tank of your toilet—the space that it takes up is water saved each time the toilet is flushed.

24. Compost garbage. Even high-volume establishments can make this happen. Keep separate cans for all food-based waste, and dump it in a compost bin out back. A common misconception about compost is that it smells bad—this is not true!

25. Recycle! Be strict about kitchen and bar staff recycling glass and plastic receptacles. Recycle cardboard and wood boxes used for produce, and any newspapers or magazines sent to the restaurant.

26. Cut down on linens. Tablecloths and napkins require a large amount of chemical cleaners, bleaches, and starches. Stay away from white, if possible. If it's not imperative, consider eliminating tablecloths all together. Go for soft cloth napkins instead of starched.

27. Ice = water + energy. Don't waste it! Don't automatically refill ice bins—wait until they truly get low, and only add as much as you need to get through the crush. Ice is expensive to produce, both in terms of money and resources.

28. If you're a small restaurant or café, without huge needs or storage space, look into joining (or forming) a local co-op for purchasing green items. Cleaning supplies, paper products, and so on are all cheaper in bulk.

29. Educate yourself! From agricultural philosophy to the specifics of restaurant operations, the number of resources for green issues and practices is ever growing. Pick up *The Omnivore's Dilemma* by Michael Pollan, the Green Restaurant Association's *Dining Green: A Guide to Creating Environmentally Sustainable Restaurants and Kitchens*, and *Sourcing Seafood: A Professional's Guide to Procuring Ocean-friendly Fish and Shellfish* by Seafood Choices Alliance.

30. Last but not least, educate your staff! They need to know *why* you're doing what you're doing, so that they can spread the word—to the diners, and beyond!

▶ Check Your Knowledge

1. Name at least two ways to practice sustainability in a restaurant operation.

LEARNING OBJECTIVE 4
Describe front- and back-of-the-house systems.

Front-of-the-House Restaurant Systems

Point-of-Sale Systems

POS systems are very common in restaurants and other foodservice settings, such as stadiums, theme parks, airports, and cruise ships. These systems are used by hotel properties that have food and beverage and retail outlets. They are used to track food and beverage charges and other retail charges that may occur at a hotel or restaurant. A POS system is made up of a number of POS terminals that interface with a remote central processing unit. A POS terminal may be used as an electronic cash register, too.

MICROS, a leading software, hardware, and enterprise systems provider, offers the MICROS 3700 point-of-sale system, a modular suite of applications that encompasses front-of-the-house, back-of-the-house, and enterprise systems. The popular 3700 POS is a Microsoft Windows–based touch-screen system where client terminals are networked to a central POS server. Transactions are rung at the terminal and posted into the database for later analysis and reporting. The 3700 POS will support a network of kitchen printers so that orders can be presented to line cooks and chefs for food preparation. This POS system also supports use of a wireless **personal digital assistant (PDA)** as an order-taking device so that servers can take orders directly from the guest tableside. Mobile handheld devices can greatly speed the processing of orders to the kitchen and ultimately increase revenues as a result of faster table turns.

A point-of-sale system.

Kitchen Display Systems

Kitchen display systems further enhance the processing of orders to and in the kitchen. Printers in the kitchen may be replaced with video monitors and present orders to kitchen associates along with information on how long orders are taking to be prepared. Orders change color or flash on the monitor, which alerts kitchen associates to orders that are taking too long. Kitchen monitors are widely used in quick-service restaurants but are also gaining momentum in table service restaurants. Kitchen video systems also post order preparation time to a central database for later reporting and analysis by management to determine how the kitchen is performing.

Guest Services Solutions

Guest services solutions are applications that are designed to help a restaurateur develop a dining relationship with guests. Applications include a frequent-diner management program, delivery management with caller ID interface, and guest-accounts receivable to manage home accounts and gift certificates. All these applications are accessed through the POS system and give restaurateurs the opportunity to offer their guests convenience, while allowing the restaurateurs to track who their best customers are. Guest activity is posted into the central database and management can develop targeted marketing programs based on this information.

Back-of-the-House Restaurant Systems

Back-of-the-house systems are also known as product management systems and include inventory control and food costing, labor management, and financial reporting features. SoftCafe develops software for restaurants and foodservice operations, allowing them to create menus on personal computers. SoftCafe MenuPro® creates professional menus at a fraction of the cost of print shop menus, with more than 175 predesigned menu styles; 1,500 menu graphics, watermarks, borders, and food illustrations; more than 100 font types; and a culinary spelling checker.[5] Beverage inventory systems are discussed in Chapter 9.

Restaurant Magic, based in Tampa, Florida, has several excellent restaurant management solutions: Data Central is delivered to a desktop as an enterprise-quality, secure, and reliable, centralized business management solution to deliver powerful, user-friendly forms and reports to any Web-connected Windows PC in a restaurant organization. Data Central is a technological breakthrough in centralized application and database management because it is written entirely in the Visual C# language and is deployed as a Microsoft .NET Framework solution. Access to information is specified at the log-in level, and applications, reports, and important data are updated once available to all users automatically.[6] For a restaurant chain such as Outback Steakhouse, "Secure centralized management of enterprise data is more than a best practice, it is a necessity."[7] The benefits of programs such as Data Central are clear: Multistore managers can now view data for the enterprise. Store-level managers can view data for their store or for any group of stores they choose.

Restaurant Magic's Profit and Loss (P&L) Reporting delivers profit and loss information on demand, consolidating information from purchasing to produce accurate cost of goods sold. All the key data are collected from the POS to track all revenues, forms of payments, and complementary activity (such as data from time clocks in order to collect labor costs) and integrate it with all other data to produce P&L reporting daily, weekly, and multiperiod. The Profit and Loss Reporting allows a collaborative P&L budgeting system where the store and regional managers work together to build budgets and assess results quickly.[8]

Wireless POS Systems

Peter Perdikakis is the owner of two Skyline Chili fast-casual restaurants in Cincinnati. The restaurants are unusual in that the kitchen is open and visible to diners. Servers used to simply yell the orders across the steam table. Peter says, "You eat off china and have silverware, but it's very fast—typically you get your order about two minutes after it's ordered. Other POS systems slowed this process down because the servers had to go over to a terminal and write down the order," which is why Peter became interested in wireless. When he wanted to expand his operations, he selected a Pocket POS system from PixelPoint, consisting of two primary fixed terminals (one at a drive-through window and one at the checkout station), three handheld units for use on the dining floor, and another fixed unit for the back office.

Sample menu.

The PixelPoint wireless POS system allows the servers to use a handheld PDA, which operates on the Windows CE platform, to send orders to the kitchen. Given that wireless POS systems speed up orders, their use in restaurants is likely to increase.

Labor Management

Most front-of-the-house systems have the ability to track employee working time. A back-of-the-house labor management package adds the ability to manage all of a restaurant's payroll and human resource information. A labor management system includes a human resources module to track hiring, employee personal information, vacation, I-9 status, security privileges, tax status, availability, and any other information pertinent to employees working at the restaurant. A labor management system would also include scheduling capability so that managers can create weekly schedules based on forecasted business. Schedules can then be enforced when employees check in and out so that labor costs can be managed.

The labor management package also presents actual work time and pay rates to a payroll processor so that paychecks can be cut and distributed. It also collates tips data and receipt data from the front of the house so that proper tip allocations can be reported according to IRS guidelines.

Financial Reporting

Back-of-the-house and front-of-the-house systems post data into a relational database located on the central server. The restaurant manager uses these data for reporting and decision making. P&L reports, budget variances, end-of-day reports, and other financial reports are generated from the central database. Financial management reporting needs to be flexible so that restaurant operators can manipulate it in ways that are useful to them. It is also important to get reports during the day in real time as the day unfolds so that restaurateurs can make decisions before profit is lost. Some reporting packages provide a graphical representation of the financial data displayed continuously on a monitor so that critical restaurant data are always available. This type of reporting provides restaurants with a real-time "heartbeat" for their operations.

Both back-of-the-house and front-of-the-house systems must be reliably linked so that POS food costs, labor costs, service times, and guest activity can be analyzed on the same reports. Restaurant management can then make critical business decisions armed with all necessary information. Technology is also used to collect data throughout the day for real-time budget control and "on-the-fly" management of labor effectiveness. Budgets are tight, and this is a way for management to watch, in real time, where their labor costs are at all times.

Personal Digital Assistants

PDAs help hospitality businesses stay effective and efficient by improving time management and helping with faster service. For example, computer systems are used today in restaurants to transmit orders to the kitchen and to retrieve and post guest payments. These actions took extra time in the

A waiter uses a tablet to place an order.

past, when the computer systems were placed at a distance from the server. PDAs have been created to allow servers to control their business with their fingertips.

One leading software provider to restaurant operators is Restaurant Technologies, Inc. (RTI). RTI was founded by two restaurant owners who understood the accounting applications that operate from a central platform known as the Restaurant Financial System. Working together, their accounting programs form an integrated system, with the following modules:

- Accounts payable
- Check reconciliation
- Daily store reporting
- General ledger
- Payroll
- Time keeping

PDAs can also be used in the hotel setting. Often, PDAs can be integrated with a property management system (PMS) to give housekeepers real-time information about which rooms need to be cleaned and which rooms are not occupied. In the same way, as housekeepers complete the cleaning of a room, they can send a wireless signal to the front desk to affirm that the room is ready to be occupied.

▶ Check Your Knowledge

1. What are front- and back-of-the-house systems? Describe their purpose and function.

2. Briefly define guest services solutions.

3. Explain the ways in which advances in technology aid the inventory process in restaurants.

4. What are the benefits of using a PDA?

LEARNING OBJECTIVE 5
Outline back-of-the-house operations.

Back-of-the-House Operations

The back of the house refers to all the areas that guests do not typically come in contact with; it is generally run by the kitchen manager. The back of the house includes purchasing, receiving, storing/issuing, food production, stewarding, budgeting, accounting, and control.

One of the most important aspects to running a successful restaurant is having a strong back-of-the-house operation, particularly in the kitchen. The kitchen is the backbone of every full-service restaurant; thus, it must be well managed and organized. Some of the main considerations in efficiently operating the back of the house include staffing, scheduling, training, food cost analysis, production, management involvement, management follow-up, and employee recognition.

Food Production

Planning, organizing, and producing food of a consistently high quality are no easy tasks. The kitchen manager, cook, or chef begins the production process by determining the expected volume of business for the next few days. The same period's sales from the previous year will give a good indication of the expected volume and the breakdown of the number of sales of each menu item. As described earlier, ordering and receiving will have already been done for the day's production schedule.

The **kitchen manager** checks the head line cook's order, which will bring the prep (preparation) area up to the **par stock** of prepared items. (Par stock is the amount of stock to be on hand at any time so reordering takes place to ensure an adequate amount of stock is available.) Most of the prep work is done in the early part of the morning and afternoon. Taking advantage of slower times allows the line cooks to do the final preparation just prior to and during the actual meal service.

The kitchen layout is set up according to the business projected as well as the menu design. Most full-service restaurants have similar layouts and designs for their kitchens. The layout consists of the back door area, walk-ins, the freezer, dry storage, prep line, salad bar, cooking line, expediter, dessert station, and service bar area.

The **cooking line** is the most important part of the kitchen layout. It might consist of a broiler station, window station, fry station, salad station, sauté station, and pizza station—just a few of the intricate parts that go into the setup of the back of the house. The size of the kitchen and its equipment are all designed according to the sales forecast for the restaurant.

The kitchen will also be set up according to what the customers prefer and order most frequently. For example, if guests eat more broiled or sautéed items, the size of the broiler and sauté must be larger to cope with the demand.

Teamwork, a prerequisite for success in all areas of the hospitality and tourism industry, is especially important in the kitchen. Because of the hectic pace, pressure builds, and unless each member of the team excels, the result will be food that is delayed, not up to standard, or both.

Although organization and performance standards are necessary, it is helping each other with the prepping and the cooking that makes for teamwork. "It's just like a relay race; we can't afford to drop the baton," says Amy Lu, kitchen manager of China Coast restaurant in Los Angeles. Teamwork in the back of the house is like an orchestra playing in tune, each player adding to the harmony.

Another example of organization and teamwork is TGI Fridays five rules of control for running a kitchen:

Chefs working together as a team.

This will help management get feedback on the running of the kitchen and on how well the development program works in their particular operation. Also, this allows for internal growth and promotion.

Production Procedures

Production in the kitchen is key to the success of a restaurant because it relates directly to the recipes on the menu and how much product is on hand to produce the menu. Thus, controlling the production process is crucial. To undertake such a task, **production control sheets** are created for each station, for example, broiler, sauté, fry, pantry, window, prep, dish, and dessert. With the control sheets, levels are set up for each day according to sales. Figure 7–2 shows a production sheet for a popular seafood restaurant.

The first step in creating the production sheets is to count the products on hand for each station. After the production levels are determined, the amount of product required to reach the level for each recipe is decided. After these calculations are completed, the sheets are handed to the cooks. It is important to make these calculations before the cooks arrive, considering the amount of prep time that is needed to produce before business is conducted. For instance, if a restaurant is open only for lunch and dinner, enough product should be on hand by 11:00 A.M. to ensure that the cooks are prepared to handle the lunch crowd.

When determining production, par stock levels should be changed weekly according to sales trends. This will help control and minimize waste levels. Waste is a large contributor to food cost; therefore, the kitchen manager should determine the product levels necessary to make it through only one day. Products have a particular shelf life, and if the kitchen overproduces and does not sell the product within its shelf life, it must be thrown away. More important, this practice allows the freshest product to reach the customers on a daily basis.

After the lunch rush, the kitchen manager checks to see how much product was sold and how much is left for the night shift. (Running out of a product is unacceptable and should not happen. If proper production procedures are followed, a restaurant will not have to "86" anything—meaning that an item is no longer available on the menu.) After all production is completed on all stations, the cooks may be checked out. It is essential to check out the cooks and hold them accountable for production levels. If they are not checked out, they will slide on their production, negatively affecting the restaurant and the customer.

The use of production sheets is critical in controlling how the cooks use the products, as well, because production plays a key role in food cost. Every recipe has a particular "spec" (specification) to follow. When one deviates from the recipe, quality goes down, consistency is lost, and food cost goes up. That is why it is important to follow the recipe at all times.

Management Involvement and Follow-Up

As in any business, management involvement is vital to the success of a restaurant. Management should know firsthand what is going on in the back of

ITEM	PAR	ON HAND	PREP	INITIAL
FRESH CATCH				
Add Island Sauce to any fish				
BBQ Shrimp				
Casino				
Coconut Lobster				
Fried Lobster				
Ritz Crusted				
Seafood Kabob				
Stuffed Salmon				
SNAPPER				
Almondine				
Anna				
Broiled				
Fingers				
Stuffed				
FLOUNDER				
Allmondine				
Fried, Baked				
Stuffed				
GROUPER				
Baked				
Casino				
Coconut				
Coconut				
Floribean				
Fried Nutty				
Mexical				
Nuggets				
Nutty				
Potato Crusted				
Ritz				
Stuffed				
Wisconsin				
Holiday Specials				
DAILY APPETIZERS				
Oysters Maria (3 ea)				
Mozzereal Cheese Sticks (5 ea)				
Jammers, Jalapeno (4ea)				
Jammers, Seafood (10ea)				
Clam Strip Basket (6oz)				
Buffalo Shrimp (5ea)				
BBQ Shrimp (1 Skewer 5 Shrimp)				
Gator Gites (6oz)				

ITEM			
WRAPS			
Ham or Turkey			
Ham & turkey			
Shrimp Salad			
Chicken Caesar			
Chicken Salad			
BLT Wrap			
DAILY SALADS			
Seafood or Chicken Salad			
Shrimp			
Chicken Mediterrarean			
PIZZA			
Shrimp or B.B.Q. Chicken			
Portabello			
SOUP & SAND			
Clamwich, Mini Grouper			
Crab Cake, Chicken Salad			
EXTRA DAILY SPECIALS			
Monday AUCE Fish			
Tues Lobster			
Wed AUCE Popcorn\Crabby Night			
Thur Prime Rib			
Beef Tips and Noodles			
Chicken Pot Pie			
Salisbury Stk			
Ham & Mac & Cheese			
Chicken Oscar			
Stone Crab Mustard Sauce			
Corn Salsa			
SPECIALS ITEMS FOR CATERING			

Pull From Freezer			
Item	Par	On Hand	Pull	Initial

08/25/2003

01/12/04

Figure 7–2 • A Production Sheet for a Popular Seafood Restaurant.

(*Source:* Anna Maria Oyster Bar, Inc.)

the house. It is also important that they be "on the line," assisting the staff in the preparation of the menu and in the other operations of the kitchen, just as they should be helping when things are rushed. When management is visible to the staff, they are prone to do what they need to be doing at all times, and food quality is more apparent and consistent. Managers should constantly be walking and talking food cost, cleanliness, sanitation, and quality. This shows the staff how serious and committed they are to the successful running of the back of the house.

As management spends more time in the kitchen, more knowledge is gained, more confidence is acquired, and more respect is earned. Employee–management interaction produces a sense of stability and a strong work ethic among employees, resulting in higher morale and promoting a positive working environment. To ensure that policies and standards are being upheld, management follow-up should happen on a continual basis. This is especially important when cooks are held accountable to specifications and production and when other staff members are given duties to perform. Without follow-up, the restaurant may fold.

Employee Recognition

Employee recognition is an extremely important aspect of back-of-the-house management. Recognizing employees for their efforts creates a positive work environment that motivates the staff to excel and ultimately to produce consistently better-quality food for the guests.

Recognition can take many different forms, from personally commending a staff person for his or her efforts to recognizing a person in a group setting. By recognizing employees, management can make an immediate impact on the quality of operations. This can be a great tool for building sales, as well as assisting in the overall success of the restaurant.

▶ Check Your Knowledge

1. Outline back-of-the-house operations.
2. Explain the following terms: product specification, production control sheets.
3. Discuss the five rules for running a kitchen that TGI Fridays has implemented.

LEARNING OBJECTIVE 6
Summarize restaurant management financials.

Restaurant Management Financials

Budgeted Costs in a Restaurant

Running a good pace in the restaurant is of absolute importance. Every restaurant has different numbers to make (the following came from Chris Della-Cruz, Suso Restaurant). These numbers reflect their goals versus actual numbers run for a given week.

TECHNOLOGY SPOTLIGHT

Courtesy of **James McManemon**, M.S., University of South Florida Sarasota–Manatee

Restaurants strive for the almost impossible—to make a reasonable profit—and it is technology, and the improved efficiency it lends us, that makes that goal possible in several ways. For example, the POS system is one of the main technology items that can now provide online ordering, inventory control, wireless tableside ordering and payments, real-time alerts, mobile management capabilities, and back office management. In addition, there is an optional redundant system that mirrors the data on the server and saves it on a backup server should the main server go down. That identical data may be used until the main server is operational again.[12]

Further, restaurant owners are realizing that the 80-million-strong Millennial Generation, now the largest population group in the United States and composed of people 18–34, is dining out in droves. The POS system provides the means for restaurants to connect to these "plugged in" Millennials by offering choice, health, and adventure at an affordable price. Additionally, community involvement is very important to Millennials. They want to know how a restaurant is supporting the community—meaning, more than just recycling by supporting local farms and purchasing from local businesses and supporting local charities. Having a good social media presence is a must, but when it comes to food, Millennials like healthy choices, organic food, and they want to know where the food is coming from. All of this information can be made available to customers with the use of technology.

Restaurants are always looking for useful apps. A good example is the NoWait app, a waitlist-management program that enables guests to compare the wait times at certain restaurants in their areas, put their names on lists, and monitor the times at which they'll be seated.

Hotel restaurants are "connecting" in fun ways. In July 2012, the restaurants at 19 various Four Seasons hotels participated in a National Ice Cream Day when chefs created ice cream treats that reflected their locale and posted pictures on Instagram. The hotels held live "Insta-Meets" and encouraged guests to share their own photos. Posts came in from around the world. Repeats of this event occurred in July of 2013 and 2014.[13]

INTRODUCING CHRIS DELLA-CRUZ, GENERAL MANAGER OF SUSO RESTAURANT

Expectations of the General Manager

The expectations of the general manager are different in each restaurant; however, there are certain commonalities as well. Some of these commonalities are as follows:

- General managers answer directly to the owner or to regional directors of major corporations.
- General managers are expected to run good numbers for the periods. The numbers analyzed are food cost, labor cost, and beverage cost. These areas are controlled to produce sufficient profit for the restaurant.
- General managers promote good morale and teamwork in the restaurant. Having a positive environment in the restaurant is of utmost importance. This will not only keep the employees happy, but it will also contribute to providing better service to the guests.

INTRODUCING CHRIS DELLA-CRUZ, GENERAL MANAGER OF SUSO RESTAURANT *(Continued)*

Duties and Responsibilities

The general manager of a restaurant is directly in charge of all the operations in the restaurant. General managers are also in charge of the floor managers, kitchen manager, and all the remaining employees in the restaurant.

The general manager should always check on the floor managers to ensure that all policies and regulations are being met. This will keep operations running smoothly.

Another important duty is to organize and control the staffing of the restaurant. The floor managers usually write the employee schedule; however, the general manager is still directly responsible for proper staffing for the period. This will help keep labor costs to about 20 percent of sales. The general manager is also in charge of conducting employee reviews and training.

Qualifications for a General Manager

To be hired as a general manager, the following qualifications are necessary:

- The general manager should be very knowledgeable in the restaurant business.
- He or she should have previously worked all the stations in a restaurant and be very familiar with them.
- The general manager should be able to get along with all people, be fair with all employees, and not discriminate.
- Having a degree is not the most important thing in becoming a general manager. However, a degree is very useful in moving up the ladder in a company to regional manager, regional director, and so on.

	Goal (%)	Actual (%)	Variance (%)
Food Cost	27.0	27.2	+0.2
Labor Cost	19.9	20.8	+0.9
Beverage Cost	19.0	18.2	−0.8

As can be seen, this restaurant did well with the beverage cost; however, the food cost and the labor cost are two areas to focus on for the upcoming week.

Making good percentages for the restaurant is the most important focus simply because this is where the restaurant makes or does not make a profit. When the general manager runs good numbers, then he or she will receive a large bonus check for contributing to the profit of the restaurant. This is why it is so important to focus on these three key areas.

Purchasing

Purchasing for restaurants involves procuring the products and services that the restaurant needs to serve its guests. Restaurant operators set up purchasing systems that determine the following:

- Standards for each item (**product specification**)
- Systems that minimize effort and maximize control of theft and losses from other sources

- The amount of each item that should be on hand (par stock and reorder point)
- Who will do the buying and keep the purchasing system in motion
- Who will do the receiving, storage, and issuing of items[14]

It is desirable for restaurants to establish standards for each product, cal a product specification. When ordering meat, for example, the cut, weight, size, percentage of fat content, and number of days aged are all factors that are specified by the purchaser.

Establishing systems that minimize effort and maximize control of theft may be done by computer or manually. However, merely computerizing a system does not make it theft-proof. Instead, employing honest workers is a top priority because temptation is everywhere in the restaurant industry.

An efficient and effective system establishes a stock level that must be on hand at all times. This is called a par stock level. If the stock on hand falls below that specified point, the computer system automatically reorders a predetermined quantity of the item.

In identifying who will do the buying, it is most important to separate task and responsibility between the person placing the order and the person receiving the goods. This avoids possible theft. The best way to avoid losses is to have the chef prepare the order; the manager or the manager's designee place the order; and a third person, responsible for the stores, receive the goods together with the chef (or the chef's designee).

Commercial (for profit) restaurant and foodservice operators who are part of a chain may have the menu items and order specifications determined at the corporate office. This saves the unit manager from having to order individually; specialists at the corporate office cannot only develop the menu but must include specifications for the ingredients to ensure consistency. Both chain and independent restaurants and foodservice operators use similar pre-purchase functions (see Figure 7–3).

- Plan menus.
- Determine quality and quantity needed to produce menus.
- Determine inventory stock levels.
- Identify items to purchase by subtracting stock levels from the quantity required to produce menus.
- Write specifications and develop market orders for purchases.

Figure 7–3 • Food Cost Control Process.

Professor Stefanelli at the University of Nevada, Las Vegas, suggests a formal and an informal method of purchasing that includes the following steps:[15]

Formal	Informal
Develop purchase order.	Develop purchase order.
Establish bid schedule.	Quote price.
Issue invitation to bid.	Select vendor and place order.
Tabulate and evaluate bids.	
Award contract and issue delivery order.	
Inspect/receive deliveries, inventory stores, and record transactions in inventory.	Receive and inspect deliveries, store and record transaction.
Evaluate and follow up.	Evaluate and follow up.
Issue food supplies for food production and service.	Issue food supplies for food production and service.

The formal method is generally used by chain restaurant operators and the informal one by independent restaurant operators.

A **purchase order** comes as a result of the product specification. As it sounds, a purchase order is an order to purchase a certain quantity of an item at a specific price. Many restaurants develop purchase orders for items they need on a regular basis. These are then sent to suppliers for quotations, and samples are sent in for product evaluations. For example, canned items have varying amounts of liquid. Typically, it is the drained weight of the product that matters to the restaurant operator. After comparing samples from several vendors, the operator can choose the supplier that best suits the restaurant's needs.

Receiving

When placing an order, the restaurant operator specifies the day and time (e.g., Friday, 10:00 A.M. to 12:00 noon) for the delivery to be made. This prevents deliveries from being made at inconvenient times.

Receiving is a point of control in the restaurant operation. The purpose of receiving is to ensure the quantity, quality, and price are exactly as ordered. The quantity and quality relate to the order specification and the standardized recipe. Depending on the restaurant and the type of food and beverage control system, some perishable items are issued directly to the kitchen, and most of the nonperishable items go into storage.

Storing/Issuing

Control of the stores is often a problem. Records must be kept of all items going into and out of the stores. If more than one person has access to the stores, it is difficult to know where to attach responsibility in case of losses.

Items should be issued from the stores only on an authorized requisition signed by the appropriate person. One restaurateur who has been in business for many years issues stores to the kitchen on a daily basis. No inventory is kept in the production area and there is no access to the stores. To some, this may be overdoing control, but it is hard to fault the results: a good food cost percentage. All items that enter the stores should have a date stamp and be rotated using the **first in–first out (FIFO)** system.

FIFO is a simple but effective system of ensuring stock rotation. This is achieved by placing the most recent purchases, in rotation, behind previous purchases. Failure to do this can result in spoilage.

Obviously, restaurants should maintain strict controls. Among the better-known controls are taking inventory regularly, calculating food and beverage cost percentages, having receiving done by a person other than the person who orders, using a par-stock reordering system, using one entrance/exit for employees and not permitting employees to bring bags into the restaurant with them, employing a good accountant, and, yes, checking the garbage!

Budgeting

Budgeting costs fall into two categories: fixed and variable. **Fixed costs** are constant regardless of the volume of business. Fixed costs are rent/lease payments, interest, and depreciation. **Variable costs** fluctuate with the volume of business. Variable costs include controllable expenses such as payroll, benefits, direct operating expense, music and entertainment, marketing and promotion, energy and utility, administrative, and repairs and maintenance.

Regardless of sales fluctuations, variable or controllable expenses vary in some controllable proportion to sales. For example, if a restaurant is open on a Monday, it must have a host, server, cook, dishwasher, and so on. The volume of business and sales total may be $750. However, on Friday that sales total might be $2,250 with just a few more staff. The controllable costs increased only slightly in proportion to the sales, and the fixed costs did not change.

Restaurant Accounting

To operate any business efficiently and effectively, it is necessary to determine the mission, goals, and objectives. One of the most important goals in any enterprise is a fair return on investment, otherwise known as profit. In addition, accounting for the income and expenditures is a necessary part of any business enterprise. The restaurant industry has adopted a uniform system of accounts.

The **uniform system of accounts** for restaurants (USAR) outlines a standard

Restaurant managers also need to spend time with staff members.

Operating or Income Statement

From an operational perspective, the most important financial document is the operating statement. Once a sales forecast has been completed, the costs of servicing those sales are budgeted on an income statement. Figure 7–4 shows an example of an income statement for a hypothetical restaurant.

The **income statement**, which is for a month or a year, begins with the food and beverage sales. From this total, the cost of food and beverage is deducted; the remaining total is **gross profit**. To this amount, any other income is added (e.g., cigarettes, vending machines, outside catering, and telephone income). The next heading is controllable expenses, which includes salaries, wages, employee benefits, direct operating expenses (telephone, insurance, accounting and legal fees, office supplies,

A Restaurant Income Statement Year 2015		
Sales		
Food		750,000
Beverages		240,000
Other		10,000
Total sales		1,000,000
Cost of Sales		
Food	210,000	
Beverage	48,000	
Total cost of sales	258,000	
Gross profit		742,000
Controllable Expenses		
Salaries and wages	200,000	
Employee benefits	20,000	
Other	150,000	
Total Controllable Expenses	370,000	
Income before Rent, Interest, Taxes		372,000
Occupancy Costs/Rent	90,000	
Interest Depreciation	15,000	
Taxes	50,000	
Total	155,000	
Net Income/Restaurant Profit		217,000

Figure 7–4 • Sample Income Statement.

paper, china, glass, cutlery, menus, landscaping, and so on), music and entertainment, marketing, energy and utility, administrative, and general repairs and maintenance. The total of this group is called total controllable expenses. Rent and other occupation costs are then deducted from the total, leaving income before interest, depreciation, and taxes. Interest and depreciation are deducted leaving a total of net income before taxes. From this amount, income taxes are paid, leaving the remainder as net income.

Managing the money to the bottom line requires careful scrutiny of all key results, beginning with the big-ticket controllable items such as labor costs, food costs, and beverages, on down to related controllable items. Additionally, management may wish to compare several income statements representing operations over a number of different periods. The ideal method for comparing is to compute every component of each income statement as a percentage of its total sales. Then, compare one period's percentage to another to determine if any significant trends are developing. For example, a manager could compare labor as a percentage of total sales over several months, or years, to assess the impact of rising labor rates on the bottom line.

Operating Ratios

Operating ratios are industry norms that are applicable to each segment of the industry. Experienced restaurant operators rely on these operating ratios to indicate the restaurant's degree of success. Several ratios are good barometers of a restaurant's degree of success. Among the better-known ratios are the following:

- Food cost percentage
- Contribution margin
- Labor cost percentage
- Prime cost
- Beverage cost percentage

Food Cost Percentage

The basic **food cost percentage**, for which the formula is cost/sales × 100, is calculated on a daily, weekly, or monthly basis. The procedure works in the following manner:

1. An inventory is taken of all the food and the purchase price of that food. This is called the *opening inventory*.
2. The purchases are totaled for the period and added to the opening inventory.
3. The closing inventory (the inventory at the close of the week or period for which the food cost percentage is being calculated) and returns,

spoilage, complimentary meals, and transfers to other departments are also deducted from the opening inventory plus purchases.

4. This figure is the cost of goods sold. The cost of goods sold is divided by the total sales. The resulting figure is the food cost percentage.

The following example illustrates the procedure:

Food Sales	$3,000
Opening Inventory	1,000
Add Purchases	500
	1,500
Less Spoilage and Complimentary Meals	−100
Less Closing Inventory	−500
Cost of Goods Sold	$900

$$\frac{\text{Food Cost (\$900)}}{\text{Sales (\$3000)}} \times 100 = 30\% \text{ Food Cost Percentage}$$

The food cost percentage calculations become slightly more complicated when the cost of staff meals, management meals and entertaining (complimentary meals), and guest food returned are all properly calculated.

Food cost percentage has long been used as a yardstick for measuring the skill of the chef, cooks, and management to achieve a predetermined food cost percentage—usually 28–32 percent for a full-service restaurant and a little higher for a high-volume, fast-food restaurant.

Controlling food costs begins with cost-effective purchasing systems, a controlled storage and issuing system, and strict control of the food production and sales. The best way to visualize a food cost control system is to think of the food as money. Consider a $100 bill arriving at the back door: If the wrong people get their hands on that money, it does not reach the guest or the bottom line.

Contribution Margin

More recently, attention has focused not only on the food cost percentage but also on the contribution margin. The **contribution margin** is the amount that a menu item contributes to the gross profit, or the difference between the cost of the item and its sales price. Some menu items contribute more than others; therefore, restaurant operators focus more attention on the items that produce a higher contribution margin. It works like this:

The cost of the chicken dish is $2.00, and its selling price is $9.95, which leaves a contribution margin of $7.95. The fish, which costs a little more at $3.25, sells for $12.75 and leaves a contribution of $9.50. The pasta cost price of $1.50 and selling price of $8.95 leave a contribution margin of $7.45. Under this scenario, it would be better for the restaurant to sell more fish because each plate will yield $1.55 more than if chicken were sold.

Labor Cost Percentage

Labor costs are the highest single cost factor in staffing a restaurant. Fast-food restaurants have the lowest **labor costs percentage** (about 16–18 percent), with family and ethnic restaurants at about 22–26 percent and upscale full-service restaurants at about 30–35 percent.

Labor costs include salaries and wages of employees, employee benefits, and their training. Foodservice is a highly labor-intensive industry, depending on the type of restaurant. Quick-service restaurants have a lower payroll cost primarily because of their limited menu and limited service. Good managers try to manage their labor costs by accurate hiring and scheduling of staff according to the restaurant's cover turnover.

The labor cost is calculated by taking the total cost of labor for a period, say $200,000, and dividing it by the total sales for the same period, $800,000, and multiplying it by 100

$$\frac{\text{Labor Cost } \$200,000}{\text{Sales } \$800,000} \times 100 = 25\%$$

Prime Cost

Combined food and labor costs is known as **prime cost**. To allow for a reasonable return on investment, prime cost should not go above 60–65 percent of sales.

There are various methods of control, beginning with effective scheduling based on the expected volume of business. In reality, because of the high cost of labor, today's restaurateur manages by the minute. Once a rush is over, the effective manager thanks employees for doing a great job and looks forward to seeing them again. This may appear to be micromanagement, but an analysis of restaurant operations does not leave any alternatives.[17]

$$\text{Food cost + Labor cost percentage} = \text{Prime cost}$$

Beverage Cost Percentage

The **beverage cost percentage** is calculated like the food cost percentage. The method used most often is to first determine the unit cost and then mark up by the required percentage to arrive at the selling price. This is rounded up or down to a convenient figure. The actual beverage cost percentage is then compared with the anticipated cost percentage; any discrepancy is investigated.

The NRA publishes guidelines for restaurant operations. These valuable documents help provide a guide for operators to use when comparing their restaurants with other similar establishments. If the costs go above the budgeted or expected levels, then management must investigate and take corrective action.

Beverage cost is calculated by taking the costs of beverages and dividing it by the total beverage sales and multiplying by 100

$$\frac{\text{Cost of beverage sales}}{\text{Total beverage sales}} \times 100 \quad \text{For example} \quad \frac{4,250}{19,479} \times 100 = 21.82\%$$

Therefore, for a casual Italian restaurant, industry comparisons would show the following:

Labor costs at 20–24 percent of sales

Food costs at 28–32 percent of food sales

Beverage costs at 18–24 percent of beverage sales

INTRODUCING RAY KROC[18]

Of McDonald's

The world's greatest fast-food success story is undoubtedly McDonald's. Back in the 1950s, Ray Kroc was selling soda fountains. He received an order from Mr. McDonald for two soda fountains. Ray Kroc was so interested in finding out why the McDonald brothers' restaurant needed two machines (everyone else ordered one) that he went out to the restaurant. There he saw the now-familiar golden arches and the hamburger restaurant. Ray persuaded the McDonalds to let him franchise their operation. Billions of burgers later, the reason for the success may be summarized as follows: quality, speed, cleanliness, service, and value. This has been achieved by systemizing the production process and by staying close to the original concept—keeping a limited menu, advertising heavily, being innovative with new menu items, maintaining product quality, and being consistent.

Of all hospitality entrepreneurs, Ray Kroc has been the most successful financially. In 1982, he was senior chairman of the board of McDonald's, an organization intent on covering the earth with hamburgers. Among the remarkable things about Kroc is that it was not until age 52 that he embarked on the royal road to fame and fortune.

The original McDonald's concept was created by two brothers, Richard and Maurice, who had no interest in expanding. The McDonald brothers were content with their profitable yet singular restaurant in San Bernardino, California. However, the golden arches impressed Kroc, as did the cleanliness and simplicity of the operation.

Kroc's organizational skills, perseverance, and incredible aptitude for marketing were his genius. His talent also extended to selecting close associates who were equally dedicated and who added financial, analytical, and managerial skills to the enterprise. Kroc remained the spark plug and master merchandiser until he died in 1984, leaving a multimillion-dollar legacy.

Much of Kroc's $400 million has gone to employees, hospitals, and the The Field Museum. It is distributed through Kroc's own foundation. Most important, Kroc developed several operational guidelines, including the concepts of KISS—keep it simple, stupid—and QSC&V—quality, service, cleanliness, and value. Kroc's "Never Be Idle a Moment" motto was also incorporated into the business.

Enterprises such as McDonald's are not built without ample dedication, and Ray Kroc certainly had a wealth of dedication. Today, an average McDonald's franchise can net more than $1 million annually thanks to Kroc's ingenious marketing strategies. In fact, McDonald's Corporation has become so affluent that it was named *Entrepreneur* magazine's number-one franchise.

Lease and Controllable Expenses

Lease Costs

Successful restaurant operators will ensure that the restaurant's lease does not cost more than 5–8 percent of sales. Some chain restaurants will search for months or even years before they find the right location at the right price. Most leases are triple net, which means that the lessee must pay for all alterations, insurance, utilities, and possible commercial fees (e.g., landscaping or parking upkeep, security).

The best lease is for the longest time period with options for renewal and a sublease clause. The sublease clause is important because if the restaurant is not successful, the owner is still liable for paying the lease. With the sublease clause, the owner may sublease the space to another restaurant operator or any other business.

Many leases are quoted at a dollar rate per square foot per month. Depending on the location, rates may range from $2.25 per square foot up to as much as $16 or more per square foot.

Some restaurants pay a combination of a flat amount based on the square footage and a percentage of sales. This helps protect the restaurant operator in the slower months and gives the landlord a bit extra during the good months.

After a lease contract is signed, it is very difficult to renegotiate even a part of it. Only in dire circumstances is it possible to renegotiate lease contracts. The governing factor in determining lease rates is the marketplace. The marketplace is the supply and demand. If there is strong demand for space, then rates will increase. However, with a high vacancy rate, rates will be driven down by the owners in an effort to rent space and gain income.

Controllable Expenses

Controllable expenses are all the expenses over which management and ownership have control. They include salaries and wages (payroll) and related benefits; direct operating expenses such as music and entertainment; marketing, including sales, advertising, public relations, and promotions; heat, light, and power; administrative and general expenses; and repairs and maintenance. The total of all controllable expenses is deducted from the gross profit. Rent and other occupation costs are then deducted to arrive at the income before interest, depreciation, and taxes. Once these are deducted, the **net profit** remains.

Successful restaurant operators are constantly monitoring their controllable expenses. The largest controllable expense is payroll. Because payroll is about 24–28 percent of a restaurant's sales, managers constantly monitor their employees, not by the hour but by the minute. Bobby Hays, general manager of the Chart House Restaurant in Cardiff, California, says that he feels the pulse of the restaurant and then begins to send people home. Every dollar that Bobby and managers like him can save goes directly to the bottom line and becomes profit.

The actual sales results are compared with the budgeted amounts—ideally with percentages—and variances are investigated. Most chain restaurant operators monitor the key result areas of sales and labor costs on a daily basis. Food and beverage costs are also monitored closely, generally on a weekly basis.

▶ Check Your Knowledge

1. Create a recognition program that would encourage restaurant employees.

2. What is the storing/issuing process? Why is it important?

3. Briefly explain the term *contribution margin*.

Restaurant Manager Job Analysis

The NRA has formulated an analysis of the foodservice manager's job by functional areas and tasks, which follows a natural sequence of functional areas from human resources to sanitation and safety.

Human Resource Management

Recruiting/Training

1. Recruit new employees by seeking referrals.
2. Recruit new employees by advertising.
3. Recruit new employees by seeking help from district manager/ supervisors.
4. Interview applicants for employment.

Orientation/Training

1. Conduct on-site orientation for new employees.
2. Explain employee benefits and compensation programs.
3. Plan training programs for employees.
4. Conduct on-site training for employees.
5. Evaluate progress of employees during training.
6. Supervise on-site training of employees that is conducted by another manager, employee leader, trainer, and so on.
7. Conduct payroll signup.
8. Complete reports or other written documentation on successful completion of training by employees.

Scheduling for Shifts

1. Review employee work schedule for shift.
2. Determine staffing needs for each shift.
3. Make work assignments for dining room, kitchen staff, and maintenance person(s).
4. Make changes to employee work schedule.
5. Assign employees to work stations to optimize employee effectiveness.
6. Call in, reassign, or send home employees in reaction to sales and other needs.
7. Approve requests for schedule changes, vacation, days off, and so on.

Supervision and Employee Development

1. Observe employees and give immediate feedback on unsatisfactory employee performance.
2. Observe employees and give immediate feedback on satisfactory employee performance.
3. Discuss unsatisfactory performance with an employee.

4. Develop and deliver incentive for above-satisfactory performance of employees.

5. Observe employee behavior for compliance with safety and security.

6. Counsel employees on work-related problems.

7. Counsel employees on non-work-related problems.

8. Talk with employees who have frequent absences.

9. Observe employees to ensure compliance with fair labor standards and equal opportunity guidelines.

10. Discipline employees by issuing oral and/or written warnings for poor performance.

11. Conduct employee and staff meetings.

12. Identify and develop candidates for management programs.

13. Put results of observation of employee performance in writing.

14. Develop action plans for employees to help them in their performance.

15. Authorize promotion and/or wage increases for staff.

16. Terminate employment of an employee for unsatisfactory performance.

Financial Management

Accounting

1. Authorize payment on vendor invoices.

2. Verify payroll.

3. Count cash drawers.

4. Prepare bank deposits.

5. Assist in establishment audits by management or outside auditors.

6. Balance cash at end of shift.

7. Analyze profit and loss reports for establishment.

Cost Control

1. Discuss factors that affect profitability with district manager/supervisor.

2. Check establishment figures for sales, labor costs, waste, inventory, and so on.

Administrative Management

Scheduling/Coordinating

1. Establish objectives for each shift based on needs of establishment.

2. Coordinate work performed by different shifts—for example, cleanup, routine maintenance, and so on.

3. Complete special projects assigned by district manager/supervisor.

4. Complete shift readiness checklist.

Planning

1. Develop and implement action plans to meet financial goals.
2. Attend off-site workshops and training sessions.

Communication

1. Communicate with management team by reading and making entries in daily communication log.
2. Prepare written reports on cleanliness, food quality, personnel, inventory, sales, food waste, labor costs, and so on.
3. Review reports prepared by other establishment managers.
4. Review memos, reports, and letters from company headquarters/main office.
5. Inform district manager/supervisor of problems or developments that affect operation and performance of the establishment.
6. Initiate and answer correspondence with company, vendors, and so on.
7. File correspondence, reports, personnel records, and so on.

Marketing Management

1. Create and execute local establishment marketing activities.
2. Develop opportunities for the establishment to provide community services.
3. Carry out special product promotions.

Operations Management

Facility Maintenance

1. Conduct routine maintenance checks on facility and equipment.
2. Direct routine maintenance checks on facility and equipment.
3. Repair or supervise the repair of equipment.
4. Review establishment evaluations with district manager/supervisor.
5. Authorize the repair of equipment by outside contractor.
6. Recommend upgrades in facility and equipment.

Food and Beverage Operations Management

1. Direct activities for opening establishment.
2. Direct activities for closing establishment.
3. Talk with other managers at beginning and end of shift to relay information about ongoing problems and activities.
4. Count, verify, and report inventory.
5. Receive, inspect, and verify vendor deliveries.
6. Check stock levels and submit orders as necessary.
7. Talk with vendors concerning quality of product delivered.
8. Interview vendors who wish to sell products to establishment.

9. Check finished product quality and act to correct problems.

10. Work as expediter to get meals served effectively.

11. Inspect dining area, kitchen, rest rooms, food lockers, storage, and parking lot.

12. Check daily reports for indications of internal theft.

13. Instruct employees regarding the control of waste, portion sizes, and so on.

14. Prepare forecast for daily or shift food preparation.

Service

1. Receive and record table reservations.

2. Greet familiar customers by name.

3. Seat customers.

4. Talk with customers while they are dining.

5. Monitor service times and procedures in the dining area.

6. Observe customers being served to correct problems.

7. Ask customers about quality of service.

8. Ask customers about quality of the food product.

9. Listen to and resolve customer complaints.

10. Authorize complimentary meals or beverages.

11. Write letters in response to customer complaints.

12. Telephone customers in response to customer complaints.

13. Secure and return items left by customers.

Sanitation and Safety

1. Accompany local officials on health inspections on premise.

2. Administer first aid to employees and customers.

3. Submit accident, incident, and OSHA reports.

4. Report incidents to police.

5. Observe employee behavior and establishment conditions for compliance with safety and security procedures.

Recycling

At the end of the night at most restaurants, leftover food, paper, bottles, and cardboard typically are put in a dumpster in the back alley, destined for a landfill. Separating garbage is dirty; it requires people and time to do it. But several operators say making minor changes reduces trash and helps budgets. Zero waste is how Nomad Café in Berkeley, California, prefers to operate its business. It saves more than $10,000 every year by recycling and composting. Making simple changes to its daily routine of throwing out garbage also aided Scoma's in San Francisco. It color-coded the system and got staff into the habit of recycling. Scoma's saves an average of $2,000 per month.[19]

C A S E   S T U D Y *(Continued)*

beginning to "86" a great deal of product. In addition, if they do not begin production for the P.M. shift soon, they will be in deep trouble.

On Friday nights, The Pub does in excess of $12,000 in sales. However, if the problem is not immediately alleviated, the restaurant will lose many guests and a great amount in profits.

Discussion Questions

1. What immediate measures would you take to resolve the problem?
2. How would you produce the appropriate product as soon as possible?
3. Who should you call first, if anyone, to alleviate the problem?
4. What can you do to always have enough product on hand?
5. Is it important to have a backup plan for a situation like this? If so, what would it be?

Summary

1. Most restaurants forecast a budget on a weekly and monthly basis, one that projects sales and costs for a year in consideration of guest counts and the average guest check.
2. To operate a restaurant, products need to be purchased, received, and properly stored.
3. Food production is determined by the expected business for the next few days. The kitchen layout is designed according to the sales forecasted.
4. Good service is very important. In addition to taking orders, servers act as salespersons for the restaurant.

5. The front of the house deals with the part of the restaurant having direct contact with guests, in other words, what the guests see—grounds maintenance, hosts/hostesses, dining and bar areas, bartenders, bussers, and so on.
6. The back of the house is generally run by the foodservice/kitchen manager, and refers to those functional areas and tasks with which guests usually do not come in contact. This includes purchasing, receiving, storing/issuing, food production, stewarding, budgeting, accounting, and control.

Key Words and Concepts

average guest check	budgeting costs	covers
back of the house	contribution margin	curbside appeal
balance sheet	controllable expense	employee recognition
beverage cost percentage	cooking line	first in–first out (FIFO)

LEARNING OBJECTIVE 1
Outline the different managed services segments.

LEARNING OBJECTIVE 2
Describe the five factors that distinguish managed services operations from commercial ones.

fixed costs	labor costs percentage	product specification
food cost percentage	net profit	production control sheets
front of the house	operating ratios	purchase order
gross profit	par stock	receiving
guest counts	personal digital assistants	restaurant forecasting
host/hostess	(PDAs)	suggestive selling
income statement	point-of-sale (POS) systems	uniform system of accounts
kitchen manager	prime cost	variable costs

Review Questions

1. Briefly describe the two components of restaurant forecasting.
2. Explain the key points in purchasing, receiving, and storing.
3. Why is the kitchen layout an important aspect of food production?
4. Explain the purpose of suggestive selling. What characteristics make up a good server?
5. Accounting is important to determine the profitability of a restaurant. Briefly describe the following terms:

   (a) Controllable expenses
   (b) Uniform system of accounts
   (c) Prime cost

6. What is the point-of-sale system, and why is a control system important for a restaurant operation?
7. What are the differences between the back of the house and the front of the house?
8. What steps must one take in preparing production sheets?

Internet Exercises

1. Organization: **National Restaurant Association (NRA)**
   Summary: The NRA is the business association of the food industry. It consists of 40,000 members and more than 500,000 restaurants. Member restaurants represent table service and quick-service operators, chains, and franchises. The NRA helps international restaurants receive the benefits of the association and gives guidance for success to nonprofit members.

   (a) List the foodborne diseases found on the NRA site. Learn more about each disease and how the National Restaurant Association suggests you can prevent it.
   (b) What kinds of careers are available in the restaurant and hospitality industry?
   (c) What legal issues does this site advise you on if you want to start your own restaurant?

2. Organization: **Chili's**
   Summary: Chili's is a f
   place to have burgers,
   and chili. Established
   chain now has more t
   around the world.

Apply Your I

In a casual Italian restaura
of September 15 are as fol

Food sales $

Beverage sales

Total $

1. If the food cost is 30 p
   did the food actually c

Suggested Ac

1. Divide into groups of t
   roles of guest and serve
   concept of suggestive s

Endnotes

1. This section draws from Jo
   Restaurant from Concept t
   (Hoboken, NJ: John Wiley
2. Personal conversation with
   14, 2004.
3. Wikipedia, *The Inn at Littl*
   en.wikipedia.org. Search f
   Washington" (accessed Sep
4. This section is adapted fro
   .com/features/trends/30_s
   .shtml (retrieved March 10

CHAPTER 8

Managed Services

LEARNING OBJECTIVES

After reading and studying this chapter, you should be able to:

- Outline the different managed services segments.

- Describe the five factors that distinguish managed services operations from commercial ones.

- Explain the need for and trends in elementary and secondary school foodservice.

- Describe the complexities in college and university foodservice.

- Identify characteristics and trends in health care, business and industry, and leisure and recreation foodservices.

10. Richard Slawsky, "Sustainable Farming Grows on Chefs," *QSR Web*, March 8, 2007, www.qsrweb.com/article.php?id=7025 (accessed November 7, 2011).

11. www.chipotle.com, About Us, http://www.chipotle.com/en-us/company/about_us.aspx (retrieved July 22, 2014).

12. http://www.restaurantowner.com/public/department27.cmf (retrieved April 17, 2015).

13. Four Seasons, http://www.fourseasons.com/. Go to Press Room and search for "national ice cream day" to view the articles (accessed May 18, 2015).

14. This section draws from Walker, *Restaurant from Concept to Operation*, 275.

15. Walker, *Restaurant from Concept to Operation*, 275.

16. Bruce Horovitz, "Friday's, Red Lobster: Casual dining for sale," *USA Todau*, May 20, 2014, http://americasmarkets.usatoday.com/2014/05/20/fridays-red-lobster-casual-dining-for-sale/ (accessed August 3, 2015).

17. Personal conversation with Bobby Hays, general manager, Chart House Restaurant, Solana Beach, California, January 2011.

18. Wikipedia, *Ray Kroc*, http://en.wikipedia.org. Search for "Ray Kroc" (accessed September 1, 2015).

19. Jamie Popp, "Trash Talk," *Restaurants and Institutions* 116 (May 1, 2006), 75.

be quieter than weekdays in managed services and, overall, the hours and benefits may be better than those of commercial restaurants.

A company or organization might contract its food- or other services for the following reasons:

- Financial
- Quality of program
- Recruitment of management and staff
- Expertise in management of service departments
- Resources available: people, programs, management systems, and information systems
- Labor relations and other support
- Outsourcing of administrative functions[1]

Airlines and Airports

In-Flight and Airport Foodservice

When airlines do provide meals, either foodservice comes from their own *in-flight* business or they have the service provided by a contractor. In-flight food may be prepared in a factory mode at a facility close to but outside the airport. In these cases, the food is prepared and packaged; then it is transported to the departure gates for the appropriate flights. Once the food is loaded onto the aircraft, flight attendants take over serving the food and beverages to passengers.

In-flight foodservice is a complex logistical operation: The food must be able to withstand the transport conditions and the extended hot or cold holding period from the time it is prepared until the time it is served. If a food item is to be served hot, it must be able to rethermalize well on the plate. The meal should also look appetizing and taste good. Finally, all food and beverage items must be delivered on time and correctly to each departing aircraft.

Gate Gourmet is the largest in-flight food and related services provider, operating in 28 countries on six continents from 122 flight kitchens and producing 250 million meals on average annually.[2] It is estimated that sales will exceed $2 billion, supported by more than 26,000 employees.

Another major player in the in-flight foodservice market is LSG Sky Chefs, headquartered in Neu-Isenburg, Germany. The LSG Sky Chefs group has the vision to "be the global leader in airline catering and the management of all in-flight service related processes."[3] LSG Sky Chefs consists of 156 companies with more than 208 customer service centers in 54 countries. In 2013, it produced about 532 million airline meals for more than 300 airlines worldwide.[4] The in-flight food and related services management operators plan the menus, develop the product specifications, and arrange the purchasing contracts. Each airline has a representative who oversees one or more locations and checks on the quality, quantity, and delivery times of all food and beverage items. Airlines regard in-flight foodservice as an expense that needs to be controlled. To trim costs, most domestic airlines now sell snacks instead of meals on a

Airport restaurants from quick service to casual fine dining have seen an upswing in business as a result of the airlines cutting back on in-flight foodservice.

number of short flights and even on flights that span main meal times. Both Gate Gourmet and LSG Sky Chefs also now operate onboard retail solutions for most airlines.

International airlines try to stand out by offering superior food and beverages in hopes of attracting more passengers, especially the higher-paying business and first-class passengers. Others reduce or eliminate foodservice as a strategic decision to support lower fares. Because of the length of the flight and the higher price paid for the ticket, international flights have better-quality food and beverage service.

On board, each aircraft has two or three categories of service, usually coach, business, and first class. First- and business-class passengers usually receive free beverages and upgraded meal items and service. These meals may consist of such items as fresh salmon or filet mignon.

A number of smaller regional and local foodservice operators contract to a variety of airlines at hundreds of airports. Most airports have caterers or foodservice contractors who compete for airline contracts. With several international and U.S. airlines all using U.S. airports, each airline must decide whether to use its own foodservice (if it has one) or to contract with one of several independent operators.

As airlines have decreased their in-flight foodservice, airport restaurants have picked up the business. Popular chain restaurants such as TGI Fridays and Chili's are in several terminals, along with the quick-service restaurants such as McDonald's and Pizza Hut. These restaurants supplement airport foodservice offered by local restaurants.

▶ **Check Your Knowledge**

1. What are managed services?

2. Why would companies use contract management?

Military

Military foodservice is a large and important component of managed services. There are about 1.5 million soldiers, sailors, and aviators on active duty in the United States. Even with the military downsizing, foodservice sales top $6 billion per year. Base closings have prompted many military foodservice organizations to rethink services and concepts to better meet the needs of their personnel.

CORPORATE PROFILE

Sodexo

Sodexo is a leading solutions company in North America, delivering on-site service solutions in corporate, education, health care, government, and remote site segments. Sodexo's mission is twofold: Improve the quality of daily life and contribute to the economic, social, and environmental development of the cities, regions, and countries in which it operates.

Sodexo (formerly Sodexho Alliance) was founded in 1966 by a Frenchman named Pierre Bellon with its first service provider in Marseilles, France. Primarily serving schools, restaurants, and hospitals, the company soon became internationally successful by signing deals with Belgian foodservice contractors. In 1980, after considerable success in Europe, Africa, and the Middle East, Sodexho Alliance decided to expand its reach into North and South America. In 1997, the company joined with Universal Ogden Services, a leading U.S. remote-site service provider. The empire grew a year later when Sodexho and Marriott Management Services merged. The merger created a new company called Sodexho Marriott Services. Listed on the New York Stock Exchange, the new company became the market leader in food and management services in the United States. At that time, Sodexho Alliance was the biggest shareholder, holding 48.4 percent of shares on the company's capital. In 2001, however, Sodexho Alliance acquired 53 percent of the shares in Sodexho Marriott Services, which changed its name to simply Sodexo.

Today, Sodexo has more than 428,000 employees at 33,300 sites in 80 countries and serves 75 million consumers daily. In the United States, there are 125,000 employees. The goal of Sodexo is to improve the quality and life of customers and clients all over the United States and Canada. They offer outsourcing solutions to the health care, corporate, and education markets. This includes the following services: housekeeping, groundskeeping, foodservice, plant operation and maintenance, and integrated facilities management.

Sodexo's mission is to create and offer services that contribute to a more pleasant way of life for people wherever and whenever they come together. Its challenge is to continue to make its mission and values come alive through the way in which employees work together to serve the clients and customers. The values of Sodexo are service spirit, team spirit, and spirit of progress.

A leading provider of food and facilities management services in North America, Sodexo provides its services at more than 9,000 client sites, including corporations, colleges and universities, health care organizations, and school districts. They are always looking to develop talent. Sodexo offers internships in foodservice and facilities management businesses as well as in staff positions such as finance, human resources, marketing, and sales. Sodexo believes that workforce diversity is essential to the company's growth and long-term success. By valuing and managing diversity at work, Sodexo can leverage the skills, knowledge, and abilities of all employees to increase employee, client, and customer satisfaction.

Sodexo has received numerous awards; among them are as follows: top ranked in the "services" category of 2010 Global Outsourcing, recognized as a Supersector Worldwide Leader for commitment to sustainable development, named one of the world's most ethical companies, number one of World's Most Admired Companies by *Fortune* magazine, and one of the best companies for hourly workers by *Working Mother* magazine.[5]

Recent trends in military foodservice call for services such as officers' clubs to be contracted out to foodservice management companies. This change has reduced military costs because many of the officers' clubs lost money. The clubs now have moved the emphasis from fine dining to a more casual approach with family appeal. Many clubs are renovating their base concept even further, restyling according to theme concepts, such as sports or country western, for example. Other cost-saving measures include menu management, such as the use of a single menu for lunch and dinner (guests seldom eat both meals at the clubs). With proper plating techniques and portion size manipulation, a single menu (the same menu) can be created for lunch and dinner, meaning one inventory for both meals and less stock in general. To make this technique work successfully, the menu features several choices for appetizers, entrees, and desserts.

Another trend is the testing of prepared foods that can be reheated and served without much labor. Technological advances mean that field troops do not eat out of tin cans anymore; instead, they receive their food portions in plastic-and-foil pouches called meals ready-to-eat (MREs). Today, mobile field kitchens can be run by just two people, and bulk food supplies have been replaced by pre-portioned, precooked food packed in trays, which then are reheated in boiling water.

Feeding military personnel includes feeding troops and officers in clubs, dining halls, and military hospitals, as well as in the field. As both the budget and the numbers of personnel decrease, the military is downsizing by consolidating responsibilities. With fewer people to cook for, fewer cooks are required.

A model for such downsizing is the U.S. Marine Corps, which contracts out foodservice. With smaller numbers, they could not afford to take a marine away from training to work in the dining facilities without affecting military operations. Sodexo has the contract for the U.S. Marine Corps and serves seven bases in 55 barracks, plus clubs, and other related services. In addition, fast-food restaurants such as McDonald's and Burger King have opened on hundreds of bases; they are now installing Express Way kiosks on more bases. The fast-food restaurants on base offer further alternatives for military personnel on the move. One problem that may arise as a result of the downsizing and contracting out of military foodservice is that it is not likely that McDonald's could set up on the front line in a combat situation. The military will still have to do its own foodservice when it comes to mobilization.

Lately, military foodservice has been more innovative and creative in applying new ideas. For example, Naval Base San Diego Dining Services Program Director Steve Hammel revaluated the base's system in terms of overall value, quality, quick service, and their packaging to enlisted personnel. He also looked at how to individualize the system for each base when each base has its own personality. Price points are also important, so the base has a $7.50 buffet and a fixed $5 lunch with different offerings every day.[6]

At another military operation in Fort Campbell, the cafeteria received a $10 million makeover and began a program of healthy eating. Out went the deep-fat fryer and in came rotisserie chicken, so now instead of selling 75 servings of fried chicken they sell 240 portions of rotisserie chicken.[7]

Smart Choices, created by Veterans Canteen Service, is a healthy choices menu approach that gives guests more healthy meal offerings. The campaign merges value, health, and wellness that offer a side salad, a bowl of soup, and a bottle of water totaling 235 calories or a sandwich, fruit, and a bottle of water totaling 340 calories. Interestingly, the calories, grams of fat, carbs, and protein are featured alongside the price on the receipt.[8]

Elementary and Secondary Schools

LEARNING OBJECTIVE 3
Explain the need for and trends in elementary and secondary school foodservice.

The United States government enacted the National School Lunch Act in 1946. The rationale was that if students received good meals, the military would have healthier recruits. In addition, such a program would make use of the surplus food that farmers produced.

Each day, millions of children are fed free or low-cost breakfast or lunch, or both, in approximately 101,000 schools to more than 31 million children each school day.[9] Many challenges currently face elementary and secondary school foodservice. One major challenge is to balance salability with good nutrition. Apart from cost and nutritional value, the broader social issue of the universal free meal arises. Proponents of the program maintain that better-nourished children have a better attention span, are less likely to be absent from school, and will stay in school longer. Offering free meals to all students also removes the poor-kid stigma from school lunch. Detractors from the universal program say that if we learned anything from the social programs that were implemented during the 1960s, it was that throwing money at problems is not always the best answer. Both sides agree that there is serious concern about what young students are eating. It's probably no surprise that the percentage of children who eat one serving or less of fruits and vegetables each day (excluding french fries) is as high as it is. These percentages are shown in Figure 8–1. One example of a school system encouraging a healthier meal program is in Texas, where fried chicken will

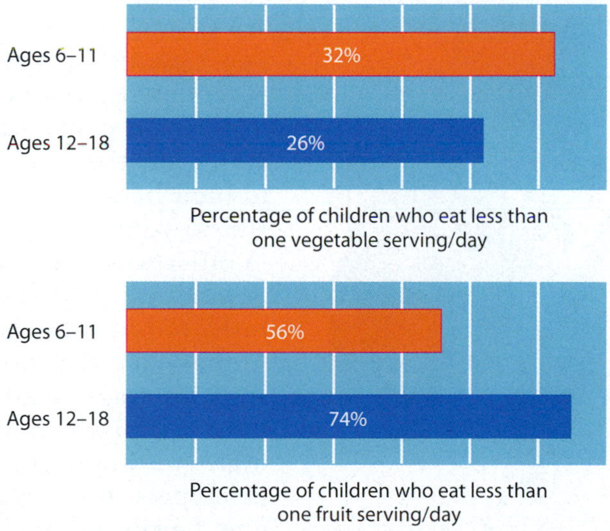

Figure 8–1 • Numbers of Servings of Fruit and Vegetables That Children Eat.
(*Source*: National Center Institute.)

no longer be a lunchtime staple and deep-fat frying is being eliminated. Instead, all potatoes, including french fries, must be oven baked, and no food item can exceed 28 grams of fat. Fruits and vegetables, preferably fresh, must be offered every day for lunch and breakfast. Sodas will not be offered during the school day in middle school. The aim is to provide a healthy environment in which children can grow.[10]

The preparation and service of school foodservice meals varies. Some schools have on-site kitchens where the food is prepared and dining rooms where the food is served. Many large school districts operate a central commissary that prepares the meals and then distributes them among the schools in that district. A third option is for schools to purchase ready-to-serve meals that require only assembly at the school.

Schools may decide to participate in the **National School Lunch Program (NSLP)** or operate on their own. In reality, most schools have little choice because participating in the program means that federal funding is provided in the amount of approximately $2.72 per meal per student. Contract companies such as ARAMARK and Sodexo are introducing more flexibility in choices for students.

Meeting dietary guidelines is also an important issue. Much work has gone into establishing the nutritional requirements for children. It is difficult to achieve a balance between healthy food and costs, taking children's eating habits into account. Under the NSLP regulations, students must eat from what is commonly known as the type A menu. All the items in the type A menu must be offered to all children at every meal. The children have to select a minimum of three of the five meal components for the school to qualify for funding. However, U.S. Department of Agriculture (USDA) regulations have established limits on the amount of fat and saturated fat that can be offered: Fat should not exceed 30 percent of calories per week, and saturated fat was cut down to 10 percent of calories per week.

The government-funded NSLP, which pays in excess of $11.6 billion per year[11] for the meals given or sold at a discount to schoolchildren, is a huge potential market for fast-food chains. Chains are extremely eager to penetrate into the elementary and secondary school markets, even if it means a decrease in revenues. However, they believe that it is to their benefit to introduce Pizza Hut to young people very early—in other words, the aim is to build brand loyalty. For example, in Duluth, Minnesota, James Bruner, foodservice director for the city schools, was forced into offering branded pizza in several junior high and high schools. The local principals, hungry for new revenue, began offering Little Caesar's in direct competition to the cafeteria's frozen pizzas.

Getting kids to eat proper food is a challenge.

Taco Bell is in nearly 3,000 schools, Pizza Hut is in 4,500, and Subway is in 650. Domino's, McDonald's, Arby's, and others are well established in the market as well. Despite the positives, although it is not hard to convince the children, chains need to convince the adults. Much debate has arisen as to whether chains should enter the schools. Many parents feel that the school environment should provide a standard example of what sound nutrition should be, and they believe that with fast food as an option, that will not be the case.

At a school lunch challenge at the American Culinary Federation (ACF) conference, chefs from around the country developed nutritious menus geared to wean children away from junk food to healthy foods. An 80-cent limit on the cost of raw ingredients was placed on the 11 finalists. Innovation and taste, as well as healthfulness, were the main criteria used to evaluate the winning entry: turkey taco salad, sausage pizza bagel, and stuffed potatoes.

Nutrition Education Programs

Nutrition education programs are now a required part of the nation's school lunch program. As a result of this program, children are learning to improve their eating habits, which, it is hoped, will continue for the rest of their lives. To support the program, nutritional education materials are used to decorate the dining room halls and tables. Perhaps the best example of this is the food guide called MyPlate developed by the Food and Nutrition Service of the USDA. Figure 8–2 shows the MyPlate food guide, which illustrates what to eat each day to follow a healthy diet.

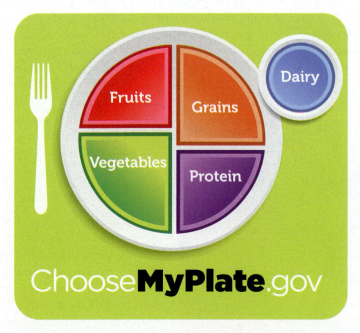

Figure 8–2 • The MyPlate icon featuring the five food groups.

Many schools are now developing unique ways to expose children to nutrition and proper eating guidelines. Planting a garden has sparked the interest of 1,500 elementary school students at Veterans Park Academy in Florida where students were involved with the planting of a vegetable garden as a result of a $10,000 grant. Students have increased their vegetable consumption as a result of their involvement with the program and have learned firsthand the value of good nutrition by participating in after-school cooking classes to learn how to prepare the vegetables they helped grow.[12]

LEARNING OBJECTIVE 4
Describe the complexities in college and university foodservice.

Colleges and Universities

College and university foodservice operations are complex and diverse. Among the various constituents of foodservice management are residence halls, sports concessions, conferences, cafeterias/student unions, faculty clubs, convenience stores, administrative catering, and outside catering.

On-campus dining is a challenge for foodservice managers because, as you well know, the clients live on campus and eat most of their meals at the campus dining facility. If the manager or contractor is not creative, students, staff, and faculty will quickly become bored with the sameness of the surroundings and menu offerings. Most campus dining is cafeteria style, offering cyclical menus that rotate every 10 or 14 days.

However, a college foodservice manager does have some advantages when compared with a restaurant manager. Budgeting is made easier because the on-campus students have already paid for their meals and their numbers are easy to forecast. When the payment is guaranteed and the guest count is predictable, planning and organizing staffing levels and food quantities are relatively easy and should ensure a reasonable profit margin. For instance, the **daily rate** is the amount of money required per day from each person to pay for the foodservice. Thus, if foodservice expenses for one semester of 98 days amount to $650,000 for an operation with 1,000 students eating, the daily rate is calculated as follows:

$$\frac{\$650,000 \div 98 \text{ days}}{1,000 \text{ students}} = \$6.63$$

College foodservice operations now offer a variety of meal plans for students. Under the old board plan, when students paid one fee for all meals each day—whether they ate them or not—the foodservice operator literally made a profit from the students who did

College foodservice.

INTRODUCING HADYN HAYWARD

Operations Director for Dining Services

Hadyn began his career at a small university in North Carolina in 2004 as a shift manager. He quickly moved up to become the location manager of that operation and then became the location manager of the largest dining hall on campus. In 2007, Hadyn transferred to a larger Connecticut university as the assistant food service director, managing many locations across the campus. In 2008, Hadyn was again promoted to food service director when he transferred to a state university in Georgia. In 2009, Hadyn was promoted to the operations director, managing all retail operations on campus.

Hadyn's major responsibilities included planning and managing high-volume, complex, multilocation foodservice operations. He planned, directed, and controlled all retail unit foodservice and resources in order to meet operating and financial goals, client objectives, retail brand franchise relations, audits, and customer needs. He analyzed all financial reports for the retail operations, along with all financial measurements to ensure achievement of financial goals. Hadyn also had to ensure compliance with the company's operation standards in all retail and catering operations. Daily interaction with university clients helped him maintain effective client and customer relations at all levels within the university and its dining services.

There is no such thing as a typical day for Hadyn at USF as he oversees over 10 locations on the campus, in addition to the catering department for the university. Hadyn's workweek involves meetings with various departments and groups ranging from HR, marketing, finance, clients, catering events, customers, and his management team. In between these tasks, he also attends monthly meetings with students, who voice their opinions and offer suggestions about the services on campus. Hadyn then meets with his operations team to review the student meeting notes along with operational goals, successes, and opportunities.

not actually eat the meals for which they had paid. More typically now, students match their payments to the number of meals eaten: Monday through Friday, breakfast, lunch, dinner; dinner only; and prepaid credit cards that allow a student to use the card at any campus outlet and have the value of the food and beverage items deducted from his or her credit balance.

Leaders of the National Associations of College Auxiliary Services (NACAS), which represents 600 member institutes, have noticed that on-campus services and activities are undergoing continuous change.[13] The environment has become a critical part of policy and implementation that transcends parochial interests for those that best meet the needs of the institution and, ultimately, its students.

The driving forces of change on campuses are the advent and growth of branded concepts, privatization, campus cards, and computer use. A college foodservice manager today must have greater skills in retail marketing and merchandizing as students are given more discretion in how they may spend their money for food on campus.

Student Unions

As you know, the college student union offers a variety of managed services that cater to the needs of a diverse student body. Among the services offered are cafeteria foodservice, beverage services, branded quick-service restaurants, and take-out foodservice.

The cafeteria foodservice operation is often the "happening" place in the student union where students meet to socialize as well as to eat and drink. The cafeteria is generally open for breakfast, lunch, and dinner. Depending on the volume of business, the cafeteria may be closed during the nonmeal periods and weekends, and the cafeteria menu may or may not be the same as the residence foodservice facility. Offering a menu with a good price value is crucial to the successful operation of a campus cafeteria.

On campuses at which alcoholic beverage service is permitted, beverage services mainly focus on some form of a student pub where beer and perhaps wine and spirits may be offered. Not to be outdone, the faculty will undoubtedly have a lounge that also offers alcoholic beverages. Other beverages may be served at various outlets such as a food court or convenience store. Campus beverage service provides opportunities for foodservice operators to enhance profits.

In addition, many college campuses have welcomed branded, quick-service restaurants as a convenient way to satisfy the needs of a community on the go. Such an approach offers a win-win situation for colleges. The experience and brand recognition of chain restaurants such as Chick-fil-A, Moe's Southwest Grill, Au Bon Pain, Ben & Jerry's, Einstein Bros Bagels, Burger King, Smokehouse Bar-B-Q, Starbucks, Beef 'O' Brady's, Pizza Hut, McDonald's, Subway, and Wendy's attract customers; the restaurants pay a fee either to the foodservice management company or the university directly. Obviously, there is a danger that the quick-service restaurant may attract customers that the cafeteria might then lose, but competition tends to be good for all concerned. To create interest, an Iron Chef competition was held at the University of Missouri, where it gave students and chefs the opportunity to come up with innovative menu ideas, while creating a tighter knit campus community.[14]

Take-out foodservice is another convenience for the campus community. At times, students—and staff—do not want to prepare meals and are thankful for the opportunity to take meals with them. And it is not just during examination time that students, friends, and staff have a need for the take-out option. For example, tailgate parties prior to football and basketball games or concerts and other recreational/sporting events allow entrepreneurial foodservice operators to increase revenue and profits. The type of contract that a managed services operator signs varies depending on the size of the account. If the account is small, a fee generally is charged. With larger accounts, operators contract for a set percentage (usually about 5 percent) or a combination of a percentage and a bonus split. Figure 8–3 shows a typical college menu for the dining hall where students usually eat on campus.

Week 1

	Monday	Tuesday	Wednesday	Thursday	Friday

Breakfast- Cold Cereal, Fruit and Yogurt Bar, Toast, English Muffins, Belgium Waffles, Juices, Milks, Coffee, Tea, Hot Chocolate, Whole Fruit

	Monday	Tuesday	Wednesday	Thursday	Friday
Entrees	French Toast	Chocolate Chip Buttermilk Pancakes	Bacon, Egg & Cheese English Muffin	Southwestern Egg Wrap	Made to Order Omelets
	Egg, Ham & Cheese Bagel	Breakfast Taco	Made to Order Omelets	French Toast	Blueberry Buttermilk Pancakes
	Scrambled Eggs	Scrambled Eggs	Biscuits & Gravy	Scrambled Eggs	Cheddar Biscuits
	Hashbrowns	Home Fries	O' Brein Potatoes	Crispy Tater Tots	Rosemary Potatoes
	Turkey Sausage Links	Bacon	Turkey Sausage Patty	Sausage Patty	Turkey Bacon
Hot Cereal	Old Fashioned Oatmeal	Cream of Rice	Grits	Cream of Wheat	Old Fashioned Oatmeal
Bakery	Blueberry Muffins	Apple Cinnamon Scones	Peach Almond Crumb Cake	Chocolate Chip Scone	Iced Cinnamon Roll
	Assorted Donut Bites	Double Chocolate Chip Muffins	Bananas Foster Muffin	Blueberry Muffin	Banana Nut Muffin
	Cherry Cobbler Sweet Bread	Buttermilk Biscuits	Chocolate Donut Bites	Cinnamon-Sugar Donut	Caramel Apple Sweet Bread

Lunch- Salad Bar, Specialty Pizzas, Cereal, Build-Your-Own Sandwich Bar, Fresh Fruit

	Monday	Tuesday	Wednesday	Thursday	Friday
Entrees	Bistro Chicken Sandwich	Grilled Lemon Chicken	Roast Beef	Shrimp Pad Thai	Grilled Ham & Cheese Sandwich
	French Fries	Basmati Rice	French Dip Au Jus	Steamed Broccoli	French Fries
	Celery Sticks	Carrots	Steakhouse Potatoes		Carrot Sticks
	Char Sui Pork	Ham & Swiss Panini	Chicken, Broccoli & Mushroom Stir-Fry	Country-Style Meatloaf	BBQ Grilled Turkey
	White Rice	Pasta Salad	Jasmine Rice	Mashed Potatoes with Gravy	Baked Sweet Potatoes
	Orange Spiced Carrots	Homemade Chips		Glazed Carrots	Grilled Zucchini & Squash Medley
	Bruschetta Calzones	Cheesy Lasagna	Pepperoni Melt	Meat Lover's Mini Calzone	Meatball Stromboli
	Garlic Toast	Garlic Breadsticks	Mini Italian Sandwich	Farfalle & Sausage Alfredo Bake	Cheesy Toast
Vegetarian Feature	Vegetable Enchilada	Moroccan Vegetable Stew	Quinoa & Red Pepper Slider	Grilled Veggie & Black Bean Wrap	Blackened Tofu Taco Salad
Soup	Cheddar Cauliflower	Chicken & Rice Florentine	Beef Mushroom Barley	Split Pea	Broccoli Cheddar
	Chicken Noodle	Hearty Vegetable	Curried Tomato Lentil	Two Bean Chili	Minestrone
Dessert	Chocolate Chip Cookies	Banana Pudding Parfait	Duce de Leche Brownies	Spiced Pumpkin Blondies	Oreo Brownie Pudding Parfait
	Peanut Butter & Devil's Food Parfait	Double Chocolate Brownie	Strawberry Jell-O Parfaits	Peanut Butter Swirl Brownies	Rice Krispy Treats
	Vegan Oatmeal Cookies	Peanut Butter Cookies	M&M Cookies	Sugar Cookies	Double Chocolate Chip Cookies

Dinner- Salad Bar, Specialty Pizzas, Cereal, Build-Your-Own Sandwich Bar, Fresh Fruit

	Monday	Tuesday	Wednesday	Thursday	Friday
Entrees	Chicken Fresca Quesadilla	Beef Teriyaki	Crispy Fried Chicken	Roasted Turkey	Top Your Own Burger
	Brown Rice	Lo Mein Noodles	Baked Macaroni & Cheese	Homemade Stuffing	French Fries
	Black Beans	Ginger Honey Glazed Carrots	Fresh Collard Greens	Sweet Cornbread	Corn on the Cob
	Roast Beef	Stuffed Pork Chops	BBQ Beef Brisket	Spaghetti and Meatballs	Rotisserie Lemon-Garlic Chicken
	Garlic Mashed Potatoes	Baked Potato Wedges	Scalloped Potatoes Au Gratin	Garlic Breadsticks	Whipped Cheddar Mashed Potatoes
	Sautéed Sugar Snap Peas	Seasonal Mixed Vegetables	Steamed Green Beans	Fresh Steamed Broccoli	Roasted Carrots
	Grilled Basa Bruschetta	Crispy Asiago-Crusted Chicken	Blackened Fish Sandwich	Slow Roasted BBQ Ribs	Crispy Tilapia with Tropical Salsa
	Oven Roasted Sea Salt Potatoes	Rice Pilaf	Hand Cut French Fries	Savory Baked Beans	Cilantro-Lime Rice
	Steamed Broccoli	Grilled Asparagus	Creamy Coleslaw	Sautéed Brussel Sprouts	Steamed Green Peas
Vegetarian Feature	Grilled Portobello Sandwich	Tofu Fajita	Eggplant Parmesan	BBQ Tofu Sliders	Vegetable Quesadilla
Soup	Cheddar Cauliflower	Chicken & Rice Florentine	Beef Mushroom Barley	Split Pea	Broccoli Cheddar
	Chicken Noodle	Hearty Vegetable	Curried Tomato Lentil	Two Bean Chili	Minestrone
Dessert	Caramel Pecan Cupcake	Blueberry Crumb Cupcake	Banana Chocolate Chip Cupcake	Red Velvet Cream Cheese Cupcake	Vanilla Sprinkle Cupcakes
	Strawberry Shortcake Parfait	Ginger-Spiced Rice Pudding	Oreo Pudding Parfait	Peanut Butter Pie	Banana Pudding Parfait
	Sugar Cookies	Double Chocolate Chunk Cookies	Vegan Oatmeal Cookies	Chocolate Chip Cookies	M&M Cookies

Figure 8–3 ● Sample College Menu.

(Courtesy: Sodexo Foodservice Management.)

Employee Relations

- Team development
- Rewards/recognition
- Drug alcohol abuse/prevention
- Positive work environment
- Coaching/facilitating versus directing

Human Resource Management

- Recruitment/training/evaluating
- Wage/salary administration
- Benefits administration
- Compliance with federal/state laws/EEOC (Equal Employment Opportunity)/Senate Bill 198
- Harassment/OSHA (Occupational Safety and Health Administration)
- Disciplinary actions/terminations
- Unemployment/wrongful disclosure

Financial/Budgeting

- Project budgets
- Actual versus projected budget monitoring (weekly)
- Controlling food cost, labor, expenses, and so on
- Record-keeping requirements/audit
- Monitoring accounts payable/receivable
- Billing/collecting
- Compliance with contracts
- Cash procedures/banking

Safety Administration

- Equipment training/orientation
- Controlling workers' compensation
- Monthly inspections/audits (federal/state/OSHA requirements/Senate Bill 198)

Safety Budget

- Work on the expensive injuries
- Reduce lost time frequency rate and injury frequency rate

Food Production/Service

- Menu/recipe development
- Menu mix versus competition
- Food waste/leftovers utilization

- Production records
- Production control
- Presentation/merchandising

Sanitation/Foodborne Illness Prevention

- Foodborne illness (FBI) prevention
- Sanitation/cleaning schedule
- Proper food handling/storage
- Daily prevention/monitoring
- Monthly inspection
- Health department compliance

Purchasing/Recruiting

- Ordering/receiving/storage
- Food and beverage specifications/quality
- Inventory control
- Vendor relation/problems

Staff Training/Development

- On-the-job versus structured
- Safety/sanitation/food handling and so on
- Food preparation/presentation
- Guest service

Figure 8–4 shows an organization chart for a large university foodservice operation.

Sustainable Managed Services

Hospital foodservice directors often say that offering healthy choices in their cafeterias is a key department mission. But many operators are quick to add that they still offer the so-called unhealthy options to prevent a drop in participation and revenues. However, Raquel Frazier, former food-service director at La Rabida Children's Hospital in Chicago, did not have that luxury. She was mandated by the hospital's administration to make the cafeteria 100 percent healthy.[18] To meet new nutritional guidelines, food items could not exceed 450 calories, with 10 grams of fat or three grams of saturated fat, and had to contain at least three grams of fiber. In addition, nutritional information for all items had to be posted on the menu and at the point of service. The outcome was that most employees reported losing weight and keeping it off and leading a healthier lifestyle.[19]

DESCRIPTION		%	STUDENT UNION	%	TOTAL	%
SALES						
FOOD REGULAR	$ 951,178				$ 951,178	
FOOD SPECIAL FUNCTIONS	40,000				40,000	
PIZZA HUT EXPRESS			$ 100,000		100,000	
BANQUET & CATERING	200,000				200,000	
CONFERENCE	160,000				160,000	
BEER			80,000		80,000	
SNACK BAR			300,000		30,000	
A LA CARTE CAFE	60,000				60,000	
** TOTAL SALES	$1,411,178		$ 480,000	100.0%	$1,891,178	100.0%
PRODUCT COST						
BAKED GOODS	$ 9,420		$ 4,700		$ 14,120	
BEVERAGE	10,000		8,000		18,000	
MILK & ICE CREAM	11,982		2,819		14,801	
GROCERIES	131,000		49,420		180,420	
FROZEN FOOD	76,045		37,221		113,266	
MEAT, SEAFOOD, EGGS, & CHEESE	129,017		48,000		177,017	
PRODUCE	65,500		26,000		91,500	
MISCELLANEOUS					0	
COLD DRINK	0		0		0	
** TOTAL PRODUCT COST	$ 432,964		$ 176,160	36.7%	$ 609,124	32.2%
LABOR COST						
WAGES	$ 581,000		$ 154,000		$ 735,000	
LABOR—OTHER EMPLOYEES	101,500		545,000		156,000	
BENEFITS + PAYROLL TAXES	124,794		50,657		175,451	
MANAGEMENT BENEFITS	58,320		6,000		64,320	
WAGE ACCRUALS	0				0	
** TOTAL LABOR COST	$ 865,614		$ 265,157	55.2%	$1,130,771	59.8%
FOOD OPERATING COST— CONTROLLABLE						
CLEANING SUPPLIES	$ 24,000		$ 6,000		$ 30,000	
PAPER SUPPLIES	9,000		46,000		55,000	
EQUIPMENT RENTAL					0	
GUEST SUPPLIES					7,000	
PROMOTIONS	4,500		2,500		40,000	
SMALL EQUIPMENT	35,000		5,000		0	
BUSINESS DUES & MEMBERSHIP					3,000	
VEHICLE EXPENSE	3,000				4,300	
TELEPHONE	3,600		700		22,000	
	$ 17,000		$ 5,000		$ 22,000	

Figure 8–5 • An Operating Statement.

▶ Check Your Knowledge

1. In your own words, define in-flight foodservice.

2. What are some of the challenges faced by in-flight foodservice operators? What can be done to solve these problems?

3. Name the foodservice operations that constitute managed services.

4. How is each foodservice operation characterized?

5. In small groups, discuss the differences between the foodservice operations and then share with the class.

DESCRIPTION		%	STUDENT UNION	%	TOTAL	%
LAUNDRY & UNIFORMS					0	
MAINTENANCE & REPAIRS	$ 1,200		$ 200		$ 1,400	
FLOWERS	10,000		4,000		140,000	
TRAINING					0	
SPECIAL SERVICES	18,000		3,000		21,000	
MISCELLANEOUS						
** TOTAL CONTROLLABLE SUPPLIES	$ 125,300	8.9%	$ 72,400	15.1%	$ 197,700	10.5%
OPERATING COSTS— NONCONTROLLABLE						
AMORTIZATION & DEPRECIATION	$ 13,500		$ 7,000		$ 20,500	
INSURANCE	55,717		14,768		70,485	
MISCELLANEOUS EXPENSE	12,400		4,100		16,500	
ASSET RETIREMENTS					0	
RENT/COMMISSIONS	48,000		40,000		88,000	
PIZZA HUT ROYALTIES			7,000		7,000	
PIZZA HUT — LICENSING MARKETING			7,000		7,000	
TAXES, LICENSE & FEES	5,000		500		5,500	
VEHICLE — DEPRECIATION & EXPENSE	4,000				4,000	
ADMINISTRATION & SUPERVISION						
** TOTAL NONCONTROLLABLE COST	$ 138,617	9.8%	$ 80,368	16.7%	$ 218,985	11.6%
** TOTAL COST OF OPERATIONS	$ 1,562,495	110.7%	$ 594,085	123.8%	$2,156,580	114.0%
EXCESS OR (DEFICIT)	(151,317)	(10.7%)	(114,085)	(23.8)	(265,402)	(14.0%)
PARTICIPATION-CONTRACTOR						
*** NET EXCESS OR (DEFICIT)						
STATISTICS						
CUSTOMER COUNT						
HOURS WORKED						
AVERAGE FOOD- SALES/CUSTOMER						

Figure 8–5 • An Operating Statement. (*continued*)

Health Care Facilities

LEARNING OBJECTIVE 5
Identify characteristics and trends in health care, business and industry, and leisure and recreation foodservices.

Health care managed services operations are remarkably complex because of the necessity of meeting the diverse needs of a delicate clientele. Health care managed services are provided to hospital patients, long-term care and assisted living residents, visitors, and employees. The service is given by tray, cafeteria, dining room, coffee shop, catering, and vending.

The challenge of health care managed services is to provide many special meal components to patients with very specific dietary requirements. Determining which meals need to go to which patients and ensuring that they reach their destinations involve especially challenging

TECHNOLOGY SPOTLIGHT

Data Mining

Courtesy of Allie Hire

Understanding your guests in the hospitality industry, where they are from, and what they seek in terms of value and quality is strategic to maximizing profits. Success or failure can often depend upon how much data a company can collect, or mine, and translate that data into useful information for marketing, retention, and overall guest experience improvements. Data mining is a traditional approach in the hospitality industry, and it has proven successful in formulating hotel and restaurant customers.

More common than ever, businesses are using technology to support managed services. Managed services are the methods of outsourcing day-to-day managerial functions in efforts to improve operations and maximize profitability. Examples of outsourcing include human resource activities, employee training and improvements, and production support. The person that organizes and provides the managed service is referred to as the service provider, or MSP. The MSP is a third party and works 24/7 for the customer or client in need of the services. The MSP assumes a responsibility for constant monitoring, problem resolution, or managing of the IT (information technology) systems in an organization. The difference between an MSP and IT services is the delivery of their service and the information that is constantly monitored and provided to the client.

The MSPAlliance mission was established in 2000, with the goal of helping MSPs become better. The MSPAlliance mission states that characteristics of MSPs include the following:

- Include some form of Network Operation Center
- Have some form of service or help desk service
- Be able to remotely monitor and manage all or a majority of the IT objects for the customer
- Proactively, compared to reactively, maintain the IT objects under management for the customer
- Delivering these solutions with some form of predictable billing model, where the customer knows with great accuracy what their regular IT management expense will be

Statistics show that by the end of 2014, businesses in the United States will have spent over $13 billion on cloud computing and managed IT services, and the global market for cloud equipment is predicted to reach $79.1 billion by 2018.[20] The spending on this technology may seem high, but considering how dependent we've become on technology, especially in businesses, the spending is justified. But just how much money does a company save when using technology in managed services?

A Computing Technology Industry Association poll of 400 IT and business professionals in 2011 found that 46 percent of organizations that rely on MSPs for some or all of their IT needs say they have reduced annual IT budgets by at least 25 percent as a result of adopting managed services.[21] In the total poll, it was determined that 96 percent of all organizations that participated stated that managed services saved them money. The evidence shows that managed services makes sense, both monetarily and from a managerial standpoint.

Managed services is prominent in the hospitality industry, and particularly so in foodservice in airlines, elementary and secondary schools, colleges and universities, and health care facilities. ARAMARK is one of the largest companies that serve this industry. ARAMARK provides services to more than 1,400 colleges, universities, school systems and districts, and private schools. They also provide services to more than 2,000 health care facilities, collectively representing over 75 million patient days annually.[22] The team at ARAMARK creates dining solutions for almost any industry in need, with options that are both high quality and profitable.

TECHNOLOGY SPOTLIGHT (Continued)

In 2014, ARAMARK announced they would pilot acceptance of mobile payments from Apple Pay at certain hockey arenas during the 2015 season. ARAMARK's goal is to innovate the guest experience with concepts that work for both the client and the consumer. By allowing customers to use these apps to purchase food and beverages, they are able to have a secure and convenient way to pay for those items, using their iPhone or Apple Watch. Another innovation was a concept called Burger Studio, a retail dining experience designed for colleges and universities. Digital menu boards and electronic touch-screen ordering stations allowed students to design their own meal, from start to finish.

Sodexo is another leader in the industry of managed services. They serve more than 15 million consumers daily, and they serve 9,000 sites.[23] Sodexo manages the food and facilities for over 1,600 hospitals and health care facilities across the United States, and in 2009 expanded their partnership with Skylight Healthcare Systems, the leader in interactive patient care technology. Skylight Healthcare Systems is a pioneer in interactive patient system technology with a focus on patients and families participating in their health care. Their findings show that the more interactive a patient and their families are, the better the communication between staff and those patients, thus creating a more seamless and comfortable hospital stay. A recent example of this joint venture is turning the hospital televisions into interactive patient information stations—a small change that makes a large impact for patients and staff alike.

Managed foodservices aren't just on land. If you've recently travelled on an airline and received a beverage, snack, or meal, you've witnessed the managed service of airline foodservice from companies like Gate Gourmet and LSG Sky Chefs. LSG Sky Chefs use retail technology to maximize revenues for airlines. They advertise that their point-of-sale hand-held terminals allow an airline to change prices and offer promotions, accept credit cards, loyalty cards, and coupons. The terminals communicate information that is then useful for marketing, sales predictions, and controlling stock levels.

advantage of being able to introduce changes immediately without having to support layers of regional and corporate employees.

Another trend in health care managed services is the arrival of the major quick-service chains. McDonald's, Pizza Hut Express, Burger King, and Dunkin' Donuts are just a few of the large companies that have joined forces with the contract managed services operators. Using branded quick-service leaders is a win-win situation for both the contract foodservice operator and the quick-service chain.

The chains benefit from long-term leases at very attractive rates compared with a restaurant site. Chains assess the staff size and patient and visitor count to determine the size of unit to install. Thus far, they have found that weekday lunches and dinners are good, but the numbers on weekends are disappointing.

In contrast, several hospitals are entering the pizza-delivery business: They hook up phone and fax ordering lines, and they hire part-time employees to deliver pizzas made on the premises. This ties in with the increasing emphasis on customer service. Patients' meals now feature comfort foods, based on the concept that the simpler the food is, the better—hence, the resurgence of meat loaf, pot pies, meat and potatoes, and tuna salad, which contributes to customer satisfaction and makes patients feel at home and comfortable.

B&I foodservice may be characterized in the following ways:

1. Full-service cafeteria with *straight line*, *scatter*, or *mobile systems*
2. *Limited-service cafeterias* offering parts of the full-service cafeteria, fast-food service, cart and mobile service, fewer dining rooms, and executive dining rooms

▶ Check Your Knowledge

1. What roles other than those strictly related to foodservice does the foodservice manager perform?
2. Briefly explain some of the tasks the foodservice manager performs. What makes each task so important?

Managed Services Other Than Food

Many companies such as Sodexo have recognized the potential to increase their market opportunities by developing service capabilities beyond food. This also offers hospitality managers the opportunity to expand their career paths as well. Typically, hospitals, colleges, schools, and businesses outsource other service departments the same as they do for food. Companies on the cutting edge are able to offer clients broader packages of services. These services often come under the area of facilities management[25] and offer the following services:

- Housekeeping/custodial/environment services
- Maintenance and engineering
- Grounds and landscaping
- Procurement and materials management
- Office and mail services
- Concierge services
- Patient transportation services (hospitals)

Many colleges and universities recognize that this is an area for career opportunities and are developing courses and programs surrounding the area of facilities management. Managers who work in the managed services segment of the industry have the advantage of learning about several disciplines. In doing so, they increase their career growth potential and can find career paths similar to those available in the lodging segment of the industry.

Leisure and Recreation

The leisure and recreation[26] segment of managed services may be the most unique and the most fun part of the foodservice industry in which to work.

Leisure and recreation foodservice operations include stadiums, arenas, theme parks, national parks, state parks, zoos, aquariums, and other venues where food and beverage are provided for large numbers of people. The customers are usually in a hurry, so the big challenge of the foodservice segment is to offer the product in a very short period of time. The average professional sporting event lasts for only two to three hours of time.

What makes this segment unique and fun is the opportunity to be part of a professional sporting event, a rock concert, a circus, or other event in a stadium or arena. There is also the choice of working in a national or state park and being part of the great outdoors. The roar of the crowd and the excitement of the event make this a very stimulating place to work. Imagine *getting paid* to see the Super Bowl versus *paying* to see the Super Bowl.

Stadium Points of Service

Leisure and recreation facilities usually have several points of service where food and beverage are provided. In the typical stadium, a vendor yells, "Here, get your hot dog here!" to the fans in the stands, while on the concourse other fans get their food and beverage from concession stands. These stands offer everything from branded—meaning well-known brands—foods to hot dogs and hamburgers to local cuisine. For example, in Philadelphia the cheesesteak sandwich is popular, whereas in Baltimore, crabcake sandwiches are favored by fans. Another place for people to get food is in a restaurant, which most stadiums have as a special area. In some cases, fans must be members of the restaurant; in other cases, fans can buy special tickets that provide them with access to this facility. These restaurants are like any other except that they provide unobstructed views of the playing area.

The other major point of service is the food and beverage offered in the premium seating areas known as superboxes, suites, and skyboxes. These premium seating areas are usually leased by corporations to entertain corporate guests and customers. In each of these areas, branded and gourmet food and beverage service is provided for the guests. These facilities are capable of holding 30–40 guests and usually have an area where the food is set up buffet style and a seating area where the guests can see the sporting or other event. In a large, outdoor stadium, there could be as many as 60 or 70 of these superbox-type facilities. For stadium foodservices, more tickets are being placed on mobile devices to enter the stadium/arena; once in the stadium, there are promotions texted to fans, and GPS locations are used in stadiums for vendor ordering.

In summary, a large stadium or arena could have vendors in the stands, concession outlets, restaurants, and superboxes all going at once and serving upward of 60,000–70,000 fans. Feeding all these people takes tremendous planning and organization on the part of the foodservice department. The companies that have many of the contracts for stadiums and arenas are ARAMARK, Sodexo, Compass Group, and Delaware North.

Other Facilities

Besides stadiums and arenas, food and beverage service is provided in several other types of facilities by the same major managed services companies that service stadiums. Most of the U.S. national parks are contracted to these companies. These parks have hotels, restaurants, snack bars, gift shops, and a

CASE STUDY *(Continued)*

4. How should Jane handle the president's function, knowing that the requested desserts have not been delivered?

5. If the special dessert cannot be purchased in time, how should the catering supervisor approach this situation when speaking with the president's office?

6. What can be done to ensure that mistakes, such as the one made by the bakery employee, do not happen again?

Summary

1. Managed services operations include segments such as airlines, military, schools and colleges, health care facilities, and businesses.

2. Food has become scarce on short and medium domestic flights. Most airlines have food prepared by a contractor, such as Gate Gourmet or LSG Sky Chefs.

3. Service to the military includes feeding troops and officers in clubs, dining halls, and hospitals as well as out in the field. Direct vendor delivery, menu management, prepared foods, and fast-food chains located on the base have met new trends in military foodservice.

4. Schools are either equipped with on-site kitchens and dining rooms or receive food from a central commissary. They try to balance salability with good nutrition. Today, nutrition education is a required subject in school.

5. College and university managed services operations include residence halls, cafeterias, student unions, faculty clubs, convenience stores, and catering.

6. The responsibilities of a foodservice manager are very complex. He or she is in charge of employee relations, human resource management, budgeting, safety administration, sanitation, and inventory.

7. Health care managed services operations need to provide numerous special meals to patients with very specific dietary requirements and nutritious meals in a limited time period for employees. The main areas of concern for health care managed services operations are tray lines and help-yourself food stations.

8. Business and industry managed services operations either operate with a full-service cafeteria or limited-service cafeteria. The type of service is determined by money, space, and time available.

9. Leisure and recreation foodservice offers yet more career opportunities. It is often available at several points of service.

Key Words and Concepts

batch cooking
commercial foodservice
contractors
daily rate

liaison personnel
managed services
National School Lunch Program (NSLP)

nutrition education programs
self-operators
tray line

Review Questions

1. What are managed services operations?
2. List and explain features that distinguish managed services operations from commercial ones.
3. Describe the issues that schools are currently facing concerning school foodservice.
4. Explain the term *National School Lunch Program* (NSLP).
5. Identify recent trends in college foodservice management.
6. What are the pros and cons concerning fast-food chains on campus?
7. Briefly explain the complex challenges for health care managed services operations.

Internet Exercises

1. Organization: **ARAMARK**
   Summary: ARAMARK is "a global leader in managed services" according to its web site. ARAMARK is an outsourcing company that provides services ranging from everyday catering to corporate apparel.
   (a) Go to ARAMARK's web site and see what they are doing under the Social Responsibility heading.
   (b) What are some of the characteristics that make a star of the month?

2. Organization: **Sodexo**
   Summary: Sodexo offers a full range of outsourcing solutions and is a leading food and facilities management services company in North America.
   (a) What corporate services does Sodexo offer?
   (b) Look at the current opportunities (at Sodexo or **ARAMARK**) within your area.

Apply Your Knowledge

1. From the sample operating statement (Figure 8–5), calculate the labor cost percentage by taking total labor cost and dividing by total sales × 100. Remember the formula:

$$\frac{\text{Cost}}{\text{Sales}} \times 100$$

2. Consider a retail operation at a local college where a grilled chicken combo, which consists of a grilled chicken breast, fries, and a 20-oz. soda, is on the menu. Find out the cost of the ingredients and write out everything needed for the combo, including its service. What is your cost price? How much would you charge customers for the item to make a reasonable profit?

Suggested Activity

1. Create a sample menu for a day at an elementary or high school. Then, compare your items to the MyPlate food guide and the recommended daily servings. How does your menu measure up?

Endnotes

1. Personal conversation with Susan Pillmeier, ARAMARK, and John Lee, Sodexo, July 28, 2005.

2. Gate Gourmet, *About Gate Gourmet*, www.gategourmet.com. Click on About (accessed May 1, 2015).

3. LSG Sky Chefs, *Who We Are*, http://www.lsgskychefs.com. Click on Who we are (accessed July 29, 2014).

4. Ibid.

5. This content is based on material from the following sites: Sodexo, *Group profile*, http://www.sodexo.com. Click on Group (accessed February 29, 2015); Sodexo, *About Us*, http://www.sodexousa.com. Click on About Us (accessed March 4, 2015).

6. "Channeling the College Environment: Viewing a Military Installation Like a College Campus Can Help Foodservice Enhance the Retail Experience," *Foodservice Director* (March 15, 2011):

7. "Cafeteria Boot Camp: Fort Campbell's Hospital Cafeteria Focuses on Healthy Dining after Renovation," *Foodservice Director* (March 15, 2011): 8.

8. "Smart Choices," *Foodservice Director* (April 15, 2011): 10.

9. United States Department of Agriculture, Food and Nutrition Service. *National School Lunch Program*, September 2013, www.fns.usda.gov. Go to Programs, click on National School Lunch Program (NSLP), and then click on Program Fact Sheet (accessed April 28, 2015).

10. Sahra Bahari, "Students can Expect Healthier Selection," *Fort Worth Star-Telegram*, August 12, 2007.

11. United States Department of Agriculture, Food and Nutrition Service. *National School Lunch Program*, September 2013, www.fns.usda.gov. Go to Programs, click on National School Lunch Program (NSLP), and then click on Program Fact Sheet (accessed November 24, 2014).

12. "Teaching Moments: School's Garden Spurs Nutrition Program for Students," *Foodservice Director* (December 15, 2010): 8.

13. The National Association of College & University Food Services, *About NACUFS*, www.nacufs.org. Click on About NACUFS (accessed April 28, 2015).

14. "Smart Choices," *Foodservice Director* (April 15, 2011): 1.

15. Based on an interview with Steve Dobrowolski, Retail Operations Director, ARAMARK, University of South Florida, April 27, 2011.

16. ARAMARK, *About Us*, www.aramark.com. Click on About Us (accessed July 29, 2014).

17. ARAMARK, *Food Services*, http://www.aramark.com. Go to Services and then click on Food Services (accessed May 27, 2015).

18. FSD Staff, "Environmental Awareness," *Foodservice Director* 22(8), August 15, 2009, 58.

19. Ibid.

20. Nate Teplow, "29 Statistics Every MSP Needs to Know," *MSP Blog*, April 29, 2014 (8:30 A.M.), http://blog.continuum.net/29-statistics-every-msp-needs-to-know.

21. Pedro Pereira, "Do Managed Services Really Save Money?," December 1, 2011, http://www.channelinsider.com. Search for "Do Managed Services Really Save Money" to view the article (accessed May 27, 2015).

22. ARAMARK, *Food Services*, http://www.aramark.com. Go to Services and then click on Food Services (accessed May 27, 2015).

23. Sodexo, *About Us*, http://www.sodexousa.com. Click on About Us (accessed March 4, 2015).

24. Personal correspondence with John Lee, Director of College and External Relations, Sodexho, September 13, 2005.

25. Ibid.

26. Courtesy of David Tucker.

P A R T III
Tourism, Recreation, Attractions, Clubs, and Gaming

CHAPTER 9

Tourism

LEARNING OBJECTIVES

After reading and studying this chapter, you should be able to:

- Summarize the historical impact of transportation on tourism.
- Define tourism and describe the important international tourism organizations.
- Describe the benefits and prospects of tourism.
- Describe the economic impact of tourism.
- Identify the promoters of tourism.
- Summarize the sociocultural impact of tourism.
- Describe ecotourism.

Highlights of Tourism

It is difficult to determine when tourism began because, centuries ago, very few people traveled for pleasure or business as they do today. We can trace some travel destinations since ancient times as follows:

- In the fourth century B.C. (before Christ), work started on the Great Wall of China and continued for centuries until the 1600s. Although not a tourist destination (or attraction) back then, it certainly is today.

- In 776 B.C., athletic games were held on the plain of Olympia in Greece (the modern Olympic Games were inspired by these games), and presumably people traveled there to participate or to watch.

- The Romans liked to visit the Bay of Naples, so they built a road there from Rome in 312 A.D. (*anno Domini*, after Christ). The road was 100 miles long and took four days by litter to get there (in which a nobleperson sat on a platform and was carried by some unfortunate servants).

- Religious pilgrimages to Rome and the Holy Land (now Israel) began in the 1200s, so inns sprang up to feed and accommodate the pilgrims.

- Marco Polo became the first noted European business traveler as he pioneered trade routes from Europe to China from 1275 to 1292, staying at primitive inns called *khans* along the way.

- In the 1600s, during the age of horse-drawn coach travel in England, posthouses were set up to feed and shelter travelers and change the teams of horses every few miles. The journey from London to Bristol took three days—it now takes less than two hours by rail.

- In 1841, Thomas Cook organized a group tour for 570 people to a religious meeting in England.

- Cruising began in the 1840s with the Cunard Line crossing the Atlantic between England and North America.

- In the 1840s, the Peninsular and Oriental Steam Navigation Company (P&O) cruised the Mediterranean.

- In the 1850s, Monaco (a principality in the south of France) decided to cure its economic woes by becoming a winter haven for the rich as a health resort and a casino.

- During the age of the grand tour, from the 1880s through the 1930s, wealthy Europeans toured Europe as a part of their education.

- Rail travel began in the 1800s.

- Auto and air travel began in the 1900s.

- American Airlines introduced its first transcontinental flight between New York and Los Angeles in 1959.

- In 1970, the Boeing 747 began flying 450 passengers at a time across the Atlantic and Pacific Oceans.

- In the 1970s, ecotourism and sustainable tourism became important topics.

- In the 1980s, cruising became popular.

- In 1986, the United States established the Visa Waiver Program to eliminate unnecessary barriers to travel to the United States. Currently, 38 countries are part of the program.

- In the 2000s, international tourism temporarily declined as a result of the September 11 attacks, severe acute respiratory syndrome (SARS), bird flu, and war. However, tourism is projected to grow at a rate of between 3.0 and 3.5 percent a year, according to the World Travel & Tourism Council.[1]

- In 2008, there were over 922 million international tourist arrivals, but as a result of the 2007–2010 recession, tourism was down 4 percent in 2009. However, it was expected to and did rise since then.[2]

- International tourism arrivals grew by almost 5 percent in the first half of 2011, consolidating the nearly 7-percent growth rate from 2010.[3]

- China's expenditure on travel abroad reached US $102 billion in 2012, making it the first tourism source market in the world.

- In 2012, international tourism produced $1.3 trillion in export earnings for the United States, while international tourist arrivals increased by 4 percent. This number is expected to increase an additional 4.3 percent in 2014.[4]

Transportation: Its Historical Impact on Tourism

LEARNING OBJECTIVE 1
Summarize the historical impact of transportation on tourism.

The historical development of tourism has been divided into five distinct ages (or periods),[5] four of which paralleled the advent of a new means of transportation:

Pre–Industrial Revolution (prior to 1840)

The railway age

The automobile age

The jet aircraft age

The cruise ship age

Pre–Industrial Revolution

As early as 5,000 years ago, some ancient Egyptians sailed up and down the Nile River to construct and visit the pyramids. Probably the first journey ever made for the purposes of peace and tourism was made by Queen Hatshepsut to the Land of Punt (believed to be on the east coast of Africa) in 1480 B.C. Descriptions of this tour have been recorded on the walls of the temple of Deir el-Bahari at Luxor.[6] These texts and bas-reliefs are among the world's rarest artworks and are universally admired for their wondrous beauty and artistic qualities. The Colossi of Memnon at Thebes have on their pedestals the names of Greek tourists of the fifth century B.C.[7] The Phoenicians were among the early travelers. They traveled in both the Mediterranean and the Orient (now called Southeast Asia), and travel was motivated by trade. Later, the Roman Empire provided safe passage for travelers via a vast road system that stretched from Egypt to Britain. Wealthy Romans traveled to Egypt and Greece to baths, shrines, and seaside resorts.[8] The Romans were as curious as are today's tourists. They visited the attractions of their time, trekking to Greek temples and places where Alexander the Great slept, Socrates lived, Ajax committed suicide, and Achilles was buried, and to the pyramids, the Sphinx, and the Valley of the Kings—just as today's tourists do.[9] The excavated ruins of the Roman town Pompeii, which was buried by the volcanic eruption of Mount Vesuvius, revealed some 20-plus restaurants, taverns, and inns that tourists visit even today.

The earliest Olympic Games for which we still have written records were held in 776 B.C. (though it is generally believed that the games had been going on for many years before that).[10] Thus, sports have been a motivation for tourism for a long time.

Travel via land and sea in the Middle Ages was mostly for religious or trade reasons. People made pilgrimages to various shrines: Muslims to Mecca and Christians to Jerusalem and Rome. The Crusades (which began in 1095 and lasted for the next 200 years) stimulated a cultural exchange that was in part responsible for the Renaissance.

Marco Polo (1254–1324) traveled the Silk Road, which was anything but a road, as we know it, from Venice to Beijing, China. He was the first European to journey all the way across Asia to Beijing, and his journey, which lasted 24 years, and the tales from it became the most well known travelogue in the Western world.[11]

Marco Polo's father and uncle had traveled extensively in Asia before Marco joined them. The journey was both difficult and dangerous (excerpts of Marco's account can be read at several Marco Polo web sites). One time, to make sure the Polo brothers would be given every assistance on their travels, Kublai Khan presented them with a golden tablet (or *paiza*, in Chinese; *gerege*, in Mongolian) a foot long and three inches wide and inscribed with the words "By the strength of the eternal Heaven, holy be the Khan's name. Let him that pays him not reverence be killed." The golden tablet was a special VIP passport, authorizing the travelers to receive throughout the Great Khan's dominions such horses, lodging, food, and guides, as they required.[12] This was an early form of passport.

The Hall of Supreme Harmony in Beijing's Forbidden City.

Coach, Rail, and Automobile Travel

Changes in the technology of travel have had widespread implications for society. In the United States, travel was principally by horse and wagon or stagecoach until the advent of rail travel, which greatly advanced opening up the West. Along with the growth of towns and cities, came hotels near rail depots to accommodate travelers. Likewise, auto travel produced the motel and a network of highways, and the commercial jet created destination resorts in formerly remote and exotic locations, made the rental car business a necessity, and changed the way we look at geography. Although long-distance travel has always been fairly comfortable for the wealthy, it was not until the development of the railroad in the 1830s that travel became comfortable and cheap enough to be within reach of the masses.

Traveling by Train

Coast to coast, the United States has a lot of land with a fair share of mountains, canyons, forests, deserts, rivers, and other natural barriers to travel. One of the main factors that led to the development of railroads in the United States was the need to move goods and people from one region of the country to another. Farmed goods needed to be transported to industrial areas, and people wanted a quicker route to the West, especially after the discovery of gold in California. Those who already lived at the frontier wanted the same conveniences as their neighbors in the East, such as efficient postal service.

The train made mass travel possible for everyone. Long-distance travel became both cheaper and faster, making the horse and ship seem like overpriced snails. The vast rail networks across North America, Asia, Australia, and Europe made the train station a central part of nearly every community. Naturally, entrepreneurs soon built hotels conveniently close to train stations.

Although hugely important and popular for many years, the popularity of rail travel started to decline as early as the 1920s. Why did people stop using the train? For two main reasons: the bus and the car. In addition, the Great Depression of the 1930s certainly deterred travelers. Although World War II brought a new surge in passenger numbers, people were seldom traveling for pleasure, and at the close of the war, the decline continued. Automobiles were again available, and people had the money to buy them. By 1960, airplanes, which made faster travel possible, had taken over much of the long-distance travel market, further reducing the importance of the train.

Facing a possible collapse of passenger rail services, the U.S. Congress passed the Rail Passenger Service Act in 1970 (amended in 2001). Shortly after, the National Railroad Passenger Corporation began operation as a semipublic corporation established to operate intercity passenger trains, a move in the direction of seminationalization of U.S. railroads. The corporation is known today as Amtrak.

An Amtrak train at its station.

Rail Travel Abroad

While the United States tries to rejuvenate rail travel under the direction of Amtrak, rail service in other parts of the industrialized world is far ahead in progress. Taking the train makes good sense in densely populated areas such as those in Western Europe and parts of Asia, and high-speed networks are already well developed, often drawing most of the traffic that formerly went by air. One good example is the Eurostar, connecting the United Kingdom with mainland Europe via the 31-mile-long underwater Channel Tunnel. France's TGV (Train à Grande Vitesse) trains are perhaps the best known of them all, serving more than 150 cities in France and Europe, and traveling at about 201 mph (although they have the capacity of running at 250 mph). The TGV's most spectacular feature is the smoothness of the ride: It is like sitting in your armchair at home. Because of their importance, all trains—high speed or not—run frequently and on time. Fares are generally reasonable, and service levels are high.

Japan's Shinkansen, the bullet train system, makes the 550-mile run between Tokyo and Osaka in 3 hours and 10 minutes, down from the former rail time of 18 hours. In addition, it provides a ride so smooth that a passenger can rest a coffee cup on the windowsill and not a drop will spill, just like on the TGV.

Do you dream of exploring Europe? As a student, you have probably heard of the famous Eurail Pass. Several European nations have banded together to offer non-European visitors unlimited first-class rail service for a reduced lump sum. However, if you want to use the Eurail Pass, be sure to purchase a pass before you leave home because not all types of passes are available in Europe and the ones that are cost on average 20 percent more when bought in Europe. When visiting Europe, you can choose to travel in one country, in a few selected ones, or in all with Eurail Pass; it's up to you to choose between the different passes available. In other parts of the world, Australia offers the Austrail Pass, India the Indrail Pass, and Canada the Canrailpass. The new rail line in China linking Beijing to Nepal is of interest because it is one of the longest and highest rail lines in the world, and, according to some, it is going to dilute the Tibetan culture. This is one of the dilemmas of tourism: Travel and tourism can bring an economic and social development; yet it can also damage local cultures and environments.

Traveling by Car

The internal combustion engine automobile was invented in Germany, but it quickly became America's obsession. In 1895, there were about 300 horseless carriages of one kind or another in the United States, including gasoline buggies, electric cars, and steam cars. In 1914, Henry Ford began making the Model T on the first modern assembly line, making the car available to many more Americans because of its low cost. Even during the Great Depression, almost two-thirds of American families had automobiles. Henry Ford's development of the assembly line and the gradual construction of good, solid roads helped make the automobile the symbol of American life that it is today.

Rental cars offer business and leisure travelers the convenience of fly–drive or drive-only to facilitate tourists' needs.

The auto changed the American way of life, especially in the leisure area, creating and satisfying people's urge to travel. The automobile remains the most convenient and rapid form of transportation for short and medium distances. Without question, it has made Americans the most mobile people in history and has given them options not otherwise possible. Whereas many Europeans ride their bikes or use the bus or train to get to school or work, Americans cannot seem to function without their cars. In fact, it is not uncommon for an American to drive 20,000 miles a year.

Road trips are a must for most Americans—college students, families, and retirees alike. Travel by car is by far the largest of all segments in the ground transportation sector of the travel and tourism industry. It is no wonder, then, that the highways and byways of the United States and Canada play such important roles in tourism. The advantages of car travel are that a car can take you to places that are otherwise inaccessible. Mountain resorts, ski destinations, dude ranches, and remote beaches are just a few examples. This kind of travel generates millions of dollars, and in certain places the local economy depends on the car tourist.

Rental Cars

Some 5,000 rental car companies operate in the United States. Waiting at nearly every sizable airport in the world are several highly competitive rental car agencies, a significant segment of the travel/tourism business. About 75 percent of their sales take place at airport counters that are leased from the airport, the cost of which is passed on to the customer. The larger companies do 50 percent or more of their business with large corporate accounts, accounts that receive sizable discounts under contract. The hurried business traveler is likely to rent a car, speed out of the airport, do his or her business in a day or two, return to the airport, and hop on a plane to return home. The pleasure traveler, however, is more likely to rent a small car for a week or more. This group constitutes about 30 percent of the rental car market. Some of the top rental car companies in the United States are Hertz, Avis, Enterprise, National, and Budget. The agencies maintain between 300,000 and 900,000 rental cars that are usually new and are sold after six months to reduce maintenance costs and help avoid breakdowns.

Traveling by Bus

Although scheduled bus routes aren't as competitive as scheduled service for airlines, buses still play an important role in the travel and tourism industry, especially with regard to charter and tour services. Some bus companies even offer services such as destination management, incentive programs, and planning of meetings, events, and conferences. Some companies to check out are Gray Line Worldwide, Contiki Tours, and Canadian Tours International.

The major reasons for selecting the bus over other modes of travel are convenience and economy. Many passengers are adventurous college students from the United States and abroad or senior citizens, both with limited funds but plenty of time on their hands. Most people don't choose bus travel for long trips, however, because a flight is much quicker and often just as economical. However, in places such as the heavily populated northeast corridor, regular bus service between most sizable communities in New England and New York often makes it easier and safer for travelers to ride the bus than to drive their cars into the city. Anyone who has experienced New York City traffic will probably agree.

Another reason why buses are popular is because they allow the leisure traveler to sit back, relax, and enjoy the scenery. In addition, they are hassle free and provide an opportunity to make new friends and stop along the way. Long-distance buses offer a variety of amenities similar to an airplane, with an extra benefit of almost door-to-door service! Buses travel to small and large communities, bringing with them tourist dollars and thus a boost to the local economy.

Types of Bus Service

In addition to routes between towns and cities, bus travel includes local route service, charter service, tour service, special services, commuter service, airport service, and urban and rapid transit service. The largest and most recognized of all of the specialized travel services is Gray Line. Founded in 1910, Gray Line is a franchise operation based in Colorado. The company assembles package tours and customized tours, arranges rail and air transfers, and even provides meeting and convention services. Its major service, however, is sightseeing trips by bus. When a traveler arrives at a destination and wishes to see the town and the major tourist attractions, Gray Line is usually ready to serve. The 150-member organization carries about 28 million passengers a year at more than 200 destinations. Their trips are widely diversified, such as "around-the-town" in Paris and "around-the-country" in Thailand. In the

United States, Gray Line's biggest market is Los Angeles, followed by San Francisco and then Manhattan.

▶ Check Your Knowledge

1. In what locations does rail travel make the most sense?
2. What is the future of rail travel?
3. Who are the major users of buses?

Travel by Air and Sea

Air travel has made it possible to build great resorts on remote islands, it has fostered multinational enterprises, and it has broadened the horizons of hundreds of millions of people. Without the airplane, most resort destinations would have been virtually impossible to build. The number of international travelers would be far fewer because of the time, money, and difficulty involved in travel. The airplane makes travel easier and more convenient because even the most remote location is just a few hours away by plane, and reasonable airfares make it possible for more people to travel by air.

Air transport has become an integral factor in the travel and tourism industry. Hotels, car rental agencies, and even cruise lines depend heavily on airplanes for profits. For instance, lower airfares result in more passengers and hence a higher occupancy at hotels. Whole towns and cities can and do benefit from this concept by receiving more taxes from tourists, which leads to better public facilities, better schools, and even lower local and property taxes.

In the United States, there are, at any one time, about 5,500 airplanes in the skies.[13] In recent years, the airline has become the preferred means of travel for the long haul. The jet aircraft has made previously inaccessible places such as Bali, Boracay, and Bangkok easily accessible, for a reasonable price. Today millions of Americans travel within the United States and abroad, and millions more visit the United States because of air travel.

Over the past few years—with the exception of Southwest, AirTran, and JetBlue—major U.S. airlines have lost billions of dollars. One reason is competition from low-cost domestic and international airlines.

Since the economic recession, business travelers continue to spend less, and airlines' pension, fuel, and security costs have risen. The major airlines have laid off employees, delayed delivery of new jets, and closed some hubs, reservations, and maintenance centers in an effort to reduce costs. Several of the major U.S. airlines have been and are in financial trouble, so they are charging an additional fuel surcharge on tickets and charging for checked bags, food, beverages, and selected seats just so that they can stay in the air.

For example, in efforts to promote passenger loyalty and operating effectiveness, the major U.S. airlines have formed strategic alliances with

American Airlines and its 15 oneworld® alliance partner airlines go just about anywhere. The oneworld partners include British Airways, Cathay Pacific, and Japan Airlines.

partner airlines to provide passengers with easier ticket purchases and transportation to destinations in countries not served by U.S. airlines. Many of the world's major airlines are grouped with Star Alliance, SkyTeam, or oneworld. The SkyTeam Alliance network includes Delta from the United States, Aeroflot from Russia, AeroMexico, Air Europa, Air France, Alitalia from Italy, China Airlines, China Southern, KLM from the Netherlands, Korean Air, and others. Alliances of this nature will allow airlines access to each other's feeder markets and to resources that will enable them to compete in what will ultimately be a worldwide deregulation. A *feeder market* is a market that provides the source—in this case, passengers for the particular destination. Ultimately, any major European airline without a strategic alliance in the United States will only limit its own horizons and lose market share. Airlines have merged or taken over others to increase their scope of operations and reduce costs in an effort to stay competitive. Delta acquired Northwest Airlines and Continental was acquired by United.

Another example is Southwest Airlines. Southwest operates more efficiently than the competition does despite the fact that its workforce is unionized. Southwest gets more flight time from its pilots than does American Airlines—672 hours a year versus 371—and racks up 60 percent more passenger miles per flight attendant. These efficiencies have resulted in annual profits for 30 consecutive years as a result of Southwest's dedication to a low-cost, high-customer-satisfaction strategy.

Carriers such as Southwest, AirTran, and JetBlue have lower operating costs because they use only one type of aircraft, fly point to point, and offer a no-frills service. Their lower fares have forced many larger airlines to retreat. In 2012, the industry's fuel bill had risen to 33 percent of operating costs—a huge factor to consider when airlines decide to put older, less fuel-efficient aircrafts into storage.

To reduce losses brought about by deregulation and high labor, pension plan, and fuel costs, major carriers have eliminated unprofitable routes, often those serving smaller cities. New airlines began operating shuttle services between the smaller cities and the nearest larger or hub city. This created the hub-and-spoke system (see Figure 9–1).

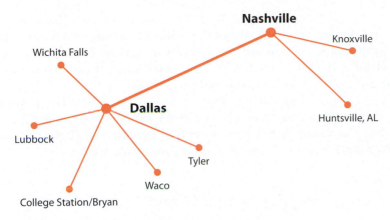

Figure 9–1 • The Hub-and-Spoke System.

The Hub-and-Spoke System

To remain efficient and cost effective, major U.S. airlines have adopted a **hub-and-spoke system**, which enables passengers to travel from one smaller city to another smaller city via a hub or even two hubs. Similarly, passengers may originate their travel from a small city and use the hub to reach connecting flights to destinations throughout the world.

The hub-and-spoke system has two main benefits: (1) Airlines can service more cities at a lower cost and (2) airlines can maximize passenger loads from small cities, thereby saving fuel. The airlines have also used deregulation to their advantage to save money whenever possible, for instance, by cutting nonprofitable routes from some smaller cities.

New Airplanes

Boeing's first new airplane model in several years, the 787 Dreamliner, takes advantage of huge advances made in aviation technology in the past decade and is capable of flying long-haul routes using up to 20 percent less fuel than today's similar-sized airplanes. Up to 50 percent of the primary structure of the plane, including the fuselage and wing, is made of components such as carbon fiber, which reduces the weight of the plane.[14]

Able to fly up to 9,400 miles without refueling, the Boeing 787 Dreamliner could easily manage

The Boeing 787 Dreamliner is able to fly up to 9,400 miles without refueling.

a flight between New York and Moscow, Manila, or Sao Paulo or between Boston and Athens. Richard Aboulafia, Vice President of Analysis with Teal Group, comments, "If you look at it from an airline standpoint: you don't have a choice. If you don't have a 787-class aircraft and your competitor does, he can under price you and out-profit you."[15]

Boeing's competitor, Airbus, makes the Airbus A380. The giant double-decker Airbus A380 can carry up to 525 passengers for a distance of up to 8,000 miles. Singapore Airlines flew the first commercial flight of this aircraft in October 2007 between Singapore and Sydney, Australia.

Components of Airline Profit and Loss

Have you ever wondered why air travel is so expensive? You might find some answers in this section, where we look at the different costs included when you buy an air ticket. Airlines have both fixed and variable costs. *Fixed costs* are constant and do not change regardless of the amount of business. Examples are the lease of airplanes, the maintenance of airline-owned or leased terminals, interest on borrowed money, insurance, and pensions. *Variable costs* tend to rise and fall with the volume of sales or the number of flights. They include wages and salaries, advertising and promotion, fuel costs, passenger food and drink, and landing fees.

The biggest single cost for airline operations is labor, which is typically 30–45 percent of total operating costs. Senior pilots for airlines such as United and Delta can receive as much as $150,000 or more a year.[16] The median salary for a flight attendant is $67,000 or more a year, plus benefits.[17] Additionally, landing and takeoff charges charged to airlines by airports can add up to thousands of dollars per plane, depending on the airport and time of day. Passenger servicing costs such as reservations, ticketing, food, baggage handling, and an amount for additional security and fuel must also be accounted for in the ticket price. Once a schedule is set and the break-even point is reached, selling tickets to extra passengers produces large profits for airlines. Being able to offer just the right amount of discount tickets that are needed to fill a plane then becomes highly important. Capacity control is one yield-management technique for maximizing sales income by lowering the price of seats according to expected demand.

The Load Factor

A key statistic in analyzing an airline's profitability is the **load factor**, which means the percentage of seats filled on all flights, including planes being flown empty to be in position for the next day's schedule. The load factor, like the occupancy rate of a hotel, is an indicator of efficient or inefficient use. The current U.S. commercial air carrier load factor is around 79.76 percent.[18] The break-even point, the point at which carriers neither lose money nor make a profit, is likely to be unique on any given flight. This point is determined by the rate structure in effect, the length of the flight, the time spent on the ground, and other costs such as wages and salaries. An airline with a long-haul, high-density route—for example, from New York to Los Angeles—has a decided cost advantage over another airlines' short-haul, low-density routes. The cost of flying a plane is sharply reduced once it reaches cruising altitude. A short flight thus costs more per mile than a long one does because a greater proportion of flight time and fuel is consumed in climbing to and descending from the cruising altitude.

In busy airports such as Atlanta, O'Hare, Los Angeles, and Kennedy, planes may spend much time waiting to take off or land. Every minute's wait adds dollars to personnel, fuel, and other costs. To keep costs down, the airlines have shifted to newer two-engine planes such as the Boeing 767, which enables them to reduce fuel consumption by as much as 30 percent. Airlines have also reconfigured seat arrangements to include more seats, but this results in seats that are smaller and have less legroom for passengers. Claustrophobic? You'd better travel business class! A few years ago, American Airlines removed some rows of seats to give more legroom by spacing the remaining seats farther apart. This has proven to be a popular decision, and many others have followed.

Cruise Ships

More than 200 cruise lines offer a variety of vacations, from a Carnival cruise to freighters that carry only a few passengers. Travelers associate a certain romance with cruising to exotic locations and being pampered all day.

Being on a cruise ship is like being on a floating resort. For example, the *Diamond Princess* is a kind of "super love boat," weighing in at 116,000 tons with 18 decks and costing $500 million to build. This ship is longer than two football fields and is capable of carrying up to 2,670 passengers.[19] The largest cruise ships can carry over 6,000 passengers. Cruise ship accommodations range from luxurious suites to cabins that are even smaller than most hotel rooms. Attractions and distractions range from early morning workouts to fabulous meals and nightlife consisting of dancing, cabarets, and casinos. Day life might involve relaxation, visits to the hair salon or spa, organized games, or simply reclining in a deck chair by the pool. Nonstop entertainment includes language lessons, charm classes, port-of-call briefings, cooking demonstrations, dances, bridge, table tennis, shuffleboard, and more.

The cruise market has increased dramatically in recent years. About 20 million people take a cruise each year. Rates vary from a starting point of about $95 per person per day on Carnival Cruise Lines to $850 on Seabourn Cruise Line. Rates typically are quoted per diem (per day) and are cruise-only figures based on double occupancy. Some 215 ships provide lake and river cruises, but most cruises are oceangoing. Casual ships cater to young couples, singles, and families with children. At the other end of the spectrum, ships that appeal to the upscale crowd draw a mature clientele that prefers a more sedate atmosphere, low-key entertainment, and dressing up for dinner. The spectacular new ships with multideck atriums and razzle-dazzle entertainment cater to the tourist markets that have a median income of $109,000 a year.[20]

Carnival Cruise Line is the most financially successful of the cruise lines, netting about 20 percent of cruise sales. It targets adults between the ages of 25 and 54 and expects to attract millions of passengers with its spectacular atriums

In addition, cruise ships sail under foreign flags (called flags of convenience) because registering these ships in countries such as Panama, the Bahamas, and Liberia means fewer and more lax regulations and little or no taxation.

Employment opportunities for Americans are mainly confined to sales, marketing, and other U.S. shore-based activities, such as reservations and supplies. Onboard, Americans sometimes occupy certain positions, such as cruise director and purser.

The reasons that few Americans work onboard cruise ships are because the ships are at sea for months at a time with just a few hours in port. The hours are long and the conditions for the crew are not likely to be acceptable to most Americans. No, you don't get your own cabin! Still interested? Try www.crewunlimited.com.

The Cruise Market

There are marked differences between the segments of the cruise industry:

Mass Market—Generally, people with incomes in the $35,000–$75,000 range, interested in an average cost per person of between $99 and $195 per day, depending on the location and size of the cabin.

Middle Market—Generally, people with incomes in the $75,000–$89,000 range, interested in an average cost per person of about $175–$350 per day. These ships are capable of accommodating about 750–2,500 passengers. The middle-market ships are stylish and comfortable, with each vessel having its own personality that caters to a variety of different guests. Among the cruise lines in the middle market are Princess Cruises, Norwegian Cruise Line, Royal Caribbean International, Holland America Line, Windstar Cruises, Cunard Line, and Celebrity Cruises.

Luxury Market—Generally, people with incomes higher than $100,000, interested in an average cost per person of more than $300 per day. In this market, the ships tend to be smaller, averaging about 700 passengers, with superior appointments and service. What constitutes a luxury cruise is partly a matter of individual judgment, partly a matter of advertising and public relations. The ships that received the top accolades from travel industry writers and others who assign such ranks cater only to the top 5 percent of North American income groups. Currently, the ships considered to be in the very top category are *Seabourn Spirit*, *Seabourn Legend*, *Crystal Serenity*, and *Silver Wind*. These six-star vessels have sophisticated cuisine, excellent service, far-reaching and imaginative itineraries, and highly satisfying overall cruise experiences.

The rising demand for cruising means larger ships with a resort-like design, numerous activities, and amenities such as virtual golf, pizzerias, and caviar bars. Significant growth opportunities still exist for the industry. With only about 10 percent of the cruise market tapped and with an estimated market potential of billions, the cruise industry is virtually assured of a bright future.

▶ Check Your Knowledge

1. What measures have the major U.S. airlines taken in recent years to combat the tough economic conditions?

2. Why do most cruise ships sail under foreign flags?

3. Summarize the cruise market.

4. Summarize the historical impact of transportation on tourism.

What Is Tourism in the Twenty-First Century?

LEARNING OBJECTIVE 2
Define tourism and describe the important international tourism organizations.

Tourism is a dynamic, evolving, consumer-driven force and is the world's largest industry, or collection of industries, when all its interrelated components are placed under one umbrella: tourism and travel; lodging; conventions, expositions, meetings, and events; restaurants and managed services; assembly, destination, and event management; and recreation. Tourism plays a foundational role in framing the various services that hospitality companies perform.

The leading international organization in the field of travel and tourism, the **World Tourism Organization (UNWTO)** is vested by the United Nations with a central and decisive role in promoting the development of responsible, sustainable, and universally accessible tourism, with the aim of contributing to economic development, international understanding, peace, prosperity, and universal respect for and observance of human rights and fundamental freedoms. In pursuing this aim, the organization pays particular attention to the interests of the developing countries in the field of tourism. The UNWTO's definition of tourism is, "Tourism comprises the activities of persons traveling to and staying in places outside their usual environment for not more than one consecutive year for leisure, business, and other purposes."[23]

The UNWTO plays a catalytic role in promoting technology transfers and international cooperation, stimulating and developing public–private-sector partnerships, and encouraging the implementation of the Global Code of Ethics for Tourism. The UNWTO is dedicated to ensuring that member countries, tourist destinations, and businesses maximize the positive economic, social, and cultural effects of tourism and fully reap its benefits, while minimizing its negative social and environmental impacts. Francesco Frangialli, secretary general of the UNWTO from 1998 to 2008, writes:

The Global Code of Ethics for Tourism sets a frame of reference for the responsible and sustainable development of world tourism. It draws inspiration from many similar declarations and industry codes that have come before and it adds new thinking that reflects our changing society at the beginning of the 21st century.

Waikiki Beach is a popular tourist destination.

With international tourism forecast to reach 1.6 billion arrivals by 2020, members of the World Tourism Organization believe that the Global Code of Ethics for Tourism is needed to help minimize the negative impacts of tourism on the environment and on cultural heritage while maximizing the benefits for residents of tourism destinations. The Global Code of Ethics for Tourism is intended to be a living document. Read it. Circulate it widely. Participate in its implementation. Only with your cooperation can we safeguard the future of the tourism industry and expand the sector's con-tribution to economic prosperity, peace and understanding among all the nations of the world.[24]

The UNWTO membership includes 156 countries, six Associate Members, and some 400 affiliate members representing the private sector, educational institutions, tourism associations, and local tourism authorities.[25] Unfortunately, the United States is not a member, but it may soon be.

The UNWTO and the World Travel and Tourism Council (WTTC) declare the travel and tourism industry to have the following characteristics:

- A 24-hour-a-day, 7-day-week, 52-week-a-year economic driver
- Total contribution to world gross domestic product (GDP) of 9 percent
- Employer of more than 272 million people, or 1 in 11 of the world's total jobs, and is expected to be 1 in 10 by 2021[26]
- Leading producer of tax revenues

Given declining manufacturing and agricultural industries, and in many countries the consequent rise in unemployment, world leaders should turn to the service industries for real strategic employment gains. For many developing nations, tourism represents a large percentage of gross national product and a way of gaining a positive balance of trade with other nations.

▶ **Check Your Knowledge**

1. What role does the UNWTO play in the tourism industry?

2. Define tourism.

3. How is tourism categorized?

Benefits and Prospects of Tourism

LEARNING OBJECTIVE 3
Describe the benefits and prospects of tourism.

Tourism is firmly established as the number one industry in many countries and the fastest-growing economic sector in terms of foreign exchange earnings and job creation. International tourism is the world's largest export earner and an important factor in the balance of payments of most nations.

Tourism has become one of the world's most important sources of employment. It stimulates enormous investment in infrastructure, most of which helps to improve the living conditions of residents as well as tourists. Tourism also provides governments with substantial tax revenues. Most new tourism jobs and businesses are created in the developing countries, helping to equalize economic opportunities and keep rural residents from moving to overcrowded cities. Intercultural awareness and personal friendships fostered through tourism are powerful forces for improving international understanding and contributing to peace among all the nations of the world.

The UNWTO encourages governments, in partnership with the private sector, local authorities, and nongovernmental organizations, to play a vital role in tourism. The UNWTO helps countries throughout the world to maximize the positive impacts of tourism, while minimizing its possible negative consequences on the environment and societies.[27] Tourism is a collection of industries, or segments, that when combined, form the world's largest industry. Tourism offers the greatest global employment prospects. This trend is caused by the following factors:

1. The opening of borders: Despite security concerns, we can travel to more countries now than 10 years ago. The United States has a Visa Waiver Program with 38 countries, which means citizens of these countries with machine-readable passports do not require a visa to visit the United States.

2. An increase in disposable income and vacation taking

3. Reasonably affordable airfares

4. An increase in the number of people with more time and money to travel

5. More people with the urge to travel

The Economic Impact of Tourism

The World Travel and Tourism Council, a London-based organization, suggests that the revenue from travel and tourism was $7 trillion (approximately 3 percent) of GDP in 2013 and will rise by 4.2 percent annually through 2023. The total contribution of travel and tourism to GDP, including its wider economic impacts, is forecast to be $10.4 trillion by 2023.[32] Total contribution of travel and tourism to employment, including jobs indirectly supported by the industry, was $266 million in 2013 and is forecasted to rise to 323,826,000 jobs (9.7 percent) by 2021.[33]

Tourism accounts for 7.72 million jobs in the United States. The United States is second to France in the number of tourists (59.7 million) but first in tourism revenues (see Figure 9–3).

World international arrivals, according to the UNWTO, will reach 1.8 billion by 2030, more than triple the 475 million people who traveled abroad in 1992. Nearly every state publishes its own tourism economic impact study indicating billions of dollars in tourism revenue. The U.S. Travel Association's *U.S. Travel Answer Sheet*[35] shows travel's impact on America. Statistics for 2014 include the following:[36]

- International travelers spent about $137 billion on travel-related expenses (e.g., lodging, food, entertainment), thereby supporting over 1 million U.S. jobs.

- There were about 8 million people directly employed in the travel industry, ranking travel among the top 10 industries.

- Travel generated more than $140 billion in tax receipts. If it were not for tourism, each U.S. household would have paid over $1,000 more in taxes.

International Tourism Receipts (US $ billion)		
Rank		**2012**
1	United States	128.6
2	Spain	55.9
3	France	53.7
4	China	50.0
5	Italy	41.2
6	Macao (China)	38.6
7	Germany	38.1
8	United Kingdom	36.4
9	Hong Kong (China)	31.7
10	Australia	31.5

Figure 9–3 • World's Top Ten Tourism Receipts 2012.[34]
Source: World Tourism Organization (WTO)©.

- Spending by international visitors in the United States was $40 billion more than travel-related spent by Americans outside the United States.

- Approximately 73.9 million international travelers visited the United States.

By employing approximately one out of every 10 workers, travel and tourism is the world's largest employer and is the world's largest industry grouping.

The Multiplier Effect

Tourists bring new money into the economy of the place they are visiting, and this has effects beyond the original expenditures. When a tourist spends money to travel, to stay in a hotel, or to eat in a restaurant, that money is recycled by those businesses to purchase more goods, thereby generating further use of the money. In addition, employees of businesses who serve tourists spend a higher proportion of their money locally on various goods and services. This chain reaction, called the **multiplier effect**, continues until there is a leakage, meaning that money is used to purchase something from outside the area. Figure 9–4 illustrates the multiplier effect.

In most economic impact studies to date, developed economies have a multiplier effect of between 1.5 and 2.0.[37] This means that the original money spent is used again in the community between 1.5 and 2.0 times. If tourism-related businesses spend more money on locally produced goods and services, it benefits the local economy.

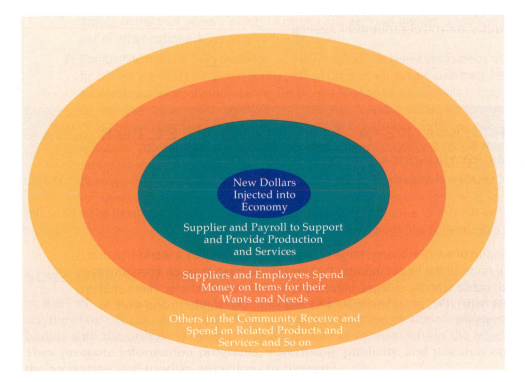

New Dollars Injected into Economy

Supplier and Payroll to Support and Provide Production and Services

Suppliers and Employees Spend Money on Items for their Wants and Needs

Others in the Community Receive and Spend on Related Products and Services and So on

Figure 9–4 • The Multiplier Effect.

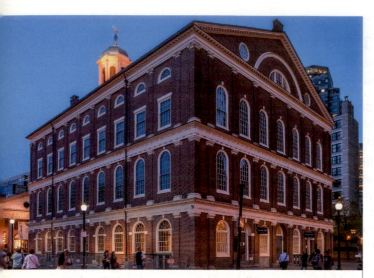

State offices of tourism promote places of interest, such as Faneuil Hall and Quincy Market in Boston.

City-Level Offices of Tourism and Convention Centers

Cities have also realized the importance of the new money that tourism brings. Many cities have established **convention and visitor bureaus (CVBs)**, whose main function is to attract and retain visitors to the city. The CVBs are staffed by representatives of the city's attractions, restaurants, hotels and motels, and transportation system. These bureaus are largely funded by the transient occupancy tax (TOT) that is charged to hotel guests. In most cities, the TOT ranges from 8 to 18 percent. The balance of funding comes from membership dues and promotional activities. In recent years, convention centers have sprung up in a number of large and several smaller cities. Spurred on by expectations of economic and social gain, cities operate both CVBs and convention centers. Both CVBs and convention centers are discussed in detail in Chapter 12.

National Offices of Tourism (NOTs)

NOTs seek to improve the economy of the country they represent by increasing the number of visitors and consequently their spending in the country. Connected to this function is the responsibility to oversee and ensure that hotels, transport systems, tour operators, and tour guides maintain high standards in the care and consideration of the tourist. The main activities of NOTs are as follows:

- Publicizing the country
- Assisting and advising certain types of travelers
- Creating demand for certain destinations
- Supplying information
- Ensuring that the destination is up to expectations
- Advertising[39]

Tour Operators

Tour operators promote tours and trips that they plan and organize. A *tour* is a trip taken by an individual or group of people who travel together with a professional tour manager/escort and follow a preplanned itinerary. Most tours include travel, accommodations, meals, land transportation, and sightseeing. The tour operator negotiates discounted travel, accommodation, meals, and sightseeing and then adds a markup before advertising the package. Tour operators also offer **vacation packages** to people traveling alone. Vacation packages include a combination of two or more travel services—hotel, car rental, and air transportation—offered at a package price. Most vacation packages offer a choice of components and options, allowing the client to customize his or her package to personal interests and budget.

Travel Agencies

A *travel agent* is a middleperson who acts as a travel counselor and sells travel services on behalf of airlines, cruise lines, rail and bus transportation companies, hotels, and auto rental companies. Agents may sell individual parts of the overall system or several elements, such as air and cruise tickets. The agent acts as a broker, bringing together the client (buyer) and the supplier (seller). Agents have quick access to schedules, fares, and advice for clients about various destinations.

The American Society of Travel Agents (ASTA) is the world's largest travel trade association, with more than 26,000 members in more than 140 countries. Agents use central reservation systems (CRSs) to access service availability and make bookings. In the United States, the main vendors of CRSs are Amadeus, Sabre, TravelSky, Worldspan, and Galileo.

A travel agent is more than a ticket seller. Agents serve their clients in the following ways:

- Arranging transportation by air, sea, rail, bus, car rental, and so on
- Preparing individual itineraries, personally escorted tours, group tours, and prepared package tours
- Arranging for hotel, motel, and resort accommodations; meals; sightseeing tours; transfers of passengers and luggage between terminals and hotels; and special features such as tickets for music festivals, the theater, and so forth
- Handling and advising on many details involved with travel, such as insurance, foreign currency exchange, documentary requirements, and immunizations and other inoculations needed
- Using professional know-how and experience (e.g., schedules of air, train, and bus connections, rates of hotels, quality of accommodations)
- Arranging reservations for special-interest activities, such as group tours, conventions, business travel, gourmet tours, and sporting trips

Travel agents have knowledge of destinations and can make air, ground, and hotel reservations for clients to visit popular destinations such as Venice, Italy.

Each sales manager has a staff or team that includes people in the following positions:

- Special events manager, who has expertise in sound, lighting, staging, and so on
- Accounts manager, who is an assistant to the sales manager
- Operations manager, who coordinates everything, especially on-site arrangements, to ensure that what is sold actually happens

For example, Patti Roscoe's DMC organized meetings, accommodations, meals, beverages, and theme parties for 2,000 Ford Motor Company dealers in nine groups over three days per group.

Roscoe also works closely with incentive houses, such as Carlson Marketing or Maritz Travel. These incentive houses approach a company and offer to evaluate and set up incentive plans for the sales team, including whatever it takes to motivate them. Once approved, Carlson contacts a DMC and asks for a program.

In conclusion, thousands of companies and associations hold meetings and conventions all over the country. Many of these organizations use the services of professional meeting planners, who in turn seek out suitable destinations for the meetings and conventions. Some larger hotels and resorts now have a destination management department to handle all the arrangements for groups and conventions.

▶ Check Your Knowledge

1. Describe at least three ways in which tourism has a significant economic impact upon society.
2. Is it better to have a higher or lower multiplier effect, and why?
3. Identify the promoters of tourism.

Business Travel

In recent years, business travel has declined due to[41] the general economic climate; in addition, increases in airfares, incidences in terrorism, and businesses reducing their travel budgets have negatively affected business travel.

Yet, a good percentage of the guests who check into upscale hotels around the world are traveling for business reasons. Much **business travel** is hard work, whether it is travel in one's own automobile or in the luxury of a first-class seat aboard an airplane. A good portion of business travel, however, is mixed with pleasure.

Counted as business travelers are those who travel for business purposes, such as for meetings; all kinds of sales, including corporate, regional, product, and others; conventions; trade shows and expositions; and combinations of more than one of these purposes. In the United States, meetings and conventions alone attract millions of people annually. Sometimes the distinction between business and leisure travel becomes blurred. If a convention attendee in Atlanta decides to stay on for a few days after the conference, is this person to be considered a business or leisure traveler? Business travelers, when compared to leisure travelers, tend to be younger, spend more money, travel farther, and travel in smaller groups, but they do not stay as long as leisure travelers do.

Social and Cultural Impact of Tourism

From a social and cultural perspective, tourism can have both positive and negative impacts on communities. Undoubtedly, tourism has made significant contributions to international understanding. World tourism organizations recognize that tourism is a means of enhancing international understanding, peace, prosperity, and universal respect for and observance of human rights and fundamental freedom for all without distinction as to race, sex, language, or religion. Tourism can be a very interesting sociocultural phenomenon. Seeing how others live is an interest of many tourists, and the exchange of sociocultural values and activities is rewarding.

LEARNING OBJECTIVE 6
Summarize the sociocultural impact of tourism.

Provided that the number of tourists is manageable and that they respect the host community's sociocultural norms and values, tourism provides an opportunity for a number of social interactions. A London pub or a New York café are examples of good places for social interaction. Similarly, depending on the reason for the tourist visit, myriad opportunities are available to interact both socially and culturally with local people. Even a visit to another part of the United States can be both socially and culturally stimulating. For example, New Orleans has a very diverse social and cultural heritage. Over the years, the city has been occupied by the Spanish, French, British, and Americans, so the food, music, dance, and social norms are unique to the area. The competitiveness of international destinations is based on attributes such as service quality, value for the price, safety, security, entertainment, weather, infrastructure, and natural environment.[42] Political stability is also important in determining the desirability of a destination for international tourism. Imagine the feelings of an employee in a developing country who earns perhaps $5 per day when he or she sees wealthy tourists flaunting money, jewelry, and an unobtainable lifestyle.

At beaches in Cannes, France there may be standing room only.

Just imagine what will happen when another 500 million people become tourists by virtue of increasing standards of living and the ability of more people to obtain passports. Currently, only about 39 percent of the U.S. population has passports, although that may increase because everyone returning to the United States from Mexico and Canada must now have a passport.[43] The population of Eastern Europe and the new rich of the Pacific Rim countries will substantially add to the potential number of tourists.

is to provide tourists with new knowledge about a certain natural area and the culture that is found in it, along with a little bit of adventure. As for the local inhabitants, ecotourism aims to help improve the local economy and conservation efforts. All parties are to gain a new appreciation for nature and people.

Generally, most of the more popular ecotourism destinations are located in underdeveloped and developing countries. As vacationers become more adventurous and visit remote, exotic places, they are participating in activities that should affect nature, host communities, and themselves in a positive manner. And because of the growing interests of travelers, many developed countries are following the trend and developing ecotourism programs. Ecotourism can be a main source of worldwide promotion of sustainable development geared toward tourists and communities in all countries.

Thus far, ecotourism projects tend to be developed on a small scale. It is much easier to control such sites, particularly because of limits that are normally set on the community, the local tourism business, and the tourists. Limitations may include strict control of the amount of water and electricity used, more stringent recycling measures, regulation of park and market hours, and more important, caps on the number of visitors to a certain location at one time, and the size of the business. Another reason ecotourism projects are kept small is to allow more in-depth tours and educational opportunities.

Sustainable Tourism

The increasing number of tourists visiting destinations has heightened concerns about the environment, physical resources of the place, and sociocultural degradation. The response of tourism officials has been to propose that all tourism be sustainable. The concept of **sustainable tourism** places a broad-based obligation on society, especially those involved in making tourism policy, planning for development, and harmonizing tourism and tourism development by improving the quality of a place's environment and physical and sociocultural resources. According to the UNWTO definition, sustainable tourism refers to the environmental, economic, and sociocultural aspects of tourism development, with the establishment of a suitable balance between these three dimensions to guarantee its long-term sustainability.[46]

The United Nations Environment Programme (UNEP) says that sustainability principles refer to the environmental, economic, and sociocultural aspects of tourism. Sustainable tourism should (1) make optimal use of environmental resources that constitute a key element in tourism development; (2) respect the sociocultural authenticity of host communities, conserve their built and living cultural heritage and traditional values, and contribute to intercultural understanding

The Great Barrier Reef off the coast of Australia is one of the world heritage sites.

and tolerance; and (3) ensure viable, long-term economic operations, providing socioeconomic benefits to all stakeholders that are fairly distributed, including stable employment and income-earning opportunities and social services to host communities, and contributing to poverty alleviation.

The two key factors are community-based tourism and quality tourism. Community-based tourism ensures that a majority of the benefits go to locals and not to outsiders. Quality tourism basically offers tourists good value for their money. This also serves as a protection of local natural resources and as an attraction to the kinds of tourists who will respect the local environment and society. All tourism should be sustainable, but the problem is that all too frequently it is not.

Let's look around the world and see how the concept of sustainable tourism is applied. Europe has been criticized for lack of sustainability, but apart from the congested areas of, for example, London, Rome, and Paris, there are plenty of destinations focusing on sustainable tourism. In particular, tours to explore the ancient ruins, architecture, and cultures of Turkey and Greece are popular choices. Also, the largely untouched nature and distinctive culture of the Scandinavian countries are growing in recognition and importance.

If you want to explore Asia, join an ecotour to the snow-capped Himalayas in Nepal or the sultry jungles of Thailand. More and more places, such as Malaysia, Thailand, and the Philippines, are developing their tourism programs based on environmental conservation and protection. Looking for Shangri-La? The former hidden kingdom of the Hunza Valley in Pakistan has been opened for ecotourism, allowing a select number of tourists to see the 700-year-old Baltit Fort and village. The project has been internationally acclaimed as an outstanding example of sustainable tourism.

More adventures await you in Africa, where the tourism industry, especially ecotourism, has been growing tremendously over the past years. The most popular activity is the safari, which lets you get up close and personal with exotic wildlife such as elephants, gazelles, lions, tigers, cheetahs, and countless others. Kenya is an important destination for safaris, as are Tanzania, South Africa, Botswana, and Malawi.

Australia is home to an impressive variety of eco-friendly places. The Great Barrier Reef is perhaps the most famous spot. The Leave No Trace program, originally an American initiative, ensures that visitors to the reef act in a responsible manner. As a visitor to the Great Barrier Reef, you can enjoy activities such as snorkeling, fishing, diving, hiking, camping, and much more with many certified eco-friendly companies. Another area that is subject to increasing interest and attention is the massive glaciers of Antarctica.

These days, many regions of the world are designating their attractions as ecotourism sites. Vacationers are becoming more adventurous and are visiting remote, exotic places. They are participating in activities that hopefully affect nature, host communities, as well as themselves, in a positive manner.

From Yellowstone National Park in the United States to the Mayan ruins of Tikal in Guatemala, from the Amazon River in Brazil to the vast safari lands of Kenya, from the snow-capped Himalayas in Nepal to the sultry jungles of Thailand, and from the Great Barrier Reef in Australia to the massive ice glaciers in Antarctica, it seems that sustainable tourism is taking place in all corners of the world. Quite frankly, some sort of ecotourism activity is happening in almost every country.

in international travel and are more likely to travel for leisure than non-Millennials. They are also twice as likely to use their mobile phones to share travel photos and experiences to friends on social media, blogs, as well as post travel reviews. The Matures target group, however, is estimated between 1.3 and 1.6 billion worldwide and 59 percent are aged 55 and over. This group is known to love to travel and most have the time to travel and explore new places. While both segments offer travel and tourism providers great opportunities, each differs in their attitudes, preferences, and intentions toward travel.

- *Green Tourism.* Green tourism will continue to develop in response to consumer interest in patronizing tourism organizations who adopt and manifest sustainable practices with the idea of being green and staying green. Consumers are more interested now on the environmental impact of the industry. An increasing number of destinations and travel supplier web sites highlight their positions and practices of sustainable tourism. Tourism currently produces 5 percent of global emissions through transportation and service accommodations. As a result, green initiatives are constantly increasing in the tourism sector.[50]

- *Travel Experiences.* Many travelers nowadays are looking for real travel experiences that enrich their knowledge, understanding, and culture. More consumers are seeking travel experiences that require some sort of mission or learning opportunity such as voluntourism, language tourism, culinary tourism, and music tourism. Global athletic events and spectator sports are drivers of economic activity and tourism, and as a result are constantly on the rise.

- *Destination Management Companies.* With the tourism industry being so competitive, destination management companies and marketers will continue to find ways to compete with other destination brands. Focusing on service, professionalism, and pride of place are three ways the industry has drawn toward competition.

- *Marketing Strategies.* Tourism destinations require an integrated marketing strategy to include online and traditional media including interactive maps and brochures that can be seen on mobile apps or the brand's web site, along with product development in changing a want to a need for the customer.

- *Unique Experiences.* The travel industry will continue to find ways to personalize and customize the visitor experience as consumers look for more relevant and unique experiences. Marketers will drive customer engagement and influence in the inspiration, research, planning and booking, and postpurchase phases of consumer buying behavior.

- *Technology.* As technology keeps becoming more affordable and accessible, and consumers embrace the power of video, there's more support for tourism advertising spend around video, and there are many forms to choose from, such as micro video on Instagram and Vine to more traditional longer-form videos.

- *Social Media.* Tourism organizations will continue to profile and segment their target audiences. There is a wealth of data that can make marketers more efficient in developing new audiences or segmenting deeper targets within their current audiences. It will be required knowledge to be efficient and fiscally responsible in future social and online ad campaigns. For smaller destinations, a key will be working with bloggers to help those with limited budgets spread their message. And, if possible, working with niche bloggers would be even better for these destinations.

- *Near Field Communications (NFC)*. Tourism destinations and organizations will embrace NFC technology in combination with mobile apps to deliver a more immersive experience in the destination. NFC is a set of ideas and technology that enables smartphones and other devices to establish radio communication with each other by touching them together or bringing them into proximity. Being able to arrive at a destination waypoint where the mobile phone in your pocket can interact with the push of a single button and start a multitude of interfaces for the consumer in your city can be indispensable. With NFC chips now in all iPhone 6 devices, and the fact that Android phones have already had them for some time, the percentage of phones capable of this type of technology will only increase; 90 percent of phones by 2016 will have this technology built in. Proximity and interaction can launch a host of things, such as informative videos, interactive maps, and spoken narratives.

- *Destination Marketing Organizations (DMOs)*. DMOs will have to learn to be more personable and time-sensitive across all facets of the organization—sales, service, and marketing. Being able to peel back the layers of the destination brand to be more authentic and connect with consumers in a personal and emotional way will be key. In the destination meeting environment, a key success factor is personalized service over sales, meaning that DMOs will have to find a way to make meetings and groups have successful shows and move beyond the discussion over rates, dates, and space. Meeting planners will rely on DMOs more than ever to make their shows and attendee experiences a success, starting with the initial planning phases once that group is booked.

- *Alternative Lodging Sites*. Hospitality and travel organizations will be challenged by the emerging sharing economy based businesses such as alternative lodging and transportation options (e.g., Airbnb and Uber). How DMOs work with consumers and these companies to ensure that visitor experiences are safe and excellent and appropriate revenues are calculated and taxes collected is the foremost challenge. By 2017, the mobile device outlet is expected to include more than 30 percent of online consumer travel sales.[51] Group specials on sites such as Groupon and Living Social have allowed travelers to make travel arrangements in a more cost efficient way. Group deals allow the industry to offer a service for a limited time at a certain price. The bulk selling and purchasing concept is becoming increasingly popular for both the seller and the consumer.

- *Record Numbers*. International tourist travel will continue to rise. Throughout 2013, international tourist arrivals increased by approximately 5 percent to reach a record high 747 million worldwide, which amounts to 38 million more than in the same time period of 2012.[52] Online travel sales, which increased 8.4 percent in 2012, reaching $524 billion globally, are expected to continue to increase.[53] Culinary tourism has seen an increase in interest with 27 million Americans traveling for culinary purposes in the last three years. American culinary tourists have spent nearly $12 billion on culinary activities while traveling.[54]

CASE STUDY

Congratulations! You have just been appointed to your city's council. You discover that a hot topic soon to be presented to the council is the construction of a convention center. Your initial research shows that several mid-sized cities are considering the convention center as a way to increase economic activity, including job creation. The challenge these cities face is how to finance the convention center; projected costs are $100 million. Voters may resist a ballot to increase local taxes (either property or sales), but there is still the TOT—that is, taxes paid by people staying in local hotels—to consider. However, that tax is already earmarked for various local charities, and as we all know, good politicians want to be reelected; so voting against several worthy causes would not be popular. How can the center be financed and built? The city could float a bond on the market or could raise the TOT, but that might dissuade some groups from coming to your city because other cities have lower TOTs.

Discussion Questions

1. What would you do?
2. What information do you need in order to decide whether to support or oppose the convention center?

Summary

1. Tourism can be defined as the idea of attracting, accommodating, and pleasing groups or individuals traveling for pleasure or business. It is categorized by geography, ownership, function, industry, and travel motive.

2. Tourism involves international interaction and, therefore, government regulation. Several organizations, such as the World Tourism Organization, promote environmental protection, tourism development, immigration, and cultural and social aspects of tourism.

3. Tourism is a collection of industries that, when combined, form the world's largest industry and employer. It affects other industry sectors, such as public transportation, foodservice, lodging, entertainment, and recreation. In addition, tourism produces secondary impacts on businesses that are affected indirectly, which is known as the multiplier effect.

4. Travel agencies, tour operators, travel managers, wholesalers, national offices of tourism, and destination management companies serve as middlepersons between a country and its visitors.

5. Physical needs, the desire to experience other cultures, and an interest in meeting new people are some of the motives of travelers. Because of flexible work hours, early retirement, and the easy accessibility of traveling, tourism is constantly growing.

6. From a social and cultural perspective, tourism can further international understanding and economically improve poorer countries. However, it can also disturb a culture by presenting it with mass tourism and the destruction of natural sites. A trend in avoiding tourism pollution is ecotourism.

7. Business travel has increased in recent years as a result of the growth of convention centers in several cities. As a result, business travelers have given a boost to hotels, restaurants, and auto rental companies. The number of female business travelers is rising as well.

8. Ecotourism is tourism with a conscience, or responsible travel to natural areas that conserve the environment and improve the well being of the local people.

9. The concept of sustainable tourism places a broad-based obligation on society, especially those involved with tourism policy, planning, and development.

Key Words and Concepts

business travel
convention and visitors bureaus (CVBs)
cultural tourism
ecotourism
hub-and-spoke system
interdependency

load factor
multiplier effect
Pacific Area Travel Association (PATA)
sustainable tourism
tourism

United Nations Educational, Scientific and Cultural Organization (UNESCO)
vacation package
volunteer tourism
World Tourism Organization (UNWTO)

Review Questions

1. Give a broad definition of tourism and explain why people are motivated to travel.
2. Give a brief explanation of the economic impact of tourism. Name two organizations that influence or further the economic impact of tourism.
3. Choose a career in the tourism business and give a brief overview of what your responsibilities would be.
4. Discuss the positive and negative impacts that tourism can have on a country in relation to tourism pollution and ecotourism.

Internet Exercises

1. Organization: **World Tourism Organization (UNWTO)**
   Summary: The UNWTO is the only intergovernmental organization that serves in the field of travel and tourism and is a global forum for tourism policy and issues. It has about 156 member countries and six territories. Its mission is to promote and develop tourism as a significant means of fostering international peace and understanding, economic development, and international trade.
   (a) How much is spent on international tourism?
   (b) What does *Tourism Toward 2030 Vision* predict?

2. Organization: **World Travel and Tourism Council**
   Summary: The World Travel and Tourism Council is the forum for business leaders in the travel and tourism industry. With chief executives of some 100 of the world's leading travel and tourism companies as its members, the WTTC has a unique mandate and overview on all matters related to travel and tourism.
   (a) What is your opinion of the blueprint for new tourism?

Apply Your Knowledge

1. Analyze your family's and friends' recent or upcoming travel plans and compare them with the examples in the text for reasons why people travel.

2. Suggest some ecotourism activities for your community.
3. How would you promote or improve tourism in your community?

Suggested Activities

1. Go online and get prices for an airline round-trip ticket between two cities for a flight that is as follows:
   (a) More than 60 days out
   (b) 30–59 days out
   (c) 15–29 days out
   (d) 7–14 days out
   (e) For tomorrow

2. Compare the prices and share the results with your class.

Endnotes

1. Jennifer Blanke and Thea Chiesa, The Travel & Tourism Competitiveness Report 2011, *World Economic Forum*, http://www.weforum.org. Search for "Travel & Tourism 2011" to view the report (accessed November 13, 2011).

2. World Tourism Organization (UNWTO), "In Focus: Transport," *UNTO World Tourism Barometer* 7 (June 2009), 42–46.

3. World Tourism Organization (UNWTO), *Press Release: Healthy Growth of International Tourism in First Half of 2011*, September 7, 2011, http://media.unwto.org. Search for "healthy growth of international tourism in first half of 2011" (accessed November 14, 2011).

4. World Travel and Tourism Council, *Economic Impact of Travel & Tourism 2014*, http://www.wttc.org. Search for "economic impact 2014" to view the article (accessed July 29, 2014).

5. Charles R. Goeldner and J. R. Brent Ritchie, *Tourism: Principles and Practices*, 9th ed. (New York: John Wiley and Sons, 2003), 42–48.

6. Goeldner and Ritchie, *Tourism: Principles and Practices*, 43.

7. Ibid.

8. Donald E. Lundberg, *The Tourist Business*, 6th ed. (New York: Van Nostrand Reinhold, 1990), 16.

9. Lundberg, *The Tourist Business*, 17.

10. N. S. Gill, "101 on the Ancient Olympic Games," *About.com*, www.about.com. Search for "101 on the Ancient Olympic Games" to view this article (accessed April 6, 2011).

11. TravelChinaGuide, *Marco Polo*, www.travelchina guide.com. Click on Silk Road, click on History, click on Famous Travellers, and then click on Marco Polo (accessed April 6, 2011).

12. Ibid.

13. Federal Aviation Administration, *Air Traffic: NextGen Briefing*, http://www.faa.gov. Click on Air Traffic and then NextGen (accessed November 14, 2011).

14. "Boeing Unveils Ambitious 787 Dreamliner Passenger Jet," *Philippine Star*, July 10, 2007, B8.

15. Ibid.

16. Salary.com, *Salary Wizard: Captain/Pilot in Command (Large Jet)*, http://www.salary.com. Go to Salary and click on Browse Salaries by Category, click on Aviation and Airlines, and choose Captain/Pilot in Command (accessed November 14, 2011).

17. Salary.com. *Salary Wizard: Flight Attendant*, http://www.salary.com. Go to Salary and click on Browse Salaries by Category, click on Aviation and Airlines, and choose Flight Attendant (accessed July 29, 2014).

18. United States Department of Transportation, Office of the Assistant Secretary for Research and Technology, *U.S. Air Carrier Traffic Statistics through February 2015*, http://www.rita.dot.gov/. Go to Programs and click on Bureau of Transportation Statistics, and then search for "U.S. Air Carrier Traffic Statistics" (accessed April 13, 2015).

19. Princess Cruises, *Diamond Princess*, http://www.princess.com. Click on Cruise Ships & Deck Plans, and then click on Diamond Princess (accessed November 14, 2011); Dori Saltzman, "Diamond Princess Overview," *Cruise Critic*, www.cruisecritic.com. Search for "Diamond Princess Review" (accessed November 14, 2011).

20. "Cruise Ship Industry Statistics–Statistic Brain," *2014 Statistic Brain Research Institute, publishing as Statistic Brain*, Research Date: March 3, 2015, http://www.statisticbrain.com/cruise-ship-industry-statistics/ (accessed May 17, 2015).

21. Ibid.

22. "Maritime Industry Background," *Cruise Lines International Association*, www.cruising.org. Click on enter under regulatory, click on Industry Resources, and then click on Maritime Industry Background to view this page (accessed May 28, 2015).

23. "Understanding Tourism: Basic Glossary," *World Tourism Organization UNWTO*, http://www2.unwto.org/. Search for "basic glossary" to view glossary terms (accessed November 14, 2011).

24. "Background of the Global Code of Ethics for Tourism," *World Tourism Organization UNWTO*,

http://www2.unwto.org. Go to What We Do and click on Ethics and Social Responsibility Programme and then go to Global Code of Ethics for Tourism and click on Background Information to access this page (accessed November 13, 2011).

25. "Who we are," *World Tourism Organization UNWTO*, http://www2.unwto.org. Go to About and click on About UNWTO (accessed November 24, 2013).

26. World Travel and Tourism Council, *Travel & Tourism: Economic Impact 2015 World*, http://www.wttc.org. Go to Research and click on Economic Research, click on Regional Reports, click on World, and then click on View Full Report (accessed July 29, 2014).

27. "Who we are," *World Tourism Organization UNWTO*, http://www2.unwto.org. Go to About and click on About UNWTO (accessed November 24, 2013).

28. World Travel and Tourism Council, *Travel & Tourism: Economic Impact 2015 World*, http://www.wttc.org. Go to Research and click on Economic Research, click on Regional Reports, click on World, and then click on View Full Report (accessed July 29, 2014).

29. World Tourism Organization UNWTO, *Tourism towards 2030: Global Overview*, http://www2.unwto.org (October 10, 2011). Click on Media, search for "2030 Korea" under the UNWTO Archive tab to view this report (accessed May 15, 2015).

30. Ibid.

31. Op Cit.

32. World Travel and Tourism Council, *Travel & Tourism: Economic Impact 2015 World*, http://www.wttc.org. Go to Research and click on Economic Research, click on Regional Reports, click on World, and then click on View Full Report (accessed July 29, 2014).

33. Ibid.

34. Adapted from http://dtxtq4w60xqpw.cloudfront.net/sites/all/files/pdf/unwto_receipts_1995_2012_graph.pdf.

35. U.S. Travel Association, *U.S. Travel Answer Sheet*, http://www.ustravel.org. Click on U.S. Travel Answer Sheet to view this report (accessed May 28, 2015).

36. Ibid.

37. Personal conversation with Dr. Greg A. Dunn, Vice President, Y Partnership, April 12, 2011.

38. "Asia Pacific travel market to reach almost US $352 billion in 2013," *ITB Asia*, October 23, 2013, http://www.itb-asia.com. Go to Press and click on Press Releases and News to locate this article (accessed July 29, 2014).

39. Personal correspondence with Karen Smith and Claudia Green, June 28, 2005.

40. NTA, *Home Page*, http://ntaonline.com (accessed November 14, 2011).

41. Personal correspondence with Edward Inskeep, June 4, 2007.

42. Personal conversation with Dr. Greg A. Dunn, September 14, 2007.

43. Matt Stabile, "How Many Americans Have a Passport?" *The Expeditioner* (blog), February 9, 2014, http://www.theexpeditioner.com/2010/02/17/how-many-americans-have-a-passport-2 (accessed November 24, 2014).

44. The International Ecotourism Society, *What Is Ecotourism?* www.ecotourism.org. Go to About and click on What is Ecotourism? (accessed November 14, 2014).

45. Ibid.

46. World Tourism Organization UNWTO, *Sustainable Development of Tourism: Definition*, http://www2.unwto.org. Go to What We Do and click on Sustainable Development of Tourism Programme, and then click on Definition (accessed May 15, 2015).

47. United Nations Educational, Scientific and Cultural Organization, World Heritage Convention, *World Heritage Centre*, http://whc.unesco.org. Click on About World Heritage and then click on About World Heritage (accessed November 16, 2014).

48. Ibid.

49. "Volunteer Tourism Beckons," University of Technology, Sydney, January 1, 2002, http://www.uts.edu.au. Search for "Volunteer Tourism Beckons" to view this article (accessed April 18, 2011).

50. Chris Fair, "2014 Trends in Travel and Tourism," *Slideshare.net*, November 12, 2013, http://www.slideshare.net. Search for "2014 Trends in Travel and Tourism" to view this content (accessed January 4, 2015).

51. World Travel Market, "WTM Global Trends Report," *Hospitality Net*, November 5, 2013, http://www.hospitalitynet.org. Search for "World Travel Market Global Trends Report 2013" to view this report (accessed January 4, 2015).

52. World Tourism Organization UNWTO, *International Tourism on the Rise Boosted by Strong Performance in Europe*, October 17, 2013, http://www2.unwto.org. Search for "international tourism on the rise" to view this article (accessed May 15, 2015).

53. Euromonitor International, "Travel and Tourism in a Fast-Changing World: New Trends for 2014," *Marketwired*, November 4, 2013, http://www.marketwired.com. Search for "Travel and Tourism in a Fast-Changing World: New Trends for 2014" to view this article (accessed January 4, 2015).

54. Chris Fair, "2014 Trends in Travel and Tourism," *Slideshare.net*, November 12, 2013, http://www.slideshare.net. Search for "2014 Trends in Travel and Tourism" to view this content (accessed January 4, 2015).

Recreational activities include both active and passive activities. Passive activities include all kinds of sports—team and individual. Baseball, softball, football, basketball, volleyball, tennis, swimming, jogging, skiing, hiking, aerobics, rock climbing, and camping are all active forms of recreation. Passive recreational activities include reading, fishing, playing and listening to music, gardening, playing computer games, and watching television or movies. **Recreation** *is an integral part of our nation's total social, economic, and natural resource environment. It is a basic component of our lives and well being.*[1]

LEARNING OBJECTIVE 1
Discuss the relationship of recreation and leisure to wellness.

Recreation, Leisure, and Wellness

As postindustrial society has become more complex, life has become more stressed. The need to develop the wholeness of the person has become increasingly important. Compared to a generation ago, the stress levels of business executives are much higher. The term *burnout*—and indeed the word *stress*—has become a part of our everyday vocabulary only in recent years. Recreation is all about creating a balance, a harmony in life that will maintain wellness and wholeness.

Recreation allows people to have fun together and to form lasting relationships built on the experiences they have enjoyed together. This recreational process is called *bonding*. Bonding is hard to describe, yet the experience of increased interpersonal feeling for friends or business associates as a result of a recreational pursuit is common. These relationships result in personal growth and development.

The word *recreation* implies the use of time in a manner designed for therapeutic refreshment of one's body or mind.[2] Recreation is synonymous with lifestyle and the development of a positive attitude. An example of this is the increased feeling of well being experienced after a recreational activity. Some people make the mistake of trying to pursue happiness as a personal goal. It is not enough for a person to say, "I want to be happy; therefore, I will recreate." Nathaniel Hawthorne wrote in the mid-nineteenth century: "Happiness in this world, when it comes, comes incidentally. Make it the object of pursuit, and it leads us a wild-goose chase, and is never attained. Follow some other object, and very possibly we may find that we have caught happiness without dreaming of it."[3]

Recreation is a process that seeks to establish a milieu conducive to the discovery and development of characteristics that can lead to happiness. Happiness and well being, therefore, are incidental outcomes of recreation. Thus, happiness may be enhanced

Windsurfing is definitely an active recreational activity.

by the pursuit of recreational activities. Personal recreational goals are equally as important as any other business or personal goals. These goals might include running a mile in under six minutes or maintaining a baseball batting average above .300. The fact that a person sets and strives to achieve goals requires personal organization. This helps improve the quality of life.

Leisure is best described as time free from work, or discretionary time. Some recreation professionals use the words *leisure* and *recreation* interchangeably, while others define leisure as the productive, creative, or contemplative use of free time. History, by this latter definition, shows again and again a direct link between leisure and the advancement of civilization. Ironically, however, much of the leisure we, as a society, enjoy is the direct result of increased technological and productivity advancements or just plain hard work.

Hiking is a great exercise and an ideal way to get back to nature.

▶ Check Your Knowledge

1. Discuss the relationship of recreation and leisure to wellness.

Government-Sponsored Recreation

LEARNING OBJECTIVE 2
Explain the origins and extent of government-sponsored recreation.

Various levels of government that constitute **government-sponsored recreation** are intertwined, yet distinct, in the parks, recreation, and leisure services. The founding fathers of America said it best when they affirmed the right to life, liberty, and the pursuit of happiness in the Declaration of Independence. Government raises revenue from income taxes, sales taxes, and property taxes. Additionally, government raises special revenue from recreation-related activities such as automobile and recreational vehicles, boats, motor fuels, **transient occupancy taxes (TOTs)** on hotel accommodations, state lotteries, and others. The monies are distributed among the various recreation- and leisure-related organizations at the federal, state/provincial, city, and town levels. Recreation and leisure activities are extremely varied, ranging from cultural pursuits such as museums, arts and crafts, music, theater, and dance to sports (individual and team), outdoor recreation such as hiking and camping, amusement parks, theme parks, community centers, playgrounds, libraries, and gardens. People select recreational pursuits based on their interests and capabilities.

Parks and recreation groups are up against numerous challenges, especially as leisure and recreational resources become more highly valued assets in the community. Funding for staff and services is one area these groups find challenging. Following are some other issues with which recreation professionals must deal:

- Comprehensive recreation planning
- Land classification systems
- Federal revenue sharing
- Acquisition- and development-funding programs
- Land-use planning and zoning
- State and local financing
- Off-road vehicle impacts and policy
- Use of easements for recreation
- Designation of areas (such as wilderness, wild and scenic rivers, national trails, nature preserves)
- Differences in purposes and resources (of the numerous local, state/provincial, and federal agencies that control more than one-third of the nation's land, much of which is used for recreation)

National Parks in the United States

The prevailing image of a **national park** is one of grand natural playgrounds, such as Yellowstone National Park, but there is much more to parks than that.[4] The United States has 407 designated areas throughout the country and the U.S. territories. The **National Park Service** was founded in 1916 by Congress to conserve park resources and to provide for their use by the public in a way that leaves them unimpaired for the enjoyment of future generations. In addition to the better-known parks such as Yellowstone and Yosemite, the park service also manages many other heritage attractions, including the Freedom Trail in Boston, Independence Hall in Philadelphia, the Antietam National Battlefield in Sharpsburg, Maryland, and the USS *Arizona* Memorial at Pearl Harbor in Hawaii. The park service is also charged with caring for myriad cultural artifacts, including ancient pottery, sailing vessels, colonial-period clothing, and Civil War documents.

The ever-expanding mandate of the park service also calls for understanding and preserving the environment. It monitors the ecosystem from the Arctic tundra to coral atolls, researches the air and water quality around the nation, and participates in global studies

The splendor of nature awaits us in our national parks.

on acid rain, climate change, and biological diversity. The idea of preserving exceptional lands for public use as national parks arose after the Civil War when America's receding wilderness left unique national resources vulnerable to exploitation. Recent years have seen phenomenal growth in the system, with three new areas created in the last 20 years. These include new kinds of parks, such as urban recreational areas, free-flowing rivers, long-distance trails, and historic sites honoring our nation's social achievements. The system's current roster of 407 areas covers more than 80 million acres of land, with individual areas ranging in size from the 13-million-acre Wrangell–St. Elias National Park and Preserve in Alaska to the Thaddeus Kosciuszko National Memorial (a Philadelphia row house commemorating a hero of the American Revolution), which covers two one-hundredths of an acre.

Annual visitation to the national park system approaches 300 million visitors, who take advantage of the full range of services and programs.[5] The focus once placed on preserving the scenery of the most natural parks has shifted as the system has grown and changed. Today, emphasis is placed on preserving the vitality of each park's ecosystem and on the protection of unique or endangered plant and animal species.

National Park Management

The National Park Service is in the Department of the Interior and is overseen by a director who reports to the Secretary of the Interior. The director of the National Park Service establishes and approves service-wide natural resource policies and standards. The director is ultimately responsible for establishing natural and cultural resource programs that conserve natural resources unimpaired for the enjoyment of future generations and for ensuring that such programs are in compliance with directives, policies, and laws.[6]

Each national park has a superintendent, and the superintendent is responsible for understanding the park's resources and their condition. The superintendent is responsible for establishing and managing park backcountry-management programs and ensuring that they comply with directives, policies, and laws. The superintendent initiates the development of backcountry recreational use plans as necessary. The superintendent should coordinate the visitor use-management plans with neighboring land managers as appropriate. Each superintendent with designated or eligible wilderness should designate a wilderness coordinator to review all activities ongoing in the wilderness.[7]

The National Park Service budget request for 2014 and 2015 was around $3 billion, employing a staff of 22,000 permanent, temporary, and seasonal employees. Beyond these appropriated funds, the National Park Service is also authorized to collect and retain revenue from the following specified sources:[8]

- Recreation fees: approximately $172.9 million per year
- Park concessions franchise fees: approximately $60 million per year

- Filming and photography special use fees: approximately $1.2 million per year
- Additional funding comes from individual donations.

Managing a national park is a complex task that involves skilled professionals from many fields. Park management is not achieved by merely relying on experience and instincts. Whenever possible, it is based on solid scientific research, conducted not only by park staff, but by universities and independent researchers as well. Financial constraints are always an issue while managing our national parks.[9]

The Great Smoky Mountains National Park is the most visited of the national parks, receiving over 9 million visitors a year. This park has the following main operating departments:

Ranger—rangers provide the chief response and visitor protection and are the sole law enforcement in the park. Rangers operate the campgrounds, perform search and rescue, and provide emergency medical services.

Resource Education—creates curriculum and delivers courses ranging from elementary students to adults and seniors. Known as "walks, talks, and tours," they cover pre-visitation to guided tours of the park.

Resource Management and Science—is responsible for the ongoing health of the natural and cultural resources.

Facility Management—responsible for a $2 billion infrastructure of roads, 350 nonhistoric buildings, and 72 bathrooms.

Administration—takes care of human resources, purchasing, contracts, and property management.

Remember that the park service has the mission to conserve natural resources. This can prove very challenging, as nonnative pests and diseases threaten the biological diversity of the park, such as the case of the woolly adelgid, an aphid-like pest that kills hemlock trees. The Great Smoky Mountains National Park has over 90,000 acres of hemlock trees that are likely to be killed by these pests unless something can be found to stop the pests quickly.

Let's look at another national park, Cape Lookout National Seashore. There are natural and cultural resources and numerous historic structures that are managed within the 56 miles of seashore. In all national parks, the need for efficient, innovative park management is especially important in order to protect the very best of this nation's rich heritage. And the law of the land dictates that, in turn, these resources, and the American public that owns them, deserve the very best that the National Park Service can give them.[10]

The National Park Service is required to maintain an up-to-date general management plan (GMP) for each unit of the park system. The purpose of each GMP is to ensure that the park has a clearly defined direction for asset preservation and visitor use. This foundation for decision-making is to be developed by an interdisciplinary team, in consultation with relevant offices within the park service, other federal and state agencies, interested parties, and the general public. The GMP should be based on use of scientific information related to existing and potential asset conditions, visitor experiences, environmental impacts, and relative costs of alternative courses of action. The GMP should take the long view, which may project many years into the future, when dealing with time frames. The plan should consider the park in its full ecological, scenic, and cultural contexts as a unit of the National Park Service and as part of a surrounding region.[11]

No two days are alike in the park service. On one day, a meth lab may be discovered; on another, a tornado may create havoc or visitors may get lost and need rescuing. Yet every day at the Great Smoky Mountains National Park there are thousands of visitors to take care of at the visitor center. Each visitor has questions ranging from "Where are the bathrooms?" to "Can I see a bear?"

Public Recreation and Parks Agencies

During the early part of the nineteenth century in the United States, the parks movement expanded rapidly as a responsibility of government and voluntary organizations. By the early 1900s, 14 cities had made provisions for supervised play facilities, and the playground movement gained momentum. Private initiative and financial support were instrumental in convincing city government to provide tax dollars to build and maintain new play areas.

About the same time, municipal parks were created in a number of cities. Boston established the first metropolitan park system in 1892. In 1898, the New England Park Association (predecessor of the American Institute of Park Executives) was established to bring together park superintendents and promote their professional concerns. Increasingly, the concept that city governments should provide recreation facilities, programs, and services became widely accepted. Golf courses, swimming pools, bathing beaches, picnic areas, winter sports facilities, game fields, and playgrounds were constructed.

Street basketball is a great team sport.

▶ Check Your Knowledge

1. Name a few parks in the United States and in Canada. What are some characteristics that make the parks you named special?

2. Explain the origins and extent of government-sponsored recreation.

3. Name your favorite park. Share with your classmates why it is your favorite.

LEARNING OBJECTIVE 3
Distinguish between commercial and noncommercial recreation.

LEARNING OBJECTIVE 4
Name and describe various types of recreational clubs.

Commercial Recreation—Attractions

Recreation management came of age in the 1920s and 1930s, when recreation and social programs were offered as a community service. Colleges and universities began offering degree programs in this area. Both public and private sector recreation management has grown rapidly since 1950.

Commercial recreation, often called eco- or adventure tourism, provides residents and visitors with access to an area's spectacular wilderness through a variety of guided outdoor activities. Specifically, commercial recreation is defined as outdoor recreational activities provided on a fee-for-service basis, with a focus on experiences associated with the natural environment.[12] Commercial recreation includes theme parks, attractions, and clubs.

Theme Parks

The idea of theme parks all began in the 1920s in Buena Park, California, with a small berry farm and tea room. As owner Walter Knott's restaurant business grew, different attractions were added to the site to keep waiting customers amused. After a gradual expansion, over 80 years after its humble beginnings, Knott's Berry Farm has become one of the largest independent theme parks in the United States.

Today, Knott's Berry Farm is 160 acres of rides, attractions, live entertainment, historical exhibits, dining, and specialty shops. The park features four themes—Ghost Town, Fiesta Village, the Boardwalk, and Camp Snoopy, which is the official home of Snoopy and the Peanuts characters. In addition, the California Marketplace is located right outside the park, and offers 15 unique shops and restaurants.

Knott's Berry Farm has truly been a great influence on the American theme park industry. Hundreds of parks, both independent and corporate owned, started to develop following the birth of Knott's. Creator Walter Knott may have figured out why amusement parks became so popular so quickly. He was quoted as saying, "The more complex the world becomes, the more people turn to the past and the simple things in life. We [the amusement park operators] try to give them some of those things."[13] Even with the ever-increasing competition, Knott's continues to attract guests with its authentic historical artifacts, relaxed atmosphere, emphasis on learning, famous food, varied entertainment, innovative rides, and specialty shopping.[14]

Knott's Berry Farm is now owned and operated by Cedar Fair Entertainment Company.

Size and Scope of the Theme Park Industry

Visiting **theme parks** has always been a favorite tourist activity. Theme parks attempt to create an atmosphere of another place and time, and they usually emphasize one dominant theme around which architecture, landscape, rides, shows, foodservices, costumed personnel, and retailing are orchestrated. In this definition, the concept of *themes* is crucial to the operation of the parks,

A water park is an example of a single-themed park.

with rides, entertainment, and food all used to create several different environments.[15]

Theme parks and attractions vary according to theme, which might be historical, cultural, geographical, and so on. Some parks and attractions focus on a single theme, such as the marine zoological SeaWorld parks. Other parks and attractions focus on multiple themes, such as Kings Island in Ohio, a family entertainment center divided into seven theme areas: Action Zone, Coney Mall, X-Base, International Street, Oktoberfest, Planet Snoopy, Rivertown, and Soak City. Another example is California's Great America, a 100-acre family entertainment center that includes the following areas and attractions: Action Zone, All American Corners, Celebration Plaza, County Fair, Orleans Place, Planet Snoopy, and Boomerang Bay.

Roller coasters are staples at most amusement parks.

There is an abundance of theme parks located throughout the United States, visited by more than 300 million people each year. The estimated 400 theme parks and attractions throughout the United States generate more than $12 billion in revenue and account for an estimated 600,000 jobs annually, which significantly contributes to the country's economic activity. These parks have a variety of attractions, from animals and sea life to thrill rides and motion simulators. There are parks with educational themes and parks where people go simply to have a good time.[16]

HOW TO MANAGE THEME PARK DAY-TO-DAY OPERATIONS

Courtesy of **James McManemon**, M.S., University of South Florida Sarasota–Manatee

There are hundreds of theme parks in the United States alone, and while we commonly think of popular Florida theme parks such as Disney World, Universal Studios, SeaWorld, and Busch Gardens, the majority of theme parks are lesser-known and smaller parks throughout the country like Little Amerricka in Wisconsin, Dutch Wonderland in Pennsylvania, and Holiday World & Splashin' Safari in Indiana. Mark Froman, the manager of a smaller under-the-radar North Carolina theme park, shared some of his responsibilities for overseeing the day-to-day operations of the theme park when it is active during the busy spring and summer season.

Walt Disney.

incorporated music and sound, on November 18, 1928. Huge audiences were ecstatic about the work of the Disney Brothers, who became overnight successes.

During the next few years, Walt and Roy made many Mickey Mouse films, which earned them enough to develop other projects, including full-length motion pictures in Technicolor.

According to Disney, "Disneyland really began when my two daughters were very young. Saturday was always Daddy's Day, and I would take them to the merry-go-round and sit on a bench eating peanuts while they rode. And sitting there alone, I felt there should be something built, some kind of family park where parents and children could have fun together."[17]

Walt's original dream was not easy to bring to reality. During the bleak war years, not only was much of his overseas market closed, but the steady stream of income that paid for innovation dried up. However, even during the bleak years, Walt never gave up. Instead, he was excited to learn of the public's interest in movie studios and the possibility of opening the studios to allow the public to visit the birthplace of Snow White, Pinocchio, and other Disney characters.

After its creation, Disneyland had its growing pains—larger-than-expected opening day crowds, long lines at the popular rides, and a cash flow that was so tight that the cashiers had to rush the admission money to the bank to make payroll. Fortunately, since those early days, Disneyland and the Disney characters have become a part of the American dream.

By the early 1960s, Walt had turned most of his attention from film to real estate. Because he was upset when cheap motels and souvenir shops popped up around Disneyland, for his next venture, Walt Disney World, he bought 27,500 acres around the park. The center of Walt Disney World was to be the Experimental Prototype Community of Tomorrow (Epcot). Regrettably, Epcot and Walt Disney World were his dying dreams; Walt Disney succumbed to cancer in 1966.

However, Walt's legacy carries on. The ensuing years since Walt's death have included phenomenal Disney successes with Epcot, movies, a TV station, the Disney Channel, Disney stores, and Disney's Hollywood Studios theme park (formerly Disney-MGM Studios). In April 1992, Euro Disneyland, now Disneyland Paris, opened near Paris. For a variety of reasons (location, cost, climate, and culture), it was initially a failure, until his Royal Highness Prince Alwaleed Bin Talal of Saudi Arabia purchased up to 25 percent of the Disneyland Paris Resort.

Both Walt Disney World and Disneyland have excellent college programs that enable selected students to work during the summer months in a variety of hotel, foodservice, and related park positions. Disney has also introduced a faculty internship that allows faculty to intern in a similar variety of positions.

Walt Disney World is composed of four major theme parks: Magic Kingdom, Epcot, Disney's Animal Kingdom, and Disney's Hollywood Studios, with more than 100 attractions, 31 resort hotels, spectacular nighttime entertainment, and vast shopping, dining, and recreation facilities that cover thousands of acres in this tropical paradise.

Walt Disney World includes tennis courts, championship golf, marinas, swimming pools, jogging and bike trails, water skiing, and motor boating. Walt Disney World is always full of new surprises: It now features an unusual water adventure park—a "snow-covered" mountain with a ski resort theme called Blizzard Beach.

The Disney hotels are architecturally exciting and offer a number of amenities. The fun-filled Disney's All-Star Sports Resort and Disney's colorful All-Star Music Resort are categorized as value-class hotels. Disney's Wilderness Lodge is one of the park's jewels, with its impressive tall-timber atrium lobby and rooms built around a Rocky Mountain–like geyser pool. In all, the park has a cast of thousands of hosts, hostesses, and entertainers famous for their warm smiles and commitment to making every night an especially good one for Disney guests.

Walt Disney World.

There is more to enjoy than ever at Walt Disney World in Mickey's PhilharMagic, which incorporates new 3D movie technology in the Fantasyland area of the Magic Kingdom; Splash Mountain, a popular log flume ride in Frontierland at the Magic Kingdom; Mission: SPACE, a motion simulator ride at Epcot that mimics what an astronaut experiences; and, at Disney's Hollywood Studios, the ultimate thriller, the Twilight Zone Tower of Terror.

Magic Kingdom

The heart of Walt Disney World and its first famous theme park is the Magic Kingdom. It is a giant theatrical stage where guests become part of exciting Disney adventures. It is also the home of Mickey Mouse, Snow White, Peter Pan, Tom Sawyer, Davy Crockett, and the Swiss Family Robinson.

More than 40 major shows and ride-through attractions, not to mention shops and unique dining facilities, fill its six lands of imagination. Each land carries out its theme in fascinating detail—architecture, transportation, music, costumes, dining, shopping, and entertainment are designed to create a total atmosphere where guests can leave the ordinary world behind. The six lands are as follows:[18]

Main Street, USA Experience turn-of-the-century charm with horse-drawn trolleys, horseless carriages, plenty of souvenir shops, a penny arcade, and a grand-circle tour of the park on the Walt Disney World Railroad.

Adventureland Explore exotic places with the Pirates of the Caribbean, the Swiss Family Treehouse, the Magic Carpets of Aladdin, and Walt Disney's Enchanted Tiki Room.

Frontierland Experience thrills on Splash Mountain and Big Thunder Mountain Railroad, musical fun in the Country Bear Jamboree, recreation in the Frontierland Shootin' Arcade, and adventure in the Tom Sawyer Island caves and its raft rides.

Liberty Square Go steam boating on the Rivers of America, find mystery in the Haunted Mansion, and view the impressive Hall of Presidents with the addition of President Barack Obama in a speaking role.

The monorail track at Walt Disney World.

Fantasyland Cinderella Castle is the gateway to Fantasyland, where you'll find the Enchanted Tales with Belle and Main Street Philharmonic at Storybook Circus. Take the Journey of the Little Mermaid and go Under the Sea with Ariel, dine at Be Our Guest Restaurant and Gaston's Tavern, or ride the Seven Dwarfs Mine Train. Storybook Circus includes attractions like Dumbo the Flying Elephant, Walt Disney World Railroad, and Casey Jr. Splash 'N' Soak Station.

Tomorrowland Travel to a sci-fi city of the future with the whirling Astro Orbiter, the shoot-em-up Buzz Lightyear's Space Ranger Spin, the interactive Monsters, Inc. Laugh Floor, the adventurous Stitch's Great Escape!, the speedy Space Mountain, the Tomorrowland Speedway, the elevated Tomorrowland Transit Authority People Mover, and Walt Disney's Carousel of Progress, one of Disney's oldest productions.

Epcot

Epcot is a unique, permanent, and ever-changing world's fair with two major themes: Future World and World Showcase. Highlights include IllumiNations: Reflections of Earth, a nightly spectacle of fireworks, fountains, lasers, and classical music.

Future World shows an amazing exposition of technology for the near future for home, work, and play in Innoventions. The newest consumer products are continually added. Major pavilions exploring past, present, and future are shown in the Spaceship Earth story of communications (Spaceship Earth is the geosphere symbol of Epcot). The Universe of Energy giant dinosaurs help explain the origin and future of energy. There are also Mission: SPACE, which launches visitors into a simulated space adventure; Test Track, a high-speed vehicle-simulation ride; Journey Into Imagination, a tour through various sensory labs; and The Seas with Nemo & Friends, which houses the world's second-largest indoor ocean with thousands of tropical sea creatures.[19]

The Epcot World Showcase are pavilions centered around a reflective lagoon where guests can see replicas of world-famous landmarks and sample the native foods, entertainment, and culture of 11 nations:[20]

Mexico Mexico's fiesta plaza and boat trip on Gran Fiesta Tour Starring The Three Caballeros, plus La Hacienda de San Angel for authentic Mexican cuisine

Norway Stave Church Gallery, an exhibit centered on the origins of the movie *Frozen*, and the Akershus Royal Banquet Hall restaurant

China Reflections of China Stunning Circle-Vision 360° film tours and ancient and modern China, plus the Nine Dragons Restaurant

Germany An authentic Biergarten restaurant

Italy St. Mark's Square street players and Tutto Italia Restaurant

United States The American Adventure's stirring historical drama

Japan Replica of Japan's Imperial Palace plus the Teppan Edo restaurant

Morocco Morocco's palatial Restaurant Marrakesh

France "Impressions de France" film tour of the French countryside, plus Les Chefs de France and Monsieur Paul restaurants

United Kingdom Shakespearean street players, plus the Rose and Crown Dining Room pub

Canada "O Canada!," a 360° Circle-Vision film narrated by Martin Short

Each showcase has additional snack facilities and a variety of shops featuring arts, crafts, and merchandise from each nation.

Disney's Hollywood Studios

With over 100 major shows, shops, restaurants, ride-through adventures, and backstage tours, Disney's Hollywood Studios combines real working motion picture, animation, and television studios with exciting movie attractions. The reproduction of Grauman's Chinese Theatre on Hollywood Boulevard houses the Great Movie Ride.

Other major attractions include the Twilight Zone Tower of Terror, a stunning 13-story elevator fall; fast-paced adventure on the Rock 'n' Roller Coaster Starring Aerosmith; New York Street of Streets of America; exciting shows at Indiana Jones Epic Stunt Spectacular! and Muppet*Vision 3D; plus a thrilling *Star Wars* adventure on Star Tours.

Especially entertaining for Disney fans is The Magic of Disney Animation, where guests can visit the Animation Academy and sit in on a class hosted by a Disney artist. Favorite Disney films become entertaining stage presentations in the Voyage of the Little Mermaid theater and in Beauty and the Beast, a live, 25-minute musical revue at Theater of the Stars. The best restaurants at Disney's Hollywood Studios include the Hollywood Brown Derby, Hollywood & Vine, 50's Prime Time Café, Sci-Fi Dine-In Theater Restaurant, and Mama Melrose's Ristorante Italiano.[21]

Disney's Animal Kingdom Theme Park is the newest addition to Walt Disney World. Animal Kingdom focuses on nature and the animal world around us. Guests can go on time-traveling rides and come face to face with animals from the prehistoric past to the present. Shows are put on featuring Disney's most popular animal-based films, such as *Lion King* and *A Bug's Life*. Safari tours that bring guests up close and personal with live giraffes, elephants, and hippopotamuses are also offered at Animal Kingdom.

Walt Disney World's two water parks are Disney's Blizzard Beach Water Park and Disney's Typhoon Lagoon Water Park. Blizzard Beach has a unique ski-resort theme, while Typhoon Lagoon is based on the legend that a powerful storm swept through, leaving pools and rapids in its wake. Both parks offer a variety of slides, tube rides, pools, and moving rivers that drift throughout the parks.

All this and much more are what help make Walt Disney World the most popular destination resort in the world. Since its opening in 1971, millions of guests, including kings and celebrities from around the world and all seven U.S. presidents in office since the opening (excluding President Obama), have visited the parks. What causes the most comments from guests is the cleanliness, the friendliness of its cast, and the unbelievable attention to detail—a blend of showmanship and imagination that provides an endless variety of adventure and enjoyment.[22]

Universal Studios

Universal Studios Hollywood has been giving guided tours on its famous movie sets for almost 40 years, and tens of thousands of people visit Universal every day.[23] Since its founding, Universal Studios has become the most formidable competitor facing the Walt Disney Company.

In Orlando, Florida, Universal Studios has enjoyed huge success, despite encroaching on the kingdom of Disney. In addition to its Hollywood and Orlando parks, Universal has since expanded into Singapore and Japan. Future locations are planned for Moscow, Russia and Beijing, People's Republic of China. One reason for Universal's success is its adaptation of movies into thrill rides; another is its commitment to guest participation. Guests get to help make sound effects and can participate in stunts, making Universal Studios more than just a "look behind the scenes."

Universal Studios is also a good example of what is predicted to occur in the future regarding amusement and theme parks. It is offering more realistic thrill rides by combining new technologies and state-of-the-art equipment. Also, the company has realized that visitors tend to go to theme parks just because they happen to be in the area. By greatly expanding the experience, NBC Universal is hoping that its improvements will make travelers want to visit Universal Studios Theme Parks as a one-stop destination.

Let's take a closer look at the Universal theme parks:

Universal Studios Hollywood was the first Universal park and boasts the title of the world's largest movie studio and theme park. As part of the new studio tour, visitors are taken into the tomb of the *Revenge of the Mummy*, experience a major earthquake, and are right in the middle of a Hollywood movie shoot. Afterward, guests can relax at the Universal CityWalk, a street that claims to offer the best in food, nightlife, shopping, and entertainment.

Universal Orlando is a destination in itself, with two theme parks, several themed resorts, and a bustling CityWalk. In Universal Orlando, like in the Hollywood park, you can explore the exciting world of movie making. Its newest and most exciting park, Universal's Islands of Adventure, gives you the best in roller coasters and thrill rides, whereas Wet 'n Wild Orlando gives you the opportunity to enjoy a range of cool waterslides, among other things. If you're not already exhausted by the mere thought of it, why not check out CityWalk for some food, shopping, and a taste of the hottest nightlife in town. Myriads of venues, popular with tourists and locals alike, offer an amazing variety of cool bars, hot clubs, and live music.

Universal Studios Japan features over 20 rides and shows, some brand new and others old favorites, plus great dining and shopping. The newest attraction, The Wizarding World of Harry Potter, opened in 2014 and is modeled after the areas with the same name at the Universal Orlando and Universal Studios Hollywood.

Universal Studios Singapore is the newest addition and is located within Singapore's first integrated resort.[24]

TECHNOLOGY SPOTLIGHT

Courtesy of **James McManemon**, M.S., University of South Florida Sarasota–Manatee

Use of Technology in Recreation, Attractions, and Clubs

Some of the technologies utilized in the recreation and clubs area are common to the rest of the hospitality industry. Depending on the size and amenities of an establishment, the following information technology systems can be used: call centers (for sales and customer service), point-of-sale systems (for retail distribution, food and beverage, rentals), and ticketing systems (for issuing tickets and passes). Besides these, there are some specific systems that can be implemented in the resorts and clubs.

Golf club property management systems would usually make the following functions available to users. The first is wide reservations options: online booking and group reservations. These systems usually can copy the guest's name on several tee times and thus help to save time on data entry. Another important function in golf clubs is tee-time management. This feature allows instant checking of tee-time availability to provide guests with a complete picture of what's available. Also, this module enables managing separate times and rates for different types of guests: public, member, twilight, and so forth. Besides this, club agents can relocate (drag and drop) one or multiple players from one tee time to another with ease. Some of the providers of club management software are Jonas Software, RTP|ONE, and CSI Software.

Radio-frequency identification (RFID) is rapidly entering the recreation and clubs niche of the hospitality industry. This is a technology that uses communication through radio waves for the purposes of tracking and identifying people or objects. RFID chips can be embedded in guest cards or wristbands. They enable authorization at the access points as well as retrieval of the guest's profile, picture, and membership privileges. The necessary components for this system are RFID chips and an antenna or reader. The RFID antenna picks up a unique serial number from the microchip when a ticket, pass, or wristband with the RFID chip is presented. This technology helps to enhance fraud prevention on the management side and provides hands-free convenience on the guest side. RFID access systems have been widely used at European ski resorts, and now they are also spreading to the American market. In addition, RFID systems can have electronic wallet functionality. Often, RFID is

(continued)

implemented in beach resorts, where guests receive an opportunity to pay at different retail outlets without carrying an actual wallet. This provides the convenience of electronic payment to guests and encourages shopping. Moreover, RFID wristbands can be utilized at huge resorts and amusement parks in order to track children if they are lost.

Information kiosks appear often at large parks and resorts. Usually this technology allows park visitors to purchase park passes and other services on park grounds. Kiosks can be supplemented with digital displays that provide visitors with relevant information. These technologies optimize the use of parks' personnel, maximize the use of parks' resources, and ensure information is available to park visitors. These displays can digitally present pictures or event schedules of different parts of a resort or a park. This helps to attract guests to particular areas at the right time (e.g., when there is an event taking place), as well as enables guests to plan a better recreation experience according to their interests.

SeaWorld Parks and Entertainment

SeaWorld Parks and Entertainment is a subsidiary of SeaWorld Entertainment, Inc. that also includes Busch Gardens. The animal parks not only offer guests from around the world the opportunity to see and experience the wonders of many marine and land animals, but they also have highly developed educational programs. These programs reach millions of people a year—in the parks, on TV, and over the Internet—informing them on topics such as endangered animals, the environment, and the wonders of the ocean. In addition, SeaWorld Parks and Entertainment is active in the areas of conservation, research, and wildlife assistance worldwide.

The company is dedicated to preserving marine life. It uses innovative programs to research various wildlife dilemmas. It also participates in breeding, animal rescue, rehabilitation, and conservation efforts throughout the year. What SeaWorld Parks and Entertainment does for the preservation of animals is important to the existence of its theme parks because the research and rescue programs are subsidized through guest revenue. Also, each park offers unique shows and attractions that combine entertainment and education with a strong commitment to research and conservation.

Currently, SeaWorld Parks and Entertainment[25] runs the following parks in the United States:

SeaWorld The three SeaWorld parks are located in California (San Diego), Florida

Bottlenose dolphins can be seen performing at SeaWorld.

(Orlando), and Texas (San Antonio). Each park has various themes, marine and animal attractions, shows, rides, and educational exhibits. SeaWorld is based on the creatures of the sea. Guests can pet dolphins and other fish; watch shows featuring Shamu, the famous killer whale; and learn all about the mysteries of the sea. Several rides are also available at SeaWorld, and countless exhibits feature everything from stingrays to penguins.

Busch Gardens These theme parks, located in both Tampa, Florida, and Williamsburg, Virginia, feature exciting thrill rides and attractions in addition to large zoos and safari parks. The theme for the Williamsburg Park is classic Europe. It re-creates the seventeenth-century charm of the Old World European atmosphere with a journey through nine authentically detailed European hamlets. Busch Gardens in Tampa has a distinctly African theme.

Adventure Island Also located in Tampa, Adventure Island is the only splash park in the Tampa Bay area. It is also the only water theme park on Florida's west coast featuring several unique water play areas and thrilling splash rides. The water park comprises more than 30 acres of fun-filled water rides, cafés, and shops.

Water Country USA Also located in Williamsburg, Water Country USA is Virginia's largest family water park, featuring state-of-the-art water rides and attractions, all set to a retro surf theme, plus live entertainment, shopping, and restaurants.[26] Like Adventure Island, Water Country has an educational atmosphere to help guests, especially children, learn water safety techniques.

Aquatica These water parks are located in Orlando, San Antonio, and San Diego. They are known as SeaWorld's water parks. Aquatica Orlando's theme is the southern Pacific and features Australian- and New Zealand-based mascots. The park also features dolphins, which you ride by on one of the attractions.

Sesame Place This 14-acre park is located in Langhorne, Pennsylvania, and is dedicated totally to a Sesame Street theme. It was designed with the goal of stimulating children's natural curiosity to learn and explore, while building self-confidence as they interact with other children.

Discovery Cove Adjacent to SeaWorld in Orlando, Florida, Discovery Cove is where you can immerse yourself in adventure. It offers up-close encounters with dolphins and other exotic sea life. Guests can swim with dolphins and snorkel through a coral reef, a tropical river, waterfalls, and an amazing freshwater lagoon, among other things.[27]

Hershey's

What does the name Hershey bring to mind?[28] It was at the 1893 World's Columbian Exposition in Chicago that Hershey first became fascinated with the art of chocolate. Then, Milton Hershey, a small-time candy manufacturer, decided he wanted to make chocolate to coat his caramels. He opened his new establishment in Lancaster, Pennsylvania, and named it the Hershey Chocolate Company. In the 1900s, the company started to produce mass quantities of milk chocolate, which resulted in immediate success. Soon after, Hershey decided that there was a need to increase his production facilities. He built a new factory on the farmland of south-central Pennsylvania in Derry Township. The following decades brought many product-line expansions. In 1968, the company was renamed the Hershey Foods Corporation. Today, the company is the leading manufacturer of chocolate, nonchocolate confectionery, and grocery products in North America.

In 1907, Milton Hershey opened Hershey Park as a leisure park for employees of Hershey's company. He wanted to create a place for his employees to relax and have some fun when they were not on the job. The park was small and simple, offering employees a place to picnic, canoe, and walk around the beautifully landscaped grounds. In 1908, the park started its soon-to-be huge expansion with the addition of a merry-go-round.

In the years to come, the park continued to add more rides and attractions. As the park continued to expand, the company decided to open the park's doors to the public. It became a small regional park with a pay-as-you-ride policy.

In 1971, the park underwent redevelopment to turn the small regional park into a large theme park. In addition, the company decided to add a one-time admission fee to eliminate the pay-as-you-ride policy and changed its name from Hershey Park to Hersheypark. Today, the park sits on more than 110 acres and is the home of more than 60 rides and attractions.

▶ Check Your Knowledge

1. Distinguish between commercial and noncommercial recreation.
2. Why did Walt Disney really create Disneyland?
3. Discuss your favorite theme park with your class. Explain why it is your favorite.

LEARNING OBJECTIVE 5
Identify some of the major attractions in the United States.

Regional Theme Parks

Just to show how varied the attractions industry is, consider the state of Florida and its attractions association. The Florida Attractions Association, founded in 1949, is a trade association representing over 90 leading attractions, including astronautical, historical, cultural, military, and scientific museums; botanical gardens; castles; collections of the unique and different; dinner entertainments; dolphin and marine parks; exhibitions of alligators, lions, monkeys, parrots, butterflies, and manatees; Native American villages; musical entertainment complexes; sightseeing trains, cruises, and boat tours; state parks; theme parks; towers; water parks; and zoological parks.

In addition to some of the larger theme parks mentioned in the preceding section, there are others that cater to thousands of visitors each year.

The Miami Seaquarium is a 38-acre tropical paradise, a place where dolphins walk on water, killer whales fly through the air, and endangered sea turtles and manatees find a safe haven.

There are several different marine animal shows and an educational program that focuses on the mysteries of the sea even top marine scientists can't explain. In order to broaden its appeal and bring in additional revenue, the Miami Seaquarium has developed a company program for events and a schools and Scouts program to appeal to the youth market.

Marineland Dolphin Adventure in Miami began in 1938 in an effort to duplicate the variety of marine life as it exists in the wild for the purpose of making films. It was a hit with Hollywood and was used in a number of movies. Today, the park offers an array of dolphin adventures including opportunities to touch and feed the dolphins, to simulate being a trainer for the day, to make art with the dolphins, and take kayak tours in the local estuary.

Dollywood

In 1961, a small attraction with a Civil War theme called Rebel Railroad opened its doors to the public.[29] In the 1970s, the name Rebel Railroad was changed to Goldrush Junction, and the theme was changed to resemble the Wild West. This attraction is now known all across the world as Dollywood. The name came about in 1986 when Dolly Parton became a co-owner of the park. The park sits on 150 acres in the foothills of the Smoky Mountains in Pigeon Forge, Tennessee. In addition to having all the rides of an amusement park, Dollywood is enriched by the culture of the Smoky Mountains. The park includes crafts such as blacksmithing, glass blowing, and woodcarving. It also hosts several festivals, concerts, and musical events. Today, Dollywood brings in more than 3 million visitors during its operating season and continues to be Tennessee's number one tourist attraction. Additionally, Dollywood's DreamMore Resort opened in July 2015 and is expected to double in the number of visitors it attracts each year.[30]

Legoland

Legoland is a theme park partly owned by the Lego Group.[31] In 1968, Legoland Billund Resort in Denmark opened and now has over 1 million visitors annually. The parks are themed after—you guessed it—Legos, the brightly colored plastic bricks, gears, minifigures, and other pieces that are assembled to create models of almost anything. The parks are marketed toward young families. This is emphasized in the rides: All the parks have roller coasters that are not quite as extreme as the roller coasters found in other theme parks. Today there are six Legoland parks located in Billund, Denmark; Windsor, United Kingdom; Carlsbad, California; Günzburg, Germany; Winter Haven, Florida; and Malaysia. Each park features a miniland, which is made up of millions of bricks that create models of landmarks and scenes from all around the world. Legoland Windsor is one of Britain's most popular attractions. Legoland's theme parks are owned and operated by Merlin Entertainments.[32]

Gatorland

Gatorland is a 110-acre theme park and wildlife preserve located in Orlando, Florida.[33] It all started when Owen Godwin built an alligator pit in his backyard. After World War II, Godwin bought a 16-acre plot located off Florida's second-most-traveled highway. He decided that he wanted to build an attraction on his land that would provide a close-up view of Florida's animals in their native habitat. In 1949, Godwin opened the attraction's doors to the public under the name of the Florida Wildlife Institute, which he shortly after changed to the Snake Village and Alligator Farm. In 1954, Godwin once again changed the name of the attraction to its current name, Gatorland.

The 1960s brought growth to the tourism industry in Florida. As the industry grew, Gatorland continued to expand by adding a number of exhibits and attractions. Today, Gatorland features alligators, crocodiles, a breeding marsh, reptilian shows, a petting zoo, a swamp walk, educational programs, and train rides. In addition, it offers the following shows: Gator Jumparoo, which features alligators jumping four to five feet out of the water to retrieve food; Gator Wrestlin', an alligator wrestling show in which wranglers catch an alligator by hand; and Up Close Encounters, where visitors meet wildlife from around the globe. One of the oldest attractions in the area, Gatorland continues to be privately owned by Godwin's family.

Wet 'n Wild

Wet 'n Wild was founded by George Millay in Orlando, Florida, in 1977.[34] George Millay is also known as the creator of SeaWorld. Wet 'n Wild is considered the first major water park to be opened in the United States. Millay received the first Lifetime Achievement Award from the World Waterpark Association for creation of Wet 'n Wild. The association named him the official "Father of the Waterpark."

Today, Wet 'n Wild is a chain of water parks with locations in Florida and North Carolina. The Wet 'n Wild located in Emerald Pointe, North Carolina features more than 36 rides and attractions that are classified from mild to wild. Wet 'n Wild Orlando also offers something for everyone. The rides fall into three categories: Super Thrills, Group Thrills, and Family Fun. In 1998, Millay sold the Orlando park to the Universal Studios Recreation Group.

Animal Attractions

Another sector that has been growing substantially is the one of animal attractions. Although they are usually not the main reason people visit a state or city, zoos, aquariums, and wild animal parks attract millions of visitors every year.

Zoos

Every kid's dream, and just as much fun for parents, zoos are one of those things that just don't seem to go out of style. They are forms of tourist attractions that people may visit when in a destination city such as New York, Chicago, or San Diego. Approximately 181 million people visit a U.S. zoo every year.[35] The first zoo in the United States was the Philadelphia Zoo, built in 1859. Even today, zoos are extremely popular in the United States and Canada, and almost every major city has one. In fact, the popularity of zoos was proven when the Walt Disney Company unveiled its Animal Kingdom as one way to combine the effects of visiting a zoo with the attractions of a theme park. Busch Gardens and SeaWorld also have similar parks.

Following are examples of two of the most popular and noteworthy American zoos.

San Diego Zoo, California

The San Diego Zoo attracts many tourists from across the country for a variety of reasons. It may be in part because of the favorable climate that allows the zoo to operate all year round. Also, the zoo has a large collection of animals, interactive programs, and educational programs for children.

The world-famous San Diego Zoo is located in historic Balboa Park in downtown San Diego, California. Founded in 1916 by Dr. Henry Wegeforth, the zoo's original collection totaled 50 animals. Today, it is home to over 3,700 animals of more than 650 different species. The zoo also features a prominent botanical collection with more than 700,000 exotic plants.[36] The zoo's breeding programs help not only to enhance the zoo, but also to provide hope for the survival of many endangered animals. The first giant panda born in the United States to survive to adulthood, Hua Mei, was born at the San Diego Zoo.[37]

The National Zoo

The National Zoological Park in Washington, D.C., is part of the respected Smithsonian Institution. More than 2,000 animals from nearly 400 species make their home in this zoo.[38] Among the rare animals featured at the National Zoo are a giant panda, komodo dragons, rare Sumatran tigers, and Asian elephants.

The National Zoo is located in a quiet residential area only minutes away from other Smithsonian museums, the Capitol, and the White House. It is not only a place to observe the behavior of certain animals, but also a place that works actively to educate visitors on conservation issues and the various interactions among living organisms. The National Zoo breeds endangered species and reintroduces the animals into their natural habitats. The zoo also participates in other visitor education programs and biological research.[39]

Aquariums

Aquariums are attractions that provide thrilling educational experiences to millions of tourists each year. They are also multimillion-dollar showpieces, displaying creatures vastly different from us who dwell on land. For example, each year, 1.8 million visitors pass through the doors of the National Aquarium in Baltimore.[40] This impressive aquarium seeks to stimulate public interest in and knowledge about the aquatic world, focusing on the beauty of these species in their natural environments. It uses only the most modern interpretative techniques to engage and get an emotional response from visitors. In fact, many visitors walk out with a desire to become more environmentally responsible.[41]

▶ Check Your Knowledge

1. Name at least two regional theme parks and discuss similarities and distinctive differences.

2. Identify some of the main attractions found in the United States.

3. Name some rare animals you can find at the National Zoo.

Historic Places and Sites

Travelers and tourists have visited historic sites for thousands of years. The first sites visited in recorded history were the Seven Wonders of the Ancient World, which included the Great Pyramid of Giza (Egypt), the Hanging Gardens of Babylon (modern-day Iraq), the Statue of Zeus at Olympia (Greece), the Temple of Artemis at Ephesus (modern-day Turkey), the Mausoleum at Halicarnassus (modern-day Turkey), the Colossus of Rhodes (Greece), and the Lighthouse of Alexandria (Egypt). Historic places, sites, and museums are a part of what is now called **heritage tourism**. Heritage tourism has gained prominence in recent years, particularly with baby boomers and older adults. These groups are less likely to engage in adventure tourism and usually prefer more passive activities. Tourists visiting historic places/sites and museums are interested in the national culture. The various historic attractions appeal to a broad spectrum of the community because they are diverse and located throughout the nation.

The Great Pyramid of Giza, Egypt.

The National Park Service maintains properties listed in the National Register of Historic Places. The **National Register of Historic Places** is the United States' official list of districts, sites, buildings, structures, and objects worthy of preservation. The more than 90,000 listings represent significant icons of American culture, history, engineering, and architecture.[42] Historic sites include buildings that have been restored and that are now being used as private houses as well as hotels, inns, churches, libraries, galleries, and museums.

Because of declining funds, galleries, museums, and heritage sites have had to become creative in raising money. They have not only had to cover operating costs but also cater to an increasing number of visitors. To self-generate revenues, they have had to become more entrepreneurial while continuing to meet their heritage preservation and educational goals. Revenue generation has often been achieved through an increased concentration on partnerships, promotions, and packages in which the sites team up with other operators in the tourism industry, such as tour companies, hotels, restaurants, and car rental companies.

Heritage tourism is discussed more in depth in Chapter 9, but consider the following for a look at a few of the most important U.S. historical attractions:

- Monticello was the home of the famous statesman Thomas Jefferson, author of the Declaration of Independence, architect of American ideals as well as noble buildings, and father of the University of Virginia. The domed mansion of Monticello is set in the beautiful Virginia countryside and is well worth a visit.

- The Alamo is a small mission in San Antonio, Texas, with a rich historical background. During Texas's fight for independence from Mexico, a vicious battle took place in this town. Almost 200 Texans held out for 13 days in a group of fortified mission buildings against General Santa Anna's army of about 2,400 soldiers. The battle resulted in a tragic Texan defeat. Not long after that, Texans everywhere united in a rallying cry: "Remember the Alamo!"[43] And people still do.

- The French Quarter in New Orleans is an original part of the city, full of life and history. Unlike historic districts in many other cities, it is still growing and evolving, regardless of the recent natural disasters. Locals constantly wrestle with the issue of balancing evolutionary changes with the need to preserve history. Visitors can have a great time when they visit during Mardi Gras.

- The Martin Luther King Jr. National Historic Site is located in the residential section of Sweet Auburn, Atlanta. Two blocks west of the home is Ebenezer Baptist Church, the pastorate of King's grandfather and father. It was in these surroundings of home, church, and neighborhood that "M. L." experienced his childhood. Here, he learned about family and Christian love, segregation in the days of Jim Crow laws, diligence, and tolerance. This important site is a reminder of King's significant contribution to the civil rights movement.

- The Grand Ole Opry in Nashville, Tennessee, is a live radio show in which country music guests are featured. Started more than 90 years ago, the Grand Ole Opry is what made Nashville "Music City." Since the Opry's start, Nashville created a theme park, Opryland (now closed), and a hotel, the Gaylord Opryland Resort. Famous musicians come from all over the world to showcase their talents, and tourists flock from everywhere to hear the sounds of the Opry and see the sites that Nashville has to offer.[44]

- The Freedom Trail is a walking tour through downtown Boston that passes through 17 points of interest, plus other exhibits, monuments, and shrines just off the trail, some of which are a part of the Boston National Historical Park. This interesting walk through a part of U.S. history includes both the Massachusetts State House and the Old South Meeting House. The Old South Meeting House was the site of many important town meetings concerning the British colonial rule, including those that sparked the Boston Tea Party. Today, there is a multimedia exhibition depicting the area's 300-year history. The building and two other restored structures today house a bustling marketplace of more than 100 specialty shops, restaurants, and bars. Paul Revere's house is the only seventeenth-century structure left in downtown Boston. It was from this house that the silversmith left for his historic ride on April 18, 1775. Another site on the Freedom Trail is the Bunker Hill Monument.

- The Liberty Bell is housed on Market Street in Philadelphia. The bell's inscription reads, "Proclaim Liberty throughout All the Land unto All the Inhabitants thereof," which in fact is taken from the Bible, Leviticus 25:10. For many years, it was known as the State House bell. Its popularity rose when a group of abolitionists, remembering its inscription, adopted the bell as a symbol of their cause; they nicknamed it their liberty bell. In the late 1800s, the bell went on tour around the United States. This trip was an effort to show the war-torn country that there had been a time in history when they had fought and died for a common cause. In 1915, when the tour ended, the Liberty Bell, as it was then known, went home to Philadelphia, where it remains to this day. Throughout American history, the Liberty Bell has served as a simple reminder, a symbol of freedom, independence, and liberty, not just in the United States but also all over the world.

▶ Check Your Knowledge

1. What were the first historic sites visited in recorded history?
2. Name some important U.S. historical attractions.

Museums

Some experts have speculated that people visit museums because of some innate fascination with the past and with diverse cultures. Nobody knows for sure, but it is a fact that the number of museums in the United States has more than quadrupled since 1950. There are many types of museums, including general, art, science and technology, natural history, history, and military. Someone has to manage these operations, and the more people that travel to experience them, the more career opportunities are available in the travel, hotel, and restaurant industries. Here are a couple of the big names in the museum sector.

The Smithsonian Institution

Established in 1846 by a man who never visited the United States, this well-known institution now holds almost 140 million artifacts, works of art, and specimens. It is composed of the following museums and galleries: the Anacostia Community Museum; the Arthur M. Sackler Gallery; the Cooper-Hewitt, Smithsonian Design Museum; the Freer Gallery of Art; the Hirshhorn Museum and Sculpture Garden; the Air and Space Museum; the African American History and Culture Museum; the African Art Museum; the American History Museum; the Natural History Museum; the American Indian Museum; the Portrait Gallery; the Postal Museum; the American Art Museum; and the Renwick Gallery. There are also nine research facilities in the United States and abroad, and 168 affiliate museums, as well as the National Zoo.[45] The institution's goal is to increase and diffuse knowledge, and it is also dedicated to public education, national service, and scholarship in the arts, sciences, and history.[46] Smithsonian museums attract approximately 30 million visitors annually, and entrance is free. The National Zoo attracts over 1.5 million visitors annually.[47] In addition to its museums and research facilities, parts of the Smithsonian collection can be viewed online at http://www.si.edu.

The Field Museum, Chicago

The Field Museum of Natural History is an institution of public learning that seeks to inspire public knowledge and curiosity by its varied collections, broad research, storied exhibits, and educational programs. The museum, located in Chicago, invites visitors to immerse themselves in scientific discovery.[48]

The museum was founded in 1893 as a place to house biological and anthropological collections for a world exposition. These types of objects continue to form the basis of the museum's collections. In addition, the museum conducts research in the areas of geology, paleontology, archaeology, and ethnography. Furthermore, the museum houses collections consisting of more than 20 million items.[49]

Permanent exhibits at the Field Museum range from dinosaurs to minerals and gems, plants, animals, and cultural exhibits. Temporary exhibits are also displayed from time to time. One example of this was a program entitled "The Art of the Motorcycle." This exhibit discussed the motorcycle as a cultural icon and also its technological design.

Performance Arts

Have you ever wished that you could just take off and follow your favorite band on tour? Although some people do, most of us do not have the money or time to do so. However, that does not stop us from enjoying an occasional concert, musical, theater production, comedy show, and so forth when we are at home or on the road. While these shows and productions are usually not the primary purpose of leisure travel, in some circumstances they might be. In Orlando or Las Vegas, for example, certain shows have taken up permanent residence. The public knows this and therefore may take a trip to Orlando or Las Vegas at their convenience so that they may see a certain production. In places like New York City and London, stopping off to see a Broadway production or a concert may be an unplanned bonus.

Theaters once were immensely important. In a time before people had access to modern inventions like radio or television, books and theater were the only entertainment available. During the industrial era of the early 1900s, the importance of theaters began to wane somewhat as people became too busy juggling work and spending time with family. In addition, many people could not afford such luxuries. In modern times, however, the theater is again gaining importance. Old theaters from the vaudeville days are now being resurrected and reopened to the public—and the public is responding. Increasing numbers of people visit the theater or opera on weekends, holidays, or just for an evening out on the town. Theater is no longer attractive only to the upper classes; affordable prices make it reasonable entertainment for almost anyone.

Concerts, musicals, and comedy shows are also becoming increasingly affordable and are included in many people's vacations schedules. As we move up the hierarchy of needs, self-actualization becomes a greater motivation, and more and more people satisfy that need with a dose of culture and performing arts.

▶ Check Your Knowledge

1. What are the goals of the Smithsonian Institution?
2. Why are theaters, concerts, musicals, and comedy shows regaining importance?

Destinations

Some destinations are major attractions in themselves. For example, a trip to Europe might include visits to cities such as London, Paris, Rome, Athens, and Madrid or just focus on one country, where visitors enjoy not only the city but also the countryside. The following sections describe some of the world's most popular destinations.

Athens, Greece

Athens, the capital city of Greece, is one of the world's oldest cities—the cradle of Western civilization and the birthplace of democracy. Classical Athens was a powerful city-state, a center for the arts, learning, and philosophy, and home of Plato's Academy and Aristotle's Lyceum.[50] History abounds in Athens, as evidenced by the Parthenon—a temple to the Greek goddess Athena built in the fifth century B.C. on the Acropolis, a flat rock above the city. Today, Athens is a bustling city of more than 3 million—all of whom seem to be on the move, hence its notorious congestion.[51]

Of the millions of tourists who go to Greece, many, after visiting Athens, take a ferryboat ride to the famed Greek Islands in the Aegean Sea. Crete, the largest island, is rugged and mountainous with beautiful beaches and a reconstruction of the palace of King Minos, which is the largest Bronze Age archeological site on Crete, dating back to between 1700 and 1400 B.C. It was probably the ceremonial and political center of Minoan civilization and culture. The strikingly beautiful island of Santorini is a remaining part of the cone of an extinct volcano that erupted some 3,500 years ago. Some of the picturesque white buildings cling to the rim of the volcano and are among the most photographed in the world. The best way up to the town on top of the hill is by donkey ride. Mykonos is a trendy island with its famed windmills and fabulous beaches, some of them nude beaches. Other often-visited islands include Rhodes, with plenty of ruins, good beaches, and nightlife, and Corfu, off the west coast of Greece, with its lush vegetation due to higher rainfall than the other islands and its excellent beaches, museum, and nightlife—including a casino—making it a favorite of package tour groups.

London

London was once the center of an empire that included approximately one-quarter of the globe. The name suggests history, pageantry, royalty, theater, shopping, museums, music, fashion, and now even food. London has several interesting areas such as Chelsea and the River Thames and Hampstead on the hill with its quaint pubs and row houses. Trafalgar Square, named after the Battle of Trafalgar in which Nelson defeated the French, is where a statue of Lord Nelson stands atop a tall column. The four large lions that guard the statue were reputedly made from the cannons of the French fleet. Nearby is Piccadilly Circus, the core of the theater and nightlife district, along with neighboring Soho, which was a former royal park and favorite hunting ground of King Henry VIII. (In Old English, the word *so* means wild boar or pig, and *ho* means there.) There are many other fascinating areas such as London's East End, originally the home of the Cockneys; the impressive buildings of the Houses of Parliament, with Big Ben, the clock tower; and of course, Buckingham Palace, the queen's London residence.

Outside London's popular tourist spots are Oxford, where travelers can visit the famous university; Stratford-upon-Avon, the birthplace of William Shakespeare, where travelers can visit the house in which Shakespeare was born in 1564 and can visit Ann Hathaway's cottage, where she lived before her marriage to Shakespeare; Bath, famous for its history of therapeutic hotsprings; and Stonehenge, a complex of Neolithic and Bronze Age monuments whose purpose

Big Ben and Westminster Abbey make London a popular destination.

is mysterious and unknown. Bath is England's most elegant city known for its Georgian architecture and, of course, its baths that date back to Roman times and that are reputed to ease the pain of arthritis. Many visitors enjoy the English countryside, with quaint villages and narrow winding roads and roundabouts. And visitors can always enjoy the British pubs.

Paris

Paris is a city of beautiful buildings, boulevards, parks, markets, and restaurants and cafés. Paris is exciting! So, for tourists, what to see first is an often-asked question over morning coffee and croissants. There are city tours, but the best way to see the real Paris is on foot, especially if people want to avoid the hordes of other tourists. A tour could begin at the Eiffel Tower or the Notre-Dame Cathedral, the Louvre or the Musée d'Orsay, the Île de la Cité, or simply with a stroll down the Champs-Élysées.

Paris began as a small island called Île de la Cité, in the middle of the River Seine. In time, Paris grew onto the Left Bank (Rive Gauche), where the Paris-Sorbonne University was founded. The university provided instruction in Latin, so it became known as the Quartier Latin, or Latin Quarter. The Latin Quarter has a Bohemian intellectual character with lots of small cafés and wine bars similar to Greenwich Village and Soho in New York. Nearby is Montparnasse, an area that is popular with today's artists and painters. On the Right Bank (Rive Droit) of the river Seine are many attractions; one favorite is the area of Montmartre, with the domes of Sacré-Cœur and the Place du Tertre. Just walking along the winding streets up to Sacré-Cœur gives visitors a feel of the special nature of Paris. Savoring the sights of the little markets with arrays of fresh fruits, vegetables, and flowers; catching the aromas wafting from the cafés; and seeing couples walking arm in arm in a way that only lovers do in Paris add to the ambiance that captivates all who go there and provide wonderful memories.

Rome

They say, "All roads lead to Rome." Rome, the Eternal City, is built on seven hills beside the Tiber River, with centuries of history that seem to exude from every building. Among the most visited sites are the Colosseum, the Pantheon, the Spanish Steps, Vatican City, and the Roman Forum. The Colosseum is the ancient stadium where gladiators fought, Christians were martyred, other sports and games were played, and thousands of men fought with ferocious animals to amuse the crowds. The Pantheon, originally built in 27 B.C. as a temple to all the gods of ancient Rome, was destroyed by fire in A.D. 80, rebuilt in 126, and is likely the best preserved building of its era. The Spanish Steps, the widest steps in Europe, are situated between the Piazza di Spagna (Plaza of Spain) and the Piazza Trinità die Monti, the Episcopal jurisdiction of the Bishop of Rome, better known as the Pope. The area is a popular hangout for tourists and residents. Vatican City is the smallest state in the world, with only 110 acres and a population of just over

800.[52] In this tiny area are St. Peter's Basilica, the Vatican Museums, and Michelangelo's *Creation*, painted on the ceiling of the Sistine Chapel, and his *Last Judgment*, on the wall behind the altar. The Roman Forum was the center of political, social, and economic life in imperial Rome, with temples, basilicas, and triumphal arches; it is the place where the Roman democratic government began. Several other interesting cities to visit in Italy include Venice, Naples, and Florence, along with the Tuscan countryside.

Managing Attractions

Managing attractions and theme parks has many similarities to managing any business. Theme park managers use the same main management functions (planning, including forecasting; organizing; decision making; and controlling).

Planning involves all types of planning that fall under two headings: strategic (long term) and tactical (short term). An example of strategic planning would be determining what kind of theme ride to build as the next major attraction or planning a new park in another country. An example of tactical planning would be forecasting the park's attendance for the next month so departments can staff correctly.

Organizing is getting everything arranged: who will do what, by whom, when, and where. For example, a theme park requires a structure to be organized for managing the process. The management team is assembled and given their assignments. Someone manages the reservations and admissions, the rides, the restaurants and foodservice, the gift shops, maintenance, marketing, human resources, and accounting and finance. Each department manager has daily, weekly, and monthly tasks that structure the organizing of the park to maximize operational efficiencies and effectiveness. Organization charts show who reports to whom and give a visual representation of the operation of the park.

Decision making can be quick and easy for the many programmed decisions—decisions that occur on a regular basis, allowing the decision to be handled with a programmed response. For example, when the inventory of an item falls below the reorder point, a programmed response is to order a predetermined quantity to bring the stock back up to par.

Another, more complicated type of decision making is nonprogrammed—which is nonrecurring and is caused by unusual circumstances. One example of a nonprogrammed decision is a situation with incomplete information—for example, which guest relations program or point-of-sale system to install.

The decision-making process consists of the following eight steps:[53]

1. Identification of the problem and definition of the problem

2. Identification of the decision criteria

3. Allocation of weights to the criteria

4. Development of alternatives

5. Analysis of alternatives

6. Selection of alternative

7. Implementation of alternative

8. Evaluation of decision effectiveness

Controlling is a key part of managing attractions and requires constant checking to make sure that the results were what they should be. Was the actual revenue what was expected? Or, was it above or below expected, and by how much? What was the labor cost and how did it compare with the expected labor cost? Control examines performance results in all the key areas of operation.

Revenue comes from entrance ticket sales, parking, vending, retail program fees, food and beverage sales, and donations. There is a great variation among attractions. Some are for profit and others are nonprofit; however, both must operate with budgets. Many attractions obtain 70 percent of their revenue from ticket sales, approximately 15 percent income from retail, and another 15 percent from food and beverage sales. Many attractions are looking to attract new revenue by staging special events such as corporate events, Father's Day or Easter celebrations, or auto shows in the parking lot.

As managers of a business, attractions managers are also trying to stay ahead of the wave and keep on top of expenditures. They also try to retain the best employees during the slow season by cross-training them to do more than one job as the need arises. Because labor costs are the highest expense item, managers do their best to reduce labor costs by boosting the volunteer base in multiple areas.[54]

Attractions management is all about keeping the quality of product and guest service at the highest levels. It boils down to revenue minus expenses equal net profit.[55]

LEARNING OBJECTIVE 6
Describe the operations of a country club.

Clubs

Private clubs are places where members gather for social, recreational, professional, or fraternal reasons. Members enjoy bringing friends, family, and business guests to their club. Their club is like a second home, but with diverse facilities and staff to accommodate the occasion. Bringing guests to one's club can be more impressive than inviting them to one's home, and there is still a level of the same personal atmosphere as there would be if guests were invited home. Many of today's clubs are adaptations of their predecessors, mostly examples from England and Scotland. For example, the North American country club is largely patterned after the Royal and Ancient Golf Club of St. Andrews, Scotland, founded in 1754 and recognized as the birthplace of golf. Many business deals are negotiated on the golf course. A few years ago, country clubs were often considered to be bastions of the social elite.

Historically, the ambiance of these clubs attracted the affluent. The character of the clubs transcended generations. Member etiquette and mannerisms developed over years to a definable point by which members could recognize each other through subtleties, and those not possessing the desired qualities were not admitted.

A golf course community in Hawaii.

Today there are more affluent people than ever, and their number continues to grow. The new rich are now targeted and recruited for a variety of new hybrid groups that also call themselves clubs. The newer clubs' cost of initiation and membership may be considerably less than some of the more established clubs. The stringent screening process and lengthy membership applications are now simplified, and cash is the key to admittance.

New clubs are born when a developer purchases a tract of land and builds a golf course with a clubhouse surrounded by homes or condominiums. The homes are sold and include a membership to the club. After all the homes are sold, the developer announces that the golf course and clubhouse will be sold to an investor who wishes to open it to the public. The homeowners rush to purchase the clubhouse and golf course to protect their investment. A board is formed, and the employees of the developer and all operations are usually transferred to and become the responsibility of the new owners or members.

Size and Scope of the Club Industry

There are a few thousand private clubs in North America, including both country and city clubs. When the total resources of all the clubs are considered, such as land, buildings, and equipment, along with thousands of employees and so forth, clubs have billions of dollars of economic impact.

Club Management

Club management is similar in many ways to hotel management, both of which have evolved in recent years. The general managers of clubs now assume the role of chief operating officer (COO), and in some cases chief executive officer of the corporation. They may also have responsibility for management of the homeowners' association and all athletic facilities, including the golf courses. In addition, they are responsible for planning, forecasting and budgeting, human resources, food and beverage operations, facility management, and maintenance. The main difference between managing a club and managing a hotel is that with clubs the guests feel as if they are the owners (in many cases they are) and frequently behave as if they are the owners. Their emotional attachment to the facility is stronger than that of hotel guests who do not use hotels with the same frequency that members use clubs. Another difference is that most clubs do not offer sleeping accommodations.

INTRODUCING EDWARD J. SHAUGHNESSY

General Manager, Belleair Country Club

For Ed Shaughnessy, working in a country club is not just a job but also a passion. Clubs feature great recreational facilities, including some fabulous golf courses, gourmet dining, the finest entertainment, and clientele who are more like family than customers. Shaughnessy has worked for three prestigious clubs in his career. He began working in clubs at the tender age of 14 as a busser. Shortly after graduating from high school, he accepted a full-time evening bar manager position at Sleepy Hollow Country Club in New York. He worked full time at night while attending college full time until he received his A.A.S. degree. Upon graduation, he was promoted to food and beverage manager, but continued his education, taking two or three courses every semester until he earned and received his B.B.A. He was subsequently promoted to assistant general manager.

After 14 years at the same club and on his 29th birthday, he was offered and accepted the general manager's position at Belle Haven Country Club in Alexandria, Virginia. He began an active role in the National Capital Club Managers Association and was elected president. He continued his education and earned his certified club manager (CCM) designation and his certified hospitality educator (CHE) designation through the Club Managers Association of America (CMAA). He stayed at Belle Haven Country Club for eight years, but wanted to live closer to sunny beaches in a warmer climate.

An opportunity at the prestigious Belleair Country Club in Belleair, Florida, was brought to Shaughnessy's attention by John Sibbald, a top recruiter in the club industry, and in 1997 Ed Shaughnessy accepted the position of general manager/chief operating officer at the Belleair Country Club. He continued his education, earning his M.B.A. in International Hotel and Tourism Management from Schiller International University, where he now teaches a variety of hospitality-related courses. Shaughnessy is still active with the CMAA and serves on the Club Foundation Allocation Committee. This committee reviews scholarship and grant applications and recommends the awarding of funds to promote education. He also serves as the ethics chair for the Florida Chapter of the CMAA.

Shaughnessy believes that there are two stages in life—growth and decay—and that we are all in one of these stages. For him, to be in the growth stage is preferred in life. He believes we are all given the choice to change our environment, and he enjoys catering to those with the highest expectations. It appears that people will always recognize and be willing to pay for great value and quality. Meticulous attention to detail and proactively providing what customers desire before they have to ask is the key to success.

No two days are the same or predictable for a general manager. One day you could be developing a strategic plan, the next you may be invited to fly on a private Lear jet to see the Super Bowl. You have to make a conscious effort to balance work and family life. A general manager should remember that although you can enjoy many of the same privileges as the elite, you are still an employee and must always set an exemplary role as a professional. A general manager's people skills are very important, as well as having a comprehensive understanding of financial statements.

The challenge for the future is finding talented and service-oriented people who are needed to exceed the constantly increasing expectations of sophisticated and discriminating club members. Shaughnessy discovered some time ago that it may be necessary to grow one's own talent among his employees, and this gives him the confidence that he will be ready to serve his customers well. Shaughnessy has a high concern for the welfare of his loyal and dedicated employees. They could lose their jobs if the club is mismanaged. These people and their families count on him to operate the club efficiently. He also recognizes that he must take proactive steps to ensure the growth and success of his club. With two waterfront golf courses, a marina, and the amenities of a full-service country club, Ed Shaughnessy is taking steps to be sure he positions the club for continued success.

second, *third*, and so on, may be used. Alternatively, vice presidents may be assigned to chair certain committees, such as membership. Board members usually chair one or more committees.

Committees play an important part in the club's activities. If the committees are effective, the operation of the club is more efficient. The term of committee membership is specified, and committee meetings are conducted in accordance with Robert's Rules of Order, which are procedural guidelines on the correct way to conduct meetings. Standing committees include the following: house, membership, finance/budget, entertainment, golf, green tennis, pool, and long-range planning. The president may appoint additional committees to serve specific functions commonly referred to as ad hoc.

The treasurer obviously must have some financial and accounting background because an integral part of his or her duties is to give advice on financial matters, such as employing external auditors, preparing budgets, and installing control systems. The general manager is responsible for all financial matters and usually signs or cosigns all checks.

It is the duty of the secretary to record the minutes of meetings and take care of club-related correspondence. In most cases, the general manager prepares the document for the secretary's signature. This position can be combined with that of treasurer, in which case the position is titled secretary–treasurer. The secretary may also serve on or chair certain committees.

The CMAA has reexamined the role of club managers, and because of ever-increasing expectations, the role of the general manager has changed from the traditional managerial model to a leadership model. (This is discussed in more detail in Chapter 14.) The new CMAA model is based on the premise that general managers or COOs are more responsible for operating assets and investments and club culture.

The basic level of competency required of a general manager or COO is management of club's operations, which includes

CMAA Code of Ethics

We believe the management of clubs is an honorable calling. It shall be incumbent upon club managers to be knowledgeable in the application of sound principles in the management of clubs, with ample opportunity to keep abreast of current practices and procedures. We are convinced that the Club Managers Association of America best represents these interests and, as members thereof subscribe to the following Code of Ethics.

We will uphold the best traditions of club management through adherence to sound business principles. By our behavior and demeanor, we shall set an example for our employees and will assist our club officers to secure the utmost in efficient and successful club operations.

We will consistently promote the recognition and esteem of club management as a profession and conduct our personal and business affairs in a manner to reflect capability and integrity. We will always honor our contractual employment obligations.

We shall promote community and civic affairs by maintaining good relations with the public sector to the extent possible within the limits of our club's demands.

We will strive to advance our knowledge and abilities as club managers, and willingly share with other Association members the lessons of our experience and knowledge gained by supporting and participating in our local chapter and the National Association's educational meetings and seminars.

We will not permit ourselves to be subsidized or compromised by any interest doing business with our clubs.

We will refrain from initiating, directly or through an agent, any communications with a director, member, or employee of another club regarding its affairs without the prior knowledge of the manager thereof, if it has a manager.

We will advise the National Headquarters, whenever possible, regarding managerial openings at clubs that come to our attention. We will do all within our power to assist our fellow club managers in pursuit of their professional goals.

We shall not be deterred from compliance with the law, as it applies to our clubs. We shall provide our club officers and trustees with specifics of federal, state, and local laws, statutes, and regulations to avoid punitive action and costly litigation.

We deem it our duty to report to local or national officers any willful violations of the CMAA Code of Ethics.

Source: The author gratefully acknowledges the professional courtesy of the Club Managers Association of America.

private club management, food and beverage, accounting and financial management, human and professional resources, building and facilities management, external and governmental influences, management, marketing, and sports and recreation (see Figure 10–1).

The second tier of the model is mastering the skills of asset management. Today's general manager or COO must be able to manage the physical property, the financial well being, and the human resources of the club. These facets of the manager's responsibilities are equally as important as managing the operations of the club.

The third and final tier of the new model is preserving and fostering the culture of the club, which can be defined as the club's traditions, history, governance, and vision. Many managers or COOs intrinsically perform this function; however, it is often an overlooked and underdeveloped quality. A job description for club manager is given in Figure 10–2. The club management competencies are shown in Figure 10–3. Additionally, you can see an example of the overall organization of a country club in Figure 10–4.

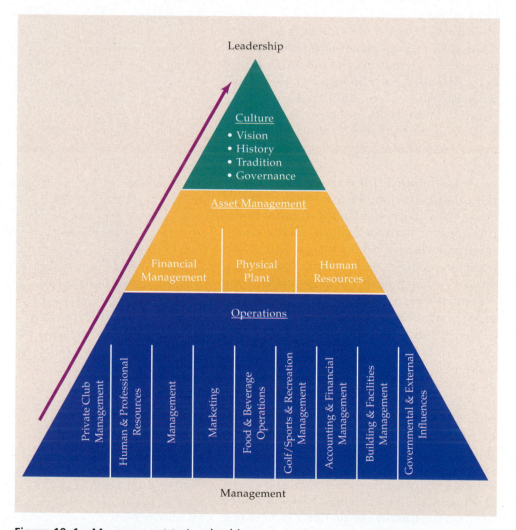

Figure 10–1 • Management to Leadership.

I. **Position:** General Manager

II. **Related Titles:** Club Manager; Club House Manager

III. **Job Summary:** Serves as chief operating officer of the club; manages all aspects of the club including its activities and the relationships between the club and its board of directors, members, guests, employees, community, government, and industry; coordinates and administers the club's policies as defined by its board of directors. Develops operating policies and procedures and directs the work of all department managers. Implements and monitors the budget, monitors the quality of the club's products and services, and ensures maximum member and guest satisfaction. Secures and protects the club's assets, including facilities and equipment

IV. **Job Tasks (Duties):**

1. Implements general policies established by the board of directors; directs their administration and execution

2. Plans, develops, and approves specific operational policies, programs, procedures, and methods in concert with general policies

3. Coordinates the development of the club's long-range and annual (business) plans

4. Develops, maintains, and administers a sound organizational plan; initiates improvements as necessary

5. Establishes a basic personnel policy; initiates and monitors policies relating to personnel actions and training and professional development programs

6. Maintains membership with the Club Managers Association of America and other professional associations. Attends conferences, workshops, and meetings to keep abreast of current information and developments in the field

7. Coordinates development of operating and capital budgets according to the budget calendar; monitors monthly and other financial statements for the club; takes effective corrective action as required

8. Coordinates and serves as ex-officio member of appropriate club committees

9. Welcomes new club members; meets and greets all club members as practical during their visits to the club

10. Provides advice and recommendations to the president and committees about construction, alterations, maintenance, materials, supplies, equipment, and services not provided in approved plans and/or budgets

11. Consistently ensures that the club is operated in accordance with all applicable local, state, and federal laws

12. Oversees the care and maintenance of all the club's physical assets and facilities

13. Coordinates the marketing and membership relations programs to promote the club's services and facilities to potential and present members

14. Ensures the highest standards for food, beverage, sports and recreation, entertainment, and other club services

15. Establishes and monitors compliance with purchasing policies and procedures

16. Reviews and initiates programs to provide members with a variety of popular events

17. Analyzes financial statements, manages cash flow, and establishes controls to safeguard funds; reviews income and costs relative to goals; takes corrective action as necessary

18. Works with subordinate department heads to schedule, supervise, and direct the work of all club employees

19. Attends meetings of the club's executive committee and board of directors

20. Participates in outside activities that are judged as appropriate and approved by the board of directors to enhance the prestige of the club; broadens the scope of the club's operation by fulfilling the public obligations of the club as a participating member of the community

V. **Reports to:** Club President and Board of Directors

VI. **Supervises:** Assistant General Manager (Club House Manager); Food and Beverage Director; Controller; Membership Director; Director of Human Resources; Director of Purchasing; Golf Professional (Director of Golf); Golf Course Superintendent; Tennis Professional; Athletic Director; Executive Secretary

Source: Club Managers Association of America.

Figure 10–2 • A Job Description for a Club Manager.

Source: The author gratefully acknowledges the professional courtesy of the Club Managers Association of America.

Types of Clubs

Country Clubs

Nearly all **country clubs** have one or more lounges and restaurants, and most have banquet facilities. Members and their guests enjoy these services

Private Club Management	*Accounting and Finance in the Private Club*	Contractors
History of Private Clubs	Accounting and Finance Principles	Energy and Water Resource Management
Types of Private Clubs	Uniform System of Accounts	Housekeeping
Membership Types	Financial Analysis	Security
Bylaws	Budgeting	Laundry
Policy Formulation	Cash Flow Forecasting	Lodging Operations
Board Relations	Compensation and Benefit Administration	
Chief Operating Officer Concept	Financing Capital Projects	*External and Governmental Influences*
Committees	Audits	Legislative Influences
Club Job Descriptions	Internal Revenue Service	Regulatory Agencies
Career Development	Computers	Economic Theory
Golf Operations Management	Business Office Organization	Labor Law
Golf Course Management	Long-Range Financial Planning	Internal Revenue Service
Tennis Operations Management		Privacy
Swimming Pool Management	*Human and Professional Resources*	Club Law
Yacht Facilities Management	Employee Relations	Liquor Liability
Fitness Center Management	Management Styles	Labor Unions
Locker Room Management	Organizational Development	
Other Recreational Activities	Balancing Job and Family Responsibilities	*Management and Marketing*
	Time Management	Communication Skills
Food and Beverage Operations	Stress Management	Marketing Through In-House Publications
Sanitation	Labor Issues	Professional Image and Dress
Menu Development	Leadership vs. Management	Effective Negotiation
Nutrition		Member Contact Skills
Pricing Concepts	*Building and Facilities Management*	Working with the Media
Ordering/Receiving/Controls/Inventory	Preventive Maintenance	Marketing Strategies in a Private Club Environment
Food and Beverage Trends	Insurance and Risk Management	
Quality Service	Clubhouse Remodeling and Renovation	*Source:* Club Managers Association of America.
Creativity in Theme Functions		
Design and Equipment		
Food and Beverage Personnel		
Wine List Development		

Figure 10–3 • The Club Management Competencies.

Source: The author gratefully acknowledges the professional courtesy of the Club Managers Association of America.

and can be billed monthly. The banquet facilities are used for formal and informal parties, dinners, dances, weddings, and so on, by members and their personal guests. Some country clubs charge what might seem to be an excessive amount for the initiation fee—as much as $250,000 in some cases—to maintain exclusivity.

Country clubs have two or more types of membership. Full membership enables members to use all the facilities all the time. Social membership allows members only to use the social facilities: lounges, bars, restaurants, and so on, and perhaps the pool and tennis courts. Other forms of membership can include weekday and weekend memberships.

City Clubs

City clubs are predominantly business oriented, although some have rules prohibiting the discussion of business and the reviewing of business-related documents in dining rooms. They vary in size, location, type of facility, and

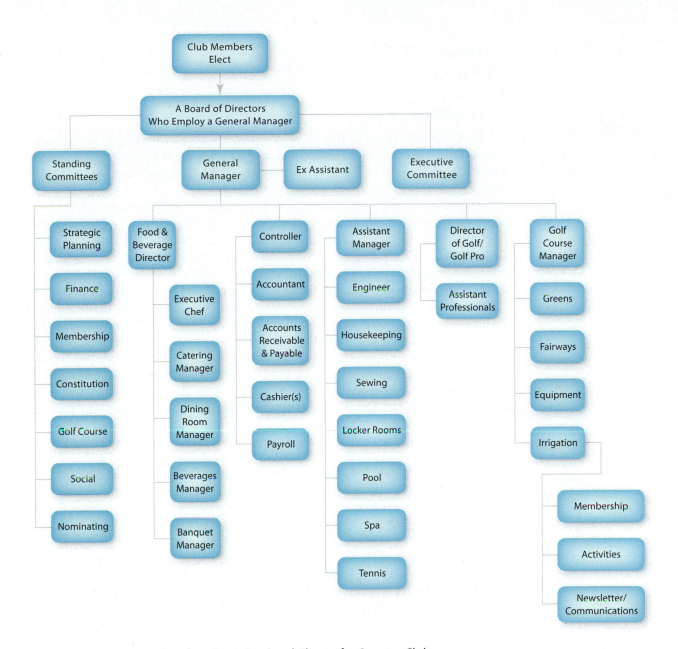

Figure 10–4 • An Example of an Organizational Chart of a Country Club.

services offered. Some of the older, established clubs own their own buildings; others lease space. Clubs exist to cater to the wants and needs of members. Clubs in the city fall into the following categories:

- Professional
- Social
- Athletic
- Dining

- University
- Military
- Yachting
- Fraternal
- Proprietary

Professional clubs, as the name implies, are clubs for people in the same profession. The National Press Club in Washington, D.C., the Lawyers Club in New York City, and the New York Friars Club for actors and other theatrical people in Manhattan are good examples.

Social clubs allow members to enjoy one another's company; members represent many different professions, yet they have similar socioeconomic backgrounds. Social clubs are modeled after the famous men's social clubs in London, such as Boodle's, St. James's, and White's. At these clubs, it is considered bad form to discuss business. Therefore, conversation and social interaction focus on companionship or entertainment unrelated to business.

The oldest social club in the United States is thought to be the Schuylkill Fishing Company of Pennsylvania, also known as the Fish House, founded in 1732. To ensure that the Fish House would always be socially oriented rather than business oriented, it was formed as a men's cooking club, with each member taking a turn preparing meals for the membership. Other social clubs exist in several major cities. The common denominator is that they all have upscale food and beverage offerings and club managers to manage them.

Athletic clubs give city workers and residents an opportunity to work out, swim, play squash and/or racquetball, and so on. Some of the downtown athletic clubs provide tennis courts and running tracks on the roof. Athletic clubs also have lounges, bars, and restaurants at which members may relax and interact socially. Some athletic clubs also have meeting rooms and even sleeping accommodations. The newest feature is known as the executive workout. This begins with a visit to the steam room, followed by a trip to the Jacuzzi, then the sauna, a massage, and a nap in the resting room before showering and returning to work.

Dining clubs are generally located in large city office buildings. Memberships are often given as an inducement to tenants who lease space in the office building. These clubs are always open for lunch and occasionally for dinner.

University clubs are private clubs for alumni. University clubs are generally located in the high-rent district and offer a variety of facilities and attractions focusing on food and beverage service.

Military clubs cater to both noncommissioned officers (NCOs) and enlisted officers. Military clubs offer similar facilities, as do other clubs for recreation and entertainment and food and beverage offerings. Some military clubs are located on base. The largest membership club in the country is the Army Navy Country Club in Arlington, Virginia. The club has more than 7,000 members, 54 holes of golf, two clubhouses, and a host of other facilities. Many of the military clubs in recent years have given over their club management to civilians.

Yacht clubs provide members with moorage slips, where their boats are kept secure. In addition to moorage facilities, yacht clubs have lounge, bar, and dining facilities similar to other clubs. Yacht clubs are based on a sailing theme and attract members with various backgrounds who have sailing as a common interest.

Fraternal clubs include many special organizations, such as the Veterans of Foreign Wars, Elks Lodges, and Shriners. These organizations foster camaraderie and often assist charitable causes. They generally are less elaborate than are other clubs, but have bars and banquet rooms that can be used for various activities.

Proprietary clubs operate on a for-profit basis. They are owned by corporations or individuals; individuals wanting to become members purchase a membership, not a share in the club. Proprietary clubs became popular with the real estate boom in the 1970s and 1980s. As new housing developments were planned, clubs were included in several of the projects. Households pay a small initiation fee and monthly dues between $30 and $50, allowing the whole family to participate in a wide variety of recreational activities.

Clearly, the opportunities for recreation and leisure abound. The goal must be to achieve a harmony between work and leisure activities and to become truly professional in both giving and receiving these services. The next few years will see a substantial increase in the leisure and recreational industries.

FOCUS ON RECREATION

Hospitality and Recreation: Inextricably Intertwined

Bart Bartlett, Ph.D., Associate Professor and Associate Director School of Hospitality Management, The Pennsylvania State University

Americans have more leisure time than ever before, and as leisure time has grown, leisure activities have evolved and grown as well. As this chapter points out, opportunities today for recreation and for careers in recreation management are vast and multifaceted. These include positions in commercial recreation (resorts, themed resorts, the ski industry), in non-commercial recreation (federal or state parks and community recreation), in clubs and sports venues, and in recreation with special populations.

Although the focus of this text is hospitality management, in many situations, recreation and hospitality go hand in hand. When a ski trip incorporates recreation on the slopes with food and beverage services in the lodge or when a hotel guest uses the hotel's business services and the spa, recreation and hospitality are both involved. When a convention center hotel provides rooms, food, and beverage; coordinates meetings and breakout sessions; and also organizes recreation and group activities during the conference, hospitality and recreation begin to merge. In fact, because our guests' total experience often involves a combination of lodging, food and beverage, and recreation, we do not want to distinguish but instead want to ensure guest satisfaction by seamlessly integrating these different elements into the total package.

As growth in leisure travel continues to outstrip growth in business travel, the growing leisure travel market will create an increasing emphasis on recreation as an integral part of hospitality. Furthermore, though hospitality and recreation may involve different emphases, the critical customer focus and customer service skills that we love about our industry are common to all aspects of hospitality and recreation.

Resorts and resort hotels are the prototypical combination of hospitality and recreation. A mega-resort such as Walt Disney World provides an ideal example of a venue that integrates hospitality and recreation skills and services. On a Disney vacation, a family may enjoy lodging and food and beverage services provided by hotel staff and management trained in hospitality, go into the park itself to enjoy attractions and shows arranged and managed by a recreation specialist, take a break to enjoy foodservice provided by a hospitality provider, and at the end of the day enjoy dinner provided by the hospitality staff and entertainment or dancing arranged by a recreation professional.

The golf industry provides other examples. At a typical golf club, the director of golf operations is primarily involved with managing recreation activities, including scheduling and supervising play, course maintenance, and the pro shop. The clubhouse manager, meanwhile, is responsible for hospitality functions, including food and beverage operations, catering events, and membership. If either were missing, the club simply could not meet guests' and members' overall expectations.

Finally, because cruise ships are essentially floating resort hotels with many features of land-based resorts, both hospitality and recreation are required. On a cruise ship, the purser and food and beverage manager are responsible for hospitality functions, while the cruise director provides recreation programming. Both are critical parts of the cruise experience, thus providing the all-around good time guests desire and deserve.

Through this text, you are learning about hotels, restaurants, and managed services and about the knowledge and skills involved in managing these operations. This chapter talks about recreation and the opportunities to apply your hospitality skills in recreation settings. Across the spectrum, from business travelers to family vacationers, from golfing outings to business banquets, from backcountry adventures to haute cuisine dining, from white-sand Caribbean beaches to black diamond ski slopes, customer service and a focus on customer satisfaction are constants, and both hospitality and recreation skills are critical to providing a memorable guest experience. The commonalities in settings, service, and focus on guest satisfaction indicate that hospitality and recreation are indeed inextricably intertwined!

Sustainable Golf Course Management

The golf course industry recognizes sustainable development as it is referenced by the Environmental Protection Agency (EPA) and the United Nations, which indicates that it "meets the needs of the present without compromising the ability of future generations to meet their own needs."[56] In an effort to appear sustainable, some courses call themselves "green." This is vague. However, it is not vague to say that a course engages in water-quality protection through the responsible use of all inputs, such as nutrients and pesticides.

The EPA gives a basic rundown of sustainability on their web site. The Environmental Institute for Golf gives information on sustainable golf management practices (www.eifg.org). Sustainable practices include the following:

- Reducing energy use especially during the peak times (a utility company's bill is much higher for consumption during peak times)
- Holding departments accountable for their energy consumption budgets by breaking down the bills by departments
- Recycling: from aluminum cans in the clubhouse to grass clippings on the course to motor oil from the golf carts[57]

Golf course facilities are prime candidates for reducing or reusing waste: As landfill disposal costs rise, recycling becomes even more important. Golf courses can improve their sustainability by improving grass and plant selection and by using well water and organic fertilization.

▶ Check Your Knowledge

1. Name all the types of clubs discussed here and briefly describe their functions.
2. List the important duties of a club manager.
3. Describe the operations of a country club.

Noncommercial Recreation

Noncommercial recreation includes voluntary organizations, campus, armed forces, and employee recreation, as well as recreation for special populations.

Voluntary Organizations

Voluntary organizations are nongovernmental, nonprofit agencies, serving the public at large or selected elements with multiservice programs that often include a substantial element of recreational opportunity. The best-known voluntary organizations include the Boy Scouts, Girl Scouts, YMCA, YWCA, and YM-YWHA.

In the early 1900s, YMCAs began to offer sporting facilities and programs. The Ys, though nonprofit, were pioneers in basketball, swimming, and weight training. Later, commercial health clubs also began to evolve, offering men's and women's exercise. As the sports and fitness movement grew, clubs appealed to special interests. Now clubs can be classified as follows: figure salons, health clubs, bodybuilding gyms, tennis clubs, rowing clubs, swim clubs, racquetball centers, or multipurpose clubs.

A DAY IN THE LIFE OF MARGIE MARTIN

Sales & Marketing Director, TPC Tampa Bay

The TPC Network was established by the PGA TOUR to provide the ultimate host venues for TOUR events—with services and amenities that met the highest standards of professional golf. Not only do the principles of excellence apply to the TOUR professionals playing our courses, they also apply to our members and guests who enjoy every aspect of our clubs. Across the country, TPC courses let golfers truly live the PGA TOUR life—by walking the same fairways as their heroes, teeing off from the very spots where history has been made, and enjoying every club detail exactly as the pros do. TPC Tampa Bay is proud to carry this brand name. As the former home of a Champions TOUR event for 21 consecutive years, TPC Tampa Bay is an industry leader in delivering exceptional golf experiences.

As Sales & Marketing Director, I oversee all aspects of Tournament and Membership Sales at TPC Tampa Bay. On the tournament side of things, I field calls from companies near and far, charity organizations, and even golf groups to assist with organizing golf events for groups as small as 12 players or as large as 144 players. I provide pricing and generate proposals, follow up and book golf events, and then keep in close contact with event organizers by managing a calendar of over 100 golf outings annually.

As a daily fee facility, we also offer membership options that provide value access to our golf course. I provide information to prospective members, assist with the membership process, and continue to keep in touch with members on a regular basis. I manage the communication to our members through our bi-weekly e-Blast that promotes events and activities at the Club. I also manage all general communications with our members at large.

Lastly, my favorite responsibility is putting a face with the name—TPC Tampa Bay. I provide that warm contact point for our local business partners promoting our local community and city as a whole to incoming travelers and convention groups. I participate in networking associations via the Convention & Visitors Bureau and act as a liaison for the TPC brand name that we so proudly carry. I truly enjoy all aspects of my job and enjoy the fact that when people visit TPC Tampa Bay, we are delivering a positive experience to their life. It's been said, "You can't have a bad day of fishing." I'd like to think the same is true of golf.

A multipurpose club has more exclusive recreation programs than a health club does. Leagues, tournaments, and classes are common for racquet sports, and most clubs offer several types of fitness classes. Some innovative clubs offer automatic bank tellers, stock market quote services, computer matching for tennis competition, auto detailing, laundry and dry cleaning services, and wine-cellar storage.

Club revenue comes from membership fees, user fees, guest fees, food and beverage sales, facility rental, and so on. Human resources account for about 66 percent of expenses at most clubs.

It is amazing to realize that in the center of a city there may be several voluntary organizations, each serving a particular segment of the population. Richard Kraus writes that a study of the city of Toronto which examined various land uses and leisure programs in the city's core found the following organizations: a Boy's Club, a mission, the Metropolitan Association for the Mentally Retarded, a Catholic settlement house, a day care center, an Indian center, a YMCA and YWCA, a service center for working people, a Chinese center, a Ukrainian center, and several other organizations meeting special needs and interests. These were all in addition to public parks, recreation areas, and 19 churches.

Campus, Armed Forces, and Employee Recreation

Campus Recreation

North America's colleges and universities provide a major setting for organized leisure and recreational programs with services involving millions of participants each year. The programs include involvement by campus recreation offices, intramural departments, student unions, residence staffs, or other sponsors. People spend much of their leisure time participating in a wide variety of organized recreational activities, such as aerobics, arts and crafts, the performing arts, camping, and sports. Recreation and fitness workers plan, organize, and direct these activities in local playgrounds and recreation areas, parks, community centers, health clubs, fitness centers, religious organizations, camps, theme parks, and tourist attractions. Increasingly, recreational and fitness workers are also found in workplaces, where they organize and direct leisure activities and athletic programs for employees of all ages.

The various recreational activities help in maintaining good morale on campus. Some use recreational activities such as sports or orchestras or theater companies as a means of gaining alumni support. Students look for an exciting and interesting social life. For this reason, colleges and universities offer a wide range of recreational and social activities that may vary from campus to campus.

Armed Forces Recreation

It is the official policy of the Department of Defense to provide a well-rounded welfare and recreational program for the physical, social, and mental well being of its personnel. Each service sponsors recreational activities under the auspices of the Morale, Welfare and Recreation (MWR) program, which is executed under the Installation Management Command. MWR activities are provided to all military personnel and civilian employees at all installations.

MWR programs include the following types of activities:

- Sports, including self-directed, competitive, instructional, and spectator programs
- Motion pictures
- Service clubs and entertainment
- Crafts and hobbies
- Youth activities for children of military families

- Special interest groups such as aero, automotive, motorcycle, and powerboat clubs, as well as hiking, skydiving, and rod and gun clubs
- Rest centers and recreation areas
- Open dining facilities
- Libraries

Recreation is perceived as an important part of the employee benefits package for military personnel, along with the G.I. Bill, medical services, commissaries, and exchanges.

Employee Recreation

Business and industry have realized the importance of promoting employee efficiency. Human resource experts have found that workers who spend their free time at constructive recreational activities have less absenteeism resulting from emotional tension, illness, excessive use of alcohol, and so on. Employee recreation programs may also be an incentive for a prospective employee to join a company. So, remember to ask for a signing bonus if you are a softball star and the company you are about to join wants to win the tournament!

In the United States and Canada, almost all the leading corporations have an employee recreation and wellness program. Some companies include recreation activities in their team-building and management-development programs.

Recreation for Special Populations

Recreation for special populations involves professionals and organizations that serve groups such as those with mental illness, mental retardation, or physical challenges. In recent years, there has been increased recognition of the need to provide recreational programs for special populations. These programs, developed for each of the special population groups, use therapeutic recreation as a form of treatment.

One sports program for people with disabilities that has received considerable attention in recent years is the Special Olympics, an international year-round program of physical fitness, sports training, and athletic competition for children and adults with intellectual disabilities. The program is unique because it accommodates competitors at all ability levels by assigning participants to competition divisions based on both age and actual performance.[58]

Today, the Special Olympics serve more than 4.4 million individuals worldwide and reach more than 170 countries. Among the 32 competitions and sports are track and field events, aquatics, gymnastics, figure skating, basketball, volleyball, soccer, softball, floor hockey, bowling, cross-country skiing, and wheelchair events. The National Recreation and Park Association and numerous state and local agencies and societies work closely with the Special Olympics in promoting programs and sponsoring competitions.[59]

Trends in Recreation and Leisure

Courtesy of Dr. Greg Dunn, Senior Lecturer & Managing Director, University of Florida, Eric Friedheim Tourism Institute

- *Rides and Attractions.* Attractions are moving toward more live, hands-on, and interactive features to provide a more personal and lifelike look and feel. Guests want to have more control over the experience.[60] Rides and attractions are constantly being developed that are geared toward the hottest pop culture movies, games and icons, replacing the outdated themes from yesterday. The most popular theme parks are always looking to make their hit attractions bigger and better.

- *Fitness Centers.* Declining membership and interest in golf has made it necessary to increase the size, scope, and quality of club facilities with state-of-the-art fitness centers featuring a wider array of indoor and outdoor recreational sports amenities, including built-in climbing walls and full body fitness classes (yoga, Pilates, Barre, Zumba, CrossFit, etc.).[61] There is also a general shift toward lowering membership and green fees and increasing services offered. The interest in health and wellness has also resulted in a shift toward healthier food and beverage options in club restaurants.

- *Reinvestment Leading to Increased Competition.* Nearly every major attractions and entertainment company is re-investing in their product to keep their service offering fresh for new and repeat visitors. Universal Orlando's the Wizarding World of Harry Potter, Walt Disney World Resort's "Frozen," and SeaWorld Orlando's Antarctica are some of the new and unique mega-attractions competing for both locals' and tourists' attention. Other notable new attractions are SeaWorld's Explorer's Reef and LEGOLAND® Florida and LEGOLAND® California Resort. As the economy continues to improve, so will the trend toward new investment in one-of-a-kind, must-see attractions.

- *Blurring the Lines.* Theme park and entertainment companies are blurring the lines in new product and program development. What traditionally used to be a theme park, water park, or nature park experience are now park experiences that combine elements of each. For instance, parks are now integrated with animal habitats, such as Cheetah Run Animal Encounter at Busch Gardens and TurtleTrek at SeaWorld Orlando. Theme park operators continue to provide compelling experiences that engage consumers and encourage repeat visits.

- *VIP Experiences.* As more and more customers seek personal and customized recreation and attraction experiences, limited availability VIP programs and behind-the-scene experiences are increasingly in demand. Examples of theme park VIP offerings include private guided tours, front-of-the-line ride privileges, valet parking, reduced theme park admission, reserved show seating, character or equity dining and autographs, all-day dining options, souvenir ride or character photos, and animal interactions and feeding. Attractions operators will also offer a broad range of interactive tour options and price levels for behind the scenes tours, up-close encounters with select animals, keeper for a day programs, coaster experience tours, and summer camps and sleepovers in the parks.

- *Shopping Entertainment Parks*. Following in the footsteps of the Mall of America, attractions developers continue to look for ways to combine elements of a theme park, shopping mall, and entertainment into one venue. Indoor theme parks are being created, combining retail pleasures with activities and rides. In some instances, new entertainment attractions are focusing on the baby boomlet market segment by targeting children, teens, young adults, and families. New family-based concepts are popping up, such as entertainment centers in malls, mini golf courses, and child-friendly themed restaurants.

- *National and State Parks*. National and state parks have long been a staple for nature enthusiasts to visit and enjoy, but by working with hospitality concessionaires and partners, parks are investing in services and facilities and promoting their locations for weddings, family reunions, corporate functions, and other similar experiences.

Career Information

Theme Parks

The operation of a theme park includes countless occupations. SeaWorld, The Walt Disney Company, and others have excellent programs for employment during college. These programs provide information on career development. Upon graduation, careers may follow a number of paths. Graduates may start in any number of levels: operations management, marketing and sales, human resources, food service, planning and development, or information systems, to name but a few.

An internship is one of the best ways to get involved in the theme park industry. An internship provides valuable work experience and is a great way to learn more about various areas of the industry. Interns are very appealing to potential employers. If you are a college student who is interested in spending a summer working for one of America's premier companies, visit the Disney College Program web site.

Remember, someone has to run the Smithsonian museums and the national parks and Walt Disney World. All of these attractions have several departments, all with management ladders that can be climbed at varying speeds. Apart from the main attractions, there are careers in accounting, marketing, maintenance, and service, in addition to professional positions for entertainers, historians, and curators. Salary levels for graduates with experience are about $30,000, and for mid-level managers in the larger attractions, salary levels are about $80,000–$120,000.[62]

Clubs

Club managers and hotel managers share many of the same responsibilities. They are in charge of preparing budgets and forecasting future sales; monitoring restaurants on the property and various internal departments, such as human resources; and making sure maintenance work is done properly. They are responsible for the overall well being of the club. The CMAA (www.cmaa.org) gives club managers certification and other membership benefits, such as professional development and networking. Its web site is worth a visit.

Club management is different from hotel management in that guests at a club are members and feel like and sometimes behave like owners because they pay a lot of money to join the club. Because of this, many feel a stronger tie to the club and therefore expect a higher level of service.

Of the many types of clubs within the club management industry, the most predominant are golf, country, city, athletic, and yacht. Country clubs are the most common. They are typically based on outdoor activities. Golf is the main draw, but other sports such as tennis and swimming are also popular. Some country clubs also offer their members a variety of classes and social activities. They typically have a lounge and/or restaurant on the property, as well. Country clubs can be private or semiprivate. If a country club is private, its facilities are only available to members; a semiprivate club offers some services to nonmembers. There is no one definite career path when it comes to club management. However, most people make the transition to club manager from positions in kitchen or bar management (see Figure 10–5). It is rare that employees move from areas such as accounting to become club managers. Depending on the level of experience, one might start out as an assistant banquet or dining room manager and then progress to a position as catering manager or assistant clubhouse manager. The next step occurs according to the amount of time in these positions, as well as the quality of the experience. For example, four to six years in a club that has a gross income of $1.5 million in food and beverage sales would most likely lead to a club management position.

Club managers do not keep regular hours. They work long hours when the club is busy, and fewer hours when the club is slow. Club managers usually create their own schedules according to fluctuations in activity. On average, they typically work five or six days a week, 10 hours a day. Most entry-level club management positions have set salaries that range from $27,000 to $30,000. Entry-level positions are usually not subject to

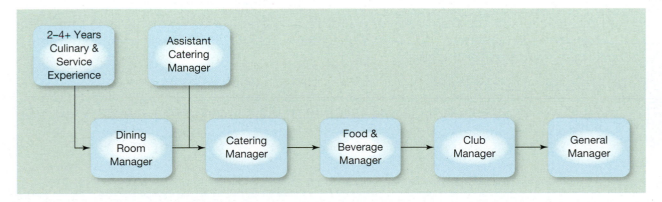

Figure 10–5 • A Career Path in Club Management.

negotiation. Mid-level position salaries, however, can be negotiated until an agreeable sum is met. The actual salary depends on the amount of experience the employee has and the strength of his or her references. The best aspect of working as club manager is that the environment and facilities are usually top notch. Managers typically have access to the club's facilities and receive meals. ClubCorp is one of the largest corporate owners of clubs, operating more than 200 country clubs, business clubs, and golf resorts. Recent expansions in corporate ownership have made it slightly easier to enter the club management profession.

If you are serious about a career in club management, you should join the local student chapter of the CMAA. CMAA meetings are a great place for networking to find a summer job or an internship. The experience you gain during your college tenure will provide you with the knowledge you need to begin your career in the recreation and leisure industries. Excellent opportunities for advancement come frequently. Club managers also often receive bonuses based on performance. These bonuses range from 5 to 15 percent of the manager's base salary of more than $100,000 annually. The highest paid country club manager makes about $1 million annually.

The following are web sites where you can gather more information:

ClubCorp: www.clubcorp.com

Club Managers Association of America: www.cmaa.org

National Park Service: www.nps.gov

National Club Association: www.nationalclub.org

CASE STUDY

Service Proposal for Guests

You recently joined the front desk of a nice resort hotel in New England, and your hotel manager has complimented you on your guest service ability. She has asked you to develop a walking/jogging trail for the guests.

Discussion Question

1. What would be some of the key elements to consider in developing a proposal for your hotel guests?

CASE STUDY

Overpopulation of National Parks

Our national parks are under serious threat from a number of sources, including congestion resulting from overvisitation, consequent environmental degradation, and pollution.

There are too many people and too many vehicles in the most popular national parks. Many visitors bring their city lifestyle, leaving garbage lying around, listening to loud music, and leaving the trails in worse shape.

Discussion Question

1. List the recommendations you have for the park superintendents to help save the parks.

Summary

1. Recreation is free time that people use to restore, rest, and relax their minds and bodies. Recreational activities can be passive or active, individual or group activities.

2. Recreational activities range from cultural pursuits such as museums or theaters, to sports or outdoor recreation such as amusement parks, community centers, playgrounds, and libraries. These services involve various levels of government.

3. National parks preserve exceptional lands for public use, emphasizing the protection of their ecosystems and endangered plant and animal species and honoring historical sites. Two of the best known of the current 407 parks in the United States include Yellowstone and Yosemite.

4. Today, city governments are increasingly expected to provide recreational facilities such as golf courses, swimming pools, picnic areas, and playgrounds as a community service.

5. Commercial recreation—for example, theme parks, clubs, and attractions—involves a profit for the supplier of the recreational activity.

6. Clubs are places where members gather for social, recreational, professional, or fraternal reasons. There are many different types of clubs such as country clubs and city clubs categorized according to the interests they represent to their members.

7. Noncommercial recreation includes governmental and nonprofit agencies, such as voluntary organization, campus, armed forces, and employee recreation, and recreation for special populations, such as the physically challenged.

Key Words and Concepts

city clubs
club management
commercial recreation
country clubs
government-sponsored recreation
heritage tourism

leisure
national park
National Park Service
National Register of Historic Places
noncommercial recreation
recreation

recreation for special populations
recreation management
theme parks
transient occupancy tax (TOT)
voluntary organizations

Review Questions

1. Define recreation and its importance to human wellness. What factors affect an individual's decision to participate in recreational activities?
2. Describe the origin of government-sponsored recreation in consideration of the origin and purpose of national parks.
3. Briefly describe the difference between commercial and noncommercial recreation.
4. Briefly explain the purpose of a theme park and the purpose of clubs.
5. Explain the concept of recreation for specific populations.

Internet Exercises

1. Organization: **Prestonwood Country Club**
   Summary: Prestonwood is a full-service country club that offers activities and fine food.
   (a) What kinds of activities are offered at the Prestonwood Country Club?

   (b) Parents may wish to take their kids on vacations. In these situations, what might this country club offer those kids?

Apply Your Knowledge

1. Create your own personal recreation goals and make a plan to reach them.
2. Describe the features of commercial versus noncommercial recreation.

Suggested Activities

1. On the Internet, research the history of Mardi Gras. Write a one-page description of the event and its cultural roots.
2. Look up your favorite theme park on the web. Think about what kind of position you would like to have at the park. If the site has job listings, tell whether any of them appeal to you.

Endnotes

1. Personal correspondence with Jay Sullivan, August 4, 2007.
2. Wikipedia, *Recreation*, http://en.wikipedia.org. Search for "recreation" (accessed November 15, 2011).
3. "Nathaniel Hawthorne at BrainyQuote," *BrainyQuote.com*, http://www.brainyquote.com. Search for Nathaniel Hawthorne quotes (accessed November 15, 2011).
4. This section draws on information supplied by the National Parks Service.
5. This section draws on information supplied by the National Parks Service.
6. National Park Service, *Backcountry Recreation Management*, http://www.nps.gov. Search for "backcountry roles" to view this page (accessed May 10, 2011).
7. Ibid.
8. National Park Service, *Budget*, http://www.nps.gov. Search for "budget request for 2014" to view these numbers (accessed July 29, 2014).
9. National Park Service, *Cape Lookout National Seashore: Management*, http://www.nps.gov. Search for "Cape Lookout" to view more information on Cape Lookout National Seashore (accessed May 10, 2011).
10. Ibid.
11. National Park Service, *Budget*, http://www.nps.gov. Click on Frequently Asked Questions to learn more (accessed May 10, 2011).
12. Wikipedia, *Recreation*, http://en.wikipedia.org. Search for "recreation" (accessed November 15, 2011).
13. Personal correspondence with Knott's Berry Farm, April 2006.
14. Knott's Berry Farm, Inside the Park, http://www.knotts.com. Click on Things to Do (accessed November 15, 2011).
15. Astrid Dorothea Ada Maria Kemperman, *Temporal Aspects of Theme Park Choice Behavior*, (Eindhoven University of Technology, 2000), http://alexandria.tue.nl/extra2/200013915.pdf (accessed November 15, 2011).
16. IAAPA.org. Amusement Park and Attractions Industry Statistics, http://www.iaapa.org. Search for "Amusement Park Industry Information" (accessed on February 12, 2015).
17. Todd D. MacCartney, *Excerpt from Walt Disney World Made Simple*, http://travelassist.com. Click on TravelASSIST MAGAZINE, and then click on the "Walt Disney World *Made Simple*" link (accessed November 15, 2011); Randy Bright, *Disneyland: Inside Story* (New York: Abraus, 1987), 33.
18. DIS, *Magic Kingdom*, http://www.wdwinfo.com. Go to Walt Disney World, Theme Parks, and then click on Magic Kingdom (accessed January 25, 2015).
19. DIS, *Epcot Future World*, http://www.wdwinfo.com. Go to Walt Disney World, Theme Parks, click on Epcot, and then click on Future World (accessed November 15, 2011).
20. DIS, *Epcot World Showcase*, http://www.wdwinfo.com. Go to Walt Disney World, Theme Parks, click on Epcot, and then click on World Showcase (accessed November 15, 2011).
21. DIS, *Disney's Hollywood Studios*, http://www.wdwinfo.com. Go to Walt Disney World, Theme Parks, and then click on Hollywood Studios (accessed January 25, 2015).

22. Atlas Cruises and Tours, *Walt Disney World Vacation Packages*, www.atlastravelweb.com/waltdisney worldpackages.shtml (site now discontinued).

23. Wikipedia, *Universal Studios Hollywood*, http://en.wikipedia.org. Search for "Universal Studios Hollywood" (accessed November 18, 2007).

24. NBC Universal, *Our History*, http://www.nbc universal.com. Click on Our History (accessed November 15, 2011).

25. Wikipedia, *SeaWorld Parks & Entertainment*, http://en.wikipedia.org. Search for "SeaWorld Parks & Entertainment" (accessed November 25, 2013).

26. Water Country USA, *Busch Gardens and Water Country USA 2015 Media Kit*, http://www.water countryusa.com. Click on Media Room, and then click on Media Kit (accessed November 15, 2011).

27. Discovery Cove, *General Park Information*, http://discoverycove.com. Click on Planning & Itineraries, and then click on General Park Information (accessed November 15, 2011).

28. Hershey's, *About the Hershey Company*, http://www.thehersheycompany.com. Click on About Hershey's, and then click on Hershey's History (accessed November 15, 2011).

29. Dollywood, *Learn More About Dolly Parton's Dollywood*, http://www.dollywood.com. Click on About Us (accessed November 15, 2011).

30. Wikipedia, *Dollywood*, http://en.wikipedia.org. Search for "Dollywood" (accessed January 29, 2015).

31. Wikipedia, *Legoland*, http://en.wikipedia.org. Search for "Legoland" (accessed November 15, 2011).

32. Ibid.

33. Gatorland, *History*, www.gatorland.com. Click on The Park link at the bottom of the page (accessed November 15, 2011).

34. Wikipedia, *Wet 'n Wild Orlando*, http://en.wikipedia.org. Search for "Wet 'n Wild Orlando" (accessed November 15, 2011).

35. Association of Zoos & Aquariums, *Home Page*, www.aza.org (accessed January 29, 2015).

36. San Diego Zoo, *About San Diego Zoo Global*, www.sandiegozoo.org. Search for "about the San Diego Zoo" (accessed November 15, 2011).

37. Wikipedia, *Hua Mei*, http://en.wikipedia.org. Search for "Hua Mei" (accessed September 19, 2009).

38. Smithsonian National Zoological Park, *About Us*, http://nationalzoo.si.edu. Click on About Us (accessed September 19, 2009).

39. Ibid.

40. National Aquarium, *In the Community*, www.aqua.org. Click on In the Community (accessed September 19, 2009).

41. Ibid.

42. National Park Service, *National Register of Historic Places Program: About Us*, www.nps.gov. Go to Working with Communities, click on National Register of Historic Place, and then click on About Us (accessed September 19, 2009).

43. Wikipedia, *Battle of the Alamo*, http://en.wikipedia.org. Search for "Battle of the Alamo" (accessed November 15, 2011).

44. Grand Ole Opry, *Backstage Tours*, http://www.opry.com. Click on Backstage Tours (accessed November 15, 2011).

45. The Smithsonian Institution, *About*, www.si.edu. Click on About Us (accessed November 15, 2011).

46. Ibid.

47. Ibid.

48. Field Museum, *Our Mission*, http://fieldmuseum.org. Click on Our Mission (accessed June 2, 2015).

49. Wikipedia, *Field Museum of Natural History*, http://en.wikipedia.org. Search for "Field Museum of Natural History" (accessed November 15, 2014).

50. Ministry of Culture, Education and Religious Affairs, *The Unification of the Archaeological Sites of Athens*, www.yppo.gr. Go to Major Projects and click on Unification of the Archaeological Sites of Athens (accessed January 20, 2009).

51. Wikipedia, *Athens*, http://en.wikipedia.org. Search for "Athens" (accessed November 15, 2011).

52. Central Intelligence Agency, *The World Factbook*, http://www.cia.gov. Search for "Vatican City" (accessed May 15, 2015).

53. John R. Walker, *Introduction to Hospitality Management*, 3rd ed. (Upper Saddle River, NJ: Pearson, 2010), 553–554.

54. Ibid.

55. Interview with Kurt Allen, General Manager, Marineland Dolphin Adventure, Miami, June 9, 2011.

56. UN Documents: Gathering a Body of Global Agreements, "Our Common Future, Chapter 2: Towards Sustainable Development," http://www.un-documents.net/index.htm. Search for "Our Common Future, Chapter 2: Towards Sustainable Development" (accessed June 2, 2015).

57. Golf Course Superintendents Association of America, "Environment: Recycling a Central Part of Golf's Sustainability Efforts," http://www.gcsaa.org. Search for "golf sustainability" (accessed November 15, 2014).

58. Special Olympics, *Changing Attitudes*, http://www
.specialolympics.org. Go to What We Do and click
on Changing Attitudes (accessed November 15,
2011).

59. Special Olympics, "Wh___ __ __," http://www
.specialolympics.org. ___
(accessed January 25, ___

60. Jack Rouse Associates___
Park Trends (and Wh___
Learn from Them)," I___
http://www.jackrous___

Theme-Park-Trends-and-What-Museums-Can-Learn-
from-Them.cfm (accessed January 2, 2015).

61. Johnson, Kelly. "Country Clubs Try to Get Out
of the Rough." *American City Business Journals:
Sacramento Business Journal*, http://www.biz
___ ___ Search for "Country clubs try to get
___ (accessed March 17, 2015).
___ ll Lupfer, CEO of the Florida
___ ation, June 9, 2011.

One of the most significant developments in the hospitality industry during the past three decades has been the astounding growth of the casino industry and its convergence with the lodging and hospitality industries. With its rapid expansion in North America and throughout the world, new opportunities have been created for hospitality careers within casino resorts.

Gaming Entertainment

While the gaming entertainment industry is a global industry, there are five types of legal gambling in the Unites States. This includes charitable gaming, commercial casinos, lotteries, Native American gaming, and parimutuel gaming. Some form of legal gaming exists in 48 of the 50 states, with commercial casinos representing the largest part of the domestic gaming market. While gaming revenues vary by the state, the industry contributes billions of dollars in tax revenue to these local governments on an annual basis. The gaming entertainment industry has seen development not only in the United States, but also internationally, particularly in the Asian destinations of Macau and Singapore. The size and scope of the global gaming industry are expected to reach $117.9 billion dollars in 2015.

When a customer places a bet in any type of gaming activity and the casino guest wins the game, he or she receives a cash payout; if the guest loses the game, the money is wagered. The total amount of the bets is called the handle, and the net amount spent by the guest is called the win by the gaming entertainment industry.

What is the difference between gambling and gaming? Gambling is playing a game of risk for the thrill of the action and the chance of making money. True gamblers spend a great deal of time learning and understanding a favorite game of risk and enjoying the subtle attributes, and, in particular, they find an enjoyable challenge in trying to beat the house, or win more than they lose from a casino. A gambler has little interest in anything other than a casino floor and the games it offers. It is true that of the nearly 40 million visitors who go to Las Vegas, the approximately 27 million people who go to Atlantic City, and the hundreds of thousands who frequent other casino operations, they love the green felt table, the whirling roulette wheels, the fall of the chips, the lottery-like game of keno, and the thrill of the game. The rows of colorful slot machines sounding out musical tones and flashing lights, the distant sounds of someone hitting the jackpot, and the ringing bells and shouting guests create an environment of excitement and anticipation that can be found only on the casino floor. The gaming industry has exploded from just two jurisdictions in 1976 to some form of legal gambling in 48 states.

Not long ago, the presence of slot machines or blackjack tables was all that was needed to lure visitors. However, with the rapid spread of casinos through North America, this is no longer true. The competitive nature of casino business has forced the creation of a bigger, better product to meet the needs of its guests. This product, gaming entertainment, has evolved over the past decade.

Games of risk are only part of the total package of entertainment and leisure time activities found in gaming entertainment. Gaming entertainment serves a customer base of social gamblers, customers who play a game of risk as a form of entertainment and social activity, thus combining gambling with other activities during their visits. Social gamblers, by this definition, are interested in many gaming entertainment amenities and take part in many diverse activities during a stay. Gaming entertainment refers to the casino gaming business and *all* its aspects, including hotel operations, entertainment offerings, retail shopping, recreational activities, and other types of operations, in addition to wagering on the gaming floor. The heart of gaming entertainment has been dubbed the "entertainment megastore" with thousands of rooms; dynamic, interesting exterior architecture; and nongaming attractions.

Gaming entertainment is the business of hospitality and entertainment with its core strength in casino gaming. According to this definition, a gaming entertainment business always has a casino floor area that offers various games of risk that serve as the focal point for marketing to and attracting guests. Next in importance to the guests are high-quality food and beverage operations.

Gaming entertainment is one of the last hospitality concepts to support the full service, tableside gourmet restaurant, in addition to the lavish buffet offerings that many casino locations offer. The number of foodservices is wide and diverse—from signature restaurants featuring famous chefs to ethnic offerings to quick service, franchised outlets. The gambling entertainment industry offers unlimited career opportunities in restaurant management and the culinary arts that were unheard of just a decade ago.

Gaming entertainment also goes hand in hand with the lodging industry because hotel rooms are part of the package. Full service hotels are part and parcel of gaming entertainment. Rooms, food and beverage, convention services, banquet facilities, health spas, recreation, and other typical hotel amenities support gaming entertainment. Most of the largest and complex hotels in the world are found in gaming entertainment venues, a number of which are described in detail later in this chapter.

Gaming entertainment offers a place where guests can gamble (the casino floor), eat and drink, sleep and relax, and maybe do some business. But there is much more: the entertainment ranges from live performances by the most famous entertainers to production shows that use high-tech wizardry. Gaming entertainment includes theme parks and thrill rides, museums, and cultural centers. The most popular gaming entertainment destinations are designed around a central theme that includes the hotel and the casino operations. Unlike its predecessor, the casino business, the gaming entertainment business has numerous revenue-generating activities. Revenue is produced from casino wins, or the money that guests spend on the casino floor. The odds of any casino game are in favor of the house, some more than others. A casino win is the cost of gambling to guests, who often win over the house in the short run and are therefore willing to place the bets and try their luck.

Nongaming revenue comes from sources that are not related to wagering on the casino floor. As the gaming entertainment concept continues to emphasize activities other than gambling, nongaming revenue is increasing in importance. This is what gaming entertainment is truly about: hospitality entertainment based on the attraction of casino.

What form does gaming entertainment take? The mega-resorts of Las Vegas and Atlantic City garner the most publicity as the meccas of the gaming entertainment industry. However, there are smaller properties throughout Nevada, and other casino-based businesses in 48 states and seven Canadian provinces. These casinos take the form of commercially operated businesses, both privately and publicly held. Some are land based, meaning casinos are housed in regular buildings. Other are in river boats that cruise up and down a river or on barges moored in water and do not cruise, called dockside casinos. Casinos are also operated by Native American tribes on their reservations and tribal lands. These are land-based casinos and are often as complex as any operations in Las Vegas. Gaming entertainment is also popular on cruise ships.

There is a strong support for gaming in the marketplace as an entertainment activity. Patrons are required to be 21 years of age to gamble in the United States, and research shows that more than a third of Americans have visited a casino in the last 12 months, and 32 percent of them have actually gambled in those 12 months. According to the market research, more than 85 percent of U.S. adults say casino entertainment is acceptable for themselves or others. Eighty-six percent of Americans report having gambled at least once.

Commercial casinos account for 36 percent of gaming revenue. Indian casinos and state lotteries tie for second place at 26 percent. The demographic makeup of the typical gaming entertainment guest has remained consistent during the past several years. In comparison to the average American, casino players tend to have higher levels of income and education and are more likely to hold white collar jobs. The customer profile of Las Vegas is a younger demographic of guests who spend money in search of total entertainment experience.

LEARNING OBJECTIVE 1
Outline the history of modern casinos.

Historical Review of Gaming Entertainment

The precise origin of gambling is still unknown today. However, according to Chinese records, the first official account of the practice dates back to as far as 2300 B.C.E.! The Romans were also gamblers. They placed bets on chariot races, cockfights, and on dice throwing. This eventually led to problems: gambling, or games of chance, was banned except for during the winter festival of Saturnalia.[1]

In the seventeenth century, casino-style gaming clubs existed in England and Central Europe. A public gambling house was legalized for the first time in 1626 in Venice, Italy, and one gambling establishment, in Baden-Baden, Germany, opened in 1948 and is still open today.[2] Soon the upper class met in so-called casinos to socialize and gamble. In the first half of the nineteenth century, organized gaming casinos started to develop.

Las Vegas—the name alone summons images of neon lights, extravagant shows, outrageous performers, and bustling casinos where millions are won and lost every night. Las Vegas is all of that and much more. This city represents the American dream. Since the state of Nevada legalized gambling in 1931, Las Vegas has been transformed into one of the most elaborate cities in the world and one of the hottest vacation spots.

The gaming entertainment business in the United States has its roots in Las Vegas. From the early 1940s until 1976, Nevada, and predominantly Las Vegas, had a monopoly on the gaming entertainment business. Casinos had no hotel rooms, entertainment, or other amenities. The hotels that existed were just places to sleep when guests were not on the casino floor.

Las Vegas is rich with tales of Benjamin Hymen Siegelbaum, better known as Bugsy Siegel. Siegel was born February 28, 1906, in Brooklyn, New York, to a poor Jewish family. It is said that he began his career at a very young age by extorting money from pushcart peddlers. Eventually he turned to a life of bootlegging, gambling rackets, and murder-for-hire operations. In 1931, Bugsy was one of four men who executed Giuseppe "Joe the Boss" Masseria. Several years later, he was sent out West to develop rackets. In California, Siegel successfully developed gambling dens and ships. He also took part in narcotics smuggling, blackmail, and other questionable operations. After developing a nationwide bookmaking wire operation, Siegel moved on to build the well-known Flamingo Hotel and Casino in Las Vegas. The casino ended up costing over $6 million, which forced Siegel to skim profits. Siegel subsequently died in Beverly Hills in June 1947, hit by a barrage of bullets fired through the window of his home. The day after his death, three mobsters walked into the Flamingo Hotel and announced that they were the new owners.[3]

During the 1970s, Atlantic City was in an impoverished state, with high rates of crime and poverty. In an effort to revitalize the city, New Jersey voters, in 1976, approved casino gambling in Atlantic City.[4] Later casino gambling was legalized in the state of New Jersey by the Casino Control Act. The state looked to the casino industry to invest capital, create jobs, pay taxes, and attract tourists, thus revitalizing the economy and creating a financial environment in which urban redevelopment could occur.

The act initiated a number of fees and taxes specific to the casino hotel business that would provide revenues to support regulatory costs, fund social services for the disabled and the elderly through the state, and provide investment funds for the redevelopment of Atlantic City. The Casino Control Act created the Casino Control Commission, whose purpose was not only to ensure the success and integrity of the Atlantic City casino industry, but also to carry out the object of reversing economic futures of cities.[5]

Sensing that the objectives of the Casino Control Act were being fulfilled in New Jersey and wanting similar benefits for its state, but not wanting land-based casino gambling, Iowa legalized riverboat casinos in the early 1990s. Illinois, Mississippi, Louisiana, Missouri, and Indiana followed suit in rapid succession. As the casino industry spread throughout the United States and Canada, its competitive nature created a need for what is now known as *gaming entertainment* and added to non casino attractions. Gaming entertainment is, therefore, a natural evolution of the casino industry.

Native American Gaming

In *California v. Cabazon Band of Mission Indians, et al.* (1987), the Supreme Court decided 6 to 3 that once a state has legalized any form of gambling, the Native Americans in that state have the right to offer and self-regulate the same games without government restrictions. This ruling came about after the state of California and the county of Riverside sought to impose local and state regulations on card and bingo clubs operated by the Cabazon and Morongo bands of Mission Indians. The Court clearly recognized the rights of tribes with regard to certain gaming activities.[6]

Congress, which some observers say was alarmed by the prospect of losing control over tribal gaming, responded to these court decisions by passing the Indian Gaming Regulatory Act of 1988 (IGRA). The IGRA provides a framework by which games are conducted in a way that protects both tribes and the general public. For example, the IGRA outlines criteria for approval of casino management contracts entered into by tribes and establishes civil penalties for violation of its provisions. The act is clearly a compromise in that it balances the rights of sovereign tribal nations to conduct gaming activities on their lands with the rights of the federal and state governments to regulate activities within state and federal borders.[7] The three objectives of the IGRA are as follows:

1. Provide a statutory basis for the operation of gaming by Native American tribes as a means of promoting tribal economic development, self-sufficiency, and strong tribal governments;
2. Provide a statutory basis for the regulations of gaming by the Native American tribe adequate to shield it from organized crime and other corrupting influence;
3. Establish an independent regulatory authority, the National Indian Gaming Commission (NIGC), for governing activity on Native American lands.[8]

IGRA defines three different kinds, or classes, of Native American gaming activities:

- Class I gaming, consisting of social games played solely for prizes of minimum value or traditional forms of Native American gaming
- Class II gaming, consisting of bingo, games similar to bingo, and called games explicitly authorized by the laws of the state

- Class III gaming, consisting of all forms of gaming that are neither class I or class II gaming, and therefore including most of what are considered casino games.[9]

The significance of the definition of class III gaming activity is that it identifies the games that must be located in a state that permits such gaming for any purpose by any person, organization, or entity and are conducted in conformance with compacts that the states are required to negotiate "in good faith" with the tribes.

While the federal gaming law precludes state taxation, the tribes in several states have voluntary payments and also negotiated payments to state governments under certain circumstances. Often tribes give local government voluntary payments in recognition of services the tribe receives, and some pay revenues in exchange of permissions to maintain a casino gambling monopoly in a state. In Michigan, Connecticut, and Louisiana, tribes have agreed to make payments to the state as a part of their comprehensive compact for casino gambling. In almost all the states, the tribes make payments to the states for costs incurred by the states in regulating the casinos as provided in the negotiated agreements.

There are over 400 gaming facilities on reservation lands in 28 states, and Native American gaming has been one of the fastest growing sectors of gaming in the United States. Foxwoods Resort Casino in Ledyard, Connecticut, operated by the Mashantucket Pequot Indian Reservation, is one of the largest casinos in the United States with more than 6,300 slot machines and 380 table games.[10]

The Casino Resort: A Hospitality Buffet

Today, **casino resorts** are among the most visible hospitality businesses in the world. Twenty of the 30 largest hotels in the world are casino resorts on the Las Vegas Strip.[11] The size and scope of the global gaming industry are expected to reach $117.9 billion dollars in 2015. Those aiming for careers in hospitality, even if they have no special interest in working on the gambling side of the operation, may find themselves considering a position in a resort that has a casino, but also a full spread of lodging, food and beverage, entertainment, and retail offerings.

Even if you don't plan on working on the casino floor itself, a rudimentary understanding of the nature of gambling—and the specifics of casino gambling—is an essential tool for those who want to pursue careers in casino resorts. Today, many casino resort presidents and key executives have come up through the lodging or food and beverage side of operations; a solid understanding of what's happening in the casino—and how casino guests are different from other hospitality patrons—makes advancing through the ranks that much easier.

What Is Gambling?

In its broadest definition, **gambling** is the act of placing stakes on an unknown outcome with the possibility of securing a gain if the bettor guesses correctly.

To be considered gambling, an act must have three elements: something wagered (the bet), a randomizing event (e.g., the spin of slot reels or the flip of a card), and a payoff.

This broad definition of gambling includes many dissimilar activities: contests between animals (horse racing, cockfighting) and between humans (team and individual sports); lotteries; and games of chance played with cards, dice, and other randomizing elements. Some of the best-known games fall into the last category: poker, blackjack, and baccarat are played with cards, and craps with dice. Slot machines, which were originally mechanical (but now are electronic) devices, award prizes based on the random stopping of reels, are also popular, and are typically the most-played games in most casinos today.

How do casinos make money from gambling? The answer lies in the kind of gambling they offer. There are two basic categories of gambling: **social** gambling and **mercantile** (or commercial) gambling. Social gambling is conducted among individuals who bet against each other; mathematically, each player has the same chance of winning. Poker is a classic social game: Every player is drawing from the same deck and has the same opportunity to check, raise, or fold. Other social forms of gambling include dominoes and Mah Jongg.

In mercantile or commercial gambling, players bet against "the house," a professional gambler or an organization that accepts wagers from the general public. Mercantile games have a mathematical advantage for the casino, or a house edge that lets professionals profit from them while still offering fair games. All lotteries are mercantile games, and every game found on the casino floor is a mercantile game. There is a small guaranteed bias toward the house that, over time, ensures the casino will win more than it pays out.

The **house edge** is best explained by looking at the game of roulette, which features a wheel with 38 slots numbered 1–36, in addition to a single zero and a double zero. On each spin, a small ball falls into one of the 38 slots. If you bet "straight up" on a number, you win 35 units for each one unit you bet. So if you bet one dollar straight on, you'd end up with 36 dollars: the one dollar you staked, plus

A casino area with slot machines.

35 more. Since the wheel has a 1-in-38 chance of hitting any number, you should be paid off at a rate of 37:1, not 35:1. That extra two dollars is the house edge; it seems slight, but over time, it adds up.

The house edge is what makes casinos possible; without it, the only way to offer games of chance to the public that can generate an income would be to cheat. The house edge allows casinos to offer their customers honest games, fairly dealt, and still remain in business.

The game of poker is an interesting exception to the rule that all casino games have built-in house edges. Many casinos have poker rooms, in which players bet against each other using a table, cards, and a dealer supplied by the house. The casino has no direct stake in the outcome of each hand but instead takes a small percentage of each pot (the rake) to defray the costs of operating the room. Though it is a popular game, poker makes little money for casinos. Poker instead is offered as an amenity for those players who will also play straight-up mercantile games or for those who are visiting with slots or table games players. The house edge is a theoretical number; it describes the amount of money wagered (handle) that the casino should keep over time. For tables and slots, casinos track the hold percentage to better understand how well the casino is performing.

To understand the hold percentage, we need to understand two other terms: handle (or buy-in) and win. The **handle** is the total amount of money bet at a game. The **win** is the handle *minus* the money paid out on winning bets—essentially, what the casino keeps. The **hold percentage** is the percentage of the total handle that is retained as win. On slot machines, the hold percentage tracks very close to the theoretical house edge. On table games, however, the hold percentage is usually considerably higher than the house edge.

Though the games offered in casinos have a statistical bias toward the house, they are still games of chance. In the short run, players can get lucky and walk away with the house's money. In small-stakes games this isn't a problem, since the sheer number of bets taken tends to drive the hold percentage toward its historically expected value.

Games played for high stakes, such as baccarat, are different. Because there are large amounts of money being spread over fewer decisions, these games have a great deal of volatility; in a given month, the hold percentage for a baccarat game in a single casino can fluctuate wildly.

As a manager of a casino resort, it is important that you have an appreciation of the nature of volatility. Just because the casino department is reporting a net loss for a shift does

This resort on the Las Vegas Strip models itself after New York City.

Casino Win Defined

Let's say you buy into a roulette game for $100 in $1 chips. You place 100 even-money bets, winning 94 and losing 6. In this case, the following are true:

The handle is $100.
The win is $6.
The winning percentage is 6 percent.

This is very close to the theoretical house edge of 5.26 percent. But if you continued playing for another 100 bets, you might lose another 6. In this case, the handle would still be $100, but the win would be $12, and the hold percentage 12 percent.

not necessarily mean that the department is inefficient or incompetent; it may just be an expression of volatility. Over time, gaming wins will tend toward their historical average.

Managers also need to understand that, because of volatility, casinos are not like other hospitality businesses. A typical hotel, running at 95-percent occupancy for the weekend and with full restaurant bookings, will certainly make a profit. Because of volatility, however, even a busy casino can end up in the red for a shift, or even a weekend, if one high-stakes player has a run of good luck.

Comps: A Usual Part of an Unusual Business

Volatility isn't the only aspect of the casino business that makes it different from most other hospitality businesses. Comps are another area that set casinos apart.

Comps are complimentary goods and services offered to casino patrons in order to attract their business. Comps are found in virtually every casino, and any casino "guest of consequence" has expectations of receiving comps. Unlike in other hospitality operations, where comps are given primarily as part of service recovery to compensate for a customer service failure or other miscue, comps are distributed as a usual part of a casino's operation.

The value of comps varies; generally speaking, higher-producing players are given higher-value comps. For example, a small-stakes slot player might receive an offer for a discounted or free buffet; a baccarat-playing high roller, betting $10,000 a hand for several hours, might receive a full RFB (room, food, beverage) comp, with all expenses in the casino's most lavish accommodations paid for. Casino guests might also receive comps for entertainment or other gifts. Many slots players receive cash back when they reach certain play thresholds.

Casinos, with thousands of guests on any given day, rely on customer **loyalty programs** to track patron play. Patrons who wish to receive comps and other offers join the casino's player loyalty club (e.g., Caesars' Total Rewards, MGM Resorts' M life, Wynn Resorts' Red Card). Slot players insert the card they receive into the machine they are playing; the card then tracks money played and won. Table games players have a pit manager swipe their card, tracking their time of play and average bet size.

Casinos use the information they gain about a player's gambling patterns to offer him or her comps, based both on theoretical wins by the player and his or her expected levels of play. Most loyalty programs have tiered rewards structures, giving patrons an incentive to play more and unlock more rewards.

Loyalty programs are an essential part of casino marketing; many guests base the money they spend gaming upon where they receive the best comps. Good casino managers know they must send out good offers to qualified players. Casinos also use sophisticated software to monitor and deliver bonuses to slot patrons as they are playing on machines. Recently, some casinos have begun tracking and rewarding nongaming spending as well, a reflection of the broadening of the casino resort revenue stream. For example, some casinos offer rewards on dining, shopping, and even staying at their hotels.

HOW TO BUILD SUCCESSFUL LONG-TERM RELATIONSHIPS WITH CASINO RESORT CUSTOMERS

Courtesy of **Nicholas Thomas**, Assistant Professor and Director of the DePaul Center for Research and Education in Hospitality Leadership

I've been fortunate enough to work at three of the largest and most successful Las Vegas casino resorts. This experience has allowed me to interact with very diverse clientele from towns and cities from around the world. The gaming floor of a casino is buzzing with patrons enjoying the varied product offerings that most casino mega-resorts possess around the clock every day of the year.

These casino operators go to great lengths to attract and retain casino players. The first step in this process is often getting the player signed up for the casino players club, also referred to as a rewards program. Very similar to frequent customer programs at airlines or hotel chains, casinos use their player's club memberships to track, analyze, and market to their various players. In many cases, these clubs can track players across multiple casinos within the company's portfolio. For example, M life, the rewards program for MGM Resorts, tracks casino patron play at all 15 of their destination resort casinos. Similar programs exist with competing companies such as the Total Rewards program at Caesars Entertainment and the Wynn Las Vegas & Encore Red Card.

Traditionally, when joining one of these clubs, a player receives a membership card (similar in size to a credit card), which can be used to track play. When playing a slot machine, the card is inserted directly into the machine and can track how much money is spent and won, and for what duration the machine was played. Tracking play at casino table games, such as blackjack and roulette, is a little bit more hands on and requires a casino supervisor or host to monitor betting quantity, frequency, and duration. As a result of play, customers are tiered and awarded points and/or comps. To encourage this play, there are a myriad of ways that the casino markets to individual players. Casinos can send very specific marketing collateral customized to players' particular interests, via traditional mail or e-mail, in order to entice players to visit and play. For example, customers who are interested in country music may be invited to Las Vegas during the National Finals Rodeo held in the city every year. Some strategies also include sending promotional material to customers reminding them of how much they have won in the past, or how much someone from their town may have won recently.

When casino players reach a certain level of play, they are likely to be assigned a casino host. The casino host is a great resource in building a relationship with casino customers, and can usually be a wonderful tool to get players to visit and gamble. Casino hosts can encourage more gambling by providing comps to the customer in the form of discounted (or free) food, beverages, hotel rooms, show tickets, and other desirable incidentals. The more valuable a player is to a casino (valuable in terms of how much money is potentially gambled), the more comps a host could potentially extend. This may include the use of private jet travel to pick up players from their homes and bring them to the casino.

(Continued)

HOW TO BUILD SUCCESSFUL LONG-TERM RELATIONSHIPS WITH CASINO RESORT CUSTOMERS *(Continued)*

According to Dr. Lisa Thomas, a hospitality marketing researcher, slot tournaments create vibrant social scenes for customers to interact with each other, and of course, enjoy gambling. A slot tournament is held in a special roped-off area of the casino or in the casino's ballroom space. Event décor is used to enhance the slot tournament's specific theme around rows of identical slot machines programmed to generate high jackpots and point accumulation rates, which increases the excitement for the tournament experiences.

Slot tournaments are traditionally divided into several sessions with machines that start with a preset number of credits. Each time the spin button is hit, the maximum bet is deducted from the starting credits. The credits won are shown on a separate meter, with the player unable to replay those credits. Once the tournament session time limit is up, the machine will lock, and any original credits not played are lost. The goal is to accumulate the most points in the won meter during each of the slot tournament sessions.

Most slot tournaments end with a player award party, which increases the ability for casino hosts to strengthen their relationships with their slot clients. The top prize goes to the participant who accumulates the highest point total during the slot tournament's duration. Prizes can range from a few thousand to over several hundred thousand dollars. Customized tournament participation gifts are typically given to all participants as an event memento so that everyone walks away a winner. These events are often held in conjunction with national holidays (the Fourth of July), sporting events (the Super Bowl), or cultural festivities (Chinese New Year).

Types of Casino Operations

There are several different kinds of casino operations, operating on vastly different scales. At one end of the spectrum is the Nevada-style gaming tavern, which is a typical bar and restaurant that has less than 16 electronic gaming devices, usually bar-top video poker and slot machines. At the other is a fully developed casino resort, with (on average) a 100,000-square-foot casino that features thousands of slot machines and dozens of table games, approximately 3,000 hotel rooms, at least a dozen bars and restaurants, meeting and convention facilities, entertainment venues, retail shopping, and pool and spa facilities.

Between these two extremes, which are both found in Las Vegas, there are several other kinds of operations. Stand-alone casinos are not very common in the United States or elsewhere in the world. Where they are found, they usually consist of only slot machines; this type of operation might be called a slot *parlor.* In Europe, the Middle East, Africa, and South America, casinos located in hotels might be extremely small and ancillary to the general hospitality operation.

In the United States, casinos on Indian reservations can take many forms, from bingo parlors in prefabricated buildings to fully functional casino resorts with lodging, dining, and entertainment that are indistinguishable from resorts on the Las Vegas Strip. Some states allow gambling only on riverboats, which originally cruised the waterways but today are usually "boat in a moat" operations that are permanently moored and connected almost seamlessly with a hotel and resort facility. Other states allow slot machines at racetracks (called racinos), and in some cases these have evolved to include hotel and resort operations as well. Finally, many cruise lines have casinos as part of the amenities available to guests on their ships.

FOCUS ON CASINO RESORTS

Casino Resorts and Hospitality

David G. Schwartz, Director, Center for Gaming Research, University of Nevada, Las Vegas

Casino resorts combine virtually every strand of the hospitality business. They've come a long way since the dusty saloons of frontier Nevada and the grimy illegal slot routes and bookmaking operations of American cities. Today, funded by mainstream capital, staffed by trained hospitality managers, and promoted globally, there is little that one can't find in a major casino resort.

It's important to note that casino resorts are so all-inclusive because it makes good economic sense. Originally, most revenues were generated on the casino floor. Yet the nature of casino gambling—games that, over time, have a slight bias in favor of the house—demanded that casinos offer more than just gambling. To discourage spot play, in which a lucky player cashes out and leaves, casino resorts developed a number of attractions to lure and keep players near the casino. Lodging, food, beverage, and entertainment were offered as "loss leaders" to get players through the doors.

In the 1990s, following the opening of Steve Wynn's Mirage, the rules of the game changed. Though the old approach—offering loss leaders and focusing on gaming revenues—was profitable, there was more growth potential in a more balanced approach. Shifting the revenue center from exclusively gaming to also including rooms and particularly restaurants proved to be a lucrative decision. Guests got the chance to stay in more luxurious accommodations and sample a variety of dining experiences.

Now, major casino resorts earn most of their money from things other than gambling. But gambling is still central to their identity, and many high-value guests are primarily focused on gambling. Even if your job isn't directly on the gaming floor, it's important to remember that without gambling, the resort wouldn't exist.

At the same time, many smaller resorts still get most of their revenues from gambling, so managers of other departments may face an uphill battle for respect—and resources. If this is the case, it will be important to remind everyone that your department can help increase revenues, both by earning money itself and by contributing to an environment to which gamblers will flock.

At the end of the day, despite the sometimes obscure jargon and hard-to-figure-out gameplay, casino gambling is really no different from other hospitality operations: The idea is to help guests enjoy themselves. Guests pay for that privilege, and there are many other places where they can do so.

That's an important fact to remember: Today there are a wealth of choices for casino customers; any oversight or cut corner gives your customers an excuse to spend their money with your competition, who will gladly take it. A good casino manager, no matter what the department, will never lose sight of that fact, and will start and end each day with a single question: "What can I do to help my guests have a better time with us?" Anyone who can continue to come up with innovative but not budget-busting answers to this simple question will enjoy a long, successful career in the gaming and hospitality industry.

LEARNING OBJECTIVE 2
Describe the various components of modern casino hotels.

Components of Casino Resorts

The best example of the modern casino resort can be found on the Las Vegas Strip. These destination resorts are centered on casinos that have several types of games available:

- Slot machines
- Table games, including twenty-one (blackjack), craps, roulette, baccarat, and carnival games such as three-card poker
- Race and sports books, which accept wagers on horseracing and sporting events
- Poker rooms, where players bet against each other and where the house only keeps a portion of each pot
- Live keno games

In most parts of the United States, slot machines produce the bulk of the revenue; on the Las Vegas Strip, due to high-stakes table play, it is closer to a 50/50 split. Among table games, blackjack is most popular nationally, while on the Strip baccarat has recently become a favorite. In Macau casinos, nearly all revenue comes from high-stakes baccarat; slot machines are negligible.

Casino resorts also include the following components:

- Lodging (on average, 3,000 hotel rooms)
- Food and beverage outlets, ranging from fast food to gourmet eateries
- Entertainment venues, including lounges but also purpose-built theaters for Cirque du Soleil and similar spectaculars
- Retail shopping: several casinos have shopping esplanades or even attached malls (Caesars Palace, The Venetian, Planet Hollywood)
- Convention facilities, ranging from a few small rooms to the 2.25-million-square-foot Sands Expo and Convention Center connected to the Venetian and Palazzo hotels

- Nightclubs, which are an increasingly lucrative part of the casino resort package
- Pool and spa facilities, which may be branded as "dayclubs" with DJ entertainment and bottle service available in cabanas

Casino resorts in other jurisdictions may have some, but not all, of these features. For example, outside of Nevada, sports betting is currently illegal, so those casinos will have, at most, a race book. Most casinos outside of Las Vegas, with a few notable exceptions, have smaller hotel and entertainment components.

Gamblers playing poker at the Foxwoods Resort Casino in Mashantucket, Connecticut.

Evolution of Gambling and Casinos

LEARNING OBJECTIVE 3
Explain how casinos have been integrated into larger hospitality operations.

Gambling is among the oldest of human behaviors; archaeological evidence of gambling stretches back into prehistory, and purpose-built dice have been discovered at sites dating back to 7,000 years before the present. Gambling developed in nearly every ancient civilization of consequence and has been part of Western life since the days of Ancient Greece.

Casino resorts, as they are currently operated, are much younger, dating back only to 1941, though the casino industry has its antecedents in several earlier developments, both legal and illegal. Legal public gambling in casinos dates back to 1638, when the Great Council of Venice awarded a franchise for a single legal casino in that city. Though that casino was closed in 1774, other European states—mostly small, resource-poor jurisdictions—also permitted gambling, usually as part of a larger spa complex; spas were Europe's first true tourist destination, and gambling was considered an essential part of many European spa communities. By 1872, however, casino-style gambling had been banned in all European countries except in the tiny Mediterranean enclave of Monaco, whose Monte Carlo would grow wealthy on a decades-long monopoly.

In the United States, public gambling at cards and dice was legal intermittently during the nineteenth century in several states, including Louisiana, California, and Nevada, but by 1910 this kind of gambling—and playing at slot machines—had been outlawed everywhere in the United States. Both before and after the criminalization of all casino-style gambling, illegal gambling halls flourished in most of the major American cities.

Yet the tide soon turned toward legalization, at least in Nevada. When legislators authorized "wide open" commercial gambling there in 1931, the state was in the throes of the Great Depression. By allowing taverns and hotels to conduct games of chance, they hoped to increase tourism slightly. There was initially no state tax on gambling, and the economic impact was thought to be negligible. Reno and Las Vegas soon developed thriving downtown gambling districts, with small clubs offering slot machines and table games. These were usually simple, storefront operations with no real amenities.

The real creation of the modern casino came in 1941, with the opening of the **El Rancho Vegas**, the first casino resort on what would become the **Las Vegas Strip**. As a spa-like, self-contained destination with fine dining, entertainment, and gambling, the El Rancho Vegas appealed to casual tourists in a way that the smoky downtown gambling halls did not. Within a decade, a half-dozen other resorts joined the El Rancho Vegas, and the Las Vegas Strip was becoming a force.

These casinos were superior to gambling halls because, with rooms and a full range of amenities, they offered a diverse set of options for travelers–gamblers and nongamblers alike—and because they allowed casinos to keep visitors near the casino. Although in the short run the players might get lucky thanks to volatility, the longer they remained near the tables and slots, the more likely the casino was to end up with their money. Casinos in resorts therefore proved more profitable than stand-alone casinos, and they soon proliferated, particularly along the Strip.

Indian Gaming Regulatory Act codified the rules under which Indian tribes could open Las Vegas–style casinos with slot machines and bank games: To do so, the tribes needed to sign a compact, or treaty, with the state in whose land the reservation sat. Frequently, these compacts specified fees that tribes would remit to state governments, often pegged to slot machine revenues, but states had no power to tax tribes; these payments were instead the result of negotiation. As of 2010, over 200 tribes in more than 30 states have some form of gambling operation, with combined annual revenues of more than $25 billion.

Casinos opened elsewhere, as well. Major cities like Detroit (in 1996) legalized a limited number of casinos within their borders, partly to spur tourism, partly to prevent the outflow of gambling dollars to neighboring jurisdictions. States like West Virginia and Delaware balked at authorizing new casino development but legalized slot machines at racetracks, businesses that came to be known as racinos. The horseracing industry, which began to decline as track attendance fell in the 1970s, embraced the racino concept, and slot machines helped to stave off the demise of live racing in several states. In 2004, Pennsylvania authorized slot machines at racetracks, destination resorts, and urban slot parlors, signaling a further expansion of slot gaming. Gambling has proven to be a growth industry, even in areas of the country that have experienced an overall economic decline.

In addition, American-run casino operators have found that Asia is an even more lucrative market for casinos than the United States. Both Macau (concession awarded in 2002; first U.S.-owned casino opened in 2004) and Singapore (franchises awarded 2006; first U.S.-owned casino opened in 2010) have become casino powerhouses; since 2008, Macau's casino industry has become a leading gaming center with increasing revenues. In 2012, the total revenue from gambling at commercial casinos in the United States was $37.3 billion, not the highest it has been over the past 10 years, but a number that has risen almost $10 billion over a 10-year period.[12]

▶ Check Your Knowledge

1. Define the following:

    a. Handle

    b. Win

    c. House edge

    d. Hold percentage

    e. Volatility

2. Briefly describe why casino resorts are superior to stand-alone operations.

3. Explain the growth in casino gaming since the 1970s.

Working in a Casino Resort

LEARNING OBJECTIVE 4
Understand the basic principles of casino operations.

LEARNING OBJECTIVE 5
Discuss the different positions within the gaming industry.

Students of the industry who understand the multidisciplinary needs of the casino business find five initial career tracks in hotel operations, food and beverage operations, casino operations, retail operations, and entertainment operations.

Hotel Operations

The career opportunities in gaming entertainment hotel operations are much like the career opportunities in the full-service hotel industry, with the exception that food and beverage can be a division of its own and not part of hotel operations. The rooms and guest services departments offer the most opportunities for students of hospitality management. Because gaming entertainment properties have hotels that are much larger than nongaming hotels, department heads have a larger number of supervisors reporting to them and more responsibilities. Reservations, front desk, housekeeping, valet parking, and guest services can all be very large departments with many employees.

Food and Beverage Operations

Gaming entertainment has a foundation of high-quality food and beverage service in a wide variety of styles and concepts. Some of the best foodservice operations in the hospitality industry are found in gaming entertainment operations. There are many career opportunities in restaurant management and the culinary arts. As with hotel operations, gaming entertainment properties are typically very large and contain numerous food and beverage outlets, including a number of restaurants, hotel room service, banquets and conventions, and retail outlets. Many establishments support gourmet, high-end signature restaurants. It is not unusual to find many more executive-level management positions in both front- and back-of-the-house food and beverage operations in gaming entertainment operations than in nongaming properties.

Casino Operations

Casino operations jobs fall into five functional areas. Gaming operations staff includes slot machine technicians (approximately one technician for 40 machines), table-game dealers (approximately four dealers for each table game), and table-game supervisors. Casino service staff includes security, purchasing, and maintenance and facilities engineers. Marketing staff includes public relations, market research, and advertising professionals. Human resources staff includes employee relations, compensation, staffing, and training specialists. Finance and administration staff includes lawyers, accounts payable, audit, payroll, and income control specialists.[13]

The explosive growth of the gaming industry has increased the need for trained dealers skilled at working a variety of table games, including **blackjack**, **craps**, **roulette**, **poker**, and **baccarat**. Through the use of textbooks and videotapes combined with hands-on training at a mock casino, future dealers learn the techniques and fine points of dealing at classes offered by both colleges and private schools.

Retail Operations

The increased emphasis on nongaming sources of revenues in gaming entertainment demands an expertise in all phases of retail operations, from store design and layout to product selection, merchandising, and sales control. Negotiating with concession subcontractors may also be a part of the overall retail activities. Retail operations often support the overall theme of the property and can often be a major source of revenue; however, retail management careers are often an overlooked career path in the gaming entertainment industry.

Entertainment Operations

Because of the increased competition, gaming entertainment companies are creating bigger and better production shows to turn their properties into destination attractions. Some production shows have climbed in the million of dollars range and require professional entertainment staffs to produce and manage them. Gaming entertainment properties often present live entertainment of all sorts, with headline acts drawing huge audiences.

Casino management is hierarchical. At the top of the management structure, a property president or general manager is in charge of day-to-day operations. Internal audit and surveillance departments report directly to the president or to the casino's board of directors, bypassing the management hierarchy because of their role in maintaining controls over cash and procedures in the casino.

Below the casino president are the vice presidents (sometimes called directors) of different divisions of the casino: the casino itself; hotel; food and beverage; entertainment; marketing (for casino guests); sales (typically directed toward business travel and group sales); retail; various support functions, including finance, which include all casino cashiering operations; and security.

Within the casino, the vice president of gaming operations oversees a casino manager, who in turn oversees shift managers, one for each shift (day, swing, grave) of the casino's 24-hour day. The shift manager, in return, has authority over the managers on duty of each of the casino's departments, which may include slots, poker, keno, race and sports book, and casino hosts and marketing representatives, who work directly with high-value players, arranging comps and generally keeping them happy.

The slot department includes customer service representatives, who sign up players for the casino's loyalty program and technicians who keep the slot machines operational. Table games are organized into pits—clusters of about a dozen games—each run by a pit boss who reports directly to the casino shift manager. Below the pit boss, a floor person oversees between two and four games, while one or more dealers staff each table. The casino may have a high-limit room (also called a baccarat room) where high-stakes bets—as high as $50,000 per hand—are taken. The baccarat room frequently has its own manager who reports to the casino shift manager as well.

Other departments are managed similarly, with directors in charge of shift managers, who in turn oversee supervisors, who are then responsible for the performance of line employees.

The Mirage Effect

Since the 1990s, casino resorts on the Las Vegas Strip have seen their non-gaming operations become much more central to their bottom line. In 1993, Strip casinos earned nearly 60 percent of their revenues from the casino itself; by 2008, that number had fallen below 40 percent.[14] In the 1990s, operators enlarged and upgraded their room accommodations. Originally merely places for gamblers to seek respite from gambling, rooms became attractions in and of themselves, at least partially because convention travelers were willing to pay higher premiums for better and more comfortable accommodations. As a consequence, room accommodations have become a major revenue center.

The rooms aren't the only part of the Strip that's become a money generator. This is because in addition to paying more for higher thread-count sheets and designer finishes, Strip visitors have eagerly opened their wallets for gourmet cuisine, delivered to them in celebrity chef eateries.

In 1992, Wolfgang Puck opened Spago in The Forum Shops at Caesars. Puck, who had become famous with his restaurant of the same name in Los Angeles, brought a different sensibility to Las Vegas eating. Spago at Caesars proved successful, and a cohort of established chefs from Paris, New York, and San Francisco followed Puck to Las Vegas, leading to an explosion of both gourmet-dining opportunities for patrons and an increase in restaurant revenues for casinos.

The cost of entertainment has gone up, too, as headliner concerts and installed shows (Cirque du Soleil alone has eight) raised their production values and their prices. And with the growth of full-fledged shopping malls inside casinos, ranging from the Grand Canal Shoppes at the Venetian to the Miracle Mile Shops at Planet Hollywood, retail spending has climbed as well.

The ascendancy of nightclubs, ultra-lounges, and day clubs will further amplify the Mirage Effect. The nightclub trade, which skews to a demographic of 20- and 30-year-olds, represents a departure for Strip casinos, which traditionally considered 45-year-olds to be youngsters. Here, bottle service is the way of the future. Under this model, select patrons bypass the line and receive reserved tables along the dance floor in exchange for purchasing several bottles of liquor, at charges of up to $500 per bottle. By opening clubs and lounges along these lines, operators meet two objectives: They capture an extremely lucrative business, and they effectively orient new patrons to the casino.

Figure 11–1 shows the revenues generated by various aspects of casino resort operations.

Game	# of Units	Win Amount	Win %	Handle
Slot Machine	44,584	2,911,323	7.40	39,342,203
Table Games	2,781	3,384,579	12.56	26,947,285
Total Win		6,372,500	9.98	63,852,705

Slots detail

Game	# of Units	Win Amount	Win %	Handle
1 Cent	15,704	1,074,748	11.66	9,217,393
5 Cent	579	26,056	7.89	330,241
25 Cent	2,666	156,241	8.55	1,827,380
1 Dollar	3,454	286,281	6.40	4,473,141
Multi-Denom	20,611	1,190,174	5.84	20,379,691

Table games detail

Game	# of Units	Win Amount	Win %	Handle
Twenty-one	1,378	811,419	11.35	7,149,066
Baccarat	308	1,489,682	12.55	11,869,976
Craps	188	257,177	13.22	1,945,363
Roulette	259	292,715	17.97	1,628,909
3-Card Poker	138	104,588	31.82	328,686
Mini-Bacc	94	71,876	8.81	815,846
Let It Ride	43	25,172	24.97	100,809
Pai Gow	16	13,526	18.61	72,681
Pai Gow Poker	104	65,081	22.70	286,700
Keno	15	4,295	22.17	19,373
Bingo	3	1,921	8.59	22,363
Race Book	28	21,683	16.01	135,434
Sports Book	36	107,370	5.10	2,105,294
Poker tables	369	76,598	(rake only; no direct win)	

Figure 11–1 • The Average Strip Casino: Daily Revenues.

Sustainability in Gaming Entertainment

Sustainable initiatives are constantly gaining in popularity and prestige across the gaming industry. Gaming entertainment companies continue adapting their operations and practices to fit "green" standards. Many well-known companies in gaming entertainment are leading the way to establish sustainable initiatives as the standard practice in the industry, including Caesars Entertainment Corporation, which operates Harrah's, Caesars, and Horseshoe brands, along with Delaware North and Dover Downs Hotel & Casino.

One of the leading corporations in the gaming industry, Caesars Entertainment Corporation has undertaken a sustainable initiative in several areas of operation, including energy, waste and water conservation, as well as climate control. Caesars executives have urged their management teams to embrace a sustainable approach to their daily practices, designated "CodeGreen." This sustainable initiative involves the exchange of traditional incandescent lighting to a more resourceful energy conservative lighting, as well as ventilation controls in guest rooms, and throughout hotel and casino space in some of their larger properties. Select properties feature subsidized public transportation, habitat preservation fundraisers, recycling used oil, and composting waste products. Caesars plans to continue the future implementation of sustainable practices in select properties throughout the country.[15]

Recently, gaming entertainment companies have begun implementing sustainable initiatives into the initial construction and development of new properties. Delaware North, a well-known player in gaming industry operations has recently built a new property in Daytona Beach, Florida, which complies with all the necessary standards required to be a Leadership in Energy and Environmental Design (LEED) certified property. LEED employs a four-tier rating system for buildings, based on the level of sustainability applied during property development, and maintained upon completion. The level of certification is based on the areas of "sustainable site development, water savings, energy efficiency, materials selection, and indoor environmental quality." The Daytona property received silver certification, which is the second tier of the rating system, which followed in the footsteps of their previous sustainable site developed in West Memphis, Arkansas, in 2006.[16]

HospitalityGreen LLC, an environmental consulting firm, has taken on the task of creating a model for "green" standards that will set precedents for which existing and future initiatives will be measured. The company directed a property-wide assessment of Dover Downs Hotel & Casino's sustainable business practices in order to collect the necessary data required to provide an appropriate model. Dover Downs Hotel & Casino is one of the most noteworthy gaming and entertainment resorts in the Mid-Atlantic region. This AAA-rated Four Diamond property accepted the Silver Tier Certification Green Concierge (GC) award from HospitalityGreen in 2013.[17]

Career Information

The growth of the gaming industry has resulted in a variety of new job openings. People choose to work in the industry because it is known to place people first, whether they are employees or customers. The industry also has many opportunities for employees to learn new skills, which lead to growth and advancement in their careers.

Employees in the gaming industry may receive many tangible benefits. Most careers include impressive benefits packages and offer many career advancement opportunities. Casinos are known to hire from within, which

You also need to understand that because of the continuous operation of a casino, your work schedule will vary. It is not uncommon to work several straight 12-hour days, but the rewards for dedication and hard work can be very worthwhile: Casinos have many opportunities for advancement. Figure 11–2 shows an example of a career path in the gaming industry.

To see more of the types of jobs that are available in the gaming entertainment industry, go to **www.casinocareers.com**, where you can look up potential employers, available jobs, and areas of employment.

| Croupier | Gain Experience at All Tables | Section Supervisor | Assistant Section Manager | Game Manager | Floor Manager | Casino Manager |

Figure 11–2 • A Career Path in the Gaming Industry.

CORPORATE PROFILE

Caesars Entertainment Corporation

Harrah's Entertainment was founded in 1937 by William F. Harrah as a small bingo parlor in Reno, Nevada. The name changed to Caesars Entertainment Corporation in 2010. Today, Caesars is one of the largest gaming companies in the world, with a portfolio of nearly 40 casinos, which it owns or manages in three continents under the Harrah's, Caesars, and Horseshoe brand names.[1] Caesars has riverboat or dockside casinos, golf courses, and combination racetrack and casinos in several states, including Arizona, California, Illinois, Indiana, Iowa, Nevada, Louisiana, New Jersey, Mississippi, North Carolina, Ohio, Pennsylvania, and Missouri. Caesars grew by new property development, expansions, and acquisitions, and it now employs some 68,000 people, with a vision "to ensure Caesars is a respected leader in our industry and a trusted corporate citizen in the communities" where they operate.[2] Caesars is focused on building loyalty and value with its customers through a unique combination of guest service, excellent products, unsurpassed distribution, operational excellence, and technology leadership. The marketing strategy is designed to appeal to those who are avid players, especially those who play in more than one market.

[1]Caesars Entertainment, About Caesars, http://caesarscorporate.com/about-caesars/

[2]Caesars Corporate Citizenship Report, http://cetmeetings.com/corporate/wp-content/uploads/2014/10/CCR_Combined.04.pdf

Trends in the Gaming Entertainment Industry

Courtesy of Dr. Greg Dunn, Senior Lecturer & Managing Director, University of Florida, Eric Friedheim Tourism Institute

- *Loyalty Player Smartcards*. More casinos want players to use a ticket-voucher system, or a smartcard. Some of these systems are already in place for slot machines and video poker. A guest's winnings are not given in coins or tokens, but in a ticket that can then be inserted and played in other machines or redeemed for cash. This technology has become a way for casinos to reduce their cash inventories. The majority of gaming operations encourage all players to sign up and use their loyalty cards. Casinos can then track player participation and preferences for rewards and marketing purposes.

- *Universal Gaming Machines*. Major slot machine and video terminal manufacturers continue to develop more universally configurable game machines that can download several types of gaming software or play from a cloud configuration. Multiple types and varieties of games may be available, and players can choose from an assortment of gaming options to match their preferences. The universal gaming machines allow for more games to be available on a gaming floor, provides more options for players, and eliminates the need to constantly bring in new machines and get rid of the less popular machines since operators can just swap out game software when warranted.

- *New Generation of Gamblers*. Millennial and Generation X gamblers are much different than Baby Boomer and mature gamblers. The latest generations are known to seek higher levels of entertainment, are technologically savvy, less casino-brand loyal, and enjoy more complex games to enhance their entertainment value. Social media is also helping to shape the gaming landscape and guest experience. Millennials and Gen Xers have grown up with innovative gaming technology through connectivity—Facebook, Twitter, and Instagram allow for gaming experiences that can be personalized as well as socially interactive.

- *Candid Sky Camera Technology*. The "eye in the sky" is already in place and programmed to identify cheaters. However, as digital facial recognition technology becomes more and more advanced and sophisticated, these eye-in-the-sky cameras will be able to recognize, specifically, everyone from criminals to high rollers to regular gamblers. With the need for increased security, this opens doors for another pool of marketing data for the casino to analyze.

- *Emerging Markets*. As Las Vegas continues to develop into a hyper-entertainment destination and Atlantic City struggles to redefine itself from a gaming-only destination, casino operators are heavily pursuing emerging markets such as Asia. The potential growth stems from changes in consumer demographics, disposable income, and relaxation of government regulation on travel and in the gaming industry. Even though the Chinese government has been discouraging visitation of casinos and encouraging the Macau region to build new forms of entertainment for tourism, Macau still remains one of the most popular gambling destinations in the world. Japan is also getting closer to legalizing casinos.

- *More Than Just Gambling*. Gaming entertainment is depending less on casino revenue and more on room, food and beverage, retail, and entertainment revenues for its profitability and growth. The gaming entertainment industry and lodging industry are converging as hotel room inventory is rapidly expanding in gaming entertainment properties.

CASE STUDY

Negotiating with Convention Groups

Your convention sales department receives a call from a trip director for a large convention group. The group will use many function rooms for meetings during the day and will generate a substantial amount of convention services revenue. Likewise, the group's food and beverage needs are quite elaborate, so this will be good for the food and beverage department budget. However, the group is very sensitive concerning room price and is willing to negotiate the time of week for its three-night stay.

Discussion Question

1. What are the considerations that a gaming entertainment property must take into account when determining room rates for convention groups?

CASE STUDY

VIP

A frequent guest of the casino makes a last-minute decision to travel to your property for a weekend stay. The guest enjoys gambling as a leisure activity and is one of the casino's better customers. When he arrives at the casino, he is usually met by a casino host and is treated as a VIP due to his level of wagering at the blackjack tables. This guest is worth approximately $500,000 in casino win per year to the hotel. Due to his last-minute arrangements, however, the guest cannot notify a casino host that he is on his way to the hotel. Upon arriving, he finds a very busy registration desk. He must wait in line for 20 minutes, and when he tries to check in, he is told that the hotel is full. The front-desk clerk acts impatient when the guest says that he is a frequent customer. In a fit of frustration, the would-be guest leaves the hotel and makes a mental note that all casinos have similar odds at the blackjack table and that maybe another property will give him the respect he deserves.

Discussion Question

1. What systems or procedures could you institute to make sure this type of oversight does not happen in your property?

Summary

1. Gambling dates back to as far as 2300 B.C.E.
2. The first public gambling house was legalized for the first time in 1626 in Venice, Italy.
3. The gaming entertainment business in the United States has its roots in Las Vegas.
4. The Casino Control Act legalized gambling in New Jersey in 1976. This act led to the creation of the Casino Control Commission. The notion of gaming entertainment grew as states started to legalize other forms of non-land-based casino gambling.
5. In 1987, the Supreme Court decided that once a state had legalized any form of gambling, the Native Americans in that state had the right to offer and self-regulate the same games without government restrictions. Following that decision, Congress then passed the Indian Gaming Regulatory Act of 1988 (IGRA) in order to balance the rights of sovereign tribal nations with the rights of the federal and state governments.
6. There are three different classes of Native American gaming activities: Class I (games played solely for prizes of minimum value or traditional Native American activities), Class II (bingo or games similar to bingo), and Class III (all forms of gambling that do not fall under Class I or Class II).
7. Native American gaming has become one of the fastest growing sectors of gaming in the United States.
8. Many casino resort presidents and key executives have come up through the lodging or food and beverage side of operations.
9. Casino resorts include slots, table games, keno, race and sports books, and poker rooms as well as lodging, food and beverage outlets, entertainment venues, retail shopping, convention facilities, nightclubs, and pool and spa facilities.
10. The real creation of the modern resort casino came in 1941 with the opening of the El Rancho Vegas in Las Vegas.
11. The Gaming Control Board was created in the 1950s to regulate gambling as its popularity grew in Nevada. Different forms of casino gambling have since then opened in different states throughout the United States.
12. The casino industry is a growing international force that includes both gambling and more traditional hospitality elements. Large casino companies have started to expand their reach into the Asian market.
13. To manage a casino resort, it is necessary to understand the relationship between the casino and other departments in the operation, as well as ways that casinos are different from other businesses.
14. Casino gambling is strictly regulated by state governments, and the integrity developed over time by these regulations is necessary for the survival of the industry.
15. Nongaming revenue is increasing as a percentage of total casino resort revenue, and nongaming parts of casino resorts are gaining in prominence.
16. As Las Vegas continues to develop into a hyper-entertainment destination and Atlantic City struggles to redefine itself from a gaming only destination, casino operators are heavily pursuing emerging markets such as Asia. The potential growth stems from changes in consumer demographics, disposable income, and relaxation of government regulation on travel and in the gaming industry.

Key Words and Concepts

baccarat	gambling	mercantile
blackjack	handle	poker
casino resort	hold percentage	roulette
comps	house edge	social
craps	Las Vegas Strip	win
El Rancho Vegas	loyalty programs	

Review Questions

1. Briefly describe the history of legalized gaming in the United States.
2. What defines a gaming entertainment business?
3. Explain the attraction of gaming entertainment as a tourist.
4. Why is it necessary for strict regulations to be in force on the casino floor?
5. How are hotel operations in a gaming entertainment business different from hotel operations in a nongaming environment?

Internet Exercises

1. Organization: **Wynn Las Vegas**
   Summary: Located on the Las Vegas Strip, the Wynn Las Vegas has a lot to offer. From gaming and concerts, to hosting some of the biggest conventions, the Wynn Las Vegas will certainly keep you busy.

   (a) What are some of the gaming features that attract customers to the Wynn Las Vegas?

   (b) What are the benefits to the different packages available?

2. Pick a casino in Las Vegas and look it up on the Internet. What does it offer that sets it apart from other casinos in Las Vegas and from other casinos in the United States? In what areas is it similar to other casinos?

Apply Your Knowledge

1. Discuss how you could make a career in gaming entertainment.
2. Give examples of nongaming revenue.
3. Describe the Indian Gaming Regulatory Act of 1988 (IGRA). What did it do for Native Americans and their lands?

Suggested Activity

1. Research careers in the gaming entertainment industry. Are there more opportunities than you realized? What careers in the industry interest you the most?

Endnotes

1. History Extra, "How did the Romans celebrate 'Christmas'?" http://www.historyextra.com. Search for "Saturnalia" (accessed on May 1, 2015).
2. One for Gambling, *Complete History of Gaming: Casinos in Europe,* www.14g.com. Click on Casino, and then click on Casinos in Europe (accessed on May 1, 2015).
3. Wikipedia, *Bugsy Siegel,* http://en.wikipedia.org. Search for "Bugsy Siegel" (accessed on May 1, 2015).
4. Wikipedia, *Atlantic City, New Jersey,* http://en.wikipedia.org. Search for "Atlantic City" (accessed on May 1, 2015).
5. Ibid.
6. Julia Glick, "Cabazon Indian Leader Who Pursued Gaming Rights Dies," The Press-Enterprise, January 4, 2007 and Gaming Tribe Report National Indian Gaming Commission, July 6, 2011.
7. National Indian Gaming Commission, http://www.nigc.gov. Click on Laws & Regulations, and then click on Indian Gaming Regulatory Act (accessed on May 1, 2015).
8. Ibid.
9. Op.cit.
10. Library Index, "Casinos: Native American Tribal Casinos - The Story of Native American Casinos in Two States," http://www.libraryindex.com. Search for "Connecticut Tribal Casinos" (accessed on January 21, 2014).
11. Insider Viewpoint of Las Vegas, *20 Largest Hotels in the World,* http://www.insidervlv.com. Click on Hotels – 20 Largest in World (accessed November 18, 2011).
12. "*Casino Industry & Revenue Statistics," 2014 Statistic Brain Research Institute, publishing as Statistic Brain*, Research Date: April 8, 2015, http://www.statisticbrain.com/casino-market-and-revenue-statistics/ (accessed on April 10, 2015).
13. Wikipedia, *The Venetian Macao,* http://en.wikipedia.org. Search for "Venetian Macao" (accessed November 18, 2011).
14. American Gaming Association, "Facts at Your Fingertips: U.S. Commercial Casino Industry," http://www.americangaming.org/. Go to Industry Resource, click on Research, and then click on Facts at Your Fingertips (accessed June 3, 2015).
15. Caesars Entertainment, *Caesars Entertainment Corporation,* http://caesarscorporate.com (accessed November 18, 2014).
16. Delaware North, *Southland Park Gaming & Racing,* http://www.delawarenorth.com/. Search for "Southland Park" (accessed on November 16, 2014).
17. Dover Downs Hotel & Casino, "Press Release: Dover Downs Hotel & Casino awarded Green Concierge Silver Tier Certification," http://www.doverdowns.com. Click on Press Releases to view this article (accessed on November 16, 2014).
18. SimplyHired, http://www.simplyhired.com. Go to Salary Estimator and search for jobs (accessed June 3, 2015).

PART IV

Assemblies, Events, Attractions, Leadership, and Management

Development of the Meetings, Conventions, and Expositions Industry

People have gathered to attend **meetings**, **conventions**, and **expositions** since ancient times, mainly for social, sporting, political, or religious purposes. As cities became regional centers, the size and frequency of such activities increased, and various groups and associations set up regular expositions.

Associations go back many centuries to the Middle Ages and earlier. The guilds in Europe were created during the Middle Ages to secure proper wages and maintain work standards. In the United States, associations began at the beginning of the eighteenth century, when Rhode Island candle makers organized themselves.

Meetings, incentives, conventions, and exhibitions (MICE) represent a segment of the tourism industry that has grown in recent years. The MICE segment of the tourism industry is very profitable. Industry statistics point to the fact that the average MICE tourist spends about twice the amount of money that other tourists spend.

Size and Scope of the Industry

According to the American Society of Association Executives (ASAE), as of 2009, there were more than 90,908 trade and professional associations.[1] The association business is big business. Associations spend billions holding thousands of meetings and conventions that attract millions of attendees.

The hospitality and tourism industries consist of a number of associations, including the following:

- American Hotel & Lodging Association (AH&LA)
- National Restaurant Association (NRA)
- American Culinary Federation (ACF)
- Destination Marketing Association International (DMAI)
- Hospitality Sales & Marketing Association International (HSMAI)
- Association of Meeting Professionals (AMPs)
- Club Managers Association of America (CMAA)
- Professional Convention Management Association (PCMA)

Associations are the main independent political force for industries such as hospitality, offering the following benefits:

- A voice in government/politics
- Marketing avenues

- Education
- Member services
- Networking

Thousands of associations hold annual conventions at various locations across North America and throughout the rest of the world. Some associations alternate their venues from east to central to west; others meet at fixed locations, such as the NRA show in Chicago or the AH&LA convention and show in New York City.

Associations have an elected board of directors and an elected president, vice president, treasurer, and secretary. Additional officers, such as a liaison person or a public relations (PR) person, may be elected according to the association's constitution.

Key Players in the Industry

LEARNING OBJECTIVE 1
List the major players in the convention industry.

The need to hold face-to-face meetings and attend conventions has grown into a multibillion-dollar industry. Many major and some smaller cities have convention centers with nearby hotels and restaurants.

The major players in the convention industry are **convention and visitors bureaus (CVBs)**, corporations, associations, meeting planners and their clients, convention centers, specialized services, and exhibitions. The wheel diagram in Figure 12–1 shows the types of clients that use convention centers by percentage utilization.

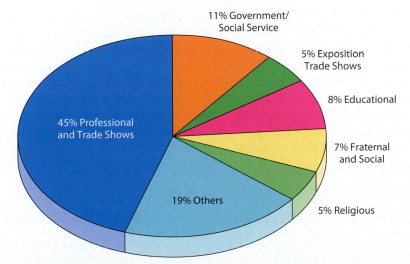

Convention Center Utilization by Market Sector

11% Government/Social Service

5% Exposition Trade Shows

8% Educational

7% Fraternal and Social

5% Religious

19% Others

45% Professional and Trade Shows

Figure 12–1 • Convention Center Clientele.

CVBs are major participants in the meetings, conventions, and expositions market. CVBs comprise a number of visitor industry organizations representing the various industry sectors:

- Transportation
- Hotels and motels
- Restaurants
- Attractions
- Suppliers

The bureau represents these local businesses by acting as the sales team for the city. A bureau has *five* primary responsibilities:

1. To enhance the image of tourism in the local/city area
2. To market the area and encourage people to visit and stay longer
3. To target and encourage selected associations and others to hold meetings, conventions, and expositions in the city
4. To assist associations and others with convention preparations and to give support during the convention
5. To encourage tourists to partake of the historic, cultural, and recreational opportunities the city or area has to offer

The outcome of these five responsibilities is for the city's tourist industry to increase revenues. Bureaus compete for business at trade shows, where interested visitor industry groups gather to do business. For example, a tour wholesaler who is promoting a tour will need to link up with hotels, restaurants, and attractions to package a vacation. Similarly, meeting planners are able to consider several locations and hotels by visiting a trade show. Bureaus generate leads (prospective clients) from a variety of sources. Associations have national and international offices in Washington, D.C. (so that they can lobby the government), and Chicago.

A number of bureaus have offices or representatives in these cities or a sales team who will make follow-up visits to the leads generated at trade shows. Alternatively, they will make cold calls to potential prospects, such as major associations, corporations, and incentive houses. The sales manager will invite the meeting, convention, or exposition organizer to make a **familiarization (FAM) trip** for a site inspection. The bureau assesses the needs of the client and organizes transportation, hotel accommodations, restaurants, and attractions accordingly. The bureau then lets the individual properties and other organizations make their own proposals to the client. Figure 12–2 shows the average expenditure per delegate per stay by convention type.

Business and Association Conventions and Meetings

Publicly held corporations are required by law to have an annual shareholders' meeting. Most also have sales meetings, incentive trips (all-expense paid trips for groups of employees that meet or exceed goals set for them),

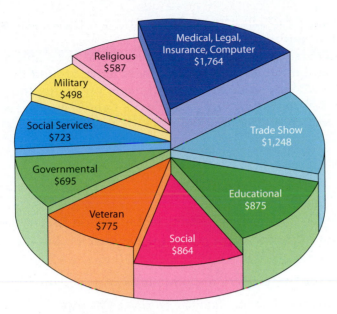

Average length of stay is 3.5 days.

Figure 12–2 • Average Expenditure per Delegate per Stay by Convention Type. The Significance of These Amounts Is That Given an Attendance of Several Hundreds to Thousands of Guests, the Economic Impact Quickly Adds Up and Benefits the Community in a Variety of Ways.

product launches, focus groups, executive retreats, seminars and training sessions, and management meetings.

Corporations are big spenders, in part because they receive tax deductions on their meeting expenditures. When a corporation decides to hold a gathering, it determines what the budget will be, where the gathering will be held, and who will attend. Since the corporation typically pays for all expenses associated with attendance at the meeting, hotels, resorts, and convention centers compete for this lucrative business. In the United States, almost 1.3 million corporate events are held annually, with a total attendance of 107 million.[2] Corporations also arrange incentive trips—paying all expenses for a special vacation for the employee or customer and a significant other at a hotel, at a resort, or on a cruise ship.

Associations represent the interests of their members and gather at the state, regional, national, and international levels for professional industry-related reasons; for annual congresses, conventions, and conferences; and for scientific, educational, and training meetings.

Conventions are a major source of income for associations, as they charge attendees a registration fee and charge vendors for booth space (this gives vendors a chance to sell their products to attendees). Association conventions and meetings attract crowds ranging from hundreds to over 100,000, which only the larger convention facilities like New York, Orlando, Las Vegas, San Francisco, and Chicago can handle. The next level of convention facilities includes cities like Washington, D.C., San Diego, Dallas/Fort Worth, Miami, Boston, and Phoenix/Scottsdale.

The larger associations book their dates several years ahead, some in the same place at the same time of year; others move around the country. For example, the AH&LA holds its annual convention during the second week of November in New York City at the Javits Center, and the NRA holds its annual convention during the third week of May in Chicago at McCormick Place.

▶ Check Your Knowledge

1. According to the American Society of Association Executives (ASAE), how many associations operate at the national level in the United States?

2. What are the five primary responsibilities of a bureau?

3. What is the purpose of a familiarization (FAM) trip?

LEARNING OBJECTIVE 2
Describe destination management companies.

Destination Management Companies (DMCs)

A DMC is a service organization within the visitor industry that offers a host of programs and services to meet clients' needs. Initially, a destination management sales manager concentrates on selling the destination to meeting planners and performance improvement companies (incentive houses).

The needs of such groups may be as simple as an airport pickup or as involved as an international sales convention with theme parties. DMCs work closely with hotels; sometimes a DMC books rooms, and another time a hotel might request the DMC's expertise on organizing theme parties. Patricia Roscoe, chairperson of Patti Roscoe and Associates (PRA), says that meeting planners often have a choice of several destinations and might ask, "Why should I pick your destination?" The answer is that a DMC does everything, including airport greetings, transportation to the hotel, VIP check-in, arranging theme parties, sponsoring programs, organizing competitive sports events, and so on, depending on budget. Sales managers associated with DMCs obtain leads, which are potential clients, from the following sources:

- Hotels
- Trade shows
- CVBs
- Cold calls
- Incentive houses
- Meeting planners

Each sales manager has a staff or team, which can include the following:

- A special events manager, who will have expertise in sound, lighting, staging, and so on

- An accounts manager, who is an assistant to the sales manager
- A theme-events creative director
- An audiovisual specialist
- An operations manager, who coordinates everything, especially on-site arrangements, to ensure that what is sold actually happens

For example, Patti Roscoe's DMC organized meetings, accommodations, meals, beverages, and theme parties for 2,000 Ford Motor Company dealers in nine groups over three days for each group.

Roscoe also works closely with incentive houses, such as Carlson Marketing and Maritz Travel. These incentive houses approach a company and offer to set up incentive plans for companies' employees, including whatever it takes to motivate them. Once approved, Carlson contacts a DMC and asks for a program.

Meeting Planners

Meeting planners may be independent contractors who contract out their services to both associations and corporations as the need arises or they may be full-time employees of corporations or associations. In either case, meeting planners have interesting careers. According to the Professional Convention Management Association (PCMA), about 212,000 full- and part-time meeting planners work in the United States.

The professional meeting planner not only makes hotel and meeting bookings but also plans the meeting down to the last minute, always remembering to check to ensure that the services that have been contracted have been delivered. In recent years, the technical aspects of audiovisual and simultaneous translation equipment have added to the complexity of meeting planning. The meeting planner's role varies from meeting to meeting, but may include some or all of the following activities:

LEARNING OBJECTIVE 3
Describe the different aspects of being a meeting planner.

Premeeting Activities

- Estimate attendance
- Plan meeting agenda
- Establish meeting objectives
- Set meeting budget
- Select city location and hotel/convention site
- Negotiate contracts
- Plan exhibition
- Prepare exhibitor correspondence and packet
- Create marketing plan
- Plan travel to and from site

A meeting planner explains to clients how a meeting will take place.

The Hawai'i Convention Center's recent list of awards includes:

- Prime Site Award from *Facilities & Destinations* magazine (1998 to present)
- Planners Choice Award—Recognition for Excellence in the Hospitality Industry—*Meeting News Magazine* (2005)
- Ranked as North America's most attractive convention center in the METROPOLL X study, Gerard Murphy & Associates (2004)
- Best Use of Nature in Design—Tradeshow Week Magazine (2003)

The Hawai'i Convention Center's Web site at http://www.meethawaii.com/ offers the following information:

- Meeting planner testimonials
- Floor plans and facility services
- News and media kit
- 12–month event calendar

TECHNOLOGY SPOTLIGHT

Meeting, Convention, and Exposition Technology

Courtesy of **James McManemon**, M.S., University of South Florida Sarasota–Manatee

Mobile technology is strongly developing in many hospitality industries. There are two types of mobile apps for events—a web-based program that may be accessed through the Internet on a mobile device, or a software program that must be downloaded to a specific device. These meeting apps allow planners to enter into web-based meeting platforms for free or for a charge. The new platforms and software are being built specifically to accommodate smartphones and tablets.

One of the market leaders of this segment is Delphi by Newmarket International. Some of the features of this software include the following:

- Providing forecast values that better estimate guestroom pickup, ensuring the desired mix between group and transient business
- Responding to requests for proposals (RFPs) from the software
- The ability to flag and determine which accounts should track transient production from the property management system
- Enhanced suite logic that enables guestroom configurations of suites for more accurate inventory reporting
- Customized guestroom security that lets you move guestrooms in and out of inventory for a specified period of time
- Configurable security settings that limit changes on key booking information
- Guestroom overblock controls that allow for specific room types to be overblocked while restricting other room types
- Simplified guestroom rate fields that drastically reduce time-consuming data entry

Similarly, there are online solutions for managing meetings. RegOnline offers online event management, registration, and planning software. This software allows anyone to create an event web site and allows registrants to self-register for the event. Additionally, it generates nametags and attendee lists.

With the advance of smartphones, a lot of conference and event-management applications were introduced for mobile phones such as the iPhone and Droid devices. Some examples are as follows:

- QuickMobile—Features include full conference schedule; personal agenda building; area guide; search capabilities for attendees, speakers, and exhibitors; integration with social media including Twitter, Facebook, and Pathable; and messaging. QuickMobile builds apps for the iPhone, iPad, Blackberry, Android, and mobile web, providing greater ease of use than companies that provide only mobile web versions.

- FollowMe from Core-apps, LLC—FollowMe was the mobile app for the 2010 Consumer Electronic Show, one of the largest shows in the tradeshow industry. Features include a full conference schedule; personal agenda builder; maps; exhibit hallway finding (you are a dot on the map); course notes and literature pickup; session alerts; Twitter integration; and sponsorship revenue sharing.

- Snipp2U from Snipp—This application allows meeting planners to send text messages (SMS) to attendees. It is a low-cost, fast communication channel.

- Foursquare—A location-aware mobile application that allows people to check in anywhere to network with others and to share with friends. Although originally used in restaurants, bars, and so forth, these applications are starting to be used for events.

Some trends in the areas of meetings and conventions involve technologies for both virtual and physical events. These hybrid events mix face-to-face encounters with virtual encounters. The SlideKlowd platform is targeted to professors and students, but can be used by businesses for training or professional courses. The interactive elements allow presenters to set up polls or surveys, ask questions, or make comments during a presentation. Presentations become more effective and engaging for learning.

Types of Meetings, Conventions, and Expositions

LEARNING OBJECTIVE 4
Explain the different types of meetings, conventions, and expositions.

Meetings

Meetings are conferences, workshops, seminars, or other events designed to bring people together for the purpose of exchanging information. Meetings can take any one of the following forms:

- *Clinic.* A workshop-type educational experience in which attendees learn by doing. A clinic usually involves small groups interacting with each other on an individual basis.

- *Forum.* An assembly for the discussion of common concerns. Usually, experts in a given field take opposite sides of an issue in a panel discussion, with liberal opportunity for audience participation.

- *Seminar.* A lecture and a dialogue that allow participants to share experiences in a particular field. A seminar is guided by an expert discussion leader, and usually 30 or fewer persons participate.

- *Symposium.* An event at which a particular subject is discussed by experts and opinions are gathered.

- *Workshop.* A small group led by a facilitator or trainer. It generally includes exercises to enhance skills or develop knowledge in a specific topic.

Conventions and Expositions

Conventions are generally larger meetings with some form of exposition or trade show included. A number of associations have one or more conventions per year. These conventions raise a large part of the association's budget. A typical convention follows a format like the following:

1. Welcome/registration
2. Introduction of the president
3. President's welcome speech, opening the convention
4. First keynote address by a featured speaker
5. Exposition booths open (equipment manufacturers and trade suppliers)
6. Several workshops or presentations on specific topics
7. Luncheon
8. More workshops and presentations
9. Demonstrations of special topics (e.g., culinary arts for a hospitality convention)
10. Vendors' private receptions
11. Dinner
12. Convention center closes

Figure 12–4 shows a convention event profile for a trade show. The profile shows brief details for all departments to see how the event will affect them. The event statistics give estimated details of check-in times and days, the space to be occupied, attendance, and food and beverage sales. The client information gives details of the billing arrangements. Event locations show the exact move in and out times, which can be critical in a fast-paced convention center.

Conventions are not always held in convention centers; in fact, the majority are held in large hotels over a three- to five-day period. The headquarters hotel is usually the one in which most of the activity takes place. Function space is allocated for registration, the convention, expositions, meals, and so on.

Expositions are events that bring together sellers of products and services at a location (usually a convention center) where they can show their products and services to a group of attendees at a convention or trade show. Exhibitors are an essential component of the industry because they pay to exhibit their products to the attendees. Exhibitors interact with attendees with the intention of making sales or establishing contacts and leads for follow-up. Expositions can take up several hundred thousand square feet of space, divided into booths for individual manufacturers or their representatives. In the hospitality industry, the two largest expositions are the AH&LA's conference, held in conjunction with the International Hotel, Motel + Restaurant Show (IHMRS) annually in November at the Javits Center in New York, and the NRA's annual exposition held every May in Chicago. Both events are well worth attending.

16:15:28

San Diego
Convention Center Corporation
EVENT PROFILE

Page: 1
9506059

EVENT STATISTICS

Event Name:	San Diego Apartment Association Trade Show	ID:	9506059
Sales Person:	Joy Peacock	Initial Contact:	8/3/2005
Event Manager:	Trish A. Stiles	Move In Date:	6/22/2009
ConVis Contact:		Move In Day:	Wednesday
Food Person:		Move In Time:	6:01 am
Event Tech.:		First Event Date:	6/23/2009
Event Attend.:		First Event Day:	Thursday
Nature of Event:	LT Local Trade Show	Start Show Time:	6:01 am
Event Parameter:	60 San Diego Convention Center	End Show Time:	11:59 pm
Business Type 1:	41 Association	# of Event Days:	1
Business Type 2:	91 LOCAL	Move Out Date:	6/23/2009
Booking Status:	D Definite	Move Out Day:	Thursday
Rate Schedule:	III Public Show, Meetings and Location	Out Time:	11:59 pm
Open to Public:	No	Date Confirmed:	8/3/2005
Number of Sessions:	1	Attend per Sesn:	3000
Event Sold By:	F Facility (SDCCC)	Tot Room Nights:	15
Abbrev. Name:	/6/Apartment Assn	Public Release:	Yes
Est Bill Amount:	Rent - 6,060.00 Equip –	0.00 Food –	0.00
Last Changed On:	8/20/05 in: Comment Maintenance	By – Joy Peacock	

This Event has been in the facility before

CLIENT INFORMATION

Company: San Diego Apartment Assn, a non-profit Corporation
  Contact Name: Ms. Leslie Cloud, Sales and Marketing Coord.
      1011 Camino Del Rio South, Suite 200, San Diego, CA 92108
      Telephone Number: (619) 297-1000
          Fax Number: (619) 294-4510
      Alternate Number: (619) 294-4510

ID: SDAA

Company: San Diego Apartment Assn, a non-profit Corporation
  Alt Contact Name: Ms. Pamela A. Trimble, Finance & Operations Director
      1011 Camino Del Rio South, Suite 200, San Diego, 92108
      Telephone Number: (619) 297-1000
          Fax Number: (619) 297-4510

EVENT LOCATIONS

ROOM	MOVE IN	IN USE	ED	MOVE OUT	BS	SEAT	RATE	EST. RENT	ATTEND
A	6/22/09 6:01 am	6/23/09	1	6/23/09 11:59 pm	D	E	III	6,060.00	5,000
AS	6/22/09 6:01 am	6/23/09	1	6/23/09 11:59 pm	D	E	III	0.00	10
R01	6/22/09 6:01 am	6/23/09	1	6/23/09 11:59 pm	D	T	III	0.00	450
R02	6/22/09 6:01 am	6/23/09	1	6/23/09 11:59 pm	D	T	III	0.00	350
R03	6/22/09 6:01 am	6/23/09	1	6/23/09 11:59 pm	D	T	III	0.00	280
R04	6/22/09 6:01 am	6/23/09	1	6/23/09 11:59 pm	D	T	III	0.00	280
R05	6/22/09 6:01 am	6/23/09	1	6/23/09 11:59 pm	D	T	III	0.00	460

FOOD SERVICES

ROOM	DATE	TIME	BS ATTEND	EST. COST FOOD SERVICE

There are No Food Services booked for this event

Figure 12–4 • Convention Event Profile for a Trade Show.
(Courtesy San Diego Convention Center.)

Types of Associations

An association is an organized body that exhibits some variety of volunteer leadership structure, which may employ an activity or purpose that the leadership shares in common. The association is generally organized to promote and enhance that common interest, activity, or purpose. The association industry is significant in many respects—total employees, payroll, and membership—but in one area, it is the undisputed leader: It's the big spender when it comes to conventions and meetings. The following sections discuss different types of associations that participate in meetings, conventions, and expositions.

INTRODUCING JILL MORAN, CSEP

Principal and Owner, JS Moran, Special Event Planning & Management

In my life, there is no typical day. As the owner of a special event company, I provide a variety of services to corporate, nonprofit, and social clients. I must be able to communicate successfully with a client at one moment, a vendor at the next, and a prospect at another. My job also involves managing the growth of my company, hiring the right staff and vendors for projects, and getting each job done from start to finish in a professional and timely manner.

As a business owner, I am required to keep my eye on many facets of the company almost daily. Some areas are a must to attend to such as billing, scheduling, and marketing. The squeakiest wheel that gets the most grease, though, is the actual ongoing projects. Once a project is secured, the contracting, planning, and execution stages quickly follow after the initial handshake. These components of meeting and event planning can be time and energy consuming as the details are planned out and put into motion. Event details may involve researching, attending meetings, generating event documents, developing creative concepts and themes, securing vendors to satisfy event details, or executing an event. In the planning of any given event or conference, I may be required to attend off-site visits with vendors, venues, or clients as well as use the computer or telephone to facilitate the planning process. Visits to art supply, furniture, fabric stores, or storerooms of linen or décor vendors are also key elements as theme and design elements are worked on. Review of entertainment or speakers, planning of room layouts or trade show and exhibition space, or discussion with graphic artists also fits into the necessary details covered during the planning phase of an event.

A typical day may involve early computer time to work on production schedules, time lines, e-mails to vendors or clients, follow-up on contracts, or focused time spent on a new proposal. I find early morning (before 9 A.M.) or evening (after 8 P.M.) to be the best time for these activities. This is when I get the least telephone interruptions, and it is before or after scheduled appointments that would require my time out of the office. During the typical business day, phone calls, planning activities, and appointments occupy most of the day. If I am working on an international project, there is more flexibility with this because of the time differences.

While the execution phase of projects and events keeps me busy moment to moment, the strategic planning and business management of my company also demand attention. The challenge for me as the owner of a small business is to carve out time for the marketing and sales arm of the business—to take time to prospect for new business at the same time that I am in the execution phase of events, so that when one project comes to an end, another will be waiting in the wings. I do this by developing fresh marketing materials using photos or components of recent meetings and events; creating video or DVD-style materials to post on my web site or to send to clients; making calls to colleagues, prospects, or venues to say "hello" or touch base; and attending luncheons or visits with past clients to keep in touch. I also try to spend time getting a pulse on new markets to explore or niche areas to develop in my business. I typically subscribe to a wide variety of industry and professional magazines and try to end my day flipping through and tearing out articles that may be useful.

Sometimes I feel I eat, sleep, and live special events, and in many ways, I do. But work doesn't take up every moment of my life. As a mother and wife, I still try to create a fun, loving home for my family by cooking dinner almost every night and by walking daily with my husband and two dogs. These breaks during the day give me downtime and a chance to regroup. I am also active in the music ministry at my local church as a youth choir director, which offers me spiritual and community involvement. I also belong to a book group, which I often attend without finishing the book. There are only so many hours in the day, and I seem to use them up very quickly. But at the end of each day, I am always looking forward to the next!

Source: Courtesy of Jill Moran.

Historical Associations

Today's associations find their roots in historical times. Ancient Roman and Asian craftsmen formed associations for the betterment of their trade. The Middle Ages found associations in the form of guilds, which were created to ensure proper wages were received and to maintain work standards.

Types of Historical Associations

Trade Associations

A trade association is an industry trade group that is generally a public relations organization founded and funded by corporations that operate in a specific industry. Its purpose is generally to promote that industry through PR activities such as advertising, education, political donation, political pressure, publishing, and astroturfing.[3]

Professional Associations

A professional association is a professional body or organization, usually nonprofit, that exists to further a particular profession and to protect both the public interest and the interests of professionals.[4]

Medical and Scientific Associations

These associations are professional organizations for medical and scientific professionals. They are based on specific specialties and are usually national, often with subnational or regional affiliates. These associations usually offer conferences and continuing education. They serve in capacities similar to trade unions and often take public policy stances on these issues.

Religious Organizations

Religious organizations include those groups of individuals who are part of churches, mosques, synagogues, and other spiritual or religious congregations. Religion has taken many forms in various cultures and individuals. These groups may come together in meeting places to further develop their faith, to become more aware of others who have the same faith, to organize and plan activities, to recognize their leaders, for fundraising, and for a number of other reasons.

Government Organizations

There are thousands of government organizations in the United States made up of numerous public bodies and agencies. These types of organizations can range from federal, state, and local organizations. There are five basic types of local governments. Three of these are general-purpose governments; the remaining two include special-purpose local governments that fall into the category of school district governments and special district governments.

Types of Meetings

There are different types of meetings and different purposes for having a meeting. Some of the types of meetings are annual meetings that are held by private or public companies, board and committee meetings, fundraisers, and professional and technical meetings. The following sections describe some of the more popular types of meetings:

Annual Meetings

Annual meetings are meetings that are generally held every year by corporations or associations to inform their members of previous and future activities. In organizations run by volunteers or a paid committee, the annual meeting is generally the forum for the election of officers or representatives for the organization.

Board Meetings, Committee Meetings, Seminars and Workshops, Professional and Technical Meetings

Board meetings for corporations must be held annually, and most corporations hold meetings monthly or four times a year. Of course, not all are held in hotels, but some are, and that brings in additional revenue at the hotel. Committee meetings are generally held at the place of business and only occasionally are held in hotels. Seminars are frequently held in hotels, as are workshops and technical meetings. To meet these needs, hotels and convention centers have convention and meeting managers who go over the requirements and prepare proposals and event orders and budgets.

Corporate Meetings, Conventions, and Expositions

Meetings are mostly held by either the corporate or nonprofit industries. Both association and corporate meeting expenditures are in the billions of dollars each year. Corporations in various industries hold lots of meetings mostly for reasons of educating, training, decision making, research, sales, team building, the introduction of a new product, organization or reorganization, problem solving, and strategic planning. Corporate meetings may be held for the employees or for the general public. For employees of a company, a corporate meeting is a command performance. The major objective of corporate meeting planners is to ensure that the meetings are successful.

SMERF (social, military, educational, religious, and fraternal) groups

Many participants in meetings, including associations and corporations, are organized and fall within this category. Often, these groups are price conscious, because of the fact that the majority of the functions sponsored by these organizations are paid for by the individual, and sometimes the fees are not tax deductible. However, SMERF groups are flexible to ensure that their spending falls within the limits of their budgets; they are a good filler business during off-peak times.

The show floor of the Environmental Quality Trade Fair and Conference.

Incentive Meetings

The **incentive market** of MICE continues to experience rapid growth as meeting planners and travel agents organize incentive travel programs for corporate employees to reward them for reaching specific targets. Incentive trips generally vary from three to six days in length and can range from a moderate trip to an extremely lavish vacation for the employee and his or her partner. The most popular destination for incentive trips is Europe, followed closely by the Caribbean, Hawaii, Florida, and California. Because incentive travel serves as the reward for a unique subset of corporate group business, participants must perceive the destination and the hotel as something special. Climate, recreational facilities, and sightseeing opportunities are high on an incentive meeting planner's list of attributes for which to look.

▶ Check Your Knowledge

1. What are three different types of meetings described in this chapter and what is their purpose?
2. What is SMERF?

Meeting Planning

Meeting planning includes not only the planning but also the successful holding of the meeting and the postmeeting evaluations. As the following sections discuss, there are a number of topics and lots of details to consider. (See Figure 12–5.)

SAN DIEGO CONVENTION CENTER

EVENT MANAGER

DEFINITION

Under moderate direction from the services manager, plans, directs, and supervises assigned events and represents services manager on assigned shifts.

KEY RESPONSIBILITIES

- Plans, coordinates, and supervises all phases of the events to include set ups, move ins and outs, and the activities themselves
- Prepares and disseminates set-up information to the proper departments well in advance of the activity, and ensures complete readiness of the facilities
- Responsible for arranging for all services needed by the tenant
- Coordinates facility staffing needs with appropriate departments
- Acts as a consultant to tenants and the liaison between in-house contractors and tenants
- Preserves facility's physical plant and ensures a safe environment by reviewing tenants plans; requests and makes certain they comply with facility, state, county, and city rules and regulations
- Prepares accounting paperwork of tenant charges, approves final billings, and assists with collection of same
- Resolves complaints, including operational problems and difficulties
- Assists in conducting surveys, gathering statistical information, and working on special projects as assigned by services manager
- Conducts tours of the facilities

MINIMUM REQUIREMENTS

- Bachelor's degree in hospitality management, business, or recreational management from a fully accredited university or college, plus two (2) years of experience in coordinating major conventions and trade shows
- Combination of related education/training and additional experience may substitute for bachelor's degree
- An excellent ability to manage both fiscal and human resources
- Knowledge in public relations; oral and written communications
- Experienced with audiovisual equipment

225 Broadway, Suite 710 • San Diego, CA 92102 • (619) 239-1989
FAX (619) 239-2030
Operated by the San Diego Convention Center Corporation

Figure 12–5 • An Event Manager's Job Description.

Needs Analysis

Before a meeting planner can start planning a meeting, a *needs analysis* is done to determine the purpose and desired outcome of a meeting. Once the necessity of the meeting has been established, the meeting planner can then work with the party to maximize the productivity of the meeting. The key to a productive meeting is a meeting agenda. The meeting agenda may not always fall under the responsibility of the meeting planner, but it is essential for the meeting planner to be closely involved with the written agenda and also with the core purpose of the agenda, which may be different from what is stated. For example, a nonprofit organization may hold a function to promote awareness of its objectives through a fun activity, but its hidden agenda is to raise funds for the organization.

The meeting agenda provides the framework for making *meeting objectives*. The meeting planner must know what the organization is trying to accomplish so as to be successful in the management of the meeting or conference. It is helpful for the meeting planner, regardless of what role he or she plays, to plan the meeting with the meeting objectives in mind. The meeting's objectives provide the framework from which the meeting planner will set the budget, select the site and facility, and plan the overall meeting or convention.

A DAY IN THE LIFE OF ALEXANDRA STOUT

Professional Meeting Planner

In most careers, organization and communication are two of the most important qualities to have. As a professional meeting planner, organization and communication define what needs to be done on a daily basis. I work with different clients every day. No client is the same, and no client will have the same request as another, so being able to listen effectively to the wants and needs of an individual or group of individuals is what I focus on first. The second step is understanding the purpose the client has for their meeting or conference and organizing the details to carry out that purpose.

When I initially meet with a client, some know exactly what they need, and others only have an idea of what they need, which is often a challenge. For the clients who only have an idea, I must cover all aspects of their meeting by asking them what message they want to send. Once I reveal that message, I can ask additional questions that will assist in creating a successful meeting. For example, will there be guest speakers, food and/or beverages, accommodations, printed material, or special audiovisual equipment?

Company A is hosting three guest speakers at its annual conference. Who will be greeting the guests on the day of the meeting? Where will they be staying? How will they be arriving at the venue?

Clients that host larger meetings or conferences often have more detailed requests, as it is not a reoccurring event. Organizations like Company A that will have guest speakers attend will also have larger requests such as catered meals, blocked hotel rooms in the area or at the venue for the duration of the conference, and transportation to and from the airport and the venue location. Other organizations have monthly or bimonthly meetings, and their needs are the same from week to week.

(Continued)

A DAY IN THE LIFE OF ALEXANDRA STOUT *(Continued)*

Company B plans on presenting a PowerPoint presentation during its monthly regional sales meeting. It will need a projector, screen, and appropriate audio and visual elements, as well as coffee and pitchers of water for its employees. Company B also asks for an assortment of fruit and breakfast pastries to be displayed by the coffee and water. Since Company B has its sales meeting on a monthly basis, its requests from month to month rarely change.

More recently, virtual meetings have been increasing in popularity. This option not only makes travel less demanding for members of an organization but also is more cost effective. "Go to" meetings allow a high volume of individuals to join a virtual conference through their computers. With a telephone, computer microphone, and speakers, everyone can communicate with one another, share ideas, and present information just the same as a conventional meeting.

By first listening and determining the purpose and impression the client wants to communicate to another organization, its own, or a group of individuals, I am then able to organize that message into a plan. Clients always have a message they want to get across; whether it be motivation to boost employee morale within a company or to make a lasting impression on a group of potential customers for a given product for sale, a meeting always has a purpose, and my job is to create and fulfill that request from start to finish.

Budget

Understanding clients and knowing their needs are both extremely important; however, the budget carries the most weight. Setting the *budget* for the meeting is more successful if the meeting planner is involved in the budget planning throughout and before making a finalized decision on how much to spend in each area. Setting the budget for the meeting is not a simple task. Knowing how much there is available to spend will help the meeting planner to better guide clients with parameters by which the event is designed. Budgets are planned for various activities and the amount of the budget needed fluctuates for different sites. Therefore, a working budget is necessary to be used as a guideline for making decisions for necessary changes. When changes in the budget are made, it is wise to communicate with the meeting planner these decisions so that the planning of activities is within budgetary constraints. Revenue and expenditure estimates must be accurate and be as thorough as possible to make certain that all possible expenditures are included in the budget prior to the event.

Income for a meeting, convention, or exposition comes from grants or contributions, event sponsor contributions, registration fees, exhibitor fees, company or organization sponsoring, advertising, and the sale of educational materials.

Expenses for a meeting, a convention, or an exposition could include, but are not limited to, rental fees; meeting planner fees; marketing expenses; printing and copying expenses; support supplies, such as office supplies and mailing; on-site and support staff; audiovisual equipment; speakers; signage; entertainment and recreational expenses; mementos for guests and attendees; tours; ground transportation; spousal programs; food and beverage; and on-site personnel.

Request for Proposal and Site Inspection and Selection

No matter how large or small a meeting, it is essential that clear meeting specifications are developed in the form of a written *request for proposal/ quote (RFP/Q)*, rather than contacting hotels by telephone to get a quote. Many larger hotels and convention centers now have online submission forms available.

Several factors are evaluated when selecting a meeting site, including location and level of service, accessibility, hotel room availability, conference room availability, price, city, restaurant service and quality, personal safety, and local attractions. Convention centers and hotels provide meeting space and accommodations as well as food and beverage facilities and service. The convention center and a hotel team from each hotel capable of handling the meeting will attempt to impress the meeting planner. The hotel sales executive will send particulars of the hotel's meeting space and a selection of banquet menus and invite the meeting planner for a site inspection. During the site inspection, the meeting planner is shown all facets of the hotel, including the meeting rooms, guest sleeping rooms, the food and beverage outlets, and any special facility that may interest the planner or the client.

Negotiation with the Convention Center or Hotel

The meeting planner has several critical interactions with hotels, including negotiating the room blocks and rates. Escorting clients on site inspections gives the hotel an opportunity to show its level of facilities and service. The most important interaction is typically with the catering/banquet/conference department associates, especially the services manager, maître d', and captains; these frontline associates can make or break a meeting. For example, meeting planners often send boxes of meeting materials to hotels expecting the hotel to automatically know for which meeting they are intended. On more than one occasion, they have ended up in the hotel's main storeroom, much to the consternation of the meeting planner. Fortunately for most meeting planners, once they have taken care of a meeting one year, subsequent years typically are very similar.

Contracts

Once the meeting planner and the hotel or conference facility have agreed on all the requirements and costs, a contract is prepared and signed by the planner, the organization, and the hotel or convention center. The *contract* is a legal document that binds two or more parties. In the case of meetings, conventions, and expositions, a contract binds an association or organization and the hotel or convention center. The components that make up an enforceable contract include the following:

1. *An offer*: The offer simply states, in as precise a manner as possible, exactly what the offering party is willing to do, and what he or she expects in return. The offer may include specific instructions for how, where, when, and to whom the offer is made.

2. *Consideration*: The payment exchanged for the promise(s) contained in a contract. For a contract to be valid, consideration must flow both ways. For example, the consideration is for a convention center to provide services and use of its facilities in exchange for a consideration of a stated amount to be paid by the organization or host.

3. *Acceptance*: The unconditional agreement to the precise terms and conditions of an offer. The acceptance must mirror exactly the terms of the offer for the acceptance to make the contract valid. The best way to indicate acceptance of an offer is by agreeing to the offer in writing.[5]

Most important to be considered legally enforceable, a contract must be made by parties who are legally able to contract, and the activities specified in the contract must not be in violation of the law. Contracts should include clauses on "attrition and performance," meaning that the contract has a clause to protect the hotel or convention facility in the event that the organizer's numbers drop below an acceptable level. Because the space reserved is supposed to produce a certain amount of money, if the numbers drop, so does the money; unless there is a clause that says something like "there will be a guaranteed revenue of $$$ for the use of the room/ space." The performance part of the clause means that a certain amount of food and beverage revenue will be charged for regardless of whether it is consumed.

Organizing and Preconference Meetings

The average lead time required for organizing a small meeting is about three to six months; larger meetings and conferences take much longer and are booked years in advance. Some meetings and conventions choose the same location each year and others move from city to city, usually from the East Coast to the Midwest or West Coast.

Conference Event Order

A conference event order has all the information necessary for all department employees to be able to refer to for details of the setup (times and layout) and the conference itself (arrival, meal times, what food and beverages are to be served, and the cost of items so that the billing can be done). An example of a conference event order is given in Figure 12–6.

Postevent Meeting

A postevent meeting is held to evaluate the event—what went well and what should be improved for next time. Larger conferences have staff from the hotel or convention center where the event will be held the following year so that they can better prepare for the event when it is held at their facility.

EVENT DOCUMENT
REVISED COPY

SAN DIEGO INTERNATIONAL BOAT SHOW
Monday, January 4, 2016–Monday, January 11, 2016

SPACE: Combined Exhibit Halls AB, Hall A - How Manager's Office, Box Office by Hall A, Hall B –
Show Manager's Office, Mezzanine Room 12, Mezzanine Room 13, Mezzanine Rooms 14 A&B, AND
Mezzanine Rooms 15 A&B

CONTACT: Mr. Jeff Hancock
National Marine Manufacturers Association, Inc.
4901 Morena Blvd.
Suite 901
San Diego, CA 92117
Telephone Number: (619) 274-9924
Fax Number: (619) 274-6760
Decorator Co.:   Greyhound Exposition Services
Sales Person: Denise Simenstad
Event Manager: Jane Krause
Event Tech.:   Sylvia A. Harrison

SCHEDULE OF EVENTS:

Sunday, January 3, 2016   5:00 am–6:00 pm   Combined Exhibit Halls AB
Service contractor move in GES,
Andy Quintena

Monday, January 4, 2016   8:00 am–6:00 pm   Combined Exhibit Halls AB
Service contractor move in GES,
Andy Quintena
12:00 pm–6:00 pm
Combined Exhibit Halls AB
Exhibitor move in

Tuesday, January 5, 2016   8:00 am–6:00 pm   Combined Exhibit Halls AB
Exhibitor move in
Est. attendance: 300

Wednesday, January 6, 2016   8:00 am–12:00 pm   Combined Exhibit Halls AB
Exhibitor final move in
                                11:30 am–8:30 pm   Box Office by Hall A
                                OPEN: Ticket prices, Adults $6, Children 12 & under $3

Figure 12–6 • Conference Event Document.
(Courtesy of the San Diego Convention Center Corporation.)

subcontractors to handle staging, construction, lighting, audiovisual, electrical, and communications.

In addition to the megaconvention centers, a number of prominent centers also contribute to the local, state, and national economies. One good example is the Rhode Island Convention Center. The $82 million center, representing the second largest public works project in the state's history, is located in the heart of downtown Providence, connected by skybridge to the Dunkin' Donuts Center. The center offers a 100,000-square-foot main exhibit hall, a 20,000-square-foot ballroom, 23 meeting rooms, and a full-service kitchen. The exhibit hall divides into four separate halls, and the facility features its own telephone system, allowing individualized billing. A special rotunda function room at the front of the building features glass walls that offer a panoramic view of downtown Providence for receptions of up to 350 people. Extensive use of glass on the façade of the center provides ample natural light throughout the entrance and prefunction areas.

Conference Centers

A conference center is a specially designed learning environment dedicated to hosting and supporting small- to medium-sized meetings, typically between 20 and 50 people.[6] The nature of a conference meeting is to promote a distraction-free learning environment. Conference centers are designed to encourage sharing of information in an inviting, comfortable atmosphere, and to focus sharply on meetings and what makes them effective. Although the groups that hold meetings in conference centers are typically small in terms of attendees, there are thousands of small meetings held every month. Increasingly, hotels are now going after executive meetings where expense is not a major issue.

Hotels and Resorts

Hotels and resorts offer a variety of locations from city center to destination resorts. Many hotels have ballrooms and other meeting rooms designed to accommodate groups of various sizes. Today, they all have web sites and offer meeting planners to help with the planning and organizing of conferences and meetings. Once the word gets out that a meeting planner is seeking a venue for a conference, there is plenty of competition among the hotels to get the business.

Cruise Ships

Meeting in a nontraditional facility can provide a unique and memorable experience for the meeting attendee. However, many of the challenges faced in traditional venues such as hotels and convention centers are also applicable to these facilities. In some cases, planning must begin much earlier for alternative meeting environments than with traditional facilities. A thorough understanding of goals and objectives, budget, and attendee profile of the meeting is essential to negotiate the best package possible. A cruise ship meeting is a uniquely different meeting setting and offers a number of advantages to the attendees such as discounts, complimentary meals, less outside distraction while at sea, entertainment, and visiting more than one destination while unpacking only once![7]

Colleges and Universities

More and more, alternative venues for meeting places include facilities such as colleges, universities, and their campuses. The paramount consideration in contemplating use of campus-based facilities is to know the nature of the target audience.[8] A certain knowledge and evaluation of the participants are inevitable and invaluable because, most of the time, the relative cost of campus-based meetings is less expensive than a medium-priced hotel.

▶ Check Your Knowledge

1. List the various venues for meetings, conventions, and expositions.

Sustainable Meetings, Conventions, and Expositions

The meetings industry is becoming more responsible in its environmental stewardship, and it makes economic sense to do so. Companies that choose to do so are reporting higher gross margins, higher return on sales, higher return on assets, and a stronger cash flow within its own organization. Although there are some upfront costs with going green, the end result is generally a significant savings.[9]

Taking small steps to go green can make an enormous difference in a company's bottom line, as well as in the environment. Simply switching from bottled water to pitchers of water for attendees saved Oracle $1.5 million at its Open World event in San Francisco. Reusing name-badge holders saved another $500 in just one year. In addition to monetary savings to these groups, the amount of waste deposited into a landfill was dramatically reduced, just by making these small changes.

Convention centers are going green by reducing the heat, light, and power consumption. LEED (Leadership in Energy and Environmental Design) buildings require far less energy to air-condition the building, less electric lighting due to increased natural lighting, and less water consumption because of low-flow toilets and faucets that supply water when a sensor is triggered.

In an effort to encourage and support sustainability, various industry certifications have been introduced, including the Sustainable Event Professional Certificate (SEPC) program and certifications to ASTM standards. Additionally, there are carbon footprint calculators.

Career Information

The MICE segment offers a broad range of career paths. Successful meeting planners are detail-oriented, organized people who not only plan and arrange meetings, but also negotiate hotel rooms and meeting spaces in hotels and convention centers.

Incentive travel careers include aspects of organizing high-end travel, hotels, restaurants, attractions, and entertainment. With big budgets, this can be an exciting career for those interested in a combination of travel and hotels in exotic locations.

Conventions and convention centers offer several career paths, from assistants to event managers to sales managers for a special type of account (e.g., associations) or territory. Senior sales managers are expected to book large conventions and expositions—yes, everyone has their quota. Event managers plan and organize the function/event with the client once the contract has been signed. Salaries range from $35,000 to $70,000 for both assistants on rise to sales or event managers. Careers are also possible in the companies that service the MICE segment.

Someone has to equip the convention center, get it ready for an exposition, and supply all the food and beverage items. Off-premise catering for special events also offers careers for creative people who like to come up with concepts and themes around which an event or function may be planned.

For all career paths, it is critical to gain experience in the areas of your interest. Ask people you respect to be your mentor. Ask questions! When you show enthusiasm, people will respond with more help and advice. Figure 12–7 illustrates a career path to becoming a meeting planner.

Figure 12–8 shows an event manager's job description at a convention center.

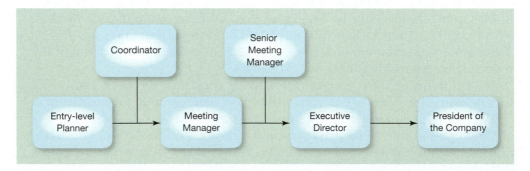

Figure 12–7 • A Career Path to Becoming a Top-Level Event Manager.

EVENT MANAGER

DEFINITION

Under moderate direction from the services manager, plans, directs, and supervises assigned events and represents services manager on assigned shifts.

KEY RESPONSIBILITIES

- Plans, coordinates, and supervises all phases of the events to include set-ups, move ins and outs, and the activities themselves
- Prepares and disseminates set-up information to the proper departments well in advance of the activity, and ensures complete readiness of the facilities
- Responsible for arranging for all services needed by the tenant
- Coordinates facility staffing needs with appropriate departments
- Acts as a consultant to tenants and the liaison between in-house contractors and tenants
- Preserves facility's physical plant and ensures a safe environment by reviewing tenants' plans; requests and makes certain they comply with facility, state, county, and city rules and regulations
- Prepares accounting paperwork of tenant charges, approves final billings, and assists with collection of same
- Resolves complaints, including operational problems and difficulties
- Assists in conducting surveys, gathering statistical information, and working on special projects as assigned by services manager
- Conducts tours of the facilities

MINIMUM REQUIREMENTS

- Bachelor's degree in hospitality management, business, or recreational management from a fully accredited university or college, plus two (2) years of experience in coordinating major conventions and trade shows
- Combination of related education/training and additional experience may substitute for bachelor's degree
- An excellent ability to manage both fiscal and human resources
- Knowledge in public relations; oral and written communications
- Experienced with audiovisual equipment

225 Broadway, Suite 710 • San Diego, CA 92102 • (619) 239-1989
FAX (619) 239-2030
Operated by the San Diego Convention Center Corporation

Figure 12–8 • Event Manager's Job Description.

Trends in Meetings, Conventions, and Expositions

Courtesy of Dr. Greg Dunn, Senior Lecturer & Managing Director, University of Florida, Eric Friedheim Tourism Institute

- *New Technologies.* Technology allows meeting planners the ability to identify and manage key markets for attracting attendees. Meeting planners will also have the ability to plan smarter and reduce costs.[10] Some event planners have taken technology to a whole new level by adding special geo-locating features to their apps to tailor the experience to the individuals. Other planners are developing apps that provide a much richer and better conference experience than a paper program guide could do, including polling, customizable agendas, gaming, video, contact exchange, social media integration, analytics, and much more. Future meetings will also incorporate and enable wearable (or everywhere) computing. New mobile technologies such as Google Glass and a range of smart watches and smart bracelets will assist meeting participants with navigation, networking, and augmented reality. Although part of a larger societal trend, this will impact events and trade shows in the next few years as attendees literally embody these devices to assist them at events.

- *Increased Use of Smartphones.* Smartphones are used by a large percent of the population, which allows meeting planners to increase audience engagement by providing them with the ability to interact directly, track activities, connect with contacts and vendors, and share their experiences with others via social media outlets.[11] This allows the organizers to listen to attendees and make some changes during the event itself to provide more value.

- *Connectivity and Lightning Speed.* The need for faster network speeds, or bandwidth, has been growing so quickly that these speeds are now estimated to double every three years. Fast and effective Wi-Fi will continue to be one of the major challenges facing meeting planning professionals and delegates. As people increasingly add new mobile devices to accomplish their computing tasks, the need for more bandwidth will continue to soar. Many conference attendees now come with up to three wireless devices, so greater bandwidth is crucial. Planners expect great Wi-Fi access to keep meeting guests connected and engaged.

- *Demand for Unique Meeting Experiences.* More and more meeting delegates are demanding out of the ordinary experiences for meeting agendas and destination decisions. For instance, some planners have partnered with unique venues such as wineries, craft breweries, attractions, museums, aquariums, and historical places and buildings to provide a memorable setting and meeting experience for their attendees. Other planners are hosting "sessions unplugged" that do not require a formal PowerPoint presentation or other audio visual equipment outdoors. Finally, some planners are creating special VIP lounges for strategic sets of attendees with special access passes and upgraded snacks, drinks, massage station, business center, and more.

- *Making Meetings Personal.* Planners are also making meetings and conferences more personal by setting up unique backdrops for attendees to be photographed, enabling attendees to share their experiences via social media or a custom event postcard. Some meeting planners are also inviting artists to sketch or paint delegates and conduct step-by-step painting classes during networking events, while others are personalizing attendee name badges with something that is interesting and unique to the attendee (e.g., baseball fanatic or yoga girl).

- *Keeping It Healthy.* Meeting planners and facilities are keeping the health and wellness of attendees in mind when developing meeting and conference agendas and functions. For instance, some planners are organizing mini-wellness programs during a conference that may include a local personal trainer for morning workouts or afternoon fitness and yoga sessions. Others recognize that several days of meetings and functions can be hazardous for those who diet, and therefore host a nutritionist to help develop menus as well encourage attendees to choose diet-friendly snacks such as granola bars, mixed fruits, and fresh vegetables. Meeting planners are starting to introduce family-style menus or sample menus that allow attendees to pick and choose what they would like to eat. Locally sourced ingredients are also becoming popular, with hometown coffee bars, local breweries or pubs, and dim sum-style cart service with cuisines specific to an area.

- *Going Greener.* The meetings industry continues to find unique ways to conduct meetings in a more sustainable, environmentally friendly manner. More planners are looking to cut a meeting's carbon footprint and reduce the negative impact that conventions and conferences can have on host communities. Convention bureaus, hotels, exposition facilities, and other vendors that service the convention industry have stepped up their sustainability efforts in recent years in response to customer demand. Most hotel chains and conference centers now have some sort of green initiative like a linen or towel reuse program, and some even offer financial incentives for groups that agree to adopt sustainability practices like creating less trash, using less energy, and incorporating locally sourced foods into menus. Many convention centers are increasingly utilizing the latest technologies in energy usage, water conservation, and waste reduction. In addition, today's attendees are wired and therefore need to constantly power their mobile devices. While some planners are adding charging stations, others are making it more fun and greener by using unique self-powered generating stations such as riding bicycles. Not only do attendees power devices by riding bikes for a period of time, they also enjoy themselves, get a little exercise, make conversation, and network. Other planners are choosing attendee giveaways or gifts that are made from recycled materials such as t-shirts, water bottles, and bags.

CASE STUDY

Double-Booked

The convention bureau in a large and popular convention destination has jurisdiction over the convention center. A seasoned convention sales manager, who has worked for the bureau for seven years and produces more sales than any other sales manager, has rebooked a 2,000-person group for a three-day exposition in the convention center. The exposition is to take place two years from the booking date.

The client has a 15-year history of holding conventions, meetings, and expositions in this convention center and has always used the bureau to contract all space and services. In fact, the sales manager handling the account has worked with the client for seven of the 15 years. The bureau considers this client a preferred customer.

The convention center group meeting planner also appeared in a magazine ad giving a testimony of praise for the convention bureau, this particular sales manager, and the city as a destination for conventions.

Shortly after the group meeting planner confirms the rebooking of the three-day exposition for two years hence, the bureau changes sales administration personnel not once but three times. This creates a challenge for the sales manager in terms of producing contracts, client files, and event profiles, and in the recording and distribution of information. The preferred customer who rebooked has a contract, purchase orders for vendor services, a move-in and setup agenda, and an event profile, all supplied by the sales manager. The sales manager has copies of these documents as well. The two hotels where the group will be staying also have contracts for the VIP group.

As is the nature of this particular bureau, other sales managers have been booking and contracting space for the same time period as the preferred customer that rebooked. In fact, the exhibit hall has been double-booked, as have the breakout rooms for seminars, workshops, and food and beverage service. The groups that contracted later with the convention bureau are all first-time users of the convention center facilities.

This situation remains undetected until 10 days prior to the groups' arrival. It is brought to the attention of the bureau and the convention center only when the sales manager distributes a memo to schedule a preconvention meeting with the meeting planner and all convention center staff.

Because of the administrative personnel changes, necessary information was not disseminated to key departments and key personnel. The convention center was never notified that space had been contracted for the preferred customer. The preferred customer has been told about this potentially catastrophic situation. Now there is a major problem to rectify.

Discussion Questions

1. Ultimately, who is responsible for decision making with regard to this situation?
2. What steps should be taken to remedy this situation?
3. Are there fair and ethical procedures to follow to provide space for the preferred customer? If so, what are they?

4. What measures, if any, should be taken in handling the seasoned sales manager?
5. What leverage does the meeting planner have to secure this and future business with the bureau?
6. What might the preferred customer do if it is denied space and usage of the convention center?
7. How can this situation be avoided in the future?

Summary

1. Conventions, meetings, and expositions serve social, political, sporting, or religious purposes. Associations offer benefits such as a political voice, education, marketing avenues, member services, and networking.

2. Meetings are events designed to bring people together for the purpose of exchanging information. Typical forms of meetings are conferences, workshops, seminars, forums, and symposiums.

3. Expositions bring together purveyors of products, equipment, and services in an environment in which they can demonstrate their products. Conventions are meetings that include some form of exposition or trade show.

4. Meeting planners contract out their services to associations and corporations. Their responsibilities include premeeting, on-site, and postmeeting activities.

5. The convention and visitors bureaus are nonprofit organizations that assess the needs of the client and organize transportation, hotel accommodations, restaurants, and attractions.

6. Convention centers are huge facilities, usually owned by the government, where meetings and expositions are held. Events at convention centers require a lot of up-front planning and careful event management. A contract that is based on the event profile and an event document is a necessary part of effective management.

Key Words and Concepts

associations
convention
convention and visitors
bureaus (CVBs)
convention center

exposition
familiarization (FAM) trip
incentive market
meeting
meeting planner

meetings, incentives, conventions, and exhibitions (MICE)
social, military, educational, religious, and fraternal (SMERF)
groups

Review Questions

1. What are associations, and what is their purpose?
2. List the primary sources of revenue and expenses involved in holding a meeting, a convention, and an exposition.
3. Describe the main types of meeting setups.
4. Explain the difference between an exposition and a convention.
5. List the duties of CVBs.
6. Describe the topics a meeting planner needs to deal with before, during, and after a meeting.

Internet Exercises

1. Organization: **Best of Boston Events**
   Summary: Best of Boston Events is an event-planning company that specializes in putting together packages for different events, such as conventions, corporate events, private parties, and weddings.
   (a) Explore this web site for events and list the different kinds of events this organization can organize.
   (b) After browsing the web site, discuss the importance of networking in the meetings, conventions, and expositions industry.

2. Organization: **M&C Online**
   Summary: This excellent web site offers in-depth information on meetings and conventions from different perspectives, ranging from legal issues to unique themes and concepts.
   (a) Click the "Latest News" heading (it's on the left side of the page). What is the latest news?

Apply Your Knowledge

1. Make a master plan with all the steps necessary for holding a meeting or seminar on careers in hospitality management.

Suggested Activity

1. Contact meeting planners in your area, and, with permission of your professor, invite them to speak to the class about their work and how they do it. Prepare questions in advance so that they may be given to the speaker ahead of time.

Endnotes

1. The Center for Association Leadership, *Associations FAQ*, http://www.asaecenter.org. Click on Advocacy, and then click on Association Frequently Asked Questions (accessed on June 4, 2015).

2. George G. Fenich, *Meetings, Expositions, and Conventions: An Introduction to the Industry*, 4th ed. (Hoboken, NJ: Pearson, 2016), 22.

3. Wikipedia, *Trade Association*, http://en.wikipedia.org. Search for "trade association" (accessed March 21, 2015).

4. Wikipedia, *Professional Association*, http://en.wikipedia.org. Search for "professionalassociation" (accessed March 21, 2015).

5. Steven Barth, *Hospitality Law: Managing Issues in the Hospitality Industry* (Hoboken, NJ: John Wiley and Sons, 2006), 26–29.

6. Professional Convention Management Association, *Professional Meeting Management*, 4th ed. (Dubuque, IA: Kendall/Hunt, 2004), 557–561.

7. Professional Convention Management Association, *Professional Meeting Management*, 564–565.

8. Ibid.

9. George G. Fenich, *Meetings, Expositions, and Conventions: An Introduction to the Industry*, 249.

10. JR Sherman, "5 meeting-tech trends to watch in 2013," January 18, 2013, *Meetings & Conventions*, http://www.meetings-conventions.com. Search for "5 meeting-tech trends to watch in 2013" (accessed January 18, 2015).

11. Ibid.

CHAPTER **13**

Special Events

LEARNING OBJECTIVES

After reading and studying this chapter, you should be able to:

- Define a special event.

- Describe what event planners do.

- Classify special events.

- Outline the skills and abilities required for event management.

- Identify the main professional organizations and associations involved with the special events industry.

LEARNING OBJECTIVE 1
Define a special event.

The **special events industry** is a dynamic and varied industry offering an array of events that fall into categories such as daily events, which normally happen spontaneously, and special events, which are planned and often motivated by a celebration such as a wedding, fair, or festival.

Special events include countless functions, such as **corporate seminars** and **workshops**, **conventions** and **trade shows**, **charity balls** and **fundraisers**, **fairs and festivals**, and **social functions** such as **weddings and holiday parties**. It is for this reason that the industry has seen such growth and presents so much potential for future careers and management opportunities.

Food, clothing, and shelter are the accepted basic physical needs that humans require. Following those needs is an emotional need to celebrate, which has a direct impact on the human spirit. All societies celebrate—whether publicly or privately, as individuals or in groups. The need to celebrate has been recognized by corporations, public and government officials, associations, and individuals. This has contributed to the rapid growth of the special events industry with a wide range of possible employment opportunities. When you consider all of the planners, caterers, producers, event sites, and others that become part of the special event, you can imagine the potential for future careers and employment possibilities.

Event management is a newcomer in the hospitality industry compared with the hotel and restaurant industries. Yet as you will soon learn, special

Someone has to manage this incredible event, the Super Bowl.

events is a field that doesn't have rigid boundaries. Closely related fields that may overlap include marketing, sales, catering, and entertainment. Future growth trends in special events management provide plenty of career opportunities in all hospitality sectors.

This chapter gives you an overview of the special events industry. You will learn about the various classifications of special events and where future career opportunities can be found. You will find information on the skills and abilities required to be successful in the field. Information on special events organizations, strategic event planning, and the future outlook of the industry will allow you to take a glimpse into this exciting, rewarding, and evolving field. As Frank Supovitz, vice president of Special Events for the National Hockey League in New York, says, "The stakes have never been higher. Sponsors are savvier. Audiences are more demanding. And, event producers and managers are held accountable by their clients to meet their financial and marketing goals more than ever before. . . . So before the lights go down and the curtain rises, reach out for the experience and expertise in these pages . . . and explore the opportunities in special events management."[1]

What Event Planners Do

LEARNING OBJECTIVE 2
Describe what event planners do.

Event planning is a general term that refers to a career path in the growing field of special events. Its forecast includes a growing demand for current and future employment opportunities. Like several other professions, event planning came about to fill a gap—someone needed to be in charge of all the gatherings, meetings, conferences, and so on that were increasing in size, number, and spectacle among the business and leisure sectors. Corporate managers had to step away from their assignments to take on the additional challenges of planning conventions and conferences. Government officials and employees were displaced from their assignments to arrange recruitment fairs and military events. Consequently, whenever a special event was to be held, the planner became a person whose job description did not include planning.

The title **event planner** was first introduced at hotels and convention centers. Event planners are responsible for planning an event, from start to finish. This includes setting the date and location, advertising the event, and providing refreshments or arranging catering services, speakers, or entertainment. Please keep in mind that this is a general list and will vary depending on the type, location, and nature of the event.

A VGM Career Book, *Opportunities in Event Planning Careers*, has the following to say about a good candidate: "In addition to good organizational skills, someone with a creative spirit, a flair for the dramatic, a sense of adventure, and a love of spectacle could expect to flourish in this field."

Highlighted skills and characteristics of a future professional in this field include the following:

Computer skills	Follow-through skills
Willingness to travel	Ability to work with high-level executives
Willingness to work a flexible schedule	Budgeting skills
Experience in delegating	Ability to initiate and close sales
Willingness to work long hours	Lots of patience
Negotiating skills	Ability to handle multiple tasks simultaneously
Verbal and written communication skills	Ability to be a self-starter
Enthusiasm	Ability to interact with other departments[2]
Project management skills	

HOW TO BECOME AN EVENT MANAGER

Courtesy of **James McManemon**, M.S., University of South Florida Sarasota–Manatee

Connie Clark, an events and creative services manager, shared her schooling and professional experience, which led her to work for a successful nonprofit tourism organization that executes 80 events each year. While there are many different paths that can lead to becoming an event manager, Connie's got her here at a young age.

In undergraduate school, she majored in Communication Studies, and then went on to receive a graduate degree in Hospitality Management. Her career began five years ago. While finishing her bachelor's degree, Connie completed an event planning internship with a gourmet grocery store chain in Minnesota. She was involved in planning and promoting corporate events such as book signings and store openings. After receiving her bachelor's degree, she got a part time job with a small wellness center in Sarasota, Florida, that was looking to hire an organized person with marketing skills to coordinate and promote free wellness classes and events at the center. The job paid very little, but Connie believed that it would help her to gain the experience needed to eventually land her dream job as an event planner. After working for a year at the wellness center, she landed a job at the University of South Florida as an event planner/administrative specialist.

While working at USF, Connie was responsible for coordinating commencement exercises for the university, as well as board meetings, public lectures, and fundraising dinners. The interactions with vendors, caterers, and local hotels helped her to realize that pursuing a master's degree in Hospitality Management was the perfect step to progress her career in event planning. After receiving her graduate degree, and having worked at USF for several years, she got a job as an event and creative services manager for a nonprofit organization in Bradenton, Florida.

In her position as event and creative services manager, Connie plans events ranging from farmers' markets and art festivals to large concerts with national headliners and thousands of attendees. She coordinates everything from lighting, sound, and staging to food and beverage concepts and menus. Moreover, she constantly references the tools and industry knowledge obtained from her schooling and previous experiences in the industry.

Connie's future plans are to complete the Convention Industry Council's Certified Meeting Professional (CMP) program to obtain the CMP credential, which can only strengthen her resume. One day, she plans to branch out and start her own event production company.

Event Management

Event management can be as small as planning an office outing, to something larger like organizing a music festival and as large as planning the Super Bowl or even the Olympics. Events can be one-off, annual (happening each year), or every four years. Things do not just happen by themselves; it takes a great deal of preparation to stage a successful event. To hold a successful event, the organizer should have a vision and leader/manager skills in the following key result areas: marketing, financial, operational, and legal. Getting good sponsorship is a big help. Sponsors provide money or in-kind contributions and receive recognition as sponsors of the event, including use or display of their logos in the event's promotion. Sponsors expect to get something in return for their sponsorship, so give them something tangible that will help their corporation or organization. Each year, thousands go to festivals and events of all kinds, and most, if not close to all, events receive some sponsorship, because it is too costly to stage an event without sponsorship.

Event management requires special skills in marketing and sales (to attract the business in the first place), planning (to ensure all details are covered and that everything will be ready on time), organization (to make sure all key staff know what to do, why, when, where, and how), financial (a budget needs to be made and kept to), human resources and motivation (the best people need to be selected and recruited, trained, and motivated), lots of patience, and attention to detail and endless checking on them. To gain business, event managers prepare a proposal for the client's approval and contract signature. There are some important how-tos in preparing an event proposal: Find out as much information as possible about the event (if it has been previously held) or what the client really has in mind. Ask organizers, attendees, providers, and others what went right and what went wrong or what could be improved on next time the event is organized. Write the proposal in business English, not elaborate or florid language. Finally, do the numbers—nobody wants a surprise—do a pro-forma invoice so that the client will know the costs, and surprise the client by being on time and on budget.

An event can be costly to put on; in addition to advertising, there is a location charge, security costs, labor costs, and production costs (this may not only be food, beverage, and service, but also staging and decor). Usually, the event manager has a good estimate of the number of ticket sales expected. He or she then budgets the costs to include the entertainment and all other costs, leaving a reasonable profit.

Event management also takes place at convention centers and hotels, where event managers handle all the arrangements after the sales manager has completed the contract. The larger convention center events are planned years in advance. As stated earlier, the convention and visitors bureau (CVB) is usually responsible for the booking of conventions more than 18 months ahead. Obviously, both the convention and visitors bureau and the convention center marketing and sales teams work closely with each other. Once the booking becomes definite, the senior event manager assigns an event manager to work with the client throughout the sequence of pre-event, event, and postevent activities.

The booking manager is critical to the success of the event by booking the correct space and working with the organizers to help them save money by allocating only the space really needed and allowing the client to begin setting up on time. A contract is written based on the event profile. The event profile stipulates in writing all the client's requirements and gives all of the relevant information, such as which company will act as decorator/subcontractor to install carpets and set up the booths.

The contract requires careful preparation because it is a legal document and will guarantee certain provisions. For example, the contract may specify that the booths may only be cleaned by center personnel or that food may be prepared for samples only, not for retail. After the contract has been signed and returned by the client, the event manager will from time to time make follow-up calls until about six months before the event, when arrangements such as security, business services, and catering will be finalized. The event manager is the key contact between the center and the client. He or she will help the client by introducing approved subcontractors who are able to provide essential services.

Two weeks prior to the event, an event document is distributed to department heads. The event document contains all the detailed information that each department needs to know for the event to run smoothly. About 10 days before the event, a WAG (week at a glance) meeting is held. The WAG meeting is one of the most important meetings at the convention center because it provides an opportunity to avoid problems—like two event groups arriving at the same time or additional security for concerts or politicians. About this same time, a preconvention or pre-expo meeting is held with expo managers and their contractors—shuttle bus managers, registration operators, exhibit floor managers, and so on. Once the setup begins, service contractors marshal the 18-wheeler trucks to unload the exhibits by using radio phones to call the trucks from a nearby depot. When the exhibits are in place, the exposition opens and the public is admitted.

The Event-Planning Process

The event-planning process has five crucial stages. It's important to note that these stages are not entirely finite—the issues the event planner must address is indeed a process of reviewing and evaluating decisions made at each previous stage.

Research

The first stage of event planning is to answer the following simple questions:

1. Why should a special event be held?
2. Who should hold it?
3. Where should it be held?
4. What should the focus of the event be?
5. What outcomes are expected?

Once answers to these questions are available, you can move to the second stage of event planning.

Design

The second stage in the event-planning process can be both the most exciting and the most challenging. This stage allows freedom in creativity and the implementation of new ideas that support the objectives of the special event. The design process is a time when an event manager or team can brainstorm new innovative ideas or develop adaptations to previous events to make them better, grander, and more exciting for the attendees. The design process seeks to obtain original and fresh ideas that will create an event in which it's worth investing. The event may be a corporate meeting or it may be a beachside wedding, yet the design of the event will have a lasting impression on those who attend it.

Planning

This event-planning stage is informed first by the budget for the event. Once the budget is established, the remaining steps in the process include contracting out services and arranging all other activities that will become part of the event. The type and size of the event will ultimately determine the steps required in the planning process, which may include the following tasks:

- Determine event budget
- Select the event site
- Select hotel accommodations
- Arrange transportation
- Negotiate contracts
- Arrange catering
- Arrange speaker, entertainment, music
- Organize audiovisual needs
- Create marketing plan for the event
- Prepare invitations or event packets

Coordination

The process of **coordination** can be compared to a director leading a band. The band may have rehearsed a piece of music countless times, and yet, during a concert, the director still has the ability to direct or control the performance. Similarly, the event manager engages in the process of coordinating the event as it unfolds. This may be a stressful time because of unforeseen problems that occur, or it may be a truly rewarding time with a flawless execution. Regardless, coordination of the event may involve decision-making skills and abilities as the event progresses.

Coordination also relates to the human resource aspect of the special event. Event managers are leaders who, through example, motivate others. As an event manager, you will engage in coordinating staff and/or volunteers to carry out the special event's planned objectives and goals. As mentioned earlier, empowering your staff will create a positive environment and will make your job of coordinating their efforts that much easier.

Evaluation

Evaluation should take place during each of the stages of the event-planning process and is a final step that can measure the success of the event in meeting the goals and objectives. If you take a look at the event-planning process diagram in Figure 13–1, you will notice that it is a continuous process. Outcomes are compared to expectations and variances investigated and corrected.

The information you learn about planning from your other courses and studies will help you if you choose to pursue a career in event management.

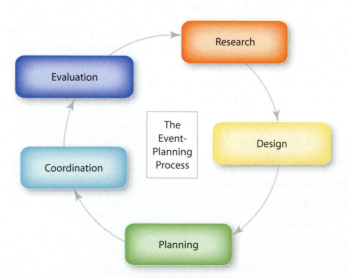

Figure 13–1 • Event-Planning Process Diagram.

Challenges and Tools for Event Planners and Managers

If you are at this point considering a professional career in event management, there are event-planning tools that you can use to your advantage as you pursue a career in this field. There are four primary challenges professional event managers face: time, finance, technology, and human resources.

Time management plays an important role in event planning, and it is an element that can be used effectively by budgeting your time the same way that you would your finances. Delegating tasks to the appropriate people, keeping accurate records and lists, preparing agendas before meetings, and focusing on what items deserve top priority are all examples of how to use time management effectively.

Financial management becomes important for an event planner when it becomes necessary for you to evaluate financial data, management fees, vendor fees, and so forth. This does not mean that you have to be a financial wizard; however, knowledge in this area will greatly enhance your opportunity to make profitable and sound decisions. There are resources that can be used in this area such as obtaining help or counsel from a financial professional and using technology that will help with event accounting.

Utilizing technology as a tool in event management can be a great opportunity to assist in the previous two areas. Software programs for word processing, financial management, and database management can help in daily tasks and event planning. Other technology products that are used by event professionals include laptop computers, cell phones, handheld devices, event management software, and the Internet.

The final tool relates to the effective management of your human resources. Empowering your employees is the key to success. As a manager and leader, you must train your employees and/or volunteers and give them the necessary information to perform their jobs. It is critical to select the right people, empower them, and develop their skills. This will ultimately help you succeed in accomplishing your goals. Empowering event staff can be used to allow them to make important decisions—successful events require many decisions to be made, and you as a manager will not have the time to

Guests mingle at a charity event in Coral Gables, Florida.

make all of them. Empowering your team is the greatest tool you can use to become an effective leader and improve the performance of your staff.

▶ **Check Your Knowledge**

1. Define a special event.
2. Give some examples to distinguish the differences between a daily event and a special event.
3. Describe the principle responsibilities of an event planner.
4. Name the stages in the event-planning process.

LEARNING OBJECTIVE 3
Classify special events.

Classifications of Special Events

The special events industry has been divided up into the following classifications:

- Corporate events (seminars, workshops, meetings, conferences)
- Association events (conventions, trade shows, meetings)
- Charity balls and fundraising events
- Social functions (weddings, engagement parties, holiday functions)
- Fairs and festivals
- Concerts and sporting events

A poll taken from a wide variety of event professionals in the industry, *Event Solutions Blackbook*, lists the following as the most popular types of event sites:

Hotel/resort	62.0 percent
Convention center	32.5 percent
Tent/structure	32.6 percent
Banquet hall	29.0 percent
Outdoors	21.8 percent
Corporate facility	28.4 percent
Museum/zoo/gardens	12.4 percent
Arena/stadium/theater	18.0 percent
Restaurant	16.1 percent
Private residence	22.8 percent
Club	16.7 percent[3]

With those figures in mind, take a closer look at the various classifications that make up this exciting industry. Each category has its own unique characteristics, rewards, and challenges. As a human resource specialist would say, "It's important to put the right person in the right position." This statement also holds true for special events. Any career selection, especially for a person seeking the management level, should look for the correct "fit." With such a vast array of options, you may find one that ignites your passion for the field, you may find several that are the wrong size before finding the right one, or you may decide that this is not the right match for your personality and goals. The events discussed below may help you to decide whether your future holds a professional career in the special events industry.

Corporate Events

Corporate events continue to lead the industry in terms of event business. About 80 percent of the event market is corporate events.

Corporate event managers are employed by the company to plan and execute the details of meetings for the corporation's employees, management, and owners. The growing use of special events in the corporate arena created the need for positions dedicated to the planning and management of them. The corporate event planners engage in the following management activities: They are involved in the planning and organizing of events, and they play a key leadership role. Additionally, the planner must possess the following skills: effective communication, ability to coordinate various activities, and attention to detail.

Corporate events include the following: annual meetings, sales meetings, new product launches, training meetings and workshops, management meetings, press meetings, incentive meetings, and awards ceremonies.

Corporate events benefit several sectors of the hospitality industry. For example, a client may hold an event at a major attraction like SeaWorld or a resort like The Breakers. Each corporate client can provide the hotel, restaurants, airlines, and other businesses in the destination's economy with tens of thousands of dollars. Corporate event planners will consider the factors most important to the attendees when using a hotel as part of the event, including corporate account rates for lodging, amenities such as fitness centers and business centers, airport transportation, and quick check-in and check-out at the hotel. Therefore, corporate event planners should have strong negotiating skills to book lodging and convention services as needed.

Microsoft Chairman Bill Gates introduces Jay Leno at a corporate function.

Association Events

There are more than 6,500 associations in the United States alone. The majority of the large association conventions are planned two to five years ahead of time, and the destination is a determining factor in the planning process. The American Medical Association and the American Dental Association are two of the most recognized examples of associations that hold large conventions. In the hospitality industry, the National Restaurant Association (NRA), the American Hotel & Lodging Association (AH&LA), and, at a global level, the International Association of Convention and Visitors Bureaus are a few of the many associations that hold conventions. Associations account for millions in generated revenue. This stems from the millions of people who attend thousands of meetings and conventions. For example, the American Marketing Association holds more than 20 conferences annually, which generates approximately a million for each hotel.

Events relating to associations can range from a monthly luncheon at a private club or hotel to a yearly convention that may comprise an educational seminar(s) with an opportunity to network with other association members. Associations generally hire full-time paid planners to manage the yearly national membership meeting that is a requirement for most associations as part of their bylaws. Larger associations with greater financial resources often hire full-time meeting and convention management professionals who are involved in the large association events as well as other association events, including board meetings, educational seminars, membership meetings, professional meetings, and regional meetings.

Other opportunities for employment are widespread. They may include a position as a convention manager, a special events manager in a hotel, a conference manager, or a special events manager at a private club for the events held by local associations.

In the event-planning industry, professional associations have a great impact in contributing to the development of their members. Professional associations provide training, certification, networking, and assistance with business plans and other consulting services for their members.

Charity Balls and Fundraising Events

Charity balls and fundraising events provide a unique opportunity for the event manager to work with the particular group or charity, and a theme is usually chosen for the event. The event manager is then responsible for selecting the location and coordinating all of the details that will determine the success of the event, which may include catering, entertainment, décor, lighting, floral arrangements, invitations, rentals, public relations, transportation, security, and technical support.

One of the key skills that a person entering this category must possess is the ability to plan the event on a set and often limited budget. Why is this skill so critical? These events are used to raise funds toward a set group or charity, and every dollar that is spent on the event is thereby one less dollar that could go toward the cause. Nevertheless, these events are expected to be extravagant—so a little creativity can go a long way in the planning and implementing of the theme. The event manager should also have strong negotiating skills to bargain with vendors on reduced rates or in some cases donated services or products. A smart planner will know how to market and sell the positive public relations that the event could provide to the vendors.

The demand for fundraising event planners/managers is one that holds solid ground. To prove this point, *Opportunities in Event Planning Careers* quoted an in-house event planner as stating, "One of the major advantages of working for a nonprofit as an in-house planner for almost six years was that I never had to look for work. There were always new events to take on."[4]

Social Events

Social function planners or managers work on a broad variety of events. This category of special events includes the traditional wedding and party planners with which most of us are already familiar. This category of event planning includes weddings, engagement parties, birthday parties, anniversary parties, holiday parties, graduation parties, military events, and all other social gatherings or events. A social event planner/manager is usually responsible for selecting the venue, determining any themes and/or design schemes, ordering or planning decorations, arranging for catering and entertainment, and having invitations printed and mailed.

SMERF, which stands for social, military, educational, religious, and fraternal organizations, is a category of organizations that also falls into the category of social events. Individuals of these organizations often pay for the events, meaning the events are price sensitive. Needless to say, budgeting skills are important for those working with these groups.

Weddings are the most widely recognized social event. Wedding planners are a key player in the social event category. The title seems glamorous and has a certain perception that most of us will hold, yet the management involved in planning a wedding involves strict attention to detail. Don't forget that the planner is responsible for creating what is considered to be the most important day of a couple's life. "Realize this is a business," says Gerard J. Monaghan, co-founder of the Association of Bridal Consultants. "A fun business to be sure, but a business nonetheless." Effective wedding planners will have contacts formed for a variety of services, such as venues like hotels, wedding locations, decorating, catering, bridal shops, musicians, photographers, florists, and so forth.

Today's weddings are more expensive than those of the past, and they are often longer. Weddings have become true "special events" because of the willingness of family and friends to travel longer distances to celebrate with the bride and groom. Many weddings today have become minivacations for those attending.

▶ Check Your Knowledge

1. What events continue to lead the industry in terms of event business?

2. When are the majority of large association conventions planned?

3. What are the key skills that a person entering the charity event category must possess?

4. What is SMERF?

Fairs and Festivals

The word *fair* is likely to evoke memories of cotton candy, funnel cakes, Ferris wheels, and other games. These memories are very important to why a fair is considered a special event, but the purpose of most fairs in the United States is usually related to the agriculture industry. A professional staff chosen by an elected committee usually produces them. Fairs are generally held at the local, county, or state level.

Festivals are planned events that are often themed to the celebration's purpose. Cultures, anniversaries, holy days, and special occasions are commonly celebrated as a festival. Mardi Gras, for example, celebrates the beginning of Lent. Food and entertainment are greatly emphasized when planning a festival. **Festivals.com** is a site that allows you to search for festivals held throughout the world. The variety of festivals is astounding—art, music, sporting, literary, performing arts, air shows, science, and even children's festivals. The web site describes cultural festivals as "Magical parades. Fabulous feasts. Dizzying dancing. The spirit of celebration crosses languages, oceans, continents and cultures, as people revel in their heritages and communities."[5]

The following is a small sampling of festivals—some are commonly known, and others are surprising:

Oktoberfest

Mardi Gras

Biketoberfest

Hispanic Heritage Festival

Street Music Festival

American Dance Festival

Polar Bear Festival

Gilroy Garlic Festival

Bagelfest

One of the key strategies in planning special events for fairs and festivals is to determine the purpose of the event early on. It is important to analyze the available manpower in the form of both professionals and volunteers who will assist in staging the event. The **International Festivals & Events Association (IFEA)** provides an opportunity for event managers from around the world to network and exchange ideas on how other festivals excel in sponsorship, marketing, fundraising, operations, volunteer coordination, and management. The IFEA is highlighted later in the chapter.

Concerts and Sporting Events

Concert promoters are an alternative career choice relating to special events. For the purpose of this text, smaller concert and music events will be the focus. Woodstock, in 1969, was a large music festival that has been labeled as a transformational event—it transformed the participants and society. Many concerts are planned as fundraisers, such as Live Aid, which raised millions of dollars to benefit starving people of Africa through a concert that included major rock performers. On a smaller scale, universities may provide a concert as a special event.

Opening ceremonies, halftime shows, and postgame shows for sporting events provide another "arena" an event manager can select as a career path. Shows such as these are highly visible because of the large number of sporting events that are televised. This provides a unique challenge for the event manager—to satisfy the millions of television viewers as well as those watching in the stadium (or whatever the venue may be).

Sporting events have historically been more popular than other forms of entertainment. This is probably because of our competitive nature and a desire to watch those who compete—a kind of flashback to the gladiator days of old. It is important to remember when planning special events in the sports environment that the primary attention should remain on the athletes and the competition. Therefore, the special event should be staged to add to and not subtract from the sport itself. Special events may even attract additional viewers and fans to the sport. The role of special events in the sports category has plenty of room for growth and expansion as professional sports become more and more competitive.

Sports entertainment is a field that will likely see considerable growth in the future. Just think, someone has to plan, organize, and run the halftime shows and the events before and after the game. A large audience awaits your Super Bowl–sized imagination, which can ensure that every sporting event is a winning experience for the most important player of all—the fan.

Mega Sporting Events

Mega sporting events are some of the biggest moneymakers in the industry. Both large and small communities embrace mega sporting events because of the positive economic impact. Activities in sports have brought forth tremendous economic impacts.

INTRODUCING SUZANNE BAILEY

Event Director

Suzanne graduated from Southern Utah University with a B.A. in Business Administration, Marketing, in 1996. Eager to get her career started, she accepted an entry-level position at Bowl Games of America (BGA), a student travel/special events production company that produces NCAA bowl game halftime shows. Within a year, Suzanne settled into the division of the company that interested her most—the tiny but growing dance division of BGA, BGA Performance, as an executive assistant.

Suzanne worked with the director of BGA Performance to create an entirely new marketing strategy, which eventually led to great success within the dance division. Rather than working with small high school dance groups exclusively, BGA Performance set up a commission system with large private dance competition

INTRODUCING SUZANNE BAILEY *(Continued)*

companies, which would market the bowl game performance opportunities to their competition winners. This marketing strategy led to 300-percent growth in the first year.

Suzanne worked her way up the ladder to associate director and eventually director of BGA Performance. Her work changed dramatically with the seasons. During dance competition season, the marketing effort was immense—that was the time to make the big sales push. Every day, Suzanne created and sent hundreds of invitation packets to private dance competition companies and made as many sales phone calls as possible. She also reviewed audition tapes and selected dancers for the bowl game halftime shows. Once she had most of the dancers signed up for the bowl game they would perform in, Suzanne's work shifted to customer service and show production. A few months prior to each event, Suzanne traveled to each city with the dance directors and/or chaperones to give them a preview of what would happen during the event with their dancers.

Finally, the events took place. Suzanne became an event director during the actual events. Suzanne traveled to the destination city a few days before the dancers arrived to confirm with hotel group sales managers, caterers, rehearsal site workers, and bowl game executives. She met and directed her on-site staff (choreography team and event staff). The workdays of the events could be long and exhausting, full of excitement and anticipation. Much of the time was devoted to rehearsals, with some fun activities also included. Catered lunches, beach parties, and evening dinner/dance parties for the group at famous spots like Mardi Gras World in New Orleans are a few examples of some activities. The dancers enjoyed every minute of their week, including the long, hard rehearsals in the sun (or rain, or even snow, depending on the city). Game day (or show day) was always the most exciting of the days. After much hard work and preparation, the dancers went out on the field for their five minutes of fame. They performed, along with famous guest stars and the BGA-recruited marching bands, to a live stadium audience in the tens of thousands and often to a national television audience. This was when the position as director of BGA Performance really pays off. The excitement of the show outweighed all the frustrations and challenges of actually putting it all together. It was extremely rewarding to watch the young people have the time of their lives! For Suzanne, the next day was usually spent traveling to the next bowl game city and starting the process all over again.

After working on bowl game halftime shows for about six years, the 2002 Olympics came to Salt Lake City, Suzanne's hometown. Having worked with the dance choreographer and other directors of the Olympic opening and closing ceremonies team for bowl game shows, she took a position as senior production coordinator, volunteer cast, with the ceremonies production team. Suzanne helped manage a team of 15 cast coordinators, who worked with more than 4,000 volunteer cast members and 200 production staff volunteers. Suzanne facilitated communication between choreographers, stage managers, producers, and the cast. She managed all aspects of casting for the ceremonies, from recruitment to auditions to performer selection to the actual live performance. This was truly an opportunity of a lifetime for Suzanne.

The *Olympic Games* is the hallmark of all sporting events, attracting more than 6 million people to the host city. That is a lot of people traveling, staying in hotels, eating in restaurants, and possibly looking at the host city's attractions. The Olympics is an international sporting event that takes place every two years, and it consists of both summer and winter games. The Olympics attract more people than any other sporting event, making it easy to see why the Olympics play an important role in the industry.

The *World Cup* features the best soccer teams in the world. It is an international competition that takes place every four years. However, the World

Cup is an ongoing competition, as the qualifying rounds take place over the three years before the final rounds in which the championship is awarded. Close to 1 million people actually attend the World Cup, and millions more tune in via television or the Internet.

The *Super Bowl* is an annual competition between the two best American football teams. It is a tradition that the game is held on "Super Bowl Sunday," typically occurring in late January or early February. Over the years, this day has become a holiday to many Americans. Super Bowl is one of the most-watched U.S. TV broadcasts of the year and not just for the game. People also tune in to see the much-discussed commercials, on which millions of advertising dollars are spent. People also tune in to watch the halftime show, during which some of the most popular musical artists perform.

The *World Series* is the fight for the title of best baseball team in the United States. The series is played every year starting in October between the champions of the American League and National League and caps off the Major League Baseball (MLB) postseason. Today, the series winner is determined through a best-of-seven playoff. The winning team is awarded the World Series Trophy, and each player receives a World Series ring.

There are four major men's golf championships known as the *Majors*. The *Masters Tournament* is an annual gathering of the world's best golf players at the Augusta National Golf Club. Champions of the Masters are automatically invited to play in the other three majors for the following five years, and earn a lifetime invitation to the Masters. The *United States Open Championship* is a men's open championship held in June of each year. The U.S. Open is on the official schedule of the PGA Tour and the European Tour. The U.S. Open takes place on a variety of golf courses. The *Open Championship* (British Open) is the oldest of the four major championships in men's golf. It is played annually on a links course (located in coastal areas causing frequent wind, on sandy soil, often amid dunes, with few water hazards and few if any trees). The *PGA Championship* is the final championship of the year, held in August. Champions of the PGA are also automatically invited to play in the other three majors for the next five years and are exempt from qualifying for the PGA Championship for life.

There are a number of boat races held on an annual basis. The *America's Cup* is perhaps the most famous of yachting races. In addition to the yacht races, it is also a test of boat design, sail design, fundraising, and managing people. The races are held in a series that currently involves a best-of-nine series of match racing (a duel between two boats).

Cruise lines are also creating specialized sports cruises, enabling spectators and participants to enhance their skills, to meet professional athletes, to attend major events, and simply to immerse themselves in their favorite sports.

Where Do Event Planners Work?

- Hotels/resorts
- Private corporations
- Associations

- Caterers
- The government
- Private clubs
- Convention centers
- Bridal businesses
- Event production companies
- Nonprofit organizations
- Advertising agencies
- Self-employed

LEARNING OBJECTIVE 4
Outline the skills and abilities required for event management.

Required Skills and Abilities for Event Management

Special events management, like any other form of management, requires certain skills and abilities. The act of carrying out a successful event takes more than just an idea—it takes leadership, communication, project management, effective negotiating and delegating skills, the ability to work within a budget, the ability to multitask, enthusiasm, social skills, and even the ability to make contacts. The following sections will provide an overview of skills critical to effective event management.

Leadership Skills

As a leader, the event manager will wear many hats. The first is to inspire the staff and volunteers by providing valid reasons as to why they should want to assist in achieving the established goals for the event. In this role, the event manager will also act as a salesperson. The second hat represents the event manager's responsibility to provide tools for the staff and volunteers to achieve the goals. This includes training and coordination. The third hat the event manager will wear will be that of a coach. The event manager as a leader will act as mentor and provide a support system to build a team. Staff and volunteer motivation is an important factor for effective event management. Leadership ability is the number-one skill for successful event managers. The goal of an event manager is to become a leader who can direct a team of employees and/or volunteers who will respect, admire, and follow your direction to accomplish the established goals.

Effective event leadership can transform the people on your team. Empowering your event team to find their own solutions will benefit both the people and the event. It will allow the team members to create new opportunities for themselves and stimulate personal growth. For the event, empowerment will enable goals and objectives to be achieved quickly.

Following are suggestions given by Dr. Joe Jeff Goldblatt, CSEP, for event leadership:

- Event leadership enables your team members to find the motivation to continue achieving the event goals and objectives.

- You cannot motivate others; they must motivate themselves by identifying clear personal goals and objectives.

- Volunteers are the lifeblood of most events. Recruiting, training, coordinating, and rewarding are critical to the success of this activity.

- The three styles of event leadership are democratic, autocratic, and laissez-faire. Each style may be used during the course of the event.

- Policies, procedures, and practices serve as the blueprint for event decision making.[6]

Ability to Communicate with Other Departments

The success of an event manager greatly depends on the ability of involved individuals to communicate effectively with one another. Communication can take different forms: oral, written, and electronic. It is very important for event managers to become effective communicators in order to maintain clear communications with all staff, volunteers, stakeholders, and other departments.

Written communications are an essential tool for record keeping and providing information to be mass distributed. Another way to communicate with other departments is through a meeting.

Delegating

One person cannot do everything, but managers seldom delegate enough. This contradiction is typical in the events business. The secret is to plan ahead of time and allow time for tasks to be delegated to others to help facilitate the smooth operation of an event. For successful delegation, a climate of trust and a positive working environment are needed. Also required is a committed associate who will complete the delegated task and who will communicate effectively throughout the process.

Project Management Skills

Event planning and management can be time consuming. Therefore, a good planner should have effective project management skills to be equipped to balance all of the elements of one event (or more if there are other events going on at the same time). Project management is the act of completing the project(s) on time and within budget. Project management is a perfect fit for the special events industry, where the entire event or components of an event can be managed as projects. Following are management tools by

Meeting planners coordinating events during a meeting.

George G. Fenich that may be used to assist in event project management:

- Flow charts and graphs are used for scheduling certain programs that will happen at the event. Look at any program of a meeting, and you will see start times and end times of a particular seminar, when the coffee break is to occur, when and where the lunch will be held, followed by the resumption of the meeting. A charting of the scheduling of the activities helps to guide your attendees and guests.

- Clearly defined work setup and breakdown schedules are necessary for any event. These provide the event manager with an opportunity to determine tasks that may have been overlooked in the initial planning process for the event.

- Policy statements will need to be developed to help guide in the decision-making process and the fulfilling of commitments to various people and groups in the course of planning and managing an event, such as human resources, sponsorships, security, ticketing, volunteers, and even to paid personnel for the event.[7]

Negotiating Skills

Negotiation is the process by which a meeting planner and supplier (e.g., hotel representative) reach an agreement on the terms and conditions that will govern their relationship before, during, and after a meeting, convention, exposition, or event. Effective negotiators will enter the negotiation with a good idea of what they want.

A seasoned negotiator gives the following tips:

- Do your homework. Develop a "game plan" of the outcomes sought, and prioritize your needs and wants. Learn as much about the other side's position as you can.

- Keep your eyes on the prize. Do not forget the outcome sought.

- Leave something on the table. It may provide an opportunity to come back later and renew the negotiations.

- Do not be the first one to make an offer. Letting the other person make the first move sets the outside parameters for the negotiation.

- Bluff, but do not lie.

- When there is a roadblock, find a more creative path. Thinking "outside the box" often leads to a solution.

- Timing is everything. Remember that time always works against the person who does not have it and that 90 percent of negotiation usually occurs in the last 10 percent of the time allocated.

- Listen, listen, listen—and do not get emotional. Letting emotions rule a negotiation will cause one to lose sight of what result is important.[8]

The planning and execution of a special event may involve the negotiation of several contracts. The most important is generally the one with the facility or event site. Contracts with other services may include destination management, entertainment, catering, temporary employees, security, and audiovisual equipment, to name a few. Event managers should keep the following two words in mind to strengthen their negotiating skills and position: information and flexibility.

A DAY IN THE LIFE OF TINA STOUGHTON

Events Assistant at the Waldorf Astoria Orlando and Hilton Bonnet Creek

A day in the life of an events assistant is never the same. While I might be doing similar tasks on a day-to-day basis, everything is very different as you encounter each client. Each day is certainly an adventure that always leaves you thinking about what will come next. This is an adventure I love.

As an events assistant at the Waldorf Astoria Orlando and Hilton Bonnet Creek, my first and most important task is to assist the events managers with anything they need. There are four managers who I assist on a daily basis: Those managers are the assistant director of events, two senior event managers, and an event manager. I report to the event manager on a daily basis.

Through our meetings, my job is to help pre-plan any event that will be taking place at one of our sites. Once I understand what the event entails, I place all of the specifications, or "specs," the client has requested onto banquet event orders, or BEOs. BEOs are like the road map for any event. The BEO will take you from point A to point B while ensuring the client's every request is fulfilled.

There are two types of BEOs: food and beverage, and meeting. If I put together a food and beverage BEO, it would consist of every food item for each meeting, reception, break, or event that will be taking place. The banquet department will use this BEO information to know when, where, and what to set up for each event. Meeting BEOs will include information regarding the setup of the room, audio visual equipment, electric services, and any other specific needs the client has requested.

While working closely with the logistics of events, I also assist with transporting VIP clients that will be staying at one of our hotels. This includes arranging appropriate modes of transportation to and from airports and our hotels, fulfilling client requests, ensuring amenities provided meet the client's expectations, and other duties such as screening the client's telephone calls.

On a monthly basis, I also set up in-house meetings for both properties. Each department has monthly meetings, and it is my job to block times, block rooms, create the space, organize BEOs, and so forth. This also includes orientation for new employees; if human resources needs a space to introduce employees to the property and begin the training process, I must ensure that their needs are met for the space.

Because each event is never the same, communication and organization are the most important qualities to have when working as an events assistant. Clients may change their mind, something may not go as originally planned, and being able to adapt to situations while satisfying the client is the core of my job. If you can multitask,

A DAY IN THE LIFE OF TINA STOUGHTON *(Continued)*

react quickly to situations that may become problematic, and balance working well with others and communicating effectively, you can become successful in this line of work.

I truly enjoy every aspect of being an events assistant. No day of work is the same, and being dedicated to what I love to do has helped me succeed with this job. My efforts as an assistant and the love for my career ensure that each event is as successful as the next.

Coordinating and Delegating Skills

The management of staff and volunteers involves coordinating their duties and job performance to enable you to accomplish the goals of the event. As the manager, you are responsible for assigning supervisors or group leaders to oversee the performance of the employees and/or volunteers. It is important to provide coaching and mentoring when working with staff and volunteers to arrive at the event's goals and objectives. When employees can see the purpose and value of their work as well as the outcomes of their work, they usually become more excited about achieving the goals and objectives.

Budgeting Skills

Budgeting is an activity that allows managers to plan the use of their financial resources. In the event industry, the event planner may be working with a fixed budget determined by an association, a SMERF group, or an individual (a wedding or an engagement). In other cases, the budget may be more flexible—a large corporation, for example, that has greater financial resources. Budgeting is a required skill in all hospitality fields, including the special events industry.

The financial history of previous identical or similar events, the general economy and your forecast of the future, and the income expenses you reasonably believe you can expect with the resources available are all factors to be considered in creating an event budget. Even though most event managers will view the budgeting aspect as the least interesting in their job, it is an area that should be carefully managed and is critical for success. The better you become in your budgeting skills, the more you will be able to use resources for other, more creative activities.

Ability to Multitask

Because of the nature of the business, an effective event manager should have the ability to multitask. During the planning and staging of the event, your ability to administrate, coordinate, market, and manage will be put to the test. Your job is ultimately to conduct and take control of whatever needs to be done to carry out your goals and objectives. You may encounter several problems arising at the same time, and an effective solution would be to delegate tasks accordingly.

Enthusiasm

As you've probably heard time and time again by now, in any hospitality field the risk of burnout is high and the work is demanding. At the same time, however, the rewards are great and so is the satisfaction when the event is a complete success. As perfectly stated by Norman Brinker, past chairman of the board of Brinker International, "Find out what you love to do and you'll never work a day in your life. . . . Make work like play and play like hell!"[9] Enthusiasm and passion, drive and determination: These are all qualities that will contribute to the success of an event manager/planner. As shown in the profile of Suzanne Bailey, the special events industry is an "exciting, exhausting, and fun place to work." For those with the right enthusiasm and passion, it can be a truly rewarding career path.

Effective Social Skills

Social skills are an important trait for any management position, including one in the special events industry. Social skills are critical in making those you do business with feel comfortable, in handling situations appropriately, and in eliminating barriers that get in the way of accomplishing your goals. Communication is a critical social skill as is another social skill—listening. Social etiquette is another skill that can make or break a career, and it is a practiced skill that can be acquired. Social etiquette is defined as exhibiting good manners established as acceptable to society and showing consideration for others. Professionals in the hospitality industry, including the special events field, must be proficient in proper social etiquette. Service is one of the largest products offered; therefore, social skills and etiquette are required to be successful. Proper social etiquette is required in planning special events, and correct social manners are key to business success.[10] Effective social skills are also critical to leading a motivated group of staff and/or volunteers. How well you communicate, coach, instruct, lead, and listen is a reflection of how well you will succeed as a manager.

Ability to Form Contacts

Many of us have heard the phrase, "It's not what you know, but who you know." Does this statement hold any value in the special events industry? It certainly does. An event may require various services, vendors, suppliers, or products. Here's how it works: An event planner prepares a specification of what is required and requests potential suppliers to submit their prices. The event planner then goes over this information with the client, and they make a decision as to who will provide the services. Over time, event planners quickly find out who is the best provider and therefore the one with whom they prefer to work.

▶ Check Your Knowledge

1. What does the International Festivals & Events Association (IFEA) provide?
2. Describe the skills and abilities needed for successful event management.
3. Define the process of negotiation.

LEARNING OBJECTIVE 5
Identify the main professional organizations and associations involved with the special events industry.

Special Event Organizations

Like other hospitality industries, professional associations are a key contributor to the professional development of the special events field. Professional associations provide training and prestigious certification to their members, and membership provides an opportunity to network with other professionals in the field. Furthermore, associations can help members connect with vendors that provide products and services relating to special events.

CORPORATE PROFILE

International Special Events Society

Members of the International Special Events Society organize events like the Macy's Thanksgiving Day Parade.

The **International Special Events Society (ISES)** was founded in 1987, and it has grown to involve nearly 5,500 members who are active in over 50 chapters around the world.[11] The organization includes professionals representing special events producers (from festivals to trade shows), caterers, decorators, florists, destination management companies, rental companies, special effects experts, audiovisual technicians, party and convention coordinators, hotel sales managers, specialty entertainers, and many others.

The ISES was founded with the objective to "foster enlightened performance through education while promoting ethical conduct. ISES works to join event and meeting professionals to focus on the 'event as a whole' rather than its individual parts."[12] The organization has formed a solid network of peers that allows its members to produce quality events for their clients while benefiting from positive working relationships with other ISES members.

The ISES awards a designation of Certified Special Events Professional (CSEP), which is considered to be the benchmark of professional achievement in the special events industry. It "demonstrates a continuous dedication to enhance individual and professional performance,"[13] as stated by ISES. Visit the ISES web site at **www.ises.com** for further information.

The mission of the International Special Events Society is to provide its members and stakeholders with:

- Collaborative networking
- Education and professional development
- Inspiration
- Outward awareness and credibility[14]

Professional associations also provide their members with help in creating a business plan and other forms of consultation. Job banks and referral services are even provided by some associations. The following sections provide a brief overview of the key associations relating to the special events industry.

International Festivals & Events Association

The IFEA has provided fundraising and modern developmental ideas to the special events industry for almost 60 years. The IFEA began the program to enhance the level of festival management training and performance with a Certified Festival and Event Executive (CFEE) program in 1983. Those seeking to achieve this distinguished title are committed to excellence in festival and event management, are using it as a tool for career advancement, and are in search of further knowledge. The CFEE program is an eight-part process that includes a core and elective curriculum as well as festival and event management experience, achievements, and assessment.[15] The organization currently has more than 2,000 plus professional members,[16] who are informed of industry developments through IFEA publications, seminars, an annual convention and trade show, and ongoing networking.[17]

The benefits of joining this association and meeting the CFEE requirements include the ability to negotiate a better income or financial package, recognition by other industry professionals, and the inside knowledge that it provides for the festival industry. Visit the IFEA web site at **www.ifea.com** for further information.

Meeting Professionals International

Meeting Professionals International (MPI) is a Dallas-based association with nearly 18,500 members.[18] MPI believes that "as the global authority and resource for the $102.3 billion meeting and event industry, MPI empowers meeting professionals to increase their strategic value through education, clearly defined career pathways, and business growth opportunities." MPI offers professional development in two certification programs:

- Certified Meeting Professional (CMP)
- Certification in Meeting Management (CMM)

The CMP program is based on professional experience and academic examination. After gaining certification, the professional may use the CMP designation after his or her name on business cards, letterheads, and other printed items. Additionally, studies show that CMPs earn up to $10,000 more annually than non-CMPs.[19]

The CMM program is directed toward senior-level meeting professionals and provides an opportunity for continuing education, global certification and recognition, potential career advancement, and a networking base.[20] Visit the MPI web site at **www.mpiweb.org** for more information.

Hospitality Sales and Marketing Association International

Hospitality Sales and Marketing Association International (HSMAI) is the largest and most active travel industry sales and marketing membership organization in the world, with over 7,000 members from 35 countries,[21] representing hotels and resorts, airlines, cruise lines, car rental agencies, theme parks and attractions, convention and visitors bureaus, destination management companies, reservations sales organizations, restaurants, golf and recreation sites, and much more. Membership is open to anyone involved in one of the sales, marketing, management, educational, planning, or reporting disciplines within the hospitality industry, including those involved in promoting, producing, or delivering support services to the travel, tourism, hospitality, convention, and meeting industries.[22]

HSMAI's mission is to be the leading source for sales and marketing information, knowledge, business development, and networking for professionals in tourism, travel, and hospitality.[23] HSMAI offers certification courses for hospitality sales executive, revenue management executive, hospitality marketing executive, hospitality digital marketer, and hospitality business acumen.

Local Convention and Visitors Bureaus

A CVB is a not-for-profit organization that is located in almost every city in the United States and Canada. Many other cities throughout the world also have a CVB or convention and visitors association (CVA). Simply stated, the CVB is an organization with the purpose of promoting tourism, meetings, and related business for its city. The CVB has three primary functions:

1. Encourage groups to hold meetings, conventions, and trade shows in the city or area it represents

2. Assist those groups with event preparations and during the event

3. Encourage tourists to visit the historic, cultural, and recreational opportunities the destination offers

The CVB does not engage in the actual planning or organizing of meetings, conventions, and other events. However, the CVB assists meeting planners and managers in several ways. First, it will provide information about the destination, area attractions, services, and facilities. Second, it provides an unbiased source of information to the planner. Finally, most of the services offered by the CVB are at no charge because they are funded through other sources, including hotel occupancy taxes and membership dues. Therefore, it can provide an array of services to event planners and managers. A sample of general services provided by a CVB includes the following:

- CVBs act as a liaison between the planner and the community.
- CVBs can help meeting attendees maximize their free time through the creation of pre- and postconference activities, spouse tours, and special evening events.
- CVBs can provide hotel room counts and meeting space statistics.
- CVBs can help with event facility availability.
- CVBs are a network for transportation—shuttle service, ground transportation, and airline information.
- CVBs can assist with site inspections and familiarization tours.
- CVBs can provide speakers and local educational opportunities.
- CVBs can provide help in securing auxiliary services, production companies, catering, security, and so forth.

TECHNOLOGY SPOTLIGHT

Courtesy of **Jay R. Schrock**, Ph.D., Professor Emeritus, School of Hotel and Restaurant Management, University of South Florida, Sarasota–Manatee

Have you ever wondered, when you've been to an event that went off extremely well, what happened to make this event so successful? The answer is hard work from dedicated people and the special events technologies that enable them to make the best use of their resources and to ensure the event is a spectacular success. Special events can range from a senior prom, a sports team's ending reception, a church gathering, or something like the National Restaurant Association's annual event in Chicago that attracts tens of thousands of people and fills thousands of hotel rooms, as well as one of the nation's largest convention centers. The technology that drives these special events range from room bookings, contacting event planners, guests, purveyors, equipment companies, multimedia companies, and companies that supply the extra bartenders and waiters for the event.

Event-planning software allows both the event sponsors and the event planner to communicate clearly and in detail about the event title, its location (ballroom A, courtyard, or waterfront lawn), the event date, as well as start and end times with time zones included for those instances where guests may be traveling long distances to attend. The event software will also include detailed descriptions of what kinds of seating and types of tables are required, types and amounts of food, service: buffet style or sit down, the number of guests, and cost per person. Additional data with regard to flowers, head tables, bands, special audio or video equipment, flip charts, or possibly champagne toasts may be needed. All of these data will be included in the planning pages of the software.

If the event is a large one like the National Restaurant Show in Chicago or the International Hotel, Motel + Restaurant Show in New York, large planning companies will work with both the event planner and the cities involved in putting on these very large special events. This is also true for large music and other themed events. At the individual hotel level, the hotel's revenue management system software will help determine how many rooms should be blocked or allocated for a particular event. This software will also allow the executive team to look at future bookings and determine how many rooms could be blocked or set aside and at what prices.

Future event management technologies will include faster check-in, live slide sharing, interactions with speakers in Google Hangout–type formats, and making events more mobile-friendly with faster Internet access.

Sustainability in Special Events

What drives hospitality and tourism companies to incorporate sustainability standards into their business practices and daily operations? What do these companies gain from employing sustainability standards?

The recent increase in special event tourism has triggered the emergence of sustainable event standards. Britain has recently developed a system of standards for event management, which highlights policies and procedures necessary to implement sustainability. Event managers can use these standards as a benchmark for how to train employees on proper sustainable practices before, during, and after events. Currently in the United States, ASTM International has created a guide for sustainable event management called the Standard Specification for Evaluation and Selection of Destinations for Environmentally Sustainable Meetings, Events, Trade Shows, and Conferences, which credits much of its content to the British system of standards.[24]

Sustainable event tourism refers to the implementation of practices and procedures that help conserve both the natural environment and the special event space. Special event tourism is one of the most lucrative and fastest growing segments of the tourism industry.[25] Special events are provided for a variety of reasons, which range from creating market demand for the host location as a desirable destination, generating publicity for the event's sponsors, achieving a specific purpose or goal, developing awareness of a particular cause or idea, and so on.[26] Whatever the reason may be, special events play an important role in consumer's images, attitudes and perceptions of host destinations.[27] Because special events bring tourism to certain locations, it is the responsibility of the event host to employ sustainable practices, in order to preserve local resources and cultural interests.[28]

Sustainable event tourism not only provides environmental advantages, but financial returns as well. The organizations who are dedicated to incorporating sustainable programs into their business plans can expect to see the greatest return on investment as a result of cost reduction, revenue increase, and so on.[29] Some practices that can result in financial gain include conserving energy such as light spill from event and security lighting, turning off lights whenever they are not in use, utilizing low carbon fuels and renewable energy, ensuring appropriate waste and cleaning procedures are followed, utilizing low emission vehicles, reducing vehicle usage, and increasing shared transportation.[30] Ultimately, the implementation of sustainable practices can increase the benefits of being in the special events business, as well as the excitement of actually hosting an event.

The Special Events Job Market

Becoming a special events consultant or an off-premise catering/event specialist requires a delicate balance of many skills. Experience gained from several avenues will propel you to the heights of success. As with any career, an "experience ladder" must be climbed.

First, allow yourself to gain all the experience you can in the food and beverage aspect of the hospitality industry. If time and resources permit, it is highly recommended that you gain knowledge from a culinary arts program. Second, experience gained as a banquet food server in a high-volume convention or resort hotel property is invaluable. Also, paying your dues as a guest service agent at a hotel front desk or as a concierge provides you with the opportunity to hone your customer service skills. Promote yourself to a banquet manager or a CSM (convention service coordinator), which provides the opportunity to learn and perfect organizational skills—to which end is the ability to multitask and deal with hundreds of details simultaneously. After all, the business of special events is the business of managing details.

The next step is obtaining a sales position. An excellent appointment to aspire to is an executive meeting manager, sometimes called a small meeting manager, in a convention or conference hotel. Here, you are responsible for booking small room blocks (usually 20 rooms or less), making meeting room arrangements, creating meal plans, and setting audiovisual requirements. On a small scale, hundreds of details are coordinated for several groups at any one time. From this position, you may laterally move to a catering sales position within a hotel.

The catering sales position in a hotel will expose you to many different kinds of events: weddings, reunions, corporate events, holiday events, and social galas and balls. In this position, one either coordinates or has the opportunity to work with various vendors. This is where the florists, prop companies, lighting experts, entertainment agencies, rental companies, and audiovisual wizards come into play. Two to three years in this capacity grooms you for the next rung on the ladder.

Figure 13–2 • A Career Path for an Event Manager.

Now, you can pursue several different angles: being promoted to a convention service manager within a hotel, moving into off-premise catering as a sales consultant, joining a production company, or perhaps affiliating yourself with a destination management company (DMC). Typically, without sales experience within a DMC, your first experience with them will be as an operations manager. Once proficient in this capacity, you then join the sales team.

After another two years creating and selling your heart out, you will be ready for the big leagues. The palette is now yours to paint your future. How about aspiring to be the next Super Bowl halftime creator and producer? Or perhaps creating the theme and schematics for the Olympics is in your future. Many avenues are available for exploring. Call on your marketing ideas, your business sense, your accounting skills, your aptitude for design, and your discriminating palette for creating unique entertaining and dining concepts. Continually educating yourself and discovering fresh ideas through adventurous experiences are essential to designing and selling special events. Don't forget to embark on as many internships as you can in the name of gaining knowledge and experience. Show your enthusiasm for what is different and unconventional. Know that creativity has no boundaries. Visualize the big picture and go for it! Figure 13–2 shows a career path for an event manager.

▶ Check Your Knowledge

1. Identify the main professional organizations and associations involved in the special events industry.

Trends in the Special Events Industry

Courtesy of Dr. Greg Dunn, Senior Lecturer & Managing Director, University of Florida, Eric Friedheim Tourism Institute

- *Multiscreen Event Experiences.* Today's special event attendees experience and share a special event in multiscreen fashion with pre-event, on-site, and postevent ac tivities performed on several devices, including a personal computer, tablet, and/or smartphone. Mobile has become the single most important part of the primary screen experience for special event attendees. Mobile device scan be used in special events for information management, registration, attendee communication, and engagement, but today's planners know that attendee technology can maximize attendee experience through enhanced engagement, connection, interaction, and participation. It makes it easy for attendees to share the experience with those not as lucky to attend the event but still want to be involved.

- *Personalization.* Special event guests want to choose and mold their own event experiences. Today's special event planners offer a choice of activities, seating, food and beverage, music, environment, and vibe in order to get their guests to talk, tweet, and post about the event. Some special event planners are taking this trend to a new level. Some have had great success with the introduction of special event pop-up stations, where the food, décor, or activity comes to the guests rather than the other way around. Other planners have adopted the drag-and-drop venue movement by reusing or reinventing existing spaces to create fresh, immersive experiences. The idea is to keep the energy of the event moving. For instance, instead of guests moving to the appetizer or dessert station or the bar or the game area, a service station pops up near the guests. Examples are food trikes or decorated metro-style push carts. Other planners are looking to serve up an "entrenched" special event experience where the attendees are put at the center of the event to make them feel they own, direct, or control the action. Activities may include special food and beverage deliveries direct to attendee seats, movie screen filming and direction, or being the event planner of the evening.

- *Integrated Special Event Technologies.* Special event developers and operators alike are embracing new integrated technology platforms that handle various event functions such as attendee and sponsor registration, web and mobile interfaces, data collection, analysis and report generation, floor plan management, abstract and speaker presentation submissions, event surveys, payment means, and delegate giveaways and promotions activities. Planners are also looking for ways to increase attendee interaction and participation by moving away from static handheld passable microphones to throwable microphones, or by developing apps that attendees can download on their smartphones to serve as mini-microphones. Some of the benefits include greater attendee control, reduced fear of speaking, and greater interaction.

- *Changing Role of the Event Planner.* Event planners will continue to evolve from a coordinator and executor of special events to more of a director and orchestrator. Some planners are moving toward a micro-location orientation that delivers greater opportunities to interact with attendees with relevant marketing initiatives. Some are integrating beacons, Wi-Fi, simple swipe and scavenger hunts via smartphone, and markers to enable attendees to have control and more fun at the event. Finally, event planners as choreographers increasingly view event guest speakers as performers. Modern speakers often fill the role of facilitator, instigator, and community leader yielding more entertaining, interactive, and richer experiences.

- *Green Events*. Environmentally conscious planning for events is in high demand, including using eco-friendly supplies and materials; recycling; providing local, sustainable, and organic food and beverages; utilizing water and energy conservations practices; and omitting pollution and waste production.

CASE STUDY

Not Enough Space

Jessica is the event planner for a large convention center. A client has requested an exhibition that would bring in not only excellent revenue, but one that is an annual event, which might lead to future revenue, and one that several other convention centers would be eager to host.

Exhibitions typically take one or two days to set up, three or four days of exhibition, and one day to break down. Professional organizations handle each part of the setup and breakdown.

When Jessica checks the space available on the days requested for the exhibition, she notices that another scheduled exhibition would be blocking part of the space needed by her client.

Discussion Question

1. What can Jessica do to get her client to use the convention center without inconveniencing either exhibitor too much?

Summary

1. Special events differ from daily events, which tend to occur spontaneously, in that they recognize a unique moment in time with ceremony and ritual to satisfy specific needs and are always planned.

2. The special events industry is a growing field that will provide many professional career opportunities in event management and planning.

3. Special events planners and managers have filled a need that was first introduced at hotels and convention centers. They are responsible for planning the event from start to finish.

4. The special events industry can be grouped into several smaller classifications, including corporate events, association events, charity balls and fundraising events, social

functions, fairs and festivals, and concert and sporting events.

5. The event-planning process includes the following steps: research, design, planning, coordination, and evaluation.
6. Special events planners can work in a variety of settings. They range from hotels and resorts, convention centers, and private clubs to self-employment.
7. Critical skills and abilities required for a career in special events management include leadership skills, effective communication, project management skills, negotiating skills, coordinating and delegating skills, budgeting skills, multitasking abilities, enthusiasm, effective social skills, and the ability to form contacts.
8. The special events industry has its own selection of professional associations that offer certification, continuing education,

and networking to their members. The International Special Events Society (ISES), International Festivals & Events Association (IFEA), and Meeting Professionals International (MPI) are three of the largest and most recognized professional associations in the field. Local convention and visitors bureaus (CVBs) are organizations that can be valuable resources to the special events industry. A CVB has the purpose of promoting tourism, meetings, and related business for its city.
9. The management of time and finances, along with technology and human resources are event-planning tools that can be utilized to your advantage as you pursue a career in this field.
10. The special events industry does not have rigid boundaries. Closely related fields that may overlap include catering, marketing, sales, and entertainment.

Key Words and Concepts

charity balls
conventions
coordination
corporate events
corporate seminars
event planner
event planning
fairs and festivals

fundraisers
International Festivals & Events Association (IFEA)
International Special Events Society (ISES)
Meeting Professionals International (MPI)
social functions

special events industry
trade shows
weddings and holiday parties
workshops

Review Questions

1. What do event planners do?
2. What are the challenges for event planners and managers?
3. Describe three of the classifications of special events.
4. Explain the skills and abilities required for event management.

Internet Exercises

1. Organization: **International Special Events Society (ISES)**
   Do an Internet search for "ISES Eventworld." What can an ISES Eventworld do for professional development, and who should attend?

2. Organization: **Meeting Professionals International (MPI)**
   Go to their web site and search on "Career Development." What types of jobs are available?

Apply Your Knowledge

1. Make a plan for a local event in your area. List all the headings and formulate a budget.

Suggested Activity

1. Attend a special event and write a brief report on the event and its planning and organization.

Endnotes

1. Frank Supovitz, "Foreword," in Joe J. Goldblatt, *Special Events: Best Practices in Modern Event Management*, 2nd ed. (New York: John Wiley and Sons, 1997), iv.
2. Blythe Cameson, *Opportunities in Event Planning Careers* (New York: McGraw-Hill, 2002), 4–7.
3. Event Solutions, *2004 Black Book* (Tempe, AZ: Event Publishing, 2004), 22.
4. Blythe Cameson, *Opportunities in Event Planning Careers*, 115.
5. Festivals.com, *Culture*, www.festivals.com (accessed March 27, 2015).
6. Goldblatt, *Special Events: Best Practices in Modern Event Management*, 129–139.
7. George G. Fenich, *Meetings, Expositions, Events, and Conventions, 3rd ed.: An Introduction to the Industry* (Upper Saddle River, NJ: Pearson Education, 2011), 181–182.
8. Fenich, *Meetings, Expositions, Events, and Conventions*, 366.
9. Norman Brinker, presentation to the National Restaurant Association, May 14, 1994.
10. Judy Allen, *Event Planning Ethics and Etiquette: A Principled Approach to the Business of Special Event Management* (Etobicoke, Ontario, Canada: John Wiley and Sons, 2003), 79.
11. International Special Events Society, *About ISES*, http://www.ises.com. Click on About ISES (accessed June 4, 2015).
12. Ibid.
13. International Special Events Society, *The CSEP Program*, http://www.ises.com. Click on CSEP (accessed June 4, 2015).
14. International Special Events Society, *Vision–Mission*, http://www.ises.com. Go to About ISES, and then click on Vision & Mission (accessed June 4, 2015).
15. International Festivals & Events Association, http://www.ifea.com/. Search for "CFEE program" (accessed June 4, 2015).

16. International Festivals & Events Association, *About IFEA*, http://www.ifea.com/. Click on About IFEA (accessed June 4, 2015).

17. Ibid.

18. Meeting Professionals International, *About MPI*, http://www.mpiweb.org. Click on About MPI (accessed on March 29, 2015).

19. Cameson, *Opportunities in Event Planning Careers*, 36–41.

20. Meeting Professionals International, *CMM*, www.mpiweb.org. Click on Professional Development, and then click on CMM Program (accessed November 27, 2014).

21. Hospitality Sales and Marketing Association International (HSMAI), *About HSMAI*, http://www.hsmai.org. Click on About HSMAI (accessed March 29, 2015).

22. Hospitality Sales and Marketing Association International (HSMAI), *Membership–HSMAI*, www.hsmai.org. Click on membership (accessed February 8, 2015).

23. Hospitality Sales and Marketing Association International (HSMAI), *HSMAI Global*, www.hsmai.org. Click on HSMAI Global (accessed March 27, 2015).

24. ASTM International, *Annual Book of ASTM Standards*, http://www.astm.org. Go to Products & Services, and then click on Book of Standards (accessed March 27, 2015).

25. S. Reid and C. Arcodia. (2002). *Understanding the Role of Stakeholders in Event Management*.

26. Michael Turney. (2009). "Special Events Generate Publicity but Are They Effective Public Relations?" http://www.nku.edu/~turney/prclass/sections/special_events.html. Retrieved on November 17, 2011.

27. L. Chalip, C. Green, and B. Hill. (2003). "Effects of Sport Media on Destination Image and Intentions to Visit." *Journal of Sport Management* 17, 214–234.

28. Roselyne N. Okech. (2011). "Promoting Sustainable Festival Events Tourism: A Case Study of Lamu Kenya." *Worldwide Hospitality and Tourism Themes*. Vol. 3, No. 3.

29. Mitchell Beer, November 14, 2011, "Commentary: New Green Standards Help Make Sustainability Sustainable," *MeetingsNet.com*, http://meetingsnet.com. Search for "New Green Standards Help Make Sustainability Sustainable" to view this article (accessed on November 17, 2014).

30. Wikipedia, *Sustainable Event Management*, http://en.wikipedia.org/. Search for "sustainable event management" (accessed on November 17, 2014).

Empower People
Inspire People
Leadership
Lead Change
Shared Vision

CHAPTER 14

Leadership and Management

LEARNING OBJECTIVES

After reading and studying this chapter, you should be able to:

- Identify the characteristics and practices of leaders.
- Define *leadership*.
- Identify the characteristics and practices of management.
- Define *management*.
- Differentiate between leadership and management.
- Discuss ethics in hospitality.

Leadership

Our fascination with **leadership** goes back many centuries. Lately, however, it has come into prominence in the hospitality, tourism, and other industries as all strive for excellence in the delivery of services and products in an increasingly competitive environment. No matter whether as a part of industry, government, school, church, a nonprofit organization, or even a neighborhood association, we all have experienced both good and poor leadership. It's also fair to say, based upon our experiences, that it is the presence of an effective leader that ultimately ensures the success of any group endeavor. Leaders can and do make a difference when measuring a company's success.

LEARNING OBJECTIVE 1
Identify the characteristics and practices of leaders.

Characteristics and Practices of Leaders

So, what are the ingredients that result in leadership excellence? If you look at the military for examples of leadership excellence, you see that leaders can be identified by certain characteristics. For example, the *U.S. Marine Guidebook* lists the following leadership traits:

- Courage
- Decisiveness
- Dependability
- Endurance
- Enthusiasm
- Initiative
- Unselfishness

- Integrity
- Judgment
- Justice
- Knowledge
- Loyalty
- Tact

A marine officer would likely choose integrity as the most important trait. Integrity, one of the Marine Corps Leadership Traits, "means that you are honest and truthful in what you say or do."[1]

In addition to these leadership traits, the following identifiable practices are common to leaders:

1. *Challenge the process.* Be active, not passive; search for opportunities; experiment and take risks.

2. *Inspire a shared vision.* Create a vision; envision the future; enlist others.

3. *Enable others to act.* Do not act alone; foster collaboration; strengthen others.

4. *Model the way.* Plan; set examples; strive for small wins.

5. *Encourage the heart.* Share the passion; recognize individual contributions; celebrate accomplishments.

Definitions of Leadership

LEARNING OBJECTIVE 2
Define *leadership*.

Because of the complexities of leadership, the different types of leadership, and individual perceptions of leaders, *leadership* has several definitions. Many definitions share commonalities, but there are also differences. In terms of hospitality leadership, the definition "Leading is the process by which a person with vision is able to influence the activities and outcomes of others in a desired way" is appropriate.[2]

Leaders know what is needed and why it is needed in a given situation—and they are able to communicate this necessity to others to gain their cooperation and support. Leadership theory and practice has evolved over time to a point where current industry practitioners may be identified as transactional or transformational leaders.[3]

INTRODUCING HORST SCHULZE

Capella Hotel Group

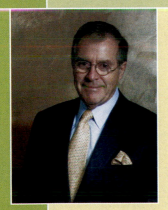

Horst Schulze is a legendary leader in the hospitality industry and one of the most influential hospitality industry leaders of our time. His vision helped reshape concepts of guest service throughout the hospitality and service industries.

Mr. Schulze grew up in a small village in Germany, and he was 11 years old when he told his parents that he wanted to work in a hotel. When he was 14, his parents took him to the finest hotel in the region, where they had an "audience" with the general manager—it lasted 10 minutes, and the general manager didn't speak to him again for the next two years! Everyone, including young Schulze's mother, the general manager, and the restaurant maître d', told him how important the guests were, and, with knees shaking, young Schulze found himself in the restaurant working as a busser. The maître d' made a favorable impression on the young man because he was respected by both guests and staff alike. So, when Horst had to do an essay for his hotel school (he attended hotel school on Wednesdays), he chose the title, "We Are Ladies and Gentlemen Serving Ladies and Gentlemen." He kept the essay because it was the only A he received, but that A also became the foundation of his philosophy to create service excellence.

Mr. Schulze now speaks on guest service to thousands every year, graciously sharing with others his knowledge and experience. He says that there are three aspects of service:[4]

1. Service should be defect free.
2. Service should be timely.
3. People should care.

It is the caring piece that exemplifies service. The guest relationship begins when a guest is greeted with a warm welcome. Mr. Schulze adds that all hospitality businesses should be doing four things:[5]

1. Keeping guests delighted equals loyalty, meaning guests trust you and are happy to form a relationship with you.
2. Find new guests.

(Continued)

INTRODUCING HORST SCHULZE *(Continued)*

3. Get as much money as you can from the guest through excellence in service.

4. Create efficiencies, meaning to provide the best services in a timely manner.

Mr. Schulze also worked with Hyatt Hotels and Hilton Hotels. After joining the Ritz-Carlton as a charter member and vice president of operations in 1983, Mr. Schulze was instrumental in creating the operating and service standards that have become world famous. He was appointed executive vice president in 1987, and president and chief operating officer (COO) in 1988. Under his leadership, the group was awarded the Malcolm Baldrige National Quality Award in both 1992 and 1999; it was the first and only hotel company to win even one such award. In 2002, Mr. Schulze, along with several former Ritz-Carlton executives, formed the Capella Hotel Group to create and operate branded hotels in several distinctive market segments. The canon of the company is as follows: "The Capella Hotel Group is in business to create value and unparalleled results for our owners by creating products that fulfill individual customer expectations."[6]

They offer significant opportunities within three profiles:[7]

1. Ultra-luxury hotel properties in gateway cities and spectacular resort destinations

2. Luxury hotel accommodations for frequent travelers

3. Management of select independent hotel properties

Capella Hotel Group has several hotels and resorts under two brands: Solís and Capella.

Transactional Leadership

Transactional leadership is viewed as a process by which a leader is able to bring about desired actions from others by using certain behaviors, rewards, or incentives. In essence, an exchange or transaction takes place between leader and follower. Figure 14–1 shows the transactional leadership model. This figure illustrates the coming together of the leader, the situation, and the followers. A hotel general manager (GM) who encourages the food and beverage director to achieve certain goals in exchange for a bonus is an example of someone practicing transactional leadership.

Transformational Leadership

Leadership involves looking for ways to bring about longer-term, higher-order changes in follower behavior. This brings us to transformational leadership. The term **transformational leadership** is used to describe the process

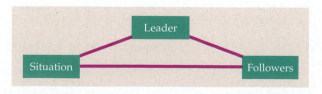

Figure 14–1 • Transactional Leadership Model.

of eliciting performance above and beyond normal expectations. A transformational leader is one who inspires others to reach beyond themselves and do more than they originally thought possible; this is accomplished by fostering a commitment to a shared vision of the future.

Transformational leaders practice a hands-on philosophy, not in terms of performing the day-to-day tasks of subordinates, but in developing and encouraging their followers individually. Transformational leadership involves three important factors:

1. Charisma
2. Individual consideration
3. Intellectual stimulation

Of course, it is also possible to be a charismatic transformational leader as well as a transactional leader. Although this does involve a measurable amount of effort, these leaders are guaranteed to rake in success throughout their careers.

Examples of Excellence in Leadership

Dr. Martin Luther King, Jr. was one of the most charismatic transformational leaders in history. Dr. King dedicated his life to achieving rights for all citizens through nonviolent methods. His dream of how society could be was shared by millions of Americans. In 1964, Dr. King won the Nobel Peace Prize.

Another transformational leader is Herb Kelleher, the co-founder, Chairman Emeritus, and former CEO of Southwest Airlines. He was able to inspire his followers to pursue his corporate vision and reach beyond themselves to give Southwest Airlines that something extra that set it apart from its competitors.

Kelleher recognized that the company does not exist merely for the gratification of its employees. He knew that Southwest Airlines must perform and must be profitable. However, he believed strongly that valuing individuals for themselves was the best way to attain exceptional performance. Passengers who fly Southwest Airlines may have seen Herb Kelleher because he traveled frequently and was likely to be found serving drinks, fluffing pillows, or just wandering up and down the aisle, talking to passengers. The success of Southwest and the enthusiasm of its employees indicate that Herb Kelleher achieved his goal of weaving together individual and corporate interests so that all members of the Southwest family benefit. Kelleher is a great transformational leader who was able to lead by visioning, inspiring, empowering, and communicating.[8]

Martin Luther King, Jr., one of the most charismatic transformational leaders of the twentieth century, giving his famous "I Have a Dream" speech.

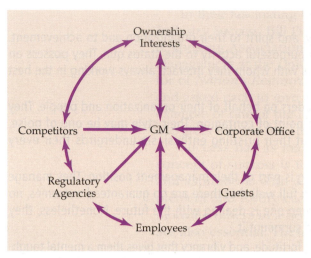

Figure 14–2 • Dynamics of Demands on Leaders in the Hospitality Industry.

Figure 14–3 • Amount of Energy the Leader Needs to Spend on Getting Results and Maintaining Relationships.

3. Orientation toward the future

4. A belief in certain fundamental principles of human behavior

5. Strong connections that they do not hesitate to display

6. Political astuteness

7. Ability to use power both for efficiency and for the larger good of the organization

Leaders vary in their values, managerial styles, and priorities. Peter Drucker, the renowned management scholar, author, and consultant of many years, has discussed with hundreds of leaders their roles, goals, and performance. These discussions took place with leaders of large and small organizations, with for-profit and volunteer organizations. Interestingly, Drucker observes the following:

All the leaders I have encountered—both those I worked with and those I watched—realized:

1. The only definition of a leader is someone who has followers. Some people are thinkers. Some are prophets. Both roles are important and badly needed. But without followers, there can be no leaders.

2. An effective leader is not someone who is loved or admired. She or he is someone whose followers do the right things. Popularity is not leadership. Results are.

3. Leaders are highly visible. They therefore set examples.

4. Leadership is not about rank, privileges, titles, or money. It is about responsibility.[10]

Drucker adds that regardless of their enormous diversity with respect to personality, style, abilities, and interests, effective leaders all behave in much the same way:

1. They did not start out with the question "What do I want?" They started out asking, "What needs to be done?"

2. Then they asked, "What can and should I do to make a difference?" This has to be something that both needs to be done and fits the leader's strengths and the way he or she is most effective.

3. They constantly asked, "What are the organization's mission and goals? What constitutes performance and results in this organization?"

4. They were extremely tolerant of diversity in people and did not look for carbon copies of themselves. It rarely even occurred to them to ask, "Do I like or dislike this person?" But they were totally—fiendishly—intolerant when it came to a person's performance, standards, and values.

5. They were not afraid of strength in their associates. They gloried in it. Whether they had heard of it or not, their motto was the one Andrew Carnegie wanted to have put on his tombstone: "Here lies a man who attracted better people into his service than he was himself."[11]

6. One way or another, they submitted themselves to the mirror test—that is, they made sure the person they saw in the mirror in the morning was the kind of person they wanted to be, respect, and believe in. This way they fortified themselves against the leader's greatest temptations— to do things that are popular rather than right and to do petty, mean, sleazy things.[12]

Finally, these leaders were not preachers; they were doers.

The most effective leaders share a number of skills, and these skills are always related to dealing with employees. The following suggestions outline an approach to becoming a hospitality industry leader rather than just a manager:

- *Be decisive.* Hospitality industry leaders are confronted with dozens of decisions every day. Obviously, you should use your best judgment to resolve the decisions that come to roost at your doorstep. As a boss, make the decisions that best meet both your objectives and your ethics, and then make your decisions known.

- *Follow through.* Never promise what you can't deliver, and never build false hopes among your employees. Once expectations are dashed, respect for and the reputation of the boss are shot.

- *Select the best.* A boss, good or bad, is carried forward by the work of his or her subordinates. One key to being a good boss is to hire the people who have the best potential to do what you need them to do. Take the time and effort to screen, interview, and assess the people

TECHNOLOGY SPOTLIGHT

Use of Social Networking Tools in the Hospitality Industry

Courtesy of **James McManemon**, M.S., University of South Florida Sarasota–Manatee

One of the most significant recent advances in consumer-based information technology is the introduction, and extremely fast adoption, of social networking tools. Today there are more than 650 million active users on Facebook, according to the site, with its popular "friending" approach to making connections. On any given day, 50 percent of these users log into their accounts. More than 250 million photos are uploaded daily; more than 350 million active users access Facebook through a mobile device; and more than 70 languages are used on the site.[1]

In the business arena, thousands, if not millions, local businesses have active pages on Facebook and those pages have created billions of fans combined. Twitter, with its 140-character "tweeting" approach to getting the word out, is powerful in its own right, with an estimated 289 million users in 2015. Marketing rules used to dictate that a happy guest would tell three friends about your establishment and an angry guest would tell 11 friends. This is no longer the case; in both instances, whether happy or displeased, guests can easily reach tens if not hundreds of contacts. Given the vastness of social media connections and networks, this can quickly multiply into thousands or more potential guests with word-of-mouth insight into your products and service.

Hotels and Restaurants in the Fray

Many hotel and restaurant operators are aware that social media tools can and should be leveraged for their businesses, but they struggle to identify specific return on investment. In fact, according to Hospitality Technology's 16th annual Restaurant Technology Study, although nearly one-half of restaurants recognize that there is value in Twitter as a marketing tool, only one-third of restaurant operators use it. There exist, however, many successful examples of hotels using social networking sites to generate awareness and additional revenue opportunities and many restaurants and hotels have thousands of fans each.

While the size of the fan base is important, the true value is in the interaction. A quick scan of these Facebook pages shows two factors for success: First, they have personality and build emotional connections, and second, people respond and interact on these pages.

Strategies for Success

Social networking tools can be used for more than connecting to external customers. Companies also use these tools to find employees and to solicit feedback from current and potential guests on menu items, decorations, room design, and more. They can even be used as a venue to prompt guests to suggest new menu items. If encouraged properly, employees can be ambassadors of a company in their own social networks.

One creative example of a hotel's use of social networking to boost guest participation is demonstrated by The Pod Hotel New York's own social networking site, Pod Social. When guests make reservations online, they are invited to become a member of the Pod Community. There they can choose a log-in and password and participate in an array of forums: Drink with Me, Eat with Me, Shop with Me, Go Out with Me, and so forth.

Though social networking tools are powerful, they must be well planned and carefully implemented to avoid pitfalls. If you ask for customers' opinions, listen to them. What's more, managing social networking

---

[1]"How many are there?" http://www.howmanyarethere.net/. Click on the tag "Facebook" (accessed April 20, 2015).

tools will take time. For this reason, each company should assign personnel to the task of monitoring and regularly updating its social networks. Some hotel companies are recruiting managers dedicated to online services and e-commerce initiatives. Many are combining this responsibility with a revenue, marketing, or front office manager.

My recommendation to all hotels and restaurants would be to connect to their guests, employees, families, and vendors through different social networking tools. If you are not doing this already, you are behind the curve.

▶ Check Your Knowledge

1. Identify the characteristics and practices of leaders.

2. Define *leadership*.

3. What three factors does transformational leadership involve?

4. Explain the demands placed on leaders.

Hospitality Management

LEARNING OBJECTIVE 3
Identify the characteristics and practices of management.

Managers plan, organize, make decisions, communicate, motivate, and control the efforts of a group to accomplish predetermined goals. Management also establishes the direction the organization will take. Sometimes this is done with the help of employees or outside consultants, such as marketing research specialists. Managers obtain the necessary resources for the goals to be accomplished, and then they supervise and monitor group and individual progress toward goal accomplishment.

Managers, such as presidents and CEOs, who are responsible for the entire company, tend to focus most of their time on strategic planning and the organization's mission. They also spend time organizing and controlling the activities of the corporation. Most top managers do not get involved in the day-to-day aspects of the operation. These duties and responsibilities fall to the middle and supervisory management. In hospitality lingo, one would not expect Bill Marriott to pull a shift behind the bar at the local Marriott hotel. Although capable, his time and expertise are better used in shaping the company's future. Thus, although the head bartender and Bill Marriott may both be considered management, they require slightly different skills to be effective and efficient managers.

What Is Management?

LEARNING OBJECTIVE 4
Define management.

Management is simply what managers do: plan, organize, make decisions, communicate, motivate, and control. *Management* is defined as "coordinating and overseeing the activities of others so that their activities are completed efficiently and effectively."[13] In looking at this statement, you can see

A DAY IN THE LIFE OF DANNA GREY

Director of Sales and Marketing

I began my career working in marketing at the local country club in Santa Monica, California. I had the fortune of working with a talented team of professionals and from them I learned the skills needed to cultivate strong business relationships. I learned how to get creative when things didn't go as planned, and I became as resilient as this field requires you to be in order to achieve success. After a few years, I moved to Los Angeles into a senior sales manager role for one of the city's most prestigious hotels.

Some interesting parts of my sales and marketing job entail hours of researching new businesses, spending countless hours on telephone calls to qualify possible leads, and the pressure to exceed revenue numbers that are set each month, each quarter, and each year. Other aspects of my job that at times are more rewarding include taking part in training new sales and marketing team members, working with the general manager of the hotel to strategize and maximize hotel revenues, and identifying the latest trends. All of these tasks, though, ensure that my days are never dull and they keep me on my toes.

Although many people choose this field because of a desire to serve people and work creatively, it is a business like any other. I feel Mr. Henry Ford said it best, "A business absolutely devoted to service will have only one worry about profits. They will be embarrassingly large."[14]

that the functions of management and working with and through the work of others are ongoing. Additionally, management involves getting efficient and effective results.

Efficiency is getting the most done with the fewest number of inputs. Managers work with scarce resources: money, people, time, and equipment. You can imagine the rush in the kitchen to be ready for a meal service. But it's not enough to just be efficient; management is also about being effective. **Effectiveness** is "doing the right thing." As an example, cooks do the right thing when they cook the food correctly according to the recipe and have it ready when needed.

Who Are Managers?

The changing nature of organizations and work has, in many hospitality organizations, blurred the lines of distinction between managers and non-managerial employees. Many traditional jobs now include managerial activities, especially when teams are used. For instance, team members often develop plans, make decisions, and monitor their own performance. This is the case with total quality management.

So, how do we define who managers are? A manager is someone who works with and manages others' activities to accomplish organizational goals

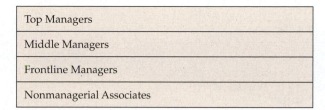

| Top Managers |
| Middle Managers |
| Frontline Managers |
| Nonmanagerial Associates |

Figure 14–4 • Three Levels of Management Plus Nonmanagerial Associates.

in an efficient and effective way. Managers are often classified into three levels: **frontline managers** are the lowest-level managers; they manage the work of line employees. They may also be called supervisors. A front-office supervisor, for example, takes charge of a shift and supervises the guest service agents on the shift.

Middle managers are akin to department heads; they fall between frontline managers and top management. They are responsible for short- to medium-range plans, and they establish goals and objectives to meet these goals. They manage the work of frontline managers.

Top managers are responsible for making medium- to long-range plans and for establishing goals and strategies to meet those goals. Figure 14–4 shows the three levels of management plus nonmanagerial employees.

Key Management Functions

The key management functions are planning, organizing, decision making, communicating, human resources and motivating, and controlling. These management functions are not conducted in isolation; rather, they are interdependent and frequently happen simultaneously or at least overlap. Figure 14–5 shows the key management functions leading to goal accomplishment.

Hospitality companies exist to serve a particular purpose, and someone has to determine the vision, mission, and strategies to reach or exceed the goals. That someone is management. The **planning** function involves setting the company's goals and developing plans to meet or exceed those goals. Once plans are complete, **organizing** is undertaken to decide what needs to be done, who will do it, how the tasks will be grouped, who reports to whom, and who makes decisions.

Decision making is a key management function. The success of all hospitality companies, whether large, multinational corporations or sole proprietorships, depends on the quality of the decision making. Decision making includes determining the vision, mission, goals, and objectives of the company. Decision making also includes scheduling employees, determining what to put on the menu, and responding to guest needs.

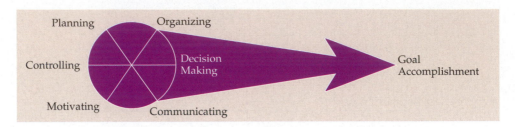

Figure 14–5 • Key Management Functions Leading to Goal Accomplishment.

Communication with and motivation of individuals and groups are required to get the job done. **Human resources and motivating** involves attracting and retaining the best employees and keeping morale high.

Controlling is the final management function that brings everything full circle. After the goals are set and the plans formulated, management then organizes, communicates, and motivates the resources required to complete the job. Controlling includes the setting of standards and comparing actual results with these standards. If significant deviations are seen, they are investigated and corrective action is taken to get performance back on target. This scientific process of monitoring, comparing, and correcting is the controlling function and is necessary to ensure that there are no surprises and that no one is guessing what should be done.

Managerial Skills

In addition to the management functions of forecasting, planning, organizing, communicating, motivating, and controlling, managers also need other major skills: conceptual, interpersonal, and technical.

Conceptual skills enable top managers to view the corporation as a complete entity and yet understand how it is split into departments to achieve specific goals. Conceptual skills allow a top manager to view the entire corporation, especially the interdependence of the various departments.

Managers need to lead, influence, communicate, supervise, coach, and evaluate employees' performances. This necessitates a high level of interpersonal human skills. The abilities to build teams and work with others are human skills that successful managers need to cultivate.

Managers need to have the technical skills required to understand and use modern techniques, methods, equipment, and procedures. These skills are more important for lower levels of management. As a manager rises through the ranks, the need for technical skills decreases and the need for conceptual skills increases.

You next need to realize the critical importance of the corporate philosophy, culture, and values, and of a corporation's mission, goals, and objectives.

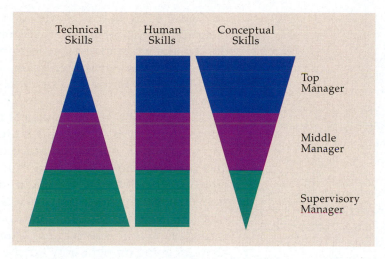

Figure 14–6 • Management Skill Areas Required by Management Level.

Figure 14–6 shows the degree of managerial skills required by top managers, middle managers, and supervisory managers.

The Manager's Changing Role

Managers may still have subordinates, but today's successful manager takes more of a team leader/coach approach. There are, of course, other ways to "slice and dice" what managers do. For example, managers don't just plan, organize, make decisions, communicate, motivate, and control. They wear a variety of hats, including the following:

- *Figurehead role.* Every manager spends some time performing ceremonial duties. For example, the president of a corporation might have to greet important business guests or clients or represent the corporation by attending dinners.

- *Leader role.* Every manager should be a leader, coaching, motivating, and encouraging employees.

- *Liaison role.* Managers spend a lot of time in contact with people in other departments both within the organization and externally. An example would be the sales manager liaising with the rooms division director.

- *Spokesperson role.* The manager is often the spokesperson for the organization. For example, a manager may host a college class visit to the property.

- *Negotiator role.* Managers spend a lot of time negotiating. For example, the head of a company along with qualified lawyers may negotiate with a union representative to establish wages and benefits for employees.

You, Too, Are a Manager

Your classmates have just voted you to be the leader/manager of the summer study-abroad trip to France. None of you knows much about France or how to get there, what to do when you get there, and so on. Where would you start? (Resist the temptation to delegate the whole trip to a travel agent, please.)

You might start by thinking through what you need to do in terms of planning, organizing, deciding, communicating, motivating, and controlling. What sort of plans will you need? Among other things, you'll need to plan the dates your group will be leaving and returning, the cities and towns you'll visit, the airline you'll take there and back, how the group will get around France, and where you'll stay when you're there. As you can imagine, plans like these are very important: You would not want to arrive at Orly Airport with a group of friends who are depending on you and not know what to do next.

Realizing how much work is involved—and that you cannot do it all and still maintain good grades—you get help. You divide up the work and create an organization by asking someone to check airline schedules and prices, another person to check hotel prices, and someone else to research the sights to see and the transportation needs. However, the job won't get done with the group members simply working by themselves. Each person requires guidance and coordination from you: The person making the airline bookings can't confirm the bookings unless she knows in what city and airport the trip will originate. Similarly, the person making the hotel arrangements can't make any firm bookings until he knows what cities are being visited. To improve communications, you could set up regular meetings, with e-mail updates between meetings. Leadership and motivation could be a challenge because two of the group members do not get along well. So, ensuring that everyone stays focused and positive will be a challenge.

Of course, you'll have to make sure the whole project remains in control. If something can go wrong, it often will, and that's certainly the case when groups of people are traveling together. Everything needs to be double-checked. In other words, managing is something managers do almost every day, often without even knowing it.

Source: Adapted from Gary Dessler, A Framework for Management *(Upper Saddle River, NJ: Prentice Hall, 2002), 8.*

These roles, together with the management functions, encompass what managers do. Remember, managers need to be many things—often in quick succession—even to the point of wearing two or more hats at once.

Twenty-first-century managers face not only a more demanding and increasingly complex world, but also a more dynamic and interdependent one. The "global village" is a reality, and sociocultural traditions and values must be understood and diversity respected and encouraged by future managers. The two most important changes going on right now are the technological advances and the internationalization of hospitality and tourism. The extent to which you as a future **leader/manager** can master these events and functions will determine your future.

The manager's role is not only internal but also external. For instance, a manager must be responsive to market needs and income generation. Managers must continually strive to be innovative by realizing efficiencies in their respective areas of responsibility through process improvement—for example, by determining how to reduce long check-in lines at airports and hotels. Some companies use innovative and creative ways to streamline the check-in procedures to make the process a more worthwhile experience for the guests. Disney, for instance, uses the creative approach of sending Mickey and the gang to entertain the guests while they stand in line.

A General Manager's Survival Kit

Ali Kasikci was a top-level manager at The Peninsula Beverly Hills, California. Under his management, he was involved in creating and implementing broad and comprehensive changes that affected the entire organization. Ali offers his list of tips:

- Know yourself, your own core competencies, and your values.
- Hire a seasoned management team.
- Build barriers of entry; that is, make yourself indispensable.
- Be very flexible.
- Get close to your guests and owners to define reality versus perception.
- Show leadership, from both the top and the bottom.
- Delegate. There is no way you can survive without delegation.
- Appeal to trends.
- Trust your instincts.
- Take risks and change the ground rules.
- Don't become overconfident.
- Look successful, or people will think you're not.
- Manage the future—it is the best thing you can do. Bring the future to the present.[15]

Sustainable Leadership

Sustainable leadership is "individual leadership that benefits the long-term good of society by positively influencing people, creating change, and demonstrating values that support the highest principles of society."[16]

The United Nations (UN) has developed a blueprint for corporate sustainability leadership. The blueprint consists of three parts[17] and is a model upon which leaders can use to make a difference within their organizations while advancing support for broader UN goals for sustainability. Participating companies and their leaders agree to implement the principles into their strategies and operations, take action in support of UN goals and issues, and commit to engage with the UN Global Compact.

Many business leaders, including hospitality ones, are becoming increasingly more concerned about sustainability. Not only are they concerned about the environment but also social responsibility. In the preceding chapters we have learned about the many ways that hospitality enterprises are becoming more sustainable in their operations. Leaders and managers need to steer the organization on a path of sustainability for all associates to follow.

If leaders stress the importance of sustainability, then others will follow. Sustainability does not happen by itself; it needs leaders to promote it. From cities that do not allow Styrofoam food containers to reducing water, paper, and electric consumption, it all comes together when leaders focus on sustainability in all the key result areas of their operations.

▶ Check Your Knowledge

1. Identify the characteristics and practices of management.

2. Explain levels of management.

LEARNING OBJECTIVE 5
Differentiate between leadership and management.

Distinction between Leadership and Management

Managing is the formal process in which organizational objectives are achieved through the efforts of subordinates. *Leading* is the process by which a person with vision is able to influence the behavior of others in some desired way. Although managers have power by virtue of the positions they hold, organizations seek managers who are leaders by virtue of their personalities, their experience, and so on. The differences between management and leadership can be illustrated as follows:

Managers

- Work in the system
- React
- Control risks
- Enforce organizational rules
- Seek and then follow direction
- Control people by pushing them in the right direction
- Coordinate effort

Leaders

- Work on the system
- Create opportunities
- Seek opportunities
- Change organizational rules
- Provide a vision to believe in and strategic alignment
- Motivate people by satisfying basic human needs
- Inspire achievement and energize people[18]

▶ Check Your Knowledge

1. What is the distinction between leadership and management?

Ethics

LEARNING OBJECTIVE 6
Discuss ethics in hospitality.

Ethics is a set of moral principles and values that people use to answer questions about right and wrong. Because ethics is also about our personal value system, there are people with value systems different from ours. Where did the value system originate? What happens if one value system is different from another? Fortunately, certain universal guiding principles are agreed on by virtually all religions, cultures, and societies. The foundation of all principles is that all people's rights are important and should not be violated. This belief is central to civilized societies; without it, chaos would reign.

Today, people have few moral absolutes; they decide situationally whether it is acceptable to steal, lie, or drink and drive. They seem to think that whatever is right is what works best for the individual. In a country blessed with so many diverse cultures, you might think it is impossible to identify common standards of ethical behavior. However, among sources from many different times and places, such as the Bible, Aristotle's *Ethics*, William Shakespeare's *King Lear*, the *Koran*, and the *Analects* of Confucius, you'll find the following basic moral values: integrity, respect for human life, self-control, honesty, and courage. Cruelty is wrong. All the world's major religions support a version of the golden rule: "Do unto others as you would have them do to you."[19]

In the foreword to *Ethics in Hospitality Management*, edited by Stephen S. J. Hall,[20] former Dean Emeritus of Cornell University, Robert A. Beck poses this question: "Is overbooking hotel rooms and airline seats ethical? How does one compare the legal responsibilities of the innkeeper and the airline manager to the moral obligation?" He also asks, "What is a fair or reasonable wage? A fair or reasonable return on investment? Is it fair or ethical to underpay employees for the benefit of investors?"

Ethics and morals have become an integral part of hospitality decisions, from employment (equal opportunity and affirmative action) to truth in menus. Many corporations and businesses have developed a code of ethics that all employees use to make decisions. This became necessary because too many managers were making decisions without regard for the impact of such decisions on others. Stephen Hall is one of the pioneers of ethics in hospitality; he has developed a code of ethics for the hospitality and tourism industry, as follows:

1. We acknowledge ethics and morality as inseparable elements of doing business and will test every decision against the highest standards of honesty, legality, fairness, impunity, and conscience.

2. We will conduct ourselves personally and collectively at all times so as to bring credit to the hospitality and tourism industry.

3. We will concentrate our time, energy, and resources on the improvement of our own products and services and we will not denigrate our competition in the pursuit of our success.

4. We will treat all guests equally regardless of race, religion, nationality, creed, or sex.

5. We will deliver all standards of service and product with total consistency to every guest.

6. We will provide a totally safe and sanitary environment at all times for every guest and employee.

7. We will strive constantly, in words, actions, and deeds, to develop and maintain the highest level of trust, honesty, and understanding among guests, clients, employees, employers, and the public at large.

8. We will provide every employee at every level all the knowledge, training, equipment, and motivation required to perform his or her tasks according to our published standards.

9. We will guarantee that every employee at every level will have the same opportunity to perform, advance, and be evaluated against the same standard as all employees engaged in the same or similar tasks.

10. We will actively and consciously work to protect and preserve our natural environment and natural resources in all that we do.

11. We will seek a fair and honest profit, no more, no less.[21]

As you can see, it is vitally important for future hospitality and tourism professionals to abide by this code. The following sections present some ethical dilemmas in hospitality. What do you think about them?

Ethical Dilemmas in Hospitality

Previously, certain actions may not have been considered ethical, but management often looked the other way. A few scenarios follow that are not seen as ethical today and are against most companies' ethical policies:

1. As catering manager of a large banquet operation, the flowers for the hotel are booked through your office. The account is worth $15,000 per month. A florist offers you a 10-percent kickback to book the account with him. Given that your colleague at a sister hotel in the same company receives a good bonus and you do not, despite having a better financial result, do you feel justified in accepting the kickback? If so, with whom would you share it?

2. As purchasing agent for a major hospitality organization, you are responsible for purchasing $5 million worth of perishable and non-perishable items. To get your business, a supplier, whose quality and price are similar to others, offers you a new automobile. Do you accept?

3. An order has come from the corporate office that guests from a certain part of the world may only be accepted if the reservation is made via the embassy of their respective countries. One Sunday afternoon, you are duty manager and several limos with people from "that part of the world" personally request rooms for several weeks. You decline, even though there are available rooms. They even offer you a personal envelope, which they say contains $1,000. How do you feel about declining their request?

▶ Check Your Knowledge

1. Discuss ethics in hospitality.

HOW TO LEAD YOURSELF

Courtesy of **James McManemon**, M.S., University of South Florida Sarasota–Manatee

Personal leadership begins with a vision, a mission, and with goals. An example of a vision might be to become president of a hospitality corporation or to open your own successful restaurant. (What is your vision?) A personal mission is a statement of purpose—perhaps to be the best student or employee that you can be. (What is your mission?) Your goals will involve how you plan to meet the mission. For example, that may mean, as a student, how you plan to achieve a certain grade point average, or, as an employee, how to achieve a high score on an employee evaluation. (What are your goals?)

A first step toward achieving personal leadership begins with developing personal self-discipline, habits, and drive. Personal self-discipline involves how we choose to conduct ourselves. Have you thought about your own strengths and weaknesses? As boring as it may sound, make a list, and then work on improving those areas of weakness that you identified. Review it, and update it regularly. As simple as it sounds, developing personal leadership abilities has to do as much with developing a routine of self-examination as with establishing goals.

Whether currently a student, or beginning a career in the world of hospitality and management, or pursuing established long-term goals in that career, each of us can lead ourselves by creating a vision, formulating a mission statement, and creating goals. Try it. Make a scorecard to record your progress toward achieving the goals you set for yourself. Among the habits you might adopt, all of which will aid you as a student and as you build your career, include the following: creating a schedule and utilizing time management, eating healthy food, exercising, studying, improving your verbal communicating skills as well as technological skills, reading widely, learning from mentors, and managing your money wisely.

Trends in Leadership and Management

Courtesy of Dr. Greg Dunn, Senior Lecturer & Managing Director, University of Florida, Eric Friedheim Tourism Institute

- *Leadership Is Walking the Talk.* For effective leadership, it is very critical to "walk the talk" and set examples. Each and every employee has something to work on or improve, and each and every employee has a special skill or ability that others may not. Forming a connection with employees and guests can improve dramatically with genuine, individual interaction. Today's leaders should look to instill the value of building relationships by sharing—whether that be in the form of knowledge or experiences. Leaders can build relationships by participating in daily or special events or functions. For instance, some managers run with their guests or employees and even participate in personal or group training sessions.

- *Uncertainty Makes Leadership Harder.* The economic and business environment in the upcoming years will continue to be unpredictable. Organizations are introducing more change initiatives than ever—as many as five each year. Today's business leaders believe that "the ability to change" is a key challenge when compared with prior years. An increased feeling of uncertainty can lead employees to lack confidence in one another and can have a derailing effect on change programs. It is important to be proactive and anticipate the future.

- *Developing First-Line Leaders.* First-line leaders (i.e., the first level of management) make up roughly half of management on average and directly supervise the majority of a workforce. However, recent research shows that there is a lack of people skills among many first-line leaders. They represent the most important group of leaders in an organization, as they are involved in all aspects of a company from strategy to customer satisfaction. Developing first-line leaders must be high on a company's agenda. First-line leaders are generally promoted to their post based on technical skills and knowledge; but it is their people skills, which often determine their effectiveness and success in their new leadership role.

- *Leadership Skills Are Vital.* Strong people-leadership skills (i.e., the ability to lead people effectively) is vital in all employees and found to be three to four times more important to a leader's career success than other skills. Better-performing companies report a much higher adoption of people-leadership practices. Effective leaders should become experts in people-leadership areas such as Loading—thinking like a leader, coaching a team, getting results through others, and engaging employees.

- *More Thoughtful Training.* Just like in the workplace, employees also need more engagement in elements of their training. Many employees feel that they have too much work to do, while others say they have little or no capacity to do more with less. Employees tend to not want to attend a one-off training day when they are pushed to work at full capacity, and still manage their regular workload. Employees will appreciate learning that is relevant, practical, and challenging; boot camp training is out.

- *Choosing a Leadership Style that Works.* We all have a preference in the way that we lead a team or an organization. It is imperative that all leaders, even in the hospitality industry, choose that leadership style and sometimes learn to adapt it for certain people. Some people might be coercive, authoritative, democratic, pacesetting, or coaching. The key to being an effective leader is learning when to use each of these techniques and, more importantly, when to switch.

- *Understand Your Organization.* Being part of the hospitality industry means being in contact with so many different types and numbers of people, including those that may be your employees, competitors, customers, suppliers, and government. It is important to understand your organization to help ensure all functions of the business are working smoothly. It is also very important that all staff know your company's organizational chart, which may display the executive staff and positions.

- *Accepting Responsibility.* As a leader in this industry you will need to make many decisions, some being tougher than others, while some also being more impactful than others. Leaders should never shift the blame from themselves onto someone else. They should be quick to accept responsibility where due and to apologize for a mistake they or their organization has made. Specifically within the hospitality industry, a good leader will be able to create a positive outlook on most situations even when dealing with an angry customer, poor decisions, or poor profit reports.

- *Exceptional Listening.* Exceptional customer service stems from exceptional listening. Although one may be a leader and ultimately be making the final decisions, it is important to listen to others. This includes the executive committee, all employees, all guests/customers, all competitors, and really everyone's voice should be heard. Not only is this important to make everyone else happy but it will help the leader grow exponentially. This can help identify all needs and be able to take care of them in a quick and professional matter. As far as employees, it is very important to meet with them regularly as well as listen to all of their ideas, thoughts, and concerns.

- *Don't Hesitate to Ask Why.* Some hospitality managers do exactly what corporate offices might tell them to do without questioning it. However, an on-site manager normally knows the facilities, functions, and employees better than anyone else in the organization. If a manager does not necessarily agree with or understand a decision, it is that person's responsibility to step up and to not hesitate to ask why.

- *Excel at Every Opportunity.* To reach the apex of this organic brand-building process, hospitality organizations are re-evaluating their services and enhancing them to match the highest standards. If you expect your customers to give you genuine positive feedback, then the customer service, in every aspect of the hospitality business, has to create a definite wow factor. While many no-frills services have emerged over the past few years in response to the economic and competitive conditions, there is a new trend toward distinctive services. We can see these in the many innovative offers like online ordering, destination specials that partner with local wineries and eateries, digital in-room dining experiences for busy executives, hiring famous chefs as brand ambassadors, and strategic tie-ups with various service providers to make their experience enjoyable. Hospitality organizations are going above and beyond to fulfill each customer's need by offering multiple amenities and services, by having a positive attitude, and by catering to each guest's needs.

CASE STUDY

Performance Standards

Charles and Nancy both apply for the assistant front-office manager position at a 300-room upscale hotel. Charles has worked for a total of eight years in three different hotels and has been with this hotel for three months as a front-office associate. Initially, he had a lot of enthusiasm. Lately, however, he has been dressing a bit sloppily and his figures, cash, and reports have been inaccurate. In addition, he is occasionally rattled by demanding guests.

Nancy recently graduated from college with honors, with a degree in hospitality management. While attending college, she worked part-time as a front desk associate at a budget motel. Nancy does not have a lot of experience working in a hotel or in customer service in general, but she is quite knowledgeable as a result of her studies and is eager to begin her career.

It appears that Charles would be considered a prime candidate for the office manager position because of his extensive experience in other hotels and his knowledge of the hotel's culture. In view of his recent performance, however, the rooms division manager will need to sit down with Charles to review his future career development track.

Discussion Questions

1. What are the qualifications for the job that should be considered for both applicants?
2. How should the discussion between the rooms division manager and Charles be handled? Make specific recommendations for the rooms division manager.
3. Who would be the better person for the job? Why?

CASE STUDY

Reluctant to Change

You have just been appointed assistant manager at an old, established, but busy, New York restaurant. Your employees respond to your suggested changes with the comment, "We have always done it this way." The employees really do not know any other way of doing things.

Discussion Questions

1. How should you handle this situation?

Summary

1. Leadership is defined as the process by which a person is able to influence the activities and outcomes of others in a desired way.
2. Contemporary leadership includes transactional and transformational types of leadership.
3. Increased demands placed on hospitality leaders include ownership, corporate, regulatory, employee, environmental, and social interests. Leaders must balance results and relationships.
4. Managing is the process of coordinating work activities so that they are completed efficiently and effectively with and through other people.
5. Leaders, according to Peter Drucker, realize four things and behave in much the same way.
   (a) A leader is someone who has followers—some people are thinkers, and some are prophets.
   (b) An effective leader is not someone who is loved or admired, but rather someone whose followers do the right things. Popularity is not leadership; results are.
   (c) Leaders are highly visible. Leaders set examples.
   (d) Leadership is not about rank, privileges, titles, or money. It is about responsibility.
6. There are six key management functions: planning, organizing, decision making, communicating, motivating, and controlling. However, in addition to these functions, managers occasionally have to fill roles such as figurehead, leader, spokesperson, and negotiator.
7. The difference between management and leadership is that the former is the formal process in which organization objectives are achieved through the efforts of subordinates, and the latter is the process by which a person with vision is able to influence the behavior of others in some desired way.

Key Words and Concepts

communication	human resources and	organizing
controlling	motivating	planning
decision making	leader/manager	top managers
effectiveness	leadership	transactional leadership
efficiency	management	transformational leadership
ethics	managing	
frontline managers	middle managers	

Review Questions

1. What kind of leader/manager will you be?
2. Give examples of the management functions as they apply to the hospitality industry.
3. Discuss the changing role of managers.
4. Define leadership and name the essential qualities of a good leader.
5. Distinguish between transactional and transformational leadership.

Internet Exercises

1. Organization: **HCareers**
   Summary: HCareers is an organization dedicated to helping you make smarter career decisions. HCareers provides a listing of posted jobs and careers for both job seekers and recruiters. By all means, take the time to check this one out! Click on the kind of job you might like in your area (hopefully you will not find your job listed). Answer the following question.

   (a) What are the positions available that interest you in your area?

2. Organization: **American Management Association**
   Summary: The American Management Association (AMA), a practitioner-based organization, offers a wide range of management development programs for managers and organizations. Find the section titled "Articles and White Papers."

Choose two current reports on leadership. Read through these and make a bullet list of the key information. Then write a description of how this information might affect the way a hospitality manager plans, organizes, makes decisions, communicates, motivates, and controls.

3. Organization: **Ritz-Carlton Hotel Company**
   Summary: Ritz-Carlton hotels are known for their superior luxury and service in the hospitality industry. This particular web exercise illustrates how Ritz-Carlton maintains its culture of service excellence. Take a look at the Ritz-Carlton Leadership Center. Click on "Leadership Center." Now answer the following questions:

   (a) What kinds of courses does the Leadership Center offer?
   (b) What are the seven habits of highly effective people?

Apply Your Knowledge

1. Your resort has management vacancies for the following positions: executive chef, executive housekeeper, and front-office manager. List the traits and characteristics that you consider essential and desirable for these positions.

Suggested Activity

1. Think of someone you admire as a leader. Make a list of the qualities that make him or her a good leader.

Endnotes

1. Strategic Leadership Studies, "Marine Corps Leadership Traits," http://www.au.af.mil/au/awc/awcgate/usmc/leadership_traits.htm (accessed June 5, 2015).

2. U.S. Marine Corps Association, Guidebook for Marines, 19th ed. (Quantico, VA: U.S. Marine Corps Association, 2009), Chapter 5, pp. 43–49.

3. For a more detailed review of the many leadership theories, consult one of the many texts on the topic and http://www.ritzcarlton.com (accessed December 8, 2014).

4. Horst Schultz, Presentation to the University of South Florida School of Hotel and Restaurant Management, March 26, 2005.

5. Ibid.

6. Capella Hotel Group, "Company Overview," http://www.capellahotelgroup.com. Click on Company Profile (accessed November 26, 2014).

7. Capella Hotel Group, http://www.capellahotel group.com (accessed November 26, 2014).

8. Jay R. Schrock, Presentation to the University of South Florida students and faculty, May 2, 2005.

9. Brainy Quote, http://www.brainyquote.com/. Search for quotes by "Vernon Law" (accessed January 1, 2012).

10. Adapted from Peter F. Drucker, "Foreword," in *The Leader of the Future*, ed. F. Hesselbein, et al. (San Francisco: Josey-Bass, 1996), xii–xiii.

11. Mark W. McCloskey, *Learning Leadership in a Changing World: Virtue and Leadership in the 21st Century* (New York: Palgrave Macmillan, 2014), 185.

12. John R. Walker and Jack E. Miller, *Supervision in the Hospitality Industry: Leading Human Resources* (New Jersey: John Wiley and Sons, 2009), 22.

13. Stephen P. Robbins and Mary Coulter, *Management*, 9th ed. (Upper Saddle River, NJ: Pearson, 2007), p. 7.

14. Brainy Quote, http://www.brainyquote.com/. Search for quotes by "Henry Ford" (accessed November 28, 2011).

15. Personal correspondence with Ali Kasiki, August 4, 2005.

16. Kelly, Sam, "Sustainable Leadership," *Prezi*, March 24, 2001, https://prezi.com/8pyr89n1k6_c/sustainable-leadership (accessed November 17, 2001).

17. United Nations Global Compact, "Blueprint for Corporate Sustainability Leadership," www .unglobalcompact.org. Search for "Blueprint for Corporate Sustainability Leadership" (accessed March 19, 2015).

18. Steve Chandler, *100 Ways to Motivate Others: How Great Leaders Can Produce Insane Results Without Driving People Crazy* (Sydney, Australia: ReadHowYouWant.com, 2008).

19. *Holy Bible, New International Version*. [Colorado Springs]: Biblica, 2011. *BibleGateway.com*. Web (accessed June 5, 2015).

20. Stephen S. Hall, ed., *Ethics in Hospitality Management: A Book of Readings* (East Lansing, MI: Educational Institute, American Hotel & Lodging Association, 1992), 75.

21. Hall, *Ethics in Hospitality Management*, 108.

CHAPTER **15**

Planning

LEARNING OBJECTIVES

After reading and studying this chapter, you should be able to:

- Describe the importance of planning.

- Discuss the merits of the different types of planning.

- Explain how goals are set and strategies are developed and give examples.

- Identify the seven steps in operational planning.

What Is Planning?

Things don't just happen by themselves—well, at least not the way we'd like them to. Remember the time, on a hot day, when you walked into an ice cream store and ordered your favorite flavor, only to be told they were out if it. You were expecting to be delighted but instead were disappointed. Your negative experience was a result of poor planning; someone, likely the manager either forgot to order the flavor of ice cream altogether or did not anticipate running short of it the day you happened to visit. This is a simple but important example of poor business planning. There are, as we shall see, more complex forms of planning.

Planning involves selecting the various **goals** that an organization wants to achieve and the **strategies** (actions) to be taken to ensure that those goals are accomplished. In business organizations, executives determine the financial and organizational health of the organization and its future goals. Goals are established for each of the **key operating areas** in the business. In the hospitality industry these would include, but not be limited to, the following key operating areas:

Guest satisfaction: The goal is 100-percent guest satisfaction. The current score may be 89 percent, so strategies must be developed for meeting the 100 percent goal.

Employee satisfaction: The goal is 100-percent employee satisfaction. Let us assume current employee satisfaction is at 87 percent; strategies will be required to bring it up to 100 percent.

Productivity: Productivity is measured in many different ways across departments. For example, the kitchen of a hotel would look at the number of meals served, and the front desk would look at the number of guests checked in and out. Another way to determine productivity is to divide the total revenue of the business by the number of full-time equivalent employees or person-hours worked. A goal might be set to increase the earnings per employee by 10 percent, and the plan would call for strategies to meet or exceed the goal. Similar examples would apply to the following key result areas: food and beverage preparation, foodservice, guest services, marketing and sales, rooms division, operating ratios, human resources, physical property, security, and finances. For each of these areas, then, strategies must be developed to ensure that the goals are met or exceeded.

All managers do some form of planning, whether informal or formal. Informal planning is often done at the last minute, and there is little or no sharing of goals and strategies with others in the organization. The owner has a vision of what he or she wants to accomplish and just goes ahead and does it. This is frequently the situation in small businesses; however, informal planning also occurs even in larger organizations. One weakness of informal planning is that it lacks continuity.

Formal planning, on the other hand, occurs when specific goals covering a period of up to several years are identified and shared with all associates, with strategies then developed stating how each goal will be reached. When planning is discussed in this chapter, we are referring to formal planning. Several types of planning exist, but we will examine the main ones used in the hospitality industry.

Think back to the summer study-abroad trip to France in the feature, "You Too, Are a Manager" that was introduced in the previous chapter. Your plans might include the following information: how you plan to get to the airport, your airline and flight times, the airport of arrival, how you'll get into Paris, your hotel, and the itinerary for each day in each city visited. Think for a moment: What if you didn't plan? The group would not know what flight to take, or, on arrival in France, how to get into central Paris and the location of your hotel. This would be chaotic and stressful, to say the least. Now think of your career plans. Perhaps your goal is to have a successful career in one of the many areas of hospitality management. Successfully completing your degree, along with having some previous work experience in the industry, would facilitate accomplishing your goal. So, we can see that planning provides direction and a sense of purpose.[1] Remember the wonderful line in *Alice's Adventures in Wonderland* when Alice is lost and asks the Cheshire Cat which way to go? The Cat asks her where she wants to go. Alice replies, "I don't much care—." The Cat replies, "Then it doesn't matter which way you go."

Planning can also help identify potential opportunities and threats. Planning helps facilitate the other functions of management—organization, decision making, communication, motivation, and especially control—because planning establishes what needs to be done and how it is to be done, and control looks at how well we have done compared to how well we expected to do.[2]

HOW TO PLAN A RESTAURANT START-UP

Courtesy of **James McManemon**, M.S., University of South Florida Sarasota—Manatee

Jan and Karen are the owners of a single unit 40-seat restaurant in Chattanooga, Tennessee, which has recently passed the three-year restaurant fail test. They shared their plan for starting the business, which they believe is the secret to initial success in the restaurant industry.

Their initial task was to establish a mission. Both expected to provide guests with an exceptional dining experience, one that would offer local fusion cuisine paired with craft beers and interesting wines, and be heightened by outstanding service and an inviting atmosphere. The planning process involved addressing three key issues, which they believe have led to their current success.

First, location. Jan and Karen believed that purchasing the right building in the right location is the first step to properly planning to open a restaurant. The restaurant is strategically located on the outskirts of downtown Chattanooga, which the owners rent at a lower cost than if they were directly downtown. The building was previously occupied by a restaurant that closed in late 2011. The building was already outfitted with an optimal restaurant

(Continued)

HOW TO PLAN A RESTAURANT START-UP *(Continued)*

layout, including a kitchen space with proper hookups that only needed equipment installed. The building is within walking distance of a large parking facility owned by the city, which offers designated free parking to restaurant patrons, in order to promote local businesses. While the building was in need of minor design renovations and cosmetic updates such as painting the entire restaurant, adding tiling to the bathrooms and bar area, installing new wood flooring and new lighting throughout and changing current light fixtures, no structural renovation was required.

Second, market analysis through environmental scanning of the competition and demographics of the area. Jan and Karen initially shared several potential ideas for concepts all centered on the general theme of crafting culinary creations using fresh, locally sourced ingredients; however, they believe market research is essential to determine the wants and needs of the surrounding neighborhood residents, as well as the demographics, before deciding on the right concept. In fact, many failed restaurateurs have made the mistake of doing the opposite and assuming that the concept will drive the market. As a consequence, they conducted multiple types of market research, including surveying and interviewing local residents, in order to gain a well-rounded perspective on a desirable concept, menu items, and an appropriate name.

Research revealed that this urban neighborhood was largely occupied by young professionals and social couples between the ages of 21 and 35, potentially a great place for business professionals working downtown to have lunch during the work week. In addition, it could be seen as a place that people could have a light dinner at a price cheaper than in a downtown restaurant, or share a few snacks over a beer or glass of wine before going downtown on the weekend for the Chattanooga nightlife scene. With the idea of a restaurant featuring a laid back atmosphere, moderately priced menu items, interesting beers and wines, and a late night snack menu, the designated young "trendy" people became the target market group.

Third, first year projections. Karen and Jan structured a plan for initial food, beverage, and labor costs along with projected annual sales goals. The planned annual food cost was 25 percent, the annual beverage cost was 30 percent, the annual labor cost was 35 percent, and the annual supplies inventory cost was 10 percent. The labor cost would be decreased once the operation was open for business for a few months and staffing needs could be better determined based on business levels. The initial hours of operation would be Monday through Saturday from 11:00 A.M. to 3:00 P.M., and dinner business from 5:00 P.M. to 10:00 P.M. They expected an average of 150 covers a day, with 75 for lunch and 75 for dinner. The average food sales per customer were expected to be $10 for lunch and $16 for dinner, while the average beverage sales were expected to be $5 for lunch and $15 for dinner. This would amount to daily sales of $3,450, weekly sales of $20,700, monthly sales of $82,800, and annual sales of $993,600.

The result. Jan and Karen actually finished the first year by sales that were 30 percent higher than what they projected. Additionally, they significantly increased sales each of the next two years and are now working on a plan for expansion in the near future.

The Purpose of Planning

Planning gives direction not only to top management but also to all associates as they focus on goal accomplishment. The purpose of planning is to determine the best goals and strategies to achieve organizational goals. Figure 15–1 shows the hierarchy of planning in organizations. Notice that

Figure 15–1 • The Hierarchy of Planning in Organizations.

top executives do most of the strategic planning and first-line managers do most of the operational planning.

Planning provides the road map of where the organization is going. Planning also helps coordinate the efforts of associates toward goal accomplishment. Planning assists in risk reduction by forcing managers to look ahead and anticipate change so that they can plan scenarios to react to those potential changes.

▶ Check Your Knowledge

1. Describe the importance of planning.

Strategic Planning and Strategic Management

LEARNING OBJECTIVE 2
Discuss the merits of the different types of planning.

The two main categories of plans are strategic (long-term) plans and operational (short-term) plans. Associated with strategic plans are business plans and feasibility studies, which deal with the structure of the plan and provide the details necessary for obtaining finance or other approvals for the operation.

Strategic planning creates the long-range plans that steer an organization toward its goals in the accomplishment of its mission and vision. The strategic planning process involves top management, who, in simple terms, identify where the organization is and where it wants to go. There is a strong link between strategic planning and strategic management. The planners figure out what to do, and management implements the plan.

How does a large hospitality company with the mission of being a global entity determine which markets to focus on? Should it focus on expansion in Canada, Europe, Latin America, or Asia? Which market would be more beneficial? And can it enter more than one market at a time? What will the method of entry into these markets be? Will a strategy appropriate for one country work in another? Pick up a copy of the *Wall Street Journal, Business*

Executive committee members planning the future direction and performance of their property.

Week, a hospitality trade magazine, or a major newspaper, and you are bound to find articles on or references to business strategy. In the hospitality industry, strategies are devised that become the road map of how to succeed in increasing guest satisfaction, gaining market share, increasing profits, and so on.

Strategic management develops the mission, goals, and strategies of the organization by identifying the business of the corporation today and the business it wants for the future, and then by identifying the course of action it will pursue, given its strengths, weaknesses, opportunities, and threats (internal and external environments).

Strategic management is a critical part of planning and the management process. There are three main strategic management tasks: (1) developing a vision and mission statement, (2) translating the mission into strategic goals, and (3) crafting a strategy (course of action) to move the organization from where it is today to where it wants to be.

Given the frequency of change in the environment, managers must conduct effective strategic planning in order to respond to the challenges of managing in a highly competitive environment. In other words, a good strategic plan should include detailed prescriptions of how a business wishes to implement its mission in the highly competitive environment, coupled with allowances for responding to extraordinary events.

A direct link exists between the mission of the organization and strategic management—they complement each other. Strategic planning involves creating a long-term strategy for how the organization will meet its mission. The job of strategic management is to translate the mission into strategic goals.

The difference between strategic planning and strategic management is that strategic planning is a systematic process whereby the top management of an organization charts the future course of the enterprise. Strategic management is the process of guiding the organizational strategic plan and acquiring the necessary resources and capabilities to ensure successful implementation of the plan in the context of emergent situations caused by the level of environmental turbulence.[3]

A strategy is the "how to" action necessary to accomplish goals and missions. In the hospitality industry, for instance, there are six steps to strategic planning:

1. Create a vision.
2. Find out what your guests want.
3. Do an environmental scan.
4. Identify critical issues.

5. Formulate strategies for the future.

6. Create your action plan and act on it, and then monitor results.

Strategic Planning/Management Process

Most of the strategic planning that takes place at the top management level is called *corporate-level strategy*. Figure 15–2 shows the strategic management process. Notice that it begins with identifying the organization's mission, goals, and objectives. The process then involves analyzing the organization's environment and resources and identifying its strengths, weaknesses, opportunities, and threats. The strategic management process then entails the organization formulating strategies, implementing them, and evaluating the results.

▶ Check Your Knowledge

1. Discuss the merits of the different types of planning.

2. What are the two main categories of planning?

3. What are the three main strategic management tasks?

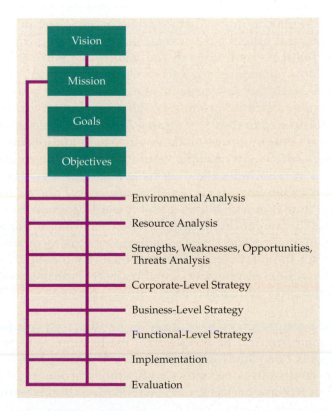

Figure 15–2 • Strategic Management Process.

LEARNING OBJECTIVE 3
Explain how goals are set and strategies are developed and give examples.

Corporate-Level Strategies

There are three corporate strategies:

1. Growth: (a) market penetration, (b) geographic expansion, (c) product development, and (d) horizontal integration
2. Strategic alliance/joint venture
3. Diversification

At the highest corporate level, many organizations consist of a portfolio of several businesses or divisions. For instance, Disney's portfolio includes movies, theme parks, and the ABC network. Hilton Worldwide's portfolio includes Conrad Hotels & Resorts, DoubleTree by Hilton, Embassy Suites Hotels, Hampton Hotels, Hilton Hotels & Resorts, Hilton Garden Inn, and Homewood Suites by Hilton. These and other companies need a corporate-level strategy to plan how best to meet the mission of the company. For example, a few years ago, after careful strategic planning, Hilton decided to form a separate company made up of its gaming entertainment hotels, and Marriott decided to sell its foodservice operations to Sodexo. This allowed both corporations to focus on best meeting their missions with their lodging operations. Hilton found that operating casino hotels was very different from operating its other hotel brands. Marriott decided that growing its hotel brands was its best strategy for meeting long-term corporate goals. Corporations choose the number of areas of business in which they want to operate. McDonald's and Panda Express are focused in one area, but Hilton, Marriott, and others have several brands, ranging from full-service hotels and extended-stay hotels all the way to vacation ownership and senior living. Most companies want to grow, and they must plan a strategy for that growth. There are four growth strategies: **Market penetration** aims to increase market share by promoting sales aggressively in existing markets. **Geographic expansion** is a strategy in which a company expands its operations by entering new markets—this is in addition to concentrating on existing markets. An example would be Hilton entering and enhancing its position in the Chinese market by entering into an agreement with Air China, China's leading air carrier. The agreement allows for cross-participation in Hilton Honors, Hilton's guest reward program, and Air China's Phoenix Miles. The aim of the partnership between one of the world's most recognized hotel brands and China's leading airline is to provide enhanced global service for the increasing number of business travelers in China, and to address the strong competitive situation with international airlines in the local business travel market after China's entry into the World Trade Organization.[4]

The third form of growth strategy is **product development**, such as Hilton Garden Inn or a new restaurant menu item. The fourth type of growth strategy is **horizontal integration**, which is the process of acquiring ownership or control of competitors with similar products in the same or similar markets. Hilton's purchase of Promus Corporation was an example of horizontal integration.

A DAY IN THE LIFE OF JESSICA LEIBOVICH

Chef/Owner, Entree Nous, San Diego, California;
"Best Personal Chef," *San Diego Magazine*

I begin planning my day as a personal chef the night before I cook for a client. Using a program called MasterCook, a recipe database software, I begin menu planning and customizing a menu for the clients that I will be cooking for the following day. I usually choose five entrées and side dishes, trying to keep a variety of one seafood, two chickens, one beef or pork, and one vegetarian selection. The side dishes are combinations of fresh vegetables, whole grains, and starches. This combination of meals may change based on the likes and dislikes of each client along with any special diets they may be on. After the menu planning, I use MasterCook to create a shopping list. This is all done the night before a cook date.

The day I am going to cook, I start my workday at approximately 8:30 A.M. I begin at my computer by printing out the shopping list for the day, along with each of the recipes I will be preparing for my client. I also type up heating instructions for the client. Before I leave the house, I go through the shopping list for the day and place all of the nonperishable items I already have into my rolling cooler. Then I go through the list and identify which stores I will need to shop at for each of the items.

Before leaving, I load my car with my cooler and my portable kitchen kit. I make sure to bring my shopping list, recipes, and heating instructions. I am in my car, ready to leave, around 9:15 A.M.

I usually need to go to at least three stores: one for my dry goods, one for my meat and produce, and one for seafood. Occasionally, I may need to visit an additional store if I cannot locate something I need at the others. As I shop, I check off my shopping list as I go.

I am finished shopping around 10:00 A.M. and begin to drive to my client's home. Each day, I go to a different client's house. Some of my clients I cook for every week, and others may only be once a month. Once I arrive, I bring in all of the groceries, my cooler from home, my portable kitchen kit, and the recipes and heating instructions.

Once everything is in from the car, I remove it from the bags and place it on the counters. I put all perishable items such as meat and dairy in the refrigerator. I then set up a cutting board and knife and wash my hands. I quickly go over my recipes and decide which ones need the longest cooking time and need to be started first. I also need to decide on the rotation of the items in the oven so I will not have more than two things in the oven at any given time. Eventually, I get in a rhythm and cook for about four to five hours, preparing each entrée and side dish. My day cooking is also spent washing, cutting, and trimming vegetables and meat. Then I may sauté, braise, roast, bake, or stew any particular dish, depending on what the menu selections are for that day. Sometimes I am preparing desserts and need to bake as well. Fresh salads are also often requested, so the blender may be buzzing with homemade salad dressings. At one time, there may be items on three burners while two different items are in the oven. One thing I always make sure to do is to clean as I go. Otherwise, I would have quite a mess at the end of the day. As I am finished with an item, I clean it up and set it aside to dry.

As I finish preparing items, I place them in ovenproof Pyrex and Corningware containers to store them in the refrigerator or freezer, depending on the client. As each item cools, I place a label identifying each item along with the date and number of servings on a sealable lid. I leave the items to cool briefly and then place them in the refrigerator. If the client will not be eating them within the next two days, they place them in the freezer to enjoy at a later date.

At the end of the day, it all comes together, and the full menu is completed. As I am finished with an item, I place it back in my cooler. That way, when I am done, there will be no more items left on the counters. Once all the

(Continued)

A DAY IN THE LIFE OF JESSICA LEIBOVICH *(Continued)*

cooking is complete, I carefully clean the kitchen and leave it exactly the way it was when I arrived. I then load up my car with my portable kitchen and rolling cooler. This is usually at about 3:00 P.M.

When I arrive back home, about 4:00 P.M., I bring in my things and unload my cooler. I place everything back in its place in the cabinets. That evening I will prepare the menu and shopping list and begin again for the next day.

For more information, including menus and background information, please visit my web site at **www .eatbreathemoveheal.com**.

Making **strategic alliances** or **joint ventures** are yet other methods for a corporation to fulfill its mission. American Airlines wanted to expand operations into Asia and Europe—the two main air travel growth areas—but lacked the resources necessary for opening up routes to several additional countries, and it was not allowed to do so by foreign governments because of the competition it would bring to national airlines. So American Airlines formed a "Oneworld" alliance with several other airlines including British Airways, Cathay Pacific, Finnair, Iberia, LAN Airlines, Qantas, and more than 30 affiliate carriers to feed each other passengers, code share some flights, and share resources, thus saving money and offering the consumer a better deal with the economy of scale.

Another strategy is **diversification**, in which companies expand into other types of business—related or unrelated. Celebrity chef Emeril "Bam!" Lagasse's expansion into TV dinners is an example of diversification.

Strengths, Weaknesses, Opportunities, and Threats Analysis

A major strategic planning technique that is widely used in the hospitality and tourism industry is a **SWOT analysis**: an analysis of *strengths*, *weaknesses*, *opportunities*, and *threats*. A SWOT analysis is used to assess the company's internal and external strengths and weaknesses, to seek out opportunities, and to be aware of and avoid threats. A SWOT analysis is conducted in comparison with a company's main competitors. This makes it easier to see the competitors' strengths, weaknesses, opportunities, and threats. It also makes it easier to plan a successful strategy. Each operator can decide what the key points are for inclusion in the SWOT analysis. The 11 P's of hospitality marketing include the traditional four P's of marketing—place (or location), product, price, promotion—but add three other P's (people, process, and physical evidence) and four new P's (personalization, participation, peer-to-peer, and predictive modeling). All plans need to be implemented; Figure 15–3 shows how plans follow goals and strategies. Notice that strategic plans are implemented through action plans, operating plans, and standing plans.

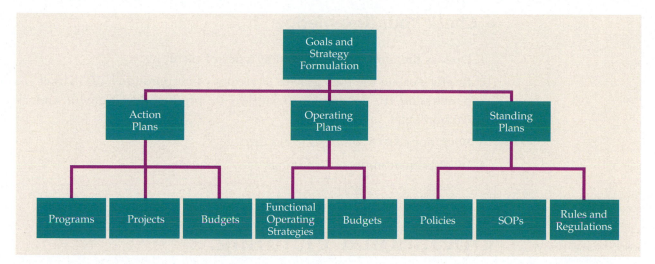

Figure 15–3 • How Plans Follow Goals and Strategies.

Environmental Scanning and Forecasting

Environmental scanning is the process of screening large amounts of information to anticipate and interpret changes in the environment. Environmental scanning creates the basis for forecasts. **Forecasting** is the prediction of future outcomes. Information gained through scanning is used to form scenarios. These, in turn, establish premises for forecasts, which are predictions of future outcomes. The two main types of outcomes that managers seek to forecast are future revenues and new technology breakthroughs. However, any component in the organization's general or specific environment may receive further attention. Both Marriott International and Disney's Magic Mountain sales levels drive purchasing requirements, production goals, employment needs, inventories, and numerous other decisions. Similarly, your university's income from tuition and state appropriations will determine course offerings, staffing needs, salaries, and so forth. These examples illustrate that predicting future revenue is a crucial first step in planning for success.

As you can imagine, the forecasting done by the president of Hilton Worldwide is very different from the forecasting done by a restaurant manager or department head. The president of Hilton needs to assess the broad economic, political, social, cultural, technological, and financial implications that may impact any forecast. For instance, should Hilton open a hotel in Providence, Rhode Island, or a different city? The desire of Hilton to have a presence in these markets must be considered along with the economic and other environmental factors in each market location. The president must also consider the probability of success of the new property. Another scenario is that of the president of a major chain restaurant corporation trying to forecast in a changing business environment. What if minimum wage is increased? What if health care is mandated? How would these changes affect the corporation?

▶ Check Your Knowledge

1. Discuss the merits of the different types of planning.

2. Briefly explain the four growth strategies of corporations: (a) market penetration, (b) geographic expansion, (c) product development, and (d) horizontal integration.

3. What does *SWOT analysis* stand for?

4. What is environmental scanning?

LEARNING OBJECTIVE 4
Identify the seven steps in operational planning.

Operational Planning

How Do Managers Plan?

Planning is the first of the management functions, so it establishes the basis for the other functions. In fact, without planning, how would managers know how or what to organize, decide on, communicate, motivate, or control? So how do managers plan? That's what this section is all about. Planning involves two main parts: goals and strategies.

We have seen that strategic planning takes place at the top management level; now we look at the operational midlevel and supervisory levels and see that most hospitality managers have a shorter planning horizon. **Operational plans** are generally created for periods of up to one year and fit in with the strategic plan. Most hotel, restaurant, and other hospitality managers plan for periods ranging from hourly, daily, weekly, or monthly to up to 90 days.

Operational plans provide managers with a step-by-step approach to accomplish goals. The overall purpose of planning is to have the entire organization moving harmoniously toward the goals. The following are the seven steps in operational planning:

1. *Setting goals.* The first step in planning is identifying expected outcomes—that is, the goals. The goals should be specific, measurable, and achievable, and should reflect the vision and mission of the organization.

2. *Analyzing and evaluating the environment.* This involves analyzing political, economic, social, and other trends that may affect the operation. The level of turbulence is evaluated in relation to the organization's present position and the resources available to achieve the goals.

3. *Determining alternatives.* This involves developing courses of action that are available to a manager to reach a goal. Input may be requested from all levels of the organization. Group work is normally better than individual input.

4. *Evaluating alternatives*. This calls for making a list of the advantages and disadvantages of each alternative. Among the factors to be considered are resources and effects on the organization.

5. *Selecting the best solution*. This analysis of the various alternatives should result in determining one course of action that is better than the others. It may, however, involve combining two or more alternatives.

6. *Implementing the plan*. Once the best solution is chosen, the manager needs to decide the following:

   a. Who will do what?

   b. By when?

   c. What resources are required?

   d. At what benefit?

   e. At what cost?

   f. What reporting procedures will there be?

   g. What authority will be granted to achieve the goals?

7. *Controlling and evaluating results*. Once the plan is implemented, it is necessary to monitor progress toward goal accomplishment.

Operational Goal Setting

Goal setting is the process of determining outcomes for each area and associate. In Chapter 1, we looked at organizational vision, mission, goals, and objectives. Once the vision and mission have been determined, organizations set goals in order to meet the mission. The goals are set for each of the key operating areas mentioned earlier. No one can work effectively without specific goals and daily, weekly, monthly, quarterly, semiannual, and annual evaluation reports to assess progress toward goal accomplishment; if progress is lacking, adjustments must be made to change course.[5] Examples of the goals and information a sales department should record and analyze each month follow.

Group Room Nights

- Booked this month and year to date by market segment and salesperson

- Actual consumed room nights this month, year to date by month, by market segment, and "on the books" for months to come

- Actual average group room rates by month, year to date, and on the books for months to come

Individual Room Nights

- Actual room nights booked by month and year to date by market segment
- Local corporate clients—actual individual and group room nights booked by month and year to date
- Occupancy—actual by month, year to date, and same time last year
- Revenue per available room (REV PAR)—actual by month, year to date, and same time last year
- Packages—number sold for each type by month, year to date, and zip code origin[6]

Another example would be setting productivity goals. Productivity refers to the amount of labor (input) it takes to do a particular task (output). Productivity is measured in labor costs, which are expressed as a percentage of sales, for each department. Because labor costs are the highest of the operational costs, it is critical to keep them in line with budget. Productivity and labor costs can be compared across similar operations to determine which is more efficient. Suppose the goal for a family restaurant's labor costs is 23 percent of sales. If sales go up, then so, too, can the labor cost—but proportionately. But what if sales go down? Then so will labor costs—again, proportionately. The skill of management is to operate efficiently and effectively. It is easier to operate a hospitality business when it is busy; however, management skill is required to run a hospitality business that is operating at only 50–60 percent capacity, or worse still, even less.

Expressing goals in specific, measurable terms is important because it allows us to measure our progress toward goal accomplishment. Goals are set for each of the key result areas (departments or elements of a business that determine its success; e.g., in a restaurant, guest satisfaction scores, sales, food costs, labor costs, and beverage costs are all key result areas).

An example would be a restaurant where guest satisfaction scores are currently 87 percent. The goal is a score of 95 percent. A time by which the goal is to be met is also identified, as is the individual who is to be responsible for its accomplishment.

Planning expert George Morrisey presents a four-point model for use in formulating goals.[7] Here is an example using Morrisey's model:

1. Increase guest satisfaction scores
2. From 87 to 95 percent
3. By December 31, 20XX
4. At a cost of $500 for training

Operational Objectives

Objectives state how the goals will be met. Objectives are operational statements of activities that should be quantifiable and attainable within a stated time. If the goal is to achieve a food cost percentage of 28.5 percent by October 15 and maintain it until further notice at a cost not to exceed $100 or 10 working hours, the food and beverage director and executive chef must do the following:

- Achieve the desired food cost percentage by having the menu items priced and their costs calculated.

- Control portion sizes by establishing an exact portion for each menu item and watching to see that it is maintained.

- Ensure that regular and spot checks are done on inventory and that the food cost is calculated correctly. Take a physical count of all food items accurately, including all items in the freezers, the kitchen, the storeroom, the banquet kitchen, and so on, and calculate their costs accurately.

- Ensure that all sales and food costs are included in the calculations. Check that all guest food charges are included in the calculations—especially any functions for the day of the inventory if the food is included—and that the sales are also included.

- Use any leftover food within 48 hours.

- Maintain a vigilant loss prevention program with security. Check bags leaving the property and do not allow any bags in the kitchen.

- Ensure that all food sales are recorded and paid for.

Collectively, these objectives ensure that the goal will be met. Each goal needs to have written step-by-step objectives that state how they will be met.

Management Concepts and Approaches

We can see from the preceding examples that it makes sense if the associates who are going to be responsible for achieving the goals are also the ones involved in setting them. Some years ago this concept lead to **management by objectives (MBO)**, a managerial process that determines the goals of the organization and then plans the objectives, that is, the how-tos of reaching the goals. With MBO, associates usually establish the goals and objectives and review them with management. MBO works because associates have been involved with setting goals and objectives and are likely to be motivated to see them successfully achieved. The MBO process consists of the following six steps:

1. *Set organizational goals.* Top management sets goals for the company in each key result area.

2. *Set departmental goals.* Department heads and their team members jointly set supporting goals for their departments' key result areas.

3. *Present goals.* Department heads present goals and gain approval from senior management.

4. *Discuss department goals.* Department heads present department goals and ask all team members to develop their own individual goals.

5. *Set individual goals.* Team members set their own goals with their supervisor, and timetables are assigned for accomplishing those goals.

6. *Give feedback.* The supervisor and team members meet periodically to review performance and to assess progress toward goals.

MBO goals need to be specific, measurable, and challenging but attainable, just like any other goals. The main purpose of an MBO program is to integrate the goals of the organization and the goals of the associates so that they are in focus. Over the years, MBO has proved very successful and has, in some organizations, been superseded by **Total Quality Management (TQM)**, which was introduced in Chapter 1. TQM not only involves planning but also touches on the other functions of management. The idea of improving efficiency and increasing productivity while placing a larger emphasis on quality has caught on fast. Originally designed by Japanese businesses to help reconstruct the economy after World War II, today TQM is widely applied in most industrialized countries. The hospitality industry has embraced quality management with open arms, asking for input from all levels of employees and calling for teamwork. Ultimately, the customer rates the team on quality, value, and product—and the customer does not lie. An example of TQM is asking a group of associates to suggest ways to improve the guest experience by addressing specific challenges (actually problems, but industry professionals prefer to be positive and use the term *challenges*) that the hospitality operation has in delivering exceptional service.

INTRODUCING TIM MULLIGAN

Chief Human Resources Officer, San Diego Zoo Global, San Diego

Meet Tim Mulligan, chief human resources officer for San Diego Zoo Global. Tim feels that the important elements in planning are knowing what the desired outcome will be, having the instructions followed by the organization, and being a good time manager to help ensure goal attainment.

Goal setting can be divided into two types: annual goals for managers, which have to be in line with career growth, annual bonuses, and so forth, and annual goals for employees, which need to be stated in terms of individual development. According to Tim, the objectives need to be in line with company objectives, individual hotel objectives, and personal growth objectives.

Operational plans are important to meet financial goals (profit), guest satisfaction goals, and employee satisfaction goals.

Specific plans are important to reach day-to-day success with goals and objectives (e.g., check-in, recruiting, hiring process, room cleaning).

Single-use plans are used only for special events, such as holiday parties or human resources (HR) receptions.

Standing plans are annual plans, such as benefit enrollment and management screening plans. They are also used for company policies, such as tuition reimbursement or training programs.

Tim gave these examples for contingency factors in planning. If the occupancy of the hotel decreases, the HR department has a plan for layoffs. On the other hand, if a need to hire a significant amount of new staff exists, then the HR department has a plan in place for a mass-hiring action.

Forecasting in the HR department differs from forecasting in other departments, according to the HR director. In the HR field, there is a need for more accurate information on a business level, to determine needs on a staffing level, and the need for dollar amounts for advertising, recruiting, background checks, drug tests, training, and so forth.

In response to a question about which benchmarking practices he believes are the most successful, Tim named turnover rates, employee retention, the employee satisfaction index, and the guest satisfaction index.

In the field of technology, a new trend in planning is the optimal business model. This model works with drivers and is based on the business practice. As an example, this model can determine the amount of hours available for scheduling and the maximum amount of money you can spend to stay within a budget. Two more trends are an online employee evaluation model and a goal-setting process called the performance management process.

Take guest check-in as an example. The TQM team would include members from the front office and guest services (bellpersons and so on.) who identify lineups for check-in from 4:00 to 7:00 P.M. The group writes a challenge or problem statement, and various ways of improving the situations are presented. They may include the following:

- Using a special desk for airport check-ins
- Handling convention and group guest check-ins in another location (the rooming list is made up in advance and rooms allocated with keys encoded and ready for distribution to guests)
- Cross-training and using associates from other departments to assist with the check-ins
- Adopting an "all hands on deck" approach to have members of management available to assist with check-ins in various ways
- Having additional help available for housekeeping to get the rooms ready more quickly

An example of TQM in the restaurant industry is asking servers in a restaurant for help solving the challenge of reducing the guests' waiting time for tables during rush periods. Once the problem or challenge statement is written, the TQM team can focus on ways to improve the guest experience by suggesting ideas to turn tables more quickly. The head chef might automatically take on the role of coach, as opposed to that of supervisor. Implementing TQM will have the natural outcome of teamwork because one employee cannot improve quality on his or her own. The chef uses motivation and inspiration to keep the team in high spirits, and each employee is important in his or her own way. Emphasis is placed on recruiting, training, and keeping quality employees to ensure that the TQM approach will be a success.

Benchmarking is a concept that identifies the best way of doing something and the companies that excel in that area (*best-practices companies*).

The best practice is noted and emulated or even improved on by other companies. In the spirit of cooperation, companies are expected to share information, so you need to give as well as receive.

The history of benchmarking begins in the 1970s.[8] Japanese companies would take trips to industrialized nations to study their large, successful industrial companies and take that knowledge home to apply to their local companies. By aggressively emulating others, they were able to supersede the company being imitated by improving on the success strategy.

CORPORATE PROFILE

Choice Hotels International, Inc.

The story of Choice Hotels began in 1968 when Gerald (Jerry) Petitt, a Dartmouth engineering and business student, was seeking summer employment with IBM.[1] He blew the roof off the company's pre-employment test scores. The test scores were brought to the attention of Robert (Bob) C. Hazard Jr., who was in charge of the Coors Brewery account. This had an appeal for the ski bum in Petitt, who was originally from Denver. Bob Hazard says that Jerry Petitt did more in one summer for IBM's efforts to design a production system for the brewery than a team of five engineers did in two years.

Bob Hazard decided then, more than 25 years ago, to keep this talented person. They progressed in their careers with spells at American Express and Best Western; they eventually went on to Silver Spring, Maryland, where they took a sleepy, stagnating lodging company called Quality Inn from 300 properties to more than 6,000 hotels in 30 countries and territories.[2] Because they had been so successful at Best Western, they were enticed to join Quality in 1980 for equity plus $500,000 annual salaries.

Bob and Jerry brought to Quality (now Choice Hotels) a combination of engineer-builders and entrepreneur-marketers. They quickly set about changing the mausoleum management style—"Where you don't get creative thinking, where you try to pit good minds against each other." Instead, you get, "What will the chairman think?" and, "We can all go along with it—or look for another job."[3]

To illustrate the change of management style, Bob Hazard draws the upside-down management organization, where the bosses are the millions of guests at 6,000 hotels worldwide. He and Jerry Petitt, of course, were on the bottom.[4]

The strategy of changing the corporate culture, of taking advantage of emerging technological and management trends with emphasis on marketing-driven management over operations, has worked for Choice Hotels. The development of brand segmentation was perhaps its best move. Choice Hotels International is now an international hotel franchisor consisting of the following brands: Comfort Inn, Comfort Suites, Quality, Sleep Inn, Clarion, Cambria Hotels &Suites, MainStay Suites, Suburban, EconoLodge, Rodeway Inn, and Ascend Hotel Collection.

More recently, Choice has reorganized, creating market area management teams strategically placed so that licensees can be closer to support staff. Each field staff manager has 45 properties and helps with sales, training, quality assurance reviews, and operations consolidations.

[1]This draws on Philip Hazard, "The Bob and Jerry Show," *Lodging* 19 (December 1993): 37–41.

[2]Choice Hotels, *Investor Information*, http://investor.choicehotels.com/phoenix.zhtml?c=99348&p=IROL-irhome (accessed October 1, 2011).

[3]Ibid., 58.

[4]Choice Hotels, *Investor Information*, http://investor.choicehotels.com/phoenix.zhtml?c=99348&p=IROL-irhome (accessed October 1, 2011).

Meanwhile, benchmarking has become a global trait. Some companies are even benchmarking companies outside their own industry. For example, IBM carefully studied Las Vegas casinos to apply their strategy of reducing employee theft at IBM.

How do you benchmark? First of all, a team is formed. The duty of this team is to identify companies to be benchmarked. Next, the team must determine the best possible way of collecting the data, which can be collected internally as well as externally. Once collected, the data must be analyzed to determine where the success lies and where the differences lie. The last step is to create an action plan on how to improve on the newly gained data—that is, what steps need to be taken to implement it.

The question to be answered is, "How do these companies obtain internal information on other companies they are benchmarking?" An initial team is formed, the members of which may have contacts among customers, suppliers, or employees of the company they are planning on benchmarking. Companies often are glad to swap success stories and information with others, not only informing about themselves but being informed about others as well. Successful companies can often be identified by the number of quality awards they have won. In addition, trade associations typically know who the successful companies are, and you can analyze financial data to help determine which companies to benchmark. Having employees who will implement the benchmarked changes helps ensure their commitment to service or product improvement.

Benchmarking is an operational tool that can be used to guide corporate strategy as well as operations strategies.[9] The process in an ideal setting is to compare company operations with those of other companies that exhibit best practices. Note that best practices are often found outside the company's industry grouping. For example, the Federal Aviation Administration has contracted with Disney to help reduce the long lines at airports occasioned by more severe security measures due to the threat of terrorism. In many instances, best practices adopted from outside the hospitality industry sometimes must be modified to fit the context.

Policies, Procedures, and Rules

Policies, procedures, and rules are examples of standing plans. **Policies** set broad guidelines for associates to use when making decisions. For example, it is the policy of most hotels to pay the room and tax at another hotel and provide a taxi or hotel limo when "walking" a guest.

Procedures specify what to do in given situations. An example would be when a former classmate calls you to request a room for the next weekend. However, the hotel is forecasting 94-percent occupancy, and company procedures, unfortunately for your friend, state that no employees or their friends may stay at complimentary or discounted rates if the hotel is forecast to be more than 90-percent occupied. Policy and procedures often go together.

A **rule** is a specific action guide that associates must follow. Consider this example: Under no circumstances shall an employee serve alcoholic beverages to minors or intoxicated guests.

Budgeting

Most of us are familiar with budgets; we learned about them when we received our first allowance as a child. Remember how often we had it spent before the week was up? That's why organizations plan the use of their financial resources. A **budget** is a plan allocating money to specific activities. There are budgets for revenues (sales) and costs (expenses) for capital equipment—equipment that has an expected life of several years.

Budgets are popular because they force managers to anticipate expected sales and to budget expenses accordingly—that is, not to spend it all before the week is up! Budgets are used extensively in all levels of hospitality organizations, from the corporate level to the smallest departments. Once an estimate of a particular department's revenues is determined, the costs are then budgeted, leaving a portion for profit. This is also called the bottom line. Here's an example of a budget: A restaurant expects 750 guests in a given week, at an average check of $15; this means sales will be $11,250 for the week. This allows management to budget labor costs, usually to a predetermined percentage of sales (normally between 18 and 24 percent, depending on the type of restaurant). Food, beverage, and other costs are budgeted in the same way. Figure 15–4 shows a detailed restaurant budget listing all the items of expenditure. Note that the column on the right-hand side is for the percentage of sales to which the dollar amount refers. This percentage is helpful in that it can be easily compared with other similar restaurant operations. In fact, restaurant companies use percentages to check on a manager's performance. If one restaurant manager gets a food cost percentage of 28.5 and another gets 33 percent, then the corporate office will be asking the latter manager questions!

Budgets are popular because they can be used with a variety of applications, all over the world. Budgets are planning techniques that force managers to be fiscally responsible. Notice that the "Actual" and "Variance" columns in Figure 15–4 have no entries in them yet. As soon as the period (usually a month) is over, the results can be totaled and any variances recorded.

Budgets are created by department heads once a year and are revised monthly or as necessary. First, the projected revenue is forecasted, and then all fixed and variable costs are allocated to ensure that the required profit is attained. Forecasting revenues is not easy—there are so many variables—but it has to be done. If the business was operating the previous year(s), there is a history. For a new business, the operator's experience, information from similar operations, environmental factors, forecasting models, and calculated guesswork equal a "guesstimate" of sales. Budgets intertwine with (1) scheduling, because scheduling equals labor costs, the largest controllable budget item; (2) purchasing, because that contributes to food, beverage, and other costs; and (3) controlling, because we want to compare budget to actual revenue and expenditure results.

▶ Check Your Knowledge

1. What is the difference between operational planning and strategic planning?

2. Define benchmarking.

3. Why is it important to have a budget?

4. Give an example of goal setting.

5. Briefly describe the six steps of the MBO process.

Restaurant Operational Budget

	Budget ($ Thousands)	%	Actual Variance +(–)
Sales			
Food	750.0	75	
Beverage	250.0	25	
Other	0.0		
Total Sales	1,000.0	100	
Cost of Sales			
Food	225.0	30.0	
Beverage	55.0	22.0	
Other	0.0		
Total Cost of Sales	280.0	28.0	
Gross Profit	720.0	72.0	
Controllable Expenses			
Salaries and wages	240.0	24.0	
Employee benefits	40.0	4.0	
Direct operating expenses	60.0	6.0	
Music and entertainment	10.0	1.0	
Marketing	40.0	4.0	
Energy and utility	30.0	3.0	
Administrative and general	40.0	4.0	
Repairs and maintenance	20.0	2.0	
Total Controllable Expenses	480.0	48.0	
Rent and other occupation costs	70.0	7.0	
Income before interest, depreciation, and taxes	170.0	17.0	
Interest	10.0	1.0	
Depreciation	20.0	2.0	
Net Income before Taxes	140.0	14.0	

Figure 15–4 • Restaurant Operational Budget.

Scheduling

Scheduling of associates is a planning activity that involves taking the business forecast and allocating an appropriate number of staff to give the necessary level of service. Because of the increasing cost of wages and benefits, schedules must be planned very carefully to avoid being overstaffed or understaffed. Because the hospitality industry mostly operates 24/7, we need to staff all departments with appropriate coverage day and night.

In Chapter 1, we briefly introduced the main shifts as morning, midshift, and evening plus night. Staffing each area or department with an adequate number of associates costs money and is necessary just to open the doors. For example, a restaurant needs a host to greet and seat guests, a server or two, a prep cook or two, a cook or two, a dishwasher, a bartender, and a manager. This is the minimum acceptable staffing level regardless of the number of guests. The same holds true for all areas of the hospitality industry. The problem is that we never know exactly how many guests we will have, and one day can be busy and the next quiet. That's why accurate forecasting, as discussed earlier, is so important.

Obviously, the level of service will vary from one lodging operation to another. A full-service hotel may have 24-hour bell service, whereas a limited-service hotel will not offer it. An amusement park may be open up to 12 hours a day and may need at least two shifts. A restaurant may be open for up to 12 hours a day and may need two shifts, depending on whether it serves breakfast, lunch, or dinner. The hospitality industry, in order to keep costs down and remain competitive, uses a large number of part-time employees. Many hospitality departments have a skeleton staff of full-time employees augmented by several part-time ones as the business needs them.

Project Management

Project management means exactly that—managing a project. Project management is the task of completing the project on time and within budget. In the hospitality industry, we have a variety of projects at each level of the corporation. At the corporate level, for instance, there is the construction of a new hotel or restaurant. At the unit level, there is the alteration or renovation of an existing building; at the department level, there is the installation of a new piece of equipment or a new point-of-sale system. But project management is broader than these examples. What about the senior prom? That's a project, too. So are most of the catering functions that take place at convention centers and hotels.

Hospitality companies are increasingly using project management because the approach fits well with the need for flexibility and rapid response to perceived market opportunities. Sometimes an organization has a specific need for a project that does not fit into a regular planning schedule, so it uses project management. Project management works like this: Say the project is for the organization to become more environmentally friendly. A hospitality organization will create a team of associates from various departments and challenge them to come up with a plan to accomplish the goal of becoming more environmentally friendly. Figure 15–5 shows the steps in the project planning process.

The process begins with clearly defining the project's goals. This step is necessary because the manager and team need to know exactly what's expected. All activities and the resources needed to do them must then be identified. What labor and materials are needed to complete the project? Once the activities have been identified, the sequence of completion needs to be determined. What activities must be completed before others can begin? Which can be done simultaneously? This step is actually done using flowchart-type diagrams such as a Gantt chart or a PERT network (see Figures 15–6 and 15–7). Next, the project activities need to be scheduled.

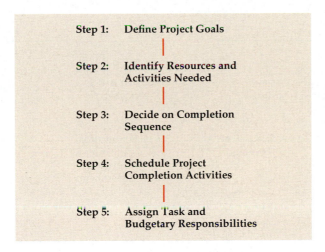

Step 1:   **Define Project Goals**

Step 2:   **Identify Resources and Activities Needed**

Step 3:   **Decide on Completion Sequence**

Step 4:   **Schedule Project Completion Activities**

Step 5:   **Assign Task and Budgetary Responsibilities**

Figure 15–5 • Steps in the Project Planning Process.

Activity	Week						
	1	2	3	4	5	6	7
Consult with beverage staff	✔						
Establish goals and determine wines to be tasted		✔					
Arrange tasting			✔				
Taste wines				✔			
Make selection and determine pricing					✔		
Prepare and print wine list						✔	✔

Figure 15–6 • A Gantt Chart for a Restaurant Owner Planning a New Wine List.

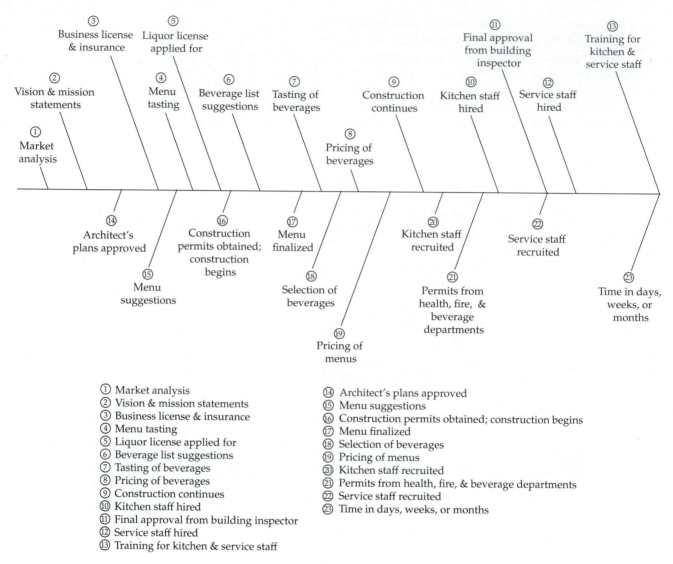

① Market analysis
② Vision & mission statements
③ Business license & insurance
④ Menu tasting
⑤ Liquor license applied for
⑥ Beverage list suggestions
⑦ Tasting of beverages
⑧ Pricing of beverages
⑨ Construction continues
⑩ Kitchen staff hired
⑪ Final approval from building inspector
⑫ Service staff hired
⑬ Training for kitchen & service staff
⑭ Architect's plans approved
⑮ Menu suggestions
⑯ Construction permits obtained; construction begins
⑰ Menu finalized
⑱ Selection of beverages
⑲ Pricing of menus
⑳ Kitchen staff recruited
㉑ Permits from health, fire, & beverage departments
㉒ Service staff recruited
㉓ Time in days, weeks, or months

Figure 15–7 • A PERT Chart for the Opening of a New Restaurant.

Time estimates for each activity are done, and these estimates are used to develop an overall project schedule and completion date.[10] Tasks and budgetary responsibilities for each step are then assigned.

▶ **Check Your Knowledge**

1. Describe the minimum acceptable staffing level for a restaurant as it relates to scheduling.

2. What are the steps in project management?

Sustainable Planning

Tourism is the largest growing segment of the hospitality industry through-out the world. The increase in tourism can be seen as having both negative and positive effects on locations, depending on what they can and choose to offer the tourist market. Tourism can provide many economic, social, cultural, and environmental benefits to a destination, but it can also incur certain costs as well. Planning for sustainable tourism requires identifying opportunities in a particular area and balancing them with possible limita-tions placed on tourism development, in order to capitalize on the strengths and diminish the negative effects that can befall on the environment. At the heart of sustainable planning is a focus on protecting the community and their environment from being misused.

Sustainable planning should be initiated with certain intentions in mind, such as using resources responsibly with an environmentally conscious approach, maintaining respect for local heritage and differ-ent cultures living in the community, improving the quality of life in the community, and encouraging the preservation of the various ways of life. Decision making should be structured by the local government, with objectives focused on long-term strategies to solve current problems and prevent future problems that might occur. Decisions should involve a strong collaboration between public and private sectors of the community. They should affect different sectors of the community, while demonstrat-ing the impact various segments have on one another as a result of tourist development.

There is a strong need for planning in sustainable tourism by way of set-ting goals and objectives, and ensuring that they are successfully achieved. In order to prevent plans from failing, it is important for the plans to be readily adaptable to changes in the environment, community, or other fac-tors involved in tourism development. Plans should include a strong "strate-gic vision," and decision making should occur from a top-down hierarchy of executives and others invested in the planning and development of the des-tination. Finally, plans must be well-defined and properly communicated in order to ensure a smooth implementation that corresponds with the overall philosophy.

The proper structure for constructing a plan includes:

1. Philosophy, or vision, and a mission statement
2. Situational analysis of environmental factors
3. Strategic goals and objectives
4. Ways you plan to achieve and implement these goals and objectives
5. How you will measure success

Based on the level of tourism planning, the goals and objectives may be smaller scale, and narrower in focus, such as for an individual site or destination property within a community, or larger in scale, and generally long-term, such as a region, a nation, or several countries. While the majority of tourism planning involves local community involvement, larger scale planning more often requires collaboration with political and legal entities, as well as different levels of government and various business organizations. Policies and procedures must be established and implemented in structured plans before they are approved for further development. The outline of the plan must highlight a number of elements depending on the size of the plan, generally including primary organizations involved, infrastructure, goods, services and facilities, financing, marketing and promotion, human resources, additional programs offered, and so on. Finally, it is necessary to provide a blueprint that physically defines the step-by-step breakdown of the plan in action. Once the plan is initiated, it is the goal of the public sector and the private sector to effectively manage the operation from start to finish.[11]

Trends in Planning

Courtesy of Dr. Greg Dunn, Senior Lecturer and Managing Director, University of Florida, Eric Friedheim Tourism Institute

- *International Visitor Planning.* In 2012, President Obama introduced the Visa Waiver Program, which has influenced international traveling exponentially. The U.S. Department of Commerce (2014) projects an annual growth rate of approximately 4 percent in international travel—this represents over 80 million visitors. This is exceptionally important to plan for in hospitality, as this growth is greater than ever before. China has been identified as one of the largest inbound markets for travel to the United States and hospitality organizations are gearing up to be "China-ready" by making adjustments to room amenities, menus, signage, and staffing to meet the growing demand and provide appropriate customer service.

- *Social Media Planning.* Social media is influencing business in all industries, including the hospitality industry. It is very important to be an active source and participant in this media channel and keep the content recent, relevant, and interesting. For instance, some businesses are creating events and hashtags for upcoming events. In addition, it is important to stay active in social media even during a not-so-busy season to stay top of consumers' minds. This may include uploading photos of the hotels and employees during soft periods or making your social media sites more interactive by asking questions or creating polls. This could be extremely helpful for your business as it is not only entertaining for your guests and followers, but also provides them a medium for their voices to be heard.

- *Social Media Marketing.* Social media can also play a huge role in the planning, organizing, and marketing departments of any hospitality organization. Managers are now not just relying on social media to attract consumers and guest, but also base many of their largest decisions on the information they gather off of social media. Managers are able to see what guests like and didn't like from their experiences shared on social media outlets and can plan ahead taking those experiences into account. Social media provides that forum to be able to communicate the latest decisions, events, and exciting information that could attract an even larger market.

- *The Continuous Job Search Culture.* Planning for new employees and dealing with a higher than average employee turnover rate is very important, especially in the hospitality industry. The hospitality industry is more complex than many may believe as sometime evidenced by long work hours, nontraditional work schedules and high numbers of customer service interactions. Recognizing that many of the Generation Y and Generation Z populations have different approaches and views toward work and jobs than their predecessors, hospitality companies must anticipate, plan for, and put in place mechanisms to handle a culture that seems to always be in the job market.

- *Diversity Planning.* It is very important to plan for having a more diverse workforce than ever before. Some hospitality companies are being proactive and open and are willing to share their diversity portfolios publicly. Other companies are being honest and showing their disappointment in not being able to attract and hire a more diverse workforce. Diversity just does not happen, it takes significant planning and effort to bring it to fruition.

- *Strengthening Stakeholder Confidence.* The saying goes, "You are only as strong as your weakest link." Strengthening ties with all business stakeholders is paramount to a company's success. This trend implies devising a robust stakeholder strategy that clearly defines the critical processes of stakeholder engagement and communication and makes sure that the organizational performance is held to a high standard as per agreed.

- *Re-evaluating Existing Business Models.* The trend of re-evaluating existing business models is not new, yet the need continues. Hospitality companies will need to focus their needs by attending to and regularly evaluating the effectiveness of existing business models. This may include conducting a close examination on how well the existing models measure up to issues of customer satisfaction, loyalty, and profitability via current routes to market, strategic pricing, capacity, and demand. Efforts may also include looking at ways to widen the business model to include new partnerships and a focus on innovation.

- *Strong Customer Focus.* Today's most successful hospitality companies work from the position of a strong customer focus and on building on their core competencies. These companies take a greater interest in the organization's operational functions and understand the makeup of their most profitable customers. They seek to answer the questions: Do we allocate our resources correctly? How do we make our clients happy?

- *Strengthen Management Talent.* When planning for how your business will be managed, you have to ask if your management has the insight and knowledge to uncover hidden leverages and identify market forces that impact on performance. Hospitality organizations must look for innovative ways to strengthen management talent and employ a diverse skilled set of people who are key factors to attaining positive future performance.

- *Beyond the Traditional Event Venue.* Meeting and event planners are seeking out alternative venues for events. Most communities have non-traditional space such as empty warehouses and airplane hangars that provide a blank canvas with perhaps fewer limitations to work with than a traditional venue. Events are being hosted in zoos, parks, restaurants, rooftops, and parking garage structures.

- *Budget Spending.* The planning structure is one that continuously changes with the changing economic environment. The struggling economy of the recession is slowly getting back on its feet and people are beginning to spend money again in areas that, over the past five to seven years, they have been cutting back on. This presents an opportunity for planners to capitalize on bigger budget spending from consumers, companies, and larger groups. Companies are bringing back budget spending on higher-end recreational and entertainment activities, amenities, lodging, and transportation.

- *Going Virtual.* Given the environment of rapid change in today's hospitality business, planning needs to be done on time, yet methodically, to keep pace with rapid environmental and global changes. Technology, especially the Internet, can be used to overcome time and distance, allowing for more people to have input into the planning process. Associates can contribute to the planning process online instead of going to meetings.

CASE STUDY

Shell's Seafood Restaurant

Shell's Seafood Restaurant caters weddings and other events in a small New England town. The following is an overview of the planning—or lack of planning—that took place last summer. Jason, the restaurant's general manager, together with the wedding couple, planned a garden wedding and reception in a town park near the restaurant. At first, it seemed as if there were too many choices and decisions to be made, but as they went through the lists they had prepared, they were all pleased with the arrangements.

They chose a wedding ceremony time of 2:00 P.M., followed by a reception at 2:30 P.M. The wedding couple and their families wanted it to be a special occasion but did not want to spend a fortune, so they decided to use Shell's Seafood Restaurant because they had enjoyed meals there in the past. Jason prepared a menu that the couple liked: cream of asparagus soup, chicken fricassee, potatoes au gratin, cauliflower Mornay, and for dessert, crème brûlée. Jason also suggested white and red house wines with an allocation of $3/4$ bottle per person. The wedding couple's aunt made the cake, and it was delivered to the park, but when Jason's staff assembled it, the weight of the top two tiers caused the cake to sink into the thin layer of icing and fall over.

The wedding ceremony was a success, but as you can imagine, the reception was less so.

Discussion Question

1. List the planning errors that were made.

Summary

1. Planning involves selecting the various goals that the organization wants to achieve and the actions (objectives) that will ensure that the organization accomplishes the goals.
2. Goals are set for each of the key operating areas.
3. Planning gives direction, not only to top managers, but also to all associates as they focus on goal accomplishment.
4. Strategic (long-term) planning and strategic management involve identifying the business of the corporation and the business it wants for the future, and then identifying the course of action it will pursue, given its strengths, weaknesses, opportunities, and threats.
5. There are three main strategic management tasks: developing a vision and mission statement, translating the mission into strategic goals, and creating a strategy or course of action to move the organization from where it is today to where it wants to be.
6. Strategic planning and management take place at the higher levels of management. This is known as corporate-level strategy.
7. There are four growth strategies: market penetration, geographic expansion, product development, and horizontal integration.
8. A strengths, weaknesses, opportunities, and threats (SWOT) analysis is a key strategic management technique.
9. Environmental scanning is the process of assessing information about the economic, social, political, and technological environment to anticipate and interpret changes in the environment.
10. Operational plans are generally for periods of up to one year and dovetail with the strategic plan.
11. There are seven steps in operational planning: setting goals, analyzing and evaluating the environment, determining alternatives, evaluating alternatives, selecting the best solution, implementing the plan, and controlling and evaluating results.
12. Benchmarking is a concept that identifies the best way of doing something and the companies that excel in the area under study.
13. Policies, procedures, and rules are examples of standing plans. Policies set broad guidelines, procedures specify what to do in given situations, and rules are specific action guides that associates must follow.

14. Budgets are plans allocating money for specific activities. They are popular because they force managers to anticipate expected sales and to budget expenses accordingly.
15. Goal setting is determining the outcomes for the organization and associates.
16. Objectives state how goals will be met. Management by objectives is a managerial process that determines the goals of the organization and then plans the objectives.
17. Project management is the task of completing a project on time and within budget.

Key Words and Concepts

benchmarking
budget
diversification
environmental scanning
forecasting
geographic expansion
goal
goal setting
horizontal integration
joint venture

key operating areas
management by objectives (MBO)
market penetration
objective
operational plans
policy
procedure
product development
project management

rule
scheduling
strategic alliance
strategic management
strategic planning
strategy
SWOT analysis
Total Quality Management (TQM)

Review Questions

1. What does planning involve?
2. How are goals and objectives different?
3. What is strategic planning?
4. What is the distinction between SWOT analysis and environmental screening analysis?
5. Why do companies use policies, procedures, and rules?

Internet Exercise

1. Organization: Any restaurant chain
   Summary: Fast-food chains need to know what their competitors are doing or going to do. In this exercise, you will select fast-food company web sites and see what you can find out about your competitors.

Apply Your Knowledge

1. Benchmarking can be an important tool and source of information for managers. It can also be useful to students, as you'll see in this team-based exercise. In your small group, discuss study habits that each of you has found to be effective from your

years of being in school. As a group, come up with a bulleted list of at least eight effective study habits in the time allowed by your professor. When the professor calls time, each group should combine with one other group and share ideas, again in the time allowed by the professor. In this larger group, be sure to ask questions about suggestions that each small group had. Each small group should make sure it understands the suggestions of the other group with which it is working. When the professor calls time, each small group will then present and explain the study habit suggestions of the other group with which it was working. After all groups have presented their suggestions, the class will come up with what it feels are the "best" study habits of all the ideas presented.

2. In groups of four, develop a plan for your formal class graduation dinner with a prominent guest speaker.

Endnotes

1. Draws on Gary Dessler, *A Framework for Management*, 2nd ed. (Upper Saddle River, NJ: Prentice Hall, 2002), 99.
2. Ibid., 100.
3. Personal conversation with Kenneth E. Crocker, Ph.D., professor, Francis Marion University College of Business, May 15, 2008.
4. Odyssey Media Group, "Hilton Joins Air China Companion Card Frequent Flyer Program," *Asia Pacific News*, January 9, 2002, http://www.odyssey mediagroup.com/apn/Editorial-Hotels-And-Resorts. asp?ReportID=31401 (accessed December 16, 2014).
5. Personal conversation with Stephen Deuker, director of marketing, Ritz-Carlton, Sarasota, Florida, April 18, 2008.
6. Ibid.
7. Dessler, *A Framework for Management*, 108.
8. Stephen P. Robbins and Mary Coulter, *Management*, 11th ed. (Upper Saddle River, NJ: Prentice Hall, 2011), 228–230.
9. Personal conversation with Kenneth E. Crocker, June 15, 2010.
10. Robbins and Coulter, *Management*, 240.
11. United Nations ESCAP. Sustainable Integrated Tourism Planning. http://www.unescap.org/ttdw /Publications/TPTS_pubs/Pub_2019/pub_2019_ch1 .pdf. Retrieved on December 2, 2014.

From Planning to Organizing

Howard Schultz, head of Starbucks Corporation, knows that with more than 20,000 Starbucks stores worldwide, organizing the company is no easy task.[1] Such an organization needs training departments to turn college students into café managers (who would know, e.g., that every espresso must be pulled within 23 seconds or be thrown away), sales departments that sell coffee to United Airlines and supermarkets, and a way to manage stores in locations as far away as the Philippines and China. How to organize is, therefore, not an academic issue to Schultz. He has discovered that planning and organizing are inseparable. When his company was small, its strategy focused on high-quality coffee drinks provided by small neighborhood coffeehouses. This strategy in turn suggested the main jobs for which Schultz had to hire lieutenants—for example, store management, purchasing, and finance and accounting. Departments then grew up around these jobs.

Starbucks has launched a number of strategic initiatives over the years aside from expanding stores throughout the United States and abroad. In 1998, with the rise of interest in the Internet, Starbucks was among the first companies to establish a company Web page, www.starbucks.com, which featured the company's history, mission, vision, goals, and product offerings. In 2002, as the interest in the Internet continued to increase, Starbucks began offering free Wi-Fi in stores to promote a sense of a "sit down and stay" culture that implored customers to frequently use the resources offered at store locations for an extended period of time while enjoying the store's products and services.

In the early 2000s, Starbucks began to heavily promote its environmentally friendly practices and sustainable initiatives both in the United States and abroad. In 2004, Starbucks opened a Farmer Support Center in San Jose, Costa Rica, to partner with local farmers working to grow coffee that would then be distributed to Starbucks.[2] In 2006, Starbucks launched an eco-friendly coffee cup product that used post consumer recycled fiber. Moving forward, Starbucks launched a series of digital promotions and social media applications to further capitalize on the Internet craze sweeping the world, which included launching My Starbucks Idea, an online community, along with a Facebook page and Twitter account in 2008. Further, in 2009 Starbucks launched a loyalty program and mobile card payment program. Moving forward, the use of mobile applications, social media, and wireless technology continues to increase within the Starbucks culture.

Finally, among the biggest strategic moves that Starbucks has made over the years, includes the acquisition of a number of other companies, which are now fully integrated into the company's brand, including Tazo Tea Company, which was acquired in 1999; Seattle Coffee Company (which includes Seattle's Best Coffee and Torrefazione Italia), which was acquired in 2003; Ethos Water, a company that produces filtered bottled water products and equipment, which was acquired in 2005; Coffee Equipment Company, which was acquired in 2008; Evolution Fresh, a company that produced fresh tasting and unique fruit juices and smoothies, which was acquired in 2011; La Boulange, a company that produces fresh baked goods, which was acquired in 2012; and Teavana, an upscale tea company, which was also acquired in 2012.[3]

As Schultz's strategy evolved over the years to include geographic expansion across the United States and abroad, his organization also needed to evolve. As a consequence, regional store management divisions were established to oversee the stores in each region. Today, with Starbucks coffee also being sold to airlines, bookstores, and supermarkets, the company's structure continues to evolve, with new departments organized to sell to, and serve, the needs of new markets. What Schultz discovered is that the organization is determined by the *plan*; that is, strategy determines structure.

Schultz talks about making sure growth doesn't dilute the company's culture. Analysts (who watch companies for investment purposes) believe the challenge for Starbucks continues to be how to contend with higher materials prices and enhanced competition from lower-priced fast-food chains, including McDonald's, Dunkin' Donuts, The Coffee Bean & Tea Leaf, Peet's Coffee & Tea, Gloria Jean's Coffees, Caribou Coffee Company, Tim Hortons, and Coffee Beanery. Schultz first announced his five-point plan on March 19, 2008, to reaffirm the chain's place as the world's coffee authority: "By embracing our heritage, returning to our core—all things coffee—and our relentless commitment to innovation, we will reignite the emotional connection we have with our customers and transform the Starbucks Experience."[4] Chris Muller, writing in *Restaurants and Institutions* magazine, says that Starbucks is a mature product offering in a significantly different marketplace. Upmarket coffee is not as relevant to every portion of the consuming public as it was 10 years ago. Energy drinks, healthy menus, and online music delivery are all factors that were not present in the market when Starbucks caught the growth wave.

The Purpose of Organizing

The purpose of **organizing** is to get a job done efficiently and effectively by completing the following tasks:

- Divide work to be done into specific jobs and departments
- Assign tasks and responsibilities associated with individual jobs
- Coordinate diverse organizational tasks
- Cluster jobs into units
- Establish relationships among individuals, groups, and departments
- Establish formal lines of authority
- Allocate and deploy organizational resources

This chapter covers these important aspects of organization, but first we need to know what organization means in terms of job function. *Organization* refers to the arrangement of activities so that they systematically contribute to goal accomplishment. No one person can do all the things necessary for a hospitality organization to be successful. Imagine just one person trying to do all the different tasks that make a restaurant meal memorable.

LEARNING OBJECTIVE 1
Describe organizational
structure and organizational
design.

LEARNING OBJECTIVE 2
Explain why structure and
design are important to an
organization.

Defining Organizational Structure

In the past few years, organizational structures have changed quite a bit. Traditional approaches were questioned and reevaluated as managers searched for structures that would best support and facilitate employees doing the organization's work. The structure needs to be efficient, but it also must have the flexibility needed in today's dynamic environment. The challenge for managers is to design an organizational structure that allows employees to efficiently and effectively do their work.

An **organizational structure** is like a skeleton in that it provides the total framework by which job tasks are divided, grouped, and coordinated within an organization. In today's leaner and meaner hospitality business environment, organizations are flatter—meaning they have fewer levels of managers. They are also structured to better fulfill the needs of the guests. A typical example is the change of mindset that turned the traditional organizational chart upside down, as shown in Figure 16–1. The general manager used to be at the top of the organizational chart and the frontline associates at the bottom—the guests never appeared on the chart! Now we have the guests at the top of the inverted pyramid and the general manager

Figure 16–1 • The "Upside-Down" Organizational Chart.

near the bottom (the president of the organization is at the very bottom of the pyramid). Given higher labor costs, there are also fewer associates to do the same amount of work. Organizations have had to become more flexible in their desire to delight the guest. Some hotels have created rapid-reaction teams of associates who respond to urgent guest needs. These teams are composed of members from several different departments who come together in an effort to please the guest. More information about this and other types of teams is discussed later in this chapter.

Work Specialization and Division of Labor

You may recall from Chapter 1 the humble beginnings of Marriott International as the Hot Shoppes restaurant chain. Mr. and Mrs. Marriott probably decided what was going to be on the menu, then purchased the food, cooked it, and served it. They also collected the money and made sure everything was to their guests' liking. It's fun and stimulating to have your own business, to see the results of food well prepared and served, and to see gratified guests returning. Now consider the organizational structure of Marriott International today.

Presently, **work specialization** is used to describe the extent to which jobs in an organization are divided into separate tasks. One person does not do the entire job. Instead, a job is broken down into steps, and a different person completes each step. In the hospitality industry, we use work specialization in various departments, but not to the extent that heavy industry does. The reason is that, in the hospitality industry, we are not producing a commodity, so the line cook is likely to continue to prepare a variety of different dishes. However, the concept does apply to a banquet kitchen when a line is created to plate the food. In such a situation, each person adds a particular part of the meal to the plate, and someone checks it and places it in the heated rolling cart. In other departments, such as housekeeping, work specialization has some application: In making up guest rooms, housekeepers may work in pairs, with each specializing in a particular task. However, because the tasks are very repetitive, housekeepers prefer to do more than one task to avoid boredom.

Departmentalization

We are all familiar with government departments such as the Department of Motor Vehicles and the Department of Labor, and your college probably has departments of admissions, financial aid, and student affairs,

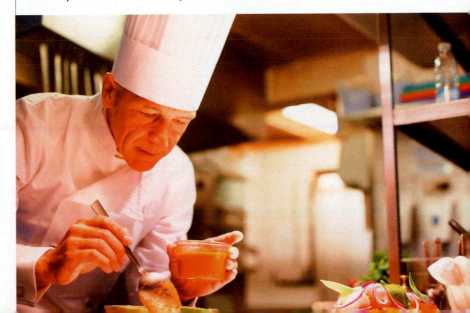

Work specialization allows professionals to focus on their specialty.

to name just a few. Once jobs have been divided up by work specialization, they have to be grouped back together so that the common tasks within each can be coordinated. This is called **departmentalization**. Every organization has its own form of departmentalization according to its needs. The organization's structure is shown in its **organization chart** (Figure 16–2).

Departments are created to coordinate the work of several associates in a given area. An example is housekeeping in a hotel or marketing and sales for a convention center. The main question facing company presidents is, "What form of organization will best meet the company's goals?" Should the company be organized by function, product, service, guest, or territory, or by a combination of these?

The simplest form of departmentalization is by **function**. A large hotel rooms division has a reservations department, uniformed service department, front desk, communications department, concierge, housekeeping, and so on—each with its own specialized function.

Choice Hotels International departmentalizes its lodging properties by **product** in the form of brands: Comfort Inn, Comfort Suites, Quality, Sleep Inn, Clarion, Cambria Hotels & Suites, MainStay Suites, Suburban, EconoLodge, Rodeway Inn, and Ascend Hotel Collection. Each brand attracts a slightly different target market, offers slightly different services, and is managed independently.

Sodexo and ARAMARK, both huge multinational corporations with billions of dollars in sales, departmentalize by **guest** needs. They have departments or divisions for education, business and industry, health care, and so on. The sales department of a convention and visitors bureau may departmentalize itself by market served: travel industry, medical, legal, insurance, leisure travel, incentive travel, or military.

Many larger companies departmentalize by **territory** when they have representation in several states, provinces, and countries. For example, Avis Rent A Car has representation in a number of states, provinces, and countries. It recognizes that each geographic market has its own nuances.

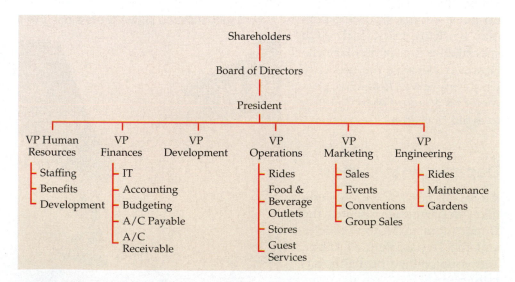

Figure 16–2 • Organization Chart for a Theme Park.

Authority and Responsibility

Authority is closely associated with chain of command (see next section) because it gives managers the right to exercise their power in a given situation. Authority should be commensurate with responsibility. In other words, managers should exercise power only in accordance with their position. In recent years, managers have increasingly empowered associates to make more decisions—particularly in the hospitality industry. We have to ensure that our guests are delighted. Some companies have empowered their employees to do whatever it takes to please the guest, even to the extent of **comping** (providing free of charge) a room if necessary.

In the hospitality industry it is very important to have not only formal authority but also respect. Associates are quick to gauge the credibility of new supervisors or managers to see how much they know and to determine whether they can help out by getting their hands dirty in an emergency. Someone who has "been there" is likely to gain the associates' respect if he or she can step in and help out during a crisis. Managers are often given authority but lack the in-depth knowledge of the department to really be able to lead by example. Simply put, "You've got to know your onions." When managers lack credibility and therefore respect, it is much more difficult for associates to work with them to get the job done. Thus, many companies require that a newly appointed manager have experience in the area or at least an accelerated apprenticeship in the area for which he or she will be responsible, thus building up his or her credibility.

When authority is delegated, so should commensurate **responsibility**. That means that you are responsible for the performance of your operation and the associates who work with you. That can sometimes be a big responsibility. What if an associate serves an alcoholic drink to a guest who is intoxicated and that guest later drives off and has an accident, injuring not only himself but also another innocent party? Are you responsible? Yes! As manager of the department or restaurant, you are not only responsible but liable, as well.

► Check Your Knowledge

1. Why is organizing important?
2. What are the drawbacks of work specialization?
3. Describe ways managers can departmentalize work activities.

Chain of Command

Organization charts show not only the structure and size of the organization but also the **chain of command** (Figure 16–3). Departments are clearly indicated, and titles may be used to show each associate's position. The chain of command begins at the top of the organization—in the case of a large, publicly traded company such as Marriott International, with the board of directors, who are elected by the shareholders. The board of directors selects

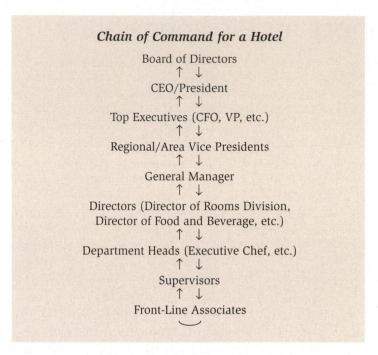

Figure 16–3 • An Example of a Hotel's Chain of Command.

a president or chief executive officer (CEO), and the president selects the top executives such as the chief financial officer (CFO) and vice president of marketing. The president and the executive team develop plans that are presented to the board for approval, and then they implement those plans. The chain of command is helpful for associates who have questions or need advice because they will know whom to ask. Similarly, they know to whom they are responsible for their work performance. The chain of command should flow from the top to the bottom of the organization and up from the bottom to the top. This is usually illustrated by lines of authority that indicate who is responsible for what or over whom.

Increasing Span of Control

How many associates can a manager supervise? The answer used to be between 8 and 12. Now, however, the answer is likely to be 12–18. The reason for this increase in span of control is that organizations need to be more competitive with not only other U.S. companies but foreign ones, too. Consider the cost savings realized by eliminating levels of management: If there are two organizations, both with 4,000 employees, and one organization has a span of control of 10 and the other 15, the organization with the wider span of control will have fewer levels of management and lower costs because there will be fewer managers.

The Guest Is God

An industry consultant was once in Japan giving a seminar with another colleague. The colleague began by saying that in business today the guest is king, and as he was saying that a gentleman rushed down from the back row and grabbed the microphone and told the audience that the guest is not king but God! The gentleman was the company president. Reflecting on this unusual happening, the consultant realized just how much the Japanese revere their guests.

But how much will this save? Well, if the average manager makes $65,000 a year, then the total savings would be $9.36 million. Having said that, many hospitality corporations have increased their span of control, it is also fair to say that they realize that there is a point when the number of people reporting to managers overburdens associates. At that point, managers don't have the time to give advice, nor do they have time to properly supervise their associates, so standards decline. So what factors determine the appropriate span of control? It depends on the type of work being done. Is it straightforward or complex? Are the associates highly skilled and well trained, or is training needed? Other factors include the degree to which standardized procedures are in place, the information technology available, the leadership style of the manager, and how experienced the manager is in the area of concern.

Empowerment allows associates to own the guest request and check to see that it has been fulfilled.

A DAY IN THE LIFE OF ANDREA KAZANJIAN

The Ritz-Carlton Members Club, Sarasota, Florida

Andrea Kazanjian serves as director of membership for The Ritz-Carlton Members Club in Sarasota, Florida. In her role, Kazanjian is charged with developing and implementing strategies that shape the membership experience for this unique and exclusive luxury-tier brand extension.

A day in the life of Andrea Kazanjian consists of conducting membership training workshops, developing professional and successful membership sales executive and members services teams, designing all membership collateral and messaging, and managing a number of marketing campaigns. These are just a few of the techniques she will use to help the organization meet the aggressive membership recruitment and sales goals outlined by the ownership.

Kazanjian earned a Bachelor of Science degree in Hotel, Restaurant, and Travel Administration from the University of Massachusetts, Amherst, on a swimming scholarship as a Division I swimmer and team captain. A native of Albany, New York, she is a board member of the Sarasota Chamber of Commerce Young Professionals Group and a volunteer for the community outreach subcommittee, a member of the Junior League of Sarasota, a representative of the Sarasota Chamber of Commerce Leadership Luncheon Series, a member of the United Way of Sarasota, and a leader of the Ritz-Carlton, Sarasota, campaign.

An extension of the Ritz-Carlton Hotel Company, The Ritz-Carlton Members Club is a luxury-tier, nonequity membership that combines the benefits of a private social club with the tradition of personalized Ritz-Carlton services and world-class amenities designed to complement the Sarasota lifestyle. Members have the opportunity to access the Members Beach Club on Lido Key, the Members Spa Club, and the Tom Fazio–designed Members Golf Club.

Empowerment

Given the increasing span of control, **empowerment** has become an industry norm. As managers delegate more authority and responsibility, associates have become empowered to do whatever it takes to delight the guest. Frontline associates are in a better position to know guests' wants and needs than management, so it makes sense to empower them to take care of satisfying guests. In the old days, associates had to check with management before making a decision to ensure guest gratification. Let's look at an example: A husband and wife check into a hotel that advertises a room rate that includes a buffet breakfast. Unfortunately, the wife catches a nasty virus and is not well enough to go down to enjoy the buffet breakfast. Her husband says that he will call her to let her know what's offered at the buffet so that she can choose something and he can bring it up for her. He goes down to the restaurant and dutifully calls her to tell her what's available. She tells him what she wants: scrambled eggs and bacon. When the husband explains to a server that his wife is sick and not able to come down for the buffet and requests a tray to carry up her breakfast, the server listens and goes to consult a more senior server, but not the manager. The husband then explains all over again and once more asks for a tray. This time he is told that food cannot be taken upstairs. The husband then says, "My wife is sick and needs something to eat and drink. We've already paid for it. . . . Get the manager here now!" The server later comes over to say that the duty manager says the husband can choose anything from the cold section of the buffet but not the hot part. That does it. The guest demands that the general manager, not the duty manager, be summoned. You get the picture. All of this could have been avoided if only the associates had been empowered to use their discretion in order to satisfy the guest's request.

Centralization and Decentralization

Some organizations make most of the decisions at the corporate office and inform unit managers of them. This process is called **centralization**. If the top managers make the organization's key decisions with little or no input from subordinates, then the organization is centralized. Other organizations make most of the decisions at the unit level or with input from associates. This is **decentralization**. In reality, organizations are never completely centralized or decentralized because they could not function if all decisions were made by the CEO, nor could they function properly if all decisions were made at the lowest level. Figure 16–4 illustrates the difference between a centralized and a decentralized organization.

Many companies become more centralized in an effort to save costs and improve service to associates. A good example is Choice Hotels' restructuring of its franchise services. However, because of rapid changes in the hospitality business, many organizations are becoming more flexible and responsive; this means the organizations are becoming more decentralized. In large companies especially, lower-level managers who are "closer to the action" and typically have more detailed knowledge about problems and how best to solve them are empowered to delight the guest.

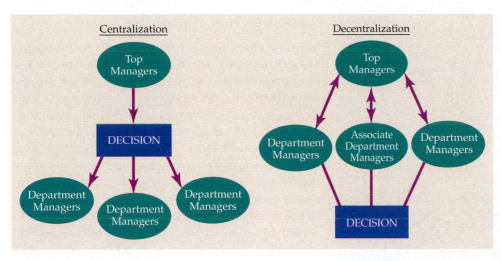

Figure 16–4 • Centralization versus Decentralization in an Organization.

▶ Check Your Knowledge

1. Describe organizational structure and organizational design.

2. How are the chain of command and span of control used in organizing?

3. Describe the factors that influence greater centralization and the factors that influence greater decentralization.

4. Explain why structure and design are important to an organization.

Organizational Design Decisions

LEARNING OBJECTIVE 3
Identify key factors that should be considered in choosing an organizational design structure, including team-based structures.

Organizations are structured in different ways, depending on which structure best suits their needs. A company with 20 associates will look very different from one with 10,000 associates. However, even organizations of comparable size don't necessarily have similar structures. What works for one organization may not work for another. How do managers decide which structure is best for them? That decision depends on certain contingency factors that we are about to discuss.

Coordination of Activities

When there are only a few associates in an operation, everyone can catch up quickly, but as a business expands, problems can and do occur unless there is good **coordination of activities**. The hospitality business is fast paced—guests want something now or even sooner! Departments need to communicate quickly and often in order to keep up with guest requests. You may have experienced an occasion when something did not go as planned—perhaps a check-out delay at your hotel or charges on your bill that were not yours, but now you're in a rush to get to the airport. You get the picture—someone made a mistake!

Coordination of various functions and areas is critical in exceeding guest expectations. Room service requires the coordination of a variety of associates, including those who take the order from the guests, kitchen staff who cook the food, and of course, those who deliver the meal and later retrieve the tray or cart.

Contingency Planning

Top managers give a lot of thought to designing an appropriate organizational structure. What that appropriate structure is depends on the organization's strategy, size, technology, and degree of environmental uncertainty. Structure should follow strategy and be closely linked.

An organization's size generally affects its structure. Larger organizations tend to have more specialization, departmentalization, centralization, and rules and regulations than do smaller organizations. If there are 30 associates at one hospitality company and 300 at another, then the one with 300 will have more departments and be more structured.

Every organization has some form of technology that relates to structure. Consider a hotel company that has a central reservations center. The central reservations center can hold the inventory of all the hotels in the chain, be far more efficient in offering available rates and rooms to callers than individual hotels, and also make the inventory available to travel agents and Internet travel organizations. A central reservations center can also do a better job of controlling and maximizing revenue for the available rooms than many decentralized centers.

Technology has enabled restaurant chains to transfer data and store menus and operations and training manuals via the Internet. In some cases, this has led to a change in organizational structure. In the hospitality industry, technology has tended to help the existing structure perform better—sometimes with fewer associates. A convention center may have the latest software program for reserving and allocating space, but it will not significantly change the organization's structure; someone must take the guest requests and enter them into the program.

Contingency factors deal with what hospitality organizations refer to as the *what-ifs*. What if such-and-such happens? The company plans and organizes for several possible outcomes. After the terrorist attacks on September 11, 2001, many hospitality companies immediately planned and organized for a drastic drop in business. Departments were greatly reduced, reorganized, or even closed in an effort to reduce losses.

Contemporary Organizational Designs

Team-Based Structures

In response to competitive market demands for organizations that are lean, flexible, and innovative, managers are finding creative ways to structure and organize work and to make their organizations more responsive to guest needs. The first of the contemporary designs is a **work team structure**; either the complete organization or a part of it is made up of teams that perform the duties necessary to delight the guest (Figure 16–5). This concept is, like many, borrowed from business but has relevance for hospitality managers. Perhaps the best use of this concept for hospitality managers is with Total Quality Management (TQM), which you may remember being introduced in Chapter 1. Basically, teams of mostly frontline associates take on the challenge of improving guest services and products. At first, these teams are often made up of associates from one department but later can be made up of associates from different departments. This actually improves coordination between departments. Sales departments can work well in teams, as can the banquet kitchen, and for that matter most departments in a hospitality operation. However, the team is more likely to consist of associates from one department as opposed to associates from several departments. In any event, teams tend to be more productive. There are two main types of work teams: integrated and self-managed. *Integrated work teams* are given a number of tasks by the manager, and the team gives specific assignments to members. *Self-managed work teams* are assigned a goal, and the team plans, organizes, leads, and controls to achieve the goal.[5]

▶ Check Your Knowledge

1. Identify the key factors in choosing an organizational structure.

Matrix and Project Structures

The matrix structure is an organizational structure that assigns specialists from different departments to work on a project—for example, a new attraction, restaurant, or hotel opening. The specialists come together to pool their

LEARNING OBJECTIVE 4
Describe matrix structures, project structures, independent business units, and boundaryless organizations.

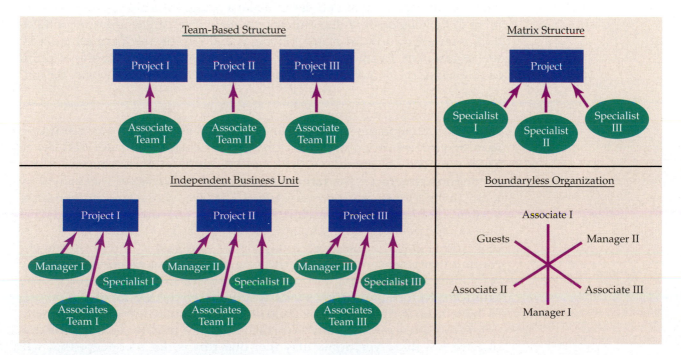

Figure 16–5 • The Four Types of Contemporary Organizational Designs.

knowledge and experience to work on the project. During this time, they may have two bosses: their department head plus the project manager. To work effectively, project managers and department heads need to communicate on a regular basis. Matrix structures are appealing to organizations that want to speed up the decision-making process or get projects accomplished more quickly.

A matrix structure, however, does not work for everyone. It can be disruptive because the participants must take leave from their current positions, and then, once the project is completed, they need to return to their original positions. Additionally, having more than one manager can be frustrating. **Project structures** are similar to matrix structures, but employees in a project structure continuously work on projects; members of a project do not return to their departments after project completion. An example of a project structure in the hospitality industry would be a preopening team for attractions, hotels, resorts, and restaurants. Teams of employees become part of the project team because they have specific knowledge and expertise. Once the project is complete, the members go on to the next project.

Independent Business Units

Some hospitality companies have adopted the concept of **independent business units (IBUs)** to encourage departments not only to delight the guest but also to watch the money all the way to the bottom line. In other words, the IBU becomes its own independent business and makes decisions accordingly, with little or no need to get approval for routine operational decisions. The unit can implement strategies that will improve guest satisfaction or reduce costs by finding a quicker or better way of doing something. Forming IBUs is an excellent strategy to get associates to realize the total picture of revenue and expenses for a department. It forces associates to engage in all elements of management in order to make a profit. IBUs also enable management to look seriously at departments not making a sufficient profit contribution, with a view toward making changes and improvements or eliminating the department. Departments that once had a loss are now making a profit as a result of the company installing an IBU system of organizational design.

Boundaryless Organizations

Another contemporary approach to organizational design is the **boundaryless organization**, an organization whose design is not defined by, or limited to, the horizontal, vertical, or external boundaries imposed by a predefined structure.[6] The term *boundaryless organization* was coined by Jack Welch, former chairman of General Electric, who wanted to eliminate vertical and horizontal boundaries within GE and break down external barriers between the company and its customers and suppliers. This idea may sound odd, yet many of today's most successful organizations are finding that they can most effectively operate in today's environment by remaining close to the guest and being flexible and unstructured. The boundaryless organization seeks to eliminate the chain of command, to have appropriate spans of control, and to replace departments with empowered teams. Hospitality organizations are moving in this direction but are not there yet. Some may feel that this is not a concept that will work for hospitality organizations, whereas others may think it's a great

INTRODUCING PATRICIA ENGFER

Area Vice President and General Manager of Hyatt Regency Grand Cypress, Orlando, Florida

Patricia Engfer began her career 37 years ago as a management trainee in Hilton Head, South Carolina. She then worked as an assistant executive housekeeper in Pittsburgh, followed by employment at a long list of Hyatt properties, including a stint as rooms executive at the Hyatt Regency Long Beach during that hotel's opening. She first became a general manager (GM) at the Hyatt City of Commerce, California, and held similar positions in Los Angeles, Edgewater, and Newport Beach, California and the Orlando International Airport. Patricia took her current position of area vice president and general manager at the Hyatt Regency Grand Cypress, Orlando, Floridain 2013. Here are Pat's answers to our questions.

How have your responsibilities changed at Hyatt?

My responsibilities as a GM have not changed. They include three areas of focus: employees, guests, and owners. What has changed are the tools and sophistication needed to succeed. Our guests, employees, and owners have higher expectations than ever. So, we have to be open to innovations that help us meet their expectations.

How did you grow into your position as a GM?

Hyatt does a great job of developing careers one position at a time. That gives each of us the opportunity to develop skills while preparing for the next step. Coming up through the rooms division and working in convention, resort, airport, and city-center hotels prepared me to manage hotels in different markets. The common thread is how you interact with people in each location.

What is the biggest challenge of your job?

We all know that the current business climate is challenging and requires focus and dedication from every member of the team to look at opportunities to drive sales and manage costs.

Do women and minorities have equal opportunities at Hyatt?

Yes. But you must have drive and determination and be willing to give 100 percent. Being a woman has never been a disadvantage. To the contrary, Hyatt has provided an environment that makes it possible to have the best of both worlds, a career and a fabulous family.

Do you have a mentor at Hyatt?

Over the years I have looked to several mentors who have helped me develop in several ways. Steve Trent hired me, and we have kept in close contact through the years. Locally, I have developed friendships with women who are true leaders, including Glenda Hood, former mayor of Orlando and former Secretary of State of Florida. Another is Linda Chaplin, our past county chairperson, who runs an economic think tank at the University of Central Florida. These women started out raising families, began volunteering time, and today are driving the vision of central Florida. That is truly inspirational.

How do you welcome new employees to your property?

I tell employees the only limits they face are the ones they put on themselves. Hyatt offers training to be successful, but only the employees can bring the personality and commitment. How many other companies offer a great work environment and the opportunity to live almost anywhere and to grow rapidly, while never having to hop from one company to another? If you put forth the effort, Hyatt provides a platform for success where employees of all races and genders are embraced.

idea. Hospitality companies recognize that it is important to stay close to the guest but are challenged to create a boundaryless organization.

Teams and Employee Involvement

Teams are task-oriented work groups; they can either be formally appointed or evolve informally. We all work with others, to a greater or lesser extent, in order to meet or exceed goals. Both formal and informal teams make important contributions to the company and to the satisfaction of associates' needs. For example, an informal team from one hotel saved the company more than $250,000 a year after the team made a proposal about energy savings. Not only did the team members receive a sizable bonus, but their employee satisfaction scores were significantly higher than those of associates who did not participate in the team.

Teams are great for doing work that is complex, interrelated, or more than one person can handle. Harold Geneen, while chairman of ITT, said, "If I had enough arms and legs, I'd do it all myself." We all know that associates cannot do everything themselves because of limitations of arms and legs, time, expertise, knowledge, and other resources. There is a certain "buzz" in a restaurant on a busy Friday night; when the kitchen is getting "slammed," you know what teamwork is or isn't!

The funny thing about teams, as you have probably experienced by now, is that you don't always get to choose who you work with—just as when you do term papers and projects in teams. And even when you do get to choose classmates, it sometimes doesn't work out. Your teammates don't do their fair share, or something else doesn't work. Yet in the hospitality industry, we are constantly working in teams to exceed guest expectations. So how can we make teams more effective?

Group Dynamics

Why are some groups more successful than others? Why does a team of mediocre players sometimes beat a team of superior players? You've probably experienced a situation in which, seemingly against all odds, a team excels. Remember the survival programs on television. A group of people was dropped off in some remote place, and over a period of time the group members had to survive as teams, *but* they could vote people "off the island." Imagine if we did that in the hospitality industry!

Why and how some teams succeed and others don't is called *group dynamics* and includes variables such as the abilities of the group's members, the size of the group, the level of conflict, and the internal pressures on members to conform to the group's norms. Sometimes external influences inhibit the group's performance. Corporate may dictate policies that make it more difficult for the group to succeed, or there may be a shortage of resources. One of the fascinating aspects of group dynamics is the members of the group. You may have experienced a group project at college. Sometimes you had to choose with whom you worked, and sometimes your group members were selected randomly. Which worked best?

How Companies Use Teams at Work

Hospitality companies use teams at work in a variety of ways. One way is to structure the organization into teams from the start. Instead of departments, they are called teams. This implies, of course, that employees must be **team players**, which is vital in the fast-paced hospitality industry. Another way management can use teams is through TQM programs that involve associates working in teams to constantly improve the guest experience. Teams are formed from either individual departments or several different departments. They choose an area of the operation that needs improvement, usually one of guest concern, and proceed to make changes that will benefit the guest. TQM teams have made important contributions to the industry and continue to do so.

Self-managed teams make decisions that were once made by managers. This saves managers time, allowing them to concentrate on more important things. We saw an example in Chapter 3; Hotel housekeepers who score highly on room inspections no longer need to have their rooms checked by a floor housekeeper. These teams of housekeepers actually receive a bonus for superior performance, and the hotel saves the salary of the floor housekeepers. Self-managed teams work successfully in several types of hospitality organizations such as theme parks and convention centers.

How to Build Productive Teams

Building productive teams is critical to the success of any organization, especially in the service-oriented hospitality industry. In recent years, the introduction of TQM processes has significantly increased the number of teams in the hospitality industry. At the heart of TQM is process improvement, and associate participation is the heartbeat. **Productive teams** are built by giving associates the authority, responsibility, and encouragement to come together to work on guest-related improvements that will not only enhance the guest experience but also make the associates' jobs easier. Teams need leadership, which is either appointed by management or chosen by the team. As with any other endeavor, goals and objectives need to be set, and the team must be given the resources it needs to accomplish those goals. It is amazing to see the enthusiasm that teams can generate as they work on improving the guest experience. Associates come up with great ideas that can save money and provide guests with better service. Team building happens when members interact to learn how each member thinks and works. Through close interaction, team members learn to develop increased trust and openness. When a team focuses on setting goals, determining who will plan on accomplishing what by when, and so on, the team should be on its way to becoming a high-achieving team.

Job Rotation

Job rotation is an excellent way to relieve the possible boredom and monotony that can be a disadvantage of work specialization because it gives associates a broader range of experiences. Once associates have mastered the jobs they were hired to do, boredom tends to set in. Job rotation creates interest and helps develop associates to take on additional responsibilities. The management training programs of some of the major hospitality corporations

HOW TO ORGANIZE RECREATIONAL RESORT ACTIVITIES

Courtesy of **James McManemon**, M.S., University of South Florida Sarasota–Manatee

In the service industry, and in particular the hospitality industry, the coordination of activities is extremely important, as there are many different departments that rely on cross-communication to operate efficiently on a daily basis. For example, the recreation department at a large resort relies on communication with the front-office department to determine the number of guests arriving and departing the resort each day in order to properly plan and schedule staff in the various recreation outlets as well as to organize recreational activities in those outlets.

Cheryl Williams, the activities manager at a beach resort in Clearwater, Florida, discussed the roles she and her staff played in planning, organizing, and executing the new Children's Enrichment Program at the resort. The Children's Enrichment Program was set up after Cheryl's team reviewed the various offerings offered at other resorts, both in and around Clearwater, as well as taking into consideration comments and suggestions provided by past guests. They found that it was necessary to offer a diverse range of activities for guests since the resort attracts many families throughout the year. Their goals were twofold: First, in order to increase guest satisfaction and to give guests a reason to visit the property during both the busy season and off season, the activities team devised a more family-friendly range of offerings than similar resorts in the local area and surrounding region; second, Cheryl wanted her team to feel empowered to do more in their current roles so she asked each team member to identify an activity that could be implemented quickly and inexpensively.

The activities they decided to institute within the Children's Enrichment Program included:

- **The Little Picasso Program** Will, a recent art graduate from one of the local universities, decided to use his connections to introduce guests to one of his favorite pastimes. Several days a week, a local artist visits the resort and co-hosts art classes with Will for the resort's younger guests in a small grassy field next to the pool deck. This provides parents the opportunity to relax and soak up the sun while their children enjoy an hour of painting with watercolors. Parents feel comfortable knowing their children are close by, kids get to bring home a unique memory of their visit, and Will has a greater sense of responsibility for helping guests enjoy their visits.

- **A Walk on the Wild Side** Julia, previously one of the front-desk associates at the resort, recently transferred to Cheryl's team. Her idea was to have the resort partner with the local nature center (located a short three miles from the property). She, along with Cheryl's help, set up daily shuttles to and from the nature center for every hour between 10:00 A.M. and 7:00 P.M. When guests arrive at the nature center, a nature center specialist hosts guided tours on foot through several miles of sandy, wooded trails that are home to a variety of birds, deer, tortoises, lizards, and other critters. After the tour, guests are welcome to peruse the gift shop or venture over to the nature center's aquatic tank and pet the gentle rays that swim past. It is Julia's responsibility to ensure that the shuttles are on time and that the guests enjoy the experience.

- **Cartoon in the Lagoon** Rachel, the assistant activities manager, wanted to offer a more laid-back activity for families. Twice a week, she hosts an animated film on the big screen at the pool deck. This allows families to enjoy an evening of poolside entertainment together while having dinner on the pool deck or lounging on pool floats. The film lineup has included favorites like *Finding Nemo*, *How to Train Your Dragon*, *Ice Age*, and *Madagascar*. Rachel feels it important to always ask for guest feedback, so she takes time before and after each movie to chat and engage with as many guests as she can.

- **Sandcastle Extravaganza** Sam, the newest team member, grew up in Clearwater. His love of the beach led him to put together the resort's sandcastle building competition. The competitions are held on the beach several times a week. Sam encourages families to work together and use their combined imaginations to construct magnificent creations. Prizes are awarded for first, second, and third place, which includes pool and beach accessories, activity rentals, and delicious sweets from the kitchen. To ensure he always has a full crowd, Sam is on the beach first thing in the morning building his own sandcastle in order to recruit guests and their families.

hospitality and tourist services.[8] Organizing a sustainable effort must take place at many levels of an organization. Beginning with a top-to-bottom approach, from the boardroom to the lowest level on the organization chart a commitment by all is required to optimize sustainability. The top level of management can make policy, plans, and procedures for the organization to follow. Middle and lower levels of management can put the plans into actions resulting in greater sustainability.

Trends in Organizing

Courtesy of Dr. Greg Dunn, Senior Lecturer & Managing Director, University of Florida, Eric Friedheim Tourism Institute

- *The Inverted Organizational Chart*. An organizational trend that continues to be prevalent in hospitality management is the inverted organization chart. It is very important to understand the role of an upside down form of organizational chart. Whereas a traditional organizational chart usually places the company leadership at the top, the inverted organizational chart places the customer at the top, followed by the frontline employees, middle management, and, then at the bottom, company leadership. This model recognizes the importance and focus of the customer or guest to the organization.

- *Responsibility vs. Authority*. In hospitality management, authority typically comes with the title and position. For instance, a general manager generally has more decision-making authority than a frontline associate, but this does not mean that an employee should not ask why they are being asked to do something or question a policy or procedure. Employees and managers should always go over expectations in the beginning of their working cycle so that both parties have a clear understanding of their responsibilities and authority. It is every single employee's responsibility to understand their job and position as well as their obligation to perform above and beyond.

- *Encouragement and Recognition for Greater Employee Involvement*. From the start, it is important for hospitality managers to organize their teams with high performance in mind. Some teams might be self-managed whereas others might work directly and closely with superiors. In order to keep employees involved and motivated, it is important to encourage them and recognize them for things they do well, and it is important to discuss things that may need improvement. A job rotation system and a clear, fair recognition program could keep employees more interested while giving them a fresh look at different departments throughout their working time period.

- *Centralized vs. Decentralized Decision Making*. When important decisions are made from the top of an organizational chart, it is recognized as being performed in a centralized manner. When frontline associates or lower management have a larger role in decision making, it is recognized as being performed in a decentralized manner. While many companies are moving toward centralized decision making, others have embraced a decentralized decision-making model to enhance employee involvement and retention in addition to providing higher levels of customer service.

- *Share Your Story.* People enter into the hospitality industry for many different reasons. When organizing your business, it is important to never forget why you got involved in this industry, how you attained the level of success you have, and who over time has been instrumental in your career development. It is important to develop your own story and share it with others. For instance, there is a trend toward managers developing personal vision, mission, values, and goals statements and sharing them with peers and colleagues in an effort to tell their story and encourage others to do the same.

- *Flattened Organizational Systems.* There is also a trend toward flattening organizational systems to allow for more flexibility. Flattening entails having fewer levels of management, where both line and staff employees are empowered to make decisions and develop fewer differences in responsibility across levels. Flattened organizational systems are also characterized by processes and people that can respond differently to different situations, fewer detailed rules and procedures, greater individual or team autonomy, and encouragement for initiative.

CASE STUDY

The Organization of Outback Steakhouse

Chris T. Sullivan, Bob Basham, Trudy Cooper, and Tim Gannon—cofounders of the Outback Steakhouse concept—began their restaurant careers as a busser, dishwasher, server, and chef's assistant, respectively. So how did they manage to build one of the all-time most successful restaurant concepts? Their careers may have had humble beginnings, but they had the money to excel. Chris and Bob met at Bennigan's. They honed their management skills under the mentorship of industry legend Norman Brinker, who later financed Chris and Bob's franchised chain of Chili's restaurants in Georgia and Florida. They later sold the Chili's restaurants back to Brinker for $3 million. This seed money allowed them to develop a restaurant concept with which they had been toying.

The concept was for a casual-themed steakhouse. Because the partners did not want to do a western theme (it had already been done by others) and because at the time there was a lot of hype about Australia, they opted for an Australian theme. Australia had just won the America's Cup (a major yacht race held every four years), and the movie *Crocodile Dundee* was popular. As with all new restaurant concepts, they searched for a suitable name. Beth Basham came up with the idea of "Outback" for the name of the steakhouse—she wrote it on a mirror in lipstick. The Outback-themed concept was just what the partners wanted—a casual, fun, family atmosphere and the highest-quality food, which is reflected in Outback's 40-percent food cost (the industry norm for steakhouses is about 36 percent). Chris and Bob

CASE STUDY *(Continued)*

asked Tim Gannon, who at the time hardly had enough money to buy the gas to drive to Tampa, to join them. Organizationally, each of the partners brought something to the table. Chris was the visionary, Bob the operations person, Tim the chef, and Trudy the trainer. Later, they realized they needed a numbers guy, and in 1990, Bob Merritt became CFO.

Instead of fancy marketing research, the partners did lots of talking and observation of what people were eating—remember, this was a time when eating red meat was almost taboo. The partners figured that people were not eating as much red meat at home, but when they dined out, they were ready for a good steak.

Initially, the partners thought of setting up one restaurant and then a few more, which would allow them to spend more time on the golf course and with their families. So the success of Outback surprised the partners as well as the Wall Street pundits. The organization grew quickly, and by the mid-1990s, more than 200 stores were open; the partners also signed a joint venture partnership with Carrabba's Italian Grill, giving them access to the high-end Italian restaurant segment.

Same-store sales increased year after year, and the partners looked forward to 500 or even 600 units. Financial analysts were amazed at the rise in Outback's stock. So, to what can we attribute Outback's success? It's a well-defined and popular concept, it has a great organizational mantra of "No Rules—Just Right," and it has the best-quality food and service in a casually themed Australian outback–decor restaurant. The typical Outback is a little more than 6,000 square feet, with about 35 tables seating about 160 guests and a bar area that has eight tables and 32 seats. In Outback's organization, servers handle only three tables at a time; this increases their guest contact time and allows for more attention to be paid to each table. Outback also offers an Australian-themed menu with a higher flavor profile than comparable steakhouses. The design of the kitchen takes up about 45 percent of the restaurant's floor space—12 percent more than other similar restaurants. This extra space represents a potential loss of revenue, but this is the way Outback wanted it done because they realized the kitchen does not run well when it's being "slammed" on a Friday or Saturday night.

There is no organizational chart at Outback Steakhouse; everyone at the unpretentious corporate headquarters in Tampa is there to serve the restaurants. There is no corporate human resources department; applicants are interviewed by two managers and must pass a psychological profile test that gives an indication of the applicant's personality. Outback provides ownership opportunities at three levels in the organization: individual restaurant level, multistore joint venture and franchises, and an employee stock ownership plan. Because there is no middle management, franchisees report directly to the president. Outback's founders had fun setting up the concept and want everyone to have fun, too—they sometimes drop in on a store and ask employees if they are having fun. Not only are they doing that—they are laughing all the way to the bank!

Discussion Questions

1. From an organizational perspective, can Outback continue to grow with so little organizational structure?
2. What kind of organizational structure would you suggest for Outback Steakhouse?

Summary

1. The purpose of organizing is to get jobs done efficiently and effectively.
2. Goals are accomplished by organizing the work to be done into specific jobs and departments; assigning tasks and responsibilities associated with individual jobs; coordinating diverse organizational tasks; clustering jobs into units; establishing relationships among individuals, groups, and departments; establishing formal lines of authority; and allocating and deploying organizational resources.
3. Organizational structure is the total framework through which job tasks are divided, grouped, and coordinated.
4. Organizational structure is divided into work specialization, departmentalization, authority and responsibility, chain of command, delegation, increasing span of control and empowerment, and centralization and decentralization.
5. Organizational designs and decisions consist of coordination, contingency factors, common organizational design, contemporary organizational design, IBUs, and the boundaryless organization.
6. Teams are task-oriented work groups; they either can be formally appointed or can evolve informally.

Key Words and Concepts

authority
boundaryless organization
centralization
chain of command
comping
contingency factors
coordination of activities
decentralization
departmentalization
empowerment

function
guest
independent business units (IBUs)
job enlargement
job enrichment
job rotation
organizational structure
organization chart
organizing

product
productive teams
project structure
responsibility
self-managed teams
teams
team players
territory
work specialization
work team structure

Review Questions

1. Looking to the future, which is the best organizational structure for a theme park? A 50-room resort? A mid-priced Italian restaurant? An economy 100-room hotel? A 3,000-room casino hotel?
2. Describe a work team structure.
3. Compare and contrast a matrix structure and a project structure.
4. When might an organization design its structure around independent business units?

Internet Exercises

1. Organization: Any company
   Summary: Pick a major corporation, such as one mentioned in the text, and go to its web site to look for answers to the following questions:
   (a) What different types of product offerings does the company have?

   (b) In how many countries or regions is the company represented?
   (c) What kind of divisions does the company have?
   (d) Have different types of guest groups been identified?

Apply Your Knowledge

1. Mini Project: This project is based on a real-life experience of the executive chef at the Sheraton Hotel in San Diego. The project is to organize an off-site event, which is an event that is planned and organized by the Sheraton staff but does not take place at the hotel itself.

2. The Sheraton typically caters the annual San Diego Zoo fund-raiser every year. The attendance for this event is roughly 1,000 people. The caterers organize and cater a reception followed by dinner. Your challenge is to plan this off-site event using the planning techniques and organizational skills you have learned so far.

Endnotes

1. Wikipedia, *Starbucks*, http://en.wikipedia.org/. Search for "Starbucks"(accessed April 25, 2015).
2. Starbucks (2014), *Starbucks Company Timeline*, www.starbucks.com. Click on our Company, and then click on Download PDF under Timeline (accessed June 8, 2015).
3. Ibid.
4. Starbucks,"Starbucks Unveils New Strategic Initiatives to Transform and Innovate the Customer Experience," March 28, 2008, www.starbucks.com. Click on Newsroom and search for "new strategic initiatives" (accessed June 8, 2015).
5. Robert N. Lussier, *Management Fundamentals* (Cincinnati, OH: South-Western, 2003), 198.
6. See, for example, G. G. Dess et al., "The New Corporate Architecture," *Academy of Management Executive*, August 1995, 7–20.
7. Abraham B.Shani, *Organizing for Sustainability*, Eds. Susan Albers Mohrman and Abraham B. Shani (China: Emerald Group Publishing, 2011), 1–33.
8. John R. Walker and Josielyn T. Walker, *Tourism: Concepts and Practices* (Hoboken: Pearson, 2011), 201.

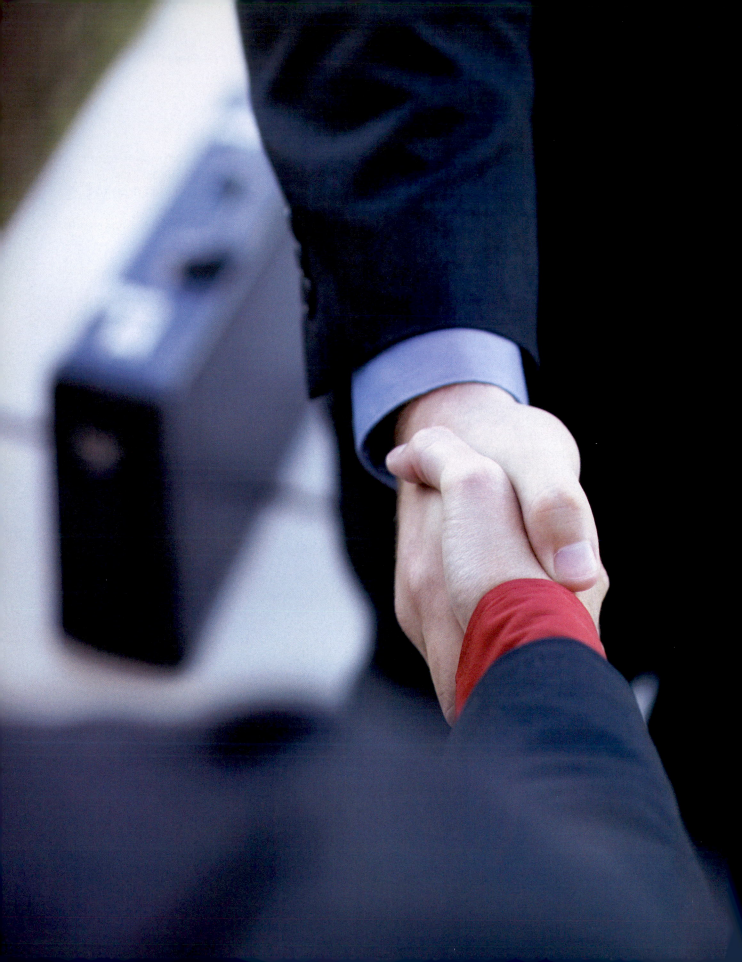

CHAPTER 17

Communication and Decision Making

LEARNING OBJECTIVES

After reading and studying this chapter, you should be able to:

- Define *communication*.

- List barriers to effective interpersonal communication and how to overcome them.

- Differentiate between formal and informal communication.

- Explain communication flows and networks.

- Outline the eight steps in the decision-making process.

- Know the difference between rational, bounded rational, and intuitive decisions.

- Identify situations in which a programmed decision is a better solution than a nonprogrammed decision.

- Differentiate the decision conditions of certainty, risk, and uncertainty.

Managerial Communication

Communication is the oil that lubricates all of the other management functions of forecasting, planning, organizing, motivating, and controlling. Additionally, because managers spend a high percentage of their time communicating, the communication function becomes doubly important. Managers interact with others throughout the day by the following means:

- Personal face-to-face meetings
- Telephone
- Mail/fax
- Memos, reports, logbooks, and other internal/external written communication
- E-mail, web sites, and online meetings such as "go-to-meetings"

The simplest method of communication involves a sender, a message, and a receiver. However, merely sending a message does not ensure that the message will be received and understood correctly. Several factors can lead to distortion of the message, such as noise interference, poor listening skills, and inappropriate tuning. The middle of a busy lunch service is not the right time to be asking the chef a question about the company's policy on sick-pay benefits. In this chapter, we explore various barriers to effective communication and the importance of good communication to a manager.

LEARNING OBJECTIVE 1
Define communication.

What Is Communication?

Communication, whether written or verbal, is the exchange of information. Successful or meaningful exchange of information between individuals requires the use of a common system of symbols or language, whether written or verbal. For instance, an employee receiving information from a manager in Spanish will find that information of little use if the employee does not understand Spanish. Successful communication is the result when a sender is able to convey a thought or idea clearly, and as a result it is perceived as the receiver intended it. The receiver may not *agree* with the message, but if the meaning of the message is clear and perceived as it was intended, the communication process may be deemed successful.

Managerial communication includes two different types: **Interpersonal communication**, which occurs between two or more individuals, and **organizational communication**, which includes all the different forms, networks, and systems of communication that occur among individuals, groups, or departments within an organization.

The Interpersonal Communication Process

Communication between two or more people is described as interpersonal communication.[1] The **interpersonal communication process** is made up of seven elements: the sender, encoding, the message, the channel, the receiver, decoding, and feedback (Figure 17–1). Before communication can take place, a *message* must exist and be conveyed. In other words, a message is sent from the sender and it is passed to the receiver. This is a process called *encoding*, whereby a message is passed on by way of a medium, a *channel*, from the sender to the receiver; because of this, the message travels in a converted form. The message is then translated by means of *decoding*. When successful communication has taken place, the receiver gives *feedback* to the sender indicating that he or she has correctly understood the message being conveyed.

"Noise" is often a part of the interpersonal communication process. Noise can consist of various activities going on in the background, such as sounds of machinery or coworkers, or it can be as simple as static in the telephone line or illegible print. Therefore, noise is considered a somewhat constant disturbance in the communications process and the cause of distortions of the message. Each element in the process can be influenced and distorted by disturbances (see Figure 17–1). The sender conveys a message by encoding it. During this process, major things could go wrong and distort the message. The sender can have too little or too much knowledge. He or she can't communicate what he or she does not know. However, if the proper explanations aren't given, the receiver could falsely interpret the message. Too much knowledge may cause the message not to be understood at all. Preexisting attitudes and the cultural system of the sender can influence the encoding of the message as well. Attitudes and

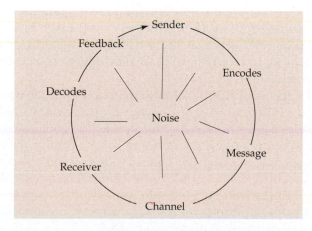

Figure 17–1 • Interpersonal Communication Process.

Source: Derived from Stephen P. Robbins and Mary Coulter, *Management*, 13th ed. (Hoboken, NJ: Pearson, 2014), 405.

beliefs about subject matters will leave their traces in the message and may be picked up by the receiver.

The message itself, such as a written document, an oral speech, or gestures and facial expressions, can be influenced by various kinds of disturbances. Noise will influence listening skills during an oral speech. Faulty equipment can lead to disruption of the message if it is conveyed through e-mail or fax. Symbols such as pictures, words, and numbers that are selected by the sender to convey his or her message can be influenced by noise.

The channel used to convey the message is important to the entire communications process. If you choose to use speech to communicate with a person who has a hearing impairment, the message may not be understood as the sender intended it to be. Whether the sender chooses to use an office memorandum, a phone call, e-mail, gestures, or pictures to convey the message will play a large role in how accurately the receiver will understand it. For this reason, using two channels can sometimes eliminate distortion—for example, oral speech followed by a written summary.

The receiver is limited by the same factors as the sender. If he or she has too little knowledge of the subject, distortions will take place. Likewise, if he or she has too much knowledge, too much can be read into a simple message. The preexisting attitudes and beliefs of the individual also play a role in how distorted the message will be after the decoding has taken place.

Communicating Interpersonally

Managers can communicate in various ways. Examples include face-to-face, telephone, e-mail, fax, group discussions and meetings, memos, formal presentations, bulletin boards, mail, employee publications, and teleconferencing. Communication experts generally agree that when two people are engaged in a face-to-face conversation, only a small fraction of the total message they share is contained in the words they use. A large portion of the message is contained in vocal elements such as tone of voice, accent, speed, volume, and inflection. The largest part of the message—and arguably the most important—is conveyed by a combination of gestures, postures, facial expressions, and clothing. Although people may listen closely to what is said, nonverbal behavior may constitute two-thirds or more of total communication. And although people have an option not to speak, they can never be uncommunicative nonverbally.[2]

Nonverbal communication is communication without words. Examples from everyday life show how important and frequent nonverbal communication is. Ambulance sirens, a honking horn, a school bell, or the sound of a ringing phone all communicate something to us without using any words. Similarly, gestures, actions, and the type of clothes worn communicate messages to us. A person wearing a police uniform tells us he or she belongs to the police force. In the same manner, the type of car a person drives or the size of his or her house conveys to others a message about that person. All of these forms of communication are nonverbal.

Body language consists of facial expressions, gestures, and any other ways of communicating a message with your body. For example, when you smile or laugh, you convey a message of joy or friendliness. In the same manner, rolling your eyes indicates disbelief or even annoyance. Emotions are typically conveyed purely by body language.

Verbal intonation is using your voice to emphasize certain parts of a phrase or certain words. For example, consider the phrase, "What are you doing?" An abrasive, loud intonation of the voice will indicate that the person is upset, angry, and even defensive. However, if the same sentence is said in a calm, soft voice, it will be perceived as genuine interest or concern or a friendly inquiry. Verbal intonation is almost more important than the words themselves. A common saying is that it is not *what* you say but *how* you say it. Managers should keep this very important fact in mind.

Facial expressions, a part of body language, convey different meanings.

▶ Check Your Knowledge

1. What is the difference between interpersonal and organizational communication?

2. What are three ways of communicating interpersonally?

3. Describe the interpersonal communication process.

Barriers to Effective Interpersonal Communication

Many elements can influence interpersonal communication.[3] The following sections discuss some of the major barriers.

LEARNING OBJECTIVE 2
List barriers to effective interpersonal communication and how to overcome them.

Perception

Everybody perceives things differently. This is due to people having different backgrounds, upbringings, personal experiences, and major influences in their lives. No two people are alike, and neither are their perceptions. Whereas one person may be optimistic and perceive a message in a positive light, another may be a pessimist and see only negative aspects of the message. Unwanted news is easily screened out and forgotten, whereas things we want to hear are remembered for a longer period of time.

Semantics

The actual meaning of words, or **semantics**, is the cause of many failed communication efforts. The literal meaning of words and the actual meaning can be two different things, but they can be expressed in the same way. For instance, if a restaurant manager tells a server to make guests feel comfortable, she doesn't necessarily mean that the server will bring pillows, blankets, or even beds into the dining area. The manager may have meant to make customers feel comfortable in a nonphysical way, by attending to them, making sure they are satisfied with their order, and making sure their water glasses are refilled promptly. Employing jargon, specialized terminology, or technical language that may be used widely within an organization may be ineffective if used with new employees or people who are not familiar with it.

Nonverbal Communication

Nonverbal communication—communication through body language—is a typical means of communication. However, it can also be considered a barrier to effective communication. The weight of decoding a message lies with the nonverbal communication rather than on the actual encoded message. For example, if a supervisor comes to work in the morning disgruntled about morning traffic, his or her subordinates may misinterpret the angry facial expression as the supervisor being dissatisfied with their work, although he or she never actually said so. The next time you have a conversation with someone, be aware of your own nonverbal communication: what you are expressing with gestures and facial expressions.

Misinterpretations of nonverbal communication are especially dominant in cross-cultural communication. Gestures and expressions mean different things in different cultures. For example, in most Asian and African countries, it is considered impolite to make direct eye contact with the person you are speaking to, whereas it is considered courteous to look the speaker in the eye in most Western cultures.

Ambiguity

Ambiguity, vagueness, or uncertainty can occur in a message being conveyed. A message may be ambiguous, meaning the person receiving the message is uncertain about the actual meaning. If a manager asks an employee to come to her office as soon as possible, it could mean immediately or next week when the employee has some free time. When the words of a message are clear but the intentions of the sender aren't, ambiguity occurs. The employee may be unclear as to why the manager wants to see him in the office now. Ambiguity may also be described as the receiver's uncertainty about the consequences of the message. The employee may think or ask, "What will happen if I don't go to her office immediately?"

Nonverbal communication is a barrier to effective communication.

Defensiveness

When people feel that they are being verbally attacked or criticized, they tend to react defensively. The reaction could be making sarcastic remarks, being overly judgmental, or simply screening out the unpleasant parts of the conversation. This often happens when employees refuse to realize personal flaws. Using defense mechanisms helps them screen out the negative image of themselves, so they can keep their self-esteem. However, acting defensively is a barrier to effective communication.

Overcoming Barriers to Effective Interpersonal Communication

Because barriers to effective interpersonal communication do exist, there are ways to improve on communication to largely overcome them. An essential part of a manager's job is to be an effective communicator. The suggestions discussed in the following sections should help make interpersonal communication more effective.

Use Feedback

Offering feedback,[4] the last step in the communication process, will eliminate misunderstandings and inaccuracies regarding the message being conveyed. The feedback can be verbal or nonverbal. After the receiver has decoded the message, the sender should make sure the message has been understood. It can be as simple as asking the employee, "Did you understand what I said?" The ideal response to this question will be more than a yes or no answer. The best form of verbal feedback is a quick restatement and summary of the message that has been conveyed: "You said you switched my shift tomorrow to the night shift." This way the sender can be sure that the message has been correctly understood.

The nonverbal form of feedback consists of various reactions to a message. First, the sender can watch for nonverbal cues as to whether the message has been understood. Eye contact, facial expression, scratching the head, or shrugging the shoulders all can indicate how accurately the message has been received and understood. Furthermore, the actions following the message can be used as feedback. A manager who is explaining a new serving procedure to the staff will know how accurately the message has been understood by observing the staff to see whether they follow the new procedure. If some servers do not follow the new procedure, the manager will have to clarify or restate the message.

Active Listening

There is a difference between hearing and actually listening.[5] You may hear what your manager is saying, but did you *really* listen? Hearing is passive, and listening is a deliberate act of understanding and responding to the words being heard. The first step to **active listening** is listening for the total meaning. For example, if a manager tells an employee that the room occupancy is down this quarter, instead of responding, "Don't worry, it'll be fine," the employee can recognize that a problem exists. The second step is to reflect the feelings. This is an important step for the sender of the message because it helps him or her communicate the emotional part of the message.

The receiver would reflect it by saying something like, "This situation must be stressful for you." The last step is to note all nonverbal cues and respond to them. These cues might include hand gestures or facial expressions.

Avoid Triggering Defensiveness

Defensiveness is one of the main barriers to effective communication. By avoiding the tendency to criticize, argue, or give advice, senders can avoid triggering defensive behavior. People don't like being criticized because it diminishes their self-image. Phrases that convey blame or finger-pointing are typically useless. The receiver will respond by arguing or storming off, and the communication will have largely failed. A solution to this is to allow a cooling-off period so that both parties can regain their composure. Generally, managers should avoid overly negative statements.

Interpersonal Dynamics

Leaders will get the best results with and through their associates if they adopt these simple suggestions: You must have a great attitude toward your associates, meaning you accept them as colleagues and treat them fairly, with respect; you establish a climate of trust; and you include your associates in as much decision making as possible. Be sensitive to cultural differences and learn more about the cultures of your associates. Learn the best ways to communicate with your associates. Make sure that your associates know what is expected of them. Actively listen to associates. Involve your associates. Train associates and develop them so they can reach their full potential. Above all, have fun!

▶ Check Your Knowledge

1. Define semantics.

2. Explain ambiguity as it relates to communication barriers.

3. What are three ways of overcoming communication barriers?

Organizational Communication

Organizational communication is necessary in managerial communication. The fundamentals include formal communication versus informal communication, communication flow patterns, and formal and informal communication networks.

LEARNING OBJECTIVE 3
Differentiate between formal and informal communication.

Formal and Informal Communication

The two major forms of organizational communication are formal and informal communication. Formal communication is used by managers to communicate job requirements to their employees. It follows the official chain of command. **Formal communication** occurs when, for instance, a manager tells an employee his or her schedule for the following week. The subject matter is always job related and is seen as essential to the employment.

Informal communication does not follow a company's chain of command or structural hierarchy. The subject matter may be job related but may not be essential to performing job duties. Examples of informal communication are employees talking at the water fountain, in the lunchroom, or at company gatherings. In every organization, employees form relationships with each other, whether as acquaintances or as friends. Employees use informal communication to satisfy their need for social interaction, and it can also improve an organization's performance by fostering better employee relationships and providing a faster, more efficient communication channel.[6] The "grapevine" is a form of informal communication.

Communication Flows and Networks

LEARNING OBJECTIVE 4
Explain communication flows and networks.

Communication flows in various directions: upward, downward, laterally, diagonally, and so on, as we will discuss in the following sections.

Upward Communication

Upward communication takes place when managers or superiors rely on their subordinates for receiving information. Information flows upward from employees to managers. This type of communication is important to managers because it helps them determine the satisfaction level of their employees, how employees feel about their jobs and the organization in general, and if employees have problems with coworkers or even with the manager. Some managers even encourage their subordinates to give them ideas about how to make improvements in the organization. Some examples of upward communication include manager performance reports, employee surveys, suggestion boxes, and informal group sessions with other coworkers.

Downward Communication

Communication flowing down from supervisor to employee is considered **downward communication**. Managers use this type of communication for various purposes: to inform employees of company policies, procedures, employee evaluations, or job descriptions and to discuss the future of the employee. Downward communication is often used to inform, direct, coordinate, and evaluate employees.

Lateral Communication

Communication that takes place between the employees of a company who are on the same hierarchical level in the organization is called *lateral communication*. This type of communication is used by employees to discuss their environment and the organization in general. Lateral communication is also used by cross-functional teams to facilitate communication.

The important thing to remember is always to let the supervisor know about decisions made through lateral communication.

Diagonal Communication

Communication that takes place between employees who are on different hierarchical levels and in different departments of the organization is called *diagonal communication*. An example of this type of communication is that of a chef communicating with a front-desk receptionist. The two employees are not on the same level, nor are they in the same department of a hotel. Through e-mail, almost every employee is able to communicate efficiently with any other employee in the same organization. However, as with lateral communication, the employees must make a point to update their managers on decisions made during this type of communication.

Two of the forms of communication flow, vertical and lateral, can be combined in various forms. These new forms are called **communication networks**. The most common are chain, wheel, and all-channel (Figure 17–2) networks, as well as the grapevine.[7]

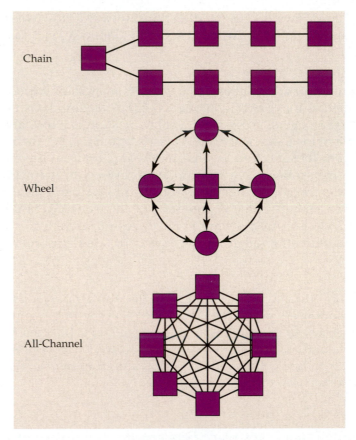

Figure 17–2 • Three Organizational Communication Networks.

Source: Derived from Stephen P. Robbins and Mary Coulter, *Management*, 13th ed. (Hoboken, NJ: Pearson, 2014), 413.

Chain, Wheel, and All-Channel Communication Networks

Communication in a chain network flows according to the existing chain of command in an organization. This includes downward as well as upward communication flows. This type of network is highly accurate; no information can be lost, and the path the message travels is precise. On the downside, the chain network is only moderately fast and moderately popular with employees.

The wheel network is a network in which communication flows between a strong leader and each individual in a group or team. In this network, the coworkers do not need to communicate with each other; they communicate solely with their leader. The advantage to this type of communication is that it is relatively speedy and accurate. However, this type of communication is usually not very popular with employees.

The all-channel communication network is differentiated from others by its freely flowing communication between all members of a group or team. This means that the leader communicates with employees, and employees all communicate with each other. This type of network is very popular with employees, and messages travel very fast. However, the accuracy of the message is not always at 100 percent.

One thing to remember is that every unique situation will require a different communication network. No one network is perfect for every situation.

The Grapevine

The grapevine may be the most popular and important communication network in an organization. One survey reported that 75 percent of employees hear about matters first through rumors on the grapevine.[8] The grapevine is an *informal* organizational communication network and an important source of communication for the managers of an organization. Through the local informal grapevine, issues that employees consider a reason for stress and anxiety are made known. This network acts as a very effective feedback mechanism and as a filter that sorts out only the issues that employees find important. The negative aspect of this communication network is the occasional rumor that travels through it. This is pretty much unavoidable; however, successful managers can eliminate the negative impact of rumors. This can be done by speaking openly and honestly with employees about any negative feelings or important decisions that are made.

▶ Check Your Knowledge

1. Define informal communication.

2. What is the difference between lateral and diagonal communication?

3. Elaborate on the wheel communication network.

The Decision-Making Process

All individuals in organizations, small or large, are faced with the task of decision making. This can involve decisions as simple as where to have lunch or as complex as the best place to locate a new franchise. A comprehensive, detailed **decision-making process** is used to make a complex decision. However, the same model can also be used for simple decisions.

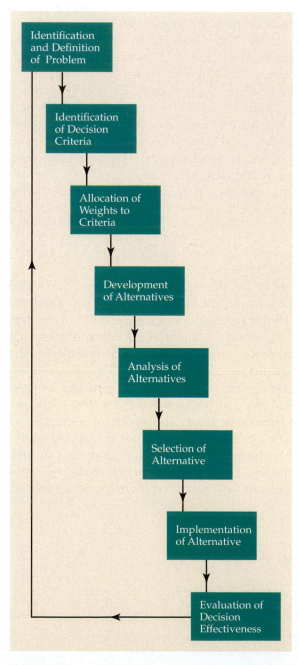

Figure 17–3 • Eight-Step Decision-Making Process.

The decision-making process consists of eight major steps (Figure 17–3):

LEARNING OBJECTIVE 5
Outline the eight steps in the decision-making process.

1. **Identification and definition of problem**
2. **Identification of decision criteria**
3. **Allocation of weights to criteria**
4. **Development of alternatives**
5. **Analysis of alternatives**
6. **Selection of alternative**
7. **Implementation of alternative**
8. **Evaluation of decision effectiveness**

This model can be used for most decisions, from simple ones such as what to buy for dinner to complex corporate decisions about new marketing strategies. So let's take a closer look at each step of the decision-making process.

Step 1: Identification and Definition of Problem

Let's say that we are experiencing a discrepancy between current and desired results. In this case, the decision-making process begins with identifying and defining the problem(s). It is not always easy to identify the problem because other issues may muddy the waters. In a hotel setting, problem situations can be identified with respect to, say, guest check-in. In some of the larger city-center, convention-oriented hotels, long lines of guests are frequently waiting to check into the hotel. Defining this problem is best done by writing a problem statement: "The problem is that it takes too long for guests to register." Once the problem has been accurately stated, it becomes easier to move to the next step in the decision-making process.

Another example comes to us from Herb Kelleher, former president of Southwest Airlines, when he decided to remove the closets at the front of Southwest planes. This was in response to a problem: It was taking too long to turn around the planes. To be competitive and successful, it is necessary to reduce the turnaround time in order to squeeze more flights into each day. The situation that caused or contributed to the turnaround problem was that the first people on the plane typically went to the closets first and then grabbed the nearest seats. On landing, the departing passengers were held up while the people in the front rows rummaged through the closets for their bags. The airline now turns around about 85 percent of its flights in 20 minutes or less and is one of the most profitable airlines.

Step 2: Identification of Decision Criteria

Once the problem has been identified and defined, we need to determine the criteria that are relevant to the decision. Suppose the problem is that we are hungry; the decision criteria might then be the following:

1. What type of food would we prefer?
2. How much time do we have to eat?
3. How much do we want to spend?

4. How convenient is parking?
5. What is the restaurant's reputation?
6. How is the food quality?
7. How is the service?
8. How is the atmosphere?

Note that the decision criteria used must be relevant to the particular situation. These criteria must have been developed by a group that wants to eat out at a restaurant. Criteria that are not identified are usually treated as unimportant.

INTRODUCING PATRICIA TAM

Chief Executive Advisor, Halekulani Corporation, Waikiki, Hawaii

Patricia Tam is a role model to everyone who wants to pursue a career in the hospitality industry. It is not hard to see why. Patricia is a woman of great ambition and ability. She has proved herself capable of succeeding at almost anything she attempts to do.[1] Patricia is of Chinese heritage and was brought up in Hawaii. During her childhood years, her ambition was to become an English teacher. Joining the hospitality industry never entered her mind. In fact, she didn't stay in a hotel until she was a young adult: "I was going along with some friends to the mainland for one of the first times I'd been off the island."

When she finished college at age 23, she became proprietor of a bakery. She was then recruited by Amfac, Inc. to open a bakeshop at its Royal Lahaina Resorton Maui in 1975. She says, "When I opened the bakeshop there, I liked the whole aura of resort life, not just because of the guests' experience, but because of the beach and the large infrastructure." She enrolled in the resort's management training program, which would be the start of a long and successful career journey in the lodging industry. Patricia started working at Halekulani in 1983. Halekulani was first constructed in 1907 as a beachfront home accompanied by five bungalows. In 1984, it reopened as a 453-room low-rise complex. It is Waikiki's premier five-diamond resort.

When Patricia became general manager of Halekulani, the situation was less than desirable. She was promoted in the post–Gulf War period, and the once-glorious Pacific destinations had stagnated. Because most of Hawaii's visitors were Asian, Japan's ongoing recession added to the difficult times. In the 1960s, Hawaii experienced its tourist boom years. But during the early 1990s, Hawaii had to fight for every bit of the global destination market it could capture. Patricia says, "We're sitting in an arena right now where the first one to the finish line is the winner. And I think that it's more exciting to be working in this business now than it would have been in the boom years, when all you had to worry about was how many people you couldn't accommodate tonight."

Patricia realizes that the hotel business can make either a profit or a loss. "I think for a lot of us who get into the business, we see the fun part of it: the bartending, the wait help, the restaurant excitement, the chance to meet really fabulous people from around the world. We see one side of the vision of what luxury properties are all about," she explains. "But there's the other side of it, which is that it is a business, and what do businesses do? They've got to make money."

---

[1] This profile draws on Tony De la Cruz, "Independent Hotelier of the World, Patricia Tam, Reaching for Resort Perfection," *Hotels*, November 1999, 64.

Patricia believes that outstanding guest services make a good hotel and maintain guest loyalty. She pays careful attention to detail and perfection and lets nothing pass her by. Even guest complaints are discussed one by one. She says, "You can get so worked up about the attention to detail that unless you're communicating with staff, it can be pretty challenging for them in terms of how to keep this hotel perfect. Not everybody knows how. But everybody tries to keep it that way." Maintaining her great reputation as a general manager as well as the hotel's reputation as a superior destination is reflected by her drive for perfection. John Sharpe, president of the Toronto-based Four Seasons hotel, nominated Patricia to be hotelier of the year. Halekulani, which means, "house befitting heaven," was voted best hotel in the world by *Gourmet* magazine. It has held its AAA five-diamond rating for years. It was a finalist for *Condé Nast Traveler's* Reader's Choice Best Tropical Resorts award and ranked in the top three hotels in the country in Zagat's U.S. hotel, resort, and spa survey. Its well-known restaurant, La Mer, is Hawaii's only AAA-rated five-diamond restaurant, and it has been known as such for years.

Patricia has served as a hotel assistant manager, rooms division director, and acting general manager, and also as general manager of Halekulani's adjacent sister property, the four-diamond Waikiki Parc hotel. In 1993, she became the general manager of Halekulani. Through it all, she always wanted more. She says, "I could work the operations in a very good management way, but I never had to be the person responsible for the final decision making on a lot of things. The challenge, the intimidation of that process, coming back over as the general manager, was quite overwhelming to me. But that was also my proudest moment because that's when I realized that I really had to buckle down." The readers of *Hotels* magazine have named Patricia Hotelier of the World.

As for her personality, Patricia is a genuine person who doesn't credit only herself. She doesn't forget that her success depends on an ongoing and mutually beneficial relationship between Halekulani's owner, Halekulani Corp., and herself. She says, "I look at it as a kind of management proposition where you can always learn every day." She adds, "Every day you can learn something new, not only about how to maintain a luxury property, but how to develop it and take it to the next level, because that's what it's all about."

Step 3: Allocation of Weights to Criteria

To decision makers, decision criteria all have different levels of importance. For instance, is the expected cost of the meal more important than the atmosphere? If so, a higher weight should be attached to that criterion.

One method used to weigh the criteria is to give the most important criterion a weight of 10 and then score the others according to their relative importance. In the meal example, the cost of the meal may receive a weight of 10, whereas the atmosphere may be awarded a weight of 6. Figure 17–4 lists a sample of criteria and weights for restaurant selection.

How much do we want to spend?	10
What type of food would we prefer?	8
How much time do we have?	6
How is the food quality?	9
How is the atmosphere?	6
How is the service?	7
How convenient is parking?	6
What is the restaurant's reputation?	6
How far do we want to go to a restaurant?	7

Figure 17–4 • Criteria and Weights in Restaurant Selection.

Step 4: Development of Alternatives

In developing alternatives, decision makers list the viable alternatives that could resolve the problem. No attempt is made to evaluate these alternatives— only to list them. The alternatives for the restaurant scenario are shown in Figure 17–5.

KFC

Taco Bell

Pizza Hut

McDonald's

Applebee's

The Olive Garden

Wendy's

Figure 17–5 • Restaurant Alternatives.

Step 5: Analysis of Alternatives

The alternatives are analyzed using the criteria and weights established in Steps 2 and 3. Figure 17–6 shows the values placed on each of the alternatives by the group for the restaurant scenario (it does not show the weighted values). The weighted values of the group's decision about which restaurant to go to are shown in Figure 17–7.

Once the weighted values are totaled, we can see that Pizza Hut and Wendy's are the restaurants with the highest scores. Notice how these are not the restaurants with the highest scores before the weighted values were included.

	KFC	Taco Bell	Pizza Hut	McDonald's	Applebee's	Olive Garden	Wendy's
Price	9	10	10	10	7	7	9
Type of food	7	8	9	8	8	9	9
How much time	9	9	7	10	7	6	10
Quality of food	7	7	8	7	8	8	8
Atmosphere	7	7	8	7	9	9	7
Service	6	6	7	7	8	9	7
Convenient parking	10	10	10	9	10	10	10
Restaurant reputation	8	8	8	7	8	9	8
How far away	8	8	8	10	7	7	8
Total	71	73	75	76	72	74	75

Figure 17–6 • Analysis of Alternatives.

	KFC	Taco Bell	Pizza Hut	McDonald's	Applebee's	Olive Garden	Wendy's
Price	90	100	100	100	70	70	90
Type of food	56	64	72	64	64	72	72
How much time	54	54	42	60	42	36	60
Quality of food	63	63	72	63	72	72	72
Atmosphere	42	42	48	42	54	54	42
Service	42	42	49	49	56	63	49
Convenient parking	60	60	60	56	60	60	60
Restaurant reputation	48	48	48	42	48	54	48
How far away	56	56	56	70	49	49	56
Total	511	529	547	546	515	530	549

Figure 17–7 • Weighted Values Analysis.

Step 6: Selection of Alternative

The sixth step is to select the best alternative. Once the weighted scores for each alternative have been totaled, it will become obvious which is the best alternative.

Step 7: Implementation of Alternative

We next need to ensure that the alternative is implemented so that the decision is put into action. Sometimes good decisions fail because they are not put into action.

Step 8: Evaluation of Decision Effectiveness

The final step in the decision loop is to evaluate the effectiveness of the decision. As a result of the decision, did we achieve the goals we set? If the decision was not effective, then we must find out why the desired results were not attained. This would mean going back to Step 1. If the decision was effective, then no action, other than recording the outcome, needs to be taken.

How Managers Make Decisions

Managers are the main decision makers in any organization. Although all employees face daily decisions, the choices a manager makes impact the future of the organization. Decision making is an integral part of all four primary managerial functions: planning, organizing, leading, and controlling.

LEARNING OBJECTIVE 6
Know the difference between rational, bounded rational, and intuitive decisions.

Making Decisions: Rationality, Bounded Rationality, and Intuition

The first criterion for making a decision is that it must be rational. Several assumptions are made to define what a rational decision really is. First, the decision itself would have to maximize value and be consistent within natural constraining limits. This means that the choice made must maximize the organization's profitability. Tying in with this is the natural assumption that the manager making the decision is pursuing the organization's values and profitability, not his or her own personal interest.

One assumption of **rationality** as it relates to the decision maker is that he or she is fully objective and logical. When making the decision, a clearly stated goal must always be kept in mind. This goes hand in hand with starting with a problem statement.

Bounded rationality means that managers make decisions based on the decision-making process that is bounded, or limited, by an individual's ability to gain information and make decisions. Managers know that their decision-making skills are based on their own competency, intelligence, and, last but not least, rationality. They are also expected to follow the decision-making process model. However, certain aspects of this model are not realistic with respect to true-life managerial decisions, which are made with respect to bounded reality. This comes into play, for example, when decision makers cannot find all of the necessary information to analyze a problem and all of its possible alternatives. Therefore, they find themselves **satisficing**, a term used by management scholar and author Peter Drucker that means accepting a solution that is just good enough, rather than maximizing. Consider this example: A chef for a major hotel chain must prepare a banquet for 50 people. On the menu is half a chicken for every guest, which means that the chef needs 25 whole chickens for this banquet. He purchases the chickens at a market 25 miles away, where he has made the same purchase before for $60. Because he has made purchases from this market before, he knows the quality of the food they sell. What the chef does not know is that there is a free-range chicken farm only 10 miles away that would have sold him the 25 chickens for the same price. Instead of researching his alternatives, the chef satisfices himself with the first option that comes to mind and settles on it, assuming it is probably not the best but is good enough. This behavior is rationally bounded because the best solution to be found is bounded by the chef's ability to research all alternatives instead of settling on the first acceptable one that comes to mind.

Most decisions that managers make are not based on perfect rationality because of various factors, such as time constraints on researching all possible solutions or lack of resources to do the research. Therefore, decisions are typically based on bounded rationality. In other words, managers make decisions based on alternatives that are just satisfactory. At the same time, though, the decision maker will be strongly influenced by an organization's culture, power considerations, internal politics, and an **escalation of commitment**. An escalation of commitment happens when the commitment to a prior decision is increased despite evidence to the contrary. For example, consider the decline of the Planet Hollywood restaurant chain. At the launch of the chain, the team of marketing professionals deemed it economically sensible to set a high price on burgers and other food items. The restaurant set out to be a novelty establishment, although the target customers were middle-class citizens. Although it was evident that the decision to have high-priced products in a middle-class establishment was doomed for failure from the beginning, the decision makers stuck with it. The inevitable took place, and Planet Hollywood went belly up and was forced to close locations all around the world. The negative consumer reaction was predictable, but the decision makers escalated their commitment to the set prices even though it was a bad decision. Rather than search for new alternatives, they did not want to admit to making a bad decision and simply increased their commitment to the original one.[9]

Using rationality and common sense to influence decision making is very important—we must not forget the role of plain and simple human intuition. Intuition is used in everyday life, such as knowing not to grab a hot baking pan with your bare hands. It ranges all the way to the corporate level, where managers often use their own intuition when making corporate decisions. **Intuitive decision making** is a subconscious process of making decisions on the basis of experience and accumulated judgment. Five different identified aspects of intuition comply with the different types of decisions made. The first is a *values-* or an *ethics-based decision*. Managers will recall the ethics system they were raised with and base their decisions on personal morals. The second is an *experience-based decision*. Through trial and error, the manager has gained experience and will base a decision on past learning. *Affect-initiated decisions* are those that are based on a manager's emotions and feelings. The fourth type is a *cognitive-based decision*. The manager's previous training, learned skills, and gained knowledge influence the decision-making process. Last, the manager may use his or her subconscious mind to retain data and process it in such a way that it will influence the type of decision he or she will make.

INTRODUCING SUZANNE SEDER

Director of Convention Services, Tampa Convention Center, Tampa, Florida

Exceeding client expectations every day! No two days are ever the same because each event is unique. The adventure of creating lasting memories and producing well-organized events is a great motivator.

Suzanne Seder manages the Convention Services Department for the Tampa Convention Center. She and her team of six convention services managers produce over 400 events a year. Her day starts as she checks-in with her staff to see how things are going with their events. She listens to the radio to hear those unexpected paramedic calls and the activities happening in the building so she can jump in when needed. Responsiveness to client's requests through e-mails, voice messages, and planning meetings is a priority.

INTRODUCING SUZANNE SEDER *(Continued)*

These things make up the daily "routine" activities. Based upon events currently in the building and upcoming events, the challenges of problem solving can quickly change the focus of the day.

Suzanne researches and assigns the events after being contracted by the Sales Department. She matches the convention services manager's skill level and their personalities while working within the team's individual schedules.

Each convention services manager creates an event document containing timelines, room assignments, setups, special instructions, and costs estimates along with AutoCAD floor plans. These documents are reviewed by Suzanne to make sure everyone is adhering to the general building policies and standard operating procedures for safety, efficiency, consistency, and accuracy of information. She works closely with the fire marshal's office in submitting floor plans for review and approval. Coming up with alternative solutions when needed to make sure policies are followed, but ensuring a positive customer experience is the creative part of the job.

It is important to make sure everyone is working from the latest information to have success in coordinating a smooth event. This is accomplished with a weekly meeting to discuss last minute changes or updates with each department. Suzanne also brings her team together on a weekly basis to work out event coverage and the opportunity to review specific event issues.

The Tampa Convention Center has a beautiful waterfront view, a Riverwalk and marina. Besides coordinating activities inside the building, Suzanne handles special boating requests and events such as the Tampa Boat Show.

Suzanne had the privilege of coordinating a variety of high-profile special events including the 2012 National Republican Convention Media Center, two NFL Super Bowl Media Centers, and several televised events including Antique Road Show, America's Got Talent, AKC Dog Shows, Oprah, and Dr. Phil. By continuing to coordinate events, she understands the issues her team experiences first-hand.

Suzanne believes that while the day never really ends in the event world because you always need to be accessible, her work is very rewarding when a client leaves with a great impression of Tampa!

Intuition and rationality are separate but are often used in combination in most decision making. The two complement each other to offer the manager an ideal solution for the decision-making process. As an example, consider a manager who has to make a decision on a situation that is similar to one he has come across in the past. Instead of using careful analytical rationality, he will make a decision based on a "gut feeling" and act quickly with what appears to be limited information. The decision is ultimately made based on his experience and accumulated judgment.

▶ Check Your Knowledge

1. List criteria for making a rational decision.

2. Give an example of satisficing.

3. What are the five aspects of intuition?

Types of Problems and Decisions

LEARNING OBJECTIVE 7
Identify situations in which a programmed decision is a better solution than a nonprogrammed decision.

Several different types of decisions match different types of problems. They are applied as solutions, depending on the various situations that arise. Managers who are aware of these differences can use them to their advantage.

The two major types of decisions are programmed decisions and nonprogrammed decisions. A **programmed decision** involves situations that recur on a regular basis, allowing the response to be handled with a "programmed" response. In a programmed decision, the response will occur on a repetitive basis; for example, when the number of New York steaks goes below a specified number, an order for more is automatically placed. Programmed decisions generally become a standard operating procedure. Alternatives are not necessary most of the time because the problem statement is familiar, and therefore the solution is in close reach because of past successful decisions made. The response to a shortage of New York steaks is simply a reorder; the alternatives are truly limited. A programmed decision is made in response to a recurring problem; the approach to dealing with it has become repetitive and therefore does not require a careful analysis.

HOW TO USE THE DECISION-MAKING PROCESS FOR PROBLEM SOLVING

Courtesy of **James McManemon**, M.S., University of South Florida Sarasota–Manatee

Susan Campbell, a food and beverage director of a Palm Beach resort, shared her story of the decision-making process that took place after the 1000-room hotel was forced to evacuate its guests shortly before Hurricane Andrew hit the coast in August 1992. The resort was at full capacity and in the middle of hosting a popular rock concert in its banquet hall when the Category 5 hurricane was suddenly projected to hit the Palm Beach coastal area.

Susan explained that after surveying a million dollars of hotel grounds damages (just a few weeks before a nationally televised golf event and celebrity/pro tennis tournament), a small team of their department heads ventured down to the Palm Beach Homestead to see, first-hand, the devastation, which was almost indescribable. There were thousands of people left homeless and without food, shelter, or any sense of security. Some of these people had been guests at the resort before it had been evacuated. In the short-term, someone had to do something to help these people until a larger scale solution could be determined. She felt that, as a company with many resources, they could assist with the short-term solution.

After returning with their report, Susan and her colleagues decided to round up their culinary team at 3 A.M., and returned to the Homestead in a convoy of pink hotel shuttle buses and maintenance vehicles to serve 1,200 hot meals a day—which turned into 2,500 meals a day within a week through word of mouth—up to a total of 60,000 meals before they had to re-open the hotel and host those major events. "As a result," Susan remarked, "I became convinced that food is the most powerful connector of community, watching people gathered around our mash-style kitchen, trying to make sense of the chaos, and draw support from each other. That experience was my inspiration for using the resources a large hotel/resort can provide to help the community when in need."

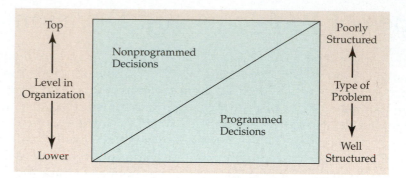

Figure 17–8 • Nonprogrammed and Programmed Decisions.

Source: Derived from Stephen P. Robbins and Mary Coulter, *Management*, 13th ed. (Hoboken, NJ: Pearson, 2014), 50.

A **nonprogrammed decision** is nonrecurring and is made necessary by unusual circumstances. The type of problem that induces a nonprogrammed decision is a poorly structured problem. These types of problems are usually new or unusual to the decision maker. More often than not, the information on the problem is incomplete or unavailable. This generally increases the difficulty gradient of finding an appropriate solution. Most important, though, the problem is unique and nonrecurring, such as which computer hardware and software a restaurant should install or whether to expand through franchising or company-owned restaurants. These distinctive decision situations are not likely to recur for several years and require a custom-made decision.

The more sophisticated a company is, the more programmed decisions are made. Many large corporations have policy and procedure manuals to guide managerial and supervisory decision making. Nonprogrammed decisions call for greater analysis, innovation, and problem-solving skills. Figure 17–8 diagrams programmed and nonprogrammed decisions according to the level in the organization and type of problem.

LEARNING OBJECTIVE 8
Differentiate the decision conditions of certainty, risk, and uncertainty.

Decision-Making Conditions

In a perfect world, we would have all the information necessary for making decisions. However, in reality, some things are unknowable. This leads us to decision-making conditions. Decisionmaking includes three major conditions: certainty, risk, and uncertainty. These three conditions each have individual characteristics.

The ideal situation for making a decision is one of **certainty**. A decision of certainty includes knowing all of the alternatives and therefore having no risk involved when making a decision, because the outcome is known. A good example for this condition is a hotel investment specialist who is allotted a share of the hotel's profit. The investor's options are clear and defined. He knows exactly how much interest is earned on bonds and how much interest is offered by various banks, the security issues, and how many years it will take for them to mature.

Making a decision that involves **risk** is one of the most common situations. Here the decision maker is not certain of the outcome of the situation. However, through personal experience, or a simple "gut feeling," she can estimate the probability of the outcome. Although not all alternatives are properly researched, by using historical data, probabilities can be assigned to various alternatives and the best probable outcome can ultimately be chosen. This is called a *risk condition* as it relates to decisionmaking and is characterized by having some knowledge of the outcome of the various alternatives, combined with the element of unpredictability.

For example, a popular hotel is thinking about adding on family apartments to its property. So far, the largest room it has is a double; the family rooms would need to have beds for four people, along with a kitchenette. Perusing past historical data helps make the decision somewhat clearer. In the past year alone, 40 percent of all customers were families of three or more. Reviewing the customer comments, managers find that the demand for a family apartment is relatively large. Although the construction of an apartment building will cut into the revenue, the rental profit made from these more expensive apartments is likely to outweigh costs in fewer than three years. In addition, the hotel is hoping to attract an even larger family crowd to its property once it offers apartments. Although all of the past data are valuable information and can to some extent predict the future, a factor of risk is involved because there is always some level of unpredictability about the future.

Uncertainty situations are characterized by having to make a decision when the outcome is not certain and when reasonable outcome estimates can't be made either. These situations often arise when alternatives to the decision are limited because of lack of adequate information. Although conditions of uncertainty are not as common as situations of risk, managers still find themselves confronted with uncertainty in decision-making situations.

Rational Decision Making

Professional managers at the Sheraton San Diego Hotel & Marina provided us with a real-life problem that deals with making rational decisions: How much space should we reserve for large parties? For example, if a group of 500 reserves a room and only 300 show up, the other 200 spaces are basically "dead space," which could have been rented out to another party of 200 people. To protect itself from this kind of dilemma, the hotel has attached a food and beverage price to each room. If you reserve the room, the food and beverage price is charged automatically, even if the guests don't show up.

Decision-Making Styles

Decision makers differ in their way of thinking; some are rational and logical, whereas others are intuitive and creative. Rational decision makers look at the information in order. They organize the information and make sure it is logical and consistent. Only after carefully studying all of the given options do they finally make the decision. Intuitive thinkers, on the other hand, can look at information that is not necessarily in order. They can make quick decisions based on their spontaneous creativity and intuition. Although a careful analysis is still required, these types of people are comfortable looking at all solutions as a whole as opposed to studying each option separately.

The second dimension in which people differ is each individual's **tolerance for ambiguity**. Managers who have a high tolerance for ambiguity are lucky in that they save a lot of time while making a decision. These individuals can process many thoughts at the same time. Unfortunately, some managers have a low tolerance for ambiguity. These individuals must have order and consistency in the way they organize and must process the information so as to minimize ambiguity.

"No … I mean yes."

A former CEO always said "no" first because he could always change his mind to "yes" later. Today it may be better to say, "Let me get back to you on that request," or, "Let's discuss this—can you meet with me on Monday at 10:00 A.M.?"

Upon review of the two dimensions of decisionmaking—way of thinking and tolerance for ambiguity—and their subdivisions, four major decision-making styles become evident:[10]

1. The **directive style** entails having a low tolerance for ambiguity as well as being a rational thinker.

Individuals who fall into the category of having a directive decision-making style are usually logical and very efficient. They also have a primary focus on the short run and are relatively quick decision makers. Directive decision makers value speed and efficiency, which can cause them to be remiss in assessing all alternatives, such that decisions are often made with minimal information.

2. Decision makers who have an **analytic style** of decision-making have a large tolerance for ambiguity. Compared to directive decision makers, these individuals require more information before making their decisions and, consequently, they consider more alternatives. Individuals with an analytic style are careful decision makers, which gives them leeway to adapt or cope to unique situations.

3. Decision makers who have a **conceptual style** of decisionmaking look at numerous alternatives and are typically very broad in their outlook. Their focus is on the long run of the decision made. These individuals are typically creative and often find creative solutions to the problem with which they are dealing.

4. Decision makers who work well with others are said to have a **behavioral style** of decision making. This entails being receptive to suggestions and ideas from others as well as being concerned about the achievements of their employees. They commonly communicate with their coworkers through meetings. These individuals try to avoid conflict as often as possible, because acceptance by others is very important to them.

At least one of these decision-making styles is always used by managers. However, decision makers often combine two or more styles to make a decision. Most often, a manager will have one dominant decision-making style and will use one or more other styles as alternates. Flexible individuals vary their decision-making styles according to each unique situation. If the style is to consider riskier options (analytic style) or if the decision is made based on suggestions

CORPORATE PROFILE

Starwood Hotels & Resorts Worldwide

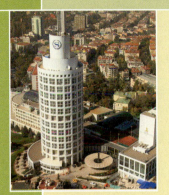

Starwood is one of the world's largest hotel and leisure companies. Its brand names include St. Regis, The Luxury Collection, Sheraton, Westin, W Hotels, Four Points by Sheraton, Le Méridien, Aloft, and Element by Westin. Through these brands, Starwood is well represented in most major markets around the world. Operations are grouped into two business segments: hotels and vacation ownership operations. Revenue and earnings are derived primarily from hotel operations, which include the operation of owned hotels, management and other fees earned from hotels managed pursuant to management contracts, and the receipt of franchise and other fees.

Starwood's hotel business emphasizes global operation of hotels and resorts primarily in the luxury and upscale segment of the lodging industry. It seeks to acquire interests in, management of, or franchise rights for properties in this segment. The hotel portfolio includes owned, leased, managed, and franchised hotels totaling over 1,200 properties, with approximately 354,200 rooms in approximately 100 countries.

Starwood's revenues and earnings are also derived from development, ownership, and operation of vacation ownership resorts, marketing and selling vacation ownerships in the resorts, and providing financing to customers who purchase such interests. Generally, these resorts are marketed under the preceding brand names. There are 22 vacation ownership resorts in the United States, Mexico, and the Bahamas.[1]

Starwood has assumed a leadership position in markets worldwide based on superior global distribution, coupled with strong brands and brand recognition. The upscale and luxury brands continue to capture market share from competitors by aggressively cultivating new customers while maintaining loyalty among the world's most active travelers. The strength of Starwood's brands is evidenced, in part, by the superior ratings received from hotel guests and from industry publications. The November 2004 edition of *Condé Nast Traveler* magazine named four Starwood properties in the top 100 Best in the World, with more than 30 properties listed in the Readers' Choice Awards list. In addition, the January 2005 issue included 51 Starwood properties among its prestigious Gold List and Gold List Reserve—more than any other hotel company.

Starwood has distinguished and diversified hotel properties throughout the world, including the St. Regis in New York City; the Phoenician in Scottsdale, Arizona; the Hotel Gritti Palace in Venice, Italy; the St. Regis in Beijing, China; and the Westin Palace in Madrid. These are among the leading hotels in the industry and are at the forefront of providing the highest quality and service.

Starwood's primary business goal is to maximize earnings and cash flow by increasing the profitability of its existing portfolio, selectively acquiring interests in additional assets, increasing the number of hotel management contracts and franchise agreements, acquiring and developing vacation ownership resorts and selling VOIs, and maximizing the value of owned real estate properties, including selectively disposing of noncore hotels and "trophy" assets that may be sold at significant premiums. Starwood plans to meet these goals by leveraging its global assets, broad customer base, and other resources and by taking advantage of scale to reduce costs. The uncertainty relating to political and economic environments around the world and consequent impact on travel in their respective regions and the rest of the world make financial planning and implementation of Starwood's strategy more challenging.

For more information, go to www.starwoodhotels.com.

---

[1] Starwood Hotels and Resorts, *2015 Proxy Statement & 2014 Annual Report*, http://www.starwoodhotels.com. Click on Investor Relations, and then click on 2014 Annual Report.

from subordinates (behavioral style), each style will eventually bring the decision maker to the optimal solution for the unique problem he or she is facing.

▶ Check Your Knowledge

1. Name the two dimensions of decision-making styles.
2. Briefly describe the conceptual style of decisionmaking.

Sustainable Communication and Decision Making

Sustainability in the hospitality industry is a trend that is constantly gaining in popularity. There is a steady increase in environmental consciousness, which has resulted in a higher demand for eco-friendly initiatives. More often we are seeing hoteliers build sustainable practices and policies into their daily operations. In order to successfully implement sustainable initiatives, it is important to effectively communicate sustainable goals internally to employees and investors, as well as to guests. Sustainable initiatives are driven from within an organization through employee encouragement and involvement. The decision to employ sustainable practices is generally made from the top of an organization; however, it must be supported by everyone in order to prevail.[11]

In communicating sustainable practices to guests, hoteliers can use a variety of informational approaches either directly or indirectly. Some hotels post their information in guestroom compendiums, while others tell guests directly upon check-in. Many hotels attempt to establish guest involvement by surveying guests to gain feedback on the effectiveness of communicating their sustainable practices. The goal is to inform guests of what the hotel advocates without being overly aggressive. Guests should feel a sense of care and commitment to their well-being, and the surrounding environment. The decision to adapt to sustainable practices is made because of the increase in interest and attractiveness from a guest perspective.[12]

The stakeholders of a company are involved in much of the decision-making, which gives them the responsibility of determining the role of sustainability within their operation. It is often necessary to establish a communication strategy, "which should identify how information, awareness creation, advocacy, network building, conflict migration, and communication platforms should be supported." In determining the level of sustainability implemented, different forms of communication are needed, which can range from meetings and conventions to e-mails, the Internet, advertisements, and forms of telecommunications. Depending on the size of the organization, "there is a need for effective communication from the central to the regional and local levels."

Because tourism heavily impacts local communities, it is important to effectively communicate sustainable initiatives by fostering a degree of participation from the local population. Some strategies to involve the local population in tourism development include training, meetings, workshops, special events, projects, and so on. It is beneficial to harbor trust by creating relationships with local communities, and considering their needs and concerns. There are also various barriers to communication with different communities, which can include differences in culture, language, perceptions, priorities, and forms of communication. These barriers can be overcome by "awareness-raising activities, and dialogue between businessmen and communities to aid in understanding different points of views, opinions and interests."[13]

Trends in Communication and Decision Making

Courtesy of Dr. Greg Dunn, Senior Lecturer & Managing Director, University of Florida, Eric Friedheim Tourism Institute

- *Maintain a Solid Business Reputation.* In today's connected, social media–prevalent world, it is as important as ever to maintain a solid and positive business reputation. Public comments and observations, both positive and negative, can be captured and shared in real time to a global audience. The status and reputation of a hospitality business is not only evaluated through articles in the popular press or on review sites such as TripAdvisor—the potential market reach is much greater. With real-time, global reach of social media, it is important for businesses to always represent their company and industry positively. "Social is Mobile" is a new saying which emphasizes how important it is to create great experiences, which ultimately result in great reviews. Just one negative review can impact a company and guest perceptions very quickly. Today's management must be able to handle all situations with an active, responsive, and positive outlook and with their customers' best interests in mind. Ignoring comments and social media postings is not an appropriate strategy in business reputation management.

- *Integrated Marketing Communications.* When marketing in hospitality, one of the most important tasks is for businesses to remain consistent in messaging across all communication channels. This includes taking an integrated approach to marketing and communications. For instance, a business shouldensure that all ofthe information and content on its website andapplications, as well as on traditional, digital, and social media platforms, are consistent. The use of supplier-based or customer-based video continues to increase in use and popularity among hospitality organizations. When done properly, video clips and campaigns on digital and social media have proven to be very successful. Many videos provide new information and perspective to a business's experience, and the best videos connect with guests. Guest or visitor videos shared on social media can prove that the experience a business presented was actually true as advertised.

- *Ethics in the Hospitality Industry.* Unfortunately, there continues to be a significant amount of discussion regarding ethical practices in the hospitality industry. Companies and managers face accusations of theft, harassment, negligence, and discrimination thatcan result in costly and public cases and lawsuits. Since the right ethical decision is not always clear, it is important for managers to gain a better understanding of the many ethical issues facing the hospitality industry. Understanding the ethical issues is just one aspect; hospitality managers also have the responsibility of maintaining the highest level of services, guest satisfaction, and optimal return on investment.

- *Employee Satisfaction Leads to Guest Satisfaction.* One of the most, if not the most, important assets of the hospitality industry are the employees. It is imperative for businesses to take great care of their employees. This includes the interview process, training, listening to them, and much more. It is the role of the manager and management team to understand what the employees think; how they perceive the culture, goals, and missions; what they think of the working environment; and overall, how satisfied they are with their jobs. Research has proven that higher levels of employee satisfaction can lead to higher levels of guest satisfaction and firm profitability.

- *New Decision-Making Models.* In many cases, people are hired into a hospitality business for their exceptional analytical and decision-making skills. Although this mostly affects managers, all staff have to be able to make decisions. Having a model for decisionmaking can ultimately help the business succeed. The first part of this model should deal with defining the problem. What is the issue, and are we capable of taking care of this problem on our own? The next part is to think about expertise. Decisionmaking often deals with thinking critically rather than consulting an expert. Next, it is important to look at the evidence, and finally, it is important to make a final decision.

- *Improved Hospitality Consumer Insights.* The saying goes, "Solid insights drive solid strategy." Top hospitality companies understand the value of solid consumer research and insights. In order to better understand hospitality consumer decisionmaking, it is imperative that we learn more about some of the choices individuals and groups make. There are several types of consumer decisions we research in hospitality. One decision theory centers on consumer financial allocation and trade-off analysis,which involves the study of how consumers budget and allocate their spend on various hospitality products and services and the related benefits received. Otherresearchers have focused on studying consumer brand and style decisions that involve consumer review and screening of specifications of the goods or services provided. This research goes into observing how a customer evaluates the value and importance of a hospitality brand and the factors that drive decisions on which brands to purchase.

- *Divergent Market Segmentation.* As the Gen Y and Millennials continue to evolve as strong consumer groups, hospitality organizations will continue to be challenged in ways to successfully serve all market segments.

For instance, as each generational cohort matures and their lifestyles evolve, their spending and travel habits typically also start to change. To attract more mature travelers, hospitality organizations may have to offer some older, experienced, or budget-conscious travelers (such as those falling in the Gen X, Boomer, and Mature segments) discounts, more value, and premium offers. On the other hand, to attract younger consumers (such as Millennials and Gen Y), hospitality organizations may have to offer experiences that include fast connectivity, high tech solutions, and novel approaches to mature products and services. We are now faced with five very different groups of travelers, each of which have unique needs and wants. Hospitality organizations will continue to be pressed to find ways to appeal to and serve each segment.

- *Innovative Technology.* Hospitality organizations will need to continue to invest in technology to help improve the guest experience, but they must also make smart investments. With limited budgets, hospitality organizations can't afford to try every new technology. They must upgrade to technologies that have been proven to add to revenues and reduce costs. For instance, hospitality organizations are offering mobile check-ins as they realize that seamless connectivity across platforms and devices are no longer the future—they are the present. Today, mobile apps are being used as everything from a digital concierge to accessing big data. Geo-location can make it easy to sell guests something that is literally right in front of them. Some hospitality organizations have developed their own apps that send offers to guests to do everything related to eating, playing, and shopping. Additionally, monitoring guest use of the Internet relative to bandwidth can provide a different data set, perhaps one that will drive down the ever-increasing costs of providing ridiculous levels of said bandwidth. Most importantly, when looking at the face of a changing consumer today, technology innovation is paramount.

CASE STUDY

Guests Complaining about Waiting Too Long for Elevators

Guests at a busy eight-story, four-star hotel are constantly complaining about having to wait too long for the elevator. At 8:00 A.M., some of the elevators are in use by the housekeeping department, whose associates are going up to begin work on the guest rooms. At the same time, room service has an elevator blocked off to serve in-room breakfasts because the kitchen and the banqueting departments are using the service elevators. Then, at about 10:30 A.M., the housekeepers use the elevators to go down for their morning break. The general manager recognizes your potential and asks you to come up with suggestions to take care of the problem/challenge.

Discussion Question

1. What suggestions do you have to remedy the situation described?

Summary

1. The definition of communication is the transfer and understanding of meaning. Managerial communication is divided into two categories: interpersonal communication and organizational communication. Interpersonal communication takes place between two or more people, and organizational communication consists of all the networks and systems of communication that exist in an organization.

2. The interpersonal communication process can be disrupted or can fail based on several factors. To improve your interpersonal communication skills, you need to eliminate as much noise during the communication process as possible; that is, close the door to your office or move to a quiet space in the building. Inform yourself about how knowledgeable the receiver is on the subject. Be sure to provide adequate explanations if the receiver's knowledge is limited. Lastly, pick the appropriate channel of communication to ensure successful conveyance of the message.

3. Barriers to effective interpersonal communication include misunderstood perception, misuse of semantics, misguided use of nonverbal communication, ambiguous messages, and defensiveness. Ways to overcome these barriers are through use of feedback, active listening, and avoiding defensiveness.

4. Managers use formal communication to communicate job requirements to their employees. It follows the official chain of command. Informal communication does not follow a company's chain of command or structural hierarchy. The subject matter is typically not job related and is not essential to performing job duties.

5. Communication flows are part of the organizational communication process. Upward communication flows from the employees to the manager. Downward communication flows from manager to employees. Lateral communication takes place among employees who are on the same organizational level. Diagonal communication cuts across organizational levels as well as work areas. The four different types of communication networks are the chain, the wheel, the all-channel, and the grapevine.

6. The decision-making process consists of eight steps: (1) identification and definition of problem, (2) identification of decision criteria, (3) allocation of weights to criteria, (4) development of alternatives, (5) analysis of alternatives, (6) selection of alternative, (7) implementation of alternative, and (8) evaluation of decision effectiveness.

7. Although all employees in a company make decisions on a regular basis, in the end it is the manager's decisions that count. His or her decisions usually represent the final word and are valued as "the right decision." Decisionmaking is a large part of all four primary managerial functions: planning, organizing, leading, and controlling. Hence, *managing* is a synonym for *decision making*.

8. A rational decision is based on the following assumptions: The decision is value maximizing and within natural limits, and the manager making the decision is fully objective and logical and has the organization's economic interest in mind. As a result, the rational decision-making is simple and has a clearly defined goal, limited alternatives, minimal time pressure, low cost for seeking and evaluating alternatives, an organizational culture that supports risk taking and innovation, and measurable and concrete outcomes. Bounded rationality suggests that managers make decisions that are bounded by an individual's ability to process information. Managers often cannot possibly analyze all available information and all alternatives, so they satisfice instead of maximize. Finally, intuitive decisionmaking is a subconscious process of making decisions on the basis of experience and accumulated judgment, including ethics learned.

9. Programmed decisions require a problem situation that is a frequent occurrence, allowing the response to be handled with a routine approach. Programmed decisions generally become standard operating procedures. A nonprogrammed decision is nonrecurring and made necessary by unusual circumstances. These types of problems are usually new or unusual to the decision maker. More often than not, the information on the problem is incomplete or unavailable.

10. The decision condition of certainty includes knowing all of the alternatives and therefore having no risk involved when making a decision, because the outcome is pretty much known. Uncertainty situations are characterized by having to make a decision when the outcome is not certain and reasonable outcome estimates can't be made

because of lack of adequate information. In risk situations, the decision maker is not certain of the outcome of the situation. However, through personal experience, historical data, or a simple "gut feeling," he or she can estimate the probability of the outcome.

11. Decision-making styles vary depending on a person's way of thinking—rational or intuitive—and a person's tolerance for ambiguity, which can be low or high. Combinations of these differences give us the directive style (low tolerance for ambiguity and rational way of thinking), the analytic style (high tolerance for ambiguity and rational way of thinking), the conceptual style (high tolerance for ambiguity and intuitive way of thinking), and the behavioral style (low tolerance for ambiguity and intuitive way of thinking).

Key Words and Concepts

active listening
allocation of weights to criteria
analysis of alternatives
analytic style
behavioral style
body language
bounded rationality
certainty
communication
communication networks
conceptual style
decision-making process
development of alternatives
directive style

downward communication
escalation of commitment
evaluation of decision
effectiveness
formal communication
identification and definition of
problem
identification of decision
criteria
implementation of alternative
informal communication
interpersonal communication
interpersonal communication
process

intuitive decisionmaking
nonprogrammed decision
nonverbal communication
organizational communication
programmed decision
rationality
risk
satisficing
selection of alternative
semantics
tolerance for ambiguity
uncertainty
upward communication
verbal intonation

Review Questions

1. The most important aspect of a manager's job is typically described as decisionmaking. Do you believe this is so? Explain.

2. When reviewing some important decisions you have made, would you describe them as mostly rational or intuitive decisions? What

are the characteristics of each? How does intuition affect the decision-making process?

3. During the communications process, if the receiver disagrees with the sender, does this always mean that the message has not been properly understood? Or could it mean something else? Explain.

4. How can the grapevine be used to a company's advantage?

5. When communication is not effective, is it always the fault of the receiver? Discuss all options.

Internet Exercise

1. Organization: **Starbucks**
   Summary: Starbucks founder Howard Schultz has resumed his role of CEO and made plans for the reorganization of Starbucks to restore what he calls the "distinctive Starbucks experience" and to focus on the guest. He has made several decisions, including focusing on espresso standards and other important tenets of coffee edu-

cation, and all Starbucks locations were closed for a three-hour training session one day. Schultz continues to communicate via his messages on the company web site.
   (a) Read about Starbucks and see if you agree with Schultz's decisions.
   (b) What do you think about his communications? How could communications be improved?

Apply Your Knowledge

1. Select a hospitality-related problem and write a problem statement. Then, using

the decision-making steps, show how you would solve the problem.

Endnotes

1. Draws on Stephen P. Robbins and Mary Coulter, *Management*, 8th ed. (Hoboken, NJ: Pearson, 2005), 282.
2. Paul Preston, "Nonverbal communication: Do you really say what you mean?" *Journal of Healthcare Management*, March/April 2005, 83.
3. Anne E. Beall, "Body language speaks," *Communication World*, March/April 2004, 18.
4. Draws on Gary Dessler, *A Framework for Management*, 3rd ed. (Hoboken, NJ: Pearson, 2004), 282.
5. Draws on Robbins and Coulter, *Management*, 265.
6. Ibid., 293–296.
7. Ibid., 294–295.
8. "Heard it through the grapevine," cited in *Forbes*, February 10, 1997, 22.
9. Personal conversation with John Horne, president, Anna Maria Oyster Bar restaurants, April 14, 2008.
10. Adapted from Robbins and Coulter, *Management*, 147.

11. Green Hotelier,"Communicating with your employees,"April 16, 2011, http://www .greenhotelier.org. Search for "communicating sustainability" to view this article(accessed December 4, 2011).

12. Maud Tixier. (November 4, 2008). "The Hospitality Business Communication and Encouragement of Guest's Responsible Behavior and Their Diverse Responses." http://www.esade.edu/cedit/pdfs/ papers/pdf7.pdf.

13. USAID. (May–June 2006)."Communication and Sustainable Tourism," http://www.usaid.gov. Search for "global e-conference 2006" to view this document (accessed June 10, 2015) .

CHAPTER 18

Control

LEARNING OBJECTIVES

After reading and studying this chapter, you should be able to:

- Define control.
- Give reasons why control is important.
- Describe the five-step control process.
- Distinguish among the three types of control.
- Explain the important financial controls.
- Describe the qualities of an effective control system.
- Outline the contemporary issues in control.

Did you ever get to the end of the week or the month and discover that you'd run out of money? Well, at one time or another, we all have, and yes, it's because we didn't exercise proper control. But control is not only about keeping our finances in order—it has a much broader and more important role to play in hospitality management. All hospitality managers need to use a variety of control measures to check whether the results they achieve are in line with expectations and, if not, to take corrective actions. The control process even sets the parameters for managerial action by setting up control by exception, meaning that managers take action only if the results are outside the acceptable range. Control is often used in conjunction with techniques such as Total Quality Management by allowing associates and management to establish guest service levels.

Control is about keeping score and setting up ways to give us feedback on how we are doing. The feedback leads to corrective action, if necessary. For instance, if a chef and restaurant manager forecast 250 covers and 320 people actually come, then they will have to prep more food items in a hurry and guide servers to recommend certain dishes in order to avoid running out of too many menu items. These and the many other examples we will read about in this chapter are all control related.

Control has close links to each of the other management functions, especially planning, which, as we know, includes setting goals and making plans on how to reach the goals.

LEARNING OBJECTIVE 1
Define control.

What Is Control?

Control provides a way to check actual results against expected results. Action can then be taken to correct the situation if the results are too far from the expected outcome. If labor costs are 26 percent and they were expected to be 23 percent, the difference is only 3 percent, but that 3 percent could add up to thousands of dollars.

Control is the management function that provides information on the degree to which goals and objectives are being accomplished. Management engages in controlling by monitoring activities and taking corrective actions whenever the goals are not being met. An effective control system ensures that activities that lead to the attainment of the organization's goals are completed.

Control is far broader than you might think. It's not just about checking on outcomes; it is also about providing guidelines and mechanisms to keep things on track by making sure there are no surprises when the results are known. Control is also about keeping your eyes and ears open. Every place seems to have someone who steals, so as a Swiss hotel manager mentor once said to me in his heavy accent, "John, before you can stop someone else stealing the chicken, you must first know how to steal the chicken." The best way to avoid these losses is to have a tight control system.

Why is Control Important?

LEARNING OBJECTIVE 2
Give reasons why control is important.

Why is control so important? Control is important because it's the final link in the management functions. It's the only way managers know whether organizational goals are being met and, if not, why not. Controlling is involved with planning, organizing, and leading. Figure 18–1 shows the relationship between controlling and the other management functions.

Goals give specific direction to managers. Effective hospitality managers need to follow up constantly to ensure that what others are supposed to do is being done and that goals are being met. Managers need to develop an effective control system—one that can provide information and feedback on employee performance. An effective control system is important because managers need to delegate duties and empower employees to make decisions. But managers are responsible for performance results, so they also need a feedback mechanism—which control provides.

Given that management involves leading, planning, organizing, communicating, motivating, and controlling, you might easily get the impression that maintaining control is just something managers do after they are finished planning, organizing, and leading. For example, controlling always requires that some desirable outcomes, such as targets, standards, or goals,

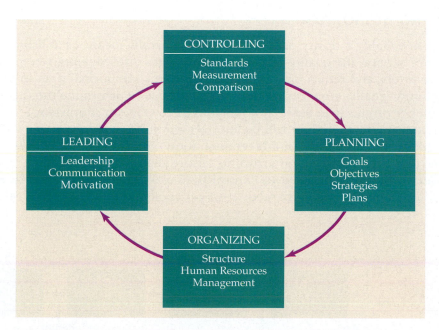

Figure 18–1 • Relationship between Controlling and the Other Management Functions.

Source: Modified from Stephen P. Robbins and Mary Coulter, *Management*, 13th ed. (Hoboken, NJ: Prentice Hall, 2014), 525.

be set. Similarly, much of what managers do when they have their leadership hats on involves making sure that employees are doing and will do the things they are supposed to do. However, the sort of self-motivation that derives from empowering teams and putting them in charge is often the better alternative.

▶ Check Your Knowledge

1. Define control.
2. Why is control important?

The Control Process

The **control process** is a five-step process of determining goals, setting standards, measuring actual performance, comparing actual performance against those standards, and taking managerial action to correct deviations or inadequate performances (Figure 18–2). These standards are the specific goals created during the planning process against which performance progress can be measured.

Setting Standards

In the hospitality industry, setting standards generally means establishing the levels of service, the quality of food and beverages offered, employee performance levels, and return on investment. Standards are normally set in terms of quantity, quality, finances, or time. A caterer has to determine the quantity or number of guests to serve at a function. If the caterer purchases food for too many guests, then food will be left over, but if he or she prepares for too few guests, then there will not be enough food. When a chef purchases food items, they are controlled on arrival to ensure that the right quality is being delivered. Budgets are used to control financial expenditures, and time is used, for example, to control labor costs—a cook should take only a certain

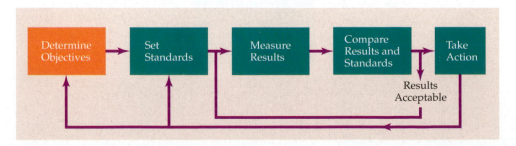

Figure 18–2 • The Control Process.

number of minutes to prepare a batch of pasta and vegetables.

A word of caution: When developing a method of **measurement**, one must be absolutely sure that the goals are indeed measurable. Now, as convoluted as that may sound, let's illustrate the point.

Suppose after careful planning, with input from staff, all agree that labor costs are too high at 28 percent. So the decision is made to reduce labor costs, and that becomes a stated goal—one to which it is hard to object. At the end of the month, the kitchen still has a labor cost of 28 percent, so it has not achieved the goal. During your discussion with the personnel responsible, they claim that their plan to reduce labor costs will not be effective until two months hence. You remind them that the goal was to reduce labor costs, they agree that

Information for control purposes can be acquired by a variety of methods, including checklists.

it was, and you point out that last month's labor cost and this month's are the same. Who is correct here? The answer: neither. The goal of reducing labor costs is inadequate and it is not measurable or attainable on your part. The kitchen staff has put a plan into effect that they feel will reduce labor costs by the end of the following month; they feel they are doing all that you asked. The dilemma is that the goal lacks *specificity*. Had the goal been to decrease labor costs to 24 percent by the end of February, it would be measurable and attainable. Then we could say to the kitchen staff that they hadn't met the stated goal, but because we didn't quantify the goal, they are correct.

Measuring

Managers must first know what they are measuring and how they are measuring it before they can measure expected performance. Personal observation—by monitoring subordinates to make sure things are done right—is the simplest and most common way of comparing actual performance to standards. So, for example, the chef can see whether the cook is cutting, slicing, and dicing correctly and whether the right amount is being prepared according to the standardized recipe.

Direct Supervision

The purpose of direct supervision is to detect problems of associate-specific actions as they occur and to make corrections immediately in order to keep associates' actions in line with management's expectations.

How We Measure

Four common sources of information frequently used by managers to measure actual performance are personal observation, statistical reports, oral reports, and written reports.

Management by walking around (MBWA) is the best way to make personal observations. MBWA is a phrase used to describe when a manager is out in the work area, interacting directly with associates and exchanging information about what is happening. MBWA can pick up factual omissions, facial expressions, and tones of voice that may be missed by other sources. Front-office managers will not be aware of how guests are being checked in during the busy early evening check-in period if they are in their offices at that time.

Statistical reports provide information in the form of data that measure results and can be used for comparative purposes. They also use charts, graphs, and other displays that are easy to visualize. Some managers keep charts on the key result areas and plot the department's progress. Others place safety charts on the associate notice board. These charts visually display the importance of safety and the number of accident-free days, which is another type of goal often sought.

Control information can be acquired through oral reports, conferences, meetings, one-on-one conversations, or telephone calls. The advantage of oral control reports is that they can be quick and allow instant feedback in

A DAY IN THE LIFE OF CHERRY CERMINARA

Dietitian and Retired General Manager, Sodexo, Gibsonia, Pennsylvania

I am a registered dietitian and a retired general manager of a K–12 school foodservice program. I worked for the management company Sodexo. Sodexo had been contracted to manage the food and nutrition program for the five-building, 4,000-student school where I served.

Sodexo School Services leads the nation in providing food and facilities management solutions that support the educational process. From nutrition education to monitoring air quality, their efforts enable students and faculty to perform at a high level consistently. Every day, Sodexo serves the needs of more than 400 school districts. Their expertise allows school administrators to focus on education leadership activities. Best of all, their partnering approach always saves money. The programs have been tested, and the results are conclusive: Sodexo's food service and facilities management solutions improve the quality of life for students, faculty, and the communities they serve.

As a general manager for a school food service operation, a day might include hiring, training, and managing employees; ordering foods; taking inventory; budget management; financial reporting; menu preparation; production; and nutrition. School meals operations are regulated by the U.S. Department of Agriculture for nutrition according to age-specific needs. Both breakfast and lunch are served. Nutrition education is also provided both in the classroom and in the lunchroom. Other areas of concentration include food safety, following hazard analysis and critical control points (HACCP), and physical safety for employees and customers. School foods ervice program sare audited every year by NSF and at least twice per year by the county health department.

As a manager, I would focus my day-to-day operations on customer service. We would look at the students, staff, parents, and administration as our customers. It was my job to train my employees to respect this aspect of their performance. If we weren't aware of our customers as a whole, we would risk losing revenue and perhaps losing the business to another company perceived to provide a better service. Providing management services to Pine-Richland School District in Gibsonia, Pennsylvania, was really a pleasure. Well-managed, trained, and enthusiastic employees worked with me at Pine-Richland. The employees and the direct relationships to our customers all contributed to the company's success.

the form of a two-way conversation. A manager can inquire about the status of a function and get immediate feedback from the banquet captain. In the often fast-paced hospitality industry, oral control communication is often more effective than other forms of communication. For example, every time a restaurant service team has an "alley rally" (a quick huddle/meeting), they are, in part, using oral control communication to let servers know what to sell, what the specials are—so guests can be encouraged to order them—instead of "slamming" the kitchen with multiple à la carte orders.

Written reports are also used to measure performance. Like statistical reports, these are slower yet more formal than personal observation or oral reports. Written reports generally have more information than oral ones and are usually easy to file and retrieve. General managers usually expect to see the daily report, which gives details of the performance results from the day before, on their desks as they walk into their offices. However, they also want a verbal report from any department they may visit on the way to the office, such as, "Did we sell out last night?"

Given the varied advantages of each of these measurement approaches, comprehensive control efforts by managers should use all four sources of information.

What We Measure

We measure results to see how they compare with expectations. What we measure is more critical than how we measure—what if we are measuring the wrong thing? The results we measure include guest satisfaction, labor costs, food and beverage costs, employee satisfaction, rooms and room rates, bed sheets, energy costs, insurance, and labor turnover.

In simple terms, we measure labor costs because they are the highest of the variable costs. Did we meet our goal of a 24-percent labor cost reduction? Next, did we meet our goal of a 28-percent food cost? To find out if we met our goals, we would need to set up control measuring procedures regarding the daily monitoring of labor costs. Estimates of sales are given to department heads, who then plan and organize their labor costs accordingly. In other words, if we know our sales we can then keep our labor costs at 24 percent. For example, for food and beverage cost control, we would scrutinize ordering, purchasing, storing, issuing, preparing, and serving of the various food items. We would take inventory, calculate the actual cost of the food, and express the cost as a percentage of sales. Remember, it's the cost over sales × 100.

Whenever performance results can be measured, it is desirable to consider a results-accountability system. Some control criteria are applicable to any management situation. For instance, because all managers, by definition, coordinate the work of others, criteria such as employee satisfaction or turnover and absenteeism rates can be measured.

Most managers have budgets set in dollar costs for their areas of responsibility. Keeping costs within budget is, therefore, a fairly common control measure. However, one of the main purposes of control is to

Effective Managers

Effective managers first control the "big ticket" items that will be costly if not controlled. Once the more costly items are under control, they can move on to other, less costly items.

influence behavior. Therefore, a results-accountability control system must be able to detect deviations from desired results quickly enough to allow for timely corrective management action.

Having timely information and acting on that information is crucial in avoiding the following situation: Why is it that at some hospitality operations, each month's income statement results take almost a month to complete? Because of the delay in producing the results, thousands of dollars are lost before any problems can be fixed.

Comparing Results

Comparing results with expectations shows the amount of variation between actual performance and the standard or expected results. Some variation is generally seen between the expected and the actual results—but how big is the variation? The range of variation is the acceptable difference between the actual and expected results.

Managers are concerned with the size and direction of the variance. Let's look at an example: If guest surveys show that one department is not performing up to expectations, then management would make decisions to have the problem fixed. But what if that didn't work? Then more drastic action would be necessary. Meanwhile, the survey scores would continue to drop. Management would quickly find out in which direction and how fast the barometer of guest satisfaction was moving.

Taking Managerial Action

The final step in the control process is taking managerial action. **Correcting actual performance** is used by managers if the source of the performance variation is unsatisfactory. For instance, **corrective action** may include changing the way the job tasks are done, changing strategy (doing different tasks), changing structure (changing supervisors'/managers' compensation practices), changing training programs, redesigning jobs, or firing employees.

A manager who decides to correct actual performance then has to make another decision: Does he or she use **immediate corrective action**, which corrects problems at once to get performance back on track, or **basic corrective action**, which looks at how and why performance has deviated and then proceeds to correct the source of deviation? Many managers say they don't have time to take corrective action, yet they are the ones perpetually "putting out fires."

Effective managers analyze deviations and, when the benefits justify it, take the time to pinpoint and correct the causes of variance. This kind of control begins with effective associate selection and training. Hiring the right person for the job and ensuring that associates are properly trained increase the chance that associates can be trusted to do the right thing.

Good communication is critical to associate control for a number of reasons. The most important reason is that good communication helps associates understand what is expected of them. Employee performance reviews take on added significance when viewed from the control perspective. Rather than a method of reviewing past performance, they become a control technique. By rewarding and praising desired behavior, management can use performance reviews to shape future behavior. The opposite will be true of undesirable behavior. Performance reviews are also a good time to consider training, reassignment, raises, and promotion decisions.

> ### Whom Do We Bill?
>
> A funny lack-of-control story happened at a five-star hotel restaurant close to Christmas, when a guest signed the check for his table's extravagant business lunch as "S. Claus." The server, thinking that the guest had signing privileges, gave the check to the restaurant cashier, who in turn sent it up to the billing office so that it would go out to the client at the end of the month. Three days later, the check came back to the restaurant with the question "Which company is he with?"

It is important to note the motivating influences of raises and promotions and how they act as a form of control. Granting raises and awarding promotions based solely on operating results criteria and desired behavior send an important message to all associates. Those actions say that performance and behavior are being monitored and are the basis for personnel decisions. In this way employee actions are controlled.

▶ Check Your Knowledge

1. Describe the five-step control process.

2. What are the four common sources of information managers use to measure employee performance?

3. Explain the difference between immediate corrective action and basic corrective action.

Types of Control

LEARNING OBJECTIVE 4
Distinguish among the three types of control.

Managers can use controls *in advance* of an activity (feedforward control), *during* the activity (concurrent control), and *after* the activity has been completed (feedback control). Figure 18–3 shows the three types of control.

Feedforward control focuses on preventing anticipated problems because it takes place in advance of the work activity. For example, by carefully explaining the policy on billing for catering functions, a catering manager uses feedforward control to explain to the client that an accurate number of people attending the function must be given in order for the correct space to be allocated for the function. A follow-up number is to be given three months, one month, and two weeks before the event, and final guaranteed numbers are required 48 hours before a function. This is the number for which food is purchased, prepared, and charged accordingly. By working closely with the client, the catering manager ensures that there are no surprises.

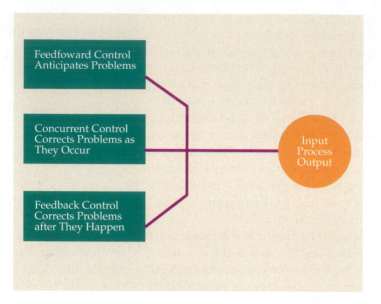

Figure 18–3 • Three Types of Control.

In the kitchen, recipes are an example of feedforward control; they prescribe the quantity of each ingredient necessary to make a particular dish. Recipes also help with consistency by making each dish look and taste the same. (That could be good or bad!) Without recipes, we know the result is going to be a disaster.

Another example of feedforward control occurred when McDonald's opened in Moscow. McDonald's sent quality control experts to help Russian farmers learn techniques for growing high-quality potatoes and bakers to teach processes for baking high-quality breads. Why? Because McDonald's strongly emphasizes product quality no matter the geographic location. It wants a McDonald's cheeseburger in Moscow to taste like one in New York.[1]

Airlines do preventive maintenance on their aircraft; restaurants do the same on their kitchen equipment to prevent any breakdowns during operation. Resorts and hotels also conduct preventive maintenance on the building, the air conditioning system, and so on. These are all examples of feedforward controls.

Feedforward controls are helpful in that they encourage managers to *prevent* problems rather than *react* to them. The challenge is that feedforward controls take more time to organize than the other types of control; however, they save time in the long run.

Concurrent control is a type of control that takes place while a work activity is in progress. When control is enacted while the work is being performed, management can correct problems before they become too costly. The best form of concurrent control is direct supervision, when a manager can concurrently monitor the actions of associates and correct problems as they occur. Although some delay results between the activity and the manager's corrective response, the delay is minimal. For instance, you may have experienced concurrent control when using word-processing software that alerts you to misspelled words or incorrect grammar. In addition, many organizational quality programs rely on concurrent controls to inform workers if their work output is of sufficient quality to meet standards. Chefs use concurrent control when checking how a recipe is being prepared; the cook can be guided on the correct consistency of a product.

Feedback control, the most popular type of control, takes place after the activity is done. For example, financial statements are examples of feedback control. If, for instance, the income statement shows that sales revenues are declining, the decline has already occurred. The manager's only option is try to determine why sales decreased and to correct the situation.

Feedback control is helpful in hospitality industry situations in which a number of activities repeat themselves: Guests make reservations, are welcomed, checked in, roomed, wined and dined, and so on, so resorts and hotels have developed several controls that help measure and report on these activities. These controls include guest surveys, comment cards, and outside checkers who stay at a property and give a detailed report to management on their findings.

Chefs frequently use concurrent control.

Feedback control has two advantages over feedforward and concurrent control. First, feedback provides managers with meaningful information on how effective their planning efforts were. Feedback that indicates little variance between standard and actual performance is evidence that the planning was generally on target. If the deviation is significant, a manager can use the information when formulating new plans to make them more effective. Second, feedback control can enhance employee motivation. Associates generally want information on how well they have performed.

Remember the profile of TGI Fridays earlier in this book, in which as the food cost percentage was expected to be 27 percent and the actual was 27.2 percent, meaning the variance was 0.2 of a percentage point? That is feedback control. When a theme park forecasts an attendance of 30,000 on a particular day and the actual comes in at 32,000, that's feedback control.

Other Types of Control

Corporate Control

The catering manager of a large convention and banqueting department received a memo stating that no overtime could be worked unless the food and beverage (F&B) director authorized it in advance. For a busy department that did thousands of dollars in business every day and was responsible for most of the F&B division's profit, that memo from the corporate office was not well received—how can we prevent clients from changing their minds at the last minute, and how dare the corporate office impose on our operation in this way? In retrospect, the department was caught up in a blanket policy to reduce labor costs by using feedforward control, and it worked because many of the not-so-profitable departments were abusing overtime payments to their associates. The convention and banqueting department services manager planned and scheduled the work more effectively, and the catering managers were able to persuade clients to avoid last-minute room changes by explaining that it would involve additional charges at overtime rates. Incentives were also given to clients to select room setups that would involve fewer complete room changes (from a dinner to a classroom setup when a cabaret might be equally as suitable). Substantial company-wide savings were made, and the convention and banqueting department reacted positively to the change (after a brief period of complaining). They also saved several thousand dollars, which, of course, went straight to the bottom line.

Food and Beverage Controls

Ask any food and beverage operator about controls and you are likely to get a serious look followed by a comment about how important control is to the operation. Lots of money can be made or lost depending on how tight the control is. Most operations take inventory and calculate the food and beverage costs expressed as a percentage of sales at least once, sometimes twice, a month. A glance at this book's index will indicate several pages where food and beverage controls are discussed in detail, so here we will look at control from a management perspective.

When you become a manager and assume responsibility for controlling food and beverage items, the first thing to do is to get the locks changed because you have no idea who has access to what. The second thing is to review all control procedures. If you really want to exercise tight control, insist that all orders have your signature or approval—that way, you know what should be received. Next, the stores need to be under the authority and responsibility of one person who is held accountable for all items under his or her control.

▶ Check Your Knowledge

1. Distinguish among the three types of control.
2. When is feedforward control used?
3. What is the difference between concurrent control and feedback control?

LEARNING OBJECTIVE 5
Explain the important financial controls.

Operational Financial Controls

At the operational level in the hospitality industry, the financial controls mainly consist of **budgets** and **income statements**. Budgets "guesstimate" the sales figure for the month or year and allow for up to a specific dollar amount to be spent on any cost of goods sold or controllable-costs item. Just preparing the budget has a control-like effect on managers. They are responsible for the financial outcome of their departments and rely heavily on budgets. Instead of just allowing departments to budget the same amount year in and year out, **zero-based budgeting** has managers begin with a budget of zero dollars and justify all the cost of goods sold, controllable costs, and capital expenditures (such as equipment) they plan on making so that there will be an appropriate amount of profit.

Income statements show the actual sales and expenditures for a month or year. They are used extensively in the hospitality industry as a means of control because they are results driven. Managers use the results for controlling the next period's performance. For example, if the results of the beverage department come in below expectations, then corrective action in the form of increased spot-checks would immediately be instigated, along with more frequent inventory checks. Figure 18–4 shows a hotel income statement.

As stated earlier, but worth repeating, good managers first control the "big ticket" items that will be most costly if not controlled. Once the most costly items are under control, managers can move on to controlling other items. Looking at the labor costs in a hospitality operation is the largest of the controllable costs. Labor costs, like any other, need to be controlled in line with sales. Each department will have its own desired labor cost expressed as a percentage of sales. If sales go up, it is easier to control labor costs. However, if sales go down, then management must control labor costs in order to avoid losing more than absolutely necessary. Management also needs to be fair with associates. After the September 11, 2001, tragedy, Marriott set an example at many of its hotels and resorts by not laying off any associates—it instead reduced everyone's hours, which did a lot to keep associates loyal.

In managerial accounting, food and beverage costs are the next largest to be controlled after labor costs. Attractions such as Sea World, clubs, resorts, hotels, and restaurants all offer food and beverages to their guests. All food and beverage items need to be costed and priced in advance to yield a certain percentage—let's say 24 percent. We all know that these percentages will vary from one organization to another; the point is both that food and beverage departments need to be controlled to produce the expected results and that income statements provide written feedback control.

Things such as recipes, portion control, proper purchasing, storage, issuing, and preparation of all food and beverage items help ensure that items reach the guest correctly. Next, we need to ensure that all monies reach the bank—no fingers in the cash register! No bags in the kitchen, no internal trades between departments. A proper system must be in place for recording all sales and ensuring that the correct amount is received from guests. Hospitality operators can choose from several point-of-sale systems and front- and back-of-the-house systems to assist the control process in making the job easier.

INCOME STATEMENT
APRIL 2015

	CURRENT MONTH						YEAR TO DATE					
	CURRENT	%	BUDGET	%	LAST YR	%	CURRENT	%	BUDGET	%	LAST YR	%
REVENUE												
ROOMS	291,371	61.5%	310,270	66.3%	312,768	66.5%	1,106,897	63.5%	1,150,835	66.1%	1,167,731	64.3%
FOOD	136,868	28.9%	111,503	23.8%	108,176	23.0%	453,192	26.0%	414,868	23.8%	449,848	24.8%
BEVERAGE	22,830	4.8%	23,717	5.1%	26,470	5.6%	90,041	5.2%	84,787	4.9%	100,355	5.5%
TELEPHONE	5,473	1.2%	4,593	1.0%	6,686	1.4%	18,634	1.1%	17,390	1.0%	28,852	1.6%
SUNDRIES	367	0.1%	651	0.1%	798	0.2%	2,020	0.1%	2,368	0.1%	2,868	0.2%
OTHER INCOME	16,605	3.5%	17,270	3.7%	15,109	3.2%	72,914	4.2%	71,108	4.1%	66,559	3.7%
TOTAL REVENUE	473,514	100.0%	468,004	100.0%	470,007	100.0%	1,743,698	100.0%	1,741,356	100.0%	1,816,213	100.0%
DEPT EXPENSES												
ROOMS	68,874	23.6%	68,671	22.1%	63,403	20.3%	272,356	24.6%	273,771	23.8%	246,979	21.2%
FOOD	138,332	101.1%	115,108	103.2%	96,580	89.3%	468,515	103.4%	427,109	103.0%	398,509	88.6%
BEVERAGE	12,809	56.1%	11,080	46.7%	11,464	43.3%	46,567	51.7%	41,676	49.2%	49,675	49.5%
TELEPHONE	4,636	84.7%	4,867	106.0%	5,628	84.2%	20,543	110.2%	19,793	113.8%	21,234	73.6%
SUNDRIES	213	58.0%	418	64.2%	990	124.1%	1,957	96.9%	1,578	66.6%	2,744	95.7%
OTHER INCOME	10,531	63.4%	12,741	73.8%	12,956	85.8%	43,047	59.0%	56,513	79.5%	44,364	66.7%
TOT DEPT EXPENSES	235,395	49.7%	212,885	45.5%	191,021	40.6%	852,985	48.9%	820,440	47.1%	763,505	42.0%
DEPT PROFIT	238,119	50.3%	255,119	54.5%	278,986	59.4%	890,713	51.1%	920,916	52.9%	1,052,708	58.0%
UNDIST EXPENSES												
ADMIN & GENL	47,054	9.9%	38,531	8.2%	43,762	9.3%	206,582	11.8%	168,784	9.7%	184,744	10.2%
MARKETING	26,619	5.6%	30,139	6.4%	15,458	3.3%	91,079	5.2%	88,953	5.1%	57,023	3.1%
REPAIR & MAINT	26,767	5.7%	39,621	8.5%	37,668	8.0%	142,323	8.2%	165,966	9.5%	130,646	7.2%
GROUNDS	22,662	4.8%	26,650	5.7%	29,897	6.4%	108,114	6.2%	107,024	6.1%	95,284	5.2%
UTILITIES	20,494	4.3%	26,785	5.7%	19,010	4.0%	85,988	4.9%	99,652	5.7%	83,380	4.6%
TOT UNDIST EXP	143,596	30.3%	161,726	34.6%	145,795	31.0%	634,086	36.4%	630,379	36.2%	551,077	30.3%
GROSS OPER PROFIT	94,523	20.0%	93,393	20.0%	133,191	28.3%	256,627	14.7%	290,537	16.7%	501,631	27.6%
FIXED EXPENSES												
PROP TAXES	5,734	1.2%	5,734	1.2%	5,099	1.1%	27,015	1.5%	26,983	1.5%	24,443	1.3%
INSURANCE	2,622	0.6%	2,622	0.6%	1,700	0.4%	10,488	0.6%	10,488	0.6%	6,800	0.4%
INTEREST	1,220	0.3%	1,252	0.3%	1,345	0.3%	4,944	0.3%	5,008	0.3%	5,442	0.3%
INCOME TAXES	0	0.0%	0	0.0%	0	0.0%	0	0.0%	0	0.0%	0	0.0%
DEPREC	26,000	5.5%	26,000	5.6%	26,000	5.5%	104,000	6.0%	104,000	6.0%	100,000	5.5%
TOT FIXED EXP	35,576	7.5%	35,608	7.6%	34,144	7.3%	146,447	8.4%	146,479	8.4%	136,685	7.5%
NET INCOME	58,947	12.4%	57,785	12.3%	99,047	21.1%	110,180	6.3%	144,058	8.3%	364,946	20.1%
ROOMS AVAIL	2,580		2,580		2,670		10,320		10,320		10,680	
ROOMS OCCUPIED	1,495		1,670		1,797		5,747		6,078		6,529	
OCCUPANCY %	57.9%		64.7%		67.3%		55.7%		58.9%		61.1%	
AVG RATE	$151.63		$147.30		$141.56		$147.84		$147.09		$142.50	

Figure 18–4 • Sample Hotel Income Statement.

HOW TO CONTROL PAYROLL THROUGH SCHEDULING AND MANAGEMENT

Courtesy of **James McManemon**, M.S., University of South Florida Sarasota–Manatee

Alejandro Rivera is the restaurant manager of a large, full-service boutique hotel. He took the time to explain the importance of controlling payroll through proper planning, scheduling, and schedule management, for the purposes of reducing overtime and unnecessary labor hours.

Alejandro pointed out that the most important part of controlling payroll is to accurately forecast your scheduling needs one week prior to creating a schedule. In this full-service hotel, the food and beverage department consists of a three-meal restaurant and a bar, which is also open for three meals, serving as a coffee bar during breakfast and a traditional bar during lunch and dinner service. Additionally, in this hotel, almost all of the restaurant guests are in-house guests.

Before setting a weekly employee schedule, Alejandro finds that it is first important to determine the forecasted number of guests expected to attend each meal period throughout the week. This can be most accurately accomplished by determining the average number of guests that dined in the restaurant during each meal period from the same month of the previous year to date.

In January 2015, the 250-room hotel had an occupancy rate of 90 percent (approximately 225 guests), and the restaurant saw an average of 90 guests during breakfast (40% of in-house guests), 68 guests during lunch (30% of in-house guests), and 68 guests during dinner (30% of in-house guests). These numbers (40% breakfast, 30% lunch, 30% dinner) provide a good estimate for calculating the expected number of guests for January 2016.

Let's say in the first week of January 2016, the hotel is expected to be 60 percent full Monday, Tuesday, and Wednesday; 70 percent full Thursday; and 85 percent full Friday and Saturday. Using these numbers, we could expect to see 60 guests for breakfast [(250 × 60%) × (40%)] and 45 guests each for lunch and dinner [(250 × 60%) × (30%)] on Monday, Tuesday, and Wednesday. So, when forecasting a schedule, you wouldlower the number of staff on Monday through Wednesday and then increase the number of staff for the weekend when the occupancy picks up.

Of course, as Alejandro points out, these numbers are estimates and do not necessarily reflect the true number of guests that the restaurant will see. It will also be necessary to manage the schedule and adjust the number of staff required as accurately as possible in *real* time, in order to ensure you control the payroll effectively.

Qualities of an Effective Control System

LEARNING OBJECTIVE 6
Describe the qualities of an effective control system.

Effective control systems tend to have certain characteristics in common.[2] The importance of these qualities varies with the situation; however, all effective control systems exhibit the following ten characteristics:

1. *Accuracy.* An effective control system is reliable and produces valid data.
2. *Timeliness.* An effective control system can be relied upon to provide information when most useful.

3. *Economy.* An effective control system is cost effective to operate.

4. *Flexibility.* An effective control system is one that adjusts relatively easy to changes and opportunities.

5. *Understandability.* The user can readily explain an effective control system.

6. *Reasonable criteria.* Control standards are both understandable and attainable.

7. *Strategic placement.* Because managers can't control everything, they must choose to control factors that are essential to the organization's performance.

8. *Emphasis on exceptions.* Managers can't control all activities; control devices call attention only to the exceptions.

9. *Multiple criteria.* Measures decrease tendencies toward a narrow focus.

10. *Corrective action.* The control system not only indicates significant deviations, but also suggests appropriate corrective action.

Experienced managers use effective controls by exception, meaning that if the results are outside the acceptable predetermined limits, then they take action; otherwise they concentrate on something else.

Contingency Plans and Control

The most important contingency plan factor that affects the design of an organization's control system is the size of the organization. The control system should vary according to the organization's size. A small organization relies more on informal and personal control approaches. Here, concurrent control (direct supervision) is probably the most cost effective. However, as organizations increase in size, direct supervision is likely to be supplemented by an expanding formal control system of reports, regulations, and rules. Very large organizations typically have highly formalized and impersonal feedforward and feedback controls. Contingency plans and control cover the *what-ifs*—what if our sales dip 8 percent? What will we do? Reduce associate hours, reduce expenditures, and attempt to boost sales.

As you move up in the organization's hierarchy, there is a greater need for several different types of control; this reflects increased operational complexities. Additionally, the greater the degree of decentralization, the more managers will need feedback on employees' decisions and performance results. Managers who delegate authority for making decisions and performing work are still ultimately responsible for the actions of those to whom the authority was delegated.

The importance of an activity influences whether and how it will be controlled. However, if a particular error can be highly damaging to the organization, extensive controls to prevent that error are likely to be implemented. It simply makes sense to control the big-ticket items.

Adjusting Controls for Cultural Differences

Control is used quite differently in other countries.[3] The differences in organizational control systems of global organizations are seen primarily in the measurement and corrective-action steps of the control process. In a global hospitality corporation, managers of foreign operations tend to be controlled less directly by the home office, for no other reason than the distance keeps managers from being able to observe work directly. Because distance creates a tendency to formalize controls, the home office of a global company often relies on extensive formal reports for control. Global companies rely on the power of information technology to provide speedy control reports of results.

Technology's impact on control can also be seen when comparing technologically advanced nations with less technologically advanced countries. In countries such as the United States, Japan, Canada, the United Kingdom, France, Germany, and Australia, managers of global companies use indirect control devices, particularly computer-related reports and analyses, in addition to standardized rules and direct supervision, to ensure that work activities are going as planned.

In less technologically advanced countries, managers tend to rely more on direct supervision and highly centralized decision making for control. Also, constraints on what corrective actions managers can take may affect managers in foreign countries because laws in some countries do not allow managers the option of choosing the facilities, laying off employees, taking money out of the country, or bringing in a new management team from outside the country.

▶ Check Your Knowledge

1. Explain the important financial controls.
2. Describe the qualities of an effective control system.

Contemporary Issues in Control

LEARNING OBJECTIVE 7
Outline the contemporary issues in control.

One issue that can arise from control systems involves information technology: Technological advances in computer hardware and software have made the process of controlling much easier, but these advances have brought with them difficult questions regarding what managers have the right to know about employee behavior.[4] Another issue is workplace privacy.

Workplace Privacy

If you work, do you think you have a right to privacy at your workplace? What can your employer find out about you and your work? You may be surprised by the answer. Why do managers feel they must monitor what employees are doing? One reason is that employees are hired to work, not to surf the Web checking stock prices, placing bets at online casinos, or shopping for presents for family or friends.

Personal on-the-job web surfing costs millions of dollars a year in wasted computer resources and billions of dollars in lost work productivity. Another reason why managers monitor employee e-mail and computer usage is that they don't want to risk being sued for creating a hostile workplace environment because of offensive messages or an inappropriate image displayed on a coworker's computer screen. Concern about sexual harassment is one of the reasons why companies may want to monitor or keep backup copies of all e-mail. This can help establish what actually happened if an incident arises and can help managers react instantly. Managers also need to be certain that employees are not inadvertently passing information on to others who could use that information to harm the company.

A Prepay Restaurant

There is a great hole-in-the-wall restaurant in New York City where arguably the best front-end control system is in place. Servers have to pay the cooks for the guest's food—so they will definitely get the money from the guests.

Employee Theft

Would it surprise you to know that a high percentage of all organizational theft and fraud is committed by employees, not outsiders? Any unauthorized taking of company property by employees for their personal use constitutes employee theft, including fraudulent filing of expense reports and removing equipment, software, and office supplies from the company premises. Hospitality businesses have long faced serious losses from employee theft caused by loose financial controls, especially at the start-up of a business.

Why do employees steal? There are several perspectives. Industrial loss-prevention professionals suggest that people steal because the opportunity presents itself through lax controls and favorable circumstances. Some people have different financial problems or pressures such as gambling debts. People steal because they can rationalize whatever they're doing as being correct and appropriate behavior. Hospitality associates also steal because they often feel underpaid, so whether it's a phone call here or a knife, fork, and spoon there, if the opportunity arises, they may take advantage of it. Notice how the concepts of feedforward, concurrent, and feedback control to identify measures for deterring or reducing employee theft apply.

Increased use of computers at the workplace poses privacy risks.

Workplace Violence

Factors contributing to workplace violence include employee stress caused by long working hours, information overload, daily interruptions, unrealistic deadlines, and uncaring managers.

You may not think that these factors apply to where you work, but some of these factors appear in a good many corporations, especially with the pressure of making a profit in the increasingly competitive 24/7/365 environment.

Control is critical in the hospitality industry because we need to know how we are doing all the time. We need to know whether goals are being met and standards reached or exceeded. According to the situation, well-managed hospitality businesses use a variety of controls to provide the necessary information to management for decision-making purposes.

INTRODUCING MICHAEL R. THORPE

The Leader of the Future Will Be a Holistic One

Michael R. Thorpe, who has earned a Bachelor of Science degree in hotel and restaurant management, is an outstanding example of the leadership skills that can be acquired throughout the school and college career.

Mike's leadership abilities developed from an early age, with his involvement in the Boy Scouts of America. Looking back at that memorable time, Mike recognizes how important it is for a leader to be a good role model. He emphasizes the fact that it is necessary to make a sharp distinction between "good" leaders and "bad" leaders, thus establishing a learning process that is based on the identification of both "shoulds" (positive examples, experiences, activities, skills) and "should nots" (mistakes, negative attitudes). Mike's experience with the Boy Scouts provided him with fundamental values and skills, which were acknowledged when he achieved the rank of Eagle Scout.

In high school as well as in college, Mike progressively developed and used his leadership skills. He believes that the key to learning is involvement. In fact, he always took part in school activities, also emphasizing the importance of maintaining a broad horizon of interests. In particular, Mike chose to actively participate in a variety of extracurricular activities, including academic, service-oriented, and sports organizations. He stressed the belief that there is a strict correlation among such fields, which shapes the overall personality of the leader. "The leader of the future will be a holistic one," Mike says.

Mike's involvement in academic organizations, such as the student body government council, in sports (as captain of the football team and vice president of the football club), and in service-oriented enterprises (such as the Hosteur's Society HRTM Club, to which he was elected president), helped him develop the necessary skills for high-quality interaction with people. He learned that a good leader is someone who can gather a group of individuals and coordinate each single talent, skill, propensity, and personality into a successful team, joining forces in the pursuit of one common goal. Each member of the team must be fulfilled in his or her need for belonging, personal satisfaction, recognition, and so on. To accomplish this task, Mike understood that a leader must also be extremely respectful of each individual's personal life, needs, problems, cultural background, and diversity, setting aside personal likes and dislikes. Diversity also provides an opportunity for the leader to learn from the people he or she guides, an opportunity that every leader must have the humility and willingness to pursue.

In Mike's words, the leader must act as the "glue" that unites people and the organizer who finds the right place for each individual, a place in which he or she will be able to excel and perform at his or her full potential.

(Continued)

INTRODUCING MICHAEL R. THORPE *(Continued)*

Work experience throughout his college career also taught Mike that workers will function at their best in a work environment that is appealing and challenging and that provides them with the right tools—in terms of knowledge, motivation, rewards, and climate—to produce the optimal outcome.

To achieve such results, Mike excludes, as much as possible, the carrot-on-a-stick approach. He feels that such a method is a superficial remedy that doesn't get to the root of the problem—and thus doesn't solve it—and doesn't consider that a leader deals with human beings intrinsically characterized by a distinct intelligence and personality. Furthermore, when dealing with subordinates' failures or mistakes, Mike prefers to approach the person(s) in question from his or her point of view, trying to understand the cause of the inefficiency and establish whether that person's poor performance is determined by his own possible leadership mistake.

Mike greatly respects a leader who creates a sense of cooperation, community, and teamwork. Just as in a family, the leader should step down from an ivory tower and be open to each member of the team, listen, and be willing to help with possible personal problems, emphasizing the importance of open communication. And, as in a family, the leader must be a caring parent who can also progressively impose discipline and obtain the results expected depending on the members' potential.

Mike understands the role of a father because he has a six-year-old who represents, among other things, the ultimate challenge for leadership. "Workers' livelihoods do depend on the employer/leader."

▶ Check Your Knowledge

1. Briefly explain zero-based budgeting.

2. Outline the contemporary issues in control.

3. What are some contributors to workplace violence?

Controlling Sustainability

One of the most important aspects of implementing sustainable practices in hospitality and tourism is the management of sustainable controls. Hotels and restaurants as well as other businesses and organizations must constantly monitor and manage the different aspects of sustainable practices, such as energy, waste, lighting, water, heating and cooling, temperature, and other sources that consume energy. More recently, focus is being placed on integrating sustainability into the planning and development of businesses in the industry. New technologies, such as management control systems, are at the forefront of sustainable practices, which provide necessary controls to monitor and conserve resources and decrease unnecessary waste production resulting in an establishment's enhanced environmental performance.[5]

Energy Management

One of the biggest trends of sustainability in hospitality establishments is energy management through temperature and lighting controls in guestrooms, and throughout hotels. There are a variety of solutions to lighting controls, including occupancy sensors, time switches, energy efficient bulbs, and so on. Panasonic Home & Environment Company recently released the Whisper Welcome ventilation system to a number of lodging establishments to install in their guest bathrooms. This new innovative technology includes both motion and humidity sensors that control the lighting and fans in the bathroom. Hotel owners can efficiently save energy resulting in an increase of money and guest satisfaction. Another feature of the product is the option to include a wall-mounted condensation sensor that controls the fan's activity by determining the level of humidity and air temperature in the room.[6]

The Westin Alexandria has recently announced their plans to install Telkonet Inc.'s new suite energy management system, EcoSmart. The EcoSmart system will be in charge of controlling the water source heat pumps in each of the hotel's guestrooms. The system will monitor the thermostat based on motion sensors and adjust the temperature when the rooms are unoccupied. The ultimate benefit of this new system is projected energy savings of 34 percent annually, which translates to approximately $42,000. Telekonet's CEO claims "Clients have been very generous with their positive feedback on the aesthetics and ease of use of our in-room thermostats. Perhaps most exciting is feedback we've received on EcoCentral, which is Telkonet's cloud-based platform for management and reporting, and is one of the most comprehensive occupancy-based management platforms available."[7]

Waste Reduction

The tourism industry serves many millions of visitors annually. The waste generated by tourists constitutes a large portion of a destination's commercial waste stream. There are many reasons lodging establishments are placing more focus on sustainable practices promoting waste reduction which include "complying with state waste management laws and regulations, improving their image among customers, saving money, and protecting the environment."[8] The increase in sustainable practices throughout the hospitality and tourism industry has resulted from an increase in the public's interest. Restaurants, lodging establishments, and other businesses are finding that promoting a "green" image provides in numerous benefits, resulting in more long-term cost-savings. Recycling waste materials has allowed many establishments to save money by decreasing garbage collection fees.[9]

There are several steps to planning and organizing a waste reduction and recycling program, which begins by arranging a team of employees dedicated to the cause. Next, your team should conduct an audit that determines what is thrown away on a consistent basis in order to evaluate the production of average weekly waste. Then your team can develop a plan with a mission and waste reduction goals to accomplish. The plan should include a system of collecting and storing recyclables. Then you should contact a facility that will collect your recycled materials and make arrangements for recyclables to be collected on a weekly basis. Your team should not only implement this program, but they should encourage all employees to implement the program as well. Finally, you should establish a way to monitor and control the waste reduction and the benefits provided by implementing the program.

Trends in Control

Courtesy of Dr. Greg Dunn, Senior Lecturer & Managing Director, University of Florida, Eric Friedheim Tourism Institute

- *Focus on Variable and Fixed Cost Control.* Hospitality organizations are increasingly challenged to find ways to reduce costs without sacrificing the quality standards imposed to consistently meet guest expectations. The idea of doing more with less requires managers to think about ways to operate more effectively (in other words to "do the right things in the right way") and to examine possibilities for cost savings that will not affect the guest's perception of value. Moreover, with the majority of leading hospitality organizations embracing the art and science of revenue management and optimization to drive the top line, the best of breed companies are also keeping a keen eye on costs and continually looking for ways to keep costs in check. In particular, many firms now use total revenue, gross operating profit, and net profit as key measures of performance. Controlling both "hard costs" and "soft costs" in a hospitality business is important for overall financial success. For instance, in the hotel industry, operating department expenses tend to be highly variable, while the majority of undistributed expenses are mostly fixed in nature. Some lodging expenses, such as utilities, property taxes, and insurance, are largely out of the day-to-day control of management, yet management is evaluated on their top and bottom lines performance.

- *Staffing Guides and Flexible Scheduling.* The best hospitality organizations continue to evaluate and refine their forecasting models, which play an integral role in staffing and labor control. Labor expenses are often the largest expense for many hospitality organizations, and top performers utilize staffing guides and detailed, yet flexible, staffing schedules to control labor use and expenses. Whether your revenues are up or down, controlling your labor costs is essential to maximizing your bottom line. Focusing on productivity as opposed to merely cutting hours or wages maintains the proper balance between labor and quality—it's not efficiency, but effectiveness. If you cut labor and diminish quality, your revenues will go down.

- *Labor Costs.* Labor costs can be controlled through careful planning, attentive scheduling, and improving the productivity of your staff. The first step in improving productivity is to have a plan in place that allocates labor hours based on actual needs and revenue sources. Some hospitality managers have a tendency to over schedule "just in case" but if the extra employees clock in, productivity automatically decreases. A proactive approach to labor control starts with examining the time it takes to perform tasks and how those tasks relate to service volumes. This approach enables an organization to build the labor forecast from the bottom up. Questions that need to be asked include, what is the absolute minimum labor needed to function, and when and why are extra people needed?Determining what those factors are, and building your schedule to them, will improve productivity. The peak time when an additional person is needed may only be three or four hours, so a four-hour overlap shift may be more productive. Alternatively, an eight-hour shift may give more labor than is necessary, and is therefore less productive, unless you can find outside tasks for that person during that shift. Cross-training your staff to perform more than one function is one of the easiest ways to improve productivity. It is common now to see hospitality employees working in two or three different areas of a property during a given shift.

- *Invest in Logistics and Equipment.* The best hospitality companies are investing in logistics and equipment to control costs and drive productivity. Many hospitality organizations still do things inefficiently because of a focus on the capital cost rather than the labor cost associated with the loss of efficiency without that item. Poor logistics and property layouts can be productivity killers. For instance, if a kitchen has an inefficient layout, it creates a need for more labor to work around the design flaw. Depending on the situation, correcting these design flaws may be cost-prohibitive; however, there are times it is simply a matter of improving organization of the work area that will immediately improve productivity. One of the first things you can do is to look at the layout and flow of your key work areas. Things to look for include whether there are labor dollars spent on team members moving items from a storeroom in one area of a facility to the kitchen located in another area or whether it takes longer to find things because storage rooms are disorganized. If so, productivity may be compromised and labor cost negatively affected.

- *Hire and Train to Reduce Turnover.* The hospitality industry, like many of its service industry peers, is faced with a skilled labor shortage. In addition, the hospitality industry is also recognized for its higher levels of employee turnover. Screening, hiring, and training are paramount to the long-term success of a hospitality venue. Many hospitality businesses are strapped looking for good people and sometimes they can get desperate and make bad hiring decisions. Hiring the wrong person may feel like it is taking some of the load off of the existing team, but it often negatively impacts productivity even more. Training is essential. For instance, hiring a new server or front-desk clerk and having that person work with someone for a day, followed by putting them on a shift alone, can be a recipe for disaster and can result in a loss of productivity while negatively impacting employee and guest satisfaction.

Proper and thorough training of your team allows them to be far more productive and also ensures that quality and service standards are maintained. Sometimes, we are pressed in operations and believe that we can't afford the time to train people. The reality is that we can't afford not to—the loss in productivity, quality, and service, in addition to the costs of employee turnover, is far more than the cost of hiring and training right.

CASE STUDY

The Ritz-Carlton

The Ritz-Carlton is an outstanding hotel providing luxury service to its guests. In contrast with the standard goals of typical business hotels—to provide a home away from home—the Ritz-Carlton decided to take it a step further and provide luxury accommodation to industry executives, meeting and corporate travel planners, and other affluent travelers. The chain is based in Chevy Chase, Maryland, and runs 87 luxury hotels that pursue excellence in each market.

The hotel company was awarded the U.S. government's Malcolm Baldrige National Quality Award. The award praised Ritz-Carlton for its participatory leadership, thorough information gathering, coordinated planning and execution, and trained workforce that was ready "to move heaven and earth" to satisfy its customers. Thinking about control, what types of control mechanisms did Ritz-Carlton need to achieve excellence?

Ritz-Carlton's corporate motto is "Ladies and gentlemen serving ladies and gentlemen." All employees are expected to practice the company's "Gold Standards." These standards are made up of a service credo and the basics of premium service, including processes for solving any problem guests may have.

The difference between this luxury chain and other hotel companies is that its employees are "certified" after the common basic orientation followed by an on-the-job training. This certification to work for Ritz-Carlton is reinforced daily by frequent recognition for achievement, performance appraisal, and daily "lineups." Annual surveys are given to make sure the employees know the quality standards the hotel company expects of them as well as to determine their level of satisfaction with the company. One year, 96 percent of the employees surveyed ranked excellence in guest services as their primary duty. Workers are empowered by the company to do whatever it takes to solve any sort of problem a customer may encounter. Employees are required to assist their coworkers in dealing with a guest satisfaction issue, leaving no room for any excuse as to why a customer problem was not solved on the spot. In this way, the guest is truly treated as a king; guest satisfaction comes first—always.[1]

Discussion Questions

1. In what ways does Ritz-Carlton use control to ensure high-quality service?
2. How does the company maintain and foster its employees' high level of commitment?

[1] Adapted from Gary Dessler, *A Framework for Management*, (Upper Saddle River, NJ: Prentice Hall, 2002), 376–377.

Summary

1. Control is the management function that provides information on the degree to which goals and objectives are being accomplished.
2. Control is important because it's the final link in the management function. An effective control system is important because managers need to delegate duties and empower employees to make decisions.
3. The control process can be described as setting standards, measuring actual performance, comparing actual performance against those standards, and taking managerial action to correct deviations or inadequate performances.
4. Managers can use controls *in advance of* an activity, which is called feedforward control; *during* the activity, which is called concurrent control; and *after* the activity, which is called feedback control.
5. Budgets and income statements are primarily used for financial control. Budgets "guesstimate" the sales figure for the month or year and allow for up to a specific dollar amount to be spent on any cost of goods sold or controllable costs item. Income statements show the actual sales and expenditures for a month or year.
6. Effective control systems have 10 characteristics: accuracy, timeliness, economy, flexibility, understandability, reasonable criteria, strategic placement, emphasis on exceptions, multiple criteria, and corrective action.
7. Contemporary issues in control include the increasing use of technological advances, which raise the issue of workplace privacy. Additionally, workplace violence and employee theft are issues in the control process.

Key Words and Concepts

basic corrective action
budget
concurrent control
control
control process

correcting actual performance
corrective action
feedback control
feedforward control
immediate corrective action

income statement
management by walking around (MBWA)
measurement
zero-based budgeting

Review Questions

1. Imagine a restaurant that is lacking any kind of control. Describe the negative and positive aspects of this environment and then answer the following question: Why is control necessary?
2. If you were a manager of a Hilton resort in the Bahamas, what way of measuring actual employee performance would you use and why? What are the pros and cons of your chosen method?
3. Explain the three different types of control. Think of a situation in which you have been controlled. Which type of control works best for you?

4. Describe how you envision an effective control system for a specific hospitality situation. What types of control would you use? How would you measure employee performance? How would you keep employee theft under control? What about workplace violence? Which operational financial control would you implement?

Internet Exercise

1. Organization: **The ePolicy Institute**
   Summary: This site summarizes e-disaster stories.
   (a) Do you think that it's fair for employers to monitor their employees' e-mails?
   (b) What would you do if you caught your boss reading your e-mails?

Apply Your Knowledge

1. You are a restaurant manager. The month-end food cost percentage has just arrived on your desk, and it shows that the actual food cost percentage is 12 percent above budget. What will you do?

Endnotes

1. Stephen P. Robbins and Mary Coulter, *Management*, 8th ed. (Upper Saddle River, NJ: Prentice Hall, 2005), 486.
2. W. H. Newman, *Constructive Control Design and Use of Control Systems* (Upper Saddle River, NJ: Prentice Hall, 1975), 33.
3. Robbins and Coulter, *Management*, 475.
4. Ibid.
5. Muhammad Jamil, CheZuriana, Lynn Hodgkinson, and Eifiona Thomas Lane. (2009). "The Effect of Management Control System on Hotel Environmental Performance." http://ijs.cgpublisher.com/product/pub.41/prod.582. Retrieved December 15, 2011.
6. Glenn Hasek. (6/20/2011). "New Bathroom Ventilation Systems Make Saving Money, Energy Easy." http://www.greenlodgingnews.com/. Search for "new bathroom ventilation systems" to view this article. Retrieved December 15, 2011.
7. Green Lodging News.(8/24/2011). "Alexandria Hotel Selects Telekonet EcoSmart Energy Management." http://www.greenlodgingnews.com. Search for "Alexandria Hotel" to view this article. Retrieved December 15, 2011.
8. Rhonda Sherman. (1996). "Waste Reduction and Recycling for the Lodging Industry." http://www.bae.ncsu.edu/programs/extension/publicat/wqwm/ag473_17.html. Retrieved December 15, 2011.
9. Florida Department of Environmental Protection."Waste Best Management Practices: Guidelines for All Hotel Areas." http://www.dep.state.fl.us. Select Green Lodging under Program Areas, click on Best Management Practices, and then click on Waste Reduction, Reuse and Recycling (accessed December 15, 2014).

Glossary

A

active listening   Listening for full meaning without making premature judgments or interpretations.

alcoholic beverage   A drink that contains a substantial amount of alcohol.

allocation of weights to criteria   Allocating different levels of importance to decision criteria according to a weighting method.

ambiance   The combined atmosphere created by the décor, lighting, service, possible entertainment (such as background music), and other amenities, which enhances the dining or lodging experience.

analysis of alternatives   Analyzing alternatives according to the "weights to criteria" method.

analytic style   A style of decision making marked by great tolerance for ambiguity and consideration of several alternatives, fostering adaptability to various situations.

application service provider (ASP)   Delivers a complete booking system tied to the hotel's inventory in real time via the Internet.

associations   A group of individuals who voluntarily enter into an agreement to accomplish a purpose.

atmosphere   The combination of mood, lighting, furnishings, and music that has an immediate conscious as well as subconscious effect on guests.

authority   The rights inherent in a managerial position to tell people what to do and to expect them to do it.

average daily rate (ADR)   One of the key operating ratios that indicates the level of a hotel's performance. The ADR is calculated by dividing the dollar sales by the number of rooms rented.

average guest check   The average amount each group spends; used primarily in a restaurant setting.

B

baccarat   A traditional table game in which the winning hand totals closest to nine.

back of the house   The support areas behind the scenes in a hotel or motel, including housekeeping, laundry, engineering, and foodservice. Also refers to individuals who operate behind the scenes to make a guest's stay pleasant and safe.

balance sheet   Itemizes a business's assets and liabilities with regard to the owner's equity at a particular moment in time.

banquet   A formal dinner.

banquet event order (BEO)   A contractual agreement between one party and another, such as a club or catering company, that details a function or event.

basic corrective action   An action that examines how and why performance deviated and then proceeds to correct the source of deviation.

batch cooking   Cooking quantities of food to be ready at a specific time; mostly used in commercial foodservice.

beer   An alcoholic drink made from yeast-fermented cereals including malted barley flavored with hops.

behavioral style   A decision-making style characterized by a low tolerance for ambiguity and an intuitive way of thinking.

benchmarking   Searching for the best practices among competitors or no competitors that lead to their superior performance.

best practices   Procedures that are accepted as being correct or most effective.

beverage cost percentage   Similar to food cost percentage, except that it relates to beverages.

blackjack   A table game in which the winning hand is determined by whether the dealer or the player gets cards that add up to a number closest to or equal to 21 without going over.

body language   Gestures, facial expressions, body postures, and other movements of the body that convey meaning, such as the emotional state and attitude of the person.

boundaryless organization   Organizations not limited to or bound by vertical or horizontal boundaries.

bounded rationality   Decision making based on or limited by an individual's ability to gain information.

brandy   A strong alcoholic spirit distilled from grapes.

brigade   A team of kitchen personnel organized into stations.

budget   An itemized listing, usually prepared annually, of anticipated revenue and projected expenses.

budgeting costs   To allocate costs of operating.

business travel   Travel for business purposes.

C

call accounting system (CAS)   A system that tracks guest room phone charges.

capital intensive   Something requiring a lot of capital.

capture rate   In hotel food and beverage practice, the number of hotel guests who use the food and beverage outlets.

career path   To chart a course for the progression of a career.

casino resort   A facility that includes gaming entertainment, hotel accommodations, and/or food and beverage venues.

casual dining   Relaxed dining; includes restaurants from several classifications.

catastrophe plans   A plan to maximize guest and property safety in the event of a disaster.

catering   The part of the food and beverage division of a hotel that is responsible for arranging and planning food and beverage functions for conventions and smaller hotel groups, and local banquets booked by the sales department.

catering coordinator   Oversees and coordinates the various aspects of catering and events operations from booking the function, allocating the space, planning, preparation, and organization for hotels, convention centers, and event companies.

catering event order (CEO)   A document detailing the client's function.

catering services manager (CSM)   Head of the catering services department.

celebrity-owned restaurant   A restaurant owned, or partially owned, by a celebrity.

central reservation office (CRO)   The central office of a lodging company where reservations are processed.

central reservation system (CRS)   A reservation system that is commonly used in large franchises to connect their reservation systems with one another; enables guests to call one phone number to reserve a room at any of the chain properties.

centralization   The degree to which decision making is concentrated at a single point in the organization.

certainty   The condition of knowing in advance the outcome of a decision.

chain of command   The continuous line of authority that extends from upper organizational levels to the lowest levels in the organization and clarifies who reports to whom.

chain restaurant   A group of restaurants owned or operated under a brand.

champagne   Sparkling wine made in the Champagne district of France.

charity balls   A gala dinner-dance event whose purpose is to raise funds toward a group or charity.

chef tournant   A chef who rotates the various stations in the kitchen to relieve the station chefs.

chief steward   The individual in a hotel, club, or foodservice operation who is responsible for the cleanliness of the back of the house and dishwashing areas and for storage and control of china, glassware, and silverware.

city clubs   Various clubs in cities.

city ledger   A client whose company has established credit with a particular hotel. Charges are posted to the city ledger and accounts are sent once or twice monthly.

classroom-style seating   A room setup where slim tables are used so meeting participants can take notes.

club management   The management of clubs.

cognac   A type of brandy made only in the Cognac region of France.

commercial foodservice   Foodservice for profit.

commercial recreation   For-profit recreation.

communication   The exchange of information and the transfer of meaning.

communication networks   Networks that enable and facilitate the communications process.

comping   Offering a complimentary service without charge.

comps   Complimentary offerings.

conceptual style   A decision-making style that involves considering numerous alternatives in order to find creative solutions to the problem.

concierge   A uniformed employee of a hotel who works at a desk in the lobby or on special concierge floors and answers questions, solves problems, and performs the services of a private secretary for the hotel's guests.

concurrent control   Control that takes place while the work is in progress.

confirmed reservations   A reservation made by a guest that is confirmed by the hotel for the dates they plan to stay.

contingency factors   Factors contingent upon various circumstances occurring; planning for the what ifs.

contractors   A company that operates a service for the client on a contractual basis.

contribution margin   Key operating figure in menu engineering, determined by subtracting food cost from selling price as a measure of profitability.

control   The provision of information to management for decision-making purposes. The process of monitoring activities to ensure that they are being accomplished as planned and of correcting any significant deviations.

control process   A five-step process of determining goals, setting standards, measuring actual performance, comparing actual performance against those standards, and taking managerial action to correct deviations.

controllable expense   Expenses that can be controlled by means of cost-effective purchasing systems, a controlled storage and issuing system, and strict control of food production and sales. These expenses are usually watched over by management.

controlling   Checking actual results against expected results.

convention   A generic term referring to any size business or professional meeting held in one specific location, which usually includes some form of trade show or exposition. Also refers to a group of delegates or members who assemble to accomplish a specific goal.

convention and visitors bureaus (CVBs)   1. An organization responsible for promoting tourism at the regional and local level. 2. A not-for-profit umbrella organization that represents a city or urban area in soliciting and servicing all types of travelers to that city or area, whether for business, pleasure, or both.

convention center   A large meeting place.

cooking line   A specific place where cooks typically work on a line, such as prep, grill, stove, vegetables, etc.

coordination   The organization of different aspects of an activity so they work together effectively and efficiently.

coordination of activities   The union of activities.

core values   The fundamental beliefs of an organization; the guiding principles that dictate behavior and action.

corporate events   Annual meetings, sales meetings, new product launches, training meetings, workshops, management meetings, press meetings, incentive meetings, and awards ceremonies.

corporate hotel   A hotel owned by a corporation.

corporate philosophy   The core beliefs that drive a company's basic organizational structure.

corporate seminars   A corporate meeting whose purpose is to exchange ideas; a conference.

correcting actual performance   Used by managers if the source of the performance variation is unsatisfactory.

corrective action   Includes changing the way the job is done, doing different tasks, changing structure, or redesigning jobs.

cost centers   Centers that cost money to operate and do not bring in revenue.

country clubs   Clubs that offer members golf and sometimes other sporting activities such as tennis and swimming along with games and social activities.

covers   The guest count of a restaurant.

craps   A dice game where players bet on the outcome of the roll or a series of rolls of a pair of dice.

culinary arts   The art of preparation, cooking, and presentation of food.

cultural tourism   Tourism related to cultural interests or pursuits.

curbside appeal   Visual appeal and cleanliness designed to encourage people to dine in a particular restaurant.

D

daily rate   The cost per day that a hotel charges for each room.

daily report   A report prepared each day to provide essential performance information for a particular property to its management.

decentralization   The degree to which lower level employees provide input or actually make decisions.

decision making   The process of deciding among alternatives.

decision-making process   The process of developing and analyzing alternatives and choosing from among them.

departmentalization   Organizing resources into departments.

development of alternatives   Listing possible alternatives that could resolve a problem.

dinner house restaurant   A restaurant with a casual, eclectic décor that may promote a particular theme.

dinner-style room seating   A type of room setup where round tables for large parties are organized; boardroom-style tables may be set up for smaller groups.

direct economic impact   The economic impact normally expressed in dollars that a hospitality business has on its area.

directive style   A decision-making style characterized by a rational way of thinking and low tolerance for ambiguity.

director of catering (DOC)   Person in charge of all catering events.

director of food and beverage   Person in charge of all food and beverage operations.

diversification   A corporate strategy whereby managers try to utilize their organization's resources more effectively by developing new products and new markets.

downward communication   Communication flow within the organization from supervisor or manager to employees.

dram shop legislation   Laws and procedures that govern the legal operation of establishments that sell measured alcoholic beverages.

E

ecotourism   Responsible travel to natural areas that conserves the environment and sustains the well-being of the local people.

effectiveness   Completing activities so that organizational goals are attained; also referred to as "doing the right things" or "getting things done."

efficiency   Getting the most output from the smallest amount of inputs; also referred to as "doing things right" or "getting things done well."

El Rancho Vegas   The first casino resort on what is now known as the Las Vegas Strip.

employee recognition   The acknowledgement of an individual's or a team's efforts and accomplishments.

Employee Right to Know   Per U.S. Senate Bill 198, information about chemicals must be made available to all employees.

empowerment   The act of giving employees the authority, tools, and information they need to do their jobs with greater autonomy.

environmental scanning   The acquisition and use of information about an organization's external environment in which policies, economics, and competition are analyzed.

escalation of commitment   Increased commitment to a previous decision despite evidence that it may have been wrong.

ethics   The study of standards of conduct and moral judgment; also, the standards of correct conduct.

ethnic restaurant   A restaurant featuring a particular cuisine such as Chinese, Mexican, or Italian.

evaluation of decision effectiveness   Determination of whether specified goals have been achieved.

event planner   An individual who is responsible for planning an event from start to finish. Duties include setting the date and location, advertising the event, providing refreshments or arranging catering services, and arranging speakers and/or entertainment.

event planning   A general term that refers to a career path in the growing field of special events.

executive chef   The head of the kitchen.

executive committee   A committee of hotel executives from each of the major departments within the hotel; generally made up of the general manager, director of rooms division, food and beverage director, marketing and sales director, human resources director, accounting and/or finance director, and engineering director.

exposition   An event held mainly to promote informational exchanges among trade people; a large exhibition in which the presentation is the main attraction, as well as being a source of revenue for an exhibitor.

F

fair return on investment   A reasonable return for the amount invested.

fairs and festivals   Planned events that are often themed to the celebration's purpose.

familiarization (FAM) trip   A free or reduced-price trip given to travel agents, travel writers, or other intermediaries to promote destinations.

family restaurant   A restaurant that targets families as patrons.

feasibility study   The assessment of the viability of a proposed venture.

feedback control   Control that takes place after the activity is done.

feedforward control   Focuses on preventing anticipated problems because it takes place in advance of the work activity.

fermentation   The chemical process in which yeast acts on sugar or sugar-containing substances, such as grain or fruit, to produce alcohol and carbon dioxide.

fine-dining restaurant   Upscale dining, usually with white tablecloths, à la carte menus, and table service.

first in–first out (FIFO)   The supplies that are ordered first are used first.

fixed cost   A cost or expense for a fixed period and range of activity that does not change in total but becomes progressively smaller per unit as volume increases.

food cost percentage   A ratio comparing the cost of food sold to food sales, which is calculated by dividing the cost of food sold during a given period by food sales during the same period.

food sales percentage   Also known as labor cost percentage.

forecasting   Predicting future outcomes.

formal communication   Communication that takes place within a prescribed organizational work agreement.

fortified wines   Wine to which brandy or other spirits have been added to stop further fermentation or to raise its alcoholic content.

franchise hotel   A hotel that is owned by an individual or company that has been granted a franchise to operate the hotel using the brand name, signage, operating methods, and reservations system.

franchising   A concept that allows a company to expand quickly by allowing qualified people to use the systems, marketing, and purchasing power of the franchiser.

front of the house   Comprises all areas with which guests come in contact, including the lobby, corridors, elevators, guest rooms, restaurants and bars, meeting rooms, and restrooms. Also refers to employees who staff these areas.

frontline manager   A low-level manager who manages the work of line employees and has guest contact.

function   An assigned duty or activity.

fundraiser   An event whose purpose is to raise funds for a group or charity.

fusion   The blending of two different cuisines.

G

gambling   Gaming entertainment that includes charitable gaming, commercial casinos, lotteries, Native American gaming, and parimutuel gaming.

geographic expansion   A strategic growth alternative of aggressively expanding into new domestic and/ or overseas markets.

global distribution system (GDS)   A system that can distribute the product or service globally.

goal   A specific result to be achieved; the end result of a plan.

goal setting   Traditionally, goals are set at the top level of an organization and then broken down into subgoals for each level of the organization so that the levels work together toward the achievement of the ultimate goals.

government-sponsored recreation   Recreation paid for by government taxes; includes monies sent to cities for museums, libraries, and municipal golf courses.

gross profit   The amount a business earns after paying to produce or buy its products but before deducting operating expenses; the difference between sales and the cost of goods sold.

guaranteed reservations   If rooms are available on guest demand, the hotel guarantees the guests rooms on those days.

guaranteed-number policy   The number of guests the hotel will prepare to serve and will charge accordingly.

guest   A person who is the recipient of hospitality in the form of entertainment—at someone's home, as a visiting participant in a program, or as a customer of an establishment such as a hotel or restaurant.

guest counts   The number of guests dining in a restaurant.

guest satisfaction   The desired outcome of hospitality services.

H

handle   The dollars wagered, or bet; often confused with *win*. Whenever a customer places a bet, the handle increases by the amount of the bet. The handle is not affected by the outcome of the bet.

haute cuisine   Elaborate or artful cuisine; contemporary cuisine.

heart of the house   The back of the house.

heritage tourism   Tourism that involves or relates to heritage.

hold percentage   The percentage of the total handle that is retained as win.

hops   The dried, conical fruit of a special vine that imparts bitterness to beer.

horizontal integration   The acquisition of ownership or control of competitors that are competing in the same or similar markets with the same or similar products.

horseshoe-style room seating   A meeting room containing tables arranged in the shape of a U.

hospitality   1. The cordial and generous reception of guests. 2. A wide range of businesses, each of which is dedicated to the service of people away from home.

hospitality industry philosophy   A philosophy in which managers counsel associates, giving them resources and helping them to think for themselves.

host/hostess   A greeter and "seater" at the entrance of a restaurant.

house edge   The advantage that a casino has over time as players play casino games.

hub-and-spoke system   A system used by airlines to transport passengers from one small city to another via a larger hub.

I

identification of decision criteria   Identifying criteria important for making decisions.

immediate corrective action   An action that corrects problems at once to get performance back on track.

implementation of alternative   Implementing the selected alternative.

incentive market   A target market of people who are rewarded a trip for reaching specific targets; the employer works with an incentive company to organize the trip, which includes expenses paid by the employer.

income statement   A report that lists the amount of money or its equivalent received during a period of time in exchange for labor or services, from the sale of goods or property, or as profit from financial investments.

independent business units (IBUs)   A business that makes decisions with little or no need to obtain approval for

independent hotel   A hotel that is independent of a group or chain ownership.

independent restaurant (indie)   A nonfranchise restaurant, privately owned.

indirect economic impact   An economic impact that is not direct.

informal communication   Does not follow a company's chain of command or structural hierarchy, and the subject matter is typically not job related or essential to performing job duties.

inseparability   The interdependence of hospitality services offered.

intangible   Something that cannot be touched.

interdependency   One hospitality entity being to some extent dependent on another; a cruise line is dependent on airlines bringing many of the passengers to the cruise ship port and to ground transportation for bringing the passengers to the ship.

International Festivals & Events Association (IFEA)   An organization that provides an opportunity for event managers from around the world to network and exchange ideas on how other festivals excel in sponsorship, marketing, fund-raising, operations, volunteer coordination, and management.

International Special Events Society (ISES)   Organization of special event planners.

interpersonal communication   Communication between two or more people.

interpersonal communication process   Communication between two or more individuals.

intuitive decision-making   A subconscious process of making decisions on the basis of experience and accumulated judgment.

inventory control   A method for keeping track of all resources required to produce a product.

J

job enlargement   A horizontal increase in the number of similar tasks assigned to a job.

job enrichment   A vertical expansion of planning and evaluating responsibilities which act as motivators and make the job more challenging.

job rotation   The systematic movement of workers from job to job to improve job satisfaction, reduce boredom, and enable employees to gain a broad perspective over the work process within the entire organization.

joint venture   An approach to going global that involves a specific type of strategic alliance in which the partners agree to form a specific, independent organization for some business purpose.

K

key operating areas   The most important functional areas of an organization that work and interact toward the achievement of the organization's goals.

kitchen manager   The individual who manages the kitchen department.

L

labor cost percentage   Similar to food cost percentage, except that it relates to labor. The formula is: Labor costs divided by net sales multiplied by 100 equals the labor cost percentage.

Las Vegas Strip   A stretch of area in Las Vegas known for international casinos and casino resorts.

leader/manager   An individual whose duties combine the functions of leadership and management.

leadership   The influence of one person over another to work willingly toward a predetermined objective.

leisure   Freedom from activities, especially time free from work or duties.

liaison personnel   Workers who are responsible for translating corporate philosophy for the contractor and for overseeing the contractor to be sure that he or she abides by the terms of the contract.

liquor   A distilled or spirited beverage.

load factor   The percentage of seats filled on all flights.

loyalty programs   Programs used to reward loyal patrons.

M

malt   Germinated barley.

managed services   Services that can be leased to professional management companies.

management   The process of coordinating work activities so that an organization's objectives are achieved efficiently and effectively with and through other people.

management by objectives (MBO)   A managerial process that determines the goals of the organization and then plans the objectives and the method to be used to reach the goals.

management by walking around (MBWA)   The best way of making personal observations; occurs when a manager is out of the office in the work area interacting with associates and guests.

management company   A company that manages properties.

management contracts   A written agreement between an owner and an operator of a hotel or motor inn by which the owner employs the operator as an agent (employee) to assume full responsibility for operating and managing the property.

managing   The formal process in which organizational objectives are achieved through the efforts of subordinates.

market penetration   A strategy to boost sales of current products by more aggressively permeating the organization's current markets.

mashing   In the making of beer, the process of grinding the malt and screening out bits of dirt.

measurement   An evaluation or basis of comparison in order to ascertain the dimensions, quantity, or capacity of something.

meeting   A gathering of people for a common purpose.

meeting planner   An individual who coordinates every detail of meetings and conventions.

Meeting Professionals International (MPI)   A Dallas-based association with nearly 19,000 members; MPI offers professional development in two certification programs: Certified Meeting Professional (CMP) and Certification in Meetings Management (CMM).

meetings, incentives, conventions, and exhibitions (MICE)   A specific segment of the tourism industry.

mercantile   Commercial gambling.

middle manager   A manager between the first-line level and the top level of the organization who manages the work of first-line managers.

mother sauce   One of five basic sauces from which many others can be developed.

multiplier effect   A concept that refers to new money that is brought into a community to pay for hotel rooms, restaurant meals, and other aspects of leisure. To some extent, that income then passes into the community when the hotel or restaurant orders supplies and services, pays employees, and so on.

N

national park   A park belonging to the nation.

National Park Service (NPS)   The service that manages to National Parks.

National Register of Historic Places   The United States' official list of districts, sites, buildings, structures, and objects worthy of preservation.

National Restaurant Association (NRA) The association representing restaurant owners and the restaurant industry.

National School Lunch Program (NSLP) The program that provides free lunches to students from a certain income level.

net profit The amount remaining when a business makes a profit, which is sales less all expenses.

niche A specific share or slot of a certain market.

night auditor The individual who verifies and balances guests' accounts.

nonalcoholic beverage A beverage that contains little to no alcohol.

noncommercial recreation Not-for-profit recreation.

nonprogrammed decision A unique decision that requires a custom made solution.

nonverbal communication Communication transmitted without words through body posture, gestures, and mimics.

nouvelle cuisine A mid-twentieth-century movement away from classic cuisine principles. Includes shortened cooking times and innovative combinations. A lighter, healthier cuisine based on more natural flavors, including herbs.

nutrition education programs Programs ensuring that food served in school cafeterias follows the nutrition standards set by government programs.

O

objective A specific result toward which effort is directed.

Occupational Safety and Health Administration (OSHA) The federal agency that enforces safety and health legislation.

operating ratios Ratios that indicate an operation's performance.

operational plans Plans for operations and organization.

organization chart A chart that illustrates the organization-wide division of work by charting who is accountable to whom and who is in charge of what department.

organizational communication All the patterns, networks, and systems of communication within an organization.

organizational structure Formal arrangement of jobs and tasks in an organization.

organizing The function of arranging order to an organization by deciding what needs to be done, who will do it, how it will be done, and who will report to whom.

P

Pacific Area Travel Association (PATA) Represents countries in the Pacific and Asia that have united behind common goals: excellence in travel and tourism growth.

par stock The level of stock that must be kept on hand at all times. If the stock on hand falls below this point, a computerized reorder system automatically reorders a predetermined quantity of the stock.

perishability The limited lifetime of hospitality products; for example, last night's vacant hotel room cannot be sold today.

perpetual inventory A running inventory that automatically updates itself.

personal digital assistant (PDA) A computer system that transmits information or orders and retrieves and posts guest payments; often used in restaurants to improve time management and allow faster service.

pilferage Stealing.

planning The process of defining the organization's goals, establishing an overall strategy for achieving those goals, and developing a comprehensive set of plans to integrate and coordinate organizational work.

point-of-sale (POS) system A system used in restaurants and outlet stores that records and posts charges; consists of a number of POS terminals that interface with a remote central processing unit.

poker A card game in which participants play against each other instead of the casino.

policy A guideline that establishes parameters for making decisions.

pour/cost percentage Similar to food cost percentage, except used in beverage control.

prime cost The cost of food sold plus payroll cost (including employee benefits). This is the largest segment of a restaurant's costs.

procedure A series of interrelated sequential steps that can respond to a well structured problem.

product A tangible good or intangible service produced by human or mechanical effort or by a natural process.

product development The strategy of improving products for current markets to maintain or boost growth.

product specification The establishment of standards for each product, determined by the purchaser. For example, when ordering meat, the product specification includes the cut, weight, size, percentage of fat content, and so forth.

production control sheets A checklist/sheet itemizing the production.

productive teams Workplace teams built by giving associates the authority, responsibility, and encouragement to come together to work on guest-related improvements that will enhance the guest experience and make the associates' jobs easier.

productivity The amount of product, goods, or services produced by employees.

programmed decision A repetitive decision that can be handled by routine approach.

Prohibition The years from 1919–1933 where alcohol was prohibited.

project management The process of completing a project's activities on time, within budget, and according to specifications.

project structure An organizational structure in which employees work continuously on projects.

proof A figure representing liquor's alcohol content.

property management system (PMS) A computerized system that integrates all systems used by a lodging property, such as reservations, front desk, housekeeping, food and beverage control, and accounting.

purchase order A document that provides specifics as to what a buyer wishes to purchases from a seller.

purée To process food to achieve a smooth pulp.

Q

quick-service restaurant (QSR) A restaurant that offers quick service.

R

rationality Consistent with or based on reason; logical. A rational decision needs to be value maximizing and consistent within natural restraining limits.

real estate investment trust (REIT) A method that enables small investors to combine their funds and protects them from the double taxation levied against an ordinary corporation or trust; designed to facilitate investment in real estate in much the same way a mutual fund facilitates investment in securities.

receiving The back-of-the-house area devoted to receiving goods.

recreation Refreshment of strength and spirits after work; a means of diversion.

recreation for special populations Recreation designed to accommodate persons with disabilities, for example the Special Olympics.

recreation management Managing recreation to deliver programs in a variety of settings.

referral associations Associations that refer guests to other participating members.

responsibility The obligation to perform any assigned duties.

restaurant forecasting The process of estimating the number of future guests, their menu preferences, and the revenue from them.

restaurant manager The head of operations in a restaurant.

return on investment (ROI) An important financial measure that determines how well management uses business assets to produce profit. It measures the efficiency with which financial resources available to a company are employed by management.

revenue centers Centers that produce revenue.

revenue management The management of revenue.

revenue per available room (REV PAR) Total Rooms Revenue for Period divided by Total Rooms Available During a Period.

risk The conditions under which the decision maker is able to estimate the likelihood of certain outcomes.

room occupancy percentage (ROP) The number of rooms occupied divided by rooms available; a key operating ratio for hotels.

room rates The various rates charged for hotel rooms.

room service The cleaning of rooms and resupplying of materials (towels, soap, etc.) by the housekeeping staff.

rooms division The departments that make up the rooms division.

roulette A traditional table game in which a dealer spins a wheel and players wager on which number a small ball will fall.

routine Operational decisions from higher up in the organization.

roux A paste for thickening sauces, made from equal quantities of fat and flour.

rule A very specific action guide that associates must follow.

S

sales volume The amount of sales.

satisficing A term coined by Peter Drucker; to pick the first alternative that appears to work rather than the best alternative.

scheduling Detailing what activities have to be done, the order in which they are to be completed, who is to do each, and when they are to be completed.

selection of alternative Choosing the alternative with the highest weighted score.

self-managed team A type of work team that operates without a manager and is responsible for a complete work process or a segment of it.

self-operators A company that manages its own foodservice operations.

semantics The study of the actual meaning of words.

service industries A business that does work for its customers.

shopper People who are paid to use a bar as regular guests would, except that they observe the operation closely.

social functions Events that include weddings, engagement parties, and holiday functions.

social, military, educational, religious, and fraternal (SMERF) A category of participants who attend meetings.

sous chef A cook who supervises food production and who reports to the executive chef; he or she is second in command of a kitchen.

sparkling wine Wine containing carbon dioxide, which provides effervescence when the wine is poured.

special events industry An industry offering an array of events that fall into categories such as daily events, which normally happen spontaneously, and special events, which are planned and often motivated by a celebration such as a wedding, fair, or festival.

spirit Distilled drink.

station chef A chef in charge of a station.

strategic alliance An approach to the expansion of a business's activities (entering new markets) that involves a partnership with another organization(s) in which both share resources, guests, and knowledge in serving existing clients and in the development of new products and services.

strategic management The process of identifying and pursuing the organization's strategic plan by aligning internal capabilities with the external demands of its environment, and then ensuring that the plan is being executed properly.

strategic planning Identifying the current business of a firm, the business it wants for the future, and the course of action it will pursue.

strategy Actions taken to achieve goals.

suggestive selling To suggest items that may be of interest to guests in order to upsell or gain more revenue.

summary operating statement Details of revenues and expenses for a period.

sustainability The ability to achieve continuing economic prosperity while protecting the natural resources of the planet.

sustainable tourism Tourism that is sustainable.

SWOT analysis A strategic planning tool for analyzing a company's strengths, weaknesses, opportunities, and threats.

T

team player An employee who is committed to the team's objectives, members, and goals.

teams A task-oriented work group that either evolves informally or is appointed formally.

territory The area for which a person is responsible as a representative or agent; a sphere of action or interest.

theater-style room seating A meeting setup usually intended for a large audience that is not likely to need to take notes or refer to documents. It generally consists of a raised platform and a lectern from which the presenter addresses the audience.

theme parks A recreational park based on a particular setting or artistic interpretation; may operate with hundreds or thousands of acres of parkland and hundreds or thousands of employees.

theme restaurant A restaurant distinguished by its combination of decor, atmosphere, and menu.

timeshare A two-bedroom suite that is owned rather than a hotel room that is rented for a transient night.

tolerance for ambiguity Individuals with a high tolerance for ambiguity are very time efficient in making decisions because they are able to process many thoughts at the same time. Those with a low tolerance for ambiguity need more time to make a decision because they process information in a consistent and ordered way in order to minimize ambiguity.

top managers A manager at or near the top level of the organization who is responsible for making organization-wide decisions and establishing the goals and plans that affect the entire organization.

total quality management (TQM) A managerial approach that integrates all of the functions and related processes of a business such that they are all aimed at maximizing guest satisfaction through ongoing improvement.

tourism Travel for recreation or the promotion and arrangement of such travel.

trade show Generally, a large display of products and services available for purchase, promoting information exchange among trade people. Trade shows frequently take place in convention centers where space is rented in blocks of 10 square feet. Also called *exposition*.

transactional leadership A type of leadership that focuses on accomplishing the tasks at hand and on maintaining good working relationships by exchanging promises of rewards for performance.

transformational leadership A type of leadership that involves influencing major changes in the attitudes and assumptions of organization members and building commitment for the organization's mission, objectives, and strategies.

transient occupancy tax (TOT) Tax paid by people staying in a city's hotels.

tray line The line of trays in hospital meal preparation where items are added to the tray to complete the meal order.

U

uncertainty A situation in which a decision maker has neither certainty nor reasonable probability estimates available.

uniform system of accounts A standard classification and presentation of operating results.

uniformed staff Front-of-the-house staff.

United Nations Educational, Scientific and Cultural Organization (UNESCO) An organization that has designated a number of world heritage sites worthy of protection and preservation due to their national and cultural heritage.

upward communication Upward information flow within the organization from employees to supervisors or managers.

V

vacation ownership Offers consumers the opportunity to purchase fully furnished vacation accommodations in a variety of forms, such as weekly intervals or points in point-based systems, for a percentage of the cost of full ownership.

vacation package A vacation that is made up of a package; may include air and ground transportation, hotel accommodation, and other goodies.

variability Capable of varying or changing.

variable cost A cost that varies according to the volume of business.

verbal intonation Use of the voice to emphasize certain parts of a phrase or certain words.

vintage The year in which a wine's grapes were harvested.

voluntary organizations A nongovernmental, nonprofit agency serving the public.

volunteer tourism A form of tourism where people volunteer to help others or projects, usually in developing countries.

W

weddings and holiday parties Of all social gatherings, weddings are the most widely recognized social event.

weighted average A method of menu pricing that takes into account the food costs, percentage contribution margin, and sales volume.

white spirits Gin, rum, vodka, and tequila.

win Dollars won by the gaming operation from its customers. The net spending of customers on gaming is called the *win*, also known as *gross gaming revenue (GGR)*.

wine Fermented juice of grapes or other fruits.

wine tasting An event in which individuals come together to sample various wines.

work specialization The degree to which tasks in an organization are divided into individual jobs; also called division of labor.

work team structure Work structure into teams of employees to delight the guest.

workshop A usually brief, intensive educational program conducted by a facilitator or a trainer, designed for a relatively small group of people, that focuses especially on techniques and skills in a particular field. Emphasizes interaction and exchange of information among a relatively small number of participants.

World Tourism Organization (UNWTO) The leading intergovernmental tourism organization.

wort In the making of beer, the liquid obtained after the mashing process.

Y

Yeast The fermenting agent used in the brewing process.

yield management The practice of analyzing past reservation patterns, room rates, cancellations, and no-shows in an attempt to maximize profits and occupancy rates and to set the most competitive room rates.

Z

zero-based budgeting Managers begin with a budget of zero dollars and justify all the costs of goods sold, controllable costs, and planned capital expenditures in order to ensure an appropriate profit after the deduction of all expenses.

Index

Credits

Part I

(p. 1): Holbox/Shutterstock

Chapter 1

pp. 2–3: Guynamedjames/Fotolia
p. 4: LENS-68/Shutterstock
p. 5: Jakrit Jiraratwaro/Shutterstock
p. 6: Daniel Schoene/Glow Images
p. 8: Greg Ward/Dorling Kindersley, Ltd.
p. 9: Angus Osborn/Dorling Kindersley, Ltd.
p. 10: Peter Wilson/Dorling Kindersley, Ltd.
p. 11: Courtesy of James MacManemon
p. 12: U.S. Census Bureau Average Lifetime Earnings—Different Levels of Education
p. 14: Kayros Studio/Shutterstock
p. 15: Walker, James R. Intro to Hospitality Management, 4e. Copyright © 2013. Pearson Education, Upper Saddle River, NJ
p. 16: Walker, James R. Intro to Hospitality Management, 4e. Copyright © 2013. Pearson Education, Upper Saddle River, NJ; Demetrio Carrasco/Dorling Kindersley, Ltd.
p. 17: Maura McEvoy/Union Square Hospitality Group
p. 18: The Increasing Importance of Technology to the Hospitality Industry, James R. Walker, Pearson Education, Inc.
p. 21: Walker, James R. Intro to Hospitality Management, 4e. Copyright © 2013. Pearson Education, Upper Saddle River, NJ
p. 22: Walker, James R. Intro to Hospitality Management, 4e. Copyright © 2013. Pearson Education, Upper Saddle River, NJ
p. 23: Walker, James R. Intro to Hospitality Management, 4e. Copyright © 2013. Pearson Education, Upper Saddle River, NJ
p. 26: Walker, James R. Introduction to Hospitality Management, 4e. Copyright © 2013. Pearson Education, Upper Saddle River, NJ; Christy Bowe/Globe Photos/ZUMAPRESS/Alamy
pp. 27–28: Courtesy of William Martin
p. 29: National Restaurant Association, www.restaurant.org
p. 31: Ryan Lashway; Chiles Group Corporation, www.groupersandwich.com; Ryan Lashway
p. 32: Imageegami/Fotolia
pp. 32–33: Walker, James R. Introduction to Hospitality Management, 4e. Copyright © 2013. Pearson Education, Upper Saddle River, NJ
p. 34: Pearson Education, Inc.
pp. 36–37: Pearson Education, Inc.
p. 37: Pearson Education, Inc.; Demetrio Carrasco/Dorling Kindersley, Ltd.
p. 40: Queendom: The Land of Tests: www.queendom.com
p. 41: International CHRIE, www.chrie.org; American Hotel & Lodging Association, www.ahla.com; The Professional Convention Management Association, www.pcma.org; The National Society of Minorities in Hospitality; The International Special Events Society, www.ises.com
pp. 41–44: Courtesy of Greg Dunn
p. 44: Walker, James R. Introduction to Hospitality Management, 4e. Copyright © 2013. Pearson Education, Upper Saddle River, NJ
pp. 45–46: Pearson Education, Inc.
p. 48: Starbucks, www.starbucks.com; Bureau of Labor Statistics, http://www.bls.gov; United States Census Bureau, http://www.census.gov; About.com, http://www.about.com; Marriott, http://www.marriott.com/
p. 49: UN Documents, http://www.un-documents.net/; Roger Williams University, www.rwu.edu' Cornell University, www.cornell.edu; W. Edwards Deming Institute, https://www.deming.org

Chapter 2

pp. 50–51: Photoman120/Fotolia
p. 55: Chad M. Gruhl
pp. 55–56: Courtesy of Chad Gruhl
p. 57: Hotel Indigo
p. 60: Walker, James R. Introduction to Hospitality Management, 4e. Copyright ©

2013. Pearson Education, Upper Saddle River, NJ

p. 60: Glow Images

p. 61: Vlas2000/Shutterstock

p. 63: Courtesy of McKibbon Hotel Management, Inc.

pp. 64–65: Walker, James R. Introduction to Hospitality Management, 4e. Copyright © 2013. Pearson Education, Upper Saddle River, NJ; AKG Images/Newscom

p. 66: Robert Mendelbaum, A Full Service Hotel Operating Statement, PFK Hospitality Group.

p. 67: © PKF Hospitality Research, a CBRE Company, Trends ® in the Hotel Industry

p. 68: The Multiplier Effect of Hotel Dollars on a Community, Courtesy of the American Hotel and Lodging Association; Courtesy of Tim Mulligan

pp. 71–72: Courtesy of James MacManemon

p. 72: Forbes

p. 73: Summary of AAA Diamond Rating Guidelines, AAA Publishing; Loews Hotels, www.loewshotels.com

p. 76: Walker, James R. Intro to Hospitality Management, 4e. Copyright © 2013. Pearson Education, Upper Saddle River, NJ; Tim Draper/Dorling Kindersley, Ltd.

p. 77: Gabbro/Stock Photo/Alamy

p. 78: Courtesy of Valerie Ferguson

p. 79: AAA, http://www.aaasouth.com

pp. 78–79: Courtesy of Valerie Ferguson

p. 81: Magnus Rew/Dorling Kindersley, Ltd.

p. 82: Paul Franklin/Dorling Kindersley, Ltd.

p. 83: Courtesy of Jason Samson; Courtesy of Jason Samson

p. 85: Josie Elias/Getty Images

p. 86: Zak Waters/Alamy

p. 87: The Use of Technology in Property Management, James R. Walker, Pearson Education, Inc.

p. 89: Gary/Fotolia

p. 91: John Dakers/Eye Ubiquitous/Alamy

p. 92: Simon Bracken/Dorling Kindersley, Ltd.

pp. 94–95: Courtesy of Greg Dunn

p. 96: Pearson Education, Inc.

p. 98: Hotelcluster.com, http://www.hotelcluster.com; American Hotel & Lodging Association, http://www.ahla.com; New York Architecture, www.nyc-architecture.com; Intercontinental Hotels Group, http://www.ihgplc.com; Hospitalitynet, http://www.hospitalitynet.org; Choice Hotels, http://www.choicehotels.com; Black Enterprise, http://www.blackenterprise.com; Wyndham Worldwide, http://www.wyndhamworldwide.com; WorldMark by Wyndham, www.worldmarkbywyndham.com

p. 99: Club Wyndham, https://www.wyndhamvacationresorts.com; Hilton Worldwide, http://www.hiltonworldwide.com; Kimpton Hotel & Restaurant Group, www.kimptonhotels.com; Marriott International, www.marriott.com; Hyatt Corporation, www.hyatt.com; AAA, http://newsroom.aaa.com; Intercontinental Hotels Group, www.ihg.com; TravelASSIST, www.travelassist.com; Advantage Travel, LLC, www.greatescapesonline.com; RCI, www.rci.com; Rhode Island Roads Magazine, http://riroads.com; Interval International; North American Free Trade Agreement (NAFTA); IndexMundi, http://www.indexmundi.com; Fairmont Hotels & Resorts, www.fairmont.com; Boutique Hotel News

Chapter 3

pp. 100–101: Plukhin/Fotolia

p. 102: Walker, James R. Introduction to Hospitality Management, 4e. Copyright © 2013. Pearson Education, Upper Saddle River, NJ; Angus Osborn/Dorling Kindersley, Ltd.

p. 103: Andrey Popov/Fotolia

p. 104: AKG Images/Newscom

p. 105: Walker, James R. Intro to Hospitality Management, 4e. Copyright © 2013. Pearson Education, Upper Saddle River, NJ

p. 107: Walker, James R. Intro to Hospitality Management, 4e. Copyright © 2013. Pearson Education, Upper Saddle River, NJ

p. 109: Dmitrijs Dmitrijevs/Fotolia

p. 110: Charlie Adams

p. 111: Walker, James R. Intro to Hospitality Management, 4e. Copyright © 2013. Pearson Education, Upper Saddle River, NJ

p. 113: Myrleen Ferguson Cate/PhotoEdit, Inc.

pp. 113–114: Walker, James R. Introduction to Hospitality Management, 4e. Copyright © 2013. Pearson Education, Upper Saddle River, NJ

p. 115: Walker, James R., Exploring the Hospitality Industry, 3e. Copyright © 2013. Pearson Education, Upper Saddle River, NJ

p. 117: Pearson Education, Inc.; Walker, James R. Intro to Hospitality Management, 4e. Copyright © 2013. Pearson Education, Upper Saddle River, NJ

p. 118: Courtesy of James MacManemon

p. 119: Supplier Deposit Photos/Glow Images

p. 122: Pearson Education, Inc.

p. 124: Walker, James R. Intro to Hospitality Management, 4e. Copyright © 2013. Pearson Education, Upper Saddle River, NJ

p. 126: Courtesy of Denny Bhakta

p. 127: michaeljung/Shutterstock

p. 129: Walker, James R. Intro to Hospitality Management, 4e. Copyright © 2013. Pearson Education, Upper Saddle River, NJ

p. 130: Diego cervo/Fotolia

pp. 131–132: Walker, James R. Intro to Hospitality Management, 4e. Copyright © 2013. Pearson Education, Upper Saddle River, NJ

p. 134: Juriah Mosin/Shutterstock

p. 136: Walker, James R. Intro to Hospitality Management, 4e. Copyright © 2013. Pearson Education, Upper Saddle River, NJ

p. 141: Courtesy of Greg Dunn

p. 143: Walker, James R. Intro to Hospitality Management, 4e. Copyright © 2013. Pearson Education, Upper Saddle River, NJ; Pearson Education, Inc.

p. 144: Walker, James R. Introduction to Hospitality Management, 4e. Copyright © 2013. Pearson Education, Upper Saddle River, NJ

p. 145: Walker, James R. Introduction to Hospitality Management, 4e. Copyright © 2013. Pearson Education, Upper Saddle River, NJ

p. 146: Walker, James R. Introduction to Hospitality Management, 4e. Copyright © 2013. Pearson Education, Upper Saddle River, NJ

p. 147: Hoteljobs.com

p. 148: STR Global, http://www.strglobal.com; WebMD, www.webmd.com; Susan Patel, Triple Bottom Line and Eco-Efficiency: Where to Start?, EcoGreenHotel, www.ecogreenhotel.com/green_hotel_news_Triple-Bottom-Line-and-Eco-Efficiency.php (accessed February 26, 2015 by Pearson); Sustainable Travel International

p. 149: New Hampshire Lodging & Restaurant Association; BUILDINGS; Hospitality Technology (HT)

Chapter 4

pp. 150–151: Maksim Shebeko/Fotolia

p. 152: Walker, James R. Intro to Hospitality Management, 4e. Copyright © 2013. Pearson Education, Upper Saddle River, NJ

p. 155: George Goldhoff

pp. 155–156: Courtesy of George Goldhoff

p. 157: Terry Vine/AGE Fotostock

p. 158: Marilyn Carlson Nelson

p. 159: Arto/Fotolia

pp. 158–159: Carlson

p. 160: Courtesy of Jose Martinez-Diaz

p. 161: Dacorum Gold/Alamy

p. 162: Catherine Rabb

p. 164: Simon Bracken/Dorling Kindersley, Ltd.

p. 166: Erwinova/Fotolia

pp. 166–167: Courtesy of James MacManemon

p. 168: XXIV/Fotolia

p. 169: Walker, James R. Intro to Hospitality Management, 4e. Copyright © 2013. Pearson Education, Upper Saddle River, NJ

pp. 169–171: Walker, James R. Introduction to Hospitality Management, 4e. Copyright © 2013. Pearson Education, Upper Saddle River, NJ

p. 172: Walker, James R. Intro to Hospitality Management, 4e. Copyright © 2013. Pearson Education, Upper Saddle River, NJ

p. 173: Courtesy of Sheraton Grande Torrey Pines

p. 175: Aastock/Shutterstock; Courtesy of James McManemon

pp. 175–176: Courtesy of James MacManemon

pp. 179–180: Courtesy of James MacManemon

p. 182: Walker, James R. Introduction to Hospitality Management, 4e. Copyright © 2013. Pearson Education, Upper Saddle River, NJ

p. 185: Carlson, http://www.carlson.com /our-company/index.do; Hotel News Now

Part II

(p. 187): Jacques Palut/Fotolia

Chapter 5

pp. 188–189: Sea Wave/Fotolia

p. 190: Pearson Education: Inc.

p. 192: Pearson Education, Inc.; Clive Streeter/ Dorling Kindersley, Ltd.

p. 191: bogdanhoda/Shutterstock

p. 193: Eddie Gerald/Dorling Kindersley Ltd.; Ian O'Leary/Dorling Kindersley, Ltd.

p. 194: Kzenon/Fotolia; Ian O'Leary/Dorling Kindersley, Ltd.

p. 195: Courtesy of J. R. Schrock

p. 196: Courtesy of J. R. Schrock; Walker, James R. Intro to Hospitality Management, 4e. Copyright © 2013. Pearson Education, Upper Saddle River, NJ

p. 197: Andrew Zarivny/Shutterstock

p. 198: Walker, James R. Introduction to Hospitality Management, 4e. Copyright © 2013. Pearson Education, Upper Saddle River, NJ

p. 200: "The French Paradox", 60 Minutes, CBS News

p. 201: Chris Laurens/Alamy

p. 205: Monty Rakusen/Cultura/Newscom

p. 207: Sergey Andrianov/Fotolia

p. 208: Halfmax.ru/Shutterstock

p. 211: Deposit Photos/Glow Images

pp. 211–212: Walker, James R. Introduction to Hospitality Management, 4e. Copyright © 2013. Pearson Education, Upper Saddle River, NJ

p. 213: Amy Etra/PhotoEdit: Inc.

pp. 215–216: Courtesy of James MacManemon

p. 218: Rob Westfall

pp. 218–219: Courtesy of Rob Westfall

pp. 219–220: Courtesy of James MacManemon

p. 221: beachfront/Fotolia

p. 223: Nightclub & Bar, www.nightclub.com; Night Club Biz, www.nightclubbiz.com

pp. 226–228: Courtesy of Greg Dunn

p. 229: Walker, James R. Introduction to Hospitality Management, 4e. Copyright © 2013. Pearson Education, Upper Saddle River, NJ

p. 232: Organic & Sustainable Wine Production Expanding Rapidly in California, Organic Consumers Association; Hottinger, Greg, Organic Beer: Tapping a New Market, http://bestnaturalfoods.com/newsletter /organic_beer.html.

p. 232: CraftBeer.com; Drink Craft Beer, http://drinkcraftbeer.com/; Brewers Association, www.brewersassociation.org; The Full Pint, http://thefullpint.com; The Beer Apostle; Hurst, Tim, "Sustainable Brewing in Colorado Not Done Impressing You Yet", Big Green Boulder, http://big-greenboulder.pmpblogs.com/2010/01/12/ sustainable-brewing-in-colorado-not-done -impressing-you-yet; E-Importz, http:// www.e-importz.com; National Coffee Association USA, http://www.ncausa.org; Starbucks Company Statistics", Starbucks, http://www.statisticbrain.com/starbucks -company-statistics

p. 233: FoodNavigator-USA, http://www .foodnavigator-usa.com/; CSPnet.com, http://www.cspnet.com/; Scannabar, http://en.scannabar.com; Azbar Plus, www.azbarplus.com

Chapter 6

pp. 234–235: Ingus Evertovskis/Fotolia

p. 238: Trotter, Charles, Ten Speed Press.

p. 239: Hulton Archive/Getty Images

pp. 240–241: Courtesy of James MacManemon

p. 243: Reprinted by permission of Richard Melman; Lettuce Entertain You Restaurants, http://www.leye.com; Used by permission of Lettuce Entertain You Enterprises.

p. 246: Mark Rasmnssen, Director, Leopold Center for Sustainable Agriculture, 209 Curtiss Hall - ISU, Ames IA 50011-1050

p. 249: Focus on Nutrition, Jim Inglis, Valencia College

p. 250: U.S. Small Business Association, www.sba.gov

p. 251: Jim Cooper/AP Images

p. 252: Courtesy of Chris Marrero

p. 253: Deposit Photos/Glow Images

p. 254: Courtesy of James MacManemon

pp. 254–255: Courtesy of Sarah Stenger

p. 257: Pearson Education, Inc.; Diane Macdonald/Moment Mobile/Getty Images

p. 258: Demetrio Carrasco/Dorling Kindersley Ltd.; Peter Bischoff/Stringer/PB Archive/Getty Images

p. 260: Walker, James R. Intro to Hospitality Management, 4e. Copyright © 2013. Pearson Education, Upper Saddle River, NJ

pp. 263–264: Courtesy of Greg Dunn

p. 266: National Restaurant Association, http://www.restaurant.org; FastCasual.com, www.fastcasual.com; NCR Blogs, http://www.ncr.com; Restaurant Hospitality; Mashable, http://mashable.com; About.com; Green Restaurant Association, http://www.dinegreen.com; Chipotle, www.chipotle.com; San Diego Free Press, www.sandiegofreepress.org; USDA, ChooseMyPlate.gov; Restaurant Resource Group, http://rrgconsulting.com/; Menu Cover Depot, http://www.menucoverdepot.com/; McDonald's, http://www.mcdonalds.com/; Yum! Brands, http://www.yum.com; Entrepreneur, http://www.entrepreneur.com/; Popeyes Louisiana Kitchen, www.popeyes.com; Subway, http://www.subway.com; Panera Bread, www.panerabread.com; QSR, http://www.qsrmagazine.com

Chapter 7

pp. 268–269: Maksim Shebeko/Shutterstock

p. 270: Panera Bread

p. 271: Kit Sen Chin/123RF

pp. 272–273: Courtesy of James MacManemon

p. 275: Kamil Macniak/Shutterstock

p. 276: Courtesy of John Self; Pearson Education, Inc.; John T. Self

p. 281: Son Hoang Nguyen/Shutterstock

p. 282: Radoma/Fotolia

p. 284: Tyler Olson/Shutterstock

p. 285: Monkey Business/Fotolia

p. 287: Courtesy of Tim Brady

p. 289: Pearson Education, Inc.

p. 291: Courtesy of James MacManemon

pp. 291–292: Pearson Education, Inc.

p. 293: Walker, James R. Intro to Hospitality Management, 4e. Copyright © 2013. Pearson Education, Upper Saddle River, NJ

p. 295: Michaeljung/Fotolia

p. 296: Greg Roden/Dorling Kindersley, Ltd.

pp. 296–297: Pearson Education, Inc.

p. 298: Walker, James R. Introduction to Hospitality Management, 4e. Copyright © 2013. Pearson Education, Upper Saddle River, NJ

p. 302: Everett Collection Historical/Alamy

p. 308: Courtesy of Greg Dunn

p. 309: Walker, James R. Introduction to Hospitality Management, 4e. Copyright © 2013. Pearson Education, Upper Saddle River, NJ

pp. 309–310: Walker, James R. Introduction to Hospitality Management, 4e. Copyright © 2013. Pearson Education, Upper Saddle River, NJ

p. 313: StarChefs.com, http://www.starchefs.com; SoftCafe, www.softcafe.com; Restaurant Magic, www.restaurantmagic.com; QSR Web, www.qsrweb.com; Chipotle, http://www.chipotle.com; RestaurantOwner.com, www.restaurantowner.com; Four Seasons, http://www.fourseasons.com/

Chapter 8

pp. 314–315: Yakov Stavchansky/Fotolia

p. 318: Peter Hansen/Shutterstock

p. 319: Walker, James R. Introduction to Hospitality Management, 4e. Copyright © 2013. Pearson Education, Upper Saddle River, NJ; Kristoffer Tripplaar/Alamy

p. 321: National Center Institute

p. 322: Cathy Yeulet/123RF

p. 323: The MyPlate icon featuring the five food groups, USDA

p. 324: Don Tran/Shutterstock

p. 327: Reprinted by permission of Sodexo Food Service

p. 329: Pearson Education, Inc.

p. 332: Walker, James R. Intro to Hospitality Management, 4e. Copyright © 2013. Pearson Education, Upper Saddle River, NJ

pp. 332–334: Nation's Restaurant News

pp. 334–335: Walker, James R. Exploring the Hospitality Industry, 3e. Copyright © 2014. Pearson Education, Upper Saddle River, NJ

p. 336: Thuansak Srilao/123RF

p. 337: Courtesy of James MacManemon

pp. 338–339: Courtesy of James MacManemon

p. 341: Courtesy of Fred DeMicco

p. 344: Courtesy of Greg Dunn

p. 345: Walker, James R. Introduction to Hospitality Management, 4e. Copyright © 2013. Pearson Education, Upper Saddle River, NJ

pp. 345–346: Walker, James R. Introduction to Hospitality Management, 4e. Copyright © 2013. Pearson Education, Upper Saddle River, NJ

p. 348: Gate Gourmet. www.gategourmet.com; LSG Sky Chefs, http://www.lsgskychefs.com; Sodexo, http://www.sodexo.com; Sodexo, http://www.sodexousa.com; United States Department of Agriculture, www.fns.usda.gov; The National Association of College & University Food Services, www.nacufs.org; Aramark, www.aramark.com; Teplow, Nate, "29 Statistics Every MSP Needs to Know", MSP Blog, http://blog.continuum.net/29-statistics-every-msp-needs-to-know; Channel Insider, http://www.channelinsider.com

Part III

(p. 349): Fotodesignhh/Fotolia

Chapter 9

pp. 350–351: Rob/Fotolia

p. 354: Chen Chao/Dorling Kindersley, Ltd.

p. 356: David Gaylor/Shutterstock

p. 357: Jeff Greenberg/AGE Fotostock

p. 360: Corbis/AGE Fotostock

p. 361: Walker, James R. Intro to Hospitality Management, 4e. Copyright © 2013. Pearson Education, Upper Saddle River, NJ; Steven May/Alamy

p. 364: E.G.Pors/Shutterstock

pp. 364–365: JT Watters

p. 367: World Tourism Organization

p. 368: Dhoxax/Shutterstock

p. 370: Reprinted by permission of World Tourism Organization (UNWTO) ©

p. 371: Courtesy of James MacManemon

p. 372: Pearson Education, Inc.

p. 373: Walker, James R. Intro to Hospitality Management, 4e. Copyright © 2013. Pearson Education, Upper Saddle River, NJ

pp. 374–375: Courtesy of James MacManemon

p. 376: Bastos/Fotolia

p. 377: Oleg Znamenskiy/Shutterstock

p. 379: Courtesy of Patti Roscoe

p. 381: Elena Elisseeva/Shutterstock

p. 382: Pcphotos/Fotolia

pp. 382–383: G Adventures Inc.

p. 384: Debra James/Shutterstock

p. 386: Courtesy of Ann-Marie Weldon

p. 387: Waring, Dr. Stephen. Volunteer Tourism Beckons," University of Technology, Sydney, January 1, 2002, http://www.uts.edu.au. Search for "Volunteer Tourism Beckons" to view this article

pp. 387–389: Courtesy of Greg Dunn

p. 390: Walker, James R. Intro to Hospitality Management, 4e. Copyright © 2013. Pearson Education, Upper Saddle River, NJ

p. 392: World Economic Forum, http://www.weforum.org; World Tourism Organization, http://media.unwto.org; World Travel and Tourism Council, http://www.wttc.org; About.com, www.about.com; TravelChinaGuide, www.travelchinaguide.com; Federal Aviation Administration, http://www.faa.gov; Salary.com, http://www.salary.com; United States Department of Transportation, Office of the Assistant Secretary for Research and Technology, http://www.rita.dot.gov; Princess Cruises, http://www.princess.com; Cruise Critic, www.cruisecritic.com; Cruise Ship Industry Statistics, American Association of Port Authorities, Florida-Caribbean Cruise Association, http://www.statisticbrain.com/cruise-ship-industry-statistics/; Cruise Lines International Association, www.cruising.org

p. 393: World Tourism Organization, http://www2.unwto.org; "World and Regions: Inbound Tourism International Tourism

Receipts", World Tourism Organization (UNWTO) ©, http://dtxtq4w60xqpw .cloudfront.net/sites/all/files/pdf/unwto _receipts_1995_2012_graph.pdf; U.S. Travel Association, http://www.ustravel. org; ITB Asia, http://www.itb-asia.com; NTA, http://ntaonline.com; Expeditioner used by permission; The International Ecotourism Society, www.ecotourism.org; United Nations Educational, Scientific and Cultural Organization, World Heritage Convention, http://whc.unesco.org; University of Technology, Sydney, http://www.uts.edu.au; Slideshare.net, http://www.slideshare.net; http://www .hospitalitynet.org; Marketwired, http:// www.marketwired.com.

Chapter 10

pp. 394–395: Dean Fikar/Shutterstock
p. 396: John R. Walker; Svtrotof/Shutterstock
p. 397: Rickyd/Shutterstock
p. 398: Bjul/Stock Photo/123RF
p. 401: Chris LeBoutillier/Shutterstock
p. 402: Alex Tihonov/Fotolia
p. 403: Urmoments/Fotolia
pp. 403–404: Courtesy of James MacManemon
p. 406: Walt Disney; Moviestore collection Ltd / Alamy
p. 407: Aroas/123RF
p. 408: Pichai Tunsuphon/123RF
p. 412: Menillo/Fotolia
p. 418: Kokhanchikov/Shutterstock
p. 423: Manamana/Shutterstock
p. 427: Global Explorer/Fotolia
p. 428: ClubCorp, Company Profile, http://www.clubcorp.com (accessed November 25, 2013).
p. 430: Courtesy of Edward J. Shaughnessy
p. 431: Text provided courtesy of the Club Managers Association of America
p. 432: Walker, James R. Intro to Hospitality Management, 4e. Copyright © 2013. Pearson Education, Upper Saddle River, NJ
p. 433: Text provided courtesy of the Club Managers Association of America
p. 434: Text provided courtesy of the Club Managers Association of America

p. 435: Walker, James R. Intro to Hospitality Management, 4e. Copyright © 2013. Pearson Education, Upper Saddle River, NJ
p. 437: Bart Bartlett
pp. 437–438: Courtesy of Bart Bartlett
p. 439: Environmental Institute for Golf, www.eifg.org
p. 440: Margie Martin; Courtesy of Margie Martin
pp. 443–444: Reprinted by permission of Dr. Greg Dunn
p. 445: Walker, James R. Intro to Hospitality Management, 4e. Copyright © 2013. Pearson Education, Upper Saddle River, NJ
p. 446: National Club Association: www .nationalclub.org; Walker, James R. Intro to Hospitality Management, 4e. Copyright © 2013. Pearson Education, Upper Saddle River, NJ; Club Managers Association of America; National Park Service; National Club Association
p. 447: Walker, James R. Intro to Hospitality Management, 4e. Copyright © 2013. Pearson Education, Upper Saddle River, NJ
p. 449: Wikipedia: http://en.wikipedia.org; BrainyQuote: http://www.brainyquote.com; National Park Service: http://www.nps.gov; Knott's Berry Farm: http://www.knotts .com; IAAPA: http://www.iaapa.org; Travel Assist: http://travelassist.com; Walt Disney World, Theme Parks: , http://www .wdwinfo.com
p. 450: Smithsonian Institution, http://www .si.edu; NBC Universal: http://www .nbcuniversal.com; Water Country USA: http://www.watercountryusa.com; Discovery Cove: http://discoverycove.com; The Hershey Company: http://www .thehersheycompany.com; Dollywood: http://www.dollywood.com; Gatorland: www.gatorland.com; Association of Zoos & Aquariums: www.aza.org; San Diego Zoo: www.sandiegozoo.org; National zoo: http:// nationalzoo.si.edu; National Aquarium: www.aqua.org; The field Museum: http:// fieldmuseum.org; Hellenic Ministry of Culture, Education and Religious Affairs: www.yppo.gr; CIA: http://www.cia.gov; UN Documents: http://www.un-documents

.net/index.htm; Golf Course Superintendents Association of America: http://www.gcsaa .org; Special Olympics: http://www .specialolympics.org; Jack Rouse Associates: http://www.jackrouse.com/2012/12/ Theme-Park-Trends-and-What-Museums -Can-Learn-from-Them.cfm; The Business Journals: http://www.bizjournals.com

Chapter 11

pp. 452–453: Andrew Moss/Fotolia

p. 460: Pavel L Photo and Video/Shutterstock

p. 461: Platinum Pictures/Fotolia

pp. 463–464: Courtesy of Nicholas Thomas

p. 465: Courtesy of David Schwartz

p. 466: Chet Gordon/The Image Works

pp. 468–469: Walker, James R. Intro to Hospitality Management, 4e. Copyright © 2013. Pearson Education, Upper Saddle River, NJ

p. 474: Walker, James R. Intro to Hospitality Management, 4e. Copyright © 2013. Pearson Education, Upper Saddle River, NJ

pp. 476–477: Courtesy of Nicholas Thomas

p. 478: Walker, James R. Intro to Hospitality Management, 4e. Copyright © 2013. Pearson Education, Upper Saddle River, NJ; Pearson Education, Inc.; Jared McMillen/Aurora Photos/Alamy

p. 480: Walker, James R. Intro to Hospitality Management, 4e. Copyright © 2013. Pearson Education, Upper Saddle River, NJ

p. 483: Casino Careers, www.casinocareers. com; Courtesy of Greg Dunn; History Extra: http://www.historyextra.com; One for Gambling: www.14g.com; Wikipedia: http://en.wikipedia.org; National Indian Gaming Commission: http://www.nigc.gov; Library Index: http://www.libraryindex .com; Insider Viewpoint of Las Vegas: http://www.insidervlv.com; Cesar Corporation: http://caesarscorporate.com; Dovers Downs: http://www.doverdowns .com; Simply Hired: http://www .simplyhired.com

Part IV

(p. 485): Monkey Business/Fotolia

Chapter 12

pp. 486–487: Pressmaster/Fotolia

p. 489: Walker, James R. Intro to Hospitality Management, 4e. Copyright © 2013. Pearson Education, Upper Saddle River, NJ

p. 493: Naka/Fotolia

p. 495: Nigel Hicks/Dorling Kindersley, Ltd.

pp. 495–496: Courtesy of Hawaii Convention Center

p. 496: Hawaii's Convention Center: http:// www.meethawaii.com/

pp. 496–497: Courtesy of James MacManemon

p. 498: Courtesy of James R. Schrock

p. 499: Courtesy of James MacManemon

p. 501: Reprinted by permission of San Diego Convention Center

p. 502: Courtesy of Jill Moran

pp. 502–503: Courtesy of Jill Moran

p. 506: Walker, James R. Intro to Hospitality Management, 4e. Copyright © 2013. Pearson Education, Upper Saddle River, NJ

pp. 507–508: Reprinted by permission of Alexandra Stout; Alexandra Stout

p. 511: Reprinted by permission of San Diego Convention Center

p. 512: Reprinted by permission of Amanda Alexander; Amanda Alexander

p. 513: Dean Allen Caron/Shutterstock

p. 516: Walker, James R. Intro to Hospitality Management, 4e. Copyright © 2013. Pearson Education, Upper Saddle River, NJ

p. 517: Walker, James R. Intro to Hospitality Management, 4e. Copyright © 2013. Pearson Education, Upper Saddle River, NJ

pp. 517–519: Courtesy of Greg Dunn

pp. 520–521: Walker, James R. Intro to Hospitality Management, 4e. Copyright © 2013. Pearson Education, Upper Saddle River, NJ

p. 523: The Center for Association Leadership: http://www.asaecenter.org; Wikipedia: http://en.wikipedia.org; Meetings and Conventions: http://www.meetings -conventions.com

Chapter 13

pp. 524: JackF/Fotolia

p. 526: Brett Coomer/AP Images

pp. 528–529: Courtesy of James MacManemon

p. 532: Walker, James R. Intro to Hospitality Management, 4e. Copyright © 2013. Pearson Education, Upper Saddle River, NJ

p. 533: Jeff Greenberg/PhotoEdit

p. 535: Jeff Christensen/Newscom

pp. 539–540: Courtesy of Suzanne Bailey

pp. 542–543: Joe J. Goldblatt, Special Events: Best Practices in Modern Event Management, 2nd ed. (New York: John Wiley and Sons, 1997), 2; Joe. J. Goldblatt, Special Events: The Art and Science of Celebration (New York: Von Nostrand Reinhold, 1990), 1-2.

p. 544: George G. Fenich, Meetings, Expositions, Events, and Conventions: An Introduction to the Industry (Upper Saddle River, NJ: Pearson Education, 2005).

p. 544: auremar/123RF

p. 545: Courtesy of Tina Stoughton

pp. 545–546: Reprinted by permission of Tina Stoughton

p. 548: A. Ramey/PhotoEdit

pp. 548–549: Courtesy of The International Special Events Society (ISES)

p. 549: International Special Events Society: http://www.ises.com

pp. 551–552: Courtesy of James R. Schrock

p. 554: Walker, James R. Intro to Hospitality Management, 4e. Copyright © 2013. Pearson Education, Upper Saddle River, NJ

pp. 554–556: Courtesy of Greg Dunn

p. 556: Walker, James R. Intro to Hospitality Management, 4e. Copyright © 2013. Pearson Education, Upper Saddle River, NJ

p. 558: International Festivals & Events Association: http://www.ifea.com

p. 559: Meeting Professionals International: http://www.mpiweb.org; Hospitality Sales and Marketing Association International (HSMAI): http://www.hsmai.org; ASTM International: http://www.hsmai.org; Meetings.Net: http://meetingsnet.com

Chapter 14

pp. 560–561: Dmitry/Fotolia

p. 563: Courtesy of Horst Schulze

pp. 563–564: Courtesy of Horst Schulze

p. 564: Walker, James R. Intro to Hospitality Management, 4e. Copyright © 2013. Pearson Education, Upper Saddle River, NJ

p. 565: Francis Miller/The LIFE Picture Collection/Getty Images

p. 566: Courtesy of William Fisher

pp. 566–567: Courtesy of William Fisher

p. 568: Walker, James R. Intro to Hospitality Management, 4e. Copyright © 2013. Pearson Education, Upper Saddle River, NJ

p. 570: F1online digitale Bildagentur GmbH/Alamy

pp. 570–571: Courtesy of Ritz Carlton Company, LLC.

p. 571: Ritz Carlton Company, LLC: http://www.ritzcarlton.com

p. 572: How Many Are There? : http://www.howmanyarethere.net/

pp. 572–573: Courtesy of James MacManemon

p. 574: Pearson Education, Inc.

p. 575: Walker, James R. Intro to Hospitality Management, 4e. Copyright © 2013. Pearson Education, Upper Saddle River, NJ

p. 576: Walker, James R. Intro to Hospitality Management, 4e. Copyright © 2013. Pearson Education, Upper Saddle River, NJ

p. 577: Walker, James R. Intro to Hospitality Management, 4e. Copyright © 2013. Pearson Education, Upper Saddle River, NJ

p. 578: Based on: Gary Dessler, A Framework for Management (Upper Saddle River, NJ: Prentice Hall, 2002), 8.

p. 581: Robert A. Beck

pp. 581–582: Stephen S. Hall, Ethics in Hospitality Management: A Book of Readings, American Hotel & Lodging Association.

p. 583: Courtesy of James MacManemon

pp. 584–586: Courtesy of Greg Dunn

p. 589: BrainyQuote: http://www.brainyquote.com; Strategic Leadership Studies: http://www.au.af.mil/au/awc/awcgate/usmc/leadership_traits.htm;The Ritz-Carlton Hotel Company: http://www.ritzcarlton.com; Capella Hotel Group: http://www.capellahotelgroup.com; Prezi: https://prezi.com; United Nations Global Compact: www.unglobalcompact.org; Walker, John R. Introduction to Hospitality Management. Pearson Education 2016

Part V

(p. 591): Erwinova/Fotolia

Chapter 15

pp. 592–593: StockRocket/Fotolia

pp. 595–596: Courtesy of James MacManemon

p. 597: Walker, James R. Intro to Hospitality Management, 4e. Copyright © 2013. Pearson Education, Upper Saddle River, NJ

p. 598: Hurst Photo/Shutterstock

p. 599: Walker, James R. Intro to Hospitality Management, 4e. Copyright © 2013. Pearson Education, Upper Saddle River, NJ

p. 603: Walker, James R. Intro to Hospitality Management, 4e. Copyright © 2013. Pearson Education, Upper Saddle River, NJ

p. 606: Walker, James R. Introduction to Hospitality Management, 4e. Copyright © 2013. Pearson Education, Upper Saddle River, NJ

p. 608:Courtesy of Tim Mulligan

pp. 608–609: Courtesy of Tim Mulligan

p. 610: Walker, James R. Introduction to Hospitality Management, 4e. Copyright © 2013. Pearson Education, Upper Saddle River, NJ

p. 613: Walker, James R. Intro to Hospitality Management, 4e. Copyright © 2013. Pearson Education, Upper Saddle River, NJ

p. 615: Walker, James R. Intro to Hospitality Management, 4e. Copyright © 2013. Pearson Education, Upper Saddle River, NJ

p. 617: Walker, James R. Intro to Hospitality Management, 4e. Copyright © 2013. Pearson Education, Upper Saddle River, NJ

pp. 618–620: Courtesy of Greg Dunn

pp. 620–621: Walker, James R. Intro to Hospitality Management, 4e. Copyright © 2013. Pearson Education, Upper Saddle River, NJ

p. 623: Odyssey Media Group: http://www.odysseymediagroup.com; United Nations ESCAP: http://www.unescap.org

p. 691: Courtesy of Jessica Liebovich

pp. 691–692: Courtesy of Jessica Lebovich

p. 692: Jessica Lebovich: www.eatbreathemoveheal.com.

Chapter 16

pp. 624–625: Yuliyagontar/Fotolia

p. 628: Walker, James R. Intro to Hospitality Management, 4e. Copyright © 2013. Pearson Education, Upper Saddle River, NJ

p. 629: Yuri Arcurs/Shutterstock

p. 630: Walker, James R. Intro to Hospitality Management, 4e. Copyright © 2013. Pearson Education, Upper Saddle River, NJ

p. 632: Walker, James R. Intro to Hospitality Management, 4e. Copyright © 2013. Pearson Education, Upper Saddle River, NJ

p. 633: Courtesy of Andrea Kazanjian; Robert Kneschke/Fotolia; Andrea Kazanjian

p. 635: Walker, James R. Intro to Hospitality Management, 4e. Copyright © 2013. Pearson Education, Upper Saddle River, NJ

p. 636: Uranov/Fotolia

p. 637:Walker, James R. Intro to Hospitality Management, 4e. Copyright © 2013. Pearson Education, Upper Saddle River, NJ

p. 639: Reprinted by permission of Patricia Engfer

p. 642: Darden Restaurants: Http://www.darden.com; Ian Dagnall/Alamy; WWW.starwoodhotels.com/corporate/company_info.html

p. 644: Courtesy of James MacManemon

pp. 645–646: Courtesy of Greg Dunn

pp. 646–647: Walker, James R. Intro to Hospitality Management, 4e. Copyright © 2013. Pearson Education, Upper Saddle River, NJ

p. 649: Wikipedia: http//en.wikipedia.org

Chapter 17

p. 650: Bellemedia/Fotolia

p. 653: Stephen P. Robbins and Mary Coulter, Management, 12th ed. (Hoboken, NJ: Pearson, 2013), 258.

p. 655: ArTo/Fotolia

p. 656: WavebreakMediaMicro/Fotolia

p. 660: Stephen P. Robbins and Mary Coulter, Management, 12th ed. (Hoboken, NJ: Pearson, 2013), 258.

p. 662: Walker, James R. Intro to Hospitality Management, 4e. Copyright © 2013. Pearson Education, Upper Saddle River, NJ

p. 664: Courtesy of Patricia Tam

pp. 664–665: Courtesy of Patricia Tam

p. 665: Walker, James R. Intro to Hospitality Management, 4e. Copyright © 2013. Pearson Education, Upper Saddle River, NJ

p. 666: Walker, James R. Intro to Hospitality Management, 4e. Copyright © 2013. Pearson Education, Upper Saddle River, NJ

p. 667: Walker, James R. Intro to Hospitality Management, 4e. Copyright © 2013. Pearson Education, Upper Saddle River, NJ

p. 669: Suzanne Seder

pp. 669–670: Suzanne Seder

p. 671: Courtesy of James MacManemon

p. 672: Derived from Stephen P. Robbins and Mary Coulter, Management, 13th ed. (Hoboken, NJ: Pearson, 2014), 50.

p. 675: Starwood Hotels and Resorts, Corporate Profile, www.starwoodhotels.com/corporate/company_info.html; Halil Erdogan/123RF

pp. 677–679: Courtesy of Greg Dunn

p. 679: Walker, James R. Intro to Hospitality Management, 4e. Copyright © 2013. Pearson Education, Upper Saddle River, NJ

Chapter 18

p. 684: Faithie/Fotolia

p. 687: Stephen P. Robbins and Mary Coulter, Management, 12th ed. (Hoboken, NJ: Pearson, 2013), 258.

p. 688: Walker, James R. Intro to Hospitality Management, 4e. Copyright © 2013. Pearson Education, Upper Saddle River, NJ

p. 689: Tyler Olson/Fotolia

p. 690: Reprinted by permission of Cherry Cerminara; Cherry Cerminara

p. 694: Walker, James R. Intro to Hospitality Management, 4e. Copyright © 2013. Pearson Education, Upper Saddle River, NJ

p. 695: Erwinova/Shutterstock

p. 698: Pearson Education, Inc.

p. 699: Courtesy of James MacManemon

p. 702: Yuliufu/Fotolia

p. 703: Courtesy of Michael R. Thorpe

pp. 703–704: Courtesy of Michael R. Thorpe

pp. 706–708: Courtesy of Greg Dunn

p. 708: Walker, James R. Intro to Hospitality Management, 4e. Copyright © 2013. Pearson Education, Upper Saddle River, NJ

p. 710: The Sustainability Collection: http://ijs.cgpublisher.com/product/pub.41/prod.582; Green Lodging News: www.greenlodgingnews.com; Waste Reduction and Recycling for the Lodging Industry: https://www.bae.ncsu.edu/topic/vermicomposting/pubs/ag473-17-lodging.html; Florida Department of Environmental Protection: http://www.dep.state.fl.us

Repeated throughout: Agsandrew/Shutterstock